The Evolving Concept of Community Citizenship

From the Free Movement of Persons to Union Citizenship

EUROPEAN MONOGRAPHS

Editor-in-Chief Prof. Dr. K.J.M. Mortelmans

1. Lammy Betten (ed.), *The Future of European Social Policy* (second and revised edition, 1991).
2. J.M.E. Loman, K.J.M. Mortelmans, H.H.G. Post, J.S. Watson, *Culture and Community Law: Before and after Maastricht* (1992).
3. Prof. Dr. J.A.E.Vervaele, *Fraud Against the Community: The Need for European Fraud Legislation* (1992).
4. P. Raworth, *The Legislative Process in the European Community* (1993).
5. J. Stuyck, *Financial and Monetary Integration in the European Economic Community* (1993).
6. J.H.V. Stuyck, A.J.Vossestein (eds.), *State Entrepreneurship, National Monopolies and European Community Law* (1993).
7. J. Stuyck, A. Looijestijn-Clearie (eds.), *The European Economic Area EC–EFTA* (1994).
8. R.B. Bouterse, *Competition and Integration–What Goals Count?* (1994).
9. R. Barents, *The Agricultural Law of the EC* (1994).
10. Nicholas Emiliou, *The Principle of Proportionality in European Law: A Comparative Study* (1996)
11. Eivind Smith, *National Parliaments as Cornerstones of European Integration* (1996)
12. Jan H. Jans, *European Environmental Law* (1996)

The Evolving Concept of Community Citizenship

From the Free Movement of Persons to Union Citizenship

Síofra O'Leary

Faculty of Law
University of Cambridge

KLUWER LAW
INTERNATIONAL

THE HAGUE · LONDON · BOSTON

Published by Kluwer Law International
Sterling House
66 Wilton Road
London SW1V 1DE
United Kingdom

Sold and distributed in the USA and Canada
by Kluwer Law International
675 Massachusetts Avenue
Cambridge MA 02139
USA

Kluwer Law International incorporates the
publishing programmes of
Graham & Trotman Ltd,
Kluwer Law & Taxation Publishers
and Martinus Nijhoff Publishers

In all other countries sold and distributed
by Kluwer Law International
P.O. Box 85889
2508 CN The Hague
The Netherlands

© Kluwer Law International 1996
First published in 1996

ISBN 90 411 0878 5

British Library Cataloguing in Publication Data is available

Library of Congress Cataloging-in-Publication Data is available

Typeset in Times by On Screen, West Hanney, Oxfordshire
Printed and bound in Great Britain by Hartnolls Ltd, Bodmin, Cornwall

Contents

Acknowledgements

This book is based on the doctoral thesis, of the same title, which I defended at the European University Institute, Florence, in October 1993. I would like to express my gratitide to Professor H.U.J. D'Oliveira, formerly of the European University Institute, Florence and now of the University of Amsterdam, for his constant supervision, guidance and encouragement of the research which I carried out during my time at the EUI. His challenging and, it must be said, unorthodox approach to legal analysis has often been the key which has helped me to open doors and attempt to resolve questions which I might otherwise have left untouched.

I must also express my thanks to Professor J. Schwarze (University of Freiburg) and Professor F. Snyder (European University Institute), who always graciously gave of their time in Florence. Thanks must also go to the remaining two members of my jury – Professor K. Lenaerts (University of Louvain) and Professor D. O'Keeffe (University College London), who patiently ploughed through the text presented to them without complaint! The structure of this book developed from some of the ideas kindly suggested to me by Professor Lenaerts. I assume all responsibility, however, for any weaknesses and errors which remain. I am also extremely grateful to both Professors Lenaerts and O'Keeffe for the interest they have shown in my work since then and the advice and support which they have always given me. It has been invaluable.

It is impossible to thank all those persons who I met and worked with at the EUI, or whose company and friendship I have enjoyed and still cherish. Mention must be made, in particular, of Peter Kennealy, Alison Tuck in the Law Faculty, Emir Lawless in the European Documentation Centre and Françoise Thauvin, who always had time for a chat or a cup of tea and who, in various ways, helped to keep me smiling! It was a pleasure working at the EUI, not least because of the excellent conditions provided by the Library and Academic Service. I would like, therefore, to thank the Irish Department of Education for enabling me to attend the Institute in the first place. It was both an honour and a privilege. Long may the governments of the European Union support the work of the Institute and long may the Institute, in response, continue in its quest for excellence.

I would also like to thank my fellow researchers and friends at the Institute who, apart from long hours in the Library and Cloister, have shared jokes, drinks and emotions in the "Bar Fiasco". Some friendships have faded with time and distance, but have not been forgotten. Special mention must be made of Declan Murphy, Peter Edurne Iraizoz, Nuno Venade, Marina Calloni and, of course, Despina.

My thanks also to the Fernández Martín family, Professor Francisco Escribano and Carmen Quintena, Inmaculada González García, Salvador Collado and Coronada Romero, for their friendship and companionship during my time in Sevilla and to the Spanish Ministry for Education and Science for sponsoring me for one year as a visiting fellow. Thanks to Carlos Closa in Madrid for always sending me the material I could not find, and to Allan Rosas and all his team in the Abo Akademi University in Turku, Finland. It has been a pleasure to meet and work with them. My thanks also to Sarah Spencer from the Institute for Public Policy Research. Finally, I would like to thank Selma Hoedt and her team at Kluwer for their constant assistance and prompt answers to my queries and for allowing me, without pressure, to complete this work past the deadline forecast.

In case they think I have forgotten, my deepest gratitude to my family – Cathal, Eithne, Aisling, Michael, Turlough, Brona and Shane – whose love and support throughout the years have been a tower of strength. These few lines would not be complete, however, without thanking Pepe – he knows what it has involved putting this together, but I don't think he realises how much it has meant to have him by my side throughout.

                                                                        Síofra O'Leary
                                                                  Sevilla, 7 July 1995

Part I

A Conceptual Framework for Community Citizenship

Chapter 1

The Concepts of Nationality and Citizenship

1.1. Introduction

We are warned that "the subject of nationality, like that of citizenship, is an elusive one ... and every author would be well advised, in order to avoid too obvious mis-understandings, to make clear from the outset, in which way s/he is going to use these terms".[1] This chapter has the unenviable task of unravelling the complex is-sues involved in any definition of nationality and citizenship. Its ultimate purpose is to devise a rough model of citizenship which incorporates a minimal series of in-gredients and which will permit discussion of the status of citizenship at Community level. This model will be used throughout the book to determine whether citizenship is an apt legal definition of the relationship between the nation-als of the Member States and the Community and whether it suitably describes the rights and/or duties which that relationship may, or does, entail. It is not intended either as an ideal model of the rights and duties connected with state membership, or simply as a description of the rights and duties contingent on the practice and definition of citizenship at Member State level. It lies somewhere between the nor-mative and the descriptive.

As a preliminary, the origins and development of the concepts of nationality and citizenship are discussed. The chapter attempts to demonstrate how divergent na-tional history, traditions and choices about the formation of the state, constitution and individual political participation combine to determine the role and signific-ance of concepts of state membership at any given time and in any given place. There is thus no single all-inclusive definition of nationality or citizenship. There

---

[1] See D'Oliveira, H.U.J., *Plural Nationality and the European Union*, forthcoming Martinus Nijhoff; O'Connell, D.P., *International Law* (1970) London, Stevens and Sons, at pp.670–672; and Heater, D., "Citizenship: A Remarkable Case of Sudden Interest", 44 *Parliamentary Affairs* (1991) 140–156, at 152.

is a multitude. This chapter does not claim to be an authoritative source on the law and politics of nationality and citizenship. It seeks simply to inform the reader of this multiplicity of meanings and to arm him or her with sufficient information to tackle the issue at hand – whether citizenship is a suitable description of a legal status established in the European Community which entails a series of rights (and duties). Having outlined the origins and development of nationality and citizenship, the chapter examines differences between these two concept. It also discusses the convergence of nationality and citizenship as a result of the democratisation of the state, the development of the idea of one nation one state, the development of an industrial and capitalist society and the consequent tendency to close off the nation state. In conclusion, it describes the development of the concept of citizenship in the European Communities from its original conception in the 1970s to the negotiations surrounding the conclusion and adoption of Article 8 in the Treaty on European Union (TEU). It also briefly suggests possible interests and ideologies which lay behind the adoption of a legal status of citizenship in the TEU. This background information should prove useful when the development of substantive citizenship-like rights in Community law is examined in the course of the book.

1.2. The Origins and Early Development of Citizenship and Nationality

In ancient Greece, citizenship was essentially a hereditary status which was used to distinguish between citizens of a city state, metics and strangers.[2] It was, even then, a prerequisite for the enjoyment of certain political rights in the public sphere, which was where men enjoyed the rights and privileges of citizenship and contributed to the development of justice and the self-government of the community. For Aristotle, the essence of being a citizen was to rule and be ruled in the context of small state units, where all those who qualified enjoyed equal liberty.[3] Over time, however, the distinction between citizens and metics diminished and Greek city states began to confer citizenship rights on their allies' populations. As a result, citizenship began to lose its original exclusive quality. In ancient Rome, citizenship was viewed as the personal and legislative status of certain persons which entailed a right to own property and a number of other ascertainable positive rights. The major social division in Roman society was between patricians and plebians. The former were property-owners who had the right to participate politically and to hold public office. The latter were landless tenants, who were forced to work for

---

[2] For a definition of metic see Meehan, E., *European Citizenship* (1993) London, Sage Publications, at p.18.

[3] See Janowitz, M., "Observations on the Sociology of Citizenship: Obligations and Rights", 59 *Social Forces* (1980) 1–29, at 2. Plato did not develop a theory of citizenship, but he did argue against the instability caused by inequality; see King, D.S. and Waldron, J., "Citizenship, Social Citizenship and the Defence of Welfare Provision", 18 *British Journal of Political Science* (1988) 415–443, at 426; and Turner, B.S., *Citizenship and Capitalism: The Debate over Reformism* (1986) Controversies in Sociology Series 21, London, Allen and Unwin, at p.13.

the land-owners and who were excluded from political life. The notion of citizenship in the early Roman empire referred to the "status of (rational) property-owners who had certain public duties and responsibilities within the city-state".[4] The Romans gradually extended parts of their *ius civile* to their neighbours and to the inhabitants of other colonies. Little by little the internal importance of the citizenship/non-citizenship distinction diminished until it finally disappeared around AD 212 when citizenship was granted to most of the Roman world.[5] The Roman conception of *civitatus* essentially meant an ensemble of citizens enjoying limited rights within a city context.[6]

From this incomplete sketch of early Greek and Roman concepts of citizenship, it is clear that essential to this status were rights of participation in the political activities of what were then small communal communities. "When in later centuries the legal bond between the 'civis' and his township widened into the much broader membership of a national community, the idea of active participation in its political life remained unabated and the title of 'citoyen' a name of honour."[7] This aspect of citizenship – active participation in public life involving a number of political rights – has survived to this day and is regarded by many authors as the essence of citizenship.[8] For Koessler, for example, citizenship "means specifically the possession by the person under consideration, of the highest or at least of a certain higher category of political rights and (or) duties established by the nation's or state's constitution".[9] In contrast to ancient Greece and Rome, political life in the Middle Ages tended to centre on the struggle for power between different political administrative entities. Members enjoyed privileges and immunities and were subject to obligations on the basis of established social hierarchies and on the basis of their relationship of allegiance with the sovereign.[10] They were treated as subjects rather than individuals.

Nationality, on the other hand, legally binds an individual to the nation, people or territory to which he or she belongs. According to Closa "nationality is, *a priori*, an undetermined attribute of a person; it is generally assigned at the moment of birth ... [and] sanctioned, thus, continuity with a determined lineage as well as a

---

[4] See Turner, B. S., "Outline of a Theory of Citizenship", 24 *Sociology* (1990) 187–217, at 202.

[5] See, in particular, Close, G., "Definitions of Citizenship" in Gardner, P. (ed.) *Hallmarks of Citizenship* (1994) Institute of Citizenship Studies/British Institute for International and Comparative Law, pp.3–18, at p.5. Plender also discusses different categories of Roman membership: (i) *cives Romani*, were the more established inhabitants of Rome and certain incorporated communities; (ii) *cives sine suffragio*, were considered too dangerous to be left independent, but were disenfranchised; (iii) *latins*; and (iv) *socii*, who were citizens of allied states. See Plender, R., *International Migration Law*, 2nd edn. (1988) Dordrecht, Martinus Nijhoff, at pp.10–11.

[6] See Turner, op. cit. note 4, at 203.

[7] See Verzijl, J.H.W., *International Law in Historical Perspective*, Vol.5 (1972) Leiden, A.J. Sijthoff, at p.14.

[8] See King and Waldron, op. cit. note 3, at 425; Schauer, F., "Community, Citizenship and the Search for National Identity", 84 *Michigan Law Review* (1985–86) 1504–1517, at 1513.

[9] See Koessler, M., "'Subject', 'Citizen', 'National'and 'Permanent Allegiance'", 56 *Yale Law Journal* (1946–47) 58–76, at 61.

[10] See Bendix, R., *Nation-Building and Citizenship: Studies of Our Changing Social Order* (1977) Berkeley, University of California.

geographical entity in which this lineage is established".[11] These two aspects of
nationality – lineage and belonging to a geographical entity – are evident in the determination of nationality in modern times on the basis of principles of *jus soli* and
jus sanguinis.[12] However, like the terms *gens* or *populus*, the Roman "nation" simply referred to a group of persons. It did not then imply the organisation of those
persons into a political entity. It referred simply to belonging.[13] Thus, unlike citizenship, nationality did not initially directly imply political participation. It was,
nevertheless, a highly political concept composed of two related but distinct
strands. On the one hand, the politico-legal aspect of nationality denoted legal
membership of a state (or organised community). On the other, nationality could
also denote the subjective corporate sentiment of unity of members of a specific
group forming a "race" or "nation". This is the historic-biological aspect of nationality.[14] The first aspect is more easily accessible and recognisable to lawyers. It is
the legal reflection of the tie which binds an individual to a particular state, or community. This positivist or formal way of perceiving nationality has two consequences. First of all, the content of the link is essentially legal. Secondly, each
state may decide as a pure question of law who can be regarded as its nationals.
The alternative historico-biological approach regards nationality in the light of the
historical, cultural and social ideal of the nation. The latter consists of an authentic,
national and organic community, formed on the basis of destiny, history and the
cultural characteristics of its components.[15] This historic-biological aspect of nationality is also sociologically determined and cannot, therefore, be qualified and
constrained simply by positive law. It will not necessarily coincide with the positive legal definitions of nationality referred to above.[16] A parallel distinction can
be sketched between the nation and the state. The former is a cultural, historical
and social concept, while the latter is generally a legal concept which refers to autonomous public institutions. In its oft-cited definition in the *Nottebohm* case the
International Court of Justice described nationality

[11]See Closa, C., "Citizenship of the Union and Nationality of the Member States", 32 *CMLRev*
(1995) 487–518, at 488.
[12]For an analysis of the development of these principles, see Plender, op. cit. note 5, at pp.11–25;
see also Habermas, J., "Citizenship and National Identity: Some Reflections on the Future of Europe",
12 *Praxis International* (1992–93) 1–19, at 5.
[13] See Habermas, op. cit. note 12, at 3.
[14]See Weis, P., *Nationality and Statelessness in International Law*, 2nd edn. (1979) Alphen aan
den Rijn, Sijthoff and Noordhoff, at p.1; Wiessner, "Blessed be the Ties that Bind: the Nexus Between
Nationality and Territory", 56 *Mississippi Law Journal* (1986) 447–450, at 448; Koessler, op. cit. note
9, at 61; Leca, J., *Une conceptualisation politique de l'Europe du Traité du Maastricht* (1993)
Barcelona, Institut de Ciències Polítiques i Socials, at pp.8 and 15.
[15]See Stuart Mill, J., *Consensus on Representative Government*, Ch. 16 (1861), cited by Vayrynen,
P., "Some Basic Concepts and Definitions", in Iivonen, J. (ed.), *The Future of the Nation State in
Europe* (1993) Aldershot, Elgar Publishing, pp.11–18, at p.13; Renan, E., *Qu'est-ce qu'une nation?*
(1882); and Smith, A., "National Identity and the Idea of European Unity", 68 *International Affairs*
(1992) 55–76, at 60. Habermas describes the nation as "communities of people of the same descent,
who are integrated geographically, in the form of settlements or neighbourhoods, and culturally by their
common language, customs and traditions, but who are not yet politically integrated in the form of a
state organisation": op. cit. note 12, at 3.
[16]See Díez-Picazo and Gullón, *Sistema de Derecho Civil* (1981) Madrid, Tecnos, at pp.321–322.

as a legal bond having as its basis a social fact of attachment, a genuine connection of existence, interests and sentiments, together with the existence of reciprocal rights and duties. It may be said to constitute the juridical expression of the fact that the individual upon whom it is conferred, either directly by the law or as a result of an act of the authorities, is in fact more closely connected with the population of the State conferring nationality than with any other state.[17]

This definition of nationality clearly reflects not only a legal bond of attachment between a national and a state, but also inferes the cultural, historical and social aspects of state membership and could even be said to incorporate aspects of what is defined here as citizenship.

1.3. The Convergence of Citizenship and Nationality

Early definitions of citizenship essentially focused on it as a personal status which conferred a number of rights, in particular, the right to participate politically in the life of the community. Nationality, on the other hand, was an undetermined attribute and a legal means to define membership of a state or community to the exclusion of non-members. The rights of political participation inherent in citizenship were enforced by the fact that certain persons did not enjoy them – aliens, persons without property and women – since the enjoyment of political rights was originally confined to a small group of (rational) male property-owners and originally functioned in the context of city states. However, once these aspects of democratic exclusion began to diminish and rights of political participation were extended to wider sections of the community, citizenship and nationality began to converge. If all, or almost all, of the persons bound to the community, state or polity (i.e. nationals) enjoyed the rights inherent in citizenship, it became difficult to distinguish whether those rights attached to them as nationals, or on the basis of their quality as citizens.

This convergence of these two aspects of state membership is best located around the time of the French Revolution, when enlightment ideas about the natural equality of human beings and the existence of a contract between the ruled and their rulers began to inform the political theories of Rousseau and Locke. Citizenship was gradually associated with a status which conveyed equal rights for all who enjoyed it. In addition, theorists began to develop the idea of a social contract, as an alternative to divine explanations for the legitimacy of government. Those opposed to the idea of an absolute sovereign with divine rights sought an explanation for why government had a right to demand obedience and they found one by constructing a contract between the government and the governed.[18] The legitimacy of this government depended on the consent of the governed and the fact

---

[17]*Liechtenstein* v. *Guatemala*, commonly known as the *Nottebohm* case, Second Phase, 6/4/1955 [1955] ICJ Reports 15, at 23.

[18]See Meehan, op. cit. note 2, at p.27.

that its powers had to be subject to restraint. For Rousseau, human nature could best be fulfilled in the context of such a civil society, where individual interests were protected by entering into a pact with one's fellow man.[19] This social contract did not necessarily flow from some collective will based on shared identity and descent, but rather from the consensus reached by free and equal men/citizens in a civil society. Modern conceptions of citizenship thus owe less to nationalist ideas about common descent and heritage and more to arguments about the rights of self-determining political communities. In this way rights became associated more with contract than with status. The development of these ideas coincided with demands for political rights from wider sections of the population, the growth and democratisation of the state and the development of the industrial, market society. Indeed some writers argue that the industrial revolution demanded the transformation of feudal status relationships, so that land and labour could be bought and sold and "[T]he individualism on which the Enlightment form of the social contract rested encouraged this, political liberalism providing a rationale and a motor for economic liberalization."[20] Habermas also traces European history from the early empires and central European federations to the development of territorial states in England, Portugal, Spain and France. These state organisations provided the infrastructure in which capitalism could develop and with the diffusion of democratic ideas following the French Revolution, they slowly developed into nation states.[21] For Habermas: "the nation state laid the foundations for cultural and ethnic homogeneity on the basis of which it then proved possible to push ahead with the democratisation of government since the late eighteenth century ... The nation state and democracy are twins born out of the French Revolution." The importance of French revolutionary ideas thus cannot be underestimated. They (i) linked the idea of citizenship rights and equality; (ii) located sovereignty within the nation, thereby emphasising national citizenship; and (iii) joined citizenship to the quest for political liberation.[22] Subjects became citizens and, as such, were the beneficiaries of a number of rights and duties and part of the foundational legitimacy of the state's exercise of authority.[23]

However, enjoyment of the rights of modern citizenship was not originally dependent on state closure, or on the exclusion of non-citizens in all cases. Indeed, following the French revolution, Article 4 of the Constitution of 1793 did not require that all those who enjoyed the political and active rights of citizenship be

---

[19]See Stevenson, L., "Conceptions of Human Nature", in Hawkesworth, M. and Kogan, M. (eds.), *Encyclopaedia of Government and Politics*, Vol.1 (1992) London, Routledge, at p.104 *et seq.*; and Russell, B., *History of Western Philosophy*, 2nd edn. (1994) London, Routledge, at p.606.

[20]See Meehan, op. cit. note 2, at p.27; and Turner (1986), op. cit. note 3, at pp.23 and 25. Ignatieff argues that the market society may require the rule of law to guarantee security of contract, but that economic man does not have to be a citizen: Ignatieff, M., "The Myth of Citizenship", 12 *Queen's Law Journal* (1987) 399–420, at 407.

[21]Habermas, op. cit. note 12, at 2.

[22]See also Turner (1986) op. cit. note 3, at p.19.

[23]See Montani, G., "Cittadinanza europea e identità europea", 36 *Il Federalista* (1994) 95–126, at 106.

French citizens.[24] Subsequent constitutions withdrew this extension of political rights. However, it should not be forgotten that one of the most important aspects of the French Declaration of the Rights of Man of 1789 was the universal nature of the text and the fact that it addressed *persons* rather than members or citizens. As such, it went beyond the "bills of rights" being discussed by the colonies on the other side of the Atlantic. The transformation of nationality and/or citizenship as mechanisms for exclusion took some time. The growth of industrial society required states to act in an increasingly protectionist manner in order to protect their economic interests. Following the First World War, the idea of one nation one state was solidified and states began to adopt passport and visa controls.[25] This need for state protection was further heightened after the Second World War when states increasingly assumed social and economic responsibilities with respect to their citizens. Freedom of movement and rights of entry and residence thus joined rights of political participation as privileges of state membership, in turn characterised variously as citizenship and/or nationality, and were used as a means to define the closure of the modern state.[26] Furthermore, in the field of political rights, the principle of equality inherent in Enlightment and revolutionary theory was only translated into legal reality early this century with the adoption of universal suffrage.

1.3.1. Legal Differences Between Citizenship and Nationality

Discussion of the meaning and content of nationality and citizenship is often obscured by the fact that jurists have tended not to differentiate between the terms "national" and "citizen".[27] Indeed, some states, such as Italy, do not distinguish between nationality and citizenship. It is also confused by the historical convergence of the two concepts around the time of the French Revolution. It is clear that both terms go to the essence of the relationship between the individual and the state. Nationality, however, could be regarded as an undetermined attribute which is used as a tool by municipal, international and even Community law to determine who belongs to what state. In other words, it identifies who enjoys what legal consequences, rather than which legal consequences they enjoy. The latter task is left to citizenship. Indeed, some authors have argued that nationality is a purely "formal frame" which gives rise to no fixed legal consequences.[28] Authors who dispute this positivist tendency to treat nationality merely as a connecting factor for the attribution of certain citizenship-like rights and obligations argue that the view that

---

[24]See Hammar, T., "Citizenship: Membership of a Nation and of a State", 24 *International Migration* (1986) 735–748, at 736; and Habermas, op. cit. note 12, at 13.

[25]See generally, Llobera, J., "The Role of the State and the Nation in Europe", in Garcia, S. (ed.), *European Identity and the Search for Legitimacy* (1993) London, The Eleni Nakou Foundation/RIIA, pp.64–80.

[26]See Layton Henry, Z.(ed.), *The Political Rights of Migrant Workers in Western Europe* (1990) London, Sage Modern Politics Series Vol.25, at p.112; and Hammar, op. cit. note 24, at 736–740.

[27]See Plender, op. cit. note 5, at p.11.

[28]See Koessler, op. cit. note 9, at 70 and 76; and Wiessner, at 447–450.

nationality is purely nominal is weakened by the fact that nationality itself can be regarded as a right and has a value of its own due to its normative and inherent entailment of rights and duties.[29] In support of this proposition Article 15 of the UN Declaration of Human Rights states that everyone has a right to a nationality, and Article 24 of the International Covenant of Civil and Political Rights provides that all children have the right to acquire a nationality.

Thus, commentators in this field are divided. Some regard nationality as a formal legal concept defining membership of a state, which entails no rights and duties. Others regard it as a substantive legal status in itself, which inheres a number of rights and entitlements. Perhaps this division is best resolved with reference to the two aspects of nationality outlined above and to the related but distinct concept of citizenship. It is not strictly accurate to say that nationality is a purely formal legal concept. The right not to be stateless is, in itself, a substantive right which may convey considerable benefits if enjoyment of the rights of citizenship are attached in a given state to the legal concept of nationality. However, the politico-legal aspect of nationality categorises it as a juridical tie or public law link between an individual and a state. This juridical link reflects a legal *relationship* which exists between the individual and a state, rather than a defined legal *status* entailing a series of rights and duties.[30] These rights and duties may flow from the primary legal (nationality) relationship between the individual and the state, but they are not the essence of that relationship. This is where the historic-biological aspect of nationality and the concept of citizenship may be considered relevant. Citizenship can be regarded as the internal reflection of state membership. Within the boundaries of the state concerned, it is a *status* which involves a series of rights and duties. It confers rights of social, political, even economic participation in the community and this is usually on the basis of some shared history, culture or group sentiment, essentially something which would entitle the individual to participate in the formation of state sovereignty and government. Viewed from this perspective, citizenship approaches the historic-biological aspect of nationality.

Nationality, therefore, can be seen as the external manifestation of state membership.[31] As a public law link between the individual and the state it may be the basis for the enjoyment of the status of citizenship, but it is not the only possible basis. Indeed, individuals may enjoy some of the rights and duties which categorise citizenship but not possess nationality,[32] and it has not been unknown for a specific

---

[29]See D'Oliveira, op. cit. note 1.

[30]See Green, L. C., "Is World Citizenship a Legal Practicality?" 25 *The Canadian Yearbook of International Law* (1987) 151–184, at 153; and Lippolis, V., *La Cittadinanza Europea* (1994) Bologna, Universale Paperbooks/Il Mulino, at p.27.

[31]See variously, Weis, op. cit. note 14, at p.29; O'Leary, S., "Nationality and Community Citizenship: A Tale of Two Uneasy Bedfellows", 12 *YEL* (1992) 353–384, at 355; Rosas, A., "Nationality and Citizenship in a Changing European and World Order", in Suksi, M. (ed.), *Law Under Exogenous Influences* (1994) Turku, pp.30–59, at p.34; and Close, op. cit. note 5, at p.5.

[32]See, for example, Clute, R.E., "Nationality and Citizenship" in Wilson *et al.* (ed.), *The International Law Standard and Commonwealth Developments* (1966) Commonwealth Studies Center, Duke University Press, pp.100–136, at p.110.

category of nationals to be deprived of some of the rights of citizenship.[33] A state is defined as "an organised community, and this implies a population occupying a defined territory which it asserts to be exclusive to it".[34] This definition is also reflected in the Montevideo Convention on the Rights and Duties of States which required that a state possess a permanent population, defined territory, government and the capacity to enter into relations with other states. Since the definition of its permanent population or personal substratum is one of the primary means by which a state defines itself, it is not surprising that the determination of nationality, or state membership, is regarded as part of the reserved domain of Member States.[35] Thus, Article 1 of the 1930 Hague Convention on Certain Questions Relating to the Conflict of Nationality Laws provides that: "It is for each State to determine under its own law who are its nationals. This law shall be recognised by other States in so far as it is consistent with international conventions, international custom, and the principles of law generally recognised with respect to nationality."[36]

García distinguishes, in this context, between formal and substantive citizenship. The former refers to citizenship as membership of a particular (political) community, the latter relates to the possession of specific rights and the obligation to comply with certain duties within the state or political community.[37] Given the convergence of the nation and the state in modern times and the close, often indistinguishable, relationship which has developed between nationality and immigration controls in some states (which in turn determine who is entitled to enjoy the rights of citizenship), nationals generally enjoy these rights as a result of their nationality. In this way, modern definitions of nationality and citizenship obscure on what basis individuals enjoy these rights and duties. International migration also complicates the distinction between them and the exclusionary rationale for the enjoyment of these rights since foreigners are increasingly admitted to an inner sanctum of rights which were previously reserved for members. However, citizenship, as distinct from legal positivist prescriptions of nationality, originally required a special bond of allegiance or attachment. It was on this basis that the individual enjoyed the right or privilege to participate in the determination of the community's sovereign affairs. With the admission of foreigners, this aspect of citizenship is more difficult to perceive, since they are increasingly able to enjoy citizenship-like rights although they remain excluded from the state's legal prescription of nationality. Nevertheless, the constitutional difficulties experienced in Spain, France and Germany with regard to the adoption of the citizenship provisions in the Union

[33]In the German law of 15 September, 1935, full political rights were only recognised for persons of German blood (and affine). Only these persons were qualified as citizens (*Staatsbürger*), the rest were only nationals (*Staatsangehörige*). See also the distinction in Belgium between *grande naturalisation*, which conferred full citizenship including citizenship rights and *petite naturalisation*, which did not include the right to vote: Koessler, op. cit. note 9, at 64.

[34]See O'Connell, op. cit. note 1, at p.284.

[35]See Weis, op. cit. note 14, at p.66.

[36]L.N. Doc. C. 24. M. 13. 1931. V.; reproduced in 63 *American Journal of International Law* (1969) 875, at 885.

[37]See García, S., *Fragmented Identities and the Frontiers of European Citizenship* (1992) RIIA Discussion Papers no.45, at p.20.

Treaty (Article 8) emphasise the survival of the political and exclusionary nature of citizenship to date.

1.3.2. Citizenship and Nationality in Context

It is essential when discussing the related but distinct concepts of nationality and citizenship to refer to their historical, political and legal contexts.[38] Their present legal significance and content are of recent origin and are closely linked to a series of historical and political developments which have varied from place to place. Turner thus warns that "a general theory of citizenship, as the crucial feature of modern political life, has to take a comparative and historical perspective on the question of citizenship rights, because the character of citizenship varies systematically between different societies".[39] Turner sketches the emergence of citizenship in different Western states.[40] A long historical struggle in France sought to break the legal and political dominance of a court society set in a rigid social system of estates. In challenging the absolute power of the king and opting for a society which permitted the general will to be expressed through parliamentary institutions, Frenchmen ceased to be subjects and became equal citizens in a national political entity. Like the French, the American Revolution based itself on a rights of man discourse and on principles of democratic representation. However, in the absence of an aristocracy and established church, it was easy to forge the American experiment on democratic foundations. In contrast, in Germany and England citizenship rights developed with respect to passive subjects who were permitted the enjoyment of certain privileges by the state. Thus, Turner points out that: "If a successful revolutionary conflict against aristocratic powers is at least one aspect of the historical emergence of democratic citizenship, then the failure of a liberal bourgeois struggle (as in Germany in 1848) provides one aspect of the peculiarly bureaucratic, authoritarian character of political life in Germany under the aristocratic dominance of the Junkers."[41]

The historical background of Community Member States, their attitude to state closure and to the development of rights of political participation, clearly influence their modern legal definitions of state membership. Modern British nationality law, for example, still betrays its feudal and monarchical origins. Nationality was, after all, developed at a time of sovereigns and subjects and it thus reflected a status dependent on allegiance, rather than a relationship conferring rights and duties. Indeed, no written code or constitution exists in the United Kingdom to date which describes the rights and duties of citizens. The historical background to the regulation of nationality law in Ireland is in sharp contrast. The struggle for independ-

---

[38]Meehan warns that "the meaning of citizenship is neither fixed in time nor the same in different societies": op. cit. note 2, at p.17.

[39]See Turner, op. cit. note 4, at 195; and van Gunsteren, H., "Notes on a Theory of Citizenship", in Birnbaum, P., Lively, J. and Parry, G. (eds.), *Democracy, Consensus and Social Contract* (1978) London, Sage Modern Politics Series Vol.2, pp.9–35, at p.10.

[40]See Turner (1990), op. cit. note 4, at 207–208.

[41]Ibid., at 210.

ence which took place in Ireland in the early part of this century and the initial position of Ireland as a dominion and member of the British Commonwealth rendered
the modern evolution of Irish nationality unique among the Member States of the
European Communities. The issue of nationality became a medium through which
the newly fledged state could assert its legal independence and its historical and
political difference. However, given the close historical relationship between the
two countries, Irish nationals are not regarded as aliens under United Kingdom law
and reciprocal privileges are afforded to British nationals resident in Ireland. A
common travel area exists between the two countries and no travel documents are
required within that area. Persons born in Britain visiting or resident in Ireland are
completely exempt from the orders controlling aliens made by the Minister for
Justice under the Aliens Act, 1935.[42] In accordance with the legislation in force in
Ireland, United Kingdom nationals may vote in local elections. In 1985, following
an amendment of Article 16 of the Constitution, they were also admitted to vote
and stand for election in parliamentary elections.[43] There is no statutory barrier to
the employment of United Kingdom nationals in the Irish Civil Service, although
Irish Civil Service commissioners may insert a nationality clause in regulations for
any competition limiting the latter to nationals. No nationality requirement attaches
to service in the Irish armed forces, although fulfilment of a period of ordinary residence is probably necessary. This extension of Irish citizenship rights to British
nationals is closely linked to the historical ties which bind the two countries and to
the privileged treatment which resident Irish nationals enjoy in the United
Kingdom. Irish nationality law is also very liberal, which can be explained in terms
of its large emigrant community and, to a certain extent, by the fact that Ireland has
never been a traditional destination for immigration.[44]

1.4. A Rough Model of Citizenship with a View to Analysing Community Citizenship

Citizenship, for the purposes of this book, is essentially regarded as a juridical
condition which describes membership of and participation in a defined community or state. This juridical condition carries with it a number of rights and duties
which are, in themselves, an expression of the political and legal link between the
state and the individual. This juridical condition or status thus makes those who
qualify the titleholders of a series of sometimes unpredictable rights and duties.[45]
To avoid circularity in this definition, however, it is necessary to answer a number
of questions. First of all, how does one qualify as a member, in order to enjoy the

[42]See the report in *Anglo Irish Joint Studies Report*, presented to both Houses of Parliament in
1981, at p.21.
[43]See *infra* Chapters 6 and 7.
[44]For further discussion of Irish nationality law see O'Leary, S., "Irish Nationality Law", in
Nascimbene, B. (ed.), *The Nationality Laws of European Community Member States*, forthcoming,
Milano, Le Giuffre.
[45]See Lippolis, op. cit. note 30, at pp.21–22.

consequent rights and duties of citizenship? One of the primary means to qualify for citizenship is the possession of state nationality. Nationality is generally acquired with reference to *jus sanguinis* or *jus soli* principles, or through naturalisation on the basis of long term residence. However, some states extend some or most of the rights of citizenship to persons legally resident in the state for a specified period of time, or on the basis of reciprocity. In all these cases, however, enjoyment of citizenship rights stems from a legal, political and even social attachment which was inherited by the individual or developed by them over time, which justifies admitting them to what is essentially a status involving a number of rights but which, in addition, is an expression or symbol of their participation in and exercise of the sovereignty of that state or community. Throughout this discussion of citizenship, however, it is useful to keep in mind that "when studying citizenship one should not assume that one knows – or after some clarification can know – what citizenship *is*, but rather treat it as an essentially contested concept that refers to a conflictual practice".[46] In other words, there is no one answer to what citizenship is, or who qualifies for it.

Secondly, one must ask what rights and duties can be enjoyed on the basis of citizenship once one has qualified? This is a disputed issue and is likely to become even more disputed as pressures on redistributive welfare systems grow, as migration flows obscure previously simple definitions of state membership and national boundaries and as international or supranational organisations extend the number of rights which individuals can enjoy beyond the boundaries of the state. It is questionable, for example, whether social rights fall within the scope of citizenship rights or what, for example, the relationship is between citizenship rights and fundamental rights. In designing a model of citizenship to assess the development of a status of citizenship in the European Union, some attention must be paid to these issues. Marshall's famous threefold definition of citizenship was based on civil, political and social rights. Civil rights were those concerning individual freedom, such as liberty of the person, free speech, thought, religion, the right to own property and to conclude contracts and the right to justice. These rights could be vindicated in courts of law and emphasised the autonomy of the citizen as a free and supposedly equal member of society. Political rights referred to democratic rights of participation as either an elector, or member of a body invested with political authority, or both. The institutions of representative democracy were central to the protection and exercise of these rights. Finally, by social rights Marshall meant economic and welfare rights, rights to a minimum standard of welfare and income. These rights were to be vindicated with reference to welfare state policies and institutions.[47] Roche suggests that the European Community seems set to disrupt Marshall's sequence for the development of the rights of citizenship since it began with civil rights, has gone on to establish a minimum of social rights and is now promising to develop political rights.[48]

[46]Van Gunsteren, op. cit. note 39, at p.10.
[47]For a more detailed list of possible rights of citizenship see Close, op. cit. note 5, at p.8.
[48]See Roche, M., *Rethinking Citizenship* (1992) Cambridge, Polity Press, at p.201.

Marshall's classification of citizenship rights has been criticised, however, for being too anglocentric and for ignoring, as a consequence, the political and historical developments which have modelled citizenship in other states.[49] Nevertheless, his model of citizenship is a useful introduction to what can be considered fundamental elements of citizenship – rights to political participation, civil rights which facilitate the exercise of these rights and which can be used generally to vindicate and protect the rights of citizenship and, more controversially, a minimum of socioeconomic rights. Furthermore, one of the essential aspects of Marshall's discourse was the central role which the principle of equality plays in the status of citizenship. He did not argue in favour of absolute equality, but rather claimed that it was more difficult to preserve inequalities once the status of citizenship was enriched and given substance. Thus civil, political and social rights of citizenship are meaningful to the extent that they even out some of the inequalities of social participation provoked, among other things, by a capitalist market economy: "Citizenship is a status which bestows upon individuals *equal* rights and duties, liberties and constraints, powers and responsibilities."[50] Theorists since ancient Greece generally agree that some sort of rough measure of equality among citizens is desirable.[51] In addition to the central importance of equality, Dahrendorf also recalls the social contract, a notion which embodies, in his view, the underlying assumptions of societies at a given time and place.[52] A basic element of the social contract is that it is one between equals and its basic function is to explain, justify and ultimately legitimate, the relationship between the individual and the body politic.

Citizenship, then, as outlined above, is comprised of a number of diverse elements. It is a juridical link implying membership, which, once possessed, confers a status involving a number of rights, duties and entitlements. In particular, it confers civil and political rights of participation which emphasise a departure from hierarchical social structures to the participation of the individual in state sovereignty. Citizenship developed, in modern times, as part of the state's redefinition of the social contract which required the participation of members in order to render legitimate the exercise of sovereignty by the state. Citizenship is also intimately linked to an extension of notions of equality between members. Without such equality, the social contract would have been null and void and the legitimacy of the modern state undermined. If one was to express the various aspects of citizenship in a number of words it would read as follows – membership, participation, rights, duties, equality and legitimacy. As a status, citizenship allows one to participate in society by conferring a number of rights and duties on an equal basis. Participation in these

[49]See in this respect Turner, op. cit. note 4, at 190 *et seq.*

[50]See Held, D., *Political Theory and the Modern State* (1989) Cambridge, Polity Press, at p.190, citing Marshall, "Citizenship and Social Class", in Marshall (ed.), *Class, Citizenship and Social Development* (1973) Westport, CT, Greenwood Press, at pp.70 and 84.

[51]See King and Waldron, op. cit. note 3, at 426 and Held, op. cit. note 50, at p.190.

[52]Dahrendorf, R., "Citizenship and the Modern Social Contract", in Holme, R. and Elliot, M., *1688–1988, Time for a New Constitution* (1988) London, Macmillan, pp.112–125, at p.116.

circumstances ultimately confers legitimacy on the state and its exercise of authority over members.[53]

With these basic notions in mind, what ingredients of the status of citizenship can be identified to help assess the development of a similar status at Community level? Clearly, rights to political participation are essential. Not simply rights to vote and stand for election, but a minimum of civil rights to ensure that those rights can be effectively exercised and vindicated before the courts if necessary. Rights to move freely, or to enter and leave the territory must also be considered relevant. This is partly the case since Marshall, in addition, called for a minimum of social rights. Some writers have argued that he added these rights with reference to what citizenship *should* look like, rather than what it actually did look like. However, given the commitment to social justice in the preamble of the SEA and to international conventions such as the ILO, which also guarantee socio-economic rights it is arguable that the Community's concept of citizenship should involve a minimum of social rights, if only with reference to the principle of equal treatment in Article 6. Once socio-economic entitlements attach to the model of citizenship, the issue of free movement is inevitably relevant since distributive justice "has to be legitimised on the basis of solidarity that comes from free common membership of a human community".[54] These social rights might include a right to engage in economic and professional activity, a right of access to education or, in certain circumstances, a right to a minimum of social assistance. A more difficult issue is the relationship of the status of citizenship with the protection and promotion of fundamental rights. As the Spanish delegation argued prior to the Maastricht Treaty, the two are distinct and independent issues. Nevertheless, it is also arguable that a notion of citizenship detached from fundamental rights is considerably impoverished. A state, or in this instance the Community, must also be obliged to respect and vindicate the fundamental rights of its citizens. Although fundamental rights are not part and parcel of a definition of citizenship, the manner in which a relationship is worked out between these two categories of rights is interesting and perhaps ultimately reflects upon the formal and social legitimacy of the state, community or legal order in question. Fundamental human rights are granted to all without distinction on grounds of nationality. Nevertheless the UN Covenant on Civil and Political Rights and the European Convention on Human Rights, to name but a few, affect the relationship between the individual (citizen and non-citizen) and the state. They guarantee and protect a number of civil, political and social and economic rights which come within the definitions of citizenship outlined above. The division between citizenship and fundamental rights is thus blurred, since the essence of these conventions is to address what individuals can expect from the

---

[53]See generally, Held, D., "Between the State and Civil Society: Citizenship", in Andrews, G. (ed.), *Citizenship* (1991), Lawrence and Wishart, pp.19–25, at pp.20–21.

[54]See Closa (1995) op. cit. note 11, at 508; Layton Henry, Z., "The Challenge of Political Rights", in Layton Henry, Z. (ed.), *The Political Rights of Migrant Workers in Western Europe* (1990) London, Sage Publications, at p.12; and Leibfried, S. and Pierson, P., "Prospects for Social Europe", 20 *Politics and Society* (1992) 333–365, at 336.

state regardless of their nationality and since these conventions do not directly concern who belongs to the political entity of the state.[55] Furthermore, though citizenship may be based on exclusionary principles in the sense that it excludes those whom it considers ineligible to participate, it should not, in defining the grounds on which it excludes non-members, infringe fundamental rights. Finally, it is essential throughout to keep respect for a broad principle of equality in mind and to assess whether some sort of social contract has been constructed between citizens and the political and legal order, which could legitimate the activities of the latter.

1.5. The Development of a Concept of Citizenship in the European Communities

It is said that the Community institutions were influenced by an evolving but ill-defined notion of European citizenship when first implementing the Treaty provisions on the free movement of persons.[56] This may have been an overestimation of the Community's legal and political disposition to alter, or interfere, with such a sensitive aspect of national sovereignty as the attribution of the rights of citizenship. Nevertheless, secondary Community legislation reflected the idea, even to a limited extent, that free movement was also a means to enable Community nationals "to pursue the activity of their choice within the Community".[57] The free movement of persons did in time develop beyond the narrow scope of the economically orientated Treaty provisions and their personal and material scope and impact was extended well beyond the strict requirements of the Treaty provisions.[58] Economic

[55]See Gardner, P., "What Lawyers Mean by Citizenship" (1990), BIICL, London, at p.4.

[56]Thus, in 1961 the Commission regarded free movement as "le premier aspect d'une citoyenneté européenne", Debs. EP. no. 48, 135, 22 November 1961; or as a "fundamental right of workers and their families" in the preamble of Regulation 1612/68, OJ 1968 L257/2. See also Commission Vice-President Sandri who spoke in terms of "an incipient form of European Citizenship", in the Free Movement of Workers in the European Communities, Bull. EC. 11-1968, 5–vbb9.

[57]See the third recital of the preamble of Regulation 1612/68, OJ 1968 L257/2; and generally Schockweiler, F., "La dimension humaine et sociale de la CE" (1993) *Revue du Marché Unique Européen* 11–45.

[58]For early discussions of the concept of European citizenship, see Evans, A.C., "European Citizenship", 45 MLR (1982) 497–515, who can be regarded as one of the pioneers in this field; "L'Europa dei cittadini", 26 *Euro Informazione* (1988) nos. 31–33, 1; Stephanou, C.A., "Identité et citoyenneté européennes", no.343 RMC (1991) 30–39; Solbes Mira, P., "La citoyenneté européenne", no.345 *RMC* (1991) 168–170; Evans, A.C., "European Citizenship: A Novel Concept in EEC Law", 32 *American Journal of Comparative Law* (1984) 679–715; Durand, A., "European Citizenship", *ELRev.* (1979) 3–14; Plender, R., "'An Incipient Form of European Citizenship'", in Jacobs, F.G. (ed.), *European Law and the Individual* (1976) North Holland, pp.39–53; Lhoest, A., "Le citoyen à la une de l'Europe", no.189 RMC (1975) 431–435; Adonnino, P., "L'Europa dei cittadini. Considerazioni e prospettive", 17 *Affari esteri* (1985) 438–449; Van den Berghe, G. and Huber, C.H., "European Citizenship", in Bieber, R., Bleckmann, A. and Capatorti, F. (eds.), *Das Europa der Zweiten Generation*, Band II (1981) Kehl-am- Rhein/Strasbourg, N.P. Engel Verlag, pp.755–774; Fransman, L., "Supranationality: the fall of empire and the rise of Europe", 4 *Immigration and Nationality Law and Practice* (1990) 28–34; Blumann, C., "L'Europe des citoyens", no.346 RMC (1991) 283–292; and Garth, B., "Migrant Workers and the Rights of Mobility in the European Community and the United States: A Study of Law, Community and Citizenship in the Welfare State", in Cappelletti, M., Seccombe, M. and Weiler, J.H.H., *Integration Through Law: Europe and the American Federal Experience*, Vol.1, Book 3 (1986) Walter de Gruyter/EUI, Berlin, pp.85–163.

integration was seen by some as the vehicle for further social and political integration. However, since the fundamental right of Community nationals to choose their place of work within the Community was regarded as essential to the notion of European citizenship at that stage, the link between the exercise of free movement and the exercise of an economic activity initially remained unaffected.

1.5.1. Special Rights and the Development of Community Citizenship

It did not take long for the non-economic strands of free movement to emerge. Commission President Mansholt in a speech before the European Parliament argued that an economic Community did not merely involve fiscal policies and the integration of a financial and budgetary nature, but that the creation of Community citizenship involved the right to move freely within the Community without being confronted by obstacles. In his view, migrants could no longer be treated as second class citizens, they must feel like citizens of the Community and enjoy the exercise of normal rights as such and the extension of voting rights to the migrant in his place of residence in elections at a municipal level would contribute to giving citizens the feeling that something concrete had been realised on their behalf.[59] The Belgian and Italian Prime Ministers at the first summit of the enlarged Communities in 1972, also spoke of bringing "the European Citizen into the construction of Europe" and proposed that "we could as of now decide to establish a European Citizenship which would be in addition to the citizenship which the inhabitants of our countries now possess."[60]

However, these were purely political statements which entailed no concrete enforceable rights for Community citizens on the basis of Community law. The first firm step towards developing the rights attendant on free movement and European citizenship was the establishment of "a working group ... to study the conditions and the timing under which the citizens of the nine Member States could be given special rights as Members of the Community" at the Paris summit in 1974.[61] This was followed in 1975 by the Tindemans Report on European Union which contained a special chapter entitled "Towards a Europe for Citizens",[62] which Mr Tindemans explicitly distinguished from a "Europe of Materials". He defined "special rights" as certain civil and political rights, in particular the right to vote and the right of eligibility and access to public office and based these rights on a principle parallel to that underlying the Community Treaties, namely the principle of equal treatment with nationals and integration into the host Member State. These rights were to be accorded to nationals of the Member States on the basis of their membership of the Community. The construction of Europe, according to the Tindemans Report, involved more than mere inter-state cooperation, "it is a rap-

[59]Debs. EP. 1972–73, no.149, at 107, 19/4/1972.
[60]Bull. EC. 11-1972, Vol.5, at 37, 39 and 43.
[61]Point 111, Bull. EC. 12-1974.
[62]Bull. EC. (8) 1975 II no.12, at 1; Bull. EC. (8) 1975 II nos. 7/8, at 12; see also Bull. EC. 1/76, at 26.

prochement of peoples who wish to go forward together, adapting their activity to the changing conditions in the world while preserving those values which are their common heritage".

The object of granting special rights to nationals of Member States resident in Member States other than their own was to integrate such nationals more fully and successfully into their host environment and to enhance their status as compared with third country nationals. The Scelba Report on behalf of the European Parliament[63] proposed that the unique development of the European Communities in the post-nation state era towards a supranational organisation of states meant that Community citizens would need special rights, specifically fundamental, civil and political rights. It characterised special rights as "subjective" public rights which the citizen possesses as a legal subject *vis-à-vis* the state, and which may be asserted at anytime. While they are not special in themselves, they are a special extension of the rights normally enjoyed by the nationals of a given Member State to the citizens of any other Community Member State who live in that state. In the context of special rights, a distinction was drawn between defensive rights which protect fundamental freedoms (fundamental rights); claims which citizens are entitled to make on the state (civil rights); and rights which guarantee the participation of the citizen in the state's institutions (political rights). Unlike Marshall's threefold typology of citizenship rights, the Scelba Report lacked any social rights for Member State nationals on the basis of Community law. Political participation at municipal level was regarded as vital, however, to the notion of special rights and the creation of a political union and the extension of democratic rights meant that citizens of the Community would inevitably be involved in all political decisions.[64]

The Commission subsequently presented a draft proposal for a Directive on a general right of residence in 1979. This proposal was a fundamental step in detaching the rights and benefits of free movement from the exercise of an economic activity. In principal, what was envisaged was a right to enter and reside irrespective of employment, establishment, or the provision of services. The preamble of the 1979 proposal for a residence Directive recognised that the Treaty "n'a toutefois pas prévu les pouvoirs d'action en ce qui concerne la libre circulation des personnes independamment de l'exercice d'une activité économique," but it invoked the Treaty aim to establish an ever closer union between the peoples of Europe and stated that the free movement of persons could not be fully realised unless a permanent right of residence be recognised for all Member State nationals. The draft Directive nevertheless insisted that its beneficiaries be in possession of sufficient resources, which considerably weakened the argument that economic activity was

---

[63]EP. Working Documents 1977–78, 25 October 77, Doc. 346/77, at 10.

[64]See also the European Parliament's resolution of the same year, OJ 1977 C299/25–26, which included civil and political rights, a right of petition, freedom of assembly and association, a right of residence for all Community citizens and trade union rights within the notion of special rights.

now no longer paramount for the enjoyment of some individual rights derived from Community law.[65]

The publication of the two Adonnino Reports in 1985 brought fresh impetus to the debate on European citizenship. The first report aimed at proposing arrangements of direct relevance to Community citizens which would visibly offer them tangible benefits in their everyday lives.[66] In particular, the report addressed Community rules and practices which caused irritation to Community citizens, such as the existence of frontier controls and formalities. The second report addressed other aspects of the special rights of Community citizens – education, culture and communication exchanges and the image and identity of the Community.[67] The Commission's 1985 Guidelines for a Community Policy on Migration also stated that "the free movement of persons should gradually become accepted in its widest sense, going beyond the concept of a Community employment market, and opening up to the notion of European citizenship".[68] In 1986 the Commission published a report entitled *Voting Rights in Local Elections for Community Nationals*.[69] The report was premised on the revolutionary basis that "the fact of being a citizen of one Member state confers rights in the other Member states too. Citizenship is thus disassociated from the national limits on rights attached to a given nationality ... There is no doubt that Community legislation has had the effect of breaking the link between national territory and the legal implications of nationality. The gradual achievement of a People's Europe will consolidate the trend."[70] The Commission subsequently presented a proposal for a Council Directive on voting rights for Community nationals in local elections in their Member State of residence.[71] The adoption of the proposal was overtaken by the intergovernmental negotiations prior to the TEU and the adoption of Article 8.

[65]See also the Thirteenth General Report on the activities of the European Communities which provided that the draft Directive would grant rights to Community nationals "no longer as persons engaged in economic activity but in their capacity as Community citizens"; and the European Parliament's resolution on the proposed Directive which regarded it as "the first step towards the creation of a European Citizenship", OJ 1980 C117/48. This issue is examined in greater detail in Chapter 4.

[66]Report of the *ad hoc* Committee on a People's Europe to the European Council, Brussels, 29–30 March 1985. Bull. EC. Suppl. 7/85, at 9.

[67]Report to the European Council, Milan, 28-29/6/1985, Bull. EC. Suppl. 7/85, at 18.

[68]See Bull. EC. Suppl. 9/85, at 5; and the European Parliament's Resolution in OJ 1985 C141/462.

[69]Bull. EC. Suppl. 7/86.

[70]On the particular issue of political rights see the Commission's 1988 Communication on a People's Europe, Bull. EC. Suppl. 2/88, at 7; and a People's Europe, COM (88) 331 Final, at 4; and *infra* Chapters 6 and 7.

[71]See COM (88) 371 Final, 11/7/88. In 1988 in "Europeans: A Universal Right to Vote in Local Elections", European File, 19/88, reference was made to the SEA and its reference to the political and democratic objectives of the Community. The time had come, it was said, for the European citizen to be recognised as such throughout the Community. The document further claimed that European citizens must have the benefit of all their democratic rights and must play their full role in the construction of Europe.

1.5.2. Supranational and Intergovernmental Approaches to the Development of Community Citizenship

Readers may wonder why this book addresses the evolving concept of *Community* citizenship, as distinct from *Union* citizenship, which is what was established in Article 8 of the EC Treaty by the TEU. It is evident with reference to the chapters in the second and third parts of this book that the rights granted to Member State nationals refer to the Community and not the Union. The TEU is constructed on three separate pillars – amendments to the EC Treaty, provisions on a common foreign and security policy and provisions on cooperation in the fields of justice and home affairs. Apart from the Committee on Petitions' disputable competence to investigate the Union's fields of activity,[72] the rights which Member State nationals enjoy on the basis of the status of citizenship have nothing to do with the remaining pillars of the TEU. Furthermore, the evolving concept of citizenship which is addressed in this book did not originate and begin to evolve following the establishment of Union citizenship. This book addresses a process whereby citizenship-like rights have gradually been extended to Member State nationals on the basis of Community law. The latest step in this process is the establishment of Union citizenship in 1992. However, reference to Community citizenship is a reference to what went on prior to the adoption of the TEU and what, it is suggested, will continue to take place thereafter, hence the subtitle, from the free movement of persons to Union citizenship.

The scope of Community citizenship depends on the legal and political approach which the Community institutions and Member States adopt. If Community citizenship is to reflect aspects of a traditional model of state citizenship, a maximalist, or supranational, approach would appear to imply, on the one hand, the existence of supranational political institutions which have been directly elected and on the other, supranational laws which create reciprocal rights and obligations between the citizens of the Member States and the supranational entity to which they also belong. Such a structure reflects the very essence of political citizenship which has pertained at national level. Since, citizenship is tied to the idea of representation, it is necessary to examine whether supranational citizenship can give rise to representative institutions. It is arguable, however, that the Community's institutions do not meet the requirements of democratic representation. Neither the Council nor the Commission are directly elected, or fulfil a representative role, and the European Parliament is still composed of national deputies elected in the context of a non-uniform electoral system. This in turn raises the essential question whether the development of Community citizenship is possible, since citizen participation to date has been confined to the level of the state. If Member States command the legal expression of national identity and are still the fora in which the basic rights of citizens can be fulfilled and protected, it is difficult to envisage the development of an effective supranational citizenship.

[72]See *infra* Chapter 8.

A minimalist approach to the concept of Community citizenship would, on the other hand, limit the extension of the benefits of each Member State's citizenship, to the citizens of the other Member States on a reciprocal basis. This approach minimalises the supranational impact on domestic law and policy and supposedly poses a lesser threat to the traditionally close relationship between the citizen and the state on which the cohesion of the latter is said to depend.[73] The relationship between Member States and their citizens is protected since the cohesion of that relationship is thought to be threatened by the wholesale introduction of rights and freedoms on the basis of Community membership in respect of persons lacking the citizenship of that state and thus not bound by its correlative duties. This minimalist approach necessarily weakens the substantive content and effect of a Community concept of citizenship, since its object is essentially to preserve the substance of the state citizenship relationship. However, even such a weak and embryonic form of citizenship at Community level excites considerable debate about which rights are entailed by it and the extent to which such a concept of citizenship threatens national sovereignty. A maximalist approach, on the other hand, extends beyond the principle of equal treatment as it operates in the Community. In such a legal context Member State boundaries and diverse national legislative standards would become increasingly anomalous.[74] This approach raises more serious questions about the scope of the Treaty, the legal competence of the Community institutions to act and the political will of Member States to accept Community action when national sovereignty and national identity are so inevitably involved.

To some extent, the Union Treaty has resolved some of these issues of competence and the extent to which Community law may impinge on national sovereignty. It establishes citizenship of the Union and enumerates a number of rights — rights of residence, electoral rights, a right of petition, etc. — which flow from Union citizenship. The approach of the Treaty seems, at a rough glance, to be minimalist. The principle of equal treatment applies, for example, in the context of rights of electoral participation and there is no suggestion of harmonisation. However, the actual or potential effect which the establishment of a concept of citizenship in Community law has on national conceptions of membership and the state will be tackled in the various chapters on nationality, involvement in an economic activity, residence, education, civil, political and fundamental rights. State closure, as we stated above, was a means of shaping the state itself. Walzer argues that: "Admissions policies are shaped partly by arguments about economic and political conditions in the host country, partly by arguments about the character and 'destiny' of the host country and partly by arguments about the character of coun-

---

[73]See Evans (1984) op. cit. note 58, at 680–681.

[74]See the Scelba Report which stated: "The assumption of sovereign rights by a supranational organisation of states is subject to the condition that a citizen should not thereby loose any of the fundamental rights which he possesses at a national level ... and the legal status enjoyed by a Community citizen in one Member State must, likewise, be accorded to him in all the other Member States". EP Working Docs. 1977–78, 25/10/77, Doc. 346/77, at 10; and the Commission's 1986 report on Voting Rights in Local Elections for Community Nationals, Bull. EC. 7/86.

tries in general."[75] By assuming a role in relation to admissions policy, freedom of movement generally, allocation of state welfare benefits and the determination of who can participate in the national "political community", the Community may weaken many of the ways in which states have traditionally set their members apart. It may be true, as some commentators have argued, that the initial extension of Community competence on the basis of the free movement provisions extended Member State obligations beyond what could originally have been expected.[76] However, in concluding the Union Treaty, Member States have made difficult constitutional choices with respect to their role in and commitment to the Community and its objectives. Although Article 8 opted, in the main, for an application of the principle of equal treatment, the choice made in the Treaty to establish supranational citizenship may lead the Community to increasingly supersede traditional conceptions of the nature and concept of state and state functions and to alter the role and content of the rights and duties of their members.

1.6. Negotiation of the Citizenship Provisions in the Treaty on European Union

The provision on citizenship in the Union Treaty developed in the context of the proposals on democratic legitimacy and reduction of the democratic deficit which were made in the preliminary stages of the intergovernmental conference negotiations. The Belgian memorandum on institutional relaunch first referred to the better-established term "People's Europe" rather than to a specific notion of citizenship.[77] The development of a People's Europe was linked in turn by the Belgians to the addition of a Treaty provision on human rights and to the accession by the Community not only to the European Convention of Fundamental Rights and Freedoms but, in addition, to agreements guaranteeing certain social rights. The Belgian memorandum also proposed more extensive use of qualified majority voting in the area of the free movement of persons in a single market,[78] the adoption of a uniform electoral procedure which would enable Community citizens to vote in European Parliament elections regardless of their nationality and the gradual adoption of a right to vote in local elections on the basis of residence along the lines of the Commission's 1988 proposed Directive. These proposals were intended, in addition to an increase in the powers of the Parliament, to redress the democratic shortfall in the Community's institutional structure. This objective of strengthening the democratic legitimation of the Union was reiterated in the

---

[75]Walzer, M. "The Distribution of Membership", in Brown, P.G. and Shue, H. (eds.), *Boundaries: National Autonomy and its Limits* (1981) Totowa, NJ, Rowman and Littlefield.

[76]In the area of social policy see, for example, Steiner, J., "The Right to Welfare: Equality and Equity under Community Law", 21 *ELRev* (1985) 21–41.

[77]Europe Documents no.1608, 29 March 1990.

[78]Although this was to be accompanied by a declaration reserving the right to Member States to act in matters relating to immigration and measures to combat terrorism and crime.

Kohl–Mitterrand letter to the Irish presidency, which called on the European Council to initiate preparations for an intergovernmental conference on political union.[79]

Defined along with the EMU and a common foreign and security policy as one of the three pillars of European political union, the term citizenship first appeared in a letter from the Spanish Prime Minister addressed to the President in office of the Council.[80] Citizenship, as proposed initially by the Spanish, entailed unlimited free movement, establishment and access to employment and the right to vote and stand for election irrespective of nationality in their country of residence. The Spanish argued that the creation of a Union at supranational level called for a definition of the rights and duties of the persons affected, which was what citizenship had achieved at national level.[81] Some Member States argued that it was too soon to treat citizenship as a constitutional element of political union, or alternatively, that rather than defining citizenship in the Treaty, it should be regarded as an objective to be gradually achieved.[82]

The question of citizenship was finally incorporated in the preparations for the Intergovernmental Conference and was included at the June 1990 European Council in Dublin in the framework of the "overall objective of political union". The Council was asked to examine the question "how will the Union include and extend the notion of Community citizenship carrying with it specific rights (human, political, social rights and the right of complete free movement and residence etc.), for the citizens of the Member States by virtue of these states belonging to the Union?" Although the Spanish were the most forthright players in the field, other Member States and Community institutions also made proposals in this regard. In its contribution to the discussions on progress towards political union, Greece insisted that that process implied a distributive process whose legitimacy must be based on representative bodies.[83] Apart from contributing to the solution of the democratic deficit in the functioning of the Community's institutions, Greece also proposed that a People's Europe be used to strengthen the feeling among citizens of Europe that they belonged to one legal community. In particular, they proposed recognition of the concepts of European citizen and human rights in the Treaty, the extension of voting rights in local elections on the basis of residence and in European Parliament elections in the context of a uniform electoral procedure. Greece also called for simplification of the means by which individuals could gain access to the Court of Justice, greater assurance that the Court's judgments be en-

---

[79]*Agence Europe*, 20 April, 1990.

[80]*Agence Europe*, 11 May 1990, at p.3.

[81]See Closa, C., "The Concept of Citizenship in the Treaty on European Union", 30 *CMLRev* (1992) 1137–1169, at 1153–1157; and Solbes Mira, op. cit. note 58, 168–170.

[82]See variously, *Agence Europe* no.5255, 16 May, 1990, at p.3 and No.5258, 19 May, 1990, at p.3.

[83]Reproduced in Laursen, F. and Van Hoonacker, S (eds.), *The Intergovernmental Conference on Political Union: Institutional Reforms, New Policies and International Identity of the European Community* (1992) Maastricht, EIPA, at p.277.

forced, introduction of a principle of solidarity and dropping the word economic in the title of the European (Economic) Community.

The first Spanish memorandum on citizenship, "The Road to European Citizenship", applauded the attempts made by the Community to date to extend and improve the benefits which Community citizens enjoyed on the basis of Community law.[84] However, it regarded these measures as an insufficient means to make Community citizens the fundamental reference point for Community action and likened the status of Community citizens to that of "privileged aliens". The creation of a political and economic union which incorporated a common foreign and security policy was seen as a radical departure from the existing position in Community law. It was necessary, as a result, to establish citizenship of the union as "the personal and indivisible status of nationals of the Member States, whose membership of the Union means that they have special rights and duties that are specific to the nature of the Union and are exercised and safeguarded specifically within its boundaries, without dismissing the possibility that such a status of European citizen may also extend beyond those boundaries". This citizenship would be a dynamic concept within the context of a dynamic Union, it would gain substance as a status as the Union developed and would help to diminish and ultimately overcome the inequalities which exist between the Community's regions. The Spanish proposal went beyond a mere extension of the principle of equal treatment to persons who had availed themselves of free movement and included proposals about greater social and economic cohesion between the Community's regions. The proposals also implicitly recognised the type of conflict which was likely to arise due to the tension between the intergovernmental and supranational perspectives of European citizenship outlined above. According to the Spanish, the content of citizenship to emerge from the conference would depend on the actual scope of the Union decided therein. No matter how modest that Union was, however, Spain argued that it was already necessary to take a qualitative leap forward with respect to European citizens beyond the rights and benefits already achieved for them to define a *status civitatis* which would involve a set of rights, freedoms and obligations for the citizens of the European Union. The flexible nature of European citizenship meant that whatever provisions were adopted did not have to be all inclusive. Although it regarded it as a matter distinct and independent from the concept of citizenship, Spain also called on the conference to review the need for uniform protection of the human rights and fundamental freedoms of persons resident in the Community, regardless of their nationality.

The Spanish memorandum identified three spheres of rights and duties for Community citizens. The first derived from national citizenship of a Member State. The second sphere of rights and duties stemmed from the Treaties for the nationals of a Member State. The object of adding a third sphere of rights was to advance the position of Community nationals resident in a Member State other than their own

---

[84]Co. Doc. SN 3940/90, 24 September, 1990.

beyond that of "privileged alien". This additional set of rights aimed to remove the negative effects of residence in another Member State. The fundamental starting point for the rights of European citizenship was the right to full freedom of movement, freedom to choose one's place of residence and the right to political participation on the basis of residence. Although most of these rights already existed on the basis of the Treaties, they were to be widened and extended. The right to political participation was to guarantee freedom of expression, association and assembly and was gradually to include participation in the electoral processes in the country of residence. This development would involve the adoption of a uniform electoral regime with respect to elections in the European Parliament. The document recognised the difficulties which had been encountered in the negotiation of the Commission's 1988 proposal on voting rights in local elections. However, it argued that the dynamic nature of the Community and of relationships between the Member States meant that the time was now right for Community action with respect to voting at local level. Ultimately, the Spanish sought "full electoral participation by the European citizen at his place of residence". The memorandum also located the adoption of new policies in the area of social relations, health, education, culture, protection of the environment and consumers, within the dynamic content of citizenship. However, it recognised that the adoption of such policies and the rights and benefits which would flow from them also depended on the model of political union which had yet to emerge. To emphasise a new developing relationship between the European Union as a whole and the European citizen as the holder of a series of rights, concrete measures were proposed in the area of diplomatic and consular protection by Member States of nationals from other Member States. The memorandum suggested that the passport of the Union could serve as a means to identify European citizens to the authorities of third countries. In addition, in order to ensure the practical functioning of this *status civitatis*, the report suggested that a European ombudsman be introduced whose function it would be, in addition to the European Parliament's Committee on Petitions and the Court of Justice, to protect and safeguard the specific rights of European citizens. The report also briefly referred to the duties of European citizens, which was essentially recognition of the validity of obligations such as military service in the Member States, or its equivalent. Apart from reiterating that citizenship was one of the three pillars of the European Union, the report reaffirmed the need to make the establishment of the European Union credible in the eyes of public opinion. As such, citizenship was "the foundation on which the democratic legitimacy of such a Union rests".

The Danish delegation tended to support the Spanish proposals on citizenship. In particular, it supported the creation of an ombudsman system, although it preferred the creation of individual European ombudsmen at national level and the extension of voting rights at local level on the basis of residence.[85] With a view to strengthening the democratic basis for Community cooperation, the Danish called

---

[85]Laursen and Van Hoonacker, op. cit. note 83, at pp.293–303.

for greater control of Community affairs by the European and national parliaments. In addition, it wanted to see greater openness in the workings of the Community institutions: "This would mean *inter alia* that certain Council meetings should be public and that citizens should be given the opportunity of obtaining direct knowledge of general administrative acts which immediately concern them." The Danish were also strongly in favour of strengthening the social dimension of the Union. They considered it a necessary means to redistribute the benefits deriving from the internal market. Furthermore, it called for the inclusion of a fundamental series of principles in the new Treaty — access to work and education, social security, protection against individual accidents and disease, etc. — and a specific reference to the Community Charter of the Fundamental Social Rights of Workers.

The Portuguese identified the need to "bring[ing] the Community closer to citizens by responding to their deepest concerns and by providing an area with genuine equality of opportunity in the framework of the harmonious development of all Community States and regions in the light of the essential strengthening of economic and social cohesion".[86] One aspect of bringing the Community closer to its citizens was identified as a need to improve the representativeness of its institutions. It also campaigned for the introduction of the assent of the European Parliament with respect to the adoption of the uniform electoral procedure. With regard to citizenship, the Portuguese memorandum wisely advised that Community citizens be informed about what exactly was entailed by the concept of European citizenship, to avoid confusion arising with respect to national citizenship. They attached particular importance to the development of free movement, a general right of residence for all Community citizens, participation in local and European Parliament elections and provision of consular and diplomatic protection of each other's nationals outside the Community. They later argued against simply maintaining the unsatisfactory status quo with respect to rights of residence and the exclusion of fundamental rights.[87]

By the time the presidency of the European Council handed down its conclusions in Rome in December in 1990, European citizenship and democratic legitimacy had been detached from each other.[88] The Presidency asked the intergovernmental conference to consider the extent to which a number of rights could be enshrined in the amended Treaty to give substance to the concept of citizenship. These rights included participation in European Parliament elections and *possible* participation in local elections on the basis of residence, freedom of movement and residence detached from the exercise of an economic activity, equality of opportunity and treatment of all Community citizens and joint protection of Community citizens outside the Community's borders. The conclusions also referred to a possible mechanism for the defence of citizens' rights and urged that with respect to the implementation of citizenship rights that problems specific to particular Member States be taken into account.

[86]Ibid., at pp.304–312.
[87]CONF-UP 1821/91.
[88]*Agence Europe*, special edition, 16 December 1990; Bull. EC. 12-1990, pt. 1.7, p.10.

Following the conclusions of the European Council meeting and with reference to its previous memorandum on citizenship, Spain proposed that a specific title of the new Treaty be devoted to citizenship.[89] The Spanish delegation reiterated that the title on citizenship would be without prejudice to proposals in other related areas, such as judicial cooperation or public health, etc. The rights and duties of citizenship were to derive from the Union and were to be the very source of its democratic legitimacy and a fundamental pillar of its construction. The proposed Title O limited Union citizenship, from the outset to nationals of the Member States (Article 1) and emphasised that Union citizenship was additional to and did not substitute or replace the rights and duties of national citizenship. However, Article 1.3 proposed that the way be left open, on the basis of unanimity in Council, to extend Union citizenship to persons who are not citizens of the Union. In other words, it envisaged granting Union citizenship to persons who were not nationals of the Member States. Although the previous memorandum had distinguished between fundamental rights and citizenship, Article 2 of the subsequent proposal specifically referred to respect for fundamental rights by the Union and Member States and provided that the Union would lay down conditions to ensure that Union citizens and others (unspecified) could avail of those fundamental rights. Article 4 guaranteed the right to equal opportunities to all citizens and provided them with a right to develop their abilities to the full. Doubt was expressed in Council about the possible justiciability of this provision,[90] although some delegations, like the Portuguese, were in favour.[91] Article 5 contained a general prohibition on all forms of discrimination on grounds of nationality "in the application of this Treaty". Such a provision would have emphasised the principle of equal treatment as part of the personal status of citizens and not simply as a means to regulate the functioning of the Treaty. Citizenship was also to involve a right of unlimited free movement, although Union citizens were obliged to comply with the laws in the host Member State and could not evade duties which were incumbent on them. They were also to be allowed to take part in political life, join political organisations and vote on the basis of residence in European Parliament and local elections. Furthermore, they were to enjoy "the protection of the Union and that of each Member State under the same conditions as the nationals of that State" while in a third country. Rather than one single ombudsman, this second Spanish document proposed individual ombudsmen in each Member State whose duty it would be to assist the citizens of the Union in the defence of the rights conferred upon them by the Treaty, although the possibility of a European Ombudsman was not totally discounted. Ombudsmen were also to inform citizens of their rights and the means to enforce them. Where the Council acted to implement these provisions on citizenship it was to do so by qualified majority and in cooperation (or co-decision) with the European Parliament. However, it was still not clear what form the notion of European citizenship would

---

[89]CONF-UP 1731/91, 20 February, 1991.
[90]SN 1059/91.
[91]CONF-UP 1821/91.

be given. On the one hand, a formulation of specific rights could have been inserted in the Treaty to be implemented over a period of time according to a timetable established therein. Alternatively, a charter of citizens rights could have been adopted which would refer to already existing rights in legal texts and conventions. Finally an obligation could have been placed on Community institutions to define a series of citizenship rights in a number of domains in conjunction with the development of the Union.

The Commission, the only institution able to directly participate in the negotiations, also submitted an opinion.[92] It also opted for the idea that citizenship was a means to emphasis the need to involve Community citizens in the Community's activities with respect to policy areas which directly affected them. Of considerable significance, however, was its position on fundamental rights, which it argued were an essential element of any definition of citizenship. The Commission wanted to introduce a reference to the European Convention in the amended Treaty and referred to the proposal already made to the Council regarding accession to that convention. The European Parliament also regarded Union citizenship as additional to citizenship of a Member State and confined its enjoyment to Member State nationals.[93] However, it also envisaged that the Union might also define the conditions for the acquisition and loss of Union citizenship, which implied that Member State nationality might not be the only condition precedent for the enjoyment of Union citizenship. The European Parliament's report reiterated, in the main, the content of citizenship which had already been proposed by the other Member States and Commission. Like the Commission, the European Parliament was adamant that fundamental rights should be included in the amended Treaty. It recalled its declaration on fundamental rights and freedoms of 1989 and asked that it be included in the Treaty on the occasion of the intergovernmental conference. It also proposed inserting further articles guaranteeing the Union's respect for such rights. It proposed that the European Parliament and national parliaments should cooperate to draw up a list of fundamental rights which would not, however, be exhaustive and would not exclude future developments. The Union, it proposed, should promote the conclusion of international agreements on the protection of fundamental rights and states would not be allowed to accede to the Union without undertaking to respect fundamental rights. Respect for fundamental rights would be amenable to judicial review by the Court of Justice and further provisions were to be concluded on social rights. In addition to this broad respect for fundamental rights, the Bindi report proposed that a definition of persons resident in the Union be devised and that a measure of equal treatment be granted those persons with respect to their economic and professional activities, employment conditions and, possibly, political rights. The Member State delegations also discussed whether a reference to fundamental rights, or their protection in the context of the European Convention,

---

[92]Commission opinion of 21 October 1990 on the proposal for an amendment of the Treaty establishing the EEC with a view to Political Union, COM (90) 600, Bull. EC. Suppl. 2/91.

[93]See EP. Doc. A3-0300/91, Bindi Report for the Committee on Institutional Affairs on Union Citizenship, 6 November 1991.

would add anything to existing Community law. Reference was also made to protection of the fundamental rights of all persons, not simply citizens, and to the possibility of introducing a clause similar to Article 4 of the Parliament's 1984 Draft Treaty Establishing the European Union.[94] Finally, the draft Treaty presented by the Luxembourg presidency considered one of the aims of the Union to reinforce the protection of the rights and interests of its Member States' nationals through the introduction of a citizenship of the Union. Articles A–F on Union Citizenship were extremely similar to the Treaty text finally adopted at Maastricht. Fundamental rights did not figure in the provisions on Union citizenship, but a reference to the Union's respect for fundamental rights as guaranteed in the European Convention appeared in the common provisions of the draft Treaty.

1.7. Conclusions

This chapter has attempted to draft a rough model of citizenship which readers can refer to throughout the course of this book to determine whether citizenship is a suitable definition of the relationship between Community or Union citizens and the Community or Union and whether it correctly describes the rights (and duties) which that status entails, or may entail in the future. The rough model which has been suggested for this purpose refers to a status of membership, which entails a number of rights and duties which Member State nationals enjoy with reference to the principle of equality. This status of citizenship has a significant social and political content, since it determines the conditions in which individuals participate in society and how they legitimate the society in which they live and the authorities which govern them. Socio-economic, civil, political and even fundamental rights are all relevant constituents of this rough definition of citizenship in modern society.

In addition to this rough model of citizenship, this chapter has also outlined the development of the citizenship debate in the Community, which culminated in the adoption of the Treaty on European Union and the establishment of the status of Union citizenship. It might also be useful, in conclusion, to keep in mind some of the objectives which persuaded Member States to establish a status of Union citizenship. It appears from the various memoranda submitted during the course of the previous intergovernmental conference, that Community citizenship was seen as a reflection of the Community's democratic legitimacy. In addition, or perhaps as a corollary, it was seen as a means to bring citizens closer to the decision-making process in the Community and, therefore, to reduce the Community's democratic deficit. As a result, greater openness, accountability and transparency were considered essential ancillary objectives of the establishment of citizenship. Citizenship

---

[94]SN 1059/91. Article 4 provided that: "l'Union protége la dignité de l'individu et reconnaît à toute personne ... les droits et libertés fondamentaux tels qu'ils resultent notamment des principes communs des constitutions des Etats membres, ainsi que de la Convention Européenne de sauvegarde des droits de l'homme et des libertés fondamentales."

was also regarded as a means to improve the legal protection of Community citizens and, at least with reference to the right of free movement and residence, a means to improve and complete the efficient functioning of the internal market. There was also some suggestion that citizenship would serve as the basis for the development of a sense of identity between citizens and the Union, a sort of European identity, and would delimit the personal scope of the nascent political union.[95] With this model of citizenship and these considerations in mind, it is time to examine whether and to what extent an effective and meaningful status of citizenship can be said to exist in the European Community or Union.

[95]See Martiniello, M., "European Citizenship, European Identity and Migrants: Towards the Post-national State?", in Miles, R. and Thranhardt, D., *Migration and European Integration* (1995) London, Pinter Publishers, pp.37–52.

Chapter 2

Member State Nationality and Community Citizenship

2.1. Introduction

Articles 48 (1) and (2) refer to "workers" and "workers of the Member States" respectively. They do not specify who qualifies as workers for the purposes of Community law. In contrast, Article 1(1) of Regulation 1612/68 refers to employed persons, a category which it confines to nationals of the Member States.[1] The Court of Justice has also confirmed in a series of judgments that the free movement of workers is to be confined to Member State nationals.[2] Articles 52 (freedom of establishment) and Article 59 (freedom to provide services), both specifically refer to Member State nationals.[3] The enjoyment of the free movement of persons in Community law is thus dependent on the possession of the nationality of one of the Member States. This reliance on Member State nationality as the basis for the enjoyment of rights derived from Community law has been repeated in the Union Treaty where Article 8(1) provides that "Every person holding the nationality of a Member State shall be a citizen of the Union."

In order to maximise the uniform application and scope of its rules, the basic concepts and parameters of Community law have generally been defined by the Court of Justice, or the Community legislator, with reference to the objectives and

---

[1]Article 1(1) Regulation 1612/68, OJ No. L257/2, 19 October 1968, provides as follows: "Any national of a Member State, shall, irrespective of his place of residence, have the right to take up an activity as an employed person, and to pursue such activity, within the territory of another Member State in accordance with the provisions laid down by law." Note that an earlier version of this chapter first appeared in 12 *YEL* (1992) 353–384.

[2]See, for example, Case 238/83 *Meade* [1984] ECR 2631.

[3]Article 52 provides for the abolition of "restrictions on the freedom of establishment of nationals of a Member State". Article 59 provides for the abolition of restrictions on freedom to provide services "in respect of nationals of Member States".

scope of Community law.[4] This is the case, for example, for charges having an effect equivalent to customs duties, or measures having an effect equivalent to quantitative restrictions under the free movement of goods provisions (Articles 9 and 30
respectively).[5] Community law also determines what is an abuse of a dominant position in competition law (Article 86), or which Member State nationals qualify as
workers for the purposes of Article 48.[6] Even when the Court of Justice has felt unable to hand down a Community definition of a concept such as the public service
(Article 48(4)) or public policy (Article 48(3)), it has warned Member States that
they may not define these concepts unilaterally, free from judicial scrutiny, and has
attempted to lay down guidelines for their future reference.[7] Since Member State
nationality plays a fundamental role in determining the personal scope of the free
movement of persons and Union citizenship in Article 8, it is important to analyse
how and by whom Member State nationality is defined for the purposes of
Community law. A declaration on nationality annexed to the Union Treaty suggests that the determination of nationality is reserved exclusively to the Member
States.[8] The Court of Justice has also denied any Community competence in this
respect in the *Micheletti* case, although its decision was somewhat ambiguous.[9]
This exclusion of nationality from the tendency in the Court of Justice to devise
teleological Community definitions is significant precisely because of the fundamental role which the nationality laws of Member States play in fixing the parameters of free movement and Community citizenship.

This peculiar position of Member State nationality in the Community context
has not gone unnoticed.[10] Having set out aspects of the nationality question which
have already been touched by other authors, this chapter then discusses the possible effects on Member State nationality laws which may result from the development of the Community's free movement regime and the concept of Community
citizenship. It is hoped to emphasise the legal paradox in nationality being determined by Member States and not the Community, or at least not subject in any significant way to Community supervision or consultation, while at the same time it
serves as one of the chosen means to define the personal scope of the free movement of persons and the Community's concept of citizenship. It is also hoped to
demonstrate how the dynamics of free movement and the development of
Community citizenship may affect traditional approaches to the determination and

---

[4]On this "Community" method of interpretation see Merten de Wilmars, J., "Refléxions sur les
méthodes d'interprétation de la Cour de Justice des Communautés Européennes", 2 *Cahiers de Droit
Européen* (1986) 5-20, at 12.
    [5]See, for example, the definition of a measure having an effect equivalent to a quantitative restric-
tion in Case 8/74 *Procureur du Roi* v. *Dassonville* [1974] ECR 837.
    [6]See *infra* Part I, Chapter 3, "The Economic Parameters of Community Citizenship", Section 3.3.1.
    [7]See, for example, Case 149/79 *Commission* v. *Belgium* [1980] ECR 3881, at paras. 10–12; and
Case 30/77 *Bouchereau* [1977] ECR 1999, at paras.33–35.
    [8]The text of the declaration is reproduced *infra* in Section 2.6.
    [9]Case C-369/90 *M.V. Micheletti* v. *Delegación del Gobierno en Cantabria* [1992] ECR I-4239.
    [10]See, for example, Greenwood, C., "Nationality and the Limits of the Free Movement of Persons
in Community Law", 7 *YEL* (1987) 185–210; and Evans, A., "Nationality Law and European
Integration", 16 *ELRev* (1991) 190–215.

content of national state membership. Though the basic proposition, which is supported by international and Community legal practice, that Member States are competent to determine their nationals remains relatively unshaken, this chapter underlines some ways in which Community law has entered areas where state nationality was previously important, thereby putting Member States' unilateral definitions of nationality under increased pressure. In conclusion, the chapter suggests that domestic concepts of state membership encapsulated in unilateral Member State definitions of nationality may become increasingly incoherent as the rights contingent on free movement mature and as the Union advances its own concept of citizenship. By preserving nationality as the foundation for Union citizenship in Article 8(1), however, the Member States have arguably sought to protect the relationship which they enjoy with their own nationals. Member State nationality has ultimately survived the Union Treaty as the basis for the enjoyment of rights. It remains to be seen whether this dependence will endanger the development of a full-bodied status of citizenship in the European Union.

2.2. Nationality and Community Law

2.2.1. Nationality and the Scope of the Free Movement of Persons and Community Citizenship

As stated above, Article 48(1) simply guarantees freedom of movement for workers. Nevertheless, this reference to workers has been taken, in secondary implementing legislation to apply to Member State nationals only. Similarly, the principle of non-discrimination in Article 6 prohibits any discrimination on grounds of nationality. Although Member State nationality is not specified, this provision is confined to the scope of application of the Treaty and is therefore taken to apply to nationals of Member States only. However, the Court of Justice has never analysed the relationship between Article 1(1) of Regulation 1612/68 and Article 48(1) and the absence of a reference to nationality in the latter provision. Take, for example, *Levin* v. *Staatssecretariat van Justitie*.[11] The Court there concluded that Community law provisions on the free movement of workers also cover a national of a Member State who pursues part-time work which yields a low income. However, it confined itself to repeating the arguably conflicting provisions of Article 48(1) and Article 1(1) Regulation 1612/68 and did not address the absence of any reference to Member State nationality in the former.[12] It has simply maintained that the nationality of a Member State and the status of worker are two essential elements for the application of the Treaty rules on free movement.[13]

[11]Case 53/81 [1982] ECR 1035.
[12]Ibid., at paras.7–9.
[13]In Case 238/83 *Meade*, op. cit. note 2, at 2641, Advocate General Mancini argued that: "I might add that the workers referred to in Article 48 must be Community citizens [in this context, Member State nationals]. That article itself confirms it. In any event there is no doubt that the authors of the Treaties of Paris and Rome intended to limit freedom of movement to citizens of the Member States: see the express provisions to that effect in Article 69 of the ECSC Treaty and Article 96 of the EAEC Treaty."

As Chapter 3 demonstrates, the Court's definition of worker does not hinge on being a national of a Member State, but on objective aspects of the employment relationship in question. Member State nationality was thus inserted in Community secondary legislation to define the beneficiaries of free movement for other reasons. It can be regarded as (i) a political choice by the drafters of early Community legislation to exclude third country nationals from the free movement regime; (ii) a legal and political choice not to interfere with Member State competence to determine nationality, despite the fact that the personal scope and application of Community rules in the area of free movement depend on that determination; and (iii) determination on the part of the Member States to maintain nationality as the ultimate basis for the enjoyment of rights in Community law. Thus, in addition to performance of an economic activity,[14] the beneficiaries of free movement generally have to be Community nationals. Union citizenship in Article 8 has also been confined to "every person holding the nationality of a Member State".[15] Non-Community nationals do not benefit from the free movement of persons regime unless they can derive rights from their relationship with a Community worker or self-employed person (Article 10, Regulation 1612/68), or pursuant to association or cooperation agreements concluded between the Community and third countries.[16] The *Rush Portuguesa* decision similarly suggested that limited rights of free movement might also exist for the third country employees of a provider of services.[17] Following the adoption of the SEA, Article 7(a) refers broadly to "an area without internal frontiers in which the free movement of ... persons is ensured". However, this provision has been the subject of considerable controversy.[18]

---

[14]See, for example, Case 36/74 *Walrave and Koch* v. *Association Union Cycliste Internationale* [1975] ECR 1405; Case 13/76 *Donà* v. *Mantero* [1976] ECR 1333; Case 196/87 *Udo Steymann* [1988] ECR 6159.

[15]See previously Article 3 of the European Parliament's Draft Treaty establishing the European Union, OJ 1984 C77/33: "The citizens of the Member States shall *ipso facto* be citizens of the Union. Citizenship of the Union shall be dependent upon citizenship of a Member State; it may not be independently acquired or forfeited"; and Article 25(3) of the Declaration of Fundamental Rights and Freedoms, OJ 1989 C120/51.

[16]See, for example, the EEC–Turkey Association Agreement, affirmed by Council Decision 64/732, OJ 1973 C113/1 and Maresceau, M., "Nationals of Third Countries in Agreements Concluded by the EC", 4 *Actualités du Droit* (1994/2) 249–263. The Commission has proposed a review of the implementation of these agreements in its Communication on immigration and asylum, COM (94) 23 final, 23 February 1994.

[17]Case 113/89 [1990] ECR 1417; Joined Cases 62 and 63/81 *SECO* v. *EVI* [1982] ECR 223; and Case C-43/93 *Van Der Elst* v. *Office des Migrations Internationales* [1995] CMLR 513. See also Verschueren, H., "L'àrret *Rush Portuguesa*: un nouvel apport au principe de la libre circulation des travailleurs dans le droit communautaire", 60 *Revue du droit des étrangers* (1990) 231–237; and Desmazières de Sechelles, "Freedom of Movement of Workers and Freedom of Services (some considerations on the employees of the provider of services with specific reference to France for illustration purposes)", in *Free Movement of Persons: Problems and Experiences* (1993) Martinus Nijhoff, Dordrecht.

[18]In Case C-445/93, *European Parliament* v. *Commission*, OJ 1994 C1/12, the European Parliament is seeking a declaration that the Commission has failed to present the necessary proposals to permit realisation of the free movement of persons in Article 7(a). The Commission has since proposed a regulation based on Article 100(c) determining the third countries whose nationals must possess a

The Commission is of the view that the free movement of persons can only operate effectively if "persons" in Article 7(a) refers also to third country nationals within the Community.[19] Some Member States have vigorously rejected this interpretation.[20] A determination to exclude third country nationals from the scope of free movement is also evident in the relegation of asylum and immigration issues to a non-Community pillar of the Union Treaty.

The restriction of free movement does not automatically follow from the text of the Treaty since Article 48(1), unlike Articles 52 and 59, refers only to freedom of movement for workers and contains no qualification on grounds of nationality.[21] Though the Common Market was aimed at the promotion of economic activity and consequently, the elimination of barriers to such activity as between Member States,[22] there seems to be no sound reason to ignore the influence and effect extra-Community elements may have on the internal situation; on the contrary, it seems unwise. Indeed, the fact that only Community nationals enjoyed equality of treatment may have rendered third country workers more attractive to prospective employers in the Community.[23] The abolition of obstacles to freedom of movement *as between Member States* in Article 3(c), could have involved the creation of an internal free movement zone between Member States, regardless of nationality, rather than the total exclusion of third country nationals from the benefits to be derived from free movement in the Community. This argument gains support from a literal reading of the text of Articles 48(1) and (2). The former refers to free movement for

visa when crossing an external frontier. There is also talk of a proposal to allow third country nationals to enter the territory of another Member State for a short stay without a visa and the Standing Committee for employment has requested that the obstacles to employment in another Member State be removed for third country nationals with permanent residence. See generally Bosscher, A., "Free Movement of Workers and Migration", in *The Future of the European Social Policy* (1994) Louvain University Press, Louvain-la-Neuve, pp.199–205, at p.200.

[19]See the Commission Communication on the lifting of border controls, SEC (92) 877 final: "The phrase `free movement ... of persons' in Article 8(a) [now 7(a)] refers to all persons, whether or not they are economically active and irrespective of their nationality."

[20]See, for example, the disagreement reported in *Agence Europe* no.5892, 7/1/1993.

[21]For a discussion of the exclusion of nationality from the text of Article 48(1), see Verschueren, op. cit. note 17 at 236 and Le Rapport Spaak, Rapport des Chefs de Délégations aux Ministères des Affaires Etrangéres, Bruxelles, 1956, pp.18 and 88–91. The authors of the Treaty thought in terms of the mobility of the available workforce, which would indicate residence in the Community, rather than nationality, as the point of reference.

[22]Article 3(c) provides that the activities of the Community shall include an internal market characterised by "the abolition, *as between Member States*, of obstacles to the free movement of goods, persons, services and capital" (emphasis added).

[23]See Evans, A., "European Citizenship", 45 *Modern Law Review* (1982) 497–515, at 498; Bohning, W.R. and Werquin, J., *Some Economic, Social and Human Rights Considerations Concerning the Future of Third Country Nationals in the Single European Market*, ILO Working Paper (1990), at p.9; Gaja, G., "I lavoratori stranieri in Italia" (1984) *Società Editrice Il Mulino* 123–155, at 154; Werner, H., "Free Movement of Labour in the Single European Market", 25 *Intereconomics* (1990) 77–81, at 79; Wihtol de Wenden, C. "The Absence of Rights: the Position of Illegal Immigrants", in Layton Henry, Z. (ed.), *The Political Rights of Migrant Workers in Western Europe* (1990) Sage Publications, at p.33; and Simon, G., "Une Europe communautaire de moins en moins mobile", 7 *Revue européenne des migrations internationales* (1991) 41–61. For details of recent intra-EC migration and migration from outside the EC see Eurostat (1993), Eurostat CD-ROM database ed. and Rapid Reports: Population and Social Conditions no.6.

workers, while the latter refers to nationality in the context of the abolition of any discrimination based on nationality, but specifies the "workers of the Member States".[24] It is perfectly conceivable that what was envisaged was a free movement zone with a common external policy towards third country labour, similar to the system instituted for the free movement of goods. Thus, once workers of whatever nationality legally entered the Community, they could move freely within that area without being subject to restriction. Meanwhile, the principles of non-discrimination and priority for Community nationals seeking employment, could have operated exclusively with respect to Community nationals.[25] Member State nationals would thus have enjoyed a right of free movement, as well as benefiting from the principle of non-discrimination, while workers from third countries would only have enjoyed a right of free movement.[26] This debate on the personal scope of Article 48 highlights the alternatives now discussed with respect to the scope of Article 7(a) and the free movement of persons in an area without internal frontiers. At this point in Community history, however, discussion of the scope of Article 48 is somewhat academic, given the restriction of the benefits of the free movement of workers to Member State nationals in secondary legislation and in the case law of the Court of Justice.

2.2.2. Nationality and the Reserved Domain of Member States in the Community Context

The personal scope of the free movement of workers, establishment and services is thus partly determined by the possession of Member State nationality. The question nevertheless arises whether the determination of nationality for the purposes of Community law remains within the reserved domain of Member States, as is traditionally the case in public international law. Although the 1930 Hague Convention mentioned the possibility of restrictions in this field, it is generally recognised that at the present stage of development of international relations states are competent to determine who their nationals are. Has the creation of the Community and the transfer of sovereignty from Member States to the Community which its establishment has entailed affected any changes in this respect? For ex-

---

[24]Article 48(2) provides that "freedom of movement shall entail the abolition of any discrimination based on *nationality* between *workers* of the Member States as regards employment, remuneration and other conditions of work and employment" (emphasis added).

[25]See Bohning, W.R., "The Scope of the EEC System of Free Movement of Workers: A Rejoinder", 10 *CMLRev* (1973) 81–84; and Plender R., "Freedom of Movement in the European Communities", in *International Migration Law*, 2nd edn. (1988) Martinus Nijhoff, Dordrecht, at p.197.

[26]Member State nationality is not specified in Article 48(3), which could be taken as support for this interpretation. Only Article 48(c)(3) embodies aspects of the principle of non-discrimination. In support of this interpretation see the Commission's communication on the lifting of border controls, op. cit., at para.6: "the free movement of persons in the common market must not be confused with the rights which flow directly from Articles 48 to 66, and in particular the taking up of economic activities as self-employed or employed persons and hence the right of residence, and which ... apply only to nationals of Member States".

ample, could the Community influence a Member State's determination of its nationals for the purposes of Community law in general and free movement in particular, by requiring such a determination to be in conformity with the objectives of the Community, or by requiring Member States to consult the Community with respect to the development or amendment of their nationality laws?[27]

Two schools of thought exist on this subject. On the one hand, it is argued that no concrete transfer of sovereignty has taken place regarding nationality and that an implicit transfer, bound up with the functional and uniform operation of free movement, would be impossible in an area which closely touches on a traditional sovereign power of the state.[28] Member States have clearly retained their statehood both in Community[29] and international law.[30] Some argue that to do away with a Member State's competence to define their personal substrata alters their autonomous status as states. This status remains relevant for international and municipal purposes regardless of Community law. On their respective accessions to the Community, the former Federal German Republic and the United Kingdom introduced declarations clarifying their definitions of nationality for Community law purposes. These declarations are seen, by those claiming that nationality remains entirely within Member State competence, as a continued assertion of state jurisdiction in this field. The ambiguity created in the Federal Republic of Germany by Article 116(1) of the Basic Law on the status of citizens of the Democratic Republic required clarification. Did nationality for the purposes of Community law involve the present holders of German nationality, or did it also involve the wider category of German national linked to the previous German Reich to which Article 116(1) referred?[31] A unilateral declaration appended to the German signature of the Treaty indicated that the wider construction was to serve for the purposes of Community law. By including all the original inhabitants of East Germany as well

[27]For an early analysis of this suggestion see Bleckmann, "The Personal Jurisdiction of the European Communities", 17 *CMLRev* (1980) 467–485, at 477.

[28]See D'Oliveira, H.U.J. and Evans, A., "Nationality and Citizenship", in Cassese, A., Clapham, A. and Weiler, J.H.H., *Human Rights and the European Community. Towards 1992 and Beyond: Methods of Protection*, Vol.2 (1991) Nomos, Baden Baden, pp.299–348.

[29]See, for example, the arrangements for the election of the European Parliament in Articles 137, 138(1) and (2), which presuppose the existence of separate Member States; and the European Parliament's Resolution on a Uniform Electoral Procedure which proposes a scheme for allocating the seats of members, OJ 1992 C176/72.

[30]A complaint cannot be directed against the European Communities as a collective in the context of the European Convention for Human Rights and Fundamental Freedoms. Complainants must sue the Member States individually in their sovereign capacity as contracting parties. The Commission has recently reiterated its proposal for the Community to jointly accede to the ECHR, SEC (90) 2087 fin, 19/11/1990; see also the European Parliament's Resolution on Accession, OJ 1994 44/32, 14 February 1994. The Court of Justice has been asked by the Council to deliver an opinion on accession. Accession to the European Convention on Human Rights would go a small way in weakening individual Member State personality in international law.

[31]Article 116(1) of the Basic Law provided: "Unless otherwise provided by law, a German within the meaning of this Basic Law is a person who possesses German citizenship or who has been admitted to the territory of the German Reich as it existed on 31 December 1937 as a refugee or expellee of German stock."

as expellees of German stock (*Aussiedler*) as potential beneficiaries of free movement, this unilateral declaration had the effect of considerably widening, at the time theoretically, the scope of free movement.[32] Following the entry into force of the British Nationality Act, 1981, the United Kingdom amended its original declaration on nationality for the purposes of Community law[33] to the effect that, only British citizens, British subjects without citizenship but possessing the right of abode and citizens of the British Dependent Territories deriving that status by virtue of a connection with Gibraltar, were to be regarded as nationals of the United Kingdom.[34]

In the alternative, there are those who argue that since nationality was chosen by the Community as a criterion for the application of Community law, it is open to the Community to make exceptions to it.[35] The Court of Justice has affirmed its pivotal role in the definition of "worker", "services" and "economic activity" – the other means by which the personal and material scope of Community law in the area of the free movement of persons is defined.[36] It has also insisted on a Community definition of public service and insists that the concept of public policy should not be unilaterally determined by Member States without being subject to the control of the Community institutions. With respect to both of these issues the Court of Justice is equally confronted with aspects of the sovereign power of Member States linked to their notions of nationality and citizenship. Since nationality is a means to define the personal scope of free movement and since it is also a means chosen by the Community,[37] it has been argued that the determination of

---

[32]In a different context in Case 14/74 *Norddeutsches Vich-und FleischkontorGmbh* [1974] ECR 899, the protocol on German Internal Trade was said not to make the GDR part of the Community.

[33]Commonwealth citizenship was considered overbroad for the purposes of Community law. The original declaration is to be found in Cmnd 4862 I (1972) 11. It covered persons who were citizens of the UK and Colonies, or a British subject not possessing that citizenship, or the citizenship of any other Commonwealth country who had a right of abode in the UK and were consequently exempt from its immigration control and persons who were citizens of the UK and Colonies by association with Gibraltar. Section 2 of the 1971 Immigration Act specified those who had the right of abode; they were known as patrials. See Hartley, T.C., *EEC Immigration Law* (1978) European Studies in Law, Amsterdam, North Holland, at p.68.

[34]Cmnd 9062 (1983); On the subject of British nationality and the European Communities, see Greenwood, op. cit. note 10; Simmonds, K., "The British Nationality Act 1981 and the Definition of the Term 'National' for Community Purposes", 21 *CMLRev* (1984) 675–686; Evans, A., "Nationality Law and the Free Movement of Persons in the EEC", 2 *YEL* (1982) 173–189; Plender, op. cit. note 25; Hartley, op. cit. note 33; MacDonald, *Immigration Law and Practice* (1983) London, Butterworths, at pp.92 *et seq.*; and Fransman, L., *British Nationality Law* (1989) London, Fourmat Publishing, at pp.134 *et seq.*

[35]See Hartley, op. cit. note 33, at p.78; Evans, op. cit. note 34, at 177; Greenwood, op. cit. note 10, at 187 *et seq.*

[36]Thus, for example, in Case 75/63 *Hoekstra (née Unger)* [1964] ECR 177, at p.184, it held that the term worker was to be given a Community scope, to avoid Member States being able to fix or vary the category of persons eligible for the protection afforded by the free movement provisions in the Treaty.

[37]The Community could alternatively have chosen to regulate free movement in terms of lawful residence and presence on the territory of the Member States, which was the means chosen to determine the application of the European Convention of Human Rights, 4/11/1950, Trb. 1951 no.154 which states in Article 1 that: "The High Contracting Parties shall secure to everyone within their jurisdiction

which nationals qualify for the enjoyment of free movement is also a question for Community law, or at least one which Member States cannot unilaterally dispose of without reference to Community law. Approached from this perspective, the aforementioned declarations are acceptable, not simply as an exercise of state competence, but as an exercise of state competence in a manner compatible with the principles of Community law. In this way, any alterations of their nationality laws by Member States will not necessarily be compatible with Community law and will be recognised by the Court of Justice only to the extent that they are.

2.2.3. Arguments in Favour of Community Competence in the Field of Nationality

It is not unknown for Community action in the area of free movement to incidentally affect matters which remain within the competence of Member States. Although Member States continue, in principle, to determine who their nationals are in accordance with domestic and international law, the Community could still be regarded as acting within its jurisdiction if, in pursuance of its policies and objectives in the area of free movement and the establishment of Union citizenship, it influences the exercise of this Member State competence. The primary actors in determining nationality would thus continue to be the Member States. The Court of Justice and Community legislator are not competent to positively impose a definition of nationality on a Member State, but they might be acting within their competence if they held that the consequences of a particular Member State definition were incompatible with the objectives of the Community and Union. This is an application of the theory of functional powers which the Court of Justice has been willing to apply in other areas of free movement, in cases concerning national demographic and educational policies, both of which remain, in principle, within the sphere of national competence.[38] Thus, in *Casagrande*, the Court held that: "Although educational and training policy is not as such included in the spheres which the Treaty has entrusted to the Community institutions, it does not follow that the exercise of powers transferred to the Community is in some way limited if it is of such a nature as to affect the measures taken in the exercise of a policy such as that of education and training."

The Union aims at the creation of an ever closer union among the peoples of Europe and the organisation, "in a manner demonstrating consistency and solidarity, relations between the Member States and between their peoples".[39] The primary aim of the Court's teleological method of interpretation is to give primacy to the general purposes of the Treaty and to construe its particular provisions in the

---

the rights and freedoms defined in Section I of this Convention. Furthermore, the EC Treaty has opted for residence, rather than nationality, as the basis for some of the rights incorporated in Union citizenship." See, in particular, Articles 8(d), 138(d) and 138(e).

[38]See Case 65/81 *Reina* v. *Landeskreditbank* [1982] ECR 33 and Case 9/74 *Casagrande* v. *Landeshauptstadt Munchen* [1974] ECR 773, respectively.

[39]Articles A TEU paras.2 and 3.

light of those purposes. D'Oliveira has cogently argued in favour of this teleological approach in the context of reverse discrimination: "Whether or not the Community legal system is brought in cannot depend, at any rate not exclusively, on some sort of catalogue of contacts or factual points of reference. It depends partly, perhaps even predominantly, on the very teleology and dynamics of the Community legal system."[40] The spirit of the Treaty and the Community's objectives should be relevant in the determination of the personal scope and application of the beneficiaries of Community citizenship and free movement to avoid unilateral restriction or expansion of their scope. Indeed, if one of the Community's objectives in establishing Union citizenship is to strengthen the rights and interests of Community citizens, as Article B suggests, it is arguable that nationality can no longer survive as the sole basis for the enjoyment of the rights of free movement and Community citizenship. Evans argues that one of the reasons for maintaining nationality in Article 8 is to preserve the direct relationship between Member States and their nationals and to foreclose any possible expansion of Community rights independent of this relationship.[41] There may, therefore, be a clash between the pro-citizen objectives in Articles A and B TEU and Article 8 and the condition of nationality which is unilaterally determined by the Member States. This type of conflict has been avoided with respect to the determination of Community "workers". If nationality is a matter to be unilaterally determined by Member States, without reference to Community law, the communitarian scope of the concept of worker is, to a certain extent, emptied of its meaning and purpose. If a conflict between Community citizenship and Member State nationality is resolved by foreclosing any possible expansion of the rights which Community citizens enjoy independently of their Member State nationality on the basis of Community law, the objectives with respect to citizenship in Title I of the Union Treaty should be read with some caution. Although "Member States cannot by means of declarations alter the meaning of expressions in the founding treaties which fall to be determined by Community law",[42] their unilateral definitions of nationality apply before those expressions in the founding treaties can come into play at all. Member States can thus restrict the scope of free movement with reference to their nationality laws and a lack of uniformity between them may exist in this respect. It is also open to Member States to considerably extend the beneficiaries of free movement and Union citizenship by generously defining their nationals. It could be argued that the Court of Justice has bowed on occasion to national definitions of certain concepts used in Community law, such as for example the definition of "spouse" in

---

[40]See D'Oliveira, "Is Reverse Discrimination Still Permissible under the SEA?", in *Forty Years On: The Evolution of Postwar Private International Law in Europe* (1990) Kluwer Academic Publishers, Dordrecht, pp.71–86, at p.75.

[41]See Evans, A.C., "Union Citizenship and the Equality Principle", in Antola, E. and Rosas, A. (eds.), *A Citizens' Europe: In Search of a New Legal Order* (1995) London, Sage Publications, pp.85–112.

[42]See Plender, op. cit. note 25, at p.199.

Reed.[43] However, the admission of national definitions in such cases does not have the same fundamental capacity to preclude the application of Community law as reliance on unilateral Member State definitions of nationality, which determine the application of Community law from the outset. In the particular case of *Reed*, at issue was the extent or application of the principle of equal treatment rather than the application of Community law as a preliminary matter.

2.3. Treatment of the Reserved Domain of Member States in Community Law

National, international and Community law generally accept, therefore, that the determination of nationality is a matter chiefly, if not exclusively, within the competence of Member States. The policy of the Court of Justice seems to have originally been to avoid controlling the correctness of the nationality of persons presenting themselves in litigation. The sensitivity of this issue was evident in the *Airola* case,[44] where the Court was confronted with an example of discrimination in the case of a Belgian woman compulsorily subject under Italian law to a change of nationality, which she was legally unable to renounce, when marrying her Italian husband. Women alone were subject to this compulsory acquisition of nationality which was clearly discriminatory. The Court could have rejected the operation of Italian nationality law as contrary to the broad notion of non-discrimination in Article 6 and the principle of equal treatment in work for men and women in Article 119 (the case was a staff case which arose in the context of an expatriation allowance). By accepting the nationality of the plaintiff, but denying its effect in the instant case,[45] the Court could be said to have recognised the primordial importance of a Member State's right to regulate its own nationality.

The question of nationality was not so easy to side-step in *Micheletti* v. *Delegación del Gobierno en Cantabria*, where the right of a dual national (Community/third country) to avail of the free movement provisions in another Member State was directly at issue.[46] The Court and Advocate General reiterated

---

[43]Case 59/85 [1986] ECR 1283, at paras.13–15: "In the absence of any indication of a general social development which could justify such a broad construction [that spouse include unmarried partners] ... the term 'spouse' in Article 10 of the Regulation refers to a marital relationship only."

[44]Case 21/74 [1975] ECR 221.

[45]It did so by undermining the importance of nationality in the Staff Regulations at issue and interpreting it in such a way as to avoid any unwarranted difference of treatment as between male and female officials so that it was "necessary to define the concept of an official's present or previous nationality under Article 4(a) of Annex VII as excluding nationality imposed by law on a female official upon her marriage with a national of another state, when she has no possibility of renouncing it"; see also Case 37/74 *Van den Broeck* v. *Commission* [1975] ECR 235.

[46]The case involved a dual Argentine/Italian national, recently arrived in Spain, who sought to rely on the Treaty provisions on the freedom of establishment in his capacity as an orthodontist. He was refused residence by the Spanish authorities which, in cases of dual nationality, referred to the last or effective *de facto* residence, which in the instant case was Argentina (Article 9(9) of the Spanish Civil Code). For a discussion of the *Micheletti* case see Bouza i Vidal, N., "El Ambito Personal de Aplicación del Derecho de Establecimiento en los Supuestos de Doble Nacionalidad", 20 *Revista de Instituciones Europeas* (1993) 563–581.

Community law's adherence to the principle that Member States determine their own nationality.[47] The Advocate General referred to Article 8 and the Union Treaty declaration on nationality and stated that no definition of Community nationality exists at the present time. The Court held that the free movement provisions do not require that a choice be made between two nationalities. Once an individual produces the appropriate documents to establish possession of the nationality of a Member State Community law may apply.[48] In its view, municipal law could not be allowed to restrict free movement by requiring that a Member State's determination of nationality be subject to additional unilaterally determined conditions. This was said to be the case independently of when or how the nationality in question is acquired and independently of the fact that the person who avails of it has another nationality. This position is supported by the Court's previous judgment in *Ministère Public* v. *Auer*, where it stated that:

> There is no provision of the Treaty which, within the field of application of the Treaty, makes it possible to treat nationals of a Member State differently according to the time at which, or the manner in which, they acquired the nationality of that State, as long as, at the time at which they rely on the benefit of the provisions of Community law, they possess the nationality of one of the Member States and that, the other conditions for the application of the rule on which they rely are fulfilled.[49]

To allow Member States to apply their diverse means of resolving which nationality should apply in cases of dual nationality would be to allow a fundamental freedom guaranteed by the Treaty in the same way to all Community citizens to be prejudiced by the internal criteria applied by Member States in such cases.

This noble defence of the uniformity of free movement skilfully ignores the fact that the personal scope of free movement and Community citizenship is generally contingent on individual Member States' determinations of nationality. In *Micheletti*, the Court would not permit a Member State to subordinate the application of a fundamental Treaty guarantee (free movement) to grounds (Article 9(9) of the Spanish Civil Code) unforeseen by the Community norms regulating that guarantee (in this case Directive 73/148). However, neither the Court nor the Commission and Council have been prepared to interfere with a Member State's ability to foreclose the applicability of free movement and Union citizenship from the outset, with reference to their definitions of nationality. There is a certain irony in the Court stating in *Micheletti* that: "Cette conclusion s'impose d'autant plus qu'admettre une telle possibilité aurait pour conséquence que le champ d'application personnel des règles communautaires portant sur la liberté d'établissement pourrait varier d'un Etat membre à l'autre."[50] As Community law stands, the extent to which the free movement rules can be applied and to whom they apply depend, from one Member State to the next, on unilateral national determinations of

[47]Ibid., at para.10.
[48]Although this does not suffice if the facts of the case are purely internal to a Member State: *Regina* v. *Immigration Appeal Tribunal* [1987] Immigration Appeal Reports 359; and *infra* Chapter 8.
[49]Case 136/78 [1979] ECR 437, at para.28; see also Case 292/86 *Gullung* [1988] ECR 111.
[50]Case C-369/90, op. cit. note 9, at para.12 and Advocate General Tesauro, at para.6.

nationality. Furthermore, by reaffirming its position in *Auer* to the effect that possession of a Member State nationality is valid regardless of when or how that nationality is acquired, the Court of Justice has left Member States no room to inspect the genuineness of nationality claims. It has been more willing, in other contexts, to protect Member States from the possibility of individuals enjoying the rights of free movement on the basis of suspicious claims.[51]

2.3.1. Consequences of Exclusive Member State Competence in the Field of Nationality Law

It should be emphasised that the consequences of this confirmation of exclusive Member State competence in the field of nationality are not academic. Recent proposals in the Netherlands seek to formally amend the naturalisation laws and to facilitate the naturalisation of legal immigrants who have been resident in the Netherlands for a certain number of years.[52] Legislation previously required that the naturalisation applicant do everything reasonably possible to get rid of his or her previous nationality.[53] To encourage immigrants to avail of the provisions of the new regime, it is proposed that they will be permitted to retain their previous nationality. A government circular presently exists regarding the acceptance of dual nationality of persons who want to acquire Dutch nationality by naturalisation and a government proposal formally abolishing Article 9 para.1 sub. b is soon expected.[54] Though the general criteria for the acquisition of nationality may not be substantially altered, this concession, allowing foreign residents to retain their nationality of origin, is fundamentally important. One of the standard reasons for low naturalisation figures is the deterrent factor involved in the loss of previous nationality.[55] In accordance with the ruling in *Micheletti*, the beneficiaries of this new naturalisation regime will qualify for free movement since they possess the nationality of a Member State of the Community. This would also entitle them to the enjoyment of the rights of Union citizenship, despite retention of their third country

---

[51]See variously Advocate General Slynn in Joined Cases 35 and 36/82 *Morson and Jhanjan* [1982] ECR 3723 (immigration controls), at 3742; and Case 61/89 *Marc Gaston Bouchoucha* [1990] ECR I-3551 (vocational training qualifications), at 3568.

[52]See the Dutch Government's Memorandum "Rechtspositie en sociale integratie" announced and summarised in St.crt. 1991, 94; and Hoogenboom, T., "Free Movement and Integration of Non-EEC Nationals and the Logic of the Internal Market", in *Free Movement of Persons in Europe: Problems and Experiences*, op. cit. note 17.

[53]Article 9 para. 1 sub. b of the nationality law of 1984.

[54]See de Groot, G.R. and Bollen, C., "Nationality Law and the Kingdom of the Netherlands", in Nascimbene, B. (ed.), *Nationality Laws of Member States in the European Union*, forthcoming, Le Giuffre, Butterworths.

[55]See Article 20 of the Spanish nationality law of 13/7/1982; Article 17 of the Swiss nationality law of 29/9/1952; and the Council of Europe Convention of 6/5/1963, which provides for the loss of original nationality on the voluntary acquisition of another. Article 7 of Luxembourg nationality law, 26/6/1975, provides that naturalisation will be refused to applicants whose countries permit them to maintain their nationality, unless they can prove that they have not availed of this facility. For details of naturalisation procedures in a number of European states see de Rham, G., "The Politics of Citizenship Acquisition", in Layton Henry, op. cit. note 23, pp.158–185, at p.158.

nationalities. This situation might give rise to particular difficulties regarding the exercise of diplomatic protection in the circumstances outlined in Article 8(c).

Furthermore, the definition of nationality in some Member States draws no distinction between nationality for municipal, international or Community law purposes. Under Portuguese nationality law, for example, persons born in Macao to a Portuguese parent acquire that nationality by birth, while naturalisation is available to aliens who reside in Macao for a particular period. Being a Portuguese national by virtue of a connection with Macao rather than Portugal does not prevent such a person from being a Portuguese national for Community purposes; 100,000 citizens of Macao are consequently eligible to avail themselves of free movement. A similar dispensation is not made with respect to the 3.25 million citizens of Hong Kong, which pursuant to Article 227(3) is not an overseas territory or country. In 1971, Portugal concluded a convention with Brazil which extended equality as regards certain civic rights and duties to all Brazilian nationals in line with Article 15 para.5 of the Portuguese Constitution. The convention did not extend to the issue of nationality and Brazilians must apply in accordance with normal Portuguese naturalisation procedure. In the event that Portugal did conclude an agreement on the issue of dual nationality, as Spain has with other South American countries, the beneficiaries of such an agreement would also qualify for the benefits of Community law in the area of free movement and citizenship.[56] If one accepts that the Community has no competence as regards nationality it would not necessarily be consulted on the conclusion of such an agreement, although the contours of the free movement of persons would be altered and the number of its beneficiaries increased.

No Community institution or Member State has objected to any national measure in this field and the declaration on nationality annexed to the TEU suggests that it is not at least their political intention to do so. The European Parliament has adopted resolutions, however, which refer to undesirable developments in municipal nationality law. Prior to the adoption of the British Nationality Act 1981, it criticised certain aspects of the nationality bill, in particular, the fact that children born of British parents in another Member State or elsewhere in the world would no longer automatically be entitled to pass British nationality on to their children should they also be born outside the United Kingdom. It pointed out with reference to the changes in British nationality legislation that "since there are differences between the Member States' nationality laws, there would be the risk that some children might be born stateless as a result of these changes, and that nationals of Member States may consequently be reluctant to exercise their rights of freedom of movement and freedom of establishment".[57] It therefore urged Member States to further harmonise their nationality laws to prevent statelessness, but it recalled from the outset that the definition of nationality for the purposes of EC law is the

---

[56]See the contribution of Duarte, M.L. (Portuguese report) to the 1992 FIDE conference, *New Aspects of the Free Movement of Persons: Towards a European Citizenship*, pp.320–364, at pp.346 and 347.
[57]OJ 1981 C260/100.

responsibility of each Member State. Indeed, the recent Imbeni Report on citizenship for the Parliamentary Civil Liberties and Internal Affairs Committee distanced itself from any proposal to abolish Member State nationality: "Such a move would, however, deprive the Member States as such of their legitimacy since they would lose the social foundation on which their legitimacy is based."[58] The persuasive effect of Parliament's intervention in the British case is evidenced in sections 2 and 3 of the British Nationality Act, 1981, which give rise to the very possibility of statelessness.[59] The European Parliament has also proposed the establishment of certain uniform rules on the acquisition and loss of Member State nationality given the creation of Union citizenship,[60] but its resolutions are not binding.

The German declaration on nationality included East German nationals and expellees of German stock within the concept of free movement even prior to reunification, thus granting them the legal right to immigrate to Member States as workers or self-employed persons. In practice, only those who entered the West as refugees were able to benefit from free movement, first, because they had no legal right under East German law at the time to leave the country, and secondly, because they lacked the requisite travel documents under Community law (although this fact was never likely to legally work against them in the actual event that they succeeded in leaving East Germany). The means by which the reunification of Germany was accommodated by the Community is of some interest in this regard.[61] The integration of the reunified Germany into the Community took place without the revision of the existing Treaties.[62] In the context of free movement, the completion of the reunification process rendered the original declaration on nationality a reality, releasing the actual benefits of free movement and a more lucrative

---

[58]EP Doc. A3-0437/93, 21/12/1993.

[59]Transmission of British citizenship is automatic to the first extra-territorially born generation (ss.2,14,16 and 23), but thereafter it depends upon the child having a grandparent born or naturalised in the UK and a parent having spent three years there before the birth of the child (ss.3(2)-(4) and 17(2)-(4)), or upon both parents and the child spending three years there after the birth; in both cases registration is required. See Killerby, M., "Nationalité et statut personnel dans la nouvelle loi sur la nationalité britannique", in Verwilghen, M. (ed.), *Nationalité et statut personnel. Leur interaction dans les traités internationaux et dans les legislations nationales* (1984) Bruylant, Brussels, pp.239–260, at p.252.

[60]See, for example, the European Parliament's Resolution on Union Citizenship following the Bindi Report (DOC A3-0300/91): "The Union may establish certain uniform conditions governing the acquisition or loss of the citizenship of the Member States, by virtue of the procedure laid down for the revision of the Treaty." See also the EP Resolution on the basis of Doc. A3-0025/93 on fundamental rights in the Community, OJ C115/178, which called for replacement of *jus sanguinis* by *jus soli* as a basis for nationality and argued that the obstacles to naturalisation in the EC were a source of discrimination.

[61]See generally, O'Keeffe, D., "The Legal Implications of East Germany's Membership of the European Community", *LIEI* (1991) 1–18.

[62]See the conclusions of the Dublin European Council of 28/4/1990, reported in Timmermans, C.W.A., "German Unification and Community Law", 27 *CMLRev* (1990) 437–449, at 438 and 440: and the Commission Communication of 21 August 1991, COM (90) 400 final Vol.1, at 27: "the principle of succession means that Community law as a whole – based on unilateral measures or treaties directly applicable or not – will apply to the territory of the former GDR from the date on which unification takes effect provided that the Community institutions do not adopt specific provisions affecting secondary legislation (primary legislation being unaffected by unification)".

Community labour market on over 10 million East Germans and other former expellees of German stock. This was done without reference to the consequent increase in the Community workforce, the possibility of large scale movement and
the economic, social and industrial problems which could ensue, though these factors were specifically addressed when Greece, Portugal and Spain had previously
acceded to the Community.[63] In *Mario Lopes da Veiga* the Court described the
purpose of the transitional arrangements for Portugal as "prevent[ing] disruption of
the labour markets of the old Member States through a massive influx of
Portuguese nationals seeking employment". Despite the enormity of this historical
event, however, the changes following reunification regarding the Community took
place without being submitted to formal parliamentary approval by either the
European or national parliaments. Though this point is not solely relevant to the
issue of nationality and is sensitive due to the complexities of the German question, it further emphasises the extent of Member State discretion when it comes to
the determination of nationality and the Community's unwillingness or political inability to interfere with such sensitive aspects of national sovereignty.

2.4. Variations on the Precondition of Member State Nationality

No detailed examination is ventured in *Micheletti* as to how or why the plaintiff
qualified for Italian nationality.[64] The "genuine or effective link" criterion, generally synonymous with the *Nottebohm* case, was rejected by the Advocate General,
who associated it with a more romantic period in international relations. A broad
use of the *Nottebohm* formula as a precedent in this context could be criticised on
the grounds that (i) the International Court of Justice thereby unnecessarily deprived the individual of diplomatic protection in a case where he only possessed
one nationality; and (ii) it unnecessarily restricted the definition of nationality for
the purposes of international law and did not accommodate the fact that an individual can legally be a national of the state in question for municipal but not international law purposes. Indeed, *Nottebohm* was later limited to the specific facts of
that case and to the circumstances of a disputed claim to exercise diplomatic protection. However, it is submitted that to dismiss *Nottebohm* as an old chestnut is to
overlook the usefulness of an effective link-type test as an equitable and logical
means to regulate the personal scope of free movement and Community citizenship.[65] Reference to an effective link could mean that some Member State nation-

---

[63]See Case 77/82 *Peskelgolou* [1983] ECR 1085 and, particularly, Advocate General Slynn, at
1098; Case 113/89 *Rush Portuguesa*, op. cit. note 17; and Case 9/88 *Mario Lopes da Veiga* v.
Staatsscretaris van Justitie [1989] ECR 2989, where the consequences of Greek, Portuguese and
Spanish accession were respectively examined in such terms.

[64]The Court simply referred, at para.2, to the relevant Italian legislation – Article 1 of Law no.555
of 13 June 1912, as modified by Article 5 of Law no.123 of 21 April 1983.

[65]See also Ruzié, D., "Nationalité, effectivité et droit communautaire", 97 *Revue General de Droit
International Public* (1993) 107–120, although the author confirms Member State sovereignty in the
field of nationality.

als, though lawfully designated as nationals for the purposes of municipal law, would not qualify as such for the purposes of Community law. Something like an "effective link" has been used by the Court of Justice when establishing the territorial scope of the free movement provisions.[66] In *Prodest* it held that "persons pursuing partially or temporarily, activities outside the territory of the Community had the status of workers employed in the territory of a Member State if the legal relationship of employment could be located within the territory of the Community or retained a *sufficiently close link* with that territory" (emphasis added). The Court in *Micheletti* may have paved the way for the development of such an approach. It held that: "La definition des conditions d'acquisition et de perte de la nationalité relève, conformément au droit international, de la compétence de chaque Etat membre, *compétence qui doit être exercée dans le respect du droit communautaire.*"[67] Although it accepted Member State competence to determine nationality, the Court arguably inferred that all Member State determinations of nationality might not be consistent with Community law. This aspect of the decision will be examined in Section 2.5.3. Use of an effective link might also reduce cases of reverse discrimination, but discussion of this phenomenon will be left to Chapter 7.[68]

Use of the "genuine link" criterion would thus mean that nationality for municipal and Community law purposes might differ. The British declaration on nationality has already demonstrated that nationality for municipal and Community law purposes need not be co-extensive.[69] The status of United Kingdom national for Community law purposes generally, does not necessarily entitle the individual to benefit from free movement. Manxmen and Channel Islanders are expressly excluded from free movement, though they are nationals of the United Kingdom within the terms of the declaration.[70] Furthermore, when Channel Islanders or Manxmen enjoy free movement they do so on the basis of ordinary residence in the United Kingdom.[71] Article 135 also establishes a special regime, to be concluded by the Member States, to govern the freedom of movement within Member States for workers from the overseas countries and territories.[72] The nationals of those countries and territories are in some cases nationals of the Member States

---

[66]Case 237/83 *Prodest* [1984] ECR 3153.

[67]Case C-369/90. op. cit. note 9, at para.10 (emphasis added).

[68]See *infra* Chapter 7.2.

[69]Bohning, op. cit. note 25, at 84, was opposed to this in the context of the British nationality declaration, which he regarded as discriminatory between Member State nationals and incompatible with the Treaty.

[70]See Article 2 of the third protocol of the United Kingdom Treaty of Accession; discussed in Case C-355/89 *Department of Health and Social Security (Isle of Man)* v. *Barr*, 20 August 1991; and the annotation of the *Barr* case by Simmonds, K.R., 29 *CMLRev* (1992) 799–806.

[71]Article 6 of the protocol. Lawful residence has also been proposed as a basis for third country nationals to enjoy Community rights, see, for example, the European Parliament's proposals with respect to the right of residence for pensioners, OJ 1990 C15/74; and Evans, op. cit. note 10, at 215.

[72]Essentially, the non-European countries and territories which have special relations with Belgium, France, Italy, the Netherlands and the UK; see Article 131 EEC and Annex IV of the Treaty. The status of these individuals is ambiguous, since the concept of worker *from* the overseas countries and territories is undefined; see Edens D.F. and Patijn, S., "The Scope of the EEC System of the Free Movement of Workers", 9 *CMLRev* (1972) 322–328; and 10 *CMLRev* (1973) 84–86.

at municipal level, but they do not automatically qualify as beneficiaries of free movement in the Community.[73] It is clear that the link required between an individual and a Member State for the enjoyment of free movement and citizenship could be defined with special reference to Community law and not simply with reference to the domestic law of the Member States. Member States could continue to determine who their nationals are in accordance with the standard principles of municipal and public international law, while Community law might, when necessary, determine which of those nationals benefit from the provisions of Community law in accordance with the establishment of an effective link between their legal position and the Community. If this proposal proves too far-reaching for some Member States, which is likely, Member States might at least be required to report developments in the field of nationality to a Community institution.[74]

2.5. The Effects of Community Law on Member State Nationality Law

This chapter has thus far addressed the established proposition that Member States are competent to determine who their nationals are for the purposes of municipal and international law. It has argued, in addition, that this competence is questionable in the context of the European Union, where the achievement of an ever closer union between peoples is based on principles of equality, uniformity and the supremacy of Community law. This section questions whether the Community's objectives with respect to free movement, the development of an internal market and the establishment of Union citizenship may affect this Member State competence to determine nationality. It seeks to show how certain aspects of free movement and Community citizenship have intentionally or inadvertently interfered with aspects of state sovereignty (issuance of passports, or the exercise of diplomatic protection), which are usually tied up with nationality in municipal and international law. The declaration on nationality annexed to the Union Treaty does not augur well for a strengthened Community role in this context. Nevertheless, on the basis of an *obiter dictum* in the *Micheletti* case it may be possible to uncover a means by which the Court may finally be prepared to assert a degree of Community competence in this field. In addition, changes which the Union Treaty might introduce in future to the determination of nationality at Member State level are examined and the possible effect which the dynamic aspect of Union citizenship may have on the nationality question is outlined herein.

---

[73]On the application of Community law to the overseas territories see Comte, H., "Jurisprudence", 29 RTDE (1993) 687–699.

[74]For alternatives to harmonisation of Member State nationality law see also Koslowski, R., "Intra-EU Migration, Citizenship and Political Union", 32 JCMS (1994) 369–402, at 396, who proposes a form of European consociationalism.

2.5.1. Passports, Identity Cards and the Right to Travel

A passport, or its equivalent, is an official document acknowledging and certifying the bearer as a national of the issuing state. Many states also provide what are known as aliens' passports for stateless persons and such like. Rather than weaken the basic proposition that passports identify the holder as a national of the issuing state, these exceptional cases could be regarded as examples of states, for whatever reason, putting stateless persons and refugees in the same position as their own nationals in this respect. A passport is recognised in international law as an official document for the primary purpose of enabling the bearer to offer some proof of his identity and nationality.[75] Passports may be issued as a matter of state prerogative as, for example, in the United Kingdom,[76] or they may be issued as of right.[77] Though the Member States meeting in Council on 23/6/1981 resolved to introduce a Community passport of uniform format, this decision took the form of an international agreement rather than binding Community legislation.[78] Consequently, the passports subsequently issued are not Community passports issued under Community law but rather, national passports issued by the individual Member States in accordance with their normal procedure, incorporating a format negotiated between the Member States.[79] The Community has not harmonised the issuing of passports and the procedure which was followed to reach agreement on the mere format of the so-called Community passport, never mind the establishment of a passport union,[80] suggests that to do so would be extremely difficult from a political perspective. Despite considerable discussion on the content and form of a passport union, the lack of concrete legal progress makes one wonder whether the Community has a role to play with reference to this aspect of state sovereignty either.

The effects of national passport regulation on free movement go without saying. The Community as a whole has not reached a point where no form of identity is necessary when crossing a border. Could a Member State, however, deny the application of Community law by refusing to grant a national a passport and therefore deny him the right to enter another Member State in accordance with Article 2

---

[75]See Turack, D.C., *The Passport in International Law* (1972) Lexington, Lexington Books, at p.21; and Lee, L.T., *Consular Law and Practice* (1991) Clarendon Press, Oxford, at p.200.

[76]See *Secretary of State* v. *Lakdawalla* [1972] Immigration Appeal Reports 26.

[77]See *Kent* v. *Dulles*, 357 US 116 (1958). Subject to exceptions, see the situation in Denmark, Germany (s.6 of Passports Act), Italy (Law no.1185 of 21 November 1967) and Greece.

[78]See OJ 1981 C241.

[79]See the Commission's response to Written Question no.990/87, OJ 1988 C61/32: "Since the European passport is, from a legal standpoint only a national passport although it is drawn up according to a uniform design"; and Denza, E., "Le passeport européen", RMC (1986) 489–493, who states that the Community passport "traduit exactement à la fois l'inspiration communautaire qui anime la résolution et les pouvoirs que les Etats continuent d'exercer en la matière".

[80]See Evans, A.C., "Entry Formalities in the European Communities", 6 *ELRev* (1981) 3–13, at 8 *et seq*. Sir Leon Brittan, "Subsidiarity in the Constitution of the EC", Robert Schuman Lecture, EUI, Florence, 11 June 1992, at p.18 suggested that the principle of subsidiarity should apply with respect to the development of a uniform passport. He questioned whether the same legitimate objective could not be achieved by means of mutual recognition of individual Member State passports.

Directive 68/360?[81] In adopting Directive 68/360, Member States have agreed to be bound by Article 2 and to comply with it in order to ensure the effective operation of free movement. Thus, although the issue of passports in the United Kingdom involves the exercise of a prerogative power,[82] the United Kingdom courts would be obliged to observe the direct effect of Community legislation. Indeed, decisions of the administration taken under the prerogative, including the issuance of passports, are amenable to judicial review in the United Kingdom.[83] In addition, the Court of Justice has handed down a decision which arguably erodes the traditional sovereign position of Member States as regards passports and their proof of nationality for the purposes of Community law. Given the Community's position on nationality as outlined above, the extent to which the Court of Justice champions the fundamental objective of free movement over Member State sovereignty in the related area of passports is remarkable.

In *Giagounidis* v. *Stadt Reutlingen*, the Court of Justice was asked whether Article 4 of Directive 68/360 must be interpreted as permitting or obliging a Member State to accord a right of residence to persons who come within Article 1 of the Directive, when they present an identity card the validity of which the issuing state has restricted to the national territory?[84] Article 3(1) obliges Member States to admit Community nationals to enter their territory simply on production of a *valid* ID card or passport. Interpreting the Directive in the light of the Treaty provisions establishing the right of free movement and the fact that a right of residence is directly conferred by the Treaty,[85] the Court reaffirmed that Member States are obliged to grant a residence permit to those individuals coming within its scope (Articles 4(1) and (2)), who prove their identity and nationality with reference to the appropriate documents – an ID card or passport.[86] An ID card, according to the Court, fulfils this condition of proof even if it does not allow an individual to leave the national territory. Furthermore, even though Articles 4(1) and (3)(a) of the Directive specifically refer to the document with which the individual entered the territory, the Court referred to the fundamental character of free

[81] Article 2(1) provides that: "Member States shall grant the nationals referred to in Article 1 the right to leave their territory in order to take up activities in the territory of another Member State. Such right shall be exercised simply on production of a *valid* ID card or passport ...".

[82] For the circumstances when the prerogative is applied to deny passport applications, see Fransman, op. cit. note 34, at p.1098, Appendix 3.

[83] See, in particular, *Regina* v. *Secretary of State for Foreign and Commonwealth Affairs, ex parte Everett* [1989] 1 All England Law Reports 655.

[84] Case C-376/89 [1991] ECR I-1069. The plaintiff was a Greek national who entered Germany in 1973 on the basis of his passport in accordance with Articles 2 and 3 of the Directive. His passport expired in 1984 and was not renewed because of his failure to complete his military service. He subsequently used his national unlimited ID card which indicated his identity and nationality. However, under Greek law, such a document is only valid internally. His request for renewal of his residence permit in Germany was refused on this basis.

[85] See Cases 48/75 *Royer* [1976] ECR 497, at para.31; Joined Cases 389/87 and 390/87 *Echternach and Moritz* [1988] ECR 723, at para.25; and Case 249/86 *Commission* v. *Germany* [1989] ECR 1263, at para.9. In the instant case the Advocate General referred to the grant of a right of residence as an obligation on Member States, not a discretionary right.

[86] See also Case 8/77 *Sagulo* [1977] ECR 1495, at para.4.

movement and the fact that its provisions should be widely interpreted to deny the consequences which a literal interpretation of the Directive entailed. If the plaintiff was obliged to rely on his passport, as Article 4(3)(a) seemed to suggest, he could be denied residence in Germany. He had entered Germany using his passport, which was now no longer valid and which no longer qualified as an appropriate document. Nevertheless, contrary to the wording of Articles 2(1) and 4(1) and (3)(a), the Court held that he could rely on his national ID card to renew his residence permit, though he could not initially have left Greece on that basis. According to the Advocate General, to allow Member States a discretionary power in this regard would have weakened the judicial protection of directly applicable individual rights afforded by the Treaty.[87] In contrast, the Court of Justice in *Commission* v. *Netherlands* has emphasised the need for the national document relied on pursuant to Article 3(1) of Directive 68/360 to be valid.[88] The Court in *Giagounidis* was unwilling to subject free movement to the possession of a valid passport, even if the latter is considered by the individual Member State as the correct means to exit and enter the national territory and the only means to verify nationality when abroad. It disregarded the wording of the Directive by emphasising that free movement constitutes one of the foundations of the Treaty and that it should be generously interpreted. The Advocate General warned, in addition, against allowing Member States to claim respect for the sovereignty of other Member States as a means to restrict free movement.[89]

If nationality is regarded as part of the reserved domain of Member States, then the means of proving it also logically fall to be regulated by Member States. However, *Giagounidis* imposes Community law restrictions on Member State reliance on passports as a means of identity and restricts this aspect of the exercise of state sovereignty. Though Article 2(3) of Directive 68/360 expressly envisages situations "where a passport is the only document on which the holder may lawfully leave the country", as was the case under Greek law, the Court rejected this concession to individual state sovereignty, preferring to fulfil the broad objectives of Community free movement. Furthermore, the reference to a valid ID card in Articles 2(1) and 3(1) of Directive 68/360 clearly presupposes validity, if not exclusively then additionally, at national level. Article 2(2) expressly refers to Member States "acting in accordance with their laws" when granting these documents. Though the plaintiff's ID card was of unlimited duration it was not valid as a means of attesting nationality outside the national territory according to national law. The Court's decision may be applauded in terms of the promotion of free movement. Nevertheless, it undermines the traditional role of the passport as a manifestation of state sovereignty whereby it facilitates the holder's right to travel and generally verifies the holder to be a national of the issuing state or an individual to be treated as such. ID cards may be a valid attestation of identity in some

---

[87]Case C-376/89, op. cit. note 84, at para.17.
[88]Case C-68/89 [1991] ECR 2637, at para.15.
[89]Case C-376/89, op. cit. note 84, at para.20.

Member States,[90] but in Greece they were valid internal to that Member State only. There is no parallel use of ID cards in the common law Member States of the Community, which traditionally rely on passports as part of their prerogative, but additionally because of the emphasis on point of entry controls in those Member States.[91] The Court of Justice may be perpetuating discrimination between those Member States' nationals who can avail of ID cards and those who can only rely on their passports, since that is the sole means by which national identity is officially regulated by their Member State of origin. If the Court goes as far as explicitly rejecting the relevance of the passport, or other chosen national means of attesting identity, then it is emptying one of the traditional fonts of state sovereignty of much of its water. The decision in *Giagounidis* may be logically acceptable in a Community where the right to travel is a fundamental pillar of the internal market and Community citizenship, but it nevertheless opposes the express provisions of Directive 68/360. The decision is rendered even more sensitive by the fact that it championed freedom of movement in the context of a national who was in difficulties with his national authorities due to his avoidance of national military service. Most states regard the latter as an essential duty of citizenship and as a particular expression of national sovereignty and identity. Article F(1) of the Union Treaty may require the Union to respect the national identities of Member States, but the effective operation of free movement may, in certain circumstances, be interpreted as outweighing the fulfilment of a national duty which is regarded as part of that. The resolution of this type of conflict will provide interesting reading in future.

2.5.2. Diplomatic Protection

Nationality has traditionally formed a basis for the international protection of the individual by a State.[92] Admittedly, it is not true to say that it is the exclusive basis upon which diplomatic protection may be extended, but neither is it irrelevant to a claim for protection. The importance of the state/individual relationship in the context of diplomatic protection is evident from the fact that it has been characterised as the only identifiable element of British citizenship: "apart from the right of entry

---

[90]That is in France, Italy, Luxembourg, Belgium (compulsory), Germany (compulsory) and Greece (compulsory), subject of course to various national legislative provisions.

[91]For details of the point of entry/post entry controls operated by Community Member States and for individual national practices regarding passports and ID cards see the Memorandum of the Foreign and Commonwealth Office, submitted to the House of Lords Select Committee on the European Communities, *Easing of Frontier Formalities*, Session 1983–84, 4th report. See also AE no.6439, 13–14 March 1995, with regard to a British High Court decision which upheld the compatability of light passport checks with Article 7(a).

[92]See O'Connell, D.P., *International Law*, Vol.2 (1970) London, Stevens and Sons, at p.672; Detter De Lupis, I., *International Law and the Independent State* (1987) Gower Publishing, Avebury; Lee, op. cit. note 75, at pp.124 *et seq.*; and Turack, op. cit. note 75, at p.19. See also *Mavrommatis*, PCIJ Ser. A no.2 at 12 (1924): "It is an elementary principle of international law that a State is entitled to protect its subjects, when injured by acts contrary to international law committed by another State."

to the UK, no right other than a claim to diplomatic protection seems to attach to British Citizenship either".[93] Thus passports were generally regarded as entitling the issuing state to exercise diplomatic or consular protection in favour of the holder.[94] Thus, in the *Everett* case, Lord Justice Taylor regarded the ready issue of a passport as the normal expectation of every citizen.[95] The functions of a diplomatic or consular mission are regarded as including protection of the interests of the sending state and of its nationals in the receiving state.[96] Outside of the legal link of nationality, the grant of diplomatic protection has also been founded on the conclusion of bilateral or multilateral conventions, or even as a means of alleviating situations thought to be contrary to international law.[97] Article 8(c) provides that: "Every citizen of the Union shall, in the territory of a third country in which the Member States of which he is a national is not represented, be entitled to protection by the diplomatic or consular authorities of any Member State, on the same conditions as the nationals of that State. Before 31 December 1993, Member States shall establish the necessary rules among themselves and start the international negotiations required to secure this protection." Cooperation between Member States as regards the provision of consular assistance has been advocated by some Community institutions since the Adonnino Report.[98] Indeed, Article 8(c) EC is similar to the provision in Article 2(3) of the European Convention on Consular Functions, which provides that:

> Upon notification to the receiving State, any Contracting Party is entitled to entrust the protection of its nationals and the defence of their rights and interests to consular officers of another Contracting Party. Nevertheless, the responsibility for protecting their own nationals by the Contracting Parties is expressed as of right and it is for them to request another Contracting Party to do so in their absence.[99]

---

[93]White R. and Hampson, F., "British Nationality Law: Proposed Changes", 31 ICLQ (1982) 849–855, at 854.

[94]See *Joyce* v. *Director of Public Prosecutions* [1946] AC 347: "[per Lord Jowitt] A well-known writer on international law said that by a universally recognised customary rule of the law of nations, every state holds the right of protection over its nationals abroad (Oppenheim). This rule thus recognised may be asserted by the holder of a passport which is for him the outward title of his rights. It is true that the measure in which the State will exercise its rights lies within its discretion. But with the issue of the passport the first step is taken. Armed with that document, the holder may demand from the State's representatives abroad ... that he be treated as a British subject". See also *United States* v. *Lamb*, 385 US 475 at 481 (1967); and *Kent* v. *Dulles,* op. cit. note 77.

[95]*Ex parte Everett*, op. cit. note 83, at 660 and further that "the grant of a passport involves a request in the name of the Queen to a foreign power to afford the holder free passage and protection. It also extends the protection and assistance of the Crown to the holder whilst he is abroad."

[96]See Article 3(1) of the Vienna Convention on Diplomatic Relations, 18/4/1961, 8 500 UNTS 95; and Article 1(1) of the European Convention on Consular Functions, 11 November 1967, ETS no.61.

[97]See the Greek contribution to the 1992 FIDE conference, Antoniou, op. cit. note 56, pp.145–197, at p.194.

[98]Bull. EC. 1985 suppl.7, 21; see also Commission Decision 88/384, OJ 1988 L183/35, advocating action by the Community Member States to improve the protection of Community nationals living and working in third countries; European Parliament Resolution of 23 October 1986, OJ 1986 C297/128; and Evans, op. cit. note 10, at 196.

[99]11 November 1967, ETS no.61.

The agreement among Member States subsequent to Article 8(c) does not give Member State nationals an enforceable right to diplomatic protection. They may be granted diplomatic protection by a Member State other than their own in the territory of a third country where the Member State of which they are nationals is not represented. The diplomatic protection afforded to them in such circumstances will be on the same basis as that enjoyed by the nationals of that Member State. The discretionary nature of diplomatic protection, which is particularly strong in the United Kingdom where the Crown prerogative continues to apply, is not unduly affected.[100] Member States were to establish the necessary rules for the operation of Article 8(c) by 31/12/1993. Guidelines for the protection of Union citizens in third countries where their Member State of origin has no diplomatic mission were adopted in the intergovernmental context of the common foreign and security policy. They address diplomatic protection in third countries in cases of death, accident or serious illness, detention or arrest, violence and aid or repatriation for Member State nationals in difficulty. Where a number of Member States do not have diplomatic missions in a third state, the remaining Member States may sort out a rota to deal with requests for assistance from Union citizens. The guidelines are based on the principle that Member State nationals in the possession of a passport or ID can solicit consular assistance from the diplomatic missions of other Member States in third states and that those Member States will treat them as they would treat their own. However, any assistance given is subject to agreement of the national authorities of that Union citizen's Member State of origin, where it can be obtained and, in any case, agreement must be established before any expense is incurred with respect to the applicant Union citizen. Thus the approval of the Foreign Affairs Ministry of the Member State of origin is necessary before expense is incurred and the applicants are generally obliged to undertake to repay the expenses incurred on their behalf to their Member State of origin, who will, in the meantime have had to repay the Member State giving the diplomatic assistance. Indeed nationals from Ireland, the Netherlands, Portugal and the United Kingdom, are to have their passport or ID confiscated if they are repatriated with public funds until they repay the sum advanced for their repatriation. These conditions make sense from an economic point of view, however, they must have been a great disappointment to the Commission, which had described citizenship in the course of the intergovernmental conference as a set of rights and duties based on *solidarity* which results from the progressive and coherent evolution of the political, economic and social evolution of the Union.[101]

This means of implementing Article 8(c) recognised that diplomatic protection is generally a matter falling within a state's reserved domain. The negotiation of agreements with third countries is necessary given that the Vienna Convention and

---

[100]See, for example, *China Navigation Company Ltd.* v. *Attorney-General* [1932] 2 King's Bench 197, where the Court held that there is no legal duty on the Crown to afford (by its military forces) protection to British subjects in foreign parts.
[101]Bull. EC Suppl.2/91.

other existing bilateral conventions only cover protection of nationals of each Member State. The development of Article 8(c) may give rise in future to disputes concerning the genuine or effective link between the Union citizen in question and the Member State extending diplomatic protection. No such effective link is necessarily present in a situation covered by Article 8(c) since all that is required for its application is that the Member State of which the Union citizen is a national, is not represented in the state against whom protection is sought. The only link between the Union citizen and the Member State seeking to diplomatically protect him, is that both are subjects of the Union, one in the capacity of citizen and the other as Member State. There will not necessarily be any connection in terms of residence, establishment, interests, activities and family ties.[102] Other states may not accept that a sufficient connection to justify a claim to exercise diplomatic protection exists. Those states against whom diplomatic protection is most essential, might not be swayed by the political consideration that to ignore the diplomatic claim in question would be to excite the collective wrath of the Community.

2.5.3. Member State Nationality and the Duty of Respect for Community Law

The *Micheletti* case is cited above in favour of the proposition that Member States are competent to regulate nationality. Yet, during the course of the decision, the Court inserted a proviso which, if brought to its logical and legal conclusion, could have considerable effect on the role of the Community in the determination of Member State nationality for the purposes of Community law. As noted above, the Court stated that the considerations for the acquisition and loss of nationality, in accordance with international law, belongs to the competence of each Member State. The latter, however, must be exercised in conformity with Community law. On the one hand, the Court concluded that to allow Member States to impose conditions beyond nominal nationality would lead to diverse application of the free movement provisions from one Member State to the next. On the other, it suggested that a determination of nationality by a Member State which does not respect Community law is not necessarily acceptable as a means to delimit the scope of free movement. In *Cowan* the Court similarly indicated that Community law may affect Member States' competence in the field of criminal law.[103] It is a difficult but nevertheless short step to introduce the objectives and effective operation of the free movement provisions and Union citizenship as a means to determine whether in fact Community law has been respected. Thus, an otherwise exorbitant or overly generous definition of nationality which could have the result of vastly extending the benefits of Community law were the Community to have no competence in the matter, might have to be tailored in accordance with its objectives and aims before being effective in the field of Community law. Spain,

---

[102]Cited as relevant factors by the Court in *Nottebohm* [1955] ICJ Reports 15, at 24, as means of establishing the necessary close connection between the two parties.

[103]See Case 186/87 [1989] ECR 216, at para.19.

for example, may find its competence to regulate dual nationality with reference to bilateral conventions limited by this need for respect for Community law.[104]

Furthermore, reflected against the duty of loyalty enunciated in Article 5, the *obiter dictum* in *Micheletti* could have considerable impact.[105] D'Oliveira claims that the absence of any protest against any national measure in this field and the declarations on nationality in particular suggest that the general prohibition in Article 5 to act in good faith "cannot be said to be of any other than a symbolic nature".[106] When the United Kingdom and Germany issued nationality declarations some years ago the Community's objectives in the field of free movement had not matured and Union citizenship, far from being constitutionalised as it is in Article 8, had hardly been conceived. Furthermore, in the past few years Article 5 has become a useful and increasingly used tool in the hands of the Court of Justice to ensure that Community law is fully enforced and effective,[107] that Community objectives are implemented, that Member States do not interfere with the operation of Community law rules or defeat its purposes and that Member States, in certain circumstances, are obliged to consult with the Commission.[108] Previous decisions of the Court of Justice such as *Airola* might now be read in accordance with the *Micheletti* line of reasoning. Thus, in the context of Community law, the Court disregarded the plaintiff's compulsory acquisition of Italian nationality specifically because such asymmetric discrimination against women was incompatible with the principle of equal treatment in Article 119. It did not question the validity of the plaintiff's nationality but disregarded it as operative in the context of Community sex equality legislation. Similarly, in *Micheletti*, the Court saw no reason to disregard the plaintiff's Member State nationality in that case. Spain had already granted him a temporary residence permit for a six month period on the basis of his Italian passport. There seemed no good reason to deny his legitimate expectations and to restrict the freedom of movement of persons by denying him the right to establish himself and exercise his profession. Indeed, given that Spain had already accepted the Italian passport for some purposes, its subsequent actions showed all the signs of protecting the national labour market from foreign labour. The case demonstrated no additional factor which counselled against acceptance of Italy's determination of

---

[104]See Iglesias Buhigues, J.S., "Doble Nacionalidad y Derecho Comunitario: A Proposito del Asunto C-369/90 *Micheletti*", in *Hacia un Nuevo Orden Internacional y Europeo. Homenaje al Profesor M. Diez de Velasco* (1993) Tecnos Madrid, pp.953–967, at p.967.

[105]Arnull points out that given the Court of Justice's adherence to the principle of precedent (it generally follows its own decisions but is not obliged to do so), the distinction between *ratio decidendi* and *obiter dicta* loses much of the significance which it enjoys in common law: Arnull, A., "Owning up to Fallibility: Precedent and the Court of Justice", 30 *CMLRev* (1993) 247–266, at 249. See also Advocate General Roemer in Case 9/61 *Netherlands* v. *High Authority* [1962] ECR 213, at 242: "the question where in judgments [of the Court of Justice] the decisive grounds of a judgment end and any *obiter dicta* begin seems to me in any case to be of secondary importance. In each case everything that is said in the text of the judgment expresses the will of the Court."

[106]D'Oliveira, *Plural Nationality and the European Union*, forthcoming, Martinus Nijhoff.

[107]See, for example, Joined Cases C-6/90 and 9/90 *Francovich and Bonifaci* [1992] ECR I-5357.

[108]See Temple Lang, J., "Community Constitutional Law: Article 5 EEC Treaty", 27 *CMLRev* (1990) 645–681, for an excellent discussion of the use of Article 5 by the Court of Justice.

nationality, or of Spain's previous acceptance of that nationality. At issue was the establishment of a qualified professional in a Community Member State.

Indeed, it appears that some Member State governments have drawn certain conclusions from this *obiter* in *Micheletti*. In February 1993 a bill was presented in the Dutch parliament to amend existing Dutch nationality law and add new provisions governing the loss of nationality. It was proposed that adult bipatriade nationals should lose their Dutch nationality once they had been abroad for over ten years. This provision was subject to a few limited exceptions. It was subsequently amended, however, and the grounds for loss of Dutch nationality was specified as over ten years residence outside the territory of the European Union.[109] It is not clear, as D'Oliveira points out, whether the Dutch government felt obliged to amend their proposed nationality legislation to bring it in line with the *Micheletti* decision. This was not explicitly stated. However, its attempts to block the loss of Dutch nationality for nationals resident in the territory of the European Union seem to stem from the possible interference the original provision might have on the free movement of persons. However, the amendment suggests that the genuine links required for the possession of nationality a la *Nottebohm* are preserved in Dutch law if the national in question is resident in the European Union. Fransman also suggests a manner in which national legislation, in this case the British Nationality Act, could be brought into line with *Micheletti*.[110] Section 6(1) of the 1981 Act provides that a person may be naturalised if "his intentions are such that, in the event of a certificate of naturalisation as a British citizen being granted to him, his home or (if he has more than one) his principal home will be in the United Kingdom". This condition of intention could be waived with respect to European Union citizens who wish to naturalise in the United Kingdom, but who wish to exercise their Article 8 rights elsewhere in the European Union. Indeed, he questions whether it is consistent with Community law to deny European Union citizens more favourable treatment with respect to naturalisation, if they comply with the remaining conditions to naturalise.

2.6. New Dimensions in the Nationality Debate Following the Treaty on European Union

Article 8 limits Union citizenship to the nationals of the Member States. The Union Treaty has not introduced any change in the means used to determine the personal scope of free movement and has posited Union citizenship on the same basis – nationality. This is emphasised by a declaration on nationality appended to the Final Act of the Union Treaty. It provides as follows: "wherever in the Treaty establishing the European Community reference is made to nationals of the Member

---

[109]See the contribution of D'Oliveira, H.U.J. at the conference on *Nationality and Citizenship Status in the New Europe*, organised by the IPPR, London, 9–10 June 1995.
[110]See the contribution of Fransman, op. cit. note 34.

States, the question whether an individual possesses the nationality of a Member State shall be settled solely by reference to the national law of the Member State concerned. Member States may declare, for information, who are to be considered their nationals for Community purposes by way of a declaration when necessary".

Like the declarations adopted at the time of the signing of the SEA,[111] the aforementioned declaration is not part of the Union Treaty. It is not incorporated in the Act, nor was it signed by the representatives of the Member States. Declarations in Community law are said to have no binding legal force, are not subject to the jurisdiction of the Court of Justice (since they generally do not form an "integral part" of the Final Act) and cannot restrict the legal effects of the Act to which they are appended.[112] Nevertheless, for the purposes of interpretation, the Vienna Convention on the Law of Treaties states that "a treaty shall comprise, in addition to the text, any agreement relating to the Treaty which was made between all the parties in connexion with the conclusion of the treaty".[113] Since the declaration was agreed upon by all Member States, it must be accepted as a legitimate means to interpret the term nationals of the Member States, used therein. Furthermore, Toth refers to a situation where a delaration may be so closely connected to the treaty that it must be regarded as an "integral part" thereof.[114] The latter is probably not the case for the nationality declaration in the Union Treaty, but the declaration may be relied on in its "context", as a legal aid to the interpretation of the Treaty provisions in which the expression "nationals of the Member States" appears and as an indication of the political will of Member States in this regard. It confirms Member State competence by confirming that questions of nationality should be settled solely with reference to the national law of the Member State concerned. As such, it supports any differences which may be perpetuated with reference to the criteria employed by Member States in the conferral of nationality for Community law purposes.

If nationality questions are to be determined *solely by reference to the national law of the Member State concerned*, the Member States may be denying themselves any right to verify the existence of an "effective nationality" which translates a genuine link between the state and the individual for the purposes of Community

---

[111]See Schermers, H.G., "The Effect of the Date 31 December 1992", 28 *CMLRev* (1991) 275–289.

[112]See Toth, A.G., "The Legal Status of the Declarations Annexed to the Single European Act", 23 *CMLRev* (1986) 803–812, at 812; Steiner, J., "The Right to Welfare: Equality and Equity under Community Law", 10 *ELRev* (1985) 21–41, at 26; and with specific reference to the declarations annexed to the Union Treaty, Jacqué, J.P., "Commentaire de la décision du Conseil constitutionnel no.92-108 DC du 9 May 1992", 28 RTDE (1992) 251–264, at 253: "ces déclarations ne font pas ... partie de l'engagement international qui sera soumis à ratification. Elles constituent soit des elements d'interprétations, soit des engagements de nature politique. Même dans le cas ou un Etat les ratifierait, on ne saurait les considerer comme faisant partie de l'engagement juridique souscrit par les Etats membres." See, however, Snyder, F., "The Effectiveness of European Community Law: Institutions, Processes, Tools and Techniques", 56 *Modern Law Review* (1993) 19–54, at 32, who accepts that declarations are political statements, but states that they may influence Community practice.

[113]Article 31(2)(a), reproduced in 63 *American Journal of Comparative Law* (1969) 875, at 885.

[114]See Toth, op. cit. note 112, at 807 who he cites *Greece* v. *United Kingdom* (the Ambatielos Case) (1952) 28 ICJRep in support of this proposition.

law into juridical terms.[115] As we stated before, the *Nottebohm* case may be severely criticised and may be restricted to cases of diplomatic protection or dual nationality. However, it can also be regarded as an aspect of a more general principle of international law that states are not bound to recognise the nationality of a state which has not been granted in accordance with international law.[116] Thus, while confirming their competence to determine nationality, the declaration on nationality may at the same time restrict, in the context of Community law, an important though limited competence stemming from international law, namely, the right to investigate the nationality of other Member States. Thus, if a Member State were to deprive some of its nationals of their rights of free movement by discontinuing their nationality status, it is arguable that those individuals could have recourse to the Community Court on the matter.[117] However, the declaration gives further force to the legal validity and sanctity of the German and British unilateral declarations on nationality by institutionalising the procedure for making such declarations. In a sense, it encourages Member States to make declarations to affirm their jurisdiction in this respect. It has become clear that nationality for municipal or international law purposes, need not bear the same meaning for Community purposes. The declaration on nationality has left the practical implementation of this possibility to the individual Member States.[118]

However, the relationship between the declaration and the *obiter* in *Micheletti* is confusing. The former negates any teleologically based Community competence as regards nationality, while the latter suggests that only those Member State determinations of nationality compatible with the Community's objectives and teleology will be effective for the purposes of Community law. If Member States begin to issue declarations on the scope of their nationality for the purposes of Community law, the value of the *Micheletti* proviso will be further confounded unless the Court is willing to assert the authority of its legal reasoning over the uncertain legal standing

[115]See generally, Parry, C., "The Duty to Recognise Foreign Nationality Law", 19 *ZaoRV* (1958); and Bleckmann, op. cit. note 27, at 477, who contended that the Community was not obliged to recognise the nationality of persons which infringe public international law or the genuine link rule.

[116]See Bleckmann, op. cit. note 27, at 477; and Article 1 of the 1930 Hague Convention, which indicates that though states are competent to determine their nationals, this determination may not be recognised by other states if it is inconsistent with international law.

[117]See Evans, op. cit. note 34, at 180, who points to s.11 of the 1981 British Nationality Act as such an example. The latter deprives a limited category of persons who had previously qualified for free movement of their right of abode and consequently of free movement.

[118]See also the decision of the Heads of State and Government, meeting within the European Council at Edinburgh, concerning certain problems raised by Denmark on the Treaty on European Union (Annex I to Part B, Bull. EC. 12-1992): "The provisions of Part Two of the Treaty establishing the European Community relating to citizenship of the Union give nationals of the Member States additional rights and protection as specified in that Part. They do not in any way take the place of national citizenship. The question whether an individual possesses the nationality of a Member State will be settled solely by reference to the national law of the Member State concerned." The Solemn Declaration of the Birmingham European Council on a Community close to its citizens, Annex I Bull. EC. 10-1992; and Curtin, D. and van Ooik, R., "Denmark and the Edinburgh Summit: Maastricht Without Tears", in O'Keeffe, D. and Twomey, P. (eds.), *Legal Issues of the Maastricht Treaty* (1994) Chancery Press, London, pp.349–365, at p.359.

of what is clearly a politically influential declaration. The dynamic aspect of Union citizenship in Article 8(e) of the Maastricht Treaty may contain the key to this puzzle.[119] Due to the paradox nationality creates in the operation of free movement and Union citizenship and the lack of uniformity which it permits as regards the basic delimitation of those two areas, Article 8(e) may facilitate greater harmonisation of Member States' nationality laws, to the limited extent necessitated by Community law. For the moment, the Court of Justice has unobtrusively indicated that Member State competence in this regard is not absolute. In addition, by extending the Community's competence to limited political rights, a general right of residence and the exercise of diplomatic protection (though the latter has been negotiated at intergovernmental level), Article 8 puts Member State definitions of nationality, particularly if they are based on jus sanguinis principles, under considerable strain. The latter are all manifestations of national sovereignty and the entry of Community law into these domains to the limited extent provided in the Union Treaty blurs the difference which the possession of an individual Member State's nationality entails.[120] Since one of the consequences of European integration, free movement and the development of a Community citizenship in particular, is a reduction in the exclusionary quality of state membership (at least as between Member State nationals), the preservation of nationality as a matter for Member State competence is not only regrettable but curious.

2.7. Conclusions

The object of this chapter is to analyse one of two criteria – nationality and economic activity – according to which the scope of the free movement of persons and Community citizenship are defined. The choice of nationality rather than residence, though unwarranted by certain provisions of the Treaty such as Article 48(1), was a political choice to restrict free movement to the nationals of the Member States. In addition, Member States were considered exclusively competent to regulate nationality. This seems inconsistent with the role which nationality plays in determining the personal scope of free movement and Union citizenship, since the enjoyment of both depend on the possession of Member State nationality. This anomaly is due to the fundamental role which nationality plays in international and municipal law. States determine their personal substratum with reference to the

---

[119]It provides that "without prejudice to the other provisions of this Treaty, the Council, acting unanimously on a proposal from the Commission and after consulting the European Parliament, may adopt provisions to strengthen or to add to the rights laid down in this part".

[120]In support of this position see O'Keeffe, D., "Judicial Interpretation of the Public Service Exception to the Free Movement of Workers", in O'Keeffe, D. and Curtin, D. (eds.), *Constitutional Adjudication in European Community and National Law* (1992) Butterworths, London pp.89–106, at p.106, who argues that the Union Treaty is bound to alter the perceptions of the state and how Member States regard the nationals of other Member States. Closa (1995), suggests that the development of Union citizenship may have an effect on naturalisation procedures for nationals from other Member States, at 516–517.

legal concept of nationality. However, since nationality was the connecting factor chosen by Community law, the Court of Justice and Community legislator could have played a more affirmative role in policing its application. They could, for example, in certain circumstances, have differentiated between nationality for municipal and Community purposes by requiring Member State nationals who wished to enjoy Community rights to demonstrate a genuine link with the objectives and operation of Community law. Nationality could have been one such genuine link, but it did not have to be the only one.

However, an *obiter dictum* in its decision in the *Micheletti* case has left open the possibility of a review of Member State determinations of nationality for their conformity with Community law. This possibility of intrusion on a traditional area of Member State sovereignty may be supported by the fact that other aspects of Community law – the creation of an internal market and the development of Community citizenship – will have consequential effects on the traditional competence of Member States to determine the rights which their nationals enjoy and consequently, on the importance of state membership. Thus, for example, in *Giagounidis*, the Court of Justice carefully phrased its judgment in terms of the *effet utile* of free movement and the purpose of the decision was clear. It would not countenance the exercise of national sovereignty in the field of passports excessively interfering with the operation of free movement. The judgment goes against the clear wording of Directive 68/360 and is in contrast to the Community's traditional approach to questions of nationality. No clear legislative position has followed this judgment, although the Court's departure from the text of the Community legislative provisions considerably clouds the existing legal position.

However, the relationship between the nationality declaration in the Union Treaty and the Court's *obiter dictum* in *Micheletti* is difficult. It may come to a head in future when the contours and scope of Community citizenship are more clearly defined and the dynamic content of this supranational concept of citizenship has been further developed pursuant to Article 8(e), or in the course of the 1996 intergovernmental conference. Indeed, by acquiring competence with respect to rights generally regarded as essential to citizenship (voting rights/rights of residence/access to the public service etc.), Union citizenship may inevitably affect the status of nationality which at national and Community level connects the individual with the enjoyment of these rights. Such an effect depends on the coordinated legislative and judicial boldness of the Community institutions and, as regards what has proved to be the sensitive issue of supranational Community citizenship, this is precisely what these institutions may lack. It is difficult to envisage the Court of Justice bringing its statement in *Micheletti* to a logical conclusion given the Member States' declaration on nationality. However, it is argued in conclusion that until specific legislative action is taken at Community level to harmonise, or rather coordinate, nationality law for the purposes of free movement, the relationship between nationality, free movement and Community citizenship, given the former's delimitation of the latter two, will continue to be awkward and the subject of considerable diversity.

Chapter 3

The Economic Parameters of Community Citizenship

3.1. Introduction

This chapter addresses the criterion of performance or involvement in an economic activity as an element in the Community's definition of its personal scope in the free movement of persons and Community citizenship. It questions whether Community law can continue to insist on participation in or performance of demonstrable economic activities as a threshold requirement for its application. This argument is phrased in terms of the inconsistent application of the criterion of economic activity to concrete cases which have been decided by the Court and the question of whether certain publicly funded sectors of activity are excluded from the scope of the Treaty on this basis. Even before the extension of the Community's competences in the Union Treaty, the requirement of an economic activity was the subject of considerable incoherence and inconsistency in the jurisprudence of the Court of Justice. In some cases the Court regarded an activity as economic in circumstances which it would not countenance in others. Indeed, it is possible to identify a number of cases with respect to the free movement of persons where the Court has ruled on the basis of the existence of an economic element, though the practical value of that economic element was weak and in order to include the activity within the scope of Community law, the Court was forced to manipulate its previous reasoning.

The Court's unsatisfactory reliance on the requirement of economic activity is also reflected in the Community's definition of worker. The latter serves as a threshold concept, admitting or denying individuals access to the benefits of the free movement provisions. In a detailed analysis of the early case law of the Court of Justice the initial criteria employed by the Court in its determination of the beneficiaries of free movement are discussed. The Court assesses an individual's position with respect to (i) existence of the elements of a classic employment relationship (service, direction and remuneration); and (ii) whether the activity in question is genuine and effective. It juggles these two criteria and variously accepts or denies the individual's status as a Community worker. An analysis of the Court's treatment of more modern variations on the traditional model of "worker" – trainees, job seekers, employees involved in statutory social employment schemes – reveal the inadequacy of these criteria in practice. It is submitted that the questions facing the Court have grown more complex in line with the growing complexity of employment relations and the employment market. Its interpretation of this notion should not be restrictive, however, since the definition of "worker" is one of the means by which the Court delimits a fundamental Treaty freedom.[1] It is suggested that its decisions have not always adequately reflected this philosophy. As the employment situation worsens and as the Court is faced with novel forms of employment, it should be careful to keep in tune with the developments in the European (un)employment and labour market on which the Community's free movement regime is so obviously dependent and its future so obviously based.

The Court's progressive judicial approach in the field of free movement may be congratulated for championing the socio-political rights of Member State nationals and their families and for affording them judicial protection detached from purely economic considerations. The fact remains, however, that the Court may and does resort to the concept of economic activity, or its equally unsatisfactory definition of worker, when necessary. The legal certainty and internal logic of Community law inevitably suffers as a result, since the determination of who is a worker and, therefore, who falls within the scope of Community law varies from case to case. The Union Treaty introduced no amendment to the present system for determining who are workers, or what constitutes an economic activity. Although Union citizenship is not based on the performance of an economic activity, recent legislation in the field of free movement and residence does not augur well for the effective operation and enforcement of purely non-economic rights in this context either.

Furthermore, certain aspects of the Union Treaty might be expected to have an effect on the Community's relative confinement to economic activities. Article 1 of the Union Treaty now simply refers to a European Community rather than a European Economic Community. This symbolic amendment gives rise to a number of questions. Is insistence on an economic element as a threshold for admission to the scope of Community law still tenable in a Community which adheres to the objectives of a broad economic and later political union? Does the establishment of a concept of citizenship in Article 8 further undermine this criterion? It seems that the criterion of economic activity may anomalously persist in the field of free movement and that this anomaly will become more pronounced as the notion of Community or Union citizenship develops. The free movement of persons and Community citizenship may, therefore, legally and substantively evolve along different lines and the rights and duties contingent on the latter may differ from the rights and legal protection enjoyed by the Community's economic agents. In the alternative, the potential of Community citizenship may remain quietly subdued by

[1] See Case 53/81 *Levin* [1982] ECR 1035, at para.13.

the continued emphasis on the economic aspects of the Community's constitution. This possibility is further discussed with respect to the substantive content of Community citizenship, in particular, the development of a general right of residence. It will be regrettable if the development of Community citizenship, which should derive from a broad principle of equality, provokes the creation of various tiers of rights and duties in the context of free movement and the evolving concept of Community citizenship. Just as the enjoyment of the rights of Community citizenship should be detached from unilateral Member State definitions of nationality, so the enjoyment of free movement and its consequent benefits should arguably be detached from the performance of an economic activity, or from the possession of economic resources in all cases. To the extent that economic activity has survived the adoption of the Union Treaty, it should do so in a more defined and legally certain manner.

3.2. Economic Activity and Free Movement

The primary and original purpose of the Community, namely, the regulation of economic activity, has acted as a considerable limitation on its power of action and on the scope of its substantive provisions.[2] The definitions attributed by the Court of Justice to concepts like economic activity, remuneration in the context of the provision of services and workers, are essential in the determination of the scope of application of the fundamental freedoms in Articles 48 to 66. Thus, a Community right of residence is said to constitute a right directly conferred by the Treaty, subject, however, to the exercise of an economic activity within the meaning of Articles 48, 52 or 59.[3] Thus, prior to the conclusion of the Union Treaty, competence with respect to the individual generally only existed to the extent that the Community citizen was involved in the free movement of persons which, in turn, demonstrated an economic element. However, as the Community intervenes in such diverse fields of activity as tourism, education, medicine, the activities of religious communities, traineeships and employment and retraining schemes for the unemployed, the essential definitions of "genuine and effective" employment, remuneration, services and economic activity have become obscured. This process is bound to continue and the

---

[2]See, for example, the decision of the Court in Case 143/87 *Stanton* v. *INASTI* [1988] ECR 3877, at para.13: "the provisions of the Treaty relating to the free movement of persons are intended to facilitate the pursuit by Community citizens of occupational activities of all kinds throughout the Community, and preclude national legislation which might place Community citizens at a disadvantage when they wish to extend their activities beyond the territory of a single Member State" and Case C-168/91 *Konstantinidis* v. *Stadt Altensteig-Standesamt* [1993] CMLR 401, where the decision of the German authorities to change the plaintiff's name only violated Community law if and to the extent that it injures his professional activities. See also Meehan, E., "European Citizenship and Social Policies", in Vogel, U. and Moran, M. (eds.), *The Frontiers of Citizenship* (1991) Macmillan, pp.125–154, at p.128; and Mattera, A., "La Libre Circulation des Travailleurs à l'Interieur de la CE" (1993) *Revue du Marché Unique Européen*, 47–108, at 58 *et seq.*

[3]See Case C-363/89 *Roux* v. *Belgian State* [1991] ECR 273, at para.9; and Bourrinet, J., "Vers une citoyenneté européenne. Aspects économiques", 362 RMC (1992) 772–776, at 773.

division between economic and non-economic spheres of competence may be increasingly difficult to delineate in the light, *inter alia*, of the provisions on citizenship, education, culture and public health, introduced by the Union Treaty.

In *Walrave and Koch* v. *Association Union Cycliste Internationale* the practice of sport was held to be subject to Community law and the principle of non-discrimination in particular, only to the extent that it constituted an economic activity within the meaning of Article 2.[4] Article 2 was also applied to the activities of professional or semi-professional football players (who were regarded as workers), if they were in the nature of gainful employment or remunerated service.[5] Rules or practices regulating sporting life and of a purely sporting concern, as for example the formation of national teams, fall outside the remit of Community law, but these rules must be restricted to their proper objective of regulating sport and not constitute obstacles to free movement. This formulation suggests that their exclusion from the application of Community law is in the nature of a derogation from the fundamental principle of free movement which must be proportionally applied. Economic activity has been defined as any gainful activity or remunerated service.[6] With respect to a distinction between work and services, the Court has held that the activities referred to in Article 59 are not to be distinguished from those in Article 48, except for the fact that they are performed outside the ties of a contract of employment.[7] The nature and frequency of the activity in question, the relationship between the person pursuing the activity and the person paying for it, and

[4]Case 36/74 [1975] ECR 1405. The plaintiffs were Dutch pacemakers who were prevented from offering their services for remuneration under agreements with the cyclists or cycling associations and sponsors, unless they were of the same nationality as the cyclists with whom they worked. In holding that the rules of an international sporting association were contrary to Article 6, the Court first had to locate those rules within the scope of Community law.

[5]Case 13/76, *Donà* v. *Mantero* [1976] ECR 1333, which involved a national sporting association restricting participation in sporting competitions to "affiliated" players who, in principle, had to be nationals. The Italian Corte di Cassazione, 2/4/1963, no.811 Giustizia Civile 1963, at 379, originally denied the status of worker under national law to professional football players; this decision was later overturned, 26 January 1971, no.174 Giustizia Civile 1971, at 89. See also Case 222/86 *Heylens* [1986] ECR 4097 (professional football trainers); and Case C-117/91 *Bosman* [1991] ECR I-4837 (transfer fees), discussed in *Boletin de la Gaceta Juridica de la CE* B-77, 23–25; and, more recently, Case C-415/93 *Bosman*, judgment of 15 December 1995 on transfer fees and UEFA rules on the number of foreign players. For a discussion of football in the context of free movement, see the Janssen van Raay Report, Doc. A2-415/88, adopted on 11/4/1989; the European Parliament's Resolution, Doc. B3-1784/91, 21 November 1991; the Commission's informal agreement with UEFA, OJ 1991 C327/25; *Le Football et l'Europe*, European University Institute/European Cultural Centre, Florence, 3–5 May 1990, in particular, D'Oliveira, H.U.J., "Football and Nationality in Europe", Colloquium Paper 119/90; Weatherill, S., "Discrimination on Grounds of Nationality in Sport", 9 *YEL* (1989) 55–92; Evans, A.C., "Freedom of Trade under the Common Law and EC Law: The Case of Football Bans", 102 *Law Quarterly Review* (1986) 510–548, at 511; Blainpain, R., *Labour Law and Industrial Relations in the European Communities* (1991) Deventer, Kluwer, at p.89, where he discusses the *de facto* disregard for the free movement rules in the case of football players in the EC.

[6]Advocate General Trabucchi in Case 13/76, op. cit. note 5, at 1343; Case 66/85 *Lawrie-Blum* [1986] ECR 2121, at para.20.

[7]See Case 36/74, op. cit. note 4, at 1419. For an alternative and, arguably, mistaken perception see Lenz, B., "The Public Service in Article 48(4) with special reference to the Law in England and in the Federal Republic of Germany", *LIEI* (1989) 75–118, at 84, where she states that "these 'services' are, of course, to be distinguished from the 'services' in Article 59ff."

whether remuneration constitutes reward for the service performed, could be regarded as factors indicating the existence, or not, of an economic activity.[8] The object of the free movement rules, namely, the establishment of a common market and the unification of economic systems, thus seems to have limited the Community's abolition of restrictions on trading activities to circumstances which promote such an eventuality.

The fact remains, however, that the Court is generally renowned for its "human" approach to the issues which have arisen in the context of the free movement of persons and its rulings are said to have gone far beyond the Treaty's economic underpinnings.[9] Thus, it has brought the recipients of services within the scope of the Treaty provisions and thereby considerably broadened their personal scope.[10] *Cowan* v. *Le Trésor Public* demonstrates one of the most far-reaching and significant aspects of this development. Though the case referred only to a tourist, whose economic role in the host Member State was minor, to say the least, the reasoning employed by the Court appears to extend access to the protection of Community law (particularly the principle of non-discrimination) to every Community national travelling within the Community, or to every individual "in a situation governed by Community law".[11] Similarly, in *Matteucci*,[12] the Court of Justice relied on Article 7(2) of Regulation 1612/68[13] to extend the principle of equal treatment to a bilateral cultural convention between Belgium and Germany which would not otherwise have fallen within the scope of the Treaty. In the opinion of the Court, Member States are under a responsibility to ensure that migrant workers and their families are equally treated in the social sphere. Indeed, Article 7(2) has been used variously to extend to migrant workers and their families all those rights "which, whether or not linked to a contract of employment, are generally granted to national workers ... and the extension of which to workers who are nationals of other Member States therefore seems suitable to facilitate their mobility".[14]

These rights include the use of a given language in judicial proceedings,[15] the right to be joined by one's partner in the Member State of residence,[16] the right to receive aid for the acquisition and use of immovable property,[17] the right to enjoy

---

[8]See Advocate General Darmon in Case 196/87 *Udo Steymann*, [1988] ECR 6159, at 6167.

[9]See, in particular, Mancini, G.F., "The Free Movement of Workers in the Case- Law of the European Court of Justice", in O'Keeffe, D. and Curtin, D. (eds.), *Constitutional Adjudication in European Community and National Law: Essays in Honour of Mr. Justice T.F. O'Higgins* (1992) Butterworths, Oxford, pp.67–77, at p.67; and O'Keeffe, D., "Trends in the Free Movement of Persons within the European Communities" in O'Reilly, J. (ed.), *Human Rights and Constitutional Law. Essays in Honour of Brian Walsh* (1992) Round Hall Press, Dublin, pp.263–291, at pp.267 *et seq.*

[10]See Joined Cases 286/82 and 26/83 *Luisi and Carbone* [1984] ECR 377; and the forebodings of Advocate General Trabucchi in Case 118/75 *Watson and Belmann* [1976] ECR 1185.

[11]Case 186/87 *Cowan* v. *Le Trésor Public* [1989] ECR 195, at para.10.

[12]Case 235/87 [1988] ECR 5589.

[13]OJ 1968 L257/2.

[14]Case 207/78 *Ministère Public* v. *Even* [1979] ECR 2019, at para.22.

[15]Case 137/84 *Ministère Public* v. *Mutsch* [1985] ECR 2681.

[16]Case 59/85 *Netherlands* v. *Reed* [1986] ECR 1283.

[17]Case 305/87 *Commission* v. *Greece* [1989] ECR 1461.

study abroad opportunities, etc.[18] This type of judicial creativity certainly points to the development of the social aspects of free movement, but in the last analysis, the cases generally demonstrate some sort of economic link (no matter how insignificant) and may be limited as future precedents on this basis.[19] It is possible to argue that the logic developed by the Court in *Cowan* and *Matteucci* could extend the principle of equal treatment to the beneficiaries of a general right of residence as regards social assistance and medical care. However, it has not yet been applied in this manner and it is unlikely, given Member State opposition, the import of the principle of subsidiarity and a general lack of social solidarity between Member States, to be so applied in the near future. The Court's judicial creativity has generally proceeded on a case by case basis and has not found a coherent or legislative basis in the scope of the Community's objectives as regards individual Community citizens, or its integrationary scheme. O'Keeffe states that "the individual exercising the right of free movement (is viewed) in a human rights or constitutional context, and not in an economic one, provided that he or she falls within the personal scope of the Treaty".[20] Therein lies the crux of the problem, however; the fact that an individual must first fall within the personal scope of the Treaty and that this may still be widened or restricted with reference to definitions of economic activity, remuneration or worker. The latter still enjoy a place of honour in the Community's legal framework. Thus, in *Bettray*, the social objectives displayed by the social employment scheme were fatal to the plaintiff's claim, given the overriding requirement of an economic activity, despite the fact that the employment activity in question was regarded as genuine and effective.[21]

3.2.1. Economic Criteria in the Context of Services

The insistence on an economic element in a transaction or activity also applies in the area of services, which are defined in the Treaty with reference to remuneration.[22] However, given the wide variety in services and the manner in which they are organised and financed, the interpretation of this criterion is not always

---

[18]Case C-308/89 *Carmina di Leo* v. *Land Berlin* [1990] ECR I- 4185; and generally, O'Keeffe, D., "Equal Rights For Migrants: The Concept of Social Advantages in Article 7(2), Regulation 1612/68", 5 YEL (1985) 93–123.

[19]Thus, Daubler, argues that "The freedoms in the Treaty are basically limited to national treatment and primarily designed to be principles of a market constitution, against which, where necessary, the interests of the individual will have to yield. This does not mean that they do not grant freedoms to the individual common market citizen, but that they do not resemble traditional fundamental rights." Daubler, W., *Market and Social Justice in the EEC: the Other Side of the Internal Market. Strategies and Options for the Future of Europe* Basic Findings 3 (1991) Bertelsmann Foundation Publishers Gutersloh, at p.93.

[20]O'Keeffe, op. cit. note 9, at p.273.

[21]Case 344/87 [1988] ECR 1621; discussed *infra* Section 3.3.2. See also Hervey, T.K., "Legal Issues Concerning the *Barber* Protocol", in O'Keeffe, D. and Twomey, P. (eds.), *Legal Issues of the Maastricht Treaty* (1993) London, Chancery Press, pp.329–337, at pp.336–337, where she discusses the triumph of market forces over the fundamental rights of individuals in the Community.

[22]Article 60 states that services within the meaning of the Treaty are *normally* provided for remuneration (emphasis added).

straightforward. It has been extended, for example, to the activities performed by members of a religious community in *Udo Steymann* v. *Staatssecretaris van Justitie*, in so far as the services provided by the community to its members were regarded as indirect consideration for the genuine and effective work performed by them. The rules of the community explicitly stated, however, that the basic services provided by it and regarded as remuneration by the Court of Justice were not related to the work performed by its members or to any other manner in which they contributed to the religious community.[23] In the *Schindler* case the Court of Justice held that a remunerated provision of services is an economic activity within the scope of the Treaty.[24] It regarded the organisation of the lottery and the participation of the individuals buying the tickets as a provision and receipt of services. The price of the ticket constituted remuneration. The fact that participants only had a chance of winning the prize did not deprive the organisation of the lottery of its economic character, nor did the recreative nature of the activity, since the participant still had a hope of winning and the organiser generally reaped a reward.[25]

In the controversial *Grogan* case,[26] the Court was asked whether the activities of abortion clinics constitute services within the meaning of Article 60 and if so, whether the Treaty provisions on the freedom to supply services preclude a national rule prohibiting the provision of information concerning abortion services legally carried on in another Member State.[27] At issue was a national prohibition on the provision of information regarding a service which was legally provided in the Member State for which it was advertised, but which was constitutionally forbidden in the Member State where the information was being provided and where the provider of information was being legally enjoined. The Court held that the medical termination of pregnancy came within the scope of the Community's definition of services.[28] In rejecting claims that the activity was immoral, the Court held that it could and should not substitute its own assessment of morality for that of a Member

---

[23]The fact that the Court subsequently rejected the application of Article 60 due to the indefinite nature of the activity is secondary. What is significant is that it broadly interpreted the requirement that the activity constitute an economic activity so as not to exclude a role for Community law from the outset.

[24]Case C-275/92 [1994] ECR I-1034, at para.19.

[25]See also *Agence Europe* no.6433, 4 March 1995, where the Commission is asking the Court of Justice to regard the organisation of pleasure boats as an economic activity.

[26]Case C-159/90 *Society for the Protection of Unborn Children* v. *Grogan* [1991] ECR I-4685.

[27]For further details of the background to *Grogan* see the annotation by O'Leary, S., "The Court of Justice as a Reluctant Constitutional Adjudicator: An examination of the abortion information case", 17 *ELRev* (1992) 138–157.

[28]This is consistent with its decision in Joined Cases 286/82 and 26/83 *Luisi and Carbone*, op. cit. note 10, at para.16, where medical services were said to come within the Community's definition of services. See also Case 131/85 *Gul* v. *Regierungsprasident Dusseldorf* [1986] ECR 1575, where the Court held that the public health sector is a sector of economic activity for the purpose of access to employment and the application of the principles of freedom of movement. The Sixth VAT Directive regards "the activities of the professions", which no doubt includes the medical profession, as services for the purposes of the Directive. Nevertheless, in Case C-61/89 *Criminal Proceedings Against Bouchoucha* [1990] ECR I-3551, at para.12, the Court held that "there is no Community definition of medical acts, the definition of acts restricted to the medical profession is, in principle, a matter for the Member States".

State where a service is legally provided.[29] The Court and Advocate General disagreed on whether the prohibition on information concerning a legally provided service was an indirect restriction on the freedom to provide services contrary to Article 59. The former held that the link between the students' associations and the clinics operating in another Member State was too tenuous for the prohibition on the distribution of information to be regarded as a restriction within the meaning of Article 59 of the Treaty.[30] The economic operators at issue were the medical clinics operating in the United Kingdom. The information distributed by the Irish students' associations was not distributed on behalf of the economic operator and was independent of the economic activity which the clinics performed. The students' associations never claimed that they themselves were provider of services, probably because of the absence of consideration from the students in return for the information provided.[31] According to the Court, however, the prohibition could not be regarded as a restriction falling within the provisions of Article 59 in the absence of a (economic) link between the providers of the information and the providers of the economic service being advertised, the implication being that the restriction could in fact impede the free provision of services, but that legally these restrictions fell outside the scope of Article 59. In contrast, the Advocate General stressed the fundamental importance of freedom to supply services in the Community framework, the need to respect this fundamental principle and further, the possibility of promoting it "by means of the provision of information, whether or not for consideration, concerning services which the provider of information supplies himself, or which are supplied by another person".[32] Thus, not only did he regard payment for publication of the information as unnecessary, but the existence of a relationship between the provider of services and the distributor of the information concerning the service at issue was not material either in his view.

The limited extent of the Court's reasoning in *Grogan* disappoints. Having held that abortion is a service under Community law, the correct inquiry was the effect of information on the free supply of services which is the concern of Community law in its attempts to create a free market in services.[33] Instead, the Court exam-

---

[29]See also Case C-275/92, op. cit. note 24, at para.32.

[30]Case C-159/90, op. cit. note 26, at para.24. See generally, O'Leary, op. cit. note 27; Wilkinson, B., "Abortion, the Irish Constitution and the EEC" (1992) *Public Law* 20–30, at 26–27; Colvin, C.M., "*SPUC* v. *Grogan*: Irish Abortion Law and the Free Movement of Services in the European Community", 15 *Fordham International Law Journal* (1991–92) 476–526, at 505 *et seq.*; and the annotation by Curtin, D., 29 *CMLRev* (1992) 585–603.

[31]The decision left open the question whether information itself could be regarded as a (related) service within the meaning of Article 60 if provided for remuneration.

[32]In this context, he relied on Case C-362/88 *GB-INNO-BM* [1990] ECR 667, which had held that restrictions on advertising compromised a consumer's freedom to shop. Extending this logic, Advocate General Van Gerven in *Grogan* said that a similar restriction on information generally would compromise the freedom of recipients of services to go to another Member State to receive a service.

[33]It is now generally accepted that the Treaty aims to positively integrate in the area of services, in the sense of prohibiting indistinctly discriminatory measures; see Advocate General Warner in Case 52/79 *Debauve* [1980] ECR 833; Collins, A., "Commercial Speech and the Free Movement of Goods and Services", in O'Reilly, op. cit. note 9, pp.319–336, at pp.329 *et seq.*; and Minor, J., "The Elimination of Non-Discriminatory Obstacles" (1994) *Actualités du Droit* 209–225.

ined the proximity and the economic content of the relationship between the defendants and the providers of the service of abortion. Since the providers of information did not act, economically and consensually, in conjunction with the providers of service, the link between the two was said to be too tenuous for Community law to apply. Thus, the criterion that an economic activity take place has been transposed to an ancillary relationship between the provider of services and the advertiser of those services, where in addition, the Court requires a direct and intentional link to be established between the two. Although the Court has never required such a link before, it did not discuss the new requirement and it distinguished *GB-INNO-BM* v. *Confédération du Commerce Luxembourgeois* by stating that that case related to a prohibition on advertisement which could have constituted a barrier to the free movement of goods. This is misleading, since the link used in *GB-INNO-BM* was one between the consumer and the advertisement and the importance of advertising was the protection of the consumer and the distribution of information to them.[34] In contrast in *Grogan* the existence of a contractual or economic relationship between the advertiser and the provider of services was of paramount importance to the Court. In *Schindler*, on the other hand, the Court refused to treat the mailing of advertising material independently from the actual lottery. The advertisement was not an end in itself, but was designed to permit the participation by the residents of the Member States where the advertisements were sent.

In the legal or commercial relationship between the provider and recipient of services some direct link could arguably be necessary, although it could also be argued that where there is a unilateral provision of a service, there must simply be deliberate conduct on the part of the person providing the service.[35] The flexibilty demonstrated by the latter approach might be the best way to promote free movement and would be more compatible with its development in the context of Community citizenship. Returning to the instant case, however, the exclusion of Community law due to the absence of a contractual or economic link between the providers of services and the advertisers of that service is misguided. If this situation is maintained, the position of many non-profit consumer or advice organisations whose function is precisely to inform Community citizens of their rights under Community law independently of the providers of those services is endangered. On the basis of *Grogan* and in the absence of any economic link, these bodies are not protected under Community law.

3.2.2. Economic Activity and the Requirement of Consideration

Remuneration in the context of Article 60 has been defined on one occasion by Advocate General Lenz as financial consideration for the service performed, normally fixed by agreement between the person providing the service and its recipient.[36] Is

---

[34]Case C-362/88, op. cit. note 32, at para.8.
[35]See, in this regard, the German submissions in Case 62/79 *Coditel* (No.1), [1980] ECR 881, and the Commission's discussion of the potentially gratuitous nature of media services.
[36]See Advocate General Lenz in Case 186/87 *Cowan*, op. cit. note 11, at 208; and Advocate General Slynn in Case 263/86 *Humbel* [1988] ECR 5635, at 5379.

it necessary that the recipient of the service furnish the remuneration directly to the person providing the service, or may payment be made by a third party to whom another service is, or is not rendered in return?[37] Such a triangular service relationship could be said to arise in the context of state or publicly funded services and economic activities. It is contended that no mutual relationship of payment should be necessary between the provider and recipient of services for Community law to apply and the fact that an individual, as a worker, taxpayer or ratepayer contributes to the local or national budget could be regarded as a sufficient causal link in certain circumstances, to create a triangle of service and remuneration between the provider, recipient and the state. This could also be the case if the state acts as the provider of services (and the payer of consideration) in the context of a national welfare system. Can consideration in these cases not be regarded as the individual's participation in and belonging to the community? After all, Article 60 refers to services *normally* provided for consideration and does not necessarily require remuneration in all circumstances. If the service is one which is *normally* paid for, then it remains a service and should still come within the scope of Community law although, in certain circumstances, it is not paid for as, for example, medical services in a state welfare system. In the context of the receipt of benefits under Regulation 1408/71 in *van Roosmalen*, the Court of Justice has held that "it is not necessary that the self-employed person should receive remuneration as a direct reward for his activity. It is sufficient if he receives, in respect of that activity, income which permits him to meet all or some of his needs, even if that income is supplied, as in this case, by third parties benefiting from the services of a missionary priest".[38] Section 3.3.1 examines the Court's decisions in *Levin* and *Kempf*, where it included workers who subsidised their incomes by other means, including recourse to public funds, within the Community definition of worker. Just as the "subsidising income by other means" reasoning in *Levin* was extended to subsidies from public funds in *Kempf*,[39] so the "third party source of remuneration" reasoning in *van Roosmalen* could be transposed to the payment for various services by the state in the field of education and health.

This type of tripartite service relationship is also demonstrated by employment agencies which operate on behalf of employers in seeking employees. Remuneration in such instances is generally paid by the employer, but the service is simultaneously provided to the employee and the employer. The Court of Justice has already touched upon such a situation in the *Rush Portuguesa* case, but its judgment does not preclude the application of Community law to such triangular service relationships.[40] The economic character of broadcasting services has also been

[37]See the submissions of the claimant and the Commission in Case 263/86, op. cit. note 36, at 5368 and 5372.
[38]See Case 300/84 [1986] ECR 3097, at para.22.
[39]See Case 139/85 [1986] ECR 1741.
[40]In the particular circumstances of that case it held that employment agencies, whose specific function is generally to recruit employees for the labour market, could not avoid the transitory restriction on free movement, such as that in the Treaty of Accession of Spain and Portugal, on the grounds that they were providers of services: Case 113/89 [1990] ECR 1417, at para.16.

discussed in the Court of Justice. The applicant in the *Coditel* case argued that the provision of services does not necessarily imply a legal relationship between the provider and the recipient and that "such a requirement is scarcely compatible with economic reality in industries in which revenue is often largely generated by advertising". The economic nature of the activity can be said to derive from advertising and not directly from the TV viewer or radio listener. Some support for this position is available in *Bond Van Adverteerders*, where the Court held, in the context of broadcasting, that Article 60 does not require that a service is paid for by its beneficiaries.[41] Furthermore, the Court of Justice has allowed the nature of the activity in question to determine the character and extent of remuneration in other cases. Thus in *Ex parte Agegate*,[42] it ruled with respect to the variable activities of fishermen that

> (they work) in very close conjunction with ... other persons performing an identical activity and where it is not possible to separate the contribution which each makes to the final result. The fisherman is in fact remunerated on the basis of the work done by the crew as a whole and his pay does not consist in the right to be able to keep the fish which he took from the sea personally and by himself or the money which such fish are worth.

3.2.3. The Public/Private Funding Distinction

The economic character of a number of sectors of state activity have also been questioned on the basis of (i) the public nature of the funding which supports them and (ii) the extra-economic social objectives which motivate their organisation. In some instances the requirement of an element of remuneration has additionally become confused, wrongly in our view, with the need for a profit-making element, so that the pursuit of a gainful or economic activity must entail an element of profit for the provider and/or the recipient, for Community law to apply.[43] The issue of private versus state funding as a criterion for the application of the Treaty has specifically arisen in the context of state education. In *Humbel*, the Court held that the essential characteristic of remuneration was absent from courses provided in the context of a public education system. Such national educational courses were said not to constitute examples of participation in a gainful activity by the students. They belonged to the sphere of national educational and social policy.[44] Their non-economic social motivation brought them outside the scope of Community law.

---

[41]Case 352/85 [1988] ECR 2085, at para.16.

[42]Case C-3/87 [1990] 3 Weekly Law Reports 226, at para.15.

[43]See the submissions of the UK government to the House of Lords Select Committee on the European Communities, *Free Movement of People and the Right of Residence in the EC*, 7th session 1989–90, which referred to the rights of recipients of services "for example, if they are staying at a hotel, or seeking private medical treatment or private education from a profit-making organisation".

[44]Case 263/86, op. cit. note 36, at para.18. See, however, Advocate General Slynn in Case 147/86 *Commission* v. *Greece* [1988] ECR 1637, at 1648, where he rejected the defendant government's claim that "being closely linked with the traditional and cultural life of a Member State, education was deliberately excluded" on the grounds that work performed or services rendered are subject to the provisions of Articles 48 and 59 whatever the sphere in which they are performed.

They were also funded from the public purse and not by arrangement between recipient and provider. Though he rejected the emphasis laid by the plaintiff state on the importance of a profit-making element, the Advocate General in *Humbel* stressed the relevant test as whether the services were provided as part of an economic activity. Though education was capable of constituting a service, this was not the case for education in state schools, which provide services without charge, or which are paid for by grants already paid for by the state. The Commission was highly critical of this emphasis on the source of remuneration in the field of state education. In the *Wirth* case the Court of Justice has confirmed the distinction between education services provided in private and public institutions of higher education. When courses are provided in institutions financed mainly out of private funds and which seek to make a commercial profit they can be classified as services within the meaning of Article 60.[45]

This public/private funding distinction is incompatible with the Court's implicit recognition of the role of the interventionary and welfare-oriented modern State in *Kempf*. The Court there held that part-time activities qualify as economic and that the individual who performs them qualifies as a Community worker even if he or she has recourse to public funds or state benefits to supplement the income he or she receives from the activity in question. Any distinction between public and privately funded services also sits uneasily with the decision of the Court in *Commission* v. *Italy*.[46] Italian legislation only permitted Italian nationals to purchase and lease housing built or renovated with the help of public funds and to obtain reduced rate mortgage loans. In holding that the said legislation infringed Articles 52 and 59, the Court extended the benefits of what was unquestionably a state social policy measure to non-nationals on an equal treatment basis without regard to the source of the funds financing the project, or the policy which lay behind the legislation. In *Bettray*, both the Court and Advocate General rejected the public source of funding as a relevant consideration in determining whether an individual involved in a public social employment scheme could be regarded as a worker for the purposes of Article 48. The source of remuneration was also considered irrelevant by the Advocate General in *Debauve*,[47] where he said that the method of financing particular broadcasting organisations or particular broadcasts could not be relevant to the decision of the Court. The decisive fact was that the services are normally paid for and not who paid for them. The distinction between private and public sectors may, however, be on the way out, given the Court's failure to refer to, or even tacit rejection of the Commission's argument in the *Grogan* case that abortion should only be considered a service within the meaning of Article 60 if it is provided privately and entirely paid for by the recipient.[48] In addition, Advocate General Gulmann rejected the argument in *Schindler* that Article 59 only applies to

---

[45]Case C-109/93 *Wirth* v. *Landes Hauptstadt Hannover*, judgment of the 7/12/1993.
[46]Case 63/86 [1988] ECR 29.
[47]Case 52/79 *Procureur du Roi* v. *Debauve* [1980] ECR 833, at 876.
[48]See Curtin, op. cit. note 30, at 592.

companies which pursue a lucrative objective. Nevertheless, the essence of the decision in *Grogan* was that the absence of remuneration between the providers of
services and the providers of information excluded the application of Community
law. Moreover, *Humbel* may be regarded as an anomaly in Community law, mit-
igated by the clear ruling in *Bettray* that public funding was not a relevant consideration in determining the applicant's status as a worker. However, the judgment in
Grogan demonstrates that the existence of an economic link or contractual and
monetary relationship is still of vital importance in determining whether a case is a
"Community" case. The fact that such a link no longer exists in the context of many
publicly-funded services has the obvious consequence that they may be excluded
from Community law, regardless of whether, as in *Humbel*, the Court explicitly ac-
knowledges the exclusion.

Community law insists, however, that the nature of legal relationships is not relevant for the application of Community law.[49] Thus, the services of a teacher employed by the state should remain services within the meaning of Community law
for the purposes of the free movement of persons and, we argue, as regards the recipients of services, despite their organisation by the state.[50] If the lessons given to
a school's pupils are of sufficient economic value for the provider to be regarded
as involved in an economic activity as in *Lawrie-Blum*, there is no need to exclude
the other side of the exchange, namely the recipients, because other social objectives inform the organisation of the exchange, in this instance the social policy of
the state to educate. Directive 73/148 proceeds on this assumption, namely, that the
rights of the providers and recipients of services are co-extensive. How can the position of the recipient of such services be excluded from the application of the
Treaty's provisions on the grounds that the organisation and funding of the exchange is public? An imbalance is created if in one sense — the position of the
provider of services (whether in a contract for services or of services) — Community
law covers this transaction, but in another sense — the position of the recipient of
such services — it does not, because of the public organisation of the activity in
question. In *Lawrie-Blum*, the Court stipulated that all that was needed to regard
education as a service in the context of Article 48 was that it was performed for remuneration. In the context of a state school system, a teacher provides services for
remuneration within the meaning of Article 48, the only difference being that the

---

[49]Case 152/73 *Sotgiu* [1974] ECR 153, at para.5: "In the absence of any distinction in the provision of Article 48(4) it is of no interest whether a worker is engaged as a blue-collar worker, a white-
collar worker or an official or even whether the terms on which he is employed come under public or
private law"; Advocate General Slynn in Case 147/86 *Commission* v. *Greece* [1988] ECR 1637, at
1648; Case 33/88 *Pillar Allué and Carmen Mary Coonan* v. *Università degli Studi di Venezia* [1989]
ECR 1591; and Case C-4/91 *Bleis* v. *Ministère de l'Education Nationale* [1991] ECR I-5627.

[50]In this context see Advocate General Lenz in Case 66/85 *Lawrie-Blum*, at 2133, where he accepted that education is not part of economic life to the extent that education policy is not part of the
market process, but stated: "However, the place of education policy must be distinguished from the activity of workers who provide services in return for remuneration. Irrespective of whether or not public
or private employers are engaged in economic activity, profiting from one's labour is undoubtedly part
of economic life ...".

remuneration comes from a source which is not the direct beneficiary.[51] Although often organised by the state and with important social policy considerations in mind, public health and education services could still be services within the meaning of Article 60, which only requires that they normally be provided for consideration.

It is possible that a distinction similar to that which has arisen in education will arise in the area of health care, although it must be said that medical services do not involve the specifically national educational and cultural factors considered relevant in *Humbel*. Advocate General Slynn also pointed out in *Humbel* that entitlement to medical care in the Community is underpinned by a complex system designed to determine which state should ultimately bear the cost of treatment.[52] If the Court's reasoning with respect to the source of funding is maintained, then public health care and other areas of state regulation and funding will fall outside the realm of the Community provisions on services. The source of funding will thus negate the economic character of the activity for the purposes of Community law. Though such activities involve economic characteristics and, at first sight, fall within the scope of Community law, the role of the state as the source of finance and organisation denies the application of Community law. As we stated above, it is to be hoped that the omission of a reference to remuneration in the context of abortion services in *Grogan*, though a distinction was urged by the Commission, is part of a judicial policy to extend a broad definition of economic activity to publicly funded services.

3.3. Further Delimitation of the Scope of Free Movement

The following section deals with the concept of worker almost exclusively in the context of Article 48, Regulation 1612/68 and the decisions of the Court of Justice handed down on that basis.[53] A distinction exists between the activities of the em-

---

[51]See Gaudemot-Tallon, H., 28 RTDE (1992) 161–180, at 171–172. Article 4(2) of the Sixth VAT Directive regards the activities of the professions generally as economic activities. Those activities are not required to be profit-making or governed by market forces, but they must be of a permanent character and be performed for consideration. Furthermore, they are assessed without regard to their purpose, whether they be linked to social policy, or to other non-economic aspects of life. See Case 235/85, *Commission* v. *Netherlands* [1987] ECR 1471, at 1487. In addition, Article 4(1) of the Directive specifically provides that a taxable person is any person who independently carries out in any place any economic activity specified in paragraph 2, whatever the purpose or results of that activity.

[52]Case 263/86, op. cit. note 36, at 5380.

[53]The terms *worker* and *employee* are also found in various contexts in Community law outside Article 48. Article 69 ECSC refers to "workers who have recognised qualifications in a coal-mining or steel occupation" and Article 96 EAEC relates to skilled employment in the field of nuclear energy. Neither of these provisions apply to job-seekers. Similar references to a particular skill or training do not appear in Article 48. Article 50, on the other hand, refers to young workers and Article 51 to migrant workers. In Title 1 of Regulation 1408/71, OJ 1971 L149/2, worker is defined in section (i) as "any person who is insured, compulsorily or on an optional basis, for one or more of the contingencies covered by the branches of a social security scheme for employed persons". This is one of the few incidents in Community law where the definition of worker is left to national law. Community law also

ployed and self-employed, but it is not dealt with in detail in the course of this chapter.[54] Our primary consideration is the determination of the applicability of the free movement rules, rather than the different manner in which they apply.

3.3.1. The Concept of Worker in Community Law

The concept of worker in Article 48 and the related concept of "activities of an employed person" in Article 1(1) of Regulation 1612/68[55] are not specifically defined in the Treaty. Nevertheless, Article 48(2) gives limited substance to the concept by pinpointing certain aspects of an employment relationship such as remuneration and employment conditions. An existing employment relationship, or the concrete possibility of such are essential aspects of the Community status of worker.[56] The Community legislator and Court were faced with the possibility of resorting to the various legislative formulations of "worker", "employee" and "employment relationships" operating in the internal legal orders of the Member States and transposing these to Community law.[57] At Member State level, however, the criteria applied in particular cases to determine the existence of a contract of employment tend to depend on the particular legislative context involved. Recourse to the various definitions of employee or worker applicable under United Kingdom employment legislation emphasise the difficulties of comparatively transposing a

variously refers to frontier workers, temporarily or permanently incapacitated persons and retired persons. Employment in the broad sense also features at various points in the Treaty – Article 118, Article 104, Article 39(1), Article 92(3). See generally, Kravaritou-Manitakis, P., "L'emploi selon le Traité de Rome et l'action communautaire. Textes et realités", 16 *Rivista di Diritto Europeo* (1976) 20–36; and Wyatt, D., "The Social Security Rights of Migrant Workers and their Families", 14 *CMLRev* (1977) 411–433, at 417.

[54]Indeed, the Court in *Walrave and Koch, Donà* and Case C-265/88 *Lothar Messner* [1989] ECR 4209, saw no need to determine whether it was dealing with a contract of service (Article 48) or a contract for services (Article 59); see also Case C-363/89 *Roux* v. *Belgian State* [1991] ECR I-273, at paras.23 and 24, where the Court held that Articles 48 and 52 ensure the same judicial protection and that if an individual exercises an economic activity, it is not necessary to qualify that activity as employed or self-employed. Different legal regimes do apply in certain contexts however. Thus, Directive 68/360 determines the conditions for the receipt of a residence permit for employed workers, while Directive 73/148 establishes the necessary and somewhat different requirements for the self-employed. In addition, Regulation 1612/68 applies to workers only; persons falling under Articles 52 and 59 must rely on the general guarantee of equal treatment in Article 6 and the second sentence of Article 52 "under the conditions laid down for its own nationals by the law of the country where such establishment is affected". See also Case C-15/90 *Middleburgh* v. *Chief Adjudication Officer* [1992] CMLR 356, at para.13, where the Court held that a person who has worked only in a self-employed capacity in a Member State before becoming unemployed cannot be regarded as a "worker" within the meaning of Article 48.

[55]Article 1(1) states that "Any national of a Member State shall, irrespective of his place of residence, have the right to take up an activity as an employed person, and to pursue such activity, within the territory of another Member State in accordance with the provisions laid down by law, regulation or administrative action governing the employment of nationals of that State."

[56]See the annotations by White, R., 17 *ELRev* (1992) 522–533.

[57]See Lenz, op. cit. note 7, at 82; Plender R., "Free Movement in the European Communities", in *International Migration Law*, 2nd edn. (1988) Martinus Nijhoff, Dordrecht, at p.195; Maestripieri, *La Libre Circulation des Personnes et des Services dans la CEE* (1972) UGA, Heule, at pp.40–42; and Advocate General Mayras unsuccessfully resorting to some comparative analysis in Case 149/79 *Commission* v. *Belgium* [1980] ECR 3881, at 3911–3912 and 3916.

definition on the basis of national legal provisions based on entirely different concepts.[58] Furthermore, if the Court had confined itself strictly to definitions of worker and employment in civil law Member States, given its initial composition, it would have faced some difficulties on being subsequently joined by their common law partners. Faced with national legal diversity and the need to act flexibly to facilitate the possible accession of new members and developments in labour law,[59] the Court could not leave the determination of who is a worker for Community purposes to national employment law definitions. Though the principle of equal treatment, which applies within a single Member State,[60] might survive the absence of a uniform definition, the broader objective of free movement and the creation of an integrated labour market, could have been rendered ineffective if Member States were able to deny the application of the Treaty by simply refusing to accord the status of worker to an individual on the basis of unilaterally determined national criteria. In the event, the Court opted for a Community interpretation partially based on a comparative and teleological approach which sought to enhance the independence and supremacy of the Community legal order over that of the Member States. In order to safeguard the *effet utile* and objectives behind the Treaty provisions on free movement, the term worker was given a Community scope.[61] To enable Member States to define worker unilaterally with reference to national minimum wage and minimum hours of work legislation would have enabled them to fix or vary the category of persons eligible for the protection afforded by the free movement provisions in the Treaty.[62] This would have upset the primary intention behind these articles – the creation of an integrated European labour market.

[58]Section 30(1) of the Trade Union and Labour Relations Act, 1974 defines employee for the purposes of the act as "an individual who has entered into or works under (or where the employment has ceased, worked under) a contract of employment" where the latter means "a contract of service or apprenticeship". The same Act defines a worker as those who normally work or who seek work under a contract of employment or under any other contract whereby the worker undertakes to do or to perform personally any work or services. See generally, Hepple, B.A., and Fredman, S., *Labour Law and Industrial Relations in Great Britain* (1986) Kluwer, Dordrecht, at p.79; and Wyatt, op. cit. note 53, at 418. We note that the UK only joined the Communities in 1973, but consider that reference to the diversity of its employment law definitions of worker is still useful with hindsight.

[59]See Mertens de Wilmars, J., "Reflexions sur les méthodes d'interprétation de la Cour de Justice des Communautés Européennes", 22 *Cahiers du Droit Européen* (1986) 5–20, at 6: "la nature même de l'ordre juridique communautaire qui est un systeme encore neuf, inachevé et destiné, à evolué et à s'adapter constamment à raison notamment des apports resultant chaque fois de l'adhésion de nouveaux membres". For comparative discussion of the evolution of labour law in Europe see Hepple, B., *The Making of Labour Law in Europe: A Comparative Study of Nine Countries up to 1945* (1986) London, Mansell Publishing,

[60]See Weatherill, S., "The Scope of Article 7", 15 *ELRev* (1990) 334–340.

[61]See generally, Vaughan, D., *The Law of the European Communities*, Vol.2 (1989) Butterworths, Oxford, para.15.08; Waelbroeck, M., *Commentaire Megret. Le Droit de la CEE Libre circulation des personnes, services et des capitaux, transports*, no.3, 2nd edn. (1990) Editions de l'Université Libre de Bruxelles, Bruxelles, at p.15; and as regards the communitarian scope of certain concepts, see Mertens de Wilmars, op. cit. note 59, at 12.

[62]See Case 75/63, *Hoekstra*, at 184.

A classical contractual working relationship, what the Court in *Bettray* referred to as a "normal working relationship", is characterised as an open-ended, daily or weekly full-time relationship with a single employer on his premises.[63] Simply stating that the notion of worker is a Community law concept and that it has to be interpreted extensively, does not determine to what extent some, or all, of these elements are considered to be applicable in Community law. In these early cases, none of the functional elements of the Community's definition of worker were elucidated and national courts were left with considerable room for manoeuvre.[64] What is clear, however, is that the Community concept of worker applied was not deduced solely with reference to labour law criteria, but additionally related to the Community's objectives of supremacy and uniformity. The Community concept of worker was designed to serve these higher objectives, in addition to the personal rights and status of the individual and the integration of the European labour market for his or her benefit. Thus, one author has argued that "it is the worker as an item in the economic processes of manufacture and distribution who was under attention, not the worker as an individual".[65] Despite magnanimous references to the Community objective of raising the standard of living of Member State nationals,[66] early cases insisted on the economic content of the activity in question. It is submitted that this was to protect the host Member States from migration detached from employment. Nevertheless, the development of the concept of worker in the jurisprudence of the Court of Justice reveals the emergence of a less strict adherence to economic aspects. The Court's response does demonstrate a general shift from a strict theory of Community nationals as economic agents of integration to one which regards them as Community citizens, if only at an embryonic stage. However, the legislative structures and legal tools of the Treaty have not changed, nor have some of the protectionist positions of the Member States. These structural legal and political obstacles set a limit to the judicial development of the non-economic and "citizenship" aspects of the free movement of persons.

---

[63]See Bouder, A., "New Forms of Employment and their Use in the Employment Policies of the Member States of the European Communities", 5 *International Journal of Comparative Labour Law and Industrial Relations* (1989) 1–16; and the elements of an employment relationship indicated by the Commission in its proposal for a Directive on the form of proof of an employment relationship which include, *inter alia*, the identity of the parties, duration of the employment relationship, remuneration and method of payment, the applicable social security system, etc. cited in Blanpain, op. cit. note 5, at pp.112 *et seq.*

[64]See, for example, the English Court's rejection of a restaurant dishwasher as a worker in *Regina v. Secchi* [1975] CMLR 383; German expulsion of an Italian national who became unfit to work shortly after arriving there in *Re Expulsion of an Italian National* [1965] CMLR 285; and *Queen of the Netherlands in Council, Re a Belgian Prostitute* [1976] CMLR 527. For a broader national interpretation see *Nijssen v. Immigration Office, London (Heathrow) Airport* (1978) Immigration Appeal Reports 226.

[65]See Mackenzie Stuart, A.J., "Problems of the European Community: Transatlantic Parallels", 36 *International Comparative Law Quarterly.* (1986) 183–197, at 191; and Mancini, G.F., "The Making of a Constitution for Europe", 26 *CMLRev* (1989) 595–614, at 596; see also Mancini in O'Keeffe and Curtin (eds.), op. cit. note 9, at p.69, who describes this approach in terms of "a hermeneutic monopoly for the purpose of counteracting the unequal and discriminatory application of the rules on freedom of movement".

[66]See, for example, Case 53/81, op. cit. note 1, at para.15.

The inapplicability of national criteria was reiterated in *Levin* v. *Staatssecretaris van Justitie*,[67] where the Court clarified the terms "worker" and "activity as an employed person" in the light of "the principles of the legal order of the Community" and reiterated the necessity that the concepts used in provisions laying down the foundations of the fundamental freedoms in the Treaty have a fixed and uniform meaning and that they be extensively interpreted.[68] It extended the protection of the Treaty provisions on free movement to part-time workers earning less than what was considered necessary at national level for subsistence. It regarded this as an acknowledgement of the widespread social reality that for many people part-time work, though yielding a lower income, was an improvement of their living conditions as required by Article 2.[69] To exclude workers whose revenue was less than the minimum level of subsistence in the host Member State would in fact have threatened the uniform personal scope of free movement, given the fact that the minimum level in question is fixed unilaterally by individual Member States and inevitably varies.[70] In *Levin* the rules on free movement covered only "the pursuit of effective and genuine activities, to the exclusion of activities *on such a small scale* as to be regarded as purely marginal and ancillary" (emphasis added). It is submitted, however, that the second part of this qualification on the remit of the Treaty provisions has subsequently been misused and taken out of the distinctly quantitative context into which it was placed in *Levin*. Similarly, though the aims which prompted an individual to seek employment in another Member State were regarded as irrelevant in *Levin*,[71] recent cases before the Court have seen the ac-

---

[67]Case 53/81, op. cit. note 1. The case involved a British subject "employed" in the Netherlands who had applied for a residence permit in accordance with the relevant provisions of Dutch law. Her application having been refused, it was held, on appeal at national level, that she could not be regarded as a worker within the meaning of the Treaty since she earned less than the nationally prescribed minimum legal wage and since she lacked the subjective will to pursue an occupation, or at least other motives lay behind her application for residence. Her employment, it was said, was to enable her non-EEC husband to benefit from the Treaty provisions.

[68]An extensive interpretation of worker in Article 48 does not equally translate to third country nationals who fall within the cooperation or association agreements concluded between the Community and third countries; see Case C-18/90 *Office National de l'emploi* v. *Kziber* [1991] ECR 199, particularly Advocate General Van Gerven, at paras.19–20. Those agreements, which seek merely to ensure equal treatment for third country workers already admitted to the Community labour market and not to facilitate the access and mobility of third country nationals generally, pursue different objectives to the EC Treaty and do not require a similar broad interpretation of their scope of application.

[69]Advocate General Slynn also regarded the question of the inclusion of part-timers as important "particularly in a time of extensive unemployment and of an increasing dependence on part-time work". The corollary, to which he also referred, was the concern of Member States that the Treaty provisions not be subject to abuse by persons not in any real or genuine sense workers (see the submissions of the Dutch and Danish governments, at 1040 and 1041, respectively). The latter is reknowned for its anxious protection of comparatively lucrative Danish welfare benefits. Given that 90 per cent of social security expenses in Denmark are levied through taxes (see Blanpain, op. cit. note 5, at p.198), this is not surprising.

[70]See Druesne, G., "Liberté de circulation des personnes, les prolongements de la libre circulation des salariés: droit de séjour et progrès social", 18 RTDE (1982) 556–567, at 558.

[71]Levin, op. cit. note 1, at para.21. Advocate General Slynn regarded only a few hours work each week as relevant in deciding whether work is "the genuine and substantial purpose of the application to reside", Case 53/81 op. cit. note 1, at 1061. See also Druesne, op. cit. note 70, at 561–563; and Plender, op. cit. note 57, at p.196.

ceptance of a purpose or intention test (i.e. an examination of the purposes or intentions of the potential or actual worker or applicant for residence), which sits uneasily with these early rulings of the Court and the developing objectives of the Treaty in the area of free movement.[72]

In *Kempf*, the Court of Justice was subsequently asked whether an individual who pursues a genuine and effective activity within the meaning of *Levin*, but supplements the income received thereunder with publicly-funded financial assistance can be regarded as a worker for the purposes of the Community's free movement provisions. The Court ruled that persons in genuine and effective part-time employment cannot be excluded from the sphere of application of the Treaty merely because they decide to supplement their low income by other lawful means.[73] In this respect the Court refused to differentiate between income from property or from other family members (which were listed as possible supplementary sources in *Levin*) or, as in the case of Mr Kempf, financial assistance drawn from public funds. The essential factor was that the work was of an effective and genuine nature. Reliance on additional funds alone did not alter the genuine and effective nature of the work in question even if those funds came from the public purse. In the view of the Advocate General, recourse to public funds could affect whether the work in question was considered genuine and effective, as for example if an individual deliberately and for no good reason took a part-time job when he could have taken a full-time one, but reliance on public funds in itself did not prevent him from being a worker.[74]

After some time the Court produced a more concrete definition of an employment relationship. Its definition illustrated its previous decision to interpret workers and employment in a Community fashion, but it implicitly drew on the various legal traditions of the Member States. In determining whether the plaintiff *stagiaire* in *Lawrie-Blum* was a worker within the meaning of Article 48, the Court held that the existence of an employment relationship must be determined in accordance with objective criteria, the essential feature being that for a certain period of time a person performs services for and under the direction of another

---

[72]See Article 2 and the preamble of Regulation 1612/68 which states that: "Whereas freedom of movement constitutes a fundamental right of workers and their families; whereas mobility of labour within the Community must be one of the means by which the worker is guaranteed the possibility of improving his living and working conditions and promoting his social advancement". Various rulings of the Court of Justice support some distinctly non-economic aspects of free movement; see, for example, Case 66/85 *Lawrie-Blum*, op. cit. note 6, at para.12, where the Court held *obiter* that, "a restrictive interpretation of Article 48(1) would reduce freedom of movement to a mere instrument of economic integration, would be contrary to its broader objective of creating an area in which Community citizens enjoy freedom of movement"; and Advocate General Jacobs in Case 344/87 *Bettray*, where he states that: "labour is not, in Community Law, to be regarded as a commodity and [the Preamble of Regulation 1612/68] notably gives precedence to the fundamental rights of workers over satisfying the requirements of the economies of Member States".

[73]The national court had already found, as a question of fact, that the occupation pursued by the plaintiff was a genuine and effective activity.

[74]Case 139/85, op. cit. note 39, at 1744.

person in return for which he receives remuneration.[75] The three criteria were satisfied in the instant case. With respect to whether the activity in question could be regarded as an economic activity thus falling within the scope of the Treaty it was said that all that is required for the application of Article 48 is that the activity should be in the nature of work performed for remuneration.[76]

3.3.2. The Concept of Worker in a Changing Employment Market

Over the years the nature of cases dealing with the question of who is a worker have changed, reflecting changes in the organisation of the labour market. The inclusion of part- time work within the scope of the Treaty provisions on free movement, for example, was the pragmatic reaction of a Court faced with the changing social reality of labour demand and organisation.[77] The following section examines the legal position of *stagiaires*, ex-workers, job-seekers and participants in sheltered employment schemes. These cases present the Court with more complicated factual and legal problems and it is contended that their judicial resolution at Community level reflects a lack of conviction about the scope of the Community's objectives in free movement and beyond. Perhaps more controversially, it is suggested that the Court has, on occasion, used its definition of worker to admit public policy considerations which have no place in this initial definition of the personal scope of free movement.

Stagiaires

Given the Court's insistence on an economic element if employment relationships are to fall within the scope of the Treaty, it was possible that a temporarily employed *stagiaire* would not qualify as a worker. The underlying purpose of a

---

[75]Case 66/85, op. cit. note 6, at para.17. Reaffirmed, *inter alia*, in Case C-3/87 *Regina* v. *Ministry for Agriculture and Fisheries, ex parte Agegate*; and Case C-179/90 *Merci convenzionali porto di Genova SPA* v. *Siderurgica Gabrielli SPA* [1991] ECR I-5889, at 5927, though the Court added that "cette qualification n'est pas affectué par le fait que le travailleur, tout en se trouvant dans le lien de subordination par rapport à l'entreprise, est lié aux autres travailleurs de celle-ci par un rapport d'association" and see the Commission's proposal for a directive on the form of proof of an employment relationship, cited in Blanpain, op. cit. note 5, at pp.112–113.

[76]The lower courts in Germany had taken the view that freedom of movement was excluded since at issue was the German state school system which was not a form of economic activity but an instrument of state education policy. The Court has addressed the peculiar character of education as a sector of state activity on other occasions; see *supra* Section 3.2.3.

[77]For some details see Manpower Services Corporate Plans, reference to whose figures for 1985–89 with respect to the UK is made in Hepple and Fredman, op. cit. note 58. In 1985, 5 million people, representing 21 per cent of the national workforce were employed in part-time employment in the UK; see also the Labour Force Survey, 1986, published in 5 *International Law Journal of Comparative Labour Law and Industrial Relations* (1989) 61, at 63; Kravaritou, Y., *New Forms of Work: Labour Law and Social Security Aspects in the European Community* (1988) European Foundation for the Improvement of Living and Working Conditions, OPOCE, Luxembourg; see also Article 5(ii) of the Community Charter of the Fundamental Social Rights of Workers.

traineeship could be regarded as a means to complete a higher education cycle rather than a means to earn a wage, or to participate in an economic transaction or activity. According to the Advocate General in *Lawrie-Blum*, however, candidates for preparatory service, who had already passed their examinations, were to be regarded not as students, but as individuals entering the first stage of their professional and economic life, and there was no reason, as such, for denying them the status of worker.[78] The Court held that the fact that during the *stage* such a person is acquiring knowledge and experience for a later, fuller activity is not sufficient to deprive stagiaires of the status of worker.[79] In the event, the Court accepted that the three criteria for the existence of an employment relationship – specified duration, remuneration and control – were fulfilled and it held that the fact that an individual follows practical preparation for the later pursuit of an occupation is not a bar to the application of Article 48(1).[80]

Whether or not an individual's *stage* will comply with the genuine and effective formula employed in *Levin* and with the criteria for an employment relationship in *Lawrie-Blum* is a question of fact for the national authorities.[81] According to the Advocate General in *Bernini*, the latter must verify that the employment relationship is not so short that the trainee concerned hardly had time to familiarise himself or herself with the concrete work which he or she had to do.[82] The authorities may be entitled to consider whether the *stagiaire* has undertaken a sufficient number of hours in order to become familiar with the work being done.[83] These guidelines are not without their difficulties in some Member States. Those who work as trainees in the United Kingdom, for example, under the Government's Youth Opportunities Programme (YOP) do not qualify under English law as apprentices or employees.[84] It will be interesting to see whether this legal position affects national judicial determinations of fact on the status of *stagiaires* for the purposes of Community law. According to the Advocate General in *Bernini*, if the services rendered by the *stagiaire* have no or a negligible economic value for the employer, or

[78]The trainees were obliged to give eleven hours of lessons a week, received a small maintenance grant, were paid at a rate fixed by federal law and were subject to the provisions of labour, tax and social security law in a manner akin to those under a "normal" employment relationship. Though at the beginning of the training, there may have been an imbalance between the work done and the pay received, according to the Advocate General this would change over time, Case 66/85 op. cit., at 2130
[79]Reiterated by the Court in Case 197/86 *Brown* [1988] ECR 3205, at paras.20–23; Case C-27/91 *URSSAF* v. *Société Hostellerie Le Manoir* [1991] ECR I-5531, at para.8.
[80]Case 66/85, op. cit. note 6, at para.19.
[81]See *MacMahon* v. *Department of Education and Science* [1982] Weekly Law Reports 1129; Advocate General Slynn in Case 139/85, op. cit. note 39, at 1743; and Advocate General Van Gerven in Case C-3/90 *Bernini* v. *Minister van Onderwijs en Wetenschappen* [1992] ECR I-1071, at para.10.
[82]Case C-3/90, op. cit. note 81, at para.12.
[83]Ibid., at para.16.
[84]*Daley* v. *Allied Suppliers Ltd* [1983] 12 Industrial Relations Law Reports 14, where the Court held that the contract at issue for the training of the applicant was not a "contract of service" or a "contract personally to execute work or labour" since the underlying purpose of any contract between the employer and trainee was not to establish the relationship of employer and employee, but to enable the applicant to acquire certain skills and experience.

if the *stagiaire* is paid a low nominal wage, one cannot speak of an employment relationship such as to confer the status of worker.[85]

Although the Court has broadly accommodated the position of trainees, its jurisprudence is nevertheless open to criticism. Remuneration, or the economic benefit derived from a transaction, should surely be a subjective matter, to be understood by the parties to the transaction themselves. For Community law to apply there need not be an exact balance between service and remuneration, since the latter may be evaluated in non-monetary terms. In *Udo Steymann*, for example, the services rendered were paid for in kind, not in cash. The long-term economic benefit derived by a trainee from a training period should not be ignored. Secondly, the objective genuine and effective status of the individual as a worker in Community law has never before been determined by the benefit which the employer may derive from the employment relationship. This philosophy surfaces in the Advocate General's opinion in *Bernini*. In *Bettray*, however, the Court denied that the productivity of the participants in the social employment scheme was relevant to the determination of their status as workers. It is hoped that this criterion will not gain general acceptance as a criterion for the application of Community law as it would give rise to unworkable and subjective determinations of when Community law should apply. In *Bernini*, the Advocate General applied the "marginal and ancillary" element of the *Levin* judgment, to assess if the traineeship was sufficiently long to be considered genuine and effective. In his view, a longer period could be required in the context of a *stage* than in the context of a normal working relationship, since the purpose of the former is to develop a certain aptitude on the part of the trainee. The Court seemed to support this reasoning. A period of ten weeks was at issue in that case, whereas eight months was considered sufficient in *Brown*. When a *stage* forms part of a study cycle is the *stagiaire* to be considered a student not a worker? In *URSSAF* v. *Société Hostellerie Le Manoir*, the Court of Justice regarded a stagiaire employed on a scheme as part of a vocational training course in her Member State of origin, as a worker within the meaning of Article 48. However, educational stagiaires were excluded from the scope of Article 48 by the Advocate General in *Bernini*.[86] The position of the Court in the former case is to be preferred since numerous professional qualifications are now acquired on the basis of mixed work experience and vocational training.[87]

---

[85]Ibid., at para.12. Cf. *Lawrie-Blum*, where the applicant stagiaire was recognised as a Community worker, though it was recognised that her remuneration was not commensurate with the work done and that the purpose of the employment was not to satisfy the employing authorities needs, but to train the applicant; and Case C-27/91, op. cit. note 79, at 4, where the Commission claimed that the fact that *stagiaires* do not accomplish complete tasks and receive inferior remuneration does not necessarily deny them the status of worker. In *Raulin* minimal wages were also rejected as a relevant criterion.

[86]Case C-3/90, op. cit. note 82, at para.12, fn.17.

[87]See, for example, Lonbay, J., "Differences in the Legal Education in the Member States of the EC", in De Witte, B. and Forder, C. (eds.), *The Common Law of Europe and the Future of Legal Education* (1992) Kluwer Law and Tax Publishers, Deventer, pp.75–83, at p.77; Watson, P., "Wandering Students: Their Rights under Community Law", in O'Keeffe and Curtin (eds.), op. cit. note 89, pp.79–88, at p.86; the House of Lords Select Committee on the ECs, *Vocational Training and Re-Training*, Session 1989–90, 21st report; and *Youth Training in the EEC*, Session 1983–84, 2nd report; and Case C-310/90 *Egle* [1992] ECR I-177.

Persons previously in employment

Situations may arise where individuals wish to avail of the provisions of Community law, though they are no longer in an existing employment relationship. May they rely on their previous status as Community workers to further enjoy the provisions of Community law? In *Lair* v. *Universitat Hannover*[88] the Court was asked whether students actually or previously pursuing a part-time or full-time employment activity could be regarded as workers for the purpose of free movement in the Treaty and secondary legislation.[89] Pointing to various examples in the Community legal order which support the view that the rights guaranteed to migrant workers do not necessarily depend on the actual or continuing existence of an employment relationship,[90] the Court held that the plaintiff retained the status of worker. Furthermore, she could benefit from equal treatment as regards social and tax advantages under Article 7(2) Regulation 1612/68, provided there was a link between the previous occupational activity and the studies subsequently pursued.[91] The Court admits an exception to this rule if the person in question has become involuntarily unemployed, or obliged by conditions in the employment market to retrain in another area of professional activity. It is remarkable that the Court subjected the enjoyment of social advantages in Article 7(2) Regulation 1612/68 to such a condition. It has denied Member States on other occasions the opportunity of making social advantages dependent on conditions such as completion of a certain period of occupational activity and its very reasoning as regards whether or not the plaintiffs in *Lair* and *Brown* were workers related to its refusal to "impose any

---

[88]Case 39/86 [1988] ECR 3161. A French national resident in Germany had been refused an education grant on the basis that she did not qualify as the child of a Community worker for the enjoyment of such benefits and in the alternative, that she had not completed five years occupational activity as was required of non-Germans.

[89]In particular, the case concerned whether a training grant for a higher education course could be considered a "social advantage" within the meaning of Article 7(2) of Regulation 1612/68 and whether the restriction of that grant to foreigners who have worked in the Member State for at least five years constituted discrimination contrary to Article 6. Applying the principle it had formulated in Case 293/83 *Gravier* v. *City of Liège* [1985] ECR 593, the Court included the grant in question within the scope of Community law and held that it could be a "social advantage" within the meaning of Article 7(2) Regulation 1612/68 if the claimant qualified as a worker. Incidentally, students do not qualify as workers in their capacity as students alone: see Cases 66/77 *Kuyken* [1977] ECR 2311, in the context of Reg. 1408/71; Case 283/83 *Meade* [1984] ECR 2631; a decision of the *Bundesverwaltungsgericht*, 5 November 1980 in *Marcel Partigny* v. *Technische Hochschule Darmstadt, Zeitschrift fur das Gesamte Familienrecht*, 1981, 406; and *MacMahon*, op. cit. note 81, at 1135–1136.

[90]Article 48(3)(d) EEC grants rights to those remaining on the territory of another Member State though their employment there is complete; see also Regulation 1251/70, OJ 1970 L142/24. In certain circumstances, Directive 68/360, OJ 1968 L257/13, prohibits the withdrawal of a residence permit for the sole reason that the holder is no longer in employment. Article 7(1) Regulation 1612/68 guarantees equal treatment with respect to reinstatement or re-employment to unemployed migrant workers. Article 7(3) also guarantees equal treatment with respect to access to vocational schools to persons not in a continuing employment relationship.

[91]Case 39/86, op. cit. note 88, at para.37; see also Case 197/86 *Brown*, op. cit. note 79, at para.26.

additional conditions for a person to be classifiable as a worker".[92] Furthermore, its insistence in *Lair* on a link between the previous employment and the subsequent course of study in the case of student/ex-workers for the enjoyment of the benefits of Regulation 1612/68 could prove problematic if the condition is strictly interpreted. Since both Ms Lair and Mr Brown were voluntarily unemployed, a fact to which the Court made no reference, it is to be expected that this condition will be generously enforced in line with "current developments in careers".[93] National courts should consider the nature and diversity of the activities undertaken and the length of time between the last activity and the beginning of the studies.[94]

In *Lair*, the Advocate General tried to resurrect the motive or intention test rejected by the Court in *Levin*. He seemed to use a worker's intentions to assess whether or not his work was genuine and effective, rather than making this decision *a priori*.[95] In his view, individuals who go to another Member State to become students, or to gain a short period of work experience before their studies begin, cannot benefit from Articles 7(2) and (3) Regulation 1612/68, even if their work is genuine and effective and satisfies the test in *Lawrie-Blum*. Furthermore, he felt that it may be relevant to have regard to how long persons have been in a Member State and what they have been doing in order to determine whether they are genuine workers. The Advocate General in *Brown* also argued that although the collateral intentions of someone doing a genuine job have been said to be irrelevant, the Court's decisions did not preclude an examination of the reasons for an individual being in a Member State. Thus, although an individual may retain the status of worker under Article 48, he or she may not necessarily be entitled to the enjoyment of all the rights conferred by Article 7(2) of Regulation 1612/68.[96] Though the Court in *Brown* accepted that the applicant was a worker, he had acquired that status as a result of his being accepted to a university course. This rendered his employment ancillary to the pursuit of his university studies and disentitled him from enjoying a maintenance grant for his studies on an equal basis with the nationals of the host Member State.

It is submitted that this is a distortion of the *Levin* test and an unnecessary introduction of subjective intention into an area which the Court has specifically said should be judged by "objective criteria".[97] If it has been established that an applicant is involved in an occupational activity then he or she should almost automatically qualify as a worker. In *Regina* v. *Pieck*, (as in *Cowan*), the fact alone that the

---

[92]See Case 196/87, op. cit. note 8, at para.22 and Case 39/86, op. cit. note 88, at para.42. See the Court's refusal to condition the right to equal treatment in Case 157/84 *Frascogna* v. *Caisse de Dépôts et Consignations* [1984] ECR 1739; Case 186/87 *Cowan*, at para.11; and Case C-326/90 *Commission* v. *Belgium*, judgment of 10/11/1992.
[93]See Case 39/86, op. cit. note 8, at para.38.
[94]See Case C-3/90, op. cit. note 82, at para.19.
[95]See Case 39/86, op. cit. note 8, at 3182.
[96]Case 197/86, op. cit. note 79, at 3232. See also Case 44/65 *Hessiche Knappschaft* v. *Maison Singer* [1965] ECR 965, where the Court held that the "notion of 'worker' may define the attributes of the beneficiary, but not the extent of his rights".
[97]Case 66/85 op. cit. note 50, at para.17.

individual was engaged in an activity regulated by Community law entitled him in that case to a right of residence.[98] It is argued that the criteria clearly established in *Lawrie-Blum* and reference to whether the activity constitutes an economic activity as broadly (but more clearly) interpreted by the Court of Justice should be sufficient to dispense of an inquiry into the genuine and effective nature of the workers' motives. If individuals are objectively workers for the purposes of entry, they should continue to be so though their original objectives on entry included other activities such as studying. A predominant intention to study or establish oneself on that territory for other purposes cannot alter that objective status.[99] If the existence of an employment relationship is established, a determination that it is "ancillary" to an individual's studies or other activity should generally be superfluous. The Court's distinction between the status of worker (Community law applies) and the genuine nature of that status (extent to which Community law applies) seems to be a means to prevent Member State nationals posing as workers in order to enjoy the benefits which the host Member State makes available to its own workers. It may be an acceptable means to prevent abuse, but it obscures the Community's definition of worker[100] and should not be allowed to permit Member States to disregard the principle of equal treatment with respect to social welfare, education or employment benefits, which they would prefer to protect for their own nationals.

Job seekers

The Treaty and secondary legislation contain no provisions explicitly dealing with the legal status of job seekers. A right to enter and move freely may be surmised, but no explicit provision is made for a right of residence.[101] Nevertheless, a declaration by Council members contained in the minutes of the meeting at which Directive 68/360 was adopted states that nationals of Member States who move into another Member State and seek employment there have a minimum of three months to achieve that purpose. At the end of that period their stay on the territory of the Member States may be terminated. The declaration also provides that if job seekers become a charge on public assistance in the host Member State during that three month period, they may be asked to leave.

---

[98]Case 157/79 [1980] ECR 2172.

[99]The *Bundesverwaltungsgericht* has held that a part-time professional could qualify as a worker though his professional occupation was ancillary to his activities as a farmer, *Raffeisenbank Gammesfeld* v. *Bundesrepublik*, B Verw. E 78, 297.

[100]See, for example, the Opinion of the Advocate General in Case 39/86, *Lair*, at 3182.

[101]Article 1 of Regulation 1612/68 refers to a right to take up an activity as an employed person which presupposes a right to search; Article 3 of Directive 68/360 confers on them a right to enter, but a certificate or confirmation of employment is needed for the grant of a residence permit under Article 4. Article 5 Regulation 1612/68 imposes an obligation on Member States to provide the same assistance to nationals of other Member States "who seek employment" as to their own. See also Case C-292/89 *Antonissen* [1991] ECR I-745, at para.14 and Advocate General Darmon, at paras.6–7; and the submissions of the German government in Case C-62/91 *Sinclair Gray* [1992] ECR I-2737.

As an agreement between Member States, the declaration confers no direct rights on individuals and its authority can only be persuasive.[102] Nevertheless, it has arguably formed part of the legal background to some decisions by the Court of Justice, in particular, *Lebon*.[103] Until recently, the rights of job seekers had not directly been at issue in the Court of Justice.[104] Reference had been made to a right of entry for job seekers, but this was *obiter* and a means of underlining the broad definition which the Court had attributed the notion of worker.[105] Job seekers enjoyed a right to "move freely" within the territory of the Member States in accordance with Article 48(3)(b), but they did not enjoy rights of residence as such and, unlike pensioners or ex-workers, they qualify for equal treatment under Regulation 1612/68 only to the extent that it relates to conditions of access to employment (Articles 2 and 5).[106] They were excluded from the principle of equal treatment enshrined in Article 7(2) of the regulation regarding tax and social advantages, although Title I of the Regulation refers to nationals as well as workers, which meant that the Court could have decided the case more extensively.[107] The *Lebon* decision, like many of the issues which arise in Community law which relate to individuals on the fringe of society and not in "normal" employment relationships, is informed by a fear of "social dumping". There is no concrete evidence, however, to suggest that job seekers have moved to Member States where social benefits are greater.[108]

As regards job seekers, Community and/or national law could distinguish between those seeking work and claiming benefit who have previously worked and those who have not.[109] This differentiation would be possible in Community law since the restrictive interpretation of the applicability of equal treatment in *Lebon* does not apply to all job seekers, but only to those who "move in search of employ-

---

[102]For a discussion of the legal status of declarations in Community law, see Advocate General Darmon in Case C-292/89, op. cit. note 101, at para.15. He ultimately concluded, as did the Court, at para. 18, that the declaration could not be relied on to fill the lacuna which so obviously existed in Directive 68/360; see also Case C-306/89 *Commission* v. *Greece* [1991] ECR I-5863, at para.8; Toth, A., "The legal status of the declarations annexed to the Single European Act", 23 *CMLRev* (1986) 803–812; Mertens de Wilmars, op. cit. note 59, at 15; and *supra* Chapter 2.6. This declaration on unemployed immigrants in search of work; see *Regina* v. *Secretary of State for the Home Department (ex parte Ayub)* [1983] CMLR 140; and Justice Nolan in *Regina* v. *Immigration Appeal Tribunal (ex parte Antonissen)* [1989] CMLR 957.

[103]Case 316/85 [1987] ECR 2811.

[104]For a number of cases addressing this issue at national level see Lasok, D., "Deporting Unemployed Immigrants" (1991) no.33, *Law Society Gazette*, 18 September 1991, 17–18.

[105]See Case 153/81, *Levin*; Case 48/75 *Royer* [1976] ECR 497 and Case 66/85, where by accepting that job-seekers came within the scope of the Treaty, the Court implicitly provided for a right of residence for job-seekers in principle without recognising its formal source.

[106]Case 316/85, op. cit. note 103, at para.26.

[107]See also Vincenzi, C., *Immigration Rights for Community Nationals: A Basis for Citizenship?* Federal Trust Workshop on European Citizenship, London, 4–6 October 1990, at p.10.

[108]See Pieters, D. (ed.), *Social Security in Europe*, Miscellanea of the ERASMUS programme of studies relating to social security in the ECs (1991) Bruylant, MAKLU Uitgevers, at p.162.

[109]See Vincenzi, C., "European Citizenship", in *The Single European Market and the Development of European Law*, W.G. Hart Legal Workshop 1989. In the UK the lack of differentiation is marked in paras.72 and 150 of the new UK immigration rules, HC 251, March 1990.

ment" and who do not have a right of residence in the country in which employment is sought. The right to remain in the territory of the host Member State presupposes that the person concerned has been previously employed there in the context of the free movement of workers.[110] Article 7(1) Directive 68/360 provides that a valid residence permit may not be withdrawn solely on grounds of unemployment if the individual concerned is temporarily incapable of work because of an accident or illness, or because he is involuntarily unemployed, a fact to be confirmed by the competent employment office.[111] The personal scope of Articles 48 and 51 is not identical and the concept of worker is defined differently in the secondary legislation designed to implement these provisions, Regulations 1612/68 and 1408/71 respectively. In the context of persons covered by the latter Regulation on the basis of compulsory contributions, the Court has held that they do not lose their status as workers by reason only of the fact that at the time when the contingency occurred they were no longer paying contributions and no longer bound to do so.[112] Unemployed workers moving in search of work who have previously worked retain the social security benefits acquired while employed under Regulation 1408/71 for three months when they move to another Member State in search of work.

In *Antonissen*, the Court was asked whether an individual seeking employment was to be treated as a "worker" for the purposes of deportation under Directive 64/221.[113] In particular, could the receiving Member State require that individual to leave its territory if after six months he had failed to enter employment? Section 143 of the British Immigration Rules allowed a job seeker to be expelled if after six months he or she had not found employment. Unable to remedy the Community legislature's failure to specify a time limit for what was clearly a limited right whose legal basis it had never specified, the Court accepted that a period of six months seemed a reasonable time to enable an individual to take all the necessary measures to secure employment. Nevertheless, if after six months the job seeker in question continues to look for work and he has a real chance of employment, he should not be obliged to leave the host Member State.[114] This pragmatic approach was justified with reference to developments in the employment market over the last two decades. Thus, an individual's right of residence may continue so long as he or she actively, persistently and seriously pursues his or her job hunting. Merely to state an intention to seek work is insufficient, because it "should be expressed in specific conduct, that is to say, the act of seeking work is evidenced by registration

---

[110]See Case C-171/91 *Tsiotras* v. *Landeshauptstadt Stuttgart*, 25 June 1993.

[111]See also Case 157/79 *Pieck*; Article 7(1) Regulation 1612/68; and Cousins, M., "Free Movement of Workers and Period of Employment Requirements in the Irish Social Welfare System", 8 *Irish Law Times* (1990) 258–262, at 261.

[112]Case 143/79 *Walsh* v. *Insurance Officer* [1980] ECR 1639.

[113]OJ 1964 L56/850.

[114]Case C-292/89, op. cit. note 101, at para.21; and Case C-171/91 *Tsiotras*, where the Court held that Community law allows the person concerned a reasonable time in which to learn of offers of employment suitable to their professional qualifications and to take, as appropriate, the necessary measures to take up the employment.

at the employment registry, calling on firms or the placing of advertisements in newspapers".[115] Merely registering for work in another Member State, however, does not bestow the status of worker according to a national court in *ex parte Ayub*. Repeated failure to take up job offers would, therefore, justify expulsion. Presumably, lack of any job offers would also be grounds for concluding that the job seeker did not have a "realistic" chance of success and would justify the termination of his temporary right of residence. However, one wonders whether the acceptance and subsequent refusal of a job after a short period in employment would stop the clock running so that the permitted job seeking period could be re-activated. In such a way, a job seeker could continue his right of residence indefinitely, without being subject to the sufficient resources requirement applicable under the 1990 Directives.[116] The vagueness of the *Antonissen* formula could mean that persons in rare occupations or with high economic expectations might be able to extend their "reasonable" time period indefinitely. The opportunity for diversity and the lack of legal precision in this judicial formula merits legislative action and the case could be an example of the Court of Justice trying to induce the Council to issue a directive expressly dealing with the legal position of job seekers and the extent to which it is prepared to respond to their position, in the absence of legislative action.

In the meantime, however, we note that the Court has carved out a broad notion of job seeker in line with its previous judgments in *Levin* and *Kempf*. However, once the period prescribed in national law has elapsed,[117] provided that period is reasonable, the job seeker's right of residence remains within the discretion of the individual Member State. The Court has sought to guarantee the freedom of movement of job seekers as a necessary means of realising the freedom of movement for workers. *Antonissen* could equally be regarded as a liberal interpretation of the rights of job seekers and a recognition of current unemployment problems in the Community, or an instrumental means to secure the effective exercise of free movement.[118] Nevertheless, the Court has identified yet another enforceable right for Member State nationals and has set limits to the exercise of Member States' previously unfettered discretion. The negative aspect of the decision is simply that its vagueness and the judicial origin of the right will permit

---

[115]See Advocate General Lenz in Case 316/85, op. cit. note 103, at para.47.

[116]In *Monteil* v. *Secretary of State* [1984] CMLR 284, the British Immigration Appeal Tribunal held that a Community national who entered a Member State, obtained employment and thereafter held various posts interspersed with periods of unemployment was a "worker". However, after the first renewal of a residence permit, its validity may be limited to a minimum of one year if the worker finds himself/herself unemployed for more than twelve consecutive months.

[117]The six month period in *Antonissen* was reiterated by the national court in *ex parte Ayub*; the German Oberverwaltungsgericht had previously specified a period of three months, *Deutsches Verwaltungsblatt* (1988) 279, 22 April 1988.

[118]See the Council's submissions in Case C-62/91, op. cit. note 101, at 14. See also Plender, op. cit. note 57, at p.197: "Supply of labour will not match demand, nor will the Community's social objectives be attained, unless those who are actively in search of work are permitted to travel to the parts of the Community where they judge that they are likely to obtain an offer of employment".

further diversity amongst the Member States, who are left to determine when or why unspecified "reasonable" time limits have elapsed. A job seeker's right to stay, like the derivative rights of the family members of the worker, can be subject to limitations, territorial limitations included. Thus in *Sinclair Gray*, the Court affirmed that the requirement that job seekers register for work in their Member State of last employment in order to receive unemployment benefit (Article 69(1) Regulation 1408/71) is compatible with Article 51. Though job seekers who immediately seek work in another Member State may consequently be put at a financial disadvantage, since their rights to claim unemployment benefit are restricted, the object of the limitations in Regulation 1408/71 is to prevent the exportation of unemployment. The absence of such a requirement might encourage job seekers to migrate to the Member States granting the highest benefits. This could not be countenanced since, as one intervening Member State put it, the Community has not yet achieved a common labour market where unemployment and other benefits are available without restriction and are organised under a common system of finance.

Persons involved in employment schemes

Do socially motivated youth employment and unemployment schemes and novel forms of employment come within the scope of the free movement provisions? If the Community institutions are successfully to achieve a common labour market they cannot ignore the difficulties created by the present climate of unemployment.[119] Many decisions of the Court on the concept of workers have attempted to come to grips with the social reality of employment and living and working conditions prevalent in the Community. Hence the *Levin* judgment on part-time workers, *Lawrie-Blum* on the inclusion of apprentice-type arrangements and *Udo Steymann* on what amounts to an economic activity. Given this record, the Court's reasoning as regards the employees in a social employment scheme in *Bettray* is surprising.

In recent years national legislatures have dealt with the worsening labour market situation and the detrimental effects of increased technology on the number of people in full time traditional employment by making contracts more flexible, in particular, by altering some of the variables of the classic employment relationship outlined in Section 3.3.1. The result has been an increase in fixed-term contracts, new forms of subcontracting and training-cum-work programmes. Although most schemes aimed at the young and unemployed involve incentives to already existing public and private enterprises ranging from exemptions from social security

---

[119]See Case 20/75 *Gaetano d'Amico* v. *Landesversicherungsanstalt* [1975] ECR 891, at 904, where Advocate General Trabucchi stated that "it is incontestable that, in whatever state it occurs, unemployment emerges as a problem of common interest in relation to the life of the worker in all Member States; it is thus a fact which assumes economic, and social importance for the Community"; and Advocate General Slynn in Case 53/81, op. cit. note 1, at 1055.

contributions to the payment of subsidies,[120] this is not always the case. Many youth employment schemes or schemes for the long-term unemployed are aimed at non-profit organisations and involve a clear element of job creation rather than access to a classic open labour market.[121] In October 1990, Eurostat estimated the seasonally adjusted unemployment rate to be 8.4 per cent. In some countries, like Spain and Ireland, figures reach 16.7 per cent. Is it preferable that such persons avail of the provisions of unemployment, training or job creation schemes within the protection of Community Law or should these modern-day (un)employment flows be left to what will, it is hoped, be a positive activism on the part of national legislatures? If the aim is to facilitate free movement within the Community, to create an area without internal frontiers (Article 7(a) SEA), to promote throughout the Community a harmonious development of economic activities and an accelerated raising of the standard of living (Article 2), the answer should be clear.

This issue came before the Court of Justice in *Bettray*, where it was asked whether a national of a Member State benefits from the provisions of free movement and consequently has a right of residence in another Member State solely by virtue of his employment under a scheme such as that provided for by the Social Employment Law.[122] The purpose of the scheme was to provide work for the purpose of maintaining, restoring or improving the capacity for work of persons who, for an indefinite period, are unable, by reason of circumstances related to their situation, to work under normal conditions. In short, to enable participants to enter or re-enter the labour market, (though the Advocate General noted that some were unlikely ever to re-enter the labour market). The scheme is specifically distinguished by the Advocate General from schemes designed for disabled persons or the unemployed, which facilitate their employment in normal commercial concerns. It is

---

[120]In Greece a job creation scheme set up in 1982, aimed at the young and long- term unemployed, entitled enterprises to a one-year subsidy. In the Netherlands a 1986 scheme (MOA) designed to re-integrate the unemployed and women out of work because of family care, involved a one-off subsidy to employers. Section 25(1) of the UK Employment Act, 1988 provides that the Secretary of State shall make such arrangements as he considers appropriate for the purpose of assisting persons to select, train for, obtain and retain employment suitable for their ages and capacities. Section 25(3) goes on to make provision for the payment of employers who participate in the scheme. For an excellent survey of new forms of employment and the existence of similar schemes in the various Member States see Bouder, op. cit. note 63.

[121]In Spain, the INEM (Instituto Nacional de Empleo) acts as both employer and trainer in a scheme aimed at unemployed youths in which they receive a daily scholarship or wage: Escuelas-Taller, Article 11 of worker's statute (Law 8/1980) modified by Law 32/1984 of 2.8. Royal Decree 1992/1984 of 31/10 Articles 2 and 3 of 1988 FIP plan Orders of 21 February 1985. In Germany an Act aimed at working and learning for job-seekers involves wage costs subsidies of 60 to 100 per cent for non-profit public and private associations: AFG s.91ff, Bildungs beihilfengesetz, Anordnung des Verwaltungsrats der BA uber die individuelle Forderung der beruflichen Ausbildung (s.13a). In Portugal, aid to the long-term unemployed comes in the form of non-profit making activities of collective interest. For further details see Bouder, op. cit. note 63, at 5–6 and 9–10 and Information published by the Mutual Information System on Employment Policies (MISEP). See also details of Community employment creation schemes in House of Lords Select Committee for the EC, *Social Policy After Maastricht*, Session 1991–1992, 7th report, at p.27.

[122]Case 344/87 *Bettray* v. *Staatssecretaris van Justitie*. The plaintiff was a German national who, having twice applied and been refused a residence permit by the Dutch authorities, applied for a permit on the basis of his employment under the provisions of the Dutch Social Employment Law.

aimed at those who, whether physically or mentally, are unable, even temporarily, to work normally and is largely financed by central and local government. Participants, who are classified on the basis of expected output, are given wages which, as far as possible, reflect equivalent wage levels for similar work in an undertaking on the open market, though remuneration does not reflect the amount of work actually done. The employment relationship is with the local authority from which participants receive their wages and to which they must turn in case of dispute. The contractual relationship is specifically governed by the Social Employment Law however, thereby excluding it from the status of employment in the public service or "ordinary" employment. The undertakings are not profit-making organisations though the work carried out must meet a social and economic need, the financial return, price and payment conditions must not be such as to compete improperly with others and the products for sale must not be offered in such a manner as to bring the scheme into disrepute.

According to the Court, the essential features of an employment relationship were present — persons employed under the scheme performed services under the direction of another person in return for which they receive remuneration. The low level of productivity of the participants and the fact that the scheme was publicly-funded did not alter the fact that it involved an employment relationship. It pointed out that there are many sectors of employment where the work performed is of a low market value, or where an individual's income is supplemented or supported by public funds. For Community law to determine the status of the worker on the basis of profit would effectively exclude persons employed in foundations, associations and other non-profit organisations. Neither was the apparently *sui generis* nature of the employment relationship relevant. What the Court did find relevant was the social objective of rehabilitation and reintegration and the readaption of the participants for work in an ordinary employment context. These social objectives meant that the work in question could not be regarded as a genuine and effective activity and the participant could not therefore be regarded as a worker for the purposes of Community Law. Although it had held that the *sui generis* nature of the employment relationship was irrelevant, the Court actually concluded that in this situation, where the activities are chosen in the light of the capabilities of the participants and where the work associations involved are artificially created solely for the purpose of the scheme, by public authorities out of public funds, the plaintiff could not be regarded as a worker.

But is this reasoning satisfactory? In the event, the abnormal work environment created by the public authorities using public funds was exactly what made the employment relationship *sui generis* and seems to be precisely why the Court denied that the plaintiff qualified as a Community worker. The Advocate General stated that if a genuine and effective activity is exercised then the individual must be regarded as a worker regardless of whether his employment relationship could be considered normal,[123] which is the basis on which the Court had reasoned *Levin*

---

[123]Ibid., at para.23.

and *Lawrie-Blum* and on which it is contended they should continue to determine these cases. However, he went on to distinguish the *Levin* case on the ground that it dealt with "a normal working relationship".[124] In his view, the elements of a normal employment relationship present in a relationship created pursuant to the Social Employment Law could be regarded as ancillary to the social aims of the legislation. Though the activity in question was substantial and not "on such a small scale as to be regarded as purely marginal and ancillary", a normal working relationship was not at issue (a criterion never before used by the Court) and the activity could therefore be regarded as ancillary as a whole. Although he recalled the broader aims of free movement and the fact that labour is not to be regarded as a commodity, the Advocate General nevertheless underlined the economic content of the free movement provisions whose purpose is "to ensure equality of access, for all Community citizens regardless of their nationality, to employment opportunities". Given this fact, those unable to accept offers of employment are not included within the purpose of the Treaty provisions or the scope of its secondary legislation. In the instant case the purely social nature of the scheme underlined that it did not serve the economic activities of the Community. The Advocate General, in conclusion, identified the decisive criterion in the case as the creation of the concern for the sole purpose of providing the participant with a near to normal working environment.

It is contended that the Advocate General and the Court in its closing submissions overemphasised the fact that the employment situation in question was created artificially. The employment relationship in question fulfilled the criteria established in *Lawrie-Blum*. Furthermore, the Court in *Lair* and *Brown* has admitted various situations where the rights guaranteed to migrant workers under Community law do not necessarily depend on the actual or continuing existence of an employment relationship. The fact that the plaintiff in *Bettray* was not as yet available for "normal employment" should not have disqualified him as a Community worker. In *Lawrie-Blum* Advocate General Lenz's view of employment and training was clear — "the fact that during the period of his engagement such a person is acquiring knowledge and experience for a later, fuller activity is not sufficient to deprive him of the status of worker". It is arguable that this is also the spirit (i.e. an appreciation of the importance of training to the success of free movement) informing judgments like *Gravier*, where the Court confirmed that vocational training comes within the scope of the Treaty provisions. Yet here the Court refused to admit Mr Bettray to the benefits of free movement because his period of rehabilitation prevented him from participating in a normal working environment. The right extended to jobseekers to enter and reside in search of work is to facilitate their integration into the labour market. Mr Bettray's training scheme was for the same purpose. Both are means of facilitating increased free movement in the Community and as such are in accordance with the objectives of the

---

[124]Ibid., at para.26; *Brown* was distinguished on the same basis.

Community as expressed in Articles 2, 48 and Regulation 1612/68. Though the Advocate General had noted that it was likely that some participants in the employment scheme would never re-enter the labour market, this did not take them outside the scope of Community law.

It is arguable that the plaintiff's past drug addiction in *Bettray* was tantamount to the Community's narrow application of the *Levin* test and its failure to apply a broad version of economic activity as, for example, it had done in *Udo Steymann*. Though drug addiction is a ground justifying, *inter alia*, Member State refusal to issue a residence permit in Directive 64/221, the Court was not asked to address the public policy issue in *Bettray*, nor was the Member State relying on it. Even if it had done, the tests carved out in the case law dealing with Article 48(3) suggest that resort to the public policy proviso would not necessarily have justified the plaintiff's exclusion.[125] Furthermore, none of the grounds listed in the annex to Directive 64/221 which can justify a state's refusal of entry or refusal to grant a residence permit can be invoked to serve economic ends.[126] *Bettray* seems a dangerous precedent in that it could mean that all job creation and youth employment schemes are excluded from Community law. It could also indicate an indirect and therefore undesirable means of applying public policy considerations under the guise of the economic activity criterion.

It has been argued that *Bettray* is confined to its facts, which were unusual, that it does not remove sheltered employment from the scope of the Treaty[127] and that the Advocate General specifically limited the scope of his opinion to the facts before him.[128] Article 177 judgments are generally declaratory of Community law and are used accordingly as precedents.[129] Limiting judgments based on suspect legal reasoning, lack of precedent and little practical sense is not the means by which one would wish to see the Court of Justice proceed. References above to new forms of employment emerging in the Member States of the Community render the Court of Justice's reasoning, which is based on the existence of a normal or classical employment relationship, misguided and untenable. "Unusual circumstances" are likely to be the order of the day in future. The Court has tended to

---

[125]See, for example, Case 67/74 *Bonsignore* [1975] ECR 297; and Case 30/77 *Bouchereau* [1977] ECR 1999. Drug offences were specifically at issue in the latter case but a previous drug addiction alone would not seem to support a denial of a residence permit.

[126]Article 2(2) Directive 64/221.

[127]The Advocate General, at para.9, phrased the scope of the question referred to the Court as "whether a national of a Member State has a right of residence ... exclusively by virtue of his employment under a scheme *such as that provided for*" (emphasis added). This does not appear to limit the import of the decision in *Bettray* to the Social Employment Law in question.

[128]Annotation by Watson, P., 14 *ELRev* (1989) 415–424; and Mancini, op. cit. note 9, at 70.

[129]See Case 112/76 *Manzoni* [1977] ECR 1647, Advocate General Warner, at 1662: "To hold that a ruling of the Court under Article 177 had no binding effect at all except in the case in which it was given would be to defeat the very purpose for which Article 177 existed which is to secure uniformity in the interpretation and application of Community law throughout Member States". See also Mackenzie Stuart A.J. and Warner, Judicial Decision as a Source of Community law, in Grewe, Rupp and Schneider, *Europaische Gerichtsbarkeit und nationale Verfassungsgerichtsbarkeit* (1981) Nomos, Baden Baden.

determine questions referred to it on a case by case basis,[130] indicating the parameters of Community law as it goes. Nevertheless, an incoherent case by case approach would be as unfortunate as an inability on the part of the Community's judiciary to accomodate, in this small but significant line of case law, the changing nature of employment and the labour market which surrounds it.

The indications are that *Bettray* will not operate as a precedent for the Court's future determination of who is a worker for the purposes of free movement. Thus in *Bernini*, Advocate General Van Gerven doubted whether the Court wished to go back on its case law and stated that "the scope of the *Bettray* judgment must be limited to the specific situation of social employment and in that case, the rehabilitation of drug addicts."[131] As stated above, this specific limitation did not emerge from the Court or Advocate General's reasoning in *Bettray*. The basis suggested by Advocate General Van Gerven for the limitation of the definition of worker, namely, the applicant's drug addiction, confirms fears that the scope of Community law was limited in *Bettray* as an indirect and unfair application of national public policy considerations. Whether or not an individual is a Community worker should not be limited in this manner and if public policy considerations are to arise, they should be disposed of by the Court when addressing the merits of the case. The scope of Community law should not be limited from the outset by the Court narrowly or broadly defining its basic concepts. The *Bettray* decision gives the impression that, in classical Dworkinian style, a hard case did make bad law.

3.4. Conclusions

Though economic integration may have been the engine intended to pull social integration subsequently in its train, the Treaty was primarily adapted for economic purposes. Nevertheless, as Community competence has expanded, inconspicuously by virtue of judicial interpretation, or more publicly, in the form of specific Treaty amendments (SEA, TEU), these criteria – economic activity, remuneration, worker – may sit uneasily with its new objectives and with the trends in the labour market. In the words of one commentator: "cette exigence [activité économique] est aujourd'hui le terrain d'une contradiction dans la mesure ou elle découle de la logique économique du marché commun en même temps qu'elle est combattue par la logique politique de l'Europe des citoyens."[132]

The judicial history of the definition of "Community workers" reflects the confusion of the Court of Justice, in particular, as to the scope, aims and objectives of the Community. Since the concept of worker defined the personal scope of one of the fundamental freedoms guaranteed by the Treaty, it was to be interpreted extens-

[130]See also Smith, L.J., "Postgraduate Degrees, Vocational Training and Reverse Discrimination: the narrow divide", 31 *CMLRev* (1994) 67–75, at 68.
[131]Case C-3/90, op. cit. note 82, at para.11.
[132]See Allopis, G., "Les migrations dans le droit européen et communautaire" Theme V in Turpin, D., *Immigrés et refugiés dans les démocraties occidentales. Défis et solutions* (1989) Economica, Presses Universitaires d'Aix Marseille, at p.242.

sively. Nevertheless, subsequent cases, in particular *Bettray*, cast doubt on the breadth of the Court's interpretation and its intention to fashion a truly Community definition. The Court's present consolidation of its position arguably applies a new and stricter approach to the question of who is a worker in Community law. This may be the natural progression of a Court with greater judicial expertise, a deeper historical evolution to support it and a greater awareness of the limits placed on its objectives by national sensibilities and the principle of subsidiarity. Nevertheless, the Court applies criteria which it continues to claim are objective and which it reiterates *verbatim*. If the demands of the Community's labour market require those criteria to be changed, then that should occur and the Community's undetermined adherence to *stare decisis* should not be the means to conceal what is in fact a qualitative difference in approach to a fundamental question which determines the beneficiaries of Community law.[133] The Community's definition of worker is still a means of shaping the European labour market and free movement and therefore a criterion affecting the development of Community citizenship and is fundamental to the subsequent activation of Community rights and the operation of the Community's legal regime.[134] The diverse criteria and differently applied tests which have emerged in these recent cases and the possibility for their diverse application at national level, by the administration and judiciary, added to the uncertain legal relevance of the economic content of the activity performed, are the antithesis however, of the clarity and flexibility required of a citizens' Europe without frontiers. For the moment, the concern of this chapter is with the fact that if economic activity continues to delimit the Community's power of action in the area of free movement, a distinction may emerge between the free movement regime as it has operated to date and the newly emerging category of Union citizens under Article 8. The body of case law which breathes life into the social advantages provisions of Regulation 1612/68 will continue to be confined to workers and their families, for example. This may be defensible in terms of economic arguments of contribution and benefit, but it does not tally with the legal and political notion of citizenship outlined in Chapter 1. Union citizenship can never effectively operate if its beneficiaries are denied equal treatment and complete free movement. If the latter are only extended under insulated economic conditions protective of welfare benefits in the host Member States, as seems to be the case in the 1990 residence Directives, then it is clear that Community citizenship offers little which is not available under the present free movement regime.

[133]On the operation of *stare decisis* in the Community see Koopmans, T., "Stare Decisis in European Law", in Schermers, H.G. and O'Keeffe, D., *Essays in European Law and Integration* (1982) Kluwer, Dordrecht, pp.11–27; Mackenzie Stuart and Warner, op. cit. note 65; Advocate General Lagrange in Cases 28–30/62 *Da Costa* [1963] ECR 31: "Clearly no one will expect that, having given a leading judgment, the Court will depart from it in another action without strong reasons, but it should retain the legal right to do so." See also Arnull, A., "Owning up to Fallibility: Precedent and the Court of Justice", 30 *CMLRev* (1993) 247–266, at 264, where he points out that the apparent reluctance of the Court of Justice to confront inconsistencies in its case-law "may be due in part to the collegiate nature of its decisions, which often embody a number of compromises".

[134]As Arnull points out, the Court must "accept that judicial decisions may constitute a source of law outside the confines of the dispute in which the decision was reached": ibid., at 265.

Part II

THE PRINCIPLE OF EQUAL TREATMENT AND COMMUNITY CITIZENSHIP

Chapter 4

Rights of Free Movement and Residence

4.1. Introduction

The growth of the modern welfare state following the Second World War and the assumption of social and economic responsibilities by the state resulted in the use of immigration controls to restrict the entry and residence of non-nationals. The rights of nationals to move and reside freely in their state of origin thus became privileges of state membership, or citizenship and became part of the state's definition of closure. This closure towards non-nationals was deemed necessary to protect the benefits granted by the welfare state.[1] Modern definitions of citizenship are thus partly related to the extent to which the benefits of membership are reserved to members and denied to non-members:

> citizenship is likely to be perceived as important to the extent that various tangible benefits or entitlements turn on its possession. The more we make significant economic and social advantages turn on citizenship, the more we will disadvantage those who are not citizens. We use citizenship to strengthen our sense of national community by making those who are citizens feel especially good about that status and we do that by investing that status with something real such as preferences for a wide range of government entitlements.[2]

The development of national welfare states is also identified with the existence of some form of common citizenship and solidarity which is thought, in turn, to depend on a degree of shared cultural, historical and social experiences. This aspect

---

[1]See Layton Henry, Z. (ed.), *The Political Rights of Migrant Workers in Western Europe* (1990) London, Sage Modern Politics Series Vol.25, at p.11; Hammar, T., "Citizenship: Membership of a Nation and of a State", 24 *International Migration* (1986) 735–748, at 736 *et seq.*; and King, D.S. and Waldron, J., "Citizenship, Social Citizenship and the Defence of Welfare Provision", 18 *British Journal of Political Science* (1988) 415–443, at 415.

[2]See Schauer, F., "Community Citizenship and the Search for National Identity", 84 *Michigan Law Review* (1985–86) 1504–1517, at 1516.

of Community citizenship is extremely immature, although the establishment of the status of citizenship in Article 8 may prompt its development. It seems, however, that the Member States, in an attempt to create the sort of social and cultural homogeneity thought to be necessary to develop the European Union and improve its legitimacy, have also opted for the exclusion of third country nationals and the creation of a "fortress Europe".[3] However, increasing state intervention via instruments of social policy and the consequent exclusion of non-nationals are of relatively recent origin and the designation of free movement, entry and residence, as privileges of state citizenship, are not as deeply rooted in the national psyche as present debates in the European Communities concerning immigration policy and free movement might suggest.[4] For example, the stricter control of immigrants from the Commonwealth was only instituted in the United Kingdom in 1962. The evolution of that country's welfare system is likely to have contributed to the subsequent removal in the British Nationality Act, 1981 of almost all immigration rights for individuals who were previously free moving Commonwealth citizens.[5]

The EC Treaty seeks to abolish obstacles to the freedom of movement of persons, services and capital (Article 3(c)) and to "promote throughout the Community ... the raising of the standard of living and quality of life, and economic and social cohesion and solidarity among the Member States" (Article 2). These objectives clearly challenge Member State sovereignty with respect to the regulation of free movement, entry and residence. In the long run they also affect national definitions of state closure and membership and, in turn, the regulation of social welfare at national level and the determination of its beneficiaries.[6] If viewed in conjunction with the far-reaching principles of direct effect and supremacy, the role of the Community in this field cannot therefore be underestimated. Following the adoption of the Union Treaty, Article 8 establishes Union citizenship and defines "the right to move and reside freely within the territory of the Member States" as one of the rights conferred by that citizenship (Article 8(a)(1)).[7] Modern defini-

---

[3]See also Leibfried, S. and Pierson, P., "Prospects for Social Europe", 20 *Politics and Society* (1992) 333–365, at 347.

4See Hammar, T., "The Emergence of Modern Citizenship", in *Democracy and the Nation State: Aliens, Denizens and Citizens in a World of International Migration* (1990) Ethnic Relations Series, Avebury, Gower Publishing, pp.41–56, at pp.42–44, where he outlines four phases of international migration: free and widespread immigration (1860–1914); control of aliens (1914–45): liberal immigration (1945–1974); and a return to strict immigration control (1974–). During these phases, the significance and meaning of citizenship and the rights it entailed underwent considerable change.

5For further details see Hartley, T.C., *EEC Immigration Law* (1978) European Studies in Law, Amsterdam, North Holland; MacDonald, I., *Immigration Law and Practice* (1983) Oxford, Butterworths; and Dummett, A. and Nicol, A., *Subjects, Citizens, Aliens and Others: Nationality and Immigration Law* (1990) Law in Context Series, London, Weidenfeld and Nicolson, at p.1.

6See Layton Henry, op. cit. note 1, at vi; and generally, Heisler, M.O., "Transnational Migration as a Small Window on the Diminished Autonomy of the Modern Democratic State", 483–485 *Annals of the American Society of Political and Social Science* (1986) 153–166.

7In a parallel context in the U.S. see Justice Jackson in *Edwards* v. *California*, 314 US 160 (1941): "It is a privilege of the US protected from state abridgement, to enter any state of the Union either for temporary sojourn or for the establishment of permanent residence therein ... If national citizenship means less than this it means nothing."

tions of citizenship have become increasingly associated with the enjoyment of a certain minimum of social rights. On the basis of Member State citizenship and sometimes simply on the basis of residence, individuals enjoy access to a state's welfare provisions and public law entitlements.[8] With the establishment of Union citizenship and the classification of residence as one of the privileges of that citizenship, one wonders whether Community citizenship should also be expected to cater for the welfare of its citizens, or whether Community citizenship means something less.

This chapter first questions the extent to which a general and meaningful right of free movement and residence forms part of the Community's definition of citizenship were further legislation to be proposed on the basis of Article 8(a)(2). It also examines the extent to which the enjoyment of such a right can be promoted within the confines of Article 8(a) and the likely political consensus among Member States. Article 8 does not explicitly provide for the enjoyment of any social rights by Union citizens. However, the scope and content of Union citizenship is not limited to the provisions of Article 8. Article 8(2) expressly provides that "Citizens of the Union shall enjoy the rights conferred by this Treaty". The fact that the rights of citizenship are not limited to the express provisions of Article 8 suggests the possibility of rights deriving from provisions situated elsewhere in the Treaty, or a possible penumbra of unenumerated rights which might benefit Union citizens. Can Community or Union citizenship boast, for example, an effective social dimension and could it entail the exercise of a right of residence by Member State nationals and a minimum of social rights detached from the exercise of an economic activity? In short, this chapter seeks to establish whether the constitutionalised status of Union citizen and the right of residence contained therein might move Member State nationals beyond market or consumer citizenship towards a more rounded political and social as well as economic Community citizen.

4.2. Rights of Free Movement and Residence and the Exercise of an Economic Activity

Article 48(3)(b) provides for a right to move freely within the territory of other Member States to accept an offer of employment "actually made" (Article 48(3)(a)). Article 52 similarly provides for the right to take up and pursue activities as self-employed persons and to set up and manage undertakings under the conditions laid down for its own nationals by the law of the country where such establishment is affected. The more provisional nature of the freedom to provide services is emphasised in Article 60 with reference to the temporary nature of the

---

[8]See Freeman, G., "Migration and the Political Economy of the Welfare State", 485 *Annals of the American Academy of Political and Social Science* (1986) 51–63.

right to reside of the provider of services.[9] These fundamental freedoms give rise to directly effective Community rights which can be invoked by individuals before their nationals courts.[10] This restricted attempt by the Treaty authors to create an integrated European labour market focused on Community nationals as workers or as self-employed persons, in short, as economically active agents. Although, as Chapter 3 demonstrated with reference to Regulation 1612/68 in particular, the translation of these Treaty provisions into secondary legislation permitted a more expansive approach to the legal rights of the individual. Nevertheless, economic activity remained a prerequisite for the enjoyment of the rights of free movement.

Recipients of services were also extended a right of residence in order to facilitate the provision of services, although the overall structure of the Treaty appeared to be limited to defined categories of persons and to exclude the recipients of services from more global and independent rights of residence.[11] Their right of residence was originally only recognised in so far as it appeared to be indissolubly connected to the right of free movement of the provider of services, who is expressly addressed in the Treaty. Nevertheless, the Court has subsequently held that freedom to provide services entails a freedom for recipients to move to another Member State unhindered by restrictions including residence restrictions.[12] Family members of the principal holder of the Community right of residence also come within the scope of the free movement provisions. Their inclusion is regarded as a means to facilitate the free movement and integration of the Community's economic actors who wish to move to another Member State.[13] The definition of family members often varies according to the legal instrument in question. In the context of free movement, however, it generally refers to the spouse of the worker and their descendants who are under the age of 21 years, or are dependents and the dependent relatives in the ascending line of the worker and his or her spouse.[14]

---

[9]See Case 196/87 *Udo Steymann* [1988] ECR 6159. The Court's decision in Case C-357/89 *Raulin* [1992] ECR I-1027, may alter this temporal limitation on the right of residence of providers and recipients of services, see *infra* Section 4.2; and O'Keeffe, D., annotation of Case C-357/89 *Raulin* and Case C-3/90 *Bernini* [1992] ECR I-1071, 29 *CMLRev* (1992) 1215–1224, at 1222.

[10]See Case 41/74 *Van Duyn* [1974] ECR 1337 (Article 48); Case 2/74 *Reyners* [1974] ECR 631 (Article 52); and Case 33/74 *Van Binsbergen* [1974] ECR 1299 (Articles 59(1) and 60(3), which were held to be directly effective notwithstanding the absence of implementing Directives).

[11]See, in this respect, the position of Advocate General Trabucchi in Case 118/75 *Watson and Belmann* [1976] ECR 1185, at 1202–1204; and Articles 1(b) Directives 64/22 and 73/148.

[12]See Joined Cases 286/82 and 26/83 *Luisi and Carbone* [1984] ECR 377; and Case 186/87 *Cowan* v. *Le Trésor Public* [1989] ECR 195.

[13]See recital 5 and Articles 10–12 Regulation 1612/68.

[14]Article 10 Regulation 1612/68. The Commission and European Parliament have sought to include "any other member of the family dependant on or living under the roof of the worker or the spouse in the country whence they came" (OJ 1989 C100/7) within the definition of family, but these proposals have met with resistance. The Commission's 1993 annual report states that this proposal, which first originated in 1988, is still before the Council. The Commission has also proposed that the rights of family members should continue after the worker's death or the dissolution of his or her marriage. For a discussion of these proposals, which so far have met with no success, see the House of Lords Select Committee on the European Communities, *Free Movement of People and the Right of Residence in the EC*, Session 1989–90, 7th Report, at p.14.

Unmarried partners of Community workers do not come within the definition of family member in Article 10 Regulation 1612/68.[15]

With reference to its teleological approach to interpretation, which examines Treaty provisions in the context of the Community's objectives, the Court has expanded Community rights of entry and residence beyond what could originally have been expected. First, although the Treaty provisions on workers, establishment and services regulate distinct legal situations as regards entry into and residence in the territory of a Member State of persons covered by Community law, the Court has said that they are based on the same principles with respect to entry and residence and the prohibition of discrimination on grounds of nationality.[16] Member State nationals have the right to enter and reside in the territory of another Member State, for the economic purposes envisaged by the Treaty and secondary legislation. This individual and subjective right is directly conferred by the Treaty and/or the measures designed to implement it.[17] It exists independently of the issue of a residence permit which serves merely to prove the Community legal status of the holder.[18] At least as regards entry, the treatment of Member State nationals under Community law is to be distinguished from the classic treatment of aliens, whose right of residence generally depends on the discretionary decision of the competent national authorities.[19] Entry by a Community national into a Member State's territory is as of right on the mere presentation of a valid identification card or passport.[20] Consequently, Community nationals who can attest their identity in accordance with Article 4(3) Directive 68/360 or Article 6 Directive 73/148 cannot be questioned as to the object of their stay or the amount of money they carry, when crossing from one Member State to another. Only when an application is lodged for a residence permit after entry may the question of sufficient resources become relevant.[21] A residence permit provided in accordance with Community secondary legislation is, however, merely declaratory in nature and in no way creates rights independently of those which directly flow from the Treaty.[22] Thus, if Community

---

[15]Case 59/85 *Netherlands State* v. *Reed* [1986] ECR 1283.

[16]See Case 48/75 *Royer* [1976] ECR 497, at para.12; and Case 118/75, op. cit. note 11, at para.9.

[17]See Case 48/75, op. cit. note 11, at para.31; Case 157/79 *Regina* v. *Pieck* [1980] ECR 2172, at para.4; Case 8/77 *Sagulo* [1977] ECR 1495, at para.4; Case C-370/90 *R.* v. *Immigration Appeal Tribunal and Surinder Singh* [1992] ECR I-4265, at para.17; Case C-68/89 *Commission* v. *Netherlands* [1991] ECR I-2637, at paras.10–12; Case 321/87 *Commission* v. *Belgium* [1989] ECR 997, at paras.11–15; Case C- 363/89 *Roux* [1991] ECR at para.9; Case 249/86 *Commission* v. *Germany* [1989] ECR 1263, at para.9.

[18]See Articles 4(1) and (2) Directive 68/360; Case 48/75, op. cit. note 11, at paras.32–33; and more recently Case C-357/89, op. cit. note 17, at para.36.

[19]See the submissions of the Commission in Case 36/75 *Rutili* [1976] ECR 1219, at 1223; Case 48/75, op. cit. note 11, at 504; Case 157/79, op. cit. note 17, at para.13; and Case 152/73 *Sotgiu* [1974] ECR 153.

[20]See Articles 3(1), 4(1) and (2) Directive 68/360; Case 157/79, op. cit. note 17, at para.8. As Chapter 3 suggested, the decision in Case C-376/89 *Giagounidis* [1991] ECR I-1069, goes farther, in that the absence of a valid ID card or passport was not allowed to limit the free movement of the applicant in that case.

[21]See Case C-68/89, op. cit. note 17, at para.13; and Advocate General Warner in Case 157/79, op. cit. note 17, at 2201.

[22]Case C-363/89, op. cit. note 17, at para.12; Case 157/79, op. cit. note 17, at para.13.

nationals fail to comply with administrative formalities regarding residence, their residence is not automatically rendered illegal, thereby justifying expulsion or temporary imprisonment.[23] Failure to comply with the legislative formalities concerning the entry, movement and residence of aliens does not, on its own, constitute a threat to public policy and as such, does not warrant expulsion, which is regarded as the very negation of free movement.[24] Sanctions may be imposed for non-compliance with administrative formalities, but they must respect the Community principles of proportionality and non-discrimination.[25] Finally, internal restrictions on free movement and residence may not be imposed on nationals of another Member State unless that Member State's own nationals are similarly treated.[26]

Articles 48 to 52 are not generally applicable to students who enter another Member State for the purposes of education, except to the extent that they qualify as workers on the basis of a stage or traineeship, or to the extent that they are registered as employed persons with a national social security system.[27] State school education is excluded from the Community's definition of a service and its recipients do not therefore come within the scope of Community law on services.[28] The gradual development of Community action in the field of education initially centred around the Court's interpretation of Articles 6 and 128 EEC.[29] In the revolutionary *Gravier* decision the Court held that conditions of access to vocational education come within the scope of application of the Treaty and, as such, are subject to the principle of non-discrimination enshrined in Article 6.[30] After *Gravier*, however, it was unclear whether students enjoyed an independent right of residence under the Treaty in their capacity as students. In other words, whether their entitlement to equal treatment as regards conditions of access to education required that they enjoy a right of residence as part of that equal treatment. Though this was regarded as the logical conclusion of *Gravier*, it was not explicitly stated to be the case until the *Raulin* decision. In that case the Court conceded that a directly ef-

---

[23]Case 48/75, op. cit. note 11, at paras.38 and 51.

[24]Case C-363/89, op. cit. note 17, at para.11; Case 157/79, op. cit. note 17, at para.18; Case 118/75, op. cit. note 11, at para.20; and the Commission's Answer to Written Question no.2781/87, OJ 1989 C24/7.

[25]See Case 118/75, op. cit. note 11, at paras.19–21; and Case 265/85 *Lothar Messner* [1989] ECR 4209, which discuss the legitimate extent to which national authorities can regulate and limit the free movement of Community nationals without recourse to the public policy, security and health exceptions in Article 48(3); see also Advocate General Mayras in Case 48/75, op. cit. note 11, at 525.

[26]Case 36/75, op. cit. note 19, at paras.49 and 50. This section describes the law as interpreted in secondary legislation and the Court of Justice. Organisations such as Advice on Individual Rights in Europe (AIRE) provide useful reports detailing how the law is not always successfully applied, see Mole, N., "Reflections Concerning the Movement of People", in *The Future of European Social Policy* (1994) Louvain, Louvain University Press, pp.225–236, at p.229.

[27]See *supra* Chapter 3.3.2; Case 66/77 *Kuyken* [1977] ECR 2311; and Case 238/83 *Meade* [1984] ECR 2631, at 2638.

[28]See Case 263/86 *Humbel* [1988] ECR 5365.

[29]Article 128 EEC previously provided that: "The Council shall, acting on a proposal from the Commission and after consulting the Economic and Social Committee, lay down general principles for implementing a common vocational training policy."

[30]Case 293/83 [1985] ECR 593.

fective right of residence was the inevitable consequence of the recognition of the principle of non-discrimination as regards access to vocational education.[31] The decision in that case rendered the adoption of the students' residence Directive somewhat redundant, since it implied that students enjoyed a right of residence directly conferred by the Treaty.

4.3. The Development of a General Right of Residence

This section first examines an early global proposal for a directive on a general right of residence and follows its passage through the Community's legislative channels. This is followed by a brief description of the adoption in 1990 of the three Directives granting a right of residence, subject to certain specific conditions, to students, retired persons and economically inactive persons generally. In a challenge to the legal basis of the students' Directive, the Court has conceded that Article 6 para.2 may serve as an independent legal basis for the adoption of Community legislation. This may prove an extremely useful legislative means to further free movement and Community citizenship, not only in the field of the free movement of students. The Court's decision lends judicial support to a division of competence as regards students between the Community and Member States which was previously unclear and contested by some Member States.

4.3.1. Early Legislative Debate

The history of the adoption of legislation on a general Community right of residence detached from the exercise of an economic activity reveals a long line of political rhetoric and attempts at legislative solutions which typify the Community's controversial and ambiguous quest for a "Citizens' Europe". A general right of residence detached from the exercise of an economic activity was regarded as an essential component of the "special rights" agenda first proposed at the Paris Summit in December 1974.[32] Following confirmation of the importance of residence by the Adonnino Report and the 1986 European Council, the Commission presented Council with a proposal for a Directive in 1979 based on Articles 235 and 56(2) for a right of residence for nationals of Member States in the territory of another Member State.[33] The proposal no longer addressed Member State nationals as persons engaged in the exercise of an economic activity, but in their capacity as

---

[31]See Case C-357/89, op. cit. note 9, at para.34.

[32]Bull. EC. 12-1974. See also the Tindemans Report with a special chapter entitled "Towards a Europe of Citizens", Bull. EC. (8) 1975 II no.7/8; Scelba Report, EP Working Documents 1977–78, 25 October 1977, Doc. 346/77, 10; the Resolution of the European Parliament, OJ 1977 C299/25. See also the Reports from the Round Table Conference in the European University Institute in Florence on "Special Rights and a Charter of the Rights of the Citizens of the EC", 26–28 October 1978.

[33]OJ 1979 C207/14. Article 56(2) was simply added as a means to ensure the application of Directive 64/221 to the provisions of the proposed Directive.

Community citizens.[34] According to the Commission, socio-economic changes since 1958, when the emphasis in migration had been on economic activity as a matter of economic necessity, justified this new legislative dimension. Reference to Article 235 as the legal basis of the proposed legislation gained support from the 1972 Paris summit and was said to be justified by the lack of explicit power of action in the Treaty with respect to economically inactive persons.[35] Article 3(c) and its reference to the abolition of obstacles to the free movement of persons generally, was also cited as recognition of the impossibility of establishing a common market and the Community objective of an ever closer union in the absence of such a general right of residence.

The proposal on residence was regarded as filling a gap in the Community system by those who, like the Parliament and ECOSOC, were in favour, in principle, of a general right of residence. As time passed, it became the subject of much debate, amendment and numerous written questions in Parliament. The legislative debate essentially revolved around (i) whether the Community could locate competence within the Treaty text to legislate in this respect; and if so, (ii) whether persons subject to it should have to prove the possession of medical coverage and sufficient financial resources before being allowed to avail of its provisions. It was felt that the unrestricted entry and residence of Community nationals into the Member State of their choice, as of right, would cause considerable economic difficulties, particularly in Member States where welfare benefits were more generous. Furthermore, or perhaps as a means of disguising these economic preoccupations, a number of Member States were unconvinced that the Community had competence to legislate in this respect at all, given the economic nature of the Community charter.[36] The original proposal thus contained economic safeguards, in that applicants for a residence permit could be required by Member States to prove that they were in possession of sufficient resources to cover their needs. These resources did not have to exceed the minimum subsistence level applicable under national legislation.[37] The European Parliament requested that the the requirement of sufficient resources be removed.[38] The question whether students, in particular, should be subject to this requirement, the difficulties generated by the disparities between the Member States' social security systems and the legal basis and scope of the proposed legislation continued to pose problems.[39] A further controversial element related to the definition of "members of the family" which was

---

[34]13th General Report on the Activities of the European Communities (1979), at point 123.

[35]Opinion of ECOSOC, OJ 1980 C182/18, at 20.

[36]Thus, Denmark considered that the Treaty related only to free movement for workers and the self-employed. In its view, an intergovernmental conference was necessary to facilitate free movement for all, see *Agence Europe* no.4991 ns. 8 April 1989; and Bolly, A., "Droit d'entrée et de séjour des ressortissants communautaire: développements récents", 3 *Actualités du droit* (1990) 735–748, at 743.

[37]See Article 4, OJ 1979 C207/15; cf. the Opinion of the ECOSOC, OJ 1980 C182/19, where it emphasised the resulting possibility of social discrimination and the difficulty of actually establishing sufficient resources.

[38]OJ 1980 C188/7, Article 4.

[39]See, for example, Written Question no.2622/87, OJ 1988 195/16.

eventually extended to "any person whom the holder of the right of residence has an obligation to support or who is, in practice, dependent on the holder".[40] The debate continued along these lines while Community actors became increasingly perturbed at what had become one of the most celebrated examples of Community inertia involving a piece of proposed legislation.[41] Indeed, one commentator correctly contended that: "The problems in adopting even this [residence] Directive, and in proposals to broaden the rights of Community workers beyond economic rights towards political and social ones, suggest difficulties in the incremental approach toward European Citizenship and what might be termed a European Welfare State."[42]

4.3.2. The Adoption of Directives 90/364, 90/365 and 90/366

After ten years of relative inactivity, the Commission regarded the Council meeting of 3 May 1989 as evidence that the legal provision on which the discussions on residence were based, namely Article 235, "was no longer the appropriate framework to enable the Council to reach positive conclusions regarding the various categories of persons covered by the proposal for a directive".[43] Consequently, the Commission withdrew the 1979 proposal with a view to reintroducing three new proposals whose provisions and legal bases were distinct and which were more closely suited to the specific situations of the categories of persons in question. It also intended that the new proposals would strengthen the legislative role of the European Parliament by introducing the cooperation procedure.[44] Completion of

---

[40]Article 2, OJ 1980 C292/3; and see the discussion in the House of Lords Select Committee on the European Communities, *Free Movement of People and Right of Residence in the EC*, Session 1980–81, 9th report, at ix of the report and pp.7 *et seq.* of the evidence.

[41]See variously, Written Question no.961/83, OJ 1983 C343/11; Written Question no.75 H-906/85, Debs. EP. no.2-339/141, 14 March 1986; Written Question no.1573/85. OJ 1986 C130/13; see the concern expressed in the Commission's 2nd report on the completion of the internal market, COM (87) 203 final, 11 May 1987; European Council meeting in Milan on the 28 and 29 June 1985; Written Question no.1573/85, OJ 1986 C130/13; Written Question no.2574/85, OJ 1986 C130/48; growing concern expressed at the European Council meetings in The Hague (26–27 June 1986), (5–6 December 1986) and Hanover (27–28 June 1988); and in the Commission's annual report on the Internal Market in 1988 where it regretted the failure on the part of some Member States to recognise the Community's competence in this respect.

[42]See Garth, B., "Migrant Workers and Rights of Mobility in the European Communities and the United States: A Study of Law, Community and Citizenship in the Welfare State", in Cappelletti, M., Seccombe, M, Weiler, J.H.H. *et al.*, *Integration Through Law*, Vol.1, Book 3 (1986) Berlin, EUI/Walter de Gruyter, pp.85–163, at p.108.

[43]See the report of the Council meeting on the internal market, 3 May 1989 cited in COM (89) 275 final, 26 February 1989. The internal market meeting of 13 April 1989 had shown that failing introduction of new elements into the debate, the residence directives were not going to succeed. The Commission had undertaken to introduce new elements to break the deadlock in the discussion, which it did in COM (89) 237 and COM (89) 275 final. On the negotiation and conclusion of the directives see Taschner, H.C., "Free Movement of Students, Retired Persons and other European Citizens: a Difficult Legislative Process", in *Free Movement of Persons in Europe: Problems and Experiences* (1993) Martinus Nijhoff, Dordrecht.

[44]See COM (89) 275, final, at 2; OJ 1989 C191/2.

the internal market, the objectives of Article 7(a) and the implications of an area "without frontiers", were all cited in support of Community action on a general right of residence.[45]

In its original proposal the Commission emphasised the importance of not burdening the social security and sickness insurance schemes of receiving Member States. Nevertheless, in its view, students are rarely beneficiaries of social assistance and thus it proposed that the financial burden for students be lower than that for retired and economically inactive persons. All they were required to prove was registration at a recognised educational establishment and coverage by a sickness insurance scheme for which they were to be eligible on the same basis as nationals.[46] If in exceptional cases the social welfare services of the host state had to intervene, the cost of such would ultimately be borne by the state of origin.[47] However, the state of origin could mean the Member State of nationality or the Member State of previous residence. The two remaining Directives required applicants to be in possession of sufficient resources and be covered by a sickness insurance scheme. In the case of employed or self-employed persons who have ceased their occupational activity (retired persons), sufficient resources could consist of proof of an invalidity pension, old age benefit or industrial or disease pension.[48] The Commission regarded the likelihood of this category requiring support as minimal, since they enjoyed a stable income.[49] With respect to other persons, Member States could require sickness insurance and adequate means of support and the level of resources was to be determined by individual Member States. Since the object was to prevent an individual becoming a burden on the host Member State's social security system,[50] the principle of proportionality would presumably apply to prevent the required level from being set too high. In all cases, except for students, where family members were confined to the spouse and dependent children, the family members entitled to accompany the applicant for residence were defined as in Article 10 of Regulation 1612/68.[51]

The students' Directive was based on Article 6 para.2, in accordance with the rulings of the Court of Justice on Article 128 EEC and Article 6, which prohibited any discrimination as regards access to vocational and professional training. Access to education on an equal basis presupposed being physically present on the

---

[45]For an excellent discussion of the legal background and content of the new proposal, see the House of Lords Select Committee Report, *Free Movement of People and Right of Residence in the EC*, op. cit. note 14, at pp.15 *et seq.*

[46]Article 1(1), OJ 1989 C191/2.

[47]Article 1(3); but not if the residence permit had originally been unconditionally granted to the student: COM (89) 275 final, at 4. In support of a system determining which Member State should bear the costs of education see Advocate General Slynn in Case 236/86 *Humbel*, op. cit. note 28, at 5380.

[48]Article 1, OJ 1989 C191/4.

[49]COM (89) 275 final, at 4.

[50]Article 1, OJ 1990 C191/5.

[51]This was criticised by the European Parliament's Estgen Report, Doc. A 3-77/89, 29 November 1989, which proposed to include the applicant's cohabiting partner or common law spouse within the scope of the Directives.

territory where instruction is given, hence the European Parliament and Commission argued that the Directive simply facilitated the regulation of a pre-existing right of residence. The proposal concerning retired persons was based on Articles 49 and 54. A right of residence was to be extended beyond the active part of their working lives and to Member States where they had not worked, in contrast to Regulation 1251/70. Finally, as an aspect of the establishment of the common market, the right of residence of economically inactive Community citizens was to be enacted on the basis of Article 100 in line with the broad definition of free movement in Articles 3(c) and 7(a).

The Commission's proposal was considerably amended during its passage through Parliament.[52] The legislative rationale behind the students' Directive was specifically linked to the promotion of vocational training and freedom of establishment.[53] Both the EEC Treaty and the SEA were said to support the right to elect one's residence without discrimination.[54] Furthermore, whereas the Commission's proposal had warned of potential problems created by the disparities existing between Member States in social welfare and student-related measures, the Parliament implicitly accepted the problem but shifted the "burden of proof" in this respect, warning that such disparities must not be allowed to act as an impediment to free movement and rights of residence. Parliament also envisaged future measures to grant similar rights of residence to third country nationals.[55] In the case of retired persons and economically inactive persons, the requirement of medical insurance coverage and possession of sufficient resources were maintained.[56] The economic resources proposed by Parliament did not have to exceed the subsistence in the host country, or in the case of retired persons, sufficient resources to ensure that they did not fall a burden on the host Member State's social security scheme.[57] Due to the greater risk and variety of medical services possibly required by the latter, medical coverage had to be *adequate* (emphasis added) for personal needs. Family members in both cases were defined in accordance with the proposed amendment of Article 10 Regulation 1612/68.[58] Death of the primary right holder or dissolution of his or her marriage was not to cause the residence rights of family members to be forfeited, which contrasts with the previous position of the Court of Justice in *Diatta* v. *Land Berlin*.[59] In the case of students, accompanying family

---

[52]See OJ 1990 C15/70.

[53]Recital 4(a), OJ 1990 C15/78; echoing the Court in Case 242/87 *Commission* v. *Council* [1989] ECR 1436 (otherwise known as the *Erasmus* case).

[54]Endorsed by the opinion of ECOSOC, OJ 1989 C329/25, pt. 1.2, at 26.

[55]Recital 6(a), OJ 1990 C15/71 (economically inactive persons); recital 5(b), OJ 1990 C15/79 (students).

[56]This was specified for retired persons as possession of an adequate invalidity pension, pre-retirement (bridging) pension, old age benefits, an adequate pension in respect of an industrial accident or sickness, entitlement to survivors benefits or other adequate resources on which to live: Article 1, OJ 1990 C15/76.

[57]Article 2(1) OJ 1990 C15/7 and Article 1 para.2, OJ 1990 C15/76 respectively.

[58]In this respect ECOSOC proposed that a proviso be inserted to prevent them from constituting an economic burden on the host Member State; also OJ 1989 C329/27.

[59]Case 267/83 [1985] ECR 567.

members were limited to the spouse and dependent children, for whom educational rights were also envisaged.[60] An applicant student was only required to prove coverage by a sickness insurance scheme and enrolment in a recognised educational establishment. Essentially Parliament wanted to reduce to a minimum the financial burden on the student[61] and extend the principle of equal treatment as widely as possible to all aspects of vocational education.[62] Although the ECOSOC preferred a global solution on a general right of residence, it approved of the intent behind the three Directives. It foresaw many practical difficulties, which it failed to specify, with respect to the extension of equal treatment to non-workers. It did not specifically comment on the choice of Article 6 para.2 as a legal basis, but it appears to have been of the view that a right of residence for students already existed in Community law. The purpose of the contested directive was simply to legislatively endorse it.[63] The Committee accepted Member States' concerns regarding the protection of the host social security system, but added that development towards the approximation of social security systems and health benefits would lead to greater social cohesion between Member States, so that citizens' rights to reside would become less dependent on economic guarantees "and more upon an open dynamic view of European societal development".[64]

In January 1990, the Council informed the European Parliament that, on the 21 December 1989, it had reached political agreement on the proposals and that it was in favour of adopting a reference to Article 235 as the legal basis for all three Directives. Nevertheless, it had been agreed in Council that further consultation would be held with the European Parliament and the text of the proposals returned to the Parliament continued to refer to the legal bases proposed by the Commission. It later transpired that this reconsultation was, in the view of the Council, part of the procedure under Article 235 and not the cooperation procedure which would have otherwise applied. Given the political agreement in Council, it was unlikely that further consultation with the Parliament would prompt inclusion of the substantively different provisions which were being proposed by the Commission and Parliament, in particular, reliance on Article 6 para.2 and rejection of the requirement that students be in possession of sufficient resources.[65] The European

[60]Articles 1(1) and 3(a), OJ 1990 C15/80.

[61]See, for example, Article 1(3) OJ 1990 C15/80, where it proposed that if the student did become a burden on the social security system of the host Member State that the costs could be met by the Member State of origin; see also the Opinion of the ECOSOC, OJ 1989 C329/26, at pt.1.6.

[62]See OJ 1990 C15/81, at recital 9a; and the Estgen Report EP Doc. A3-77/89, Article 1(1).

[63]OJ 1989 C329/26: "The existence of the Erasmus student-exchange programmes and the outcome of the *Gravier* case, recognises the right of residence for the student, spouse and dependent children. This should be endorsed." Furthermore, following the *Gravier* decision the Commission had amended its 1979 proposal to the effect that: "This Directive shall not apply to nationals of a Member State who go to another Member State for the sole purpose of vocational training at a university, or an institute of higher learning." OJ 1985 C171/8.

[64]OJ 1989 C329/27, at pt.3.1.

[65]See, for example, Article 1(1) of the Estgen Report, at 7; Article 1(1) of the Commission's amended proposals in OJ 1990 C26/17; and the European Parliament's final amendments in OJ 1990 C175/98 *et seq.*

Parliament was not happy, particularly since one of the reasons for adopting these new legal bases and introducing new elements into the debate had been the dead-lock previously encountered on the basis of Article 235. Although the Commission made it clear that it did not accept the modification of the proposed legal bases and reserved its right to take legal action,[66] the Directives were adopted on the basis of Article 235 on 28 June 1990.[67] Article 235 had clearly emerged as the lesser of two evils for Member States. It required unanimity and ensured that individual national interests could be safeguarded by the insertion of the requirement of sufficient re-sources and medical coverage. This was the ultimate price paid for unanimous Council agreement.

4.3.3. The Importance of the Legal Basis of Community Legislation

The European Parliament subsequently challenged the legal basis of Directive 90/366. It claimed that Article 6 para.2 was the appropriate legal basis and con-sequently, that the Council's reliance on Article 235 was unnecessary and disreg-arded the European Parliament's essential prerogatives in the legislative process. In addition, it challenged the adequacy of the Council's explanation of its choice of legal basis and its failure to explain why certain amendments proposed by the Parliament had not been adopted.

Case C-295/90 joined the ranks of politically unresolved institutional disputes which the Community institutions increasingly tend to bring to the attention of the Court of Justice.[68] The legal basis of Community legislation indicates the objective and nature of the legislation in question, the Community institution competent to legislate and the applicable legislative procedure, including the specific voting re-quirements in Council.[69] The choice of legal basis is relevant to the horizontal and vertical organisation of legislative powers in the Community and has emerged as a

---

[66]See the press release of Commissioner Bangemann, 20 June 1990. This view was reiterated in a letter to the President of the Council on 23 July 1990, subsequent to the adoption of the Directives; cited by Advocate General Jacobs in Case C-295/90 *European Parliament* v. *Council* [1992] CMLR 281, at para.21; see also *Agence Europe* no.5280 ns. 22 June 1990; and the opinion of the Advocate General in Case C-295/90 at paras.15–22.

[67]Directive 90/364, OJ 1990 L180/26 (others); Directive 90/365, OJ 1990 L180/28 (retired per-sons); and Directive 90/366, OJ 1990 L180/30 (students). See generally, Blumann, C., "L'Europe des Citoyens", 346 RMC (1991) 283–292, at 287; Stephanou, C.A., "Identité et citoyenneté européenne", 343 RMC 30–39, at 36; and van Nuffel, P., "L'Europe des citoyens. Vers un droit de séjour generalisé" (1991) *Revue du Marché Unique Européen* 89–108.

[68]On the subject of legal bases disputes see generally, Schwarze, J. (ed.), *Legislation for Europe 1992* (1989) Baden-Baden, Nomos; Temple-Lang, J., "European Community Constitutional Law: The Division of Powers Between the Community and Member States", 33 *Northern Ireland Law Quarterly* (1988) 209–234; and Bradley, K. St. C., "The European Court and the Legal Basis of Community Legislation", 13 *ELRev* (1988) 379–402.

[69]Article 190 requires Community legislation to state the reasons for its adoption and is the basis for the more specific requirement that it also clearly state the legal basis on which it is founded; see also Articles 11(b) and 14 of Council's Rules of Procedure, OJ 1979 L268/2; and Rule 36(3) of Parliament's Rules of Procedure which instructs the committee responsible for preparing a report on any proposal on which Parliament has been consulted, first to examine the "validity and appropriateness of the chosen legal base".

significant aspect of the institutional balance which the Court of Justice has generally championed.[70] Since the choice of legal basis is a legal and not purely a political matter it must be based on objective factors amenable to judicial review.[71] Clever use of the amendment facility in Article 149, whereby the Commission can amend its legislative proposals any time prior to their adoption enable it to present redrafted proposals which may be acceptable to a qualified majority in Council. The requirement of unanimity entails more far-reaching and fundamental redrafting and it is often the case, as with Directive 90/366, that substantial differences between the Community institutions fall by the wayside in order to secure the political consensus necessary to adopt the measure on a unanimous basis in Council. Unanimity also restricts the role of the European Parliament to consultation rather than cooperation. Legal basis cases are frequently used to contest whether the Council is able to resort to a specific or general legislative enabling provision in the Treaties.[72] The latter involves more broadly stated legislative provisions whose function is essentially to supplement the powers of action of the Community when necessary for the establishment and functioning of the common or internal market (Articles 100 and 100A), or when lacunae appear in the Treaty system (Article 235). The adoption of the residence Directives on the basis of Article 235 altered the applicable legislative procedure and voting requirements and indicated that "the necessary powers of action" to deal with a right of residence for students did not exist in the Treaty as it stood. It was a rejection of the Parliament and Commission's assessment of the Community's competence to legislate as regards the principle of non-discrimination generally and the free movement of students in particular.

In its decision in Case C-295/90, the Court of Justice reiterated that recourse to Article 235 "is justified only where no other provision of the Treaty gives the Community institutions the necessary power to adopt the measure in question".[73]

---

[70]For discussion of the Community's institutional balance see, *inter alia*, Case 45/86 *Commission v. Council* [1987] ECR 1493; Case C-11/88 *Commission* v. *Council* [1989] ECR 3799; Bradley, K. St. C., "Maintaining the Balance: The Role of the Court of Justice in Defining the Institutional Position of the European Parliament", 24 *CMLRev* (1987) 41–64; Bieber. R., "The Settlement of Institutional Conflicts on the Basis of Article 4 of the EEC Treaty", 21 *CMLRev* (1984) 505–523; and Fernández-Martín, J.M., "La Legitimación Activa Restringida del Parlamento Europeo en el Recurso de Anulación, (comentario a la sentencia del TJCE 'Chernobyl' de 22 de Mayo de 1990)", 17 *Revista de Instituciones Europeas* (1990) 911–933.

[71]See Case 45/86 [1988] CMLR 131; Case 294/83 *Les Verts* v. *European Parliament* [1986] ECR 1339, at para.23; and Case 62/88 *Greece* v. *Commission* [1990] ECR I-1527.

[72]For legal bases cases dealing with a conflict between different institutional appreciations of the scope and basis of the Community's power of action in the specific context of common policies see Case 45/86, op. cit. note 70 (common commercial policy: Articles 235 v. 113); Case C-11/88, op. cit. note 70 (common agricultural policy: Articles 235 v. 43); and Case 242/87, op. cit. (common vocational policy: Articles 235 v. 128). In the context of social policy the European Parliament has complained that "despite the possibility of adopting social directives by a qualified majority, the Council is seeking unanimity of decision-making which leads to unacceptable derogations, a lack of coherence and too low a level of social protection". See the Reding Report on the new social dimension of the TEU, Doc. A3-0091/94, 18 February 1994.

[73]See also Case 45/86, op. cit. note 70, at para.13. Article 235 provides that "If action by the Community should prove necessary to attain, in the course of the operation of the common market, one of the objectives of the Community and this Treaty has not provided the necessary powers".

To establish the appropriate legal basis the Court referred to the objective and content of the contested legislation. It held that the objective of the right of residence granted by the Directive is to "facilitate access to vocational training" (Article 1). The student beneficiaries of the right of residence must prove that they are registered at a recognised educational establishment, are sufficiently covered by medical insurance and that they are in possession of sufficient resources not to become a charge on the social assistance of the host Member State (Article 1). Though it may once have been possible to debate whether a Directive would create a new right of residence, or simply confirm a pre-existing right which, following the *Gravier* decision could be said to flow from the Treaty, the decision of the Court in Case C-295/90 was pre-empted by the judgment it had handed down some months earlier in *Raulin* v. *Minister of Education and Science*. The Court there held that equal treatment in relation to conditions of access to vocational training applied not only to conditions imposed by educational establishments, but also to any measure liable to hinder the exercise of that right.[74] To deny students a right of residence was to deny them the very right to attend vocational courses on an equal basis, which had been guaranteed in *Gravier*. Thus, the Court in *Raulin* held that the effect of the principle of non-discrimination as regards conditions of access to vocational education, which was derived from Articles 6 and 128 EEC, was that a national of a Member State admitted to a vocational training course in another Member State automatically enjoyed a right to reside there for the duration of the course.

This principle was reiterated by the Court in Case C-295/90, where it further held that although Article 6 para.1 could only apply "without prejudice to any special provisions" contained in the Treaty,[75] acts adopted pursuant to Article 6 para.2 should not necessarily be limited to regulating rights deriving from Article 6 para.1, but should cater for what appears to be necessary to ensure the effective exercise of those rights.[76] The Court pointed to the right of residence conferred by Article 1 of the Directive upon the spouse and dependent children of the student as a right essential for the effective exercise of the student's right of residence. As regards limitations on the right of residence conferred by the Directive, the Court limited itself to a reference to Article 3 to the effect that the "directive does not establish any entitlement to the payment of maintenance grants". The Advocate General was more expansive in his reference to the Directive's conditions and to the limits imposed by the Court in *Raulin* regarding the duration of the right of residence and the "legitimate interests of the host state".[77] He stressed that these matters are not covered by the principle of access on a non-discriminatory basis to vocational training courses. In conclusion, however, since the Directive prohibited discrimination on

---

[74]Case C-357/89, op. cit. note 9, at para.34.

[75]It cited Case 8/77 *Sagulo* to the effect that regulations and directives under Article 49 come within the definition of "special provisions".

[76]Case C-295/90, op. cit. note 66, at para.18.

[77]Case C-357/89, op. cit. note 9, at para.34.

grounds of nationality within a field to which the Treaty applied, namely, vocational training, both the Court and Advocate General held that the Council could have legislated on the basis of Article 6 para.2 and need not have had recourse to Article 235.[78] Directive 90/366 was subsequently readopted as Directive 93/96 on the basis of Article 6 para.2.[79]

4.4. Analysis of the Substantive Content of the Directives

If the legal position of Community citizens following the adoption of the Union Treaty is to bear any relationship to the model of citizenship outlined in Chapter 1, the rights which Community citizenship entails must have some substance and be legally enforceable. Linked to a citizen's enjoyment of the right to free movement and residence is the enjoyment of equal protection as regards fellow citizens and a minimum of social rights.[80] Admittedly, the inclusion of social rights in citizenship is contested. Marshall's threefold typology of citizenship rights arguably described what citizenship should ideally look like rather than what it does look like. King and Waldron ask whether, in fact, "our concept of citizenship provide[s] us with a reason for continuing to assure health, education, social services and income support for everyone in society?"[81] They try to answer that question in the affirmative with reference to (i) principles of equality; (ii) arguments that securing basic social standards promotes the exercise of other citizenship rights; (iii) the idea that effective political participation requires social and economic well-being; and (iv) the concept of membership or belonging. The authors do not reach one single conclusion, but demonstrate throughout their discussion the solidarity/membership/effective participation aspects of citizenship and the essential role which minimum socio-economic standards can play in this regard.

Article 8(a)(1) now provides that every Union citizen shall have the right to move and reside freely within the territory of the Member States, "subject to the limitation and conditions laid down in this Treaty and by the measures adopted to give it effect". The 1990 Directives represent part of the regulation of the rights of residence in Community law to which Article 8(a) refers. The following section

---

[78]The Court did not annul the Directive in its entirety since this would have prejudiced the exercise of a right which flowed directly from the Treaty. It noted that the essential content of the legislation was not disputed by the parties and that the date prescribed for the implementation of the Directive at national level had already passed. In the light of these circumstances and in the interests of legal certainty, the Court applied the power expressly granted to it under Article 174 in the case of regulations, to the present Directive. The Directive was to continue in force until the Council replaced it with a new Directive based on the appropriate legal basis.

[79]OJ 1993 L317/59, 29 October 1993.

[80]See also O'Keeffe, D., "The Free Movement of Persons and the Single Market", 17 *ELRev* (1992) 3–19, at 19: "If Community citizenship is to mean anything, it must entail the right to move freely within the Community, and to receive equal protection to that afforded to nationals of the host state."

[81]King and Waldron, op. cit. note 1, at 423.

analyses some substantive provisions of the 1990 Directives from this perspective.[82] In particular, certain problematic aspects of the students' Directive are discussed in the light of the Court's decision in Case C-295/90. The conclusions
drawn from this discussion are extended by analogy to the other Community citizens and the other categories of beneficiary. Discussion of the possible social dimension of citizenship is justified by the importance of the right of residence as
one of the primary characteristics of Community citizenship and the existence of a
possible penumbra of citizenship rights on the basis of Community law.
Furthermore, Article 8(a)(2) empowers the Council to "adopt provisions with a
view to facilitating the exercise of the rights referred to in para.1".

4.4.1. Possession of Sufficient Resources

With respect to economically inactive Community nationals and employed or self-
employed persons no longer pursuing their occupational activity, the grant of a
right of residence is subject to the possession of sufficient resources and medical
insurance (Article 1(1)). They must also ensure that they and their families do not
become a burden on the social assistance system of the host Member State (Article
1(1)). In addition to sickness insurance, retired persons must be in receipt of an
early retirement pension, old age benefit, an industrial accident or disease pension,
or an amount sufficient to avoid becoming a burden on the social security system
of the host Member State (Article 1(1)). Students must possess sickness insurance,
be registered at a recognised educational establishment and provide proof that they
have sufficient resources in order not to become a burden on the social assistance
system (Article 1).

One of the most remarkable aspects of the development of a general right of residence in the Community is the length of time it took the Community to concede so
little. Prior to the adoption of the three Directives, Community nationals who
wished to permanently reside in another Member State fell outside the scope of
Community law unless they exercised some sort of recognised economic activity.
Their legal position was similar to that of non-Community nationals and was regulated by national law.[83] Almost all Member States required such persons to possess
sufficient resources to support themselves and their families.[84] In the case of

---

[82]See also Kampf, R., "La directive 90/366/CEE relative au droit de séjour des étudiants communautaires: sa transposition en France", no.357 RMC (1992) 307–317, at 310; and Van Nuffel, op. cit.
note 67.
  [83]See Kampf, op. cit. note 82, at 308; Bull. EC. 7/8/1979; Written Question no.642/82, OJ 1982
C291/5, on the residence rights of Community ex-staff; Written Question no.450/87, OJ 1988 C42/60,
on the residence rights of old-age pensioners who wish to reside in a Member State other than that of
employment or origin; Written Question no.2622/87, OJ 1988 C195/16, where the Commission stated
that "for persons not covered by Community law on freedom of movement for workers, it is at present
for the Member States to determine the conditions under which they grant the right of residence";
Written Question no.1565/87, OJ 1988 C332/1; Written Question no.702/89, OJ 1990 C69/32.
  [84]See Guimezanes, N., La Circulation et l'Activité Economique des Etrangers dans la CE: Droit
Communautaire, Droits Nationaux (1990) Levallois-Perret, Nouvelles Editions Fiduciaires, at pp.34
and 93 et seq.

students, for example, all Member States, except Greece and Luxembourg, required that they prove admission to a higher educational establishment,[85] or that they possess sufficient resources to maintain themselves.[86] A medical examination was often required. Furthermore, residence permits issued to non-nationals were generally tailored to one year or less, according to the studies pursued.[87] Clearly, the 1990 Directives required Member States to amend established legal practice very little.

In any event, Member States are allowed to insist on the possession of sufficient resources with respect to all three categories. In the case of students, the requirement is limited to the applicant presenting *proof* that he or she possesses sufficient resources (emphasis added). It is not likely that national authorities will be able to go to great lengths to verify the various forms of proof presented to them, so that this distinction may lose its significance in practice. Kampf, however, points to two circulars in France which predate Directive 90/366, but which require national authorities to exercise flexibility in the determination of whether students have sufficient resources. French authorities must take any personal circumstances or advantages of which the student may avail into account and must recognise almost any form of proof.[88] He suggests that transposition of the Directive at national level should incorporate this situation and go beyond it to include declarations of honour. When the Directives were being negotiated the suggestion that students simply prove the possession of sufficient resources referred to a legally binding guarantee.[89] Given the resistance of some Member States to the Directive and their rejection of the Commission and Parliament's proposal that the Member States of origin of the students pay any additional social costs incurred, due to a fear that those costs would remain unpaid, it seems unlikely that most Member States would accept guarantees that are not legally binding. Furthermore, it should not be forgotten that France was particularly in favour of the Directive, if only as a means of regulating the growing influx of Community students. Other Member States, such

---

[85]See Danish Order on Foreigners, 18 January 1984, no.19 Article 24(1)2; Spain, Article 24 of the law of 1 July 1985 and Article 29 of the decree law of 26 May 1986; France, decree law of 30 June 1946 modified by Article 7(5) of the decree law of 4 December 1984 and decree law 81-1221, 21 December 1981 and a case of 21 December 1981 on the inscription of foreigners in universities and public establishments; FRG, AuslVwV, no.17; UK, section 21 of the Immigration Rules.

[86]See Belgium, Articles 60 of the law of 15 December 1980, the minimum level was fixed at 12 000 FB by a Royal Decree of 3 June 1983 which allowed for the annual revision of this sum in accordance with the consumer price index of the month of May preceding the beginning of the academic year; Denmark, Order on Foreigners of 18 January 1984, Article 24(1)2; Spain, Article 29 of the decree law of 26 May 1986; France, decree law of 30 June 1946 modified by decree of 4 December 1984 Article 7(5), where applicants must prove that they have resources at least equal to a monthly government grant, 1 800 F; FRG, AuslVwV, no.17; UK, Section 21 of the Immigration Rules. Please note that more recent sources were not available.

[87]For further details, in the particular context of students, see Mohr, B.(ed.), *Higher Education in the European Community: The Student Handbook*, 6th edn. (1990) Luxembourg, Commission of the European Communities.

[88]No.82-41, 5 March 1982 and 85-196, 1 April 1985; and Kampf, op. cit. note 6, at 312.

[89]See *Agence Europe* no.4991 ns. 8 April 1989.

as Denmark, did not support the Directive initially in a similar manner and opposed the extension of the Treaty to what it regarded as non-economic fields.[90]

Even if one accepts the need to incorporate economic guarantees into the Directives due to the disparity between welfare levels and welfare systems in the different Member States,[91] it must nevertheless be concluded that a general right of residence in no way follows from these Directives and that what has been adopted gives rise to the possibility of diverse national application. Sufficient resources mean resources higher than the level at which the host Member State may grant social assistance to its own nationals, or higher than the level of the minimum social security pension. This means that Member States with developed welfare systems will be able to exclude nationals of Member States who possess fewer resources due to their generally lower levels of income more easily. Community nationals not on the verge of social assistance in their Member States of origin may fall below the Article 1 threshold in other Member States and consequently be denied a right of residence there, (although the host Member State may take the personal circumstances of the applicant into account). An aspect of the *Levin* judgment, whereby a right of residence was guaranteed a worker, though he received a salary lower than the minimum level of subsistence in the host Member State, was the Court's determination to prevent the category of beneficiaries of Community law varying from one Member State to the next. Thus, it refused to allow the subsistence minimum applicable in Member States to determine the scope of application of free movement, since the latter is unilaterally and diversely determined by national authorities.[92] It is difficult to identify an objective and logical reason to distinguish between the *Levin* case and the beneficiaries of the 1990 Directives in this matter and to allow national diversity with respect to the latter and not the former. Since the *Levin* judgment does not permit the level of resources to be taken into account for the determination of the individual's status as worker and hence his right of residence, it is difficult to accept it as a condition for the recognition of a right of residence for those who do not exercise a professional activity. It could be argued that workers who come within the scope of *Levin* have some resources, even if insufficient, which may not be the case for economically inactive persons. Nevertheless, part of the rationale of the *Levin* judgment was that there are persons who live below the subsistence minimum. That rationale could equally apply to persons wishing to avail of a Community right of residence independently of their

---

[90]See *Agence Europe* no.5279 ns. 21 January 1990, where the Danish appeared to prefer an intergovernmental solution to the right of residence for "non-active" people; and *Agence Europe* no.4991 ns. 8 April 1989, where it reluctantly admitted a right of residence for students on condition that they incurred no social costs as a result.

[91]See *The EC 1992 and Beyond*, Europe on the Move Series (1991) Commission of the European Communities, at p.16, where it outlines national social welfare differences. See also Eurostat Theme 3 – Population and Social Conditions, Rapid Reports, 1990.

[92]Case 53/81 [1982] ECR 1035; and Druesne, G., "Liberté de circulation des personnes. Les prolongements de la libre circulation des salariés: droit de séjour et progrès social", 18 RTDE 556–567, at 558 *et seq.*

exercise of any economic activity.[93] The distinction (and possible discrimination) between these two situations is even less consistent with the establishment of a general right to free movement and residence for both categories of person in Article 8(a). There is an unfortunate element of truth in Commissioner Bangemann's dubbing the Directive on a general right of residence (90/364) the "playboy" Directive.

4.4.2. Medical Insurance

The diversity of national systems of social protection and Member States' desire to protect their national social policies also lie behind the insistence that applicants be covered by medical insurance in respect of all risks in the host Member State. These provisions reflect national social protectionism and do not address or resolve the difficulties caused by national diversity as regards health care. Indeed thay are more likely, in practice, to make those differences more acute. In France, for example, higher education students under 26 are compulsorily affiliated to the national social security system.[94] Non-national Community students who come within the scope of Regulation 1408/71, or who are personally insured under another Member State's social security system due to concomitant performance of some occupational or professional activity are excluded from this national regime. Other students, probably the majority, who are not personally insured under a national social security system as a result of concomitant professional activity, may fall within the provisions of the French legislation and be subject to double insurance cover in their host Member State and while resident in France. Since the Community's adoption of the ERASMUS scheme, coordination of insurance schemes at Community level, at least with respect to students, seemed necessary. Negotiations on the extension of Regulation 1408/71 to all students regardless of the performance of a professional activity have not yet been completed. Member States have, however, reached a common agreement allowing students in a Member State other than their own to receive the same treatment while abroad to that which they would be entitled if they were at home. Problems nevertheless remain with respect to students or persons covered by private insurance schemes which may not generally be favoured in some Member States. Some private insurance schemes require some sort of affiliation to a state security system and, as stated above, students do not generally fall within the categories of persons (employed, self-employed, families,

---

[93]Furthermore, Article 10 para.2 of the EC Charter of Fundamental Social Rights of Workers, COM (89) 248 final, provides that "Persons who have been unable either to enter or re-enter the labour market and have no means of subsistence must be able to receive sufficient resources and social assistance in keeping with their particular situation." Though the Charter is not legally binding, Curtin suggests that it could be used as an interpretative aid, see Curtin, D., "Prospects for a European Social Policy", in Betten, L. (ed.), *The Future of European Social Policy*, European Monographs 1 (1991) Deventer, Kluwer, at p.163; see also Case 322/88 *Grimaldi* v. *Fonds des Maladies Professionelles* [1990] ECR 4402, on the persuasive authority of recommendations in Community law.

[94]Article L381-4 of the French Social Security Code.

survivors, refugees and stateless persons) who come within the Community's co-ordination of national social security systems.[95] The national sickness insurance schemes with which they are affiliated in their Member State of origin may not cover illness in another Member State and they may be obliged to apply for further coverage in the host Member State. They will not be entitled to a residence permit until this condition is fulfilled.[96] The Directives do not specify what type of policy or coverage is necessary, implying that Member States should accept all schemes offering adequate coverage whether or not they are comparable with the national general sickness insurance schemes, as long as the coverage is adequate. It remains to be seen how this condition will operate in practice and how different national insurance schemes will be understood by the administrative authorities of the various Member States.

4.4.3. Eligible Family Members

The Directives are also restrictive in their provision of rights of residence for the family members of the applicant. Only the spouse and dependent children are allowed accompany the student (Article 1). The remaining Directives confine themselves to the current definition of family members in Article 10 of Regulation 1612/68.[97] All three seem over broad in excluding relatives, of whatever degree, who are dependent on the worker. As suggested by the House of Lords Select Committee, dependency in such cases could be verified by a document issued by the competent authority of the State of origin from whence they came.[98] Furthermore, since the Directives insist on the possession of sufficient resources to maintain the beneficiary of the right of residence and those family members who accompany him or her, it seems unnecessary to predetermine which relatives in the ascending and descending line should be included within its scope, regardless of whether they are dependent. If the sufficient resources condition were eliminated it might make some sense to restrict family members, but the economic conditions imposed on applicants are likely to restrict family members to a minimum anyway and certainly to what an applicant seems likely to be able to maintain. Since the Directives provide employment and educational rights to be enjoyed by these

---

[95]Regulation 1408/71 and Regulation 574/72, OJ 1972 L74.

[96]See Watson, P., "Wandering Students: Their Rights under Community Law", in O'Keeffe, D., and Curtin, D. (eds.), *Constitutional Adjudication in European Community and National Law: Essays in Honour of Mr Justice T.F. O'Higgins* (1992) Oxford, Butterworths, pp.79–88, at p.84.

[97]Articles 1 para.2 of Directives 90/364-5 provide: "The following shall, irrespective of their nationality, have the right to install themselves in another Member State with the holder of the right of residence: (a) his or her spouse and their descendants who are dependants; (b) dependant relatives in the ascending line of the holder of the right of residence and his or her spouse." See, however, the Opinion of Advocate General Tesauro in Case C-7/94 *Lubor Gaal*, 9 February 1995, where he held that Article 12 Regulation 1612/68 precludes the application of a national law which makes the definition of a child, for the purposes of that article, subject to age limits or conditions connected with the status of the dependent person.

[98]See *Free Movement of People and the Right of Residence in the EC*, op. cit. note 14, at p.15.

ancillary right holders,[99] these provisions seem designed to regulate if not limit the possibility of such and are the antithesis of what one would expect of a charter designed to encourage free movement in the context of a broader ideal of citizenship. Furthermore, their restrictive nature is mainly due to the fact that the eligible family members are to be admitted regardless of their nationality. Thus, Member States saw this as a means by which their immigration rules regarding third country nationals could be circumscribed and were consequently eager to reduce the possibility of this happening. Community nationals are viewed by Member States as less of a risk in this respect since at some stage, if not immediately, they can rely on their own Community rights independently of their status as family members.

However, the restriction of family members in the students' Directive is particularly excessive and could arguably be incompatible, in certain circumstances, with the respect for family life guaranteed by Article 8(1) of the European Convention on Human Rights.[100] A student's dependent parents do not qualify under Article 1 Directive 90/366. The Community respects fundamental rights as guaranteed in the Convention and as they result from constitutional traditions common to the Member States.[101] Article 8 of the European Convention is one of the few provisions of the Convention which has been expressly cited by the Court of Justice as a specific example of a principle to which it adheres.[102] Though a student's right of residence is of a less permanent nature (a fact which the House of Lords Select Committee suggested is a factor implying that considerations of family reunification do not apply to the same extent), the vital aspect, from the point of view of a successful plea for family reunification under Article 8(1), is the element of dependency on the beneficiary of residence, rather than the period of time for which residence is necessary to cater for this dependency. Furthermore, the notion of dependent person has been interpreted rather more extensively in other areas of Community law, where the status of dependent is regarded as the result of a objective factual situation. Thus in *Lebon*, the Court held that: "The person having that status is a member of the family who is supported by the worker and there is no need to determine the reasons for recourse to the worker's support or to raise the question whether the person concerned is able to support himself by taking up paid employment."[103] Given the Court's definition of spouse in *Reed*, the cohabiting partners of students, retired persons and persons of "independent means" have no entrenched rights under these Directives, even though such a status may be legally recognised for various purposes by the national legislation of their Member State of origin, or more importantly, by the host Member State with respect to its own nationals. Indeed, it seems discriminatory to exclude the common law spouses of

---

[99]Articles 2 Directives 90/364-5-6 and 1 Directive 90/366 respectively.

[100]See ETS no.5 or 213 UNTS 221; Article 8(1) provides as follows: "Everyone has the right to respect for his private and family life, his home and his correspondence."

[101]See Article F(2) and *infra* Chapter 8.

[102]See Case 249/86 *Commission* v. *Germany* [1989] ECR 1263, at para.10.

[103]See Case 316/85 [1987] ECR 2811, at para.22, in the context of dependency in Articles 10(1) and (2) of Regulation 1408/71.

residence applicants in terms of Article 8(1) of the European Convention and, in purely Community law terms, on the basis of Article 6, if the host Member States' nationals can enjoy more liberal benefits with respect to their incoming common law spouses compared to resident nationals from other Member States. Article 7(2) Regulation 1612/68 was the means used by the European Court of Justice to strike down a similarly discriminatory provision of Dutch legislation in the *Reed* case. However, that case involved workers to whom the provisions of Regulation 1612/68 are specifically addressed. The Council's refusal or failure to extend the application of that Regulation to the present Directives means that a solution may have to be found in future, possibly with reference to Article 6 para.1 of the Treaty, in conjunction with Article 8(1) of the European Convention.

4.4.4. The Legal Nature of the Right of Residence

The question remains whether the rights conferred by the 1990 Directives are similar to those extensively interpreted by the Court of Justice in *Royer* and thereafter? Sufficient resources and medical insurance may act as prior conditions for the grant of a residence permit to economically inactive individuals (though this arguably weakens any ideal of citizenship which the Community may have), but does subsequent failure to fulfil these conditions and reliance on public funds result not only in withdrawal of the residence permit,[104] but also loss of the right of residence itself and expulsion. The latter is regarded as the very negation of free movement. If residence permits are merely declaratory of individuals' rights, they may continue to enjoy a right of residence, even though their *permit* has been withdrawn for non-compliance with the conditions in Article 1 of the Directives.[105] If these rights of residence evolve by analogy with previous Community case law such as *Royer*, the negation of the right to free movement by expulsion for failure to comply with these conditions will be hard to justify. After all, public policy considerations cannot be invoked for economic reasons.[106] However, Articles 3 and 4 of Directives 90/364-365 and 90/366 respectively, state that the *right* of residence itself (and not simply the permit) shall remain as long as these conditions are fulfilled. This suggests that the conditions in the Directive are constitutive of the right of residence itself and more than mere administrative formalities and that the residence permit granted on the basis of these Directives pretends not merely to be declaratory of the citizen's rights under Article 8(a). Contrast the position in the 1990 Directives with the decision of the Court of Justice in *Commission* v. *Germany*, where it refused to permit the housing requirement in Article 10(3) of Regulation 1612/68 to continue to play a role in the subsequent validity of the residence of members of

---

[104]Article 4 Directive 90/366 and Articles 3 Directive 90/364 and 90/365.

[105]See Case C-363/89, 5 February 1991, where it stated that prior subscription to a national social insurance scheme need not be a prior condition of residence nor the grant of a residence permit; cited by Antoniou, T., Greek Report to the 1992 FIDE conference, *The New Developments of the Free Movement of Persons Towards European Citizenship* (1992) Lisbon, pp.145–197, at p.154.

[106]Article 2(2), Directive 64/221.

the migrant worker's family. Once the migrant worker's housing was established as adequate for the purposes of granting the residence permit, the national authorities' determination in this respect was said to be complete: "Once the family has been brought together, the position of the migrant worker cannot be different in relation to housing requirements from that of a worker who is a national of the Member State concerned."[107] Sanctions could only be imposed for the migrant worker's failure to maintain the housing as sufficient if they also applied to Member State nationals in similar circumstances, but a refusal to renew the residence permit was regarded as incompatible with Article 10(3) and disproportionate to the objectives sought by that provision, since sanctions of comparative severity were not imposed on nationals.

4.5. The Social Dimension of Community Citizenship

Social policy is generally taken to refer to measures in the field of social insurance, public assistance, health and welfare services, and housing. In the specific case of the European Communities it is said that: "to the framers of the Treaty 'social policy' included not only social security and interpersonal distribution of income, at least for certain groups of workers, but also interregional distribution, elements of industrial and labour market policy (vocational training, measures to improve labour mobility) and social regulation (primarily occupational health and safety and equal treatment for men and women)".[108] However, the lack of legally enforceable social rights and the weak legal nature of the Community's powers in this field are remarkable. Section 4.3.3 pointed to the fundamental principle of Community law that Community institutions can only legislate within the sphere of their express or implied powers and that all Community legislation must be based on a specific legal basis. Articles 117, 118 and 119, enable the Community institutions to act, particularly in the field of equal treatment between men and women, but the Treaty section on social policy lacks firm and uncontestable legal bases.[109]

---

[107]See Case 249/86, at para.12.

[108]See Majone, "The EC Between Social Policy and Social Regulation", 31 JCMS (1993) 153–170, at 154; and Beaumont and Weatherill, *European Community Law* (1993) London, Penguin Books, at p.541.

[109]Article 117 refers to the need for Member States to promote improved working conditions and improved standards of living for workers. The attainment of these objectives is regarded as flowing generally "not only from the functioning of the common market, which is to favour the harmonisation of social systems but also from the procedures provided for by the Treaty and from the approximation of national legislation". Article 118 assigns to the Commission the task of "promoting close cooperation between Member States in the social field". Article 119 enshrines the principle of equal pay for equal work, but again does not specify a Community power to legislate. On the scope of the Community's legisative competence in the social field see Joined Cases 281, 283–285 and 287/85, *Germany* v. *Commission* [1987] ECR 3202. For the details of the contributions by the TEU to Community social policy see variously, Szyszczak, E., "Social Policy: a Happy Ending or a Reworking of a Fairy Tale?", in O'Keeffe, D. and Twomey, P. (eds.), *Legal Issues of the Maastricht Treaty* (1993) Chancery Press, London, pp.313–327; and Shaw, J., "Twin Track Social Europe: the Inside Track", ibid., pp.295–311.

Although social policy clearly ranked amongst the Community's broad programmatic objectives, power to legislate with respect to it did not clearly figure in the specific provisions of the Treaty: "[Community social policy] is not a generalized scheme for the provision of social welfare. Nor is it designed as a means of harmonizing social security systems or levelling out social security burdens between the states by a set deadline ... Rather, it was initially tailored to the precise and immediate concerns of the three communities [viz. market integration] and focused, from the outset, on employment."[110] This emphasis on employment related social policy resurfaces in the Union Treaty, where the amended Article 118a is limited to the social security and protecion of *workers*. Community legislative activity in this domain has been slow to develop and has been fiercely contested, not least because the enjoyment of social rights at national level have generally been based on claims of access due to "traditional Community ties of autonomy and obligation".[111] An immediate difference is evident as regards social policy in the European Communities. The provisions of Title III, with the exception of Article 119, which addresses equal pay for men and women, address Member States not Community citizens and the subordination of social policy issues to the achievement of the economic objectives of the Community is evident.[112] Amendments to the Union Treaty in the field of social policy were confined to a protocol and agreement annexed to the Treaty.[113]

Controversy about the scope and content of Community social policy is fuelled principally by the vast political, legal and economic differences between the various Member States in the social field. For example, the levels and terms of coverage of social security and assistance differ from one Member State to the next. Tax and social security systems are integrated in some Member States but not in others. Continental welfare states have traditionally admitted entitlement-based benefits, while welfare systems in other Member States, such as the United Kingdom, Denmark and Ireland, also cater for need rather than entitlement and contribution. In addition, Member States use their social welfare systems to fulfil different economic, fiscal and social policies, reflecting different traditions and ideologies. According to Majone: "The 'big trade-off' between economic efficiency and a more equal distribution of income and wealth has confronted every democracy since the dawn of industrialization ... the delicate value judgments about the appropriate balance of efficiency and equity, which social policies express, can only be

---

[110]See Lodge, *The European Community and the Challenge of the Future* (1989) London, Pinter Publishers, at p.309; Leibfried, S. and Pierson, P., " Prospects for Social Europe", 20 *Politics and Society* (1992) 333–365, at 366; and Joined Cases 281/85, 283–285, 287/85, op. cit. note 109, at para.14.

[111]See Culpitt, I., *Welfare and Citizenship: Beyond the Crisis of the Welfare State?* (1992) Politics and Culture, London, Sage Publications, at p.1.

[112]See also the treatment of the issues of social policy in Case 244/87 *Bettray* [1989] ECR 1621, at paras.17–20.

[113]See *inter alia* Shaw, and Szyszczak, op. cit. note 109, and Whiteford, E., "Social Policy after Maastricht", 18 *ELRev* (1993) 202–222.

made legitimately and efficiently within homogeneous communities."[114] However, it is also arguable that it is as mistaken to defend the transposition of national-type welfare systems to the supranational level, as it is to deny any feasible social dimension at that level.[115] Thus, although Member States have accepted that the internal market can be achieved while the diversity of their social protection systems is maintained, they have also agreed to foster convergence of these policies and have fixed common objectives which will act as pointers to the way their systems are modified to take account of the challenges set by unemployment, changing family structures, ageing etc.[116] The Community created may not require the "popular legitmacy that previous modes of state-building had required",[117] but the establishment of Community citizenship in the TEU should move it beyond the market-orientated objectives of the internal market with respect to the rights of the individual. Limiting citizenship to freedom of movement and contract seems acceptable in the context of economic integration, but not when issues of greater democratic and social legitimacy are added to the Community's overall objectives.

The Community does not deny that fundamental differences exist between the Member States' social welfare systems.[118] Thus, Regulation 1408/71 does not seek to harmonise national social security systems, rather it attempts to coordinate how Member States regulate social security so that obstacles to the free movement of persons are abolished or minimised.[119] However, it is undeniable that Treaty provisions on the extent of Community competences in this field are ambiguous, as are the effects of some of its objectives, such as the abolition of borders and complete free movement in the context of the internal market, on national social regulation. Combined with the political reticence of Member States to concede more significant and far-reaching powers of action to the Community institutions, this ambiguity has marked the development of social policy from the birth of the Community. Thus, although Article 2 referred to "an accelerated raising of the

---

[114]Majone, op. cit. note 108, at 167. See also Marshall, T.H., *Social Policy* (1975) London, Hutchinson, at p.15 where he defined social policy as: "use of political power to supersede, supplement or modify operations of the economic system in order to achieve results which the economic system would not achieve on its own ... guided by values other than those determined by open market forces."

[115]See Leibfried and Pierson, op. cit. note 3, at 334, who provide an excellent overview of the present state of social Europe.

[116]See the Council recommendation on the convergence of social protection objectives and policies, 94/442/EEC, OJ L245, 26 August 1992.

[117]Streeck, "From Market-Building to State-Building? Reflections on the Political Economy of European Social Policy", DOC.IUE 76/94 (col.24) *European Law in Context: Constitutional Dimensions of European Economic Integration*, EUI, Florence, 14–15 April 1994, at p.22.

[118]See the *Commission Action Programme on the Implementation of the Community Charter of Basic Social Rights*, 8–9 December 1989: "because of great variations in nature from one Member State of the Community to another which reflect the history, traditions and social and cultural practices characteristic of each Member State and which cannot be called into question, there can be no harmonising systems of social policy." See also the Commission's White Paper on European Social Policy, COM (94) 333, at p.12.

[119]For proposals on the coordination of social security in the EC in the future see Berghman, J., "1992 and Social Security: Critique and Proposals", in Room, G. (ed.), *Towards a European Welfare State* (1991) Bristol, SAUS Publications, pp.91–103.

standard of living and closer relations between the States", which seemed to indicate common action in the social sphere, overall competence in this field is effectively seen as belonging to the Member States.[120] The Community has been caught between being committed to promoting social progress and being denied the legislative power to adopt its own independent policies. Regulation 1408/71 is increasingly outdated and is being superseded by the creation of new branches of social security at national level, the increasing importance of complementary social security schemes and a change in national methods of financing. Despite the considerable changes in free movement and employment, the basic structure of the regulation has not changed in thirty years. This is perhaps because central government in the Member States are not eager to relinquish competence in this field, since it is one of the few remaining areas where supranational and regional governments have little say and it can also be a useful tool at polling-time.

4.5.1. Social Rights Independent of the Exercise of an Economic Activity

Does Article 8(a) imply that Union citizens may enjoy a right of residence regardless of their economic status and that when doing so they are entitled to equal treatment with respect to rights which facilitate the exercise of the principal right (i.e. residence), such as access to social assistance and medical care while resident in those Member States? The answer, at first sight, appears to be no. Article 8(a)(1) also provides that the right of residence of Union citizens is "subject to the limitations and conditions laid down in this Treaty and by the measures adopted to give it effect". Thus, the traditional Article 48(3) limitations on free movement – public policy, security and health – continue to apply to Union citizens who avail of the rights of free movement and residence under Article 8(a).[121] Further limitations, or rather conditions, are to be found in the three 1990 Directives which all stipulate that the right of residence depends on the possession of sufficient resources and medical insurance. Given the express reference to the possibility of conditions in Article 8(a), the guarantees in the 1990 Directives seem to be in line with the Treaty. What, however, does this legislative framework detailing the constitutional right of residence in Article 8(a) tell us about the present or future social content of Community or Union citizenship? Free movement and residence are after all the foundations of Union citizenship and almost the only instance when the "privileged" status of Member State nationals can be clearly seen. However, it must be remembered that there is considerable disagreement about the social content of citizenship. Defining citizenship on the basis of principles of social justice, however (to which the Community is committed in the SEA), leads one to the conclusion that "market outcomes should not just be accepted with all the resulting

---

[120]See Joined Cases 281, 283–285 and 287/85, op. cit. note 109, at para.14; Case C-113/89, *Rush Portuguesa* [1990] ECR 1417, at para.45; and Vogel Polsky and Vogel, *L'Europe Sociale 1993: illusion, alibi ou réalité?* (1991) Bruxelles, Editions de l'ULB.

[121]See in this respect Demaret, p. "L'égalité de traitement", 1994–2 *Actualités du droit* 165–208.

inequalities; rather, citizenship confers a right to a central set of resources which can provide economic security, health and education – and this right exists irrespective of a person's standing in the market".[122]

4.5.2. The Social Deficit of Community Citizenship

According to Lenaerts: "Even if it could be difficult for the Community to set a financial threshold level which Member States must reach in order to comply with their obligations flowing from this provision, the latter certainly ensures that Member States will have to grant equal treatment to all Community citizens moving and residing on their territory on the basis of the national legislation organising the social and medical assistance which is due."[123] This section addresses the specific situation of students.[124] It will be remembered that equal treatment in relation to conditions of access to vocational training apply not only to conditions imposed by educational establishments, but also to any measure liable to hinder the exercise of that right (*Gravier*). The Court of Justice has held that to deny students a right of residence is to deny them the very right to attend vocational courses on an equal basis and the principle of non-discrimination thus requires that a national of a Member State admitted to a vocational training course in another Member State automatically enjoys a right to reside there for the duration of the course (*Raulin*). Article 6 para.1 only applies "within the scope of application of this Treaty" and "without prejudice to any special provisions" contained therein. Nevertheless, it is fair to say that the scope of application of the Treaty and consequently, the scope of application of Article 6 have proved far from static and the Court of Justice has been said to be "ready surreptitiously to extend the *acquis communautaire* through a broad interpretation of this phrase".[125] In the students' Directive case, the Court very broadly held that acts adopted pursuant to Article 6 para.2 need not necessarily be limited to regulating rights which derive from Article 6 para.1 and can cater for what rights appear to be necessary to ensure the effective exercise of those rights (*European Parliament v. Council*). Thus, students can be joined by their spouse and dependent children in order to facilitate the effective exercise of their right of residence and right of access to education. This interpretation of the scope of Article 6 is another aspect of the Court's general insistence on the principle of

---

[122]See Plant, R., "Citizenship, Rights and Welfare", in Coote, A. (ed.), *The Welfare of Citizens: Developing New Social Rights* (1992) London, IPPR/Rivers Oram Press, pp.15–29, at p.16.

[123]See Lenaerts, K., "Fundamental Rights to be Included in a Community Catalogue", 16 *ELRev* (1991) 367–390, at 385.

[124]For an interesting analysis of the welfare entitlements of another distinct group of Community citizens see Gruser, S., White, S. and Dorn, N., "Free Movement and Welfare Entitlement: EU Drug Users in Berlin", 5 *Journal of European Social Policy* (1995) 13–28.

[125]See Weatherill, S. "The Scope of Article 7 EEC", 15 *ELRev* (1990) 334–341, at 340; De Moor, A. "Article 7 of the Treaty of Rome Bites", 48 *Modern Law Review* (1985) 452–459, at 458–459; O'Keeffe (1992), op. cit. note 9, at pp.270 *et seq.*; and Shockweiler, F. "La Portée du Principe de Non-Discrimination de l'Article 7 du Traité CEE" (1991) *Rivista di Diritto Europeo* 3–24.

the effectiveness of Community law and the effective protection of the rights which it entails for Community nationals.[126]

The inclusion of the condition on sufficient means of support and health insurance is said to protect the "legitimate interests" of the Member States.[127] However, in the light of the Court's established case-law, it is difficult to accept the exclusion of the principle of equal treatment with respect to these conditions, or to reconcile this exclusion with the spirit of a legal instrument such as Directive 90/365 (which is actually based on the Community principle of equal treatment) or with the objective of the Union Treaty with respect to the rights and interests of Member State nationals (Article B). Furthermore, Article 8(a)(1) is said to "build(s) on the fundamental ban on discrimination on grounds of nationality" and the status of the right of residence, like the other rights of citizenship, is said to be "fundamentally altered" and on a par with other rights central to Community law.[128] These legislative conditions and this reference to "legitimate interests" in the Court's decision in *Raulin* and the Advocate General's Opinion in Case C-295/90 reflect a policy decision to prevent economically inactive Union citizens from becoming a financial burden on the host Member States.[129] Admittedly, Article 6 applies without prejudice to special provisions contained in the Treaty, but the Court of Justice has not yet identified specific Treaty provisions justifying the exclusion of medical and maintenance expenses from the scope of the principle of non-discrmination and has not sufficiently explained the legitimate interests of Member States in imposing such limitations as prior conditions of residence. Article 4(4) Regulation 1408/71 specifically excludes social and medical assistance from its scope[130] since the latter were thought to relate to the social and economic situation specific to each Member State and there was thus thought to be no justification for their exportation. But Article 8(a)(1) does not refer to the exportation of social benefits, but is instead concerned with the effective exercise by Union citizens of their constitutional right to reside in another Member State on an equal treatment basis.

If the content of Article 8 is not static, as the provisions of Article 8(a)(2) and 8(e) suggest, the essential question is whether the Community institutions and, in the short term, the Court of Justice, are willing to apply a broad interpretation of the principle of equal treatment in this context. Since the substantive provisions of the students' Directive were not altered after Parliament's successful challenge, it is possible that judicial challenges to its discriminatory provisions were considered a possibility by the European Parliament and was one of the reasons for the challenge to the legal basis in the first place. Indeed it has been argued that recourse to

---

[126]See, for example, Case 222/86 *Heylens* [1987] ECR 4097.

[127]See the Opinion of Advocate General Jacobs in Case C-295/90, op. cit. note 66, at para.34.

[128]See *Report from the Commission on Citizenship of the Union* COM (93) 702 final, at 3.

[129]See Lenaerts, K., "Education in European Community Law after 'Maastricht'", 31 *CMLRev* (1994) 7–41, at 16. Furthermore, the Court regards tuition fees as conditions of access but not maintenance grants. Lonbay regards this exclusion as a pragmatic limitation of the *Gravier* decision, based on policy rather than principle: "Education and Law: The Community Context", 15 *ELRev* (1990) 363–387, at 373.

[130]OJ 1971 L149/2.

Article 235 was motivated precisely by Member State fears that Community competence in education would be further increased if the provisions in Article 6 were allowed to apply to the right of residence of students.[131] To date, however, the Court has not been asked to bring its interpretation of the principle of equal treatment – that Article 6 para.2 is not limited to the rights in para.1, but should also cater for ancillary rights necessary to allow those rights to operate effectively – to its logical conclusion. To argue that medical coverage and sufficient resources are not conditions of access is unacceptable – without that medical coverage, for example, there is no right of residence (Article 4) and, by the Court of Justice's own admission, without a right of residence there is no access to vocational training.[132] After all, there seems to be no real difference between extending the principle of equal treatment to the residence of a students' spouse and children and extending them maintenance grants on an equal basis as the host Member State's nationals, at least as far as facilitating his or her exercise of the right of equal access to vocational training is concerned. Article 4, however, seems incompatible with Article 8(a) and with the Court's previous case law on free movement and residence pursuant to Article 48. Rather than stipulating a condition for the *exercise* of the right of residence, it actually denies the *right* itself, if Union citizens fail to fulfil the Directive's conditions.

Grounds for arguing against the exclusion of maintenance and medical restrictions are less easy to adduce with respect to the other two Directives, which are based on Article 235. Neither Directive was preceded by a *Gravier/Raulin* line of case law, which seemed to confer a right of residence directly on the basis of the Treaty. However, the scope and application of the principle of equal treatment is generally wider than is being admitted in the case of the residence Directives and the Court of Justice has proved itself willing in other circumstances to extend the personal and material scope of Community law with reference to a broad interpretation of Article 6. If economically inactive and retired persons are to be accepted as persons "in a situation governed by Community law" (*Cowan*) then Article 6 should equally apply in their respect and it is not sufficient to point vaguely to the "legitimate interests" of Member States in order to exclude social assistance, social security and medical assistance from the scope of Article 6. The Court of Justice may have to decide whether the Directives themselves constitute special provisions in the context of Article 6, or whether the proviso in Article 8(a)(1) prevents it from impugning the economic guarantees in these Directives on the basis of the principle of equal treatment.

---

[131]See Kampf, op. cit. note 82, at 310; and Lenz, C.O., "Die Rechtsprechung des EuGH im Bereich des Bildungswesens", *Europa Archiv* (1989) 125–133. The *Länder* are said to have intervened to prevent Germany from supporting the European Parliament in its attempt to annul Article 235 as the legal basis in Case C- 295/90.

[132]The author has also discussed some of these issues in the annotation of Case C-295/90 in 30 *CMLRev* (1993) 639–651 and in Antola, E. and Rosas, A. (eds.), *A Citizens' Europe: In Search of a New Order* (1995) London, Sage Publications, pp.156–181.

However, these Directives further underline the emergence of a two-tier system of free movement and the rights contingent on it and an entrenchment of the division between economically active and non-economically active Member State nationals, or Community citizens.[133] This division was also evident in the Community Charter of Fundamental Social Rights. The latter uses the criterion of employment to determine the allocation of more generous benefits. This aspect of Community legislation (which is also evident with respect to the coordinating directives and equal treatment between men and women) distinguishes the extent to which benefits are enjoyed on the basis of employment. Regulation 1612/68 has not been extended to these Directives and economically inactive Community citizens cannot enjoy the rich jurisprudence developed thereunder.

The *Kempf* judgment indicated that individuals should not be excluded from the provisions of Community law on free movement on the grounds alone that they relied on public funds. However, for the Community to apply the same policy with respect to Member State nationals generally would oblige it and Member States in their turn to adopt positive legislation to facilitate the implementation of these rights.[134] Difficult as this may seem, the future development of citizenship rights in the Community may require a perspective which recognises potential changes in the Community's jurisdiction, the quality of its legal instruments and their effects. Thus far, an individual's welfare rights depend on the scope of the Treaty provisions, his or her residence/insurance/employment status, or on being an eligible family member or dependent on a worker or self-employed person. The Court has generally proceeded on the basis that the social security rights of workers are fundamental rights,[135] but the financial implications of any decision it could make allowing the principle of equal treatment to negate the requirement of maintenance and medical coverage in the students' Directive, for example, are formidable enough to prevent it from going too far. Luckhaus, draws attention to two different perspectives of citizenship in this regard. The first emphasises a universal status of membership, territory and rights and is based on an assumption of legal equality. The second emphasises personal status rather than the idea of territory and a reciprocity of rights and duties.[136] It seems that one of the only duties of Community citizenship is the need to undertake an economic activity, since enjoyment of all of the rights of Community citizenship depends on the fulfilment of this duty. Although Community citizenship may resemble the first perspective outlined above, to the extent that it is a status with a universal content (it adheres to all Member State nationals), however, the exercise of certain rights depends on the

[133]See Van Dijk, P., Dutch report to the 1992 FIDE conference, op. cit. note 105, pp.283–306, at p.294.
[134]See Vogel-Polsky, E., "L'Acte unique ouvre-t-il l'espace social européen?" (1989) *Droit Social* 177–189, at 187.
[135]See Meehan, E., "Economic and Social Policies", in Vogel, U. and Moran, M. (eds.), *The Frontiers of Citizenship* (1991) London, Macmillan, pp.125–154, at p.145.
[136]See Luckhaus, L., "EEC Social Security and Citizenship", paper distributed at the 1990 BIICL/Federal Trust/IALS workshop on European Citizenship, at p.17.

fulfilment of certain duties such as employment, which suggests the second personal status perspective of citizenship and a reciprocity of rights and duties.

4.5.3. Social Rights as Fundamental Rights in the Context of Community Citizenship

The supremacy of Community law depends on the Community limiting itself to areas in which it is competent to act.[137] If the Court of Justice extended equal treatment with respect to maintenance grants and access to other social services to resident Member State nationals it would most probably be charged with disrespecting the limits on the competence of the Community judiciary and legislature on which supremacy is based. However, one of the objectives of the Union is to strengthen the rights and interests of Community citizens who, on the basis of Article 8, enjoy a new constitutional status and a constitutional right of residence. The Court of Justice has often reasoned according to the method of the "effect of necessity" whereby it "takes the goals of the Treaty as a first premise in order to deduce the content and the application of the obligation in question".[138] With reference to "an ever closer union" and the status of Union citizenship, the Court may be obliged in future to interpret the scope of Article 8 in a broader manner than expected by Member States and to apply Article 6 in conformity with how it has previously been interpreted in other cases. There thus seems no reason to exclude the possibility of the following scenario unravelling in a case before the Court of Justice.

Take the case of Member State nationals who are admitted to an educational course in another Member and prove that they are in possession of sufficient resources and are adequately covered by medical insurance. Having fulfilled the conditions laid down by Directive 90/366, a residence permit is awarded. During the course, through no fault of their own, it transpires that the students can no longer support themselves. On the basis of Article 4 Directive 90/366, their right to reside thereby comes to an end and consequently, as the Court itself has conceded, they will no longer have access to the education course in question. Mole cites further examples of citizens of the Union who are prevented at present from exercising rights to free movement - students with special medical conditions who cannot afford to take up a year of study in another Member State (although it may be a compulsory part of their course) because they cannot export their health service entitlements and they cannot find comprehensive health insurance at an affordable price in the Member State of destination.[139]

---

[137]See De Witte, "Fundamental Rights in Community Law and National Constitutional Values", *LIEI* (1992) 1–22, at 3: "only Community acts adopted within the sphere of Community competences can prevail over national law".

[138]See Berlin, "Interactions Between the Lawmaker and the Judiciary within the EC", *LIEI* (1992) 17–48, at 23.

[139]See Mole, N., "Reflections Concerning the Free Movement of People", in *The Future of European Social Policy*, op. cit. note 26, pp.225–236, at 227.

It is well established that fundamental rights form an integral part of the general principles of law which the Court of Justice is bound to observe[140] and that national constitutional provisions and international treaties may supply guidelines which the Court should follow in the protection of fundamental rights within the framework of the structure and objectives of the Community.[141] Various national constitutions provide for a right to education.[142] In addition, a basic right to education and non-discriminatory access figures in a number of international conventions of which some, if not all, Member States, are contracting parties.[143] The European Parliament's Draft Constitution also established a right to education and vocational training. Socio-economic rights do not simply demand, however, that states desist from certain activities, but usually require some sort of positive legislative and financial commitment on their part. Given this commitment, it is difficult to establish these rights as fundamental and enforceable.[144] In the *Belgian Linguistics* case, the European Court of Human Rights had to interpret Article 2 Protocol 1 of the Convention which provides that "No person shall be denied the right to education." The European Court of Human Rights, with reference to this provision and Article 8, held that public authorities are not obliged to educate children in the language of their parents or with their aid. These difficulties with respect to the enforcement of socio-economic rights as fundamental rights does not mean, however, that the principle of equal treatment can be denied with respect to discriminatory conditions to establish a right of residence without which there is no access to education. With reference to the essential role which education has been assigned to achieve the objectives of the Community[145] some sort of fundamental right of access to education on an equal treatment basis could be constructed on the basis of the aforementioned national constitutional provisions and conventions. Although the responsibility of Member States with respect to the content and organization of education is recognized in the Union Treaty, the Community is charged with promoting "quality education" and Articles 126 and 127 strongly emphasis the mobility of students and teachers and the importance of educational and cultural exchanges. The scope of Article 6 of the European Convention has recently been extended to include social

[140]See Case 26/69 *Stauder* [1969] ECR 419.

[141]See Case 11/70, *Internationale Handelsgesellschaft* [1970] ECR 1125; and Case 4/73 *Nold* [1974] ECR 491.

[142]See, *inter alia*, Article 27 of the Spanish Constitution and Articles 42.3.2 and 42.4 of the Irish Constitution.

[143]See Article 13 of the International Covenant on Economic, Social and Cultural Rights, 1966; Article 30 of the International Convention on the Protection of the Rights of all Migrant Workers and their Families, 1990; Article 3 of the Convention against Discrimination in Education; and Article 2, Protocol 1 of the European Convention on Human Rights.

[144]See, for example, Weston, "Human Rights", in Claude and Weston, *Human Rights in the World Community* (1989), at p.23: "the covenant [the International Covenant on Economic, Social and Cultural Rights] is essentially a 'promotional convention', stipulating objectives more than standards and requiring implementation over time rather than all at once." See also, Plant, op. cit. note 122; and generally, Drzewicki, K., Krause, K. and Rosas, A. (eds.), *Social Rights as Human Rights: A European Challenge* (1994) Institute for Human Rights, Abo Akademi University, Turku.

[145]The Commission considers that education and training are at the heart of European integration, Bull. EC. Suppl. 2/88, at 13; and see *infra* Chapter 5.

security and social welfare rights[146] and Article 13, Title VIII of the European Parliament's Draft Constitution of the EU provides that anyone lacking sufficient resources has the right to social and medical assistance. The difficulties surrounding the adoption of such a provision are evident. However, the inclusion of such a provision in the Draft constitution suggest that this may form part of the European Parliament's proposals in the 1996 intergovernmental conference and beyond.

4.6. Article 8(a) and the Directives on Residence

Article 8(a) of the Treaty on European Union provides, in the context of the establishment of Union citizenship, that every Union citizen shall have the right to move and reside freely within the territory of the Member States. This right is subject however, "to the limitations and conditions laid down in this Treaty and by the measures adopted to give it effect". Thus, although the Directives were adopted at a time and in the context of a Treaty in which Union citizenship in Article 8 did not exist, that provision expressly refers to the existing *acquis* and it must be assumed that the Directives come within the limitations and conditions proviso in Article 8(a)(1). Further restrictions might follow on the basis of arrangements or conventions concluded in accordance with Article K on Justice and Home Affairs, such as, for example, the External Frontiers Convention.[147] However, the relationship between the Directives and the constitutional right of residence which characterises Community citizenship is not without its difficulties. In the first place, the original Spanish proposal on residence was wider than Article 8(a). The right was to be unlimited, the Council was to be under an obligation to act to bring about any necessary evolution and the Parliament was to be involved in this evolutionary process on the basis of cooperation.[148] The non-draft paper on citizenship also stated that legislation implementing the right of free movement should "lay down provisions to ensure fair distribution of the resulting burden on Member States, particularly in the area of social protection".[149] This provision was subsequently dropped as was the proposal by the Commission and Spain for the inclusion of a general prohibition on discrimination on grounds of nationality.[150]

The Commission's legislative programme now includes the introduction of a new legal text to codify the existing *acquis*. The idea is to adopt one single legal text on entry and residence for Community citizens.[151] Article 8(a)(2) provides a

---

[146]See *Salesi* v. *Italy* and *Schuler-Zgraggen* v. *Switzerland*, Ser. A No.257E. 26 February 1993 and Ser. A no.263, respectively.

[147]COM (93) 684. See the House of Lords Select Committee on the European Communities, *Visas and Control of External Borders of the Member States*, Session 1993–94, 14th report.

[148]See Co. Doc. SN 3940/90, 24 September 1990 and CONF-UP 1731/91, 20 February 1991. For an account of the intergovernmental attempts to limit the right of residence see Perez González, M., Spanish report to the 1992 FIDE conference, op. cit. note 105, pp.201–233, at pp.206 and 207.

[149]See *Agence Europe* nos.1709/1710, 3 May 1991.

[150]SEC (91) 500, 85 and the Spanish memorandum cited in Laursen, F. and Van Harnackel, S., *The Intergovernmental Conference on Political Union* (1992) Maastricht, EIPA..

[151]See also the Report of the Commission on the Citizenship of the Union, COM (93) 702 final, at p.5.

new legal basis for the conclusion of legislation in the area of free movement and residence, however, it provides for a unanimous decision in Council and permits only the assent of Parliament. Existing legislation on the entry and residence of workers, self-employed persons, students, retired persons and economically inactive persons, have all been adopted with reference to legal bases which permit qualified majority or unanimity.[152] The proviso in Article 8(a)(2) "save as otherwise provided in this Treaty" suggests that the Council may still resort to these specific legal bases when adopting legislation in the field. However, the adoption of a legal instrument on the basis of Article 8(a)(2) would go a long way to making the rights of free movement and residence more coherent and to clearly establishing that they are now considered rights of citizenship and are no longer dependent on the exercise of an economic activity. Three additional issues were tackled in the Commission's legislative programme. One would rectify the fact that continued insistence on passports for entry in Directive 68/360 and 73/148 is inconsistent with an internal market without frontiers. This inconsistency has already been remedied, although not in the context of Community law, by the entry into force in March 1995 of the Schengen agreement which seven Member States have implemented. The remainder, except Britain and Ireland, are about to accede to the agreement or are discussing possible participation. The legislative programme also called for an instrument to explain the consequences of Article 7(a). It would clarify, *inter alia*, the definition of internal borders, whether Article 7(a) applies to overseas territories, its application in airports and the question whether Member States can reintroduce controls once they have been abolished. Agreement on the content of such an instrument is likely to prove difficult. Finally the programme also referred to the right to travel of third country nationals, in the sense of a Community version of Schengen, rather than the establishment of a right to take up residence and employment. Apart from difficulties likely to be encountered with respect to agreement on such an issue, it is unclear whether this issue belongs to the first pillar (Community) or the third pillar (intergovernmental). To the extent that the free movement of third country nationals is part and parcel of the abolition of Community borders and controls, the issue would seem to fall within the scope of Community law. However, Article K.1.3 deals with immigration policy and policy regarding third country nationals including "(a) conditions of entry and movement by nationals of third countries on the territory of Member States". This issue is one of many which highlights the problematic relationship between the first and third pillars of the Union.

On 12 July 1995, the Commission formally adopted three proposals for directives which would, if adopted by the Council, complete the free movement of persons in the internal market in accordance with Article 7(a). The proposals seek to amplify and communitarise the Schengen arrangements, suppress border controls for all legally resident persons regardless of nationality and establish a single visa

---

[152]Articles 49, 52, 6 and 235 respectively.

for third country nationals.[153] The adoption of these proposals is in accordance with the Commission's legislative timetable outlined above. However, in order to be adopted, these proposals require unanimity in the Council, which is unlikely to be achieved given the long-standing resistance of the United Kingdom to the suppression of border controls and Schengen-type arrangements. In order for the arrangements to be adopted, the United Kingdom may have to be conceded another "opting out" formula, which does not augur well for the development of the free movement of persons. Furthermore, even if the proposals are adopted by the Council, they permit border controls to be reestablished, albeit temporarily, in exceptional cases. Communitarisation of the Schengen agreement would, however, remedy the current absence of a supervising body, since the Court of Justice would have jurisdiction to review the operation of a Community arrangement if adopted within the scope of the first pillar.

Possibly one of the most dynamic and important aspects inherent in the establishment of Union citizenship is the possibility that the constitutional nature of citizenship itself may be judicially used in future to broadly interpret the nature and scope of the rights of Union citizenship. The implicit reliance on the 1990 Directives in Article 8(a) overlooks, for example, the unhappy fact that sufficient resources and medical coverage have been made conditions precedent for the grant and maintenance of the right of residence contained thereunder. The right of residence is withdrawn if these conditions are not fulfilled, which sits uncomfortably with the logic of Union citizenship, unless one accepts the latter as a highly circumscribed status still dependent on the fulfilment of economic criteria.[154] In addition, were the Court to decide cases in future from the perspective of a constitutionally established right of residence, it might have to alter its interpretation of permissible public policy considerations or justifiable and fundamental interests of society which it has been willing to accept to date as valid restrictions of individual rights and as a valid exercise of Member State discretion. The Court of Justice has previously held, for example, that the Community's creation of the principe of free movement and the right of access to the territory of another Member State does not exclude "the power of Member States to adopt measures enabling the national authorities to have an exact knowledge of population movements affecting their territory".[155] This national power of action was reiterated by

---

[153]See El Pais, 13 July 1995.

[154]See Misson, L., Belgian report to the 1992 FIDE conference, op. cit. note 105 pp.21–88, at p.54: "le Traité de Maastricht donne d'une main aux citoyens de l'Union ce qu'il reprend de l'autre: il ne consacre en réalité aucun progrès."

[155]Case 118/75, op. cit. note 11, at para.17. The legislative measures in question required aliens to report to the public security authorities within 3 days of entering the Italian territory in order to make his/her presence known. It further required anyone providing a foreign national with board or lodging to inform the public security authorities of that fact within twenty-four hours: Article 142 of the Consolidated Public Security Acts approved by Royal Decree no.773, 18 June 1931 and Article 2 of Decree Law no.50, 11 February 1948; Gazetta Ufficiale no. 44 at 598, 21 February 1948. See also Articles 8(2) Directive 68/360 and Article 4(2) Directive 73/148, pursuant to which national authorities may require nationals of other Member States to report their presence.

the Court in the *Lothar Messner* case.[156] The Court has held, however, that national authorities are not justified in imposing penalties, such as imprisonment, so disproportionate to the gravity of the infringement that they become an obstacle to the free movement of workers.[157] This power of Member States to supervise the movement of foreigners on their territory by means of reporting regulations is not regarded as a derogation on grounds of public policy or security within the meaning of Article 48(3). Rather, it is viewed as an accepted power of individual sovereign states to regulate their own internal order and security.[158] According to the Advocate General in *Watson and Belmann*:

> So long as there is no Community nationality, nationals of other Member States will always have a different status from that of a national of the state concerned even where he enjoys the right of free movement and residence on conditions of parity with such a national. Just as that status justifies appropriate supervision of his presence on the national territory, not by the local authorities responsible for maintaining the register of local inhabitants, but by the police authorities, it also helps to give, in each case, a varying degree of importance to failure to give information.[159]

This type of reasoning and even the margin of discretion permitted to Member States may have to be revised as Community citizens develop beyond the status of "nationals from other Member States" to "citizens" enjoying an increasingly large bundle of rights and duties on the basis of Community law.

4.6.1. The Enforceability of Article 8(a)

A directly effective provision of Community law confers rights on individuals which national courts are bound to observe.[160] A provision is directly effective insofar as it imposes an obligation which is unconditional, sufficiently clear and does not require additional action on the part of Member States.[161] The direct effect of directives has been justified on a number of grounds: (i) that preventing individuals from relying on the provisions of a directive is incompatible with their binding

---

[156]See Case C-265/88, op. cit. note 25, at para.6. The reporting requirement then only applied to persons intending to stay in Italy for three months or less. The Advocate general specifically referred to reporting in the context of the abolition of internal frontiers (para.14). In the particular case of Mr Messner, a time limit of three days was regarded as unreasonable and unnecessary for the protection of a Member State's interests.

[157]Case C-265/88, op. cit. note 25, at para.14.

[158]See Case 118/75, op. cit. note 11, at para.23 and Advocate General Trabucchi, at 1202. For a comparative analysis of the reporting regulations operative in individual Member States, see Advocate General Mischo in Case C-265/88, at paras.19 *et seq.*

[159]Case 118/75, op. cit. note 11, at 1210.

[160]On the subject of direct effect see Curtin, D., "Directives: the Effectiveness of Judicial Protection of Individual Rights", 27 *CMLRev* (1990) 709–739.

[161]See variously Case 26/62 *Van Gend en Loos* [1963] ECR 1 (Article 12 EEC); Case 13/68 *Salgoil* [1968] ECR 453; Case 93/71 *Leonesio* [1972] ECR 287 (direct effect of regulations); Cases 9/70 *Grad* [1970] ECR 825, 33/70 *SACE* [1970] ECR 1213, Case 41/74 *Van Duyn* [1974] ECR 1337, Case 148/78 *Ratti* [1979] ECR 1629, Case 8/81 *Becker* [1982] ECR 53 and Case 152/84 *Marshall* [1986] ECR 724 (direct effect of directives and decisions).

effect (Article 189); (ii) that the *effet utile* of directives would be diminished if individuals could not plead them before national courts; (iii) and that, a Member State should be estopped from denying an individual his rights due to its failure to implement a directive or comply with its Community law obligations.[162] However, the logic of estoppel and the principle of the effectiveness of Community law applies to all binding Community rules. Direct effect simply differentiates those which are sufficiently clear and precise to be justiciable by the individual at national level from those which are not.[163]

In a series of landmark decisions, the Court of Justice has championed the effectiveness of Community law obligations, even in the absence of direct effect. Thus, even when the provisions of a directive were not directly effective, national courts, in applying the applicable provisions of national law, are required to interpret national law in the light of the wording and the purpose of the directive,[164] are said to be under a general obligation to vindicate the objectives sought by the directive.[165] The Community's adherence to the principle of effectiveness, which has involved a shift from direct effect to the effective judicial protection of non-directly effective rights, is of paramount importance in Community law generally. In *Francovich and Bonifaci* the Court held that the full effect of Community norms would be put into question and the protection of the rights which they recognise would be seriously weakened if individuals did not have the possibility of obtaining restitution when their rights are damaged by a violation of Community law imputable to a Member State. This is particularly true where the operation of Community rules is subordinated to Member State action and where individuals cannot, in the absence of such action, rely on Community rules before the national courts to invoke their rights thereunder. The decision of the Court in *Francovich* further indicates that "individuals who find themselves denied a remedy in such circumstances – or in any other, since, *a fortiori*, the ruling of the Court extends to all breaches of the Treaty – can sue the state directly for the loss sustained".[166] The Court's decisions are rooted in a general obligation on Member States to repair the illicit consequences of a violation of Community law stemming from Article 5. They also stem from the general principle of Community law that rights should be

---

[162]See Case 148/78 *Pubblico Ministero* v. *Ratti* [1979] ECR 1629; Case 8/81 *Becker* v. *Finanzamst-Munster Innenstadt* [1982] ECR 53; De Burca, G., "Giving Effect to EC Directives", 55 *Modern Law Review* (1992) 215, at 215; and Snyder, F., "The Effectiveness of EC Law: Institutions, Processes, Tools and Techniques", 56 *Modern Law Review* (1993) 19–50, at 42.

[163]See, for example, Advocate General Mischo in Cases C-6/90 and 9/90, *Francovich* [1992] ECR I-5357, where he emphasised that absence of direct effect does not imply that no rights are conferred but that the rights in question are insufficiently clear, precise and unconditional to be invoked at national level.

[164]See Case 14/83 *Von Colson and Kamann* [1984] ECR 1891, which is referred to by Steiner as the "principle of indirect effect", "From Direct Effects to *Francovich*: Shifting Means of Enforcement of Community Law", 18 *ELRev* (1993) 3–22, at 5; and Case C-106/89 *Marleasing* [1990] ECR I-4135.

[165]See Case C-213/89 *Regina* v. *Secretary of State for Transport, ex parte Factortame* [1990] ECR I-2433.

[166]Curtin, D., "The Enforcement of Community Law: Judicial Snakes and Ladders", in O'Keeffe and Curtin, op. cit. note 96, pp.33–49, at 49.

effectively enforced and receive effective judicial protection at Community and national level, regardless of their direct effect. This principle is regarded as a fundamental constitutional principle of Community law which "reflects a general principle of law which underlies the constitutional traditions common to the Member States".[167] These judicial developments seem to be depriving direct effect of its monopolistic quality as a means for individuals to vindicate their rights at national level. The main question seems now to be whether in fact the individual possesses and how that right can be enforced. Member States are being required to ensure that adequate and effective means of legal redress are available at national level. The Court previously held that Community law did not require the creation of new forms of legal action at national level,[168] but its renewed emphasis on the effective protection of Community rights by Member States, now also with respect to non-directly effective provisions of Community law, may require Member States to do just that.[169]

This trend in the Court's jurisprudence, which emphasises the enforceability of rights, has been reaffirmed in *Wagner and Miret*[170] and *Faccini Dori*.[171] The overall result of this jurisprudence is that provisions without direct effect, but from which the content of subjective rights can be identified, can be invoked before national courts who are to interpret the applicable national legislation in the light of the objectives of Community law.[172] Article 8(a) is an imperfect right which does not comply with the unconditional requirement established by the Court of Justice with respect to direct effect. Nevertheless, as Fernández Martín argues, it could be invoked at national level, obliging national judges to interpret secondary legislation with respect to Article 8(a) in a manner which favours the fullest enjoyment of that right by Union citizens. Furthermore, since the right of residence in Article 8(a) is a constitutional right deriving from the Treaty, secondary legislation adopted to implement it should not contradict the substance of the right. If it does, it is arguable that national courts, or the Court of Justice, should declare the secondary legislation in question incompatible with the objective sought to be achieved by Article 8(a), which is the free movement and residence of Union citizens throughout the Union territory.[173]

However, despite the limitations and conditions permitted by Article 8(a), it could be susceptible to direct effect. The exercise of the right to free movement

[167]Case 222/84 *Johnston* [1986] ECR 1651. It also referred to Articles 6 and 13 of the European Convention on Human Rights.

[168]Case 13/68 *Salgoil* [1968] ECR 453; although nationals courts were not to permit the frustration of Community rights by this means: Case 158/80 *Rewe* v. *Hauptzollamt Kiel* [1981] ECR 1805; and generally Wyatt, D., "The Direct Effect of Community Social Law: Not Forgetting Directives", 8 *ELRev* (1983) 241–248.

[169]See Curtin (1992), op. cit. note 166, at p.35; and Snyder, op. cit. note 162, at 45.

[170]Case C-334/92 [1993] ECR I-6911.

[171]Case C-91/92 [1994] ECR I-3325.

[172]See Fernández-Martín, J.M., "El efecto directo de las directivas y la proteccion de los derchos subjetivos comunitarios en la jurisprudencia del Tribunal de Justicia. Intento de sistemización", *Noticias de la UE* (1995) 1–13.

[173]Ibid., at 13.

and residence pursuant to Article 8(a) is not dependent on further action by the Community institutions, since the Council is not obliged to adopt further measures, but may do so at its own discretion. Furthermore, any legislative action is to *facilitate* the exercise of the rights therein, which suggests that a right to free movement and residence already exists. In a discussion of policy factors affecting Member State liability, Steiner has argued that

> a number of Treaty provisions [Article 48] ... may seem to confer identifiable rights on individuals, but they may also provide for derogation, involving an element of discretion. States must be free to exercise this discretion in good faith, in the public interest. Furthermore, the nature of Community law ... is such that a particular provision which may be construed as conferring rights on individuals may be far from clear as regards its *precise* meaning and scope of application [Article 6].[174]

In such cases she regards an element of state culpability as essential in a decision to award compensation. Although it may be true that such an element should be established with respect to these more imprecise rights, the Court of Justice should nevertheless be vigilant in ensuring that these rights are as effectively protected as any other. If it does not, it will be clear that a double standard exists with respect to the enforceability of citizenship rights compared to the enforceability of economic Community rights. The question of the direct effect of Article 8(a) arose in an Article 177 reference to the Court of Justice in the *Adams* case but that case was subsequently withdrawn.[175]

4.7. The Unresolved Social Dimension of Community Citizenship

It is evident that the principle of equal treatment is being applied inconsistently with respect to the rights of Community citizens. Entitlement to social benefits still varies according to the role played by the claimant in the process of economic integration taking place in the Community, be it as a worker, a dependent, or an economically inactive individual. This is particularly evident with respect to the regulation of the constitutional right of residence in Article 8(a). This two-speed aspect of Community citizenship implies that effective enjoyment of even a minimum of social rights is not envisaged (at least for the forseeable future) as part of the Community citizenship package.

Some would argue that for the Community to attain the level of popular legitimacy necessary to forge a more political or social union, the development of an effective social policy is essential.[176] Others consider that the legitimacy of the

---

[174]Steiner, op. cit. note 164, at 17.

[175]Case C-229/94. The ban on Mr Adams's entry to the United Kingdom was lifted since the reference was made. See also OJ 1993 C264/4-5, where the Commission has stated that infringements of Article 8 will lead to Article 169 proceedings and that Union citizens can go before their national courts with respect to directly effective citizenship rights.

[176]See Leidfried, "Europe's Could-be Social State: Social Policy and Post-1992 European Integration", Contribution to a conference *Europe After 1992*, Ann Arbor MI, 6–7 September 1991, at p.16.

Community legal order stems from other sources.[177] While others still argue that the type of popular legitimacy required by previous models of state building do not apply in the Community, where national identification and sovereignty are still very strong.[178] If a more extensive Community social policy is to be developed, it must be remembered that this is not a politically and historically neutral area of policy making. The development of national social policies has been a fundamental aspect of nation building and the variety of welfare state forms in the European Communities reflect the variety of ways in which European states have developed and the economic, historical and political context in which they have done so. Majone has suggested that these differences between the traditions and background of the various Member States indicate that the Communities do not enjoy the homogeneity necessary to determine the equilibrium normally decided at state level between equity and efficiency and between the provision of goods and the redistribution of income in the determination of the content and objectives of social policy measures.[179] Furthermore, when national governments determine the standards and content of national legislative intervention in the social field, it is arguable that they do so in the context of decision-making programmes which are, on the whole, democratic, legitimate and accountable. From this perspective, the democratic deficit caused at national level by the transfer of legislative competence to the supranational level and the absence of a truly representative and legislatively dynamic representative assembly in the Community undermine its role in the development of a supranational social policy.

However, although the historical and political background experienced at Member State level may be lacking for the development of a more extensive Community social policy, it must not be forgotten that the Community's objectives are not themselves ideologically neutral. Weiler notes that the culture of the market and the principles of market efficiency and competition are fundamental to the Single Market programme.[180] The economic constitution of the Union is clearly that of a liberal economic order which therefore "gives priority to the allocation function of public policy over distributional objectives. Hence the best rationale for social initiatives at Community level is one which stresses the efficiency-improving aspects of the proposed measure".[181] Indeed Article 3(a)(1) TEU provides that the economic policy adopted by the Community and Member States will be "conducted in accordance with the principle of an open market economy with free competition". These economic objectives already contain the scope for left–right divisions and, in a sense, indicate the contours of the social policy which the Community would have to adopt to be consistent with its objectives. Social welfare rights, which are based on need as a distributive mechanism rather than work,

---

[177]See Weiler, "Problems of Legitimacy in Post 1992 Europe", 46 *Aussenwirtschaft* (1991) 411–437, at 183 *et seq.*
[178]See Streeck, op. cit. note 117, 23.
[179]See Majone, op. cit. note 108, at 167.
[180]See Weiler (1991), op. cit. note 177, at 430–431.
[181]Majone, op. cit. note 108, at 156.

seem to contradict one of the fundamental freedoms of Community law – the free movement of the factors of production.[182] It is clearly difficult to develop basic social rights free from competitive pressures in the context of a legal order which specifically seeks to promote the latter. Were the Community's competence in social policy making to be extended it would be forced to develop a clearer ideological stance on social issues which, at national level, have been the subject of years, if not decades, of fierce political debate and which have shaped the welfare systems which operate at Member State level today. Based as it is on respect for the rule of law, the Community's task is perhaps to render compatible the development of a liberal economic order with the general social well-being of its members, or its citizens.[183]

At present, the Community is not yet financially or politically equipped to interfere to a greater extent in the determination and regulation of the social policies applicable in the Member States, or to operate more extensive Community-wide social policies. This is evident from the disagreement among Member State governments regarding the development of Community social policy in Maastricht and thus explains the "policy" approach of the Court of Justice with regard to the possible financial and social consequences of a general right of residence. The British Home Office has recently been clamping down on "workshy" nationals from other Member States who are claiming income support. Two such nationals recently claimed that, given the right of free movement and residence established in the Union Treaty, Home Office letters informing them that they were not lawfully resident and that they would lose their benefits because they were out of work and not seeking employment were unlawful. The High Court, which upheld the Home Office action, refused to refer the cases to the Court of Justice and insisted that it was imperative that there be "informed debate about these crucial issues and their likely long-term effect on national life before, and not after, they have been embodied in any European Treaty".[184] Were the Court of Justice to go further it would provoke Member State resistance (some of which until recently denied Community competence to establish a right of residence independent of the exercise of an economic activity) to the financial obligations being thrust upon them with respect to nationals from other Member States. Such a scenario is dramatic indeed but it would not be the first time that the Court of Justice handed down a decision imposing far-reaching financial obligations on Member States. *Gravier* was revolutionary precisely because of the changes which it required in the organisation of

---

[182]See also Freeman, "Migration and the Political Economy of the Welfare State", 485 *The Annals of the American Academy of Political and Social Science* (1986) 51–63, at 52, who states that, "The principle that ... governs distribution in the Welfare State is that of human need. It does not replace the market principle of distribution according to economic performance, but it significantly alters it by establishing a social minimum and broadening the sphere of collective consumption ... The Welfare State is a closed system because a Community with shared social goods requires for its moral base some aspect of kinship or fellow feeling."

[183]See Diaz, *Estado de Derecho y sociedad democratica* (1981) Madrid, Taurus, at p.83.

[184]*The Guardian*, 21 March 1995.

education at Member State level. It is thus difficult to resolve the tension between the Court's propensity to widely interpret the obligations on Member States which derive from the Community's objectives and the principle of equal treatment, with its inability in other difficult cases, to dictate the logical consequences of such a wide interpretation. The overall loser in these circumstances is the development of a full-bodied and meaningful status of Community citizenship. If, as the model of citizenship in Chapter 1 suggests, distributive justice is an essential aspect of modern citizenship which is legitimated on "the basis of solidarity that comes from free common membership of a human community",[185] Community citizenship is clearly lacking.

---

[185]See Closa, C., "Citizenship of the Union and Nationality of the Member States", 33 *CMLRev* (1995) 487–518, at 508; and *infra* Chapter 1.4.

Chapter 5

Free Movement, Education and Community Citizenship

5.1. Introduction

Prior to the adoption of the Union Treaty, the Community *acquis communautaire* in the field of education was primarily based on the principle of equal treatment and promotion of the free movement of persons. Access to training and education was regarded as an important primary step to enable Community nationals to enter professional and economic life, or as part of the social integration of economically active persons and their families in the Member State in which they were established. However, on the basis of Article 6 and the former Article 128 EEC, the Court of Justice and Community legislature extended Community competence in the field of education far beyond what could originally have been expected on the basis of the relatively modest provisions in the Treaty. The assumption of this protagonistic role, by the Court of Justice in particular, with regard to education, has given rise to a number of difficulties at national level. Although the Community is not competent to legislate with respect to education and training policy, its doctrine of implied powers has harvested rich benefits for migrant workers, their families and migrant students who wish to avail themselves of the education facilities in Member States other than their own. Although the Court has tended to limit its more difficult or sensitive decisions, the consequences of its jurisprudence at national level have been far reaching. Furthermore, this occasional limitation of its powers in certain cases has arguably damaged the coherence and scope of the principle of equal treatment.

Community legislative activity has been limited, in the main, to the adoption of recommendations, resolutions proposing cooperation, or decisions establishing exchange and activity programmes. Nevertheless, the effects of these methods of Community and Member State cooperation, which attract Member States by offering significant financial incentives, or securing the mutual recognition of diplomas, should not be underestimated. By adopting binding decisions relating, for example, to the establishment of the Erasmus and now the Socrates scheme, the Community has pioneered an educational policy of sorts at the Community level.[1] It has also contributed to the creation of educational "soft law" (recommendations, resolutions, cooperation and joint programmes) which have a certain, if not considerable, impact at national level.

The Union Treaty has attempted to tackle some of the competence issues which affect the field of education and vocational training by adopting a more explicit constitutional basis for Community policy in the field. Action may now be taken with respect to education generally, whereas Article 128 EEC previously only referred to vocational training. Furthermore, the new provisions are carefully phrased in terms of subsidiarity. The authors of the Union Treaty wished to differentiate between the Member States' powers, which remain insulated from Community interference, and the powers of the Community to require or impose cooperation on Member States in other limited fields. The end result is a more useful and explicit indication of the limits of Community competence than that which previously existed on the basis of Article 128 EEC. However, the subsidiarity spirit evident in Articles 126 and 127 cannot detract from the existing *acquis*. Indeed, it is arguable that the attempt therein to clarify matters in the field of education and vocational training may not prove totally satisfactory, given the difficulties which will now be encountered in differentiating between education and vocational training and therefore the correct legal basis to be used in different circumstances. Furthermore, the guidelines with respect to Member State versus Community competence may be useful, but it is unclear whether the Community doctrine of implied powers could still be employed with the same far-reaching consequences. The principle of subsidiarity will presumably play an important role in this respect, but the legal, as distinct from the political, effects of its application are not entirely certain.

This chapter discusses the role of the Community in the field of education and the importance of education to the Community's integration process, in particular, the development of a Community concept of citizenship. The importance of education in a community of states based on a system of free movement and developing political union is undeniable. However, given the relationship between education and the formation of national social, cultural and political identity, it is not surprising that the issue of Community competence is a sensitive one, or that subsidiarity has been recruited to protect Member State competence. Although the Union professes a commitment to the protection of and respect for national identity, this commitment might conflict in future with the objectives behind the es-

---

[1] See the Conclusions of the Council and the Ministers for Education meeting within the Council on 6 October 1989, on cooperation and Community *policy* (emphasis added) in the field of education in the run up to 1993, OJ 1989 C277/5. The Commission's guidelines for Community action in the fields of education and training was one of the first documents to address general policy as regards the future of Community education cooperation, COM (93) 183 final.

tablishment of Union citizenship. However minimal that status is at present, it is ideologically suited to putting increased pressure on Member States to stress their "Europeanness".[2] Indeed, Article 3(a) of the Socrates programme identifies "develop[ing] the European dimension in education at all levels so as to strengthen the spirit of European citizenship, drawing on the cultural heritage of each Member State" as one of its objectives.[3] Furthermore, it is unclear what "spillover" effects Community action in the field of free movement and citizenship will have with respect to the content and financing of education and vocational training. It must be remembered that when Community institutions wanted to extend Community social policy beyond the limits of market-making they first "had to attach their projects to the narrow core of mobility-enhancing policies that had been placed under Community jurisdiction, invoking a broad interpretation of the Community's powers in the hope of expanding them".[4] This is precisely what the Commission and Court have done in cases like *Gravier* and *Erasmus* with respect to a Community "policy" in education. Although the principle of subsidiarity may indicate a readiness to return to national and regional decision-making, Community cooperative federalism may prove attractive in a sector which traditionally suffers in times of recession. Furthermore, the usefulness of Community subsidiarity as an instrument to contain expansive legislative and judicial policy making is far from clear, particularly in a field where spillover is an inevitable consequence of Community objectives affecting policies still within the hands of the Member States.

5.2. Community Competence in the Field of Education Prior to the Treaty on European Union

Chapter 3 demonstrates that involvement in an economic activity has generally been used as a criterion to delimit the personal scope of Community law. This insistence on an economic element is supported by those who argue that education

---

[2]See the People's Europe report adopted in 1985 at the Milan Council on the need to prepare young people for a "European" future; the resolution of the Council and Ministers for Education meeting within Council on the European Dimension of education, OJ 1988 C177; the Commission's Green Paper on the European Dimension: "the improvement of linguistic competence, the mutual understanding of the practices and cultures of other Member States, and even the ability to work with those of other nationalities, or in another setting, are among the most important factors which help young people to become more integrated into society and to accept more readily their responsibilities as European citizens." COM (93) 457 final; the Memorandum on Higher Education in the EC, COM (91) 349 final; and the Commission's proposal for a European Parliament and Council Decision establishing the Community action programme Socrates COM (93) 708, at 2.

[3]See Decision no.819/95 of the European Parliament and Council establishing the Community action programme Socrates, OJ 1995 L87/10, 20 April 1995.

[4]See Streeck, W., "From Market-Building to State-Building? Reflections on the Political Economy of European Social Policy", DOC. IUE. 76/94 (col.27), EUI, 14–15 April 1994, *European Law in Context: Constitutional Dimensions of European Economic Integration.*

does not come within the scope of Community competence.[5] Given the social and cultural objectives inherent in national education policy, Member States, Community institutions, and even the Court of Justice, maintain that the Community only enjoys limited and contingent competence in this respect. However, the Commission and Court, in particular, have been keen to emphasis the essential bridge which education and training forge between the social and economic aspects of Community law and their importance with regard to the promotion of the four freedoms. The European Council has also affirmed the importance of vocational training and education and the fact that improved access to vocational training must go hand in hand with completion of the internal market.[6]

Action in the field of education, beyond intergovernmental cooperation,[7] was initially only taken with respect to those beneficiaries of free movement and their dependants, who figured in the Treaty and early secondary legislation. Article 49 does not explicitly provide for competence to legislate with respect to education. However, like other Treaty provisions, it does incorporate a functional Community objective – the free movement of persons – which has had consequential effects on other areas of law and policy which do not strictly fall within the scope of Community law. Education is one of those areas. Article 49 thus provided a legal basis for the adoption of Regulation 1612/68, which includes members of the worker's family within its scope (Article 10), and provides certain education rights for the workers themselves and their families (Articles 7(3) and 12).[8] Article 57 also recognised the potential obstacles to freedom of establishment which resulted from the existence of differing and introspective national education policies, structures and qualifications. It provided for the adoption of Directives on the mutual recognition of diplomas, certificates and other evidence of formal qualifications in

---

[5]See the arguments put forward by the German Court and *Land* for the exclusion of educational and cultural matters from the scope of Community law in Case 9/74 *Casagrande* [1974] ECR 773, at 783 of Advocate General Warner's Opinion; Advocate General Slynn in Case 293/83 *Gravier* [1985] ECR 593, at 602; Case 66/85 *Lawrie-Blum* [1986] ECR 2121, at 2123, 2133 and 2143; the submissions of the national universities in Case 24/86 *Blaizot* [1988] ECR 379, at 386; Lachmann, "Some Danish Reflections on the Use of Article 235", *CMLRev* (1981) 447–461; Van Gerven, W. and Van den Bossche, P., "Freedom of Movement and Equal Treatment for Students in Europe: An Emerging Principle", in *Free Movement of Persons in Europe: Problems and Experiences* (1993) Martinus Nijhoff, Dordrecht; Proceedings of a workshop at Leuven, *Higher Education and Europe After 1992*, 21–23 June 89, at p.29; *EC Policies and Proposals and their Impact on Higher Education in the European Community: The Challenges of 1992*, University of Siena, 5–7 November 1990, at p.37; and LeClercq, J.M. and Rault, C., *Les systèmes educatifs en Europe. Vers un espace Communautaire?* (1990) Paris, La Documentation Française.

[6]Resolutions of the European Council at Stuttgart, 19 June 1983; Conclusions of the Council and the Ministers of Education meeting on 27 September 1985; Hanover, 27–28 June 1988; and Council Resolution on continued vocational training, OJ 1989 C148/1.

[7]See Dalichow, F., "Academic Recognition Within the EC", 22 *European Journal of Education* (1987) 39–58; and Fogg, K. and Jones, H., "Educating the EC: Ten Years On", 20 *European Journal of Education* (1985) 293–306, at 293: "In the beginning was the word 'cooperation', an innocent word, designed to reassure ministers from the Member States of the EEC that they could come together to consider common concerns in the educational field without fear of legal intervention or harmonising initiatives from Community involvement that might be justified on the basis of the Treaty of Rome."

[8]OJ 1968 L257/2.

order to make it easier for persons to take up and pursue activities as self-employed persons in another Member State. Article 52 has also been held to apply to the establishment of educational institutions.[9] In addition, the Commission is responsible for promoting close cooperation between Member States in matters relating to basic and advanced vocational training (Article 118) and vocational training figures in the Common Agricultural Policy (Article 41), implicitly with respect to the exchange of young workers (Article 50) and in the European Social Fund (Article 123). The question whether education falls within the Community's definition of services is rather more complicated. In *Luisi and Carbone* the court included students within its definition of the recipients of services who can come within the scope of the Treaty.[10] However, it has refused to include services provided in a state school within the scope of the Treaty due to the absence of remuneration and the importance of education in such a context as an instrument of national social policy.[11]

Article 128 EEC previously provided that the Council should lay down general principles for implementing a common vocational training policy which was to contribute to the development of national economies and the common market. Measures under Article 128 EC were adopted by simple majority and the European Parliament was not involved in the procedure. This fact, plus the absence of vocational training from the common policies listed in Article 3 seemed to underline the weakness of this legislative provision.[12] However, the Court interpreted the provisions of Article 128 EEC generously and left the Commission considerable room for legislative and judicial manoeuvre in the field of vocational training.

In 1987, for example, the Commission sought the annulment of Decision 87/327, which had adopted the European Community Action Scheme for the Mobility of University Students.[13] It claimed that Article 128 EEC alone provided a sufficient legal basis for the adoption of the Erasmus decision. The Court accepted that the Commission could not be denied the means of action necessary to efficiently carry out the common vocational training policy.[14] Given that the task of implementing a common vocational training policy is for the Member States and Community institutions working in cooperation, the Court held that the Council was entitled to adopt the legal measures envisaged in the Erasmus programme (in-

---

[9]Case 147/86 *Commission* v *Greece* [1988] ECR 1637.

[10]Joined Cases 286/82 and 26/83 [1984] ECR 377, at para.16.

[11]Case 263/86 *Humbel* [1988] ECR 5365, at para.18. See also Advocate General Slynn in Case 293/83 *Gravier*, at 596.

[12]See Flynn, J., "Vocational Training in Community Law and Practice", 8 *YEL* (1988) 59–85, at 60, where he suggests that "the procedure for laying down the general principles suggests lack of ambition for Article 128 on the part of the draftsmen"; Skouris, W., "La formation professionnelle dans la jurisprudence de la Cour de Justice des Communautés Européennes", in Schwarze, J. and Schermers, H.G. (eds.), *The Structure and Dimensions of EC Policy* (1988) Baden-Baden, Nomos, pp.205–213, at p.206; and the arguments adduced by the German, UK and French governments intervening on behalf of Council in Case 242/87 *Commission* v. *Council* [1989] ECR 1436, hereafter referred to as *Erasmus*.

[13]OJ 1987 L166/20.

[14]Case 242/87, op. cit. note 12, at para.9.

formation projects, promotional activity, preparation and encouragement of academic recognition, exchanges of students and teachers, etc.) and that those measures envisaged in the programme did not exceed the limits of the powers conferred by the Treaty in Article 128 EEC.[15] The Court recalled its definition of vocational training in *Gravier* – "any form of education which prepares for a qualification for a particular profession, trade or employment or which provides the necessary skills for such a profession, trade or employment".[16] This definition was said to apply even if the training programme in question includes an element of general education. University studies are generally thought to fulfil the *Gravier* criteria, as long as they are not simply aimed at improving a person's general knowledge.[17] According to the Court, the Erasmus programme applies to studies within the field of vocational training and "the mere possibility that the character of some courses would exclude them from the definition of vocational training did not justify the conclusion that the programme went beyond the scope of vocational training in Article 128 EEC.[18] The Court also repeated the consequences of its implied powers doctrine in this context: "it does not follow that the exercise of powers transferred to the Community is in some way limited if it is of such a nature as to affect the measures taken in the exercise of a policy such as that of education and training".[19] It was therefore willing to permit the adoption of the Erasmus programme on the sole basis of Article 128 EEC although it related to courses which, if identified separately, might not have come within that provision, or the Community definition of vocational training.[20] In the event, the Court only rejected sole reliance on Article 128 EEC because of the research content of the Erasmus programme.

In addition to these specific legal provisions on free movement and vocational training, the Community may also revert to a number of general legislative provisions which are designed to permit legislation which facilitates the achievement of

[15]Ibid., at para.19. Advocate General Darmon was more circumspect about the legislative scope of Article 128 EEC, which he said did not render the Community institutions responsible for the implementation of the common policy. He regarded the scheme as seeking to encourage the mobility of persons as much as the promotion of vocational training and consequently stated that recourse to Article 235 was necessary. Furthermore, in his view, the Erasmus programme imposed direct obligations on Member States in relation to the concrete measures adopted thereunder and as such, it was beyond the scope of Article 128 EEC. See Lenaerts, K., "Erasmus: Legal Basis and Implementation", in De Witte, B. (ed.), *Education and Community Law* (1989) Baden-Baden, Nomos, pp.113–125, at p.121, where he argues that the "general principles" substantive limitation in Article 128 EEC imposed inherent limits on the Community's powers in the field of education.

[16]Case 293/83, op. cit. note 5, at para.31.

[17]See also Case 24/86 *Blaizot* [1988] ECR 379, at para.20.

[18]Ibid., at para.27. See also Advocate General Tesauro in Joined Cases C-51/89, C-90/89 and C-94/89 *UK and others* v. *Council* [1991] ECR I-2757.

[19]Case 242/87, at para.31.

[20]Following the adoption of Articles 130f and 130p in the SEA, scientific research was expressly excluded from the programme, which then resorted to the single legal basis of Article 128 EEC, Decision 89/663, OJ 1989 L395/23. See also Lenaerts op. cit. note 15; and Case 56/88 *United Kingdom* v. *Council* [1989] ECR 1615, where the United Kingdom successfully attacked the adoption of Co. Decision 87/569, OJ 1987 L346/31, concerning an action programme for the vocational training of young people and their preparation for adult and working life; and Joined Cases C-51/89, C- 90/89 and C-94/89 with respect to the Comett programme.

the common and internal markets. To rely on Article 235 the Council must establish that a measure is "necessitated" by the requirements of the common market. However, it is argued that this "does not mean that Article 235 must be justifiable in terms of economic efficiency but merely that the action must have an incidence on economic activity".[21] The *Cowan* case demonstrates that relatively insignificant economic activities, such as being a tourist, activate Community law. Despite the 1985 White Paper's emphasis on mutual recognition of diplomas as an essential matter for Community law[22] and inevitable speculation that the extension of Community competences in the SEA would also result in a shift of competences with respect to education,[23] no major explicit changes were introduced in the educational context by the SEA. Articles 130f and 130g (now Articles 130f–130p) related to the promotion and improvement of research and development and singled out the training and mobility of researchers as necessary for the pursuit of the objectives laid down in the new title.[24] The introduction of provisions on economic and social cohesion also emphasised the importance of education and training as a Community priority. The impetus given to free movement by the introduction of Article 7(a) in the SEA and the dynamics of the internal market generally might be thought to require greater educational cooperation between Member States, if not harmonisation. No such bold statements emerged from the SEA, or the intergovernmental round of negotiations which preceded it.[25]

5.3. Equal Treatment in the Field of Education

Before analysing the changes adopted in the Union Treaty with respect to education, this section discusses the application of the principle of equal treatment in the field of education. It addresses three distinct categories of beneficiary who all enjoy rights on the basis of Community law. The three categories – Community workers, their family members and Community students who migrate principally, if not solely, for the purpose of studying in another Member State – derive their rights

---

[21]See De Witte, B. and Post, H., "Educational Rights and Cultural Rights", in Cassese, A., Clapham, A. and Weiler, J.H.H. (eds.), *Human Rights and the EC The Substantive Law*, Vol.3 (1992) Baden Baden, Nomos, pp.123–176, at section VI. De Witte has also questioned whether the word "necessity" does not rather indicate that recourse to Article 235 is a matter of political discretion to be freely assessed by the Council without doublechecking by the Court, De Witte, B., "The Scope of the Community Powers in Education and Culture in the Light of Subsequent Practice", in Bieber, R. and Ress, E. (eds.), *The Dynamics of European Community Law* (1987) Baden Baden, Nomos, p.261, at p.278.

[22]COM (85) 310 final.

[23]Hennis, E., "Access to Education in the European Communities", 3 *Leiden Journal of International Law* (1990) 35–44.

[24]The whole policy of research and technical development in the SEA is subject to the overall objective of strengthening the scientific and technical basis of European Industry, which could mean the exclusion of the arts and social sciences. See De Witte, B., "Higher Education and the Constitution of the EC" (1992), at 27.

[25]See De Witte and Post, op. cit. note 21, at p.139; and De Zwaan, "The SEA: Conclusion of a Unique Document", 23 *CMLRev* (1986) 747–765, at 759.

from different provisions of primary and secondary Community law and the scope of application of the principle of equal treatment consequently varies from one to the next. It is important to remember that Community law is not the source of the rights discussed in this section. The rights in question originate at national level. The principle of equal treatment in Article 6 simply intervenes to ensure that nationals from other Member States do not suffer overt or covert discrimination on the basis of their nationality. This principle may have considerable consequences within a particular Member State, but it does not oblige Member States to harmonise their treatment of Community citizens, it simply obliges them, within the scope of Community law, to treat nationals from other Member States as they do their own.

5.3.1. Members of the Worker's Family

The fifth recital of the preamble to Regulation 1612/68 provides that "the right to freedom of movement, in order that it be exercised by objective standards, in freedom and dignity, requires that ... obstacles to the mobility of workers shall be eliminated, in particular as regards the worker's right to be joined by his family and the conditions for the integration of that family into the host country". The spirit reflected in the preamble was initially used as a justification to extend the rights contingent on free movement beyond the strict confines of the employment contract and work place, first to the worker's dependants and spouse and then to benefits apparently unrelated to employment.[26]

In *Casagrande* v. *Landeshauptstadt Munchen* the Court was obliged to define the extent of its competence in education pursuant to Article 12 Regulation 1612/68, which was invoked in a case concerning discrimination in the adminstration of national educational grants.[27] The Court was unwilling to accept that the preservation of Member State competence in the field of education permitted discrimination with respect to admission grants and held that Article 12 applies to general measures designed to facilitate educational attendance. Article 12 provides that "the children of a national of a Member State who is or has been employed in another Member State shall be admitted to that State's general educational, apprenticeship and vocational training courses under the same conditions as the nationals of that State, if such children are residing in its territory". In the Court's view, "Although educational and training policy is not as such included in the spheres which the Treaty has entrusted to the Community institutions, it does not follow that the exercise of powers transferred to the Community is in some way limited if it is of such a nature as to affect the measures taken in the execution of a policy

---

[26]See *supra* Chapter 3.2.

[27]Case 9/74 [1974] ECR 773. The case involved the Italian son of a deceased worker previously resident in Germany, who sought to avail of "inducational grants" available under Article 2 of the *Bayerisches Ausbildungsforderungsgesetz* (*BAfog*), for children with insufficient means. Article 3 restricted the benefits of the legislation to German nationals, stateless persons and refugees.

such as that of education and training."[28] Although it is up to national authorities to determine the content of national educational policy, the conditions they choose must not be discriminatory. Article 12 has since been held to apply to all forms of education, whether vocational or general.[29]

De Witte regards the Court's interpretation of the scope of Article 12 as an expression of the Community's functional approach to its powers in the field of education.[30] The Community system is only partially based on the allocation of substantive policy areas. Many of its powers are defined in terms of an objective to be achieved such as, for example, the need to create a common or internal market. When the Community implements these objectives, it sometimes cuts across the boundaries between the substantive policy areas which the states internally trace for their own purposes. In this way Community law with respect to free movement and the internal market, may affect the internal division of competences between governmental institutions, or in federal states, between the national and regional levels. Given the link between free movement and education and training it is inevitable that a certain degree of spillover would occur in the exercise of the Community's competence with respect to the former. The Court's task has thus often been to establish the legitimacy and feasible limits of that spillover.

In *Casagrande* the Advocate General supported a broad interpretation of Article 12, but pointed out the fact that Member States diverged significantly as regards the treatment of non-nationals when administering educational grants.[31] He also drew attention to the important financial consequences which the ruling would have for the *Land* in question. However, the predominant concern of the Advocate General and Court was that in determining conditions for conferring educational grants Member States had to pursue a policy of equal treatment between nationals and Community migrant workers and their families. In *Alaimo*, an Italian national was refused a grant by a French department, which had claimed, in its defence, that insufficient funds prevented it from extending the scheme to non-nationals.[32] However, the Court reaffirmed its decisions in *Casagrande* with respect to equal treatment and conditions of admission. In *Gravier*, the Advocate General acknowledged the practical difficulties which a Member State might face if confronted with an influx of foreign students unaccounted for in the national distribution of public expenditure as an explanation of the stricter financial conditions imposed on

[28]Ibid., at para.12.

[29]See Joined Cases 389/87 and 390/87 *Echternach and Moritz* v. *Minister for Education and Science* [1990] CMLR 305; and Case 42/87 *Commission* v. *Belgium* [1988] ECR 5445, where it held that Article 12 applies to "courses provided by a higher education establishment not of university level".

[30]For a detailed discussion of this phenomenon in the particular context of education see De Witte in Bieber, R. and Ress, E. (eds.), *The Dynamics of European Community Law* (1987) Baden-Baden, Nomos, at pp.262 *et seq.*; the introduction by De Witte (1989), *European Community Law of Education*, op. cit. note 15, p.9, at p.10; and Handoll, J., "Foreign Teachers and Public Education", in De Witte (1989) *European Community Law of Education*, op. cit. note 15, pp.31–50, at p.35.

[31]Thus, the Commission pointed to residence requirements in Germany and Belgium (where a requirement of reciprocity additionally operated), in contrast to the assimilation already pertaining in Italy and France; see Opinion of Advocate General Warner in Case 9/74, op. cit. note 5, at 783.

[32]Case 68/74 [1975] ECR 109, at 113.

foreigners by Belgian legislation. Nevertheless, no practical steps were worked out by the Court, or subsequently by the Commission and Council in the wake of the decision, to address the very real difficulties which the requirement that non-nationals be treated equally could and did provoke.[33]

The Court should guard against Member States protecting their welfare systems from interfering untowardly with free movement. However, it is submitted that discussion of Member States' economic difficulties in coping with the consequences of the Court's decisions has been paid insufficient attention. Consideration of these difficulties should be a prerequisite for expansive Court decisions which impose obligations, financial or otherwise, on Member States, particularly if the sector remains, in principle, within national competence. In the context of the subsidiarity debate, Toth has argued against the Court of Justice having to determine whether a measure is suitable to achieve a particular objective, or how that objective can be achieved. Furthermore, he argues that "not only is this not part of the judicial function, but the Court is not equipped in terms of staff and expertise to make complex economic and political judgments of this kind".[34] Quite apart from the limits of its judicial function, the present workload of the Court probably argues against it having to assume such far- reaching obligations. Nevertheless, it should not be beyond the bounds of possibility for the Commission or ECOSOC to intervene in Court proceedings with any necessary information, or with the results of a preliminary survey. The Court's task in Article 177 references is to lay down guidelines to help the national court to adopt its ultimate decision in line with Community law. However, it is surprising that in cases like *Humbel*, it had not been informed about the source and scope of the arrangement between Belgium and Luxembourg concerning the free movement of students from those two countries.

A Member State is only required to ensure equal treatment pursuant to Article 12 Regulation 1612/68 with respect to the families of workers who work within its territory.[35] In *Humbel* the child in question was a French national who resided with his parents in Luxembourg. Having enrolled in Belgium for a general course of secondary education he was required to pay a *minerval* (a higher enrolment fee for non-nationals). Article 12 did not preclude Belgium from requiring this additional fee since the migrant worker in question resided in another Member State, despite the fact that the children of nationals of the Member State of residence would not be required to pay the fee. In the *Humbel* case the Italian government had argued that the children of migrant workers in Luxembourg should be entitled to the same educational advantages as the children of Luxembourg nationals. In the light of *Matteucci* it appears that the claimants in *Humbel* would have been more success-

---

[33]See *infra* Section 5.3.3 and Case 309/85 *Barra* [1988] ECR 309.

[34]Toth, A., "The Principle of Subsidiarity in the Maastricht Treaty", 29 *CMLRev* (1992) 1079–1105, at 1102.

[35]Case 263/86 *Humbel* [1988] ECR 5365, at para.24. The claimant was a French national, resident in Luxembourg, who had enrolled in a Belgian technical institute and refused to pay the *minerval* or enrolment fee imposed by Belgian law on non- nationals. Luxembourg nationals resident in Belgium were not required to pay such a fee as part of a reciprocal arrangement between the two states.

ful if they had been able to claim equal treatment against Luxembourg with respect to the provision of benefits for the children of nationals studying abroad. In the *Matteucci* case Articles 7(2) and 12 Regulation 1612/68 were used as alternatives to allow a worker who was also the child of a migrant worker, to benefit from the host Member State's scholarship system for study programmes abroad.[36] Advocate General Slynn regarded residence in the Member State where the application for the educational benefit is made as a condition referring to the territory from where the application for the course was made and not where the course itself took place.[37] In *Bernini* the court also held that as long as a residence condition did not apply to the children of workers in the host Member State, it could not be applied to the children of migrant workers.[38] In contrast, to determine whether an individual is a Community worker, the Court refers to economic or professional activity which took place in the host Member State, since the object of Regulation 1612/68 is to facilitate free movement and with that end in mind, to ensure the integration of the worker in the host Member State.[39]

Nevertheless, the residence criterion in Article 12 relates only to the workers not their children, since the objective of integration in Regulation 1612/68 is only fulfilled if those children are able to choose their studies under the same conditions as the children of Member State nationals.[40] This distinction *vis-à-vis* the criterion of residence between workers and their dependents can be explained by the fact that workers are regarded as the primary right-holder. The rights of family members are derivative and dependent on whether the principal subject of Community law – the worker – derives benefit from any grant or welfare benefit offered by the host state. The Court has already held that migrant workers can enjoy social welfare benefits in favour of their children as social advantages within the meaning of Article 7(2).[41] However those benefits cannot qualify as social advantages if the migrant worker in question is not responsible for the welfare and support of the child.[42] The implication is also that only the performance of economic activity in the host Member State can entitle workers to the benefits which they can derive there on the basis of Community law. However, the absence of resident parents did not deprive the applicants of their rights in *Echternach and Moritz*, since they were unable to continue their education on return to their country of origin due to non- recognition of the diplomas acquired in the Member State in which they had

[36]Case 235/87 [1988] ECR 5589.
[37]Ibid., at 5603.
[38]Case C-3/90 [1992] ECR I-1071, at para.27.
[39]See Case C-357/89 *Raulin* [1992] ECR I-1027, at paras.17–19; and Case C-3/90 *Bernini*, at para.19.
[40]See also Case C-308/89 *Carmina di Leo* [1990] ECR I-4185, at paras.12–13. The case involved an application for a grant to study abroad by the child of an Italian worker resident in Germany. An amendment to the relevant German legislation, Article 8 para.1, no.5 of the *BAfoG*, extended its benefits to the children of resident migrant workers but not with respect to education courses which took place in their Member State of origin, Article 5 para.2, line 2 of the *BAfoG*.
[41]Case 94/84 *Deak* [1985] ECR 1873.
[42]See Case C-3/90, op. cit. note 38, at para.25; and Case 316/85 *Lebon* [1987] ECR 2811.

previously resided with their parents and where they consequently wished to continue their studies.[43]

The combined effect of Articles 12 and 7(2) of Regulation 1612/68 is such that family members of migrant workers must receive equal treatment not only as regards admission to education courses but also as regards general measures intended to facilitate educational attendance including grants to cover tuition fees and admission costs and ancillary assistance such as maintenance and other costs.[44] National governments have understandably argued that to allow Articles 7(2) and 12 Regulation 1612/68 to operate with respect to study programmes not in the Member State where the worker and primary right holder is resident allows for the possibility of abuse by applicants claiming different grants.[45] The Court, however, has stated that Community law does not prevent national legislation taking account of such a possibility but it must do so in a non-discriminatory manner. The extent of the right to equal treatment, which covers all aspects of access, matriculation and maintenance for family members of migrant workers on the basis of Articles 7(2) and 12 Regulation 1612/68 is remarkable. Both provisions operate as specific applications of the principle of equal treatment in Article 6. Finally, the Council has also adopted a Directive on the education of migrant worker's children.[46] The Directive requires Member States to provide the children of migrant workers with tuition in the lanuage of the host Member State and to take appropriate measures, supported by the Member State of origin, to promote teaching of their mother tongue. The Directive applies to the children of Community workers who are, in the main, Member State nationals, but Member States also expressed a commitment to extending these provisions, wherever possible, to the children of third country migrant workers.[47]

5.3.2. Community Workers

Given that the status of worker or being the family member of a worker entails more favourable treatment as regards educational benefits than if an individual claims benefits solely as a student, it is not surprising that the Court is increasingly faced with claims by individuals who try to base their claims for educational grants on present or past activity as a worker. This trend is also the consequence of an in-

---

[43]Furthermore, Advocate General Darmon was aware that "at a time when families are less stable than before, to make the maintenance of rights derived from a parent's status of migrant worker in a host state conditional upon that parent's continuing residence in the State would place the family in a highly precarious situation" and affect free movement given the loss of rights which their departure would entail. In his view, Case 197/86 *Brown* [1988] ECR 3205, showed that the discontinued residence of parents need not be decisive.

[44]The convergence between the two provisions is noted in Case C-308/89 *Carmina di Leo*, op. cit. note 40, at para.15.

[45]See the submissions of the German government in Case C-308/89, op. cit. note 40, at para.9.

[46]Directive 77/486, OJ 1977 L199, 6 August 1977.

[47]See the recent report on the children of migrant workers "Rapport sur l'education des enfants de migrants dans l'Union européenne", COM (94) 80 final.

creasingly unstable employment market, where individuals are often required to change careers, or combine work and training programmes. Where the relevant jurisprudence in this respect has already been discussed in Chapter 3, it will not be reproduced in detail.

Article 7(2) Regulation 1612/68 applies to grants awarded for maintenance and training with a view to the pursuit of university studies.[48] Claimants are allowed to rely on previous employment relationships in order to bring themselves within the scope of Article 7(2) of the Regulation. The Court does not consider that they lose the status of worker simply because they are not presently in employment. As a result, *stagiaires* (*Bernini*), occasional contract workers (*Raulin*) and ex-teachers (*Matteucci*) have all been accorded the status of worker and have been conceded equal treatment with respect to the enjoyment of educational benefits in accordance with Article 7(2) Regulation 1612/68. Nevertheless, the Court of Justice has held that the application of equal treatment depends on the existence of a link between the previous occupational activity and the studies subsequently undertaken. The status of worker may not be retained if the individual is voluntarily unemployed, or if they have given up their employment to pursue studies unconnected with the previous employment activity.[49] However, simply because the status of worker is retained, does not entitle an individual to equal treatment in all respects, in particular, pursuant to Article 7(2) Regulation 1612/68. A link must exist and there cannot be too great a delay between the previous employment and the studies subsequently pursued. The Court has recognised that this link may not be possible where an individual pursues occupational retraining following involuntary unemployment,[50] and it seems to embrace combinations of employment and education in an attempt to respond to current developments in the employment market.[51] This link requirement was rejected in Chapter 3 on the grounds that the Court had refused in other cases to make the enjoyment of rights under Article 7(2) conditional on such contingencies. The requirement may be acceptable as a means to avoid abuse of the principle of equal treatment, but it should be applied flexibly and in the present economic climate a change of career or a delay between the employment and studies should not act as grounds for not qualifying as a Community worker.

Furthermore, in *Matteucci*, as an alternative to her claim as a migrant worker's child, the plaintiff claimed equal treatment with respect to scholarships to study

---

[48]See Case 39/86 *Lair* [1988] ECR 3161, at 3185–3186, where Advocate General Slynn felt that this was consistent with the decisions of the Court in *Casagrande* and *Alaimo*, where Article 12 was held to apply "to general measures intended to facilitate educational attendance".

[49]Ibid., at paras.37–39; see also Case 197/86 *Brown*, though on the facts of that case the plaintiff was denied the benefit of the rights in Regulation 1612/68 since his status of worker was held to be ancillary to the studies sought to be financed on that basis. See also Case C-357/89 op. cit. note 39, at para.21; and Case C-3/90 op cit., at para.19.

[50]Case 39/86 op. cit. note 48, at para.37; and Case C-357/89 op. cit. note 39, at para.18.

[51]See Advocate General Tesauro in Cases C-51/89, C-90/89 and C-94/89 *United Kingdom* v. *Council*: "training is important throughout a person's career precisely because it meets a need for continued adaptation to the requirements of working life and to occupational developments, especially as a result of economic and technological restructuring".

abroad under Article 7(2) Regulation 1612/68 on the basis of time spent as a teacher in Belgium. In the absence of the link between the studies and previous employment said to be necessary in *Lair*, Advocate General Slynn said the plaintiff could rely on Article 7(3) of Regulation 1612/68 which provides that a worker who is a national of a Member State in the territory of another Member State "shall also, by virtue of the same right and under the same conditions as national workers, have access to training in vocational schools and retraining centres". In his opinion, there is no need in the case of Article 7(3) to demonstrate a link between study and work.[52] In *Lair* and *Brown* the Court held that the term vocational school in Article 7(3) "has a narrower meaning and refers solely to establishments which provide only instruction sandwiched between periods of employment or else closely connected with employment, particularly during apprenticeship".[53] In such circumstances no link might be necessary since one of the purposes of Article 7(3) is retraining. Perhaps it would have been better if the Court in *Lair* had simply required individuals to demonstrate genuine and sufficient reasons for embarking on the new educational course regardless of the existence of a link or not. The Court did not refer to this possibility and procceded on the basis that the plaintiff had to be a worker who could rely on the provisions of Article 7(2) of the Regulation. In *Raulin*, the Commission also referred to Article 7(3) Regulation 1612/68 as a means of avoiding the requirement of a link between studies and the previous occupational activity. It concluded, however, that the definition of vocational training school in Article 7(3) could not be extended to universities. The latter had been excluded as such in *Brown* and since the provision could not provide a uniform solution it was rejected.

5.3.3. Migrant Students

The starting point for a discussion of the rights of migrant students is the *Forcheri* case, where the Court and Advocate General were confronted with the general question whether discrimination with respect to enrolment in an educational establishment and the fees charged for such come within the scope of the Treaties generally and Article 6 in particular.[54] Referring to Decision 63/266[55] which was based on Article 128 EEC, the Court concluded that "although it is true that educational and vocational training policy is not as such part of the areas which the Treaty has allotted to the competence of the Community institutions, the opportunity for such kinds of instruction falls within the scope of the Treaty".

---

[52]Advocate General Slynn in Case 235/87 op. cit. note 36, at 5600 and 5601.

[53]Case 39/86, at para.26 and Case 197/86, at para.12.

[54]Case 152/82 [1983] ECR 2323, which involved the spouse of a Community official who claimed that the imposition of an additional enrolment fee on non-nationals was unlawful and contrary to the spirit of Article 12 Regulation 1612/68 which is said to seek generally to minimise obstacles to the integration of the worker's family.

[55]OJ (Special Edition) 1963–64, 2 April 1961, at 25, which laid down the initial set of general principles designed to implement a Community common vocational training policy.

Consequently, if Member States organise courses offering vocational training, they must administer access to such courses in a non-discriminatory manner as between nationals and non-nationals. The imposition of a higher enrolment fee (minerval) on non- nationals constituted discrimination contrary to Article 6. The case did not conclude, however, which type of students, which levels of education and which type of facilities and benefits would be brought within the scope of Community law on the basis of Articles 6 and 128 EEC.[56]

This innovative use of Article 6 in conjunction with Article 128 EEC was reaffirmed in *Gravier*. The applicant in that case was a French national normally resident in France who was subject to an enrolment fee for foreign students levied by higher education institutions pursuant to the Belgian national legislation then in force. She was not normally established in Belgium under any provision of Community law (as a worker or family member) and sought instead to bring herself within the scope of the Treaty as a migrant student. The Court held that discriminatory measures relating to access to vocational training come within the scope of the Treaty and were incompatible with Article 6. It connected the gradual establishment of a common vocational policy with the free movement of persons, labour mobility and the improvement of living standards. Although access and participation in courses of instruction and apprenticeship, in particular, vocational training, are connected with Community law, the Court emphasised that the organisation and formation of education policy are not areas entrusted to Community institutions. Nevertheless, its definition of vocational training was relatively wide, extending the rationale in *Forcheri* to a wider category of students.[57] It was argued that *Gravier* established an independent right of residence for persons wishing to study in a Member State other than their own. If students were to enjoy rights of access to vocational training on an equal basis with their fellow Community nationals it was argued that a right of residence must be available, even if of temporary duration, to permit the enjoyment of such rights.[58] The Court subsequently resolved this issue in *Raulin* and *European Parliament* v. *Council*, where it held

---

[56]See Hartley, T.C., "La libre circulation des étudiants en droit communautaire", 25 *Cahiers Droits Européen* (1989) 327–344; and De Moor, A., "Article 7 of the Treaty of Rome Bites", 48 *Modern Law Review* (1985) 452–459.

[57]Case 593/83, op. cit., at para.31, where it defined vocational training as: "Any form of education which prepares for a qualification for a particular profession, trade or employment or which provides the necessary skills for such a profession, trade or employment is vocational training, whatever the age and level of training of the pupils or students, even if the training programme includes an element of general education."

[58]See, for example, Traversa, E., "L'interdiction de discrimination en raison de la nationalité en matière d'accès à l'enseignement, 25 RTDE (1989) 45–69, at 67–68; and Advocate General Slynn in Case 593/83 *Gravier*, at 599: "I do not ... read the judgment as laying down that a necessary precondition of the right to undertake a particular vocational course depends on a pre- existing right of residence." By further stating that "so far as vocational training is concerned the starting point is Article 128 and Decision 63/266" he added plenty of fuel to the Commission's subsequent amendment of the legal basis of its proposal on a general right of residence where it excluded students from the scope of the proposed directive. The implication being that they already enjoyed a right of residence on the basis of the Treaty.

that, as a result of their right of access to vocational training on an equal treatment basis, students enjoy a right of residence for the duration of their studies.

Some of the effects at national level of the *Gravier* decision are evident in the submissions of the Belgian government in *Barra*, where an individual sought to recover payment of the *minerval* which, in the light of *Gravier*, had been unduly made.[59] Following *Gravier* Belgium had adopted legislation restricting repayment to claimants who had brought an action for repayment before the decision in *Gravier* was handed down. The Belgian government relied on the innovative nature of that decision, a previous circular from the Commission suggesting that the Belgian practice of charging additional enrolment fees was unobjectionable[60] and the fact that more restrictive practices operated in other Member States, in an attempt to convince the Court that it would be unfair to oblige them to repay what had turned out to be unlawful. In particular, the Belgian authorities underlined the possible catastrophic financial effects of such an event: "in this case the damage which would be suffered by Belgian national education would be substantial, if not insupportable, and would have long-term negative effects ... For the universities and other educational institutions which charged the *minerval*, an obligation to refund such fees as from 1976 would be a complete financial catastrophe." The difficulties encountered would be rendered more acute by the fact that Belgian law merely authorised and did not oblige the *minerval* to be charged. Consequently, the individual educational institutions may have had no claim against the state for the fees they had to repay following *Gravier*. The Advocate General accepted a possible limitation of the effect of *Gravier*, given the innovative nature of that decision and its possible financial consequences.[61] The Court, however, was eager to facilitate the exercise of the rights which it had vindicated in *Gravier* and rejected the imposition of conditions by national legislation on the right of recovery, since it argued that to condition the right would render its exercise virtually impossible. Consequently, with respect to non-university vocational training, the Court held that its interpretation of Article 6 in *Gravier* was not limited in scope to applications for admission made after that judgment and that Community law precluded the application to students from other Member States who had unduly paid the supplementary enrolment fee of a national law which deprived them of the right to repayment unless they had brought such proceedings before the *Gravier* judgment.

The Court has also held that university studies fall within the Community definition of vocational training and access to such courses must consequently be administered in a non-discriminatory manner.[62] This is the case not only where the

---

[59]Case 309/85 [1988] ECR 355.

[60]Ibid., at 362, where it pointed out that no Article 169 action had been initiated against Belgium. Furthermore, the Commission had stated in two letters dated 18 April and 28 November 1984 that the minerval was not incompatible with Community law and various Council statements of 9 February 1976 and 27 June 1980 could be understood in the same vein.

[61]In support of this position see Advocate General Slynn in Case 42/87 op. cit. note 29, at 331, where he states, with respect to the abolition of the minerval, "what was required was a complete reversal of Belgian educational policy and that the decision in *Gravier* was a totally new development in Community law, since it recognised rights of persons who could not be regarded as economically active".

final academic examination directly provides the required qualification for a particular profession, trade or employment but also in so far as the studies in question provide specific training and skills needed by the student for the pursuit of a profession, trade or employment. The Court accepted in *Blaizot* that the *Gravier* decision represented a departure in its thinking on vocational training[63] and that the conduct of the Commission following *Gravier* demonstrated general confusion as to the effects of that decision,[64] "in those circumstances, pressing considerations of legal certainty preclude any opening of the question of past legal relationships where that would retroactively throw the financing of university education into confusion and might have unforseeable consequences for the proper functioning of universities".[65] The *Blaizot* decision stands out, given the previous failures by the Court to seriously contemplate the financial difficulties which its judicial inventiveness posed for national administrations and education authorities. However, the judgment was specifically limited to vocational studies at university.

A distinction operates in Community law between financial aid directed towards access to education and aid intended to maintain the student once admitted. The latter is excluded from the scope of Community law and consequently from the effects of the principle of equal treatment.[66] The rationale behind this distinction and exclusion from Article 6 is recognition of the Community's lack of competence and the unwillingness and financial inability of Member States to deal with a general Community wide system of entitlement to grants, whereby nationals of one Member State would be entitled on the basis of residence to the benefits enjoyed by the nationals of another. As a matter of law and logic, however, arguments designed to demonstrate fundamental differences between the two are weak.[67]

---

[62]Case 24/86 *Blaizot* involved seventeen or so French students following courses in veterinary medecine in Belgium. Proceedings brought by the plaintiffs for the recovery of the minerval were suspended pending the adoption of new Belgian legislation following *Gravier*, but recommenced thereafter.

[63]Ibid., at 392 and para.31.

[64]According to the Court at para.32, at an informal meeting with officials of the Belgian education ministry on 23 June 1985, the Commission stated that it had changed its position on the compatibility of the minerval due to the *Gravier* decision. Two days later, during a Council-established Education Committee meeting, it stated that it had not formed a definite opinion of the conclusions to be drawn from that judgment.

[65]Case 24/86, at para.34. See, however, the decision of the Tribunal civil de Bruxelles, 28/22/1989, reported in Lenaerts, K. and Coppenholle, K., "The application of Community law in Belgium", 17 *ELRev* (1992) 447–465, at 455, where the Court ordered the Université Libre de Bruxelles to reimburse a German medical student for higher tuition unlawfully charged him, although it recognised that there had been an evolution in Community law in terms of the inclusion of university studies within the meaning of vocational training.

[66]Thus in Case 39/86 *Lair*, though the question of independent educational rights was not directly in issue since the plaintiff could rely on her more beneficial status as a Community worker cum student, the Court was adamant that "assistance given by a Member State to its nationals when they undertake such studies nevertheless falls outside the Treaty, at the present stage of development of Community law, except to the extent to which such assistance is intended to cover registration and other fees, in particular tuition fees, charged for access to education". See also Case 197/86 *Brown*; and the Commission's answer to Written Question no.2520/90, OJ 1991 C35.

[67]See, for example, Advocate General Van Gerven in Case C-357/89, op. cit. note 39, at para.18; and *supra* Chapter 4.

Furthermore, this distinction is difficult to maintain in Member States which administer uniform grants intended to cover the various costs of higher education (tuition fees, maintenance etc.). In the Netherlands, the Wet op de Studie-financiering[68] includes a basic grant available to all and a complementary grant determined according to means. In *Raulin*, the Dutch government argued that the basic grant had no link with access and inscription and any attempt to divide the grant up according to different costs was artificial and foreign to the philosophy behind the WSF which was to give students maximum autonomy in determining their finances.[69] The Court held, however, that this aim did not prevent that part of the grant which could be deduced to apply to tuition fees from falling within the scope of Community law. Article 6 ensures equal treatment with respect to conditions of access regardless of the mode of calculating, or the philosophy behind national grant systems. This artificial distinction is an expression of policy rather than principle by the Court of Justice.[70] It is interesting to note, however, that Articles 9 and 10 of the European Social Charter recognise that the development of the individual's ability and career are for the individual to determine and for the state to help to implement even to the extent of giving "financial assistance".[71]

In the light of these decisions it is difficult to seriously assert that Community law has no effect on the organisation and financing of national education. Not only did *Gravier* constitute a "complete reversal of Belgian educational policy",[72] but the Court has extended the scope of Article 6 so that the compatibility of matters which do not otherwise come within the scope of Community law fall to be determined on an equal treatment basis. Two decisions cast further doubt on the feasability of this division between issues which come within the scope of Community law (conditions of access, tuition fees) and issues which remain within the competence of Member States (educational finance, policy, payment of maintenance grants). In 1982, Belgium adopted legislation which established a fixed quota in relation to the level of government funding for higher education.[73] Beyond a level of 2 per cent of all duly registered Belgian students, foreign students were to be excluded from financial calculations. Higher education establishments clearly had an incentive not to admit students from other Member States, since if they exceeded the 2 per cent quota they would have to finance those students without government support. The Commission lodged an Article 169 application claiming that

---

[68]Staatsblad 1986, 252.

[69]See Case C-357/89, op cit. note 39, at paras.26 *et seq.*

[70]See also Green, N., Hartley, T.C. and Usher, J.A., *The Legal Foundations of the Single Market* (1990) Oxford, Oxford University Press, at p.143; Hartley, op. cit. note 56, at 335; and Scholsem, "A propos de la circulation des étudiants. Vers un fédéralisme financier européen?", 25 CDE (1989) 306–324, at 318.

[71]See the Community Charter of Fundamental Social Rights, COM (89) 248 final, 30 May 1989.

[72]Advocate General Slynn in Case 42/87, op. cit. note 29, at 331.

[73]See Article 2 of Royal Decree of 21 July 1982, as amended by Article 1 of the Royal Decree of 12 July 1984. The Law of 21 June 1985, adopted following *Gravier*, did not alter this position. Furthermore, according to Article 64 of the Law of 21 June 1985, educational institutions were entitled to refuse to register students from other Member States beyond a quota of 2 per cent.

this was incompatible with Article 6 generally and Article 12 of Regulation 1612/68 in particular.[74] The Court and Advocate General accepted that the legislation in question had the "direct effect of excluding, in practice, students who are nationals of other Member States from such vocational training once the quota of 2 per cent is attained".[75] Such a restriction did not apply to Belgian students and as such it was discrimination contrary to Article 6 of the Treaty and Article 12 of Regulation 1612/68.

At issue in *Gravier* was a discriminatory financial barrier which obstructed non-national access to education. *Commission* v. *Belgium*, as the Advocate General rightly indicated, did not concern a direct financial barrier to access but the measure concerned the financial organisation of national education by the Belgian government.[76] Nevertheless, the Commission argued and the Court ultimately accepted that, despite the exclusion of organisation, policy and finance from its scope, Community law requires that Member States do not adopt financing arrangements which, in practice, create discrimination between nationals and non-nationals from the other Member States.[77] Article 5 also requires Members States not to act in a manner which may defeat the objectives of the Community. This duty of loyalty is a potent weapon, since in order to render a Community obligation effective (in this instance free movement, a common vocational training policy and a People's Europe), Member States may be required to take action in other fields which, in principle, fall within national competence (for example, the organisation and finance of national education). The Advocate General in *Commission* v *Belgium* claimed that this measure was not in the same category as maintenance grants and financial policies which cannot be regarded as discriminatory on the basis of Community law since, in general, they do not fall within its scope.[78] In reality, however, this is a financial policy measure and for all the Court's fine distinctions the reason why Belgium adopted the legislation was precisely to cope with the fact that Community students may no longer be required to pay additional fees and that it was difficult for the government to maintain present expenditure if the category of persons entitled to education benefits was extended immeasurably.

This situation re-emerged in *Commission* v. *Belgium*. Although Belgium had amended its legislation in the light of the *Gravier* decision, it still appeared to discriminate against non-nationals.[79] Although Belgium had amended its legislation

[74]Belgium did not contest the claim, it simply stated that the law would be changed. This is an unacceptable means of dealing with national legislation incompatible with Community law, see Case 167/73 *Commission* v. *France* [1974] ECR 359 at para.41 since: "it gives rise to an ambiguous state of affairs by maintaining, as regards those subject to the law who are concerned, a state of uncertainty as to the possibilities available to them of relying on Community law."

[75]Case 42/87 op. cit. note 29, at 5455 and 5451 respectively.

[76]Advocate General Slynn at 5451; and Flynn, op. cit. note 12, at 78.

[77]Case 42/87, op. cit. note 29, at para.8. The Court did not address the fact that for Article 6 to apply, the matter must fall within the scope of the Treaty, although in the light of the *Cowan* and *Matteucci* decisions, the Court is capable of considerably extending the scope of free movement in this respect.

[78]See Case 42/87 op. cit. note 29, at 5451.

[79]Case C-47/93 [1994] ECR I-1593.

in the light of the *Gravier* decision, it still appeared to discriminate against non-nationals. Only Member State nationals who had been admitted to courses of study in their own state and had paid enrolment fees there were excluded from the imposition of the supplementary enrolement fee.[80] Furthermore, universities were given the right to refuse students who were nationals from other Member States if they were not going to be taken into account in the state calculations for the financing of the university. Belgian legislation continued to limit those persons who could claim reimbursement of unduly paid supplementary enrolment fees to those who had commenced proceedings before *Gravier* and it only exempted persons established in Belgium who pursue, or had pursued an occupational activity and their families from the supplementary fee. The Court held that the amendment to the legislation regulating the payment of the supplementary fee which included students who had paid and registered in their host state did not remove the discrimination which it had already impugned in *Gravier* and *Blaizot*.[81] With regard to the quota of non-Belgian students in the calculation of university finances and the right to refuse to register non-nationals, the Court recalled its decision in *Commission* v. *Belgium* (Case 42/87), where it had held that in so far as the legislation in question limited the financing of vocational higher educational establishments, it had the effect of excluding in practice students who were nationals of other Member States once the 2 per cent quota was reached. This restriction did not apply to Belgian students and it amounted to discrimination contrary to Article 6.[82] The Court also held that Belgium had unlawfully discriminated against other nationals by restricting the possibility of obtaining reimbursement of the minerval.

5.4. Higher Education at National Level

The legal position of these different categories of students can therefore be cited as follows. Conditions of access to vocational training based on nationality are prohibited, though other conditions relating to qualifications, language and *numerus clausus* pass muster if they are non-discriminatory. Enrolment fees must not be higher for nationals of other Member States than for a Member State's own nationals. Unless an individual is eligible under Articles 7(2) and 12 of Regulation 1612/68, as a worker or family member, maintenance grants do not generally fall within the scope of Community law and are not subject to the provisions of Article 6 on equal treatment. What is less certain is the practical, administrative and financial impact of these decisions. According to a provisional calculation by the British Universities Central Council on Admissions, for example, 750 Irish students entered full-time university degree courses in 1986 (one year after the *Gravier* decision), a 400 per cent increase on 1985 figures and there was a 600 per cent increase

---

[80]Article 16 of the 1985 Act on education, as amended by Decree 543 of 1987.
[81]Case C-47/93, at paras.11–12.
[82]Ibid., at para.13.

in applications by Irish candidates for entry to polytechnics in the same year. The high tuition fees in the Republic of Ireland and a lack of grants to cover them encourage students to move to the United Kingdom, where they only have to meet their maintenance costs.[83] What Member States fear, in particular, is an imbalance in student mobility in the Community which will, if accentuated, cause severe difficulties for the more popular educational destinations. The question is ultimately who is to pay for the migration of students and for the consequences of the dynamic interpretations of the Community's competence in education, which have resulted from the far-reaching decisions of the Court of Justice and positive legislative participation or interference in education by Community institutions?

5.4.1. National Public Expenditure

Effective free movement and the consequences of a broad interpretation of the principle of equal treatment are clearly difficult to implement if significant differences exist between public expenditure in higher education at national level.[84] When certain macro-indicators are applied to expenditure – public expenditure as a percentage of total budget expenditure, as a percentage of the national education budget and as a percentage of gross domestic product – national preferences regarding education in general and higher education in particular are evident. Higher education has witnessed a remarkably high but declining level of expenditure in the Netherlands (4.15 per cent in 1987) compared to a much lower but increasing percentage in Luxembourg (0.42 per cent in 1988). Strictly speaking these figures are not comparable since Luxembourg does not have a fully fledged university system. Nevertheless, it is arguable that Luxembourg's failure to develop its university system is due, at least in part, to that fact that its students can be easily absorbed, without problems of mobility or language, by the universities of its neighbours.

Higher education expenditure related to the total national education budget reflects the national importance attached to third level education generally. It is ranked very highly, for example, in Denmark, the Netherlands and Germany. Although percentages are declining, however, in what may be regarded as the "richer" states and rising in their "poorer" or peripheral counterparts, the figures cited reflect distinct national choices and spending power in the financing and organisation of national higher education.[85] An examination of the level of expenditure per student also shows large differences throughout the Community. In the university sector, for ex-

---

[83]See also *The Independent* newspaper, 19 November 1987, reporting on the "influx" of Irish students to the UK following the decision in *Gravier*.

[84]See Centre for Higher Education Policy Studies, *Public Expenditure on Higher Education: A Comparative in the EC Member States (1975–1988)* (1992) Jessica Kingsley Publishers; Allington, N., "Funding arrangements for universities and students in the EC", 6 *European Access* (1991) 10–12, at 10; see also European Commission, *Higher Education in the European Union: Facts and Figures over a Decade*, 1994.

[85]Thus, there has been a decline of 13 per cent in the Netherlands and rises of 41, 43, 27 and 154 per cent in Portugal, Italy, Greece and Luxembourg, respectively.

ample, expenditure per student in Denmark, Luxembourg and the Netherlands is considerably higher than other Member States.[86] The national choice of funding mechanism is also an expression of the relationship between central or regional government and the educational institutions. Thus, in Germany, Italy and Greece, resources are strictly earmarked for specific purposes. In other Member States (Belgium, Denmark, Spain and the United Kingdom) resources are closely linked to the number of students which the authorities envisage must be catered for and in other Member States still, efficiency considerations are important.[87]

5.4.2. Student Support Systems

In 1987 the Commission published a report examining the existing provisions for student support in each Member State. A number of recommendations were proposed to overcome obstacles to mobility within the separate support systems: a special fund to cover maintenance and tuition for study abroad; modification of support systems to ensure consistent provision and exportability throughout the European Communities; review of current tuition fee policies, since fee differentials were regarded as a significant obstacle; and elimination of inconsistent treatment of students with respect to grants or loans due to internal divisions and discretionary systems.[88] A broader and more recent study concentrates on changes in the national grant systems since 1987.[89] All twelve Member States operate some sort of support system for some, or all, of their higher education institutions. Denmark, Greece, France, Italy, Luxembourg and the Netherlands operate a mixed grant/loan system.[90] The United Kingdom had previously operated a generous grants system but moved to a mixed system in 1990. Germany operates a loans only system. Belgium, Ireland, Spain and Portugal administer a grants only system, although in some of these Member States the availability of grants is relatively restricted. All Member States, except the United Kingdom and Ireland, which operate a criterion of residence, rely on nationality as the basic criterion governing eligibility. However, Section 5.3 demonstrates that if the claimant and the right being claimed come within the scope of Community law, Member States must act in a non-discriminatory manner. In all Member States some financial criteria determine eligibility, usually some system of means testing either students or their fam-

[86]In 1987, expenditure per student in the Netherlands was nine times as high as Spain. Expenditure per student is extremely low in Spain and Greece and below the EC average in Portugal. The report corrects these findings for certain distortions, at 126.
[87]In particular in the Netherlands, which operates an output funding formula based on the number of graduates.
[88]Commission, Financial Support for Students for the Purpose of Study in Another Member State of the European Communities (1987).
[89]Student Support Systems in the EC Member States, 1987/88, Task Force Human Resources, Education, Training and Youth (1989).
[90]Where known changes have been made in national legislation since 1987 they are noted. Otherwise the position is taken as stated in the report.

ilies.[91] Eligibility for grants ranged from 8 per cent in Greece and Portugal to 100 per cent in the Netherlands and the level of the yearly grant ranges from 120,000 Portuguese escudo to 36,000 Danish krona.

Thus, significant differences exist between the different Member States on the availability and extent of support. These differences reflect financial and social welfare policy choices by Member States with respect to matters which, at the present stage of development of Community law, remain within their competence.[92] A policy choice is made as to whether the system administered should be based on grants or loans or both. This choice may be based, among others, on financial considerations and/or on a cost effective and efficiency analysis of the education system. There are also considerable differences as between Member States concerning the percentage of the student body enjoying its support benefits and in the way support is administered.[93] Thus, for example, student support in Germany has consisted only of interest-free loans since 1983–84.[94] A grant element is currently being considered.[95] In contrast, student support in Spain is exclusively in the form of grants.[96] In 1985–86, 13 per cent of the total student body received a grant. No provision is made in Spanish legislation for the use of these funds abroad.[97] Since

[91]The Netherlands is unique in providing everyone with a basic grant and then determining additional benefits. The rationale is said to be, *inter alia*, to ensure student financial independence from parents. There is talk now of changes being introduced and of certain requirements being established on the basis of academic results.

[92]See the Belgian government's reliance on the contributory economic argument in Case 293/83 *Gravier* op. cit. note 5, at 596, when discussing the distribution of welfare benefits to nationals and taxpayers only; the force of the argument was recognised by AG Slynn, at 604; see also the German submissions in Case 39/86 *Lair* op. cit. note 48, at 3163, 3167 and Advocate General Slynn, at 3185.

[93]The percentage of the student population enjoying state assistance in higher education was as follows in 1987–88: UK (75 per cent), Spain (13 per cent), Germany (30 per cent), Belgium (33 per cent), Denmark (55 per cent grant, 8 per cent loan), Greece (8 per cent), France (15 per cent grants and loans), Ireland (47 per cent), Italy (no data available), Luxembourg (85 per cent), Netherlands (100 per cent) and Portugal (8 per cent).

[94]See the *Bundesausbildungs Forderungsgesetz*, *BAFog* or Federal Law on Financial Support for Education. The amount of financial support depends on the financial circumstances of the student and of the relatives who have a duty to support him or her. In 1987–88, the maximum monthly allowance was DM710, to be refunded from the fifth year following graduation and within twenty years. In 1986, approximately 30 per cent of all eligible students received an interest-free loan. In contrast, direct grants, including tuition and maintenance expenses, are available in certain circumstances for study abroad (where the course is *numerus clausus*, particularly advantageous, or capable of being subsequently credited in Germany).

[95]This follows a government investigation revealing student debts of over DM10,000 million, a decline in the number of students from low-income families, and the fact that half of the resources needed to maintain a student are provided by family support.

[96]The main conditions for support are the possession of Spanish nationality, participation in an undergraduate course, state recognition of the educational establishment concerned and the absence of any other available grant. Family income per capita and previous academic performance are also relevant to the determination of eligibility. In 1987–88, the overall amount of annual grants was between Ptas 12,000 and Ptas 332,000, which covers maintenance, travel expenses and books. Grantholders are exempt from payment of tuition fees.

[97]Through its various ministries, however, a whole range of grants and aid are available for study abroad but they generally concern postgraduate study and research. A law passed in 1989, allows Spanish Erasmus students studying abroad to enjoy an equal level of grant, but the additional costs of study abroad are not recognised.

Spanish nationality is a criterion for eligibility, the normal system of grants is not applicable to students from other Member States. Until 1990, the United Kingdom government operated a grants only system. In 1990, the government passed the Education (Students Loans) Act, 1990. Mandatory maintenance grants have been extended for study periods in other Member States if those periods are designed as a compulsory part of the course, or if the local education authority exercises its discretionary powers to that effect.[98] Support is available for students from other Member States if they are (i) ordinarily resident for the three years preceding the course, (ii) the child of an EC national who is or has been employed or so resident in the United Kingdom and who is resident in the United Kingdom on the relevant day, or (iii) is an EC national resident in the EC, who came to the United Kingdom mainly for the purpose of taking up employment and who has worked for nine months in the year preceding the course which, furthermore, must qualify as vocational training.[99]

5.4.3. Student Mobility Figures

It is clear from a study of mobility among students in the EC that there are "importing" and "exporting" countries.[100] According to the De Jonge report the major importing countries are the United Kingdom, France, Germany and, to a lesser extent, Italy and Belgium. Greece is the most important export country with 21,000 students abroad, particularly in Italy, Germany and France, compared to ninety-four foreign EC students which it receives. Luxembourg is also a prominent exporter. To a lesser extent, Portugal, Ireland and the Netherlands are exporting countries. Denmark and Spain are in balance. The report reaches a number of "qualified" conclusions on the basis of the statistics available to it.[101] Between 1987 and 1990, there has been a 16 per cent increase in the rate of student mobility. There is a growing number of students in the United Kingdom (+123 per cent), possibly due its popularity as a destination for Erasmus students and its proximity and attractiveness to Irish students. There is a decline in foreign students in Italy (–24 per cent) and Belgium (–48 per cent). The number of Greeks emigrating to study is declining (–13 per cent), as is the number of Italians (–7 per cent), Luxembourgeois (–10 per cent) and Dutch (–1 per cent). All other countries show a growth – United Kingdom (+4 per cent), Belgium (+44 per cent), Denmark (+60 per cent), Germany

---

[98]Note that some countries, Italy, Greece and Portugal, stipulate that grants/loans cannot be exported for study abroad.

[99]The relevant period for the determination of a worker's genuine status should not exceed one year according to Advocate General Slynn in Case 39/86 *Lair*, at 3183.

[100]See De Jonge, J.F.M. and Dillo, I.G., *Student Mobility Within Higher Education in the EC*, at p.29; The report also details the specific imbalances occurring between pairs of countries, at pp.32 and 33.

[101]The statistics are not entirely reliable given different definitions of foreign EC student in some Member States, different national strategies for collecting data and the unreliable nature of some of the data presented.

(+52 per cent), Spain (+19 per cent), France (+94 per cent), Portugal (+22 per cent) and Ireland (+148 per cent).[102]

Given this brief description of the organisation and financing of higher education at national level, can any conclusions be drawn about the consequences of the Community's assertion of judicial and legislative competence? Countries like Belgium and Italy, which cater for large numbers of students due to a large number of available places, operate relatively open higher education systems.[103] The limited capacity of the Portuguese and Greek systems accounts for its closed nature. An open system attracts a greater inflow of foreign students. An increase in the number of students in Belgium or Italy might be in line with the spirit of higher education in those Member States. Both are open systems which admit large numbers of students. Furthermore, the influx of Community students may be small compared to national figures on the number of higher education students, although the Belgian government in *Barra* did not seem to share this view. However, such an increase in student numbers could affect the quality of the services provided. If it worsens the quality of those services, or lessens the financial aid normally available to a Member State's own nationals, then the Court and Commission are perpetrating a situation which is arguably incompatible with the objectives of the Community.[104] After all, if generous financial policy choices by Member States in the field of higher education have the effect of penalising them in the long run because of a concentrated and unforeseen influx of students from other Member States, then something is array.[105] The Member States and the Commission recognise that imbalances in the flows of mobile students "constitute a significant burden on the resources of some of the Member States".[106] Member States have suggested evening the imbalances or providing for other compensatory measures. However, it is paradoxical that the principle of equal treatment with respect to EC students may have had some negative consequences for their mobility and access to educational institutions in other Member States. Equal treatment removes them from the special category of foreign students generally, for whom a protected quota sometimes operates. They must now compete on equal terms with a Member

---

[102]See also the foreign student statistics, broken down by country, in Mohr, B. (ed.), *Higher Education in the EC: The Student Handbook* (1990) European Commission.

[103]In *Blaizot*, op. cit. note 5, at 386, Belgian universities claimed that they received the highest number of foreign students; supported by Flynn, op. cit. note 12, at 66.

[104]See Case 167/73 *Commission* v. *France* [1974] ECR 359 and Article 2 which provides that the Community shall have as its task "an accelerated raising of the standard of living".

[105]This is the "mechanical" dynamic which Scholsem strongly criticises in the context of the distribution of social benefits, op. cit. note 70, at 314. He argues that the harmonisation of fiscal policy cannot be left to purely mechanical forces and further, at 320: "entre entités permettant une mobilité parfaite, la marge de manoeuvre de chacune d'elles est très réduite en ce qui concerne le degré de redistribution des revenus. En effet, si l'une de ces entités désire mener une politique plus redistributive, elle risque d'attirer à elle les plus demunis et de chasser les plus riches, entrant ainsi dans une spirale bien connue."

[106]Commission (Education, Training, Youth), *The Outlook for Higher Education in the EC: Responses to the Memorandum*, Studies no.2, at p.37.

State's own nationals, while national universities may be eagerly scouting for re-
cruits from third countries who are subject to higher admission fees and who therefore constitute a potentially lucrative and attractive market.[107]

5.5. Community Education Programmes

This section discusses a number of legislative initiatives which have been taken by
the Community. It attempts to further identify the manner in which Community action may affect the content, organisation and financing of education in the Member
States. At issue is the introduction of the principle of mutual recognition with respect to the recognition of qualifications and the establishment of positive legislative programmes. These developments may cast doubt, to an extent, on the
persistent claims by Community institutions that they possess limited competence
in this field and that those limitations are respected.

5.5.1. Education and the Principle of Mutual Recognition

In order to maximise the expertise and services of professionals and to promote the
fundamental principle of free movement, the recognition of professional qualifications became a major preoccupation of the Commission and Council.[108] Pursuant
to Article 57(1), which empowers the Community to issue directives for the mutual
recognition of diplomas, certificates and other evidence of formal qualifications,
the Commission initially pursued a sectoral policy whereby it introduced harmonising directives for individual professions. In order to be recognised, national diplomas in each profession had to testify to the sucessful completion of a course of
study which was compatible with the criteria set out in the coordinating directive.
The Directives harmonise the professions and national study programmes were
sometimes changed in order to comply with the common standards established in
the Directive. This sectoral approach clearly interfered with national education
policies and programmes, since it required a degree of harmonisation of national
curricula. It was not particularly successful since it took a long time to reach agreement and adopt measures in different sectors.[109]

---

[107]See, for example, Fenwick, K., "Making the Most of Overseas Students", 41 *Higher Education
Quarterly* (1987) 126–137.
    [108]See Council Resolution on the mutual recognition of diplomas, certificates and other evidence
of formal qualifications, OJ 1974 C98/1; the Fontainebleau European Council of 19 June 1984, Bull.
EC., no.6 1.1.9 para.6; the Commission's communication following Fontainebleau, COM (84) 446
final; the establishment of National Academic Research Information Centres (NARIC) in 1984; the first
Adonnino Report, Bull. EC. 1985, Suppl.7; the Brussels European Council of 19 March 1985, Bull. EC.
1985 no.3, 1.2.7; the Commission's White Paper on "Completing the Internal Market", COM (85) 310
final; and the direction of the Court in Case 222/86 *Heylens* [1987] ECR 4097 at paras.10–13.
    [109]See Lenaerts, K., "Education in EC Law After Maastricht", 31 *CMLRev* (1994) 7–41, at 17;
and Zilioli, C., "The Recognition of Diplomas and its Impact on Education Policies", in De Witte
(1989), op. cit. note 15, pp.51–70, at pp.53–57.

In 1985, in its White Paper on the completion of the internal market, the Commission announced a change in its approach to the recognition of diplomas from one of prior harmonisation to one of mutual recognition. This more general principle of mutual recognition originated in Community law in the context of the free movement of goods, where it meant that a product lawfully manufactured and marketed in one Member State should be taken in principle to be of sufficient quality to be sold throughout the Community.[110] Rather than harmonising national systems in line with common standards at Community level, national diversity was to be preserved and Member States were to mutually respect the decisions of fellow Member States that their diplomas were of a sufficiently high standard. Directive 89/48, on a general system for the recognition of higher education diplomas awarded on completion of professional education and training, disregards the prior harmonisation method previously applied in the sectoral Directives.[111] A detailed analysis of the Directive is beyond the scope of this chapter.[112] The horizontal approach employed by the Directive applies to all registered professional activities for which university level training of at least three years is required and which are not already covered by a sectoral directive (Articles 1 and 2). The system established by the Directive relies on the comparability of certificates and mutual trust between Member States and provides for compensation mechanisms (evidence of professional experience, an official adaptation period, or an aptitude test) where there are major differences in education and training between Member States (Article 4). The negotiation of the sectoral directives had been protracted. This was partly due to the difficulty in establishing a basis on which national qualifications could be compared. The House of Lords has criticised the general systems Directive because it proceeds on the assumption that there is an equivalence between the professions in the Member States and has criticised the Commission for not undertaking a comparative review of the professions covered by the Directive.[113] It felt that it was essential to define with precision what activities were restricted in each Member State, what qualifications were then required to perform each of those activities and which is the competent authority in question. The evidence which it had collected showed that there was great uncertainty on these points.

---

[110]See Case 120/78 *Rewe Zentrale* v. *Bundesmonopolverwaltung fur Branntwein* [1979] ECR 649, otherwise known as *Cassis de Dijon*.
[111]OJ 1989 L19/16.
[112]See, however, Laslett, J.M., "The Mutual Recognition of Diplomas, Certificates and Other Evidence of Formal Qualifications in the EC", 1 *LIEI* (1990) 1–66; Orzack, L.H., "The General Systems Directive: Education and the Liberal Professions", in Hurwitz, L. and Lequesne, C., (eds.), *The State of the European Community: Politics, Institutions and Debates in the Transition Years 1989–1990* (1991) Boulder, Lynne Rienner, pp.137–151, who voices the fears of professional bodies; the House of Lords Select Committee on the European Communities, *Recognition of Higher Education Diplomas*, session 1985–86, 22nd report, at pp.16 *et seq.*; and Pertek, J., "La reconnaissance mutuelle des diplômes d'enseignement supérieur", 25 RTDE (1989) 623–646.
[113]See *Recognition of Higher Education Diplomas*, op. cit. note 109, at p.33.

Recognition of professional qualifications is clearly a prerequisite of mobility. However, mutual recognition, even though it does not require prior harmonisation, has an inevitable impact on the content of national education programmes and policies. The new horizontal approach allows Member States to respond rapidly and without preconditions to the requirements of higher education certificate holders. Nevertheless, the lack of harmonisation reduces state control over national education systems as foreign qualifications are admitted and recognised on the basis of certain broad conditions outlined by the Commission and enforceable by the Community Court. The power of the state to independently evaluate these qualifications is limited.[114] The Council has subsequently adopted a second general systems directive. Directive 92/51 does not apply to higher education diplomas, to diplomas already caught by the sectoral directives, or to the public service.[115] It is aimed at recognition of vocational training and applies to courses of under three years. Mutual recognition in this context concerns (i) access to a regulated profession, (ii) this access cannot be refused to Member State nationals who have acquired their qualifications in those states and (iii) the host Member State can assure the effective competence of the candidate with reference to a *stage* or aptitude test. This Directive supplements the mutual recognition approach adopted in 1989.

Some national study programmes have been entirely refurbished as a result of Community action under Article 57.[116] These may be desirable consequences in themselves but they take place in the context of a legal order which professes a lack of competence to affect national educational policy in this way. On the one hand, the general systems Directive could be regarded as an expression of subsidiarity in that it allows Member States to determine the various criteria for mutual recognition. Nevertheless, the Directive goes beyond the mutual recognition supported by the Court of Justice in *Heylens* and *Vlassipoulou*[117] and sets limits to what Member States can do in this respect. Thus, for a qualification obtained in another Member State to be rejected, the difference in standards must be substantial. Even though the mutual recognition method affirms the role of Member States in education, the organisation and policy of national systems of education are indirectly and inevitably affected. Moreover, the fact remains that these changes originate at Community not national level indicates that: "(the) 1989 Directive shifts the locus of authority in European higher education and alters the operation of nationally based regulatory arrangements for entry to professions. These actions by the Community challenge assumptions underlying national policies concerning education and professions".[118] Moreover, the functional dynamic discussed earlier in the

---

[114]See Lonbay, J., "Education and Law: The Community context", 15 *ELRev* (1990) 363–387, at 370.

[115]Directive 92/51 on a second general system for the recognition of professional education and training to supplement Directive 89/48, OJ 1992 L209/25.

[116]Italy, for example, created a new dentistry curriculum to comply with Directive 78/87, OJ 1978 L233/70 and Belgium and France have considered upgrading their two year higher education courses to three years, although this may no longer be necessary given that the second general systems Directive applies to third level courses of less than three years and secondary level diplomas.

[117]See Case C-340/89 [1991] ECR I-2357.

[118]See Orzack, op. cit. note 112.

context of *Casagrande* is also applicable in this context, but here it can fundamentally affect the very substance of what is supposed to fall within Member State competence, namely the structure and content of education. The system established by Directive 89/48 is to be welcomed after the long years of stalemate during the sectoral negotiations, but it is argued that the impact of this legislative action should not be underestimated.[119]

5.5.2. European Community Exchange and Study Programmes

Erasmus

In 1987 Council Decision 87/327 was adopted to establish the European Community Action Scheme for the Mobility of University Students (Erasmus). The aim of the scheme was to increase student mobility and to promote greater cooperation between universities in the Community. The scheme was implemented by a number of "actions" which were described in the annex. Action 1 dealt with the establishment and operation of a European university network which required universities to conclude student and teacher exchange agreements within the Erasmus framework. In 1994, the Commission had approved over 2,300 inter-university cooperation programmes and students in participating universities were able to participate in fully recognised periods of study in other Member States as part of their diploma or academic qualification. Provision was made for financial assistance to encourage staff and student mobility and the development of integrated courses. The grant scheme in Action 2 thus involved direct Community financial support for students studying abroad. In 1994 alone, student mobility grants accounted for 70 per cent of the Erasmus budget. Action 3 related to academic recognition of diplomas and periods of study undertaken in another Member State. The scheme also involved the provision of grants for the creation of teacher and student associations with a European dimension. The Community network of national academic recognition information centres (NARIC) was later integrated into the Erasmus programme. These centres are involved in the recognition aspects of Erasmus and in the implementation of the general systems directives. Finally, the European Community course credit transfer system (ECTS) was set up as a pilot

---

[119]For the moment, Member States continue to express their distrust of qualifications from other Member States by imposing aptitude tests and adaptation measures as the rule on incoming graduates, whereas the Directive had envisaged these safeguards only in exceptional cases. For another example of the Community's influence of national education programmes see Council Directive 77/486, OJ L199/32, whereby Member States are to ensure free tuition to facilitate the reception of children in the initial period when they arrive in the host Member State (Article 2) and measures to ensure that national teachers are trained for this purpose are to be adopted if necessary. Article 3 also requires them to take appropriate measures to promote the teaching of the language and culture of the Member State of origin; and the commentary by De Witte, B., "Educational Equality for Community Workers and their Families", in De Witte (1989), op. cit. note 15, pp.71–79, at pp.74–75; and Lonbay (1990), op. cit. note 114, at 384. The Court has recently found Greece to be in contravention of the Treaty for failing to adopt the necessary legislative and administrative measures necessary to comply with the first general systems Directive in time, Case C-365/93 *Commission* v. *Greece*, judgment of 23 March 1995.

scheme within Erasmus to test how academic credits might be transferred between educational establishments in the Community.

Erasmus has acted as a catalyst for student mobility and interuniversity cooperation. However, it has also inevitably affected the organisation of education at national level, its financing and even its content. Erasmus was addressed to Member States who were required to fulfil the precise obligations it contains and to eliminate all obstacles to its implementation at national level. The Community was responsible for the organisation and coordination of the programme which made its impact on national systems considerable. Universities participated on a voluntary basis. Once they did participate, however, they had to comply with the requirements of the scheme. Action 1 required considerable changes in educational organisation, since special study courses had to be established, involving two or more universities in different Member States. This required greater flexibility in national study programmes since they had to tally with study programmes formulated by other Member States.[120] Priority in financing was given to universities which cooperated in this way. The language of the scheme was facilitative, but in Member States where the education sector was suffering increasing cutbacks, the participation of universities in the scheme and therefore its effects were, in fact, compelling.[121] The Lingua programme alone, for example, enjoyed an estimated budget of 200 million ECU between 1991 and 1994. In 1990, the Erasmus budget was raised from 85 million ECU to 192 ECU for a four-year period.[122] The financial importance of these programmes was thus considerable. Nowhere have higher education institutions benefited from such large sums from a single non-national public source.

The Court in *Erasmus* rejected the contention that national organisation of education was affected by the establishment of a European university network since the Community only set up the network, while national universities could only participate in it on the basis of national provisions governing their status and organisation. These national regulating provisions were unaffected by Erasmus.[123] However, the allocation of resources is also a system of control and the use of the financial carrot to encourage and achieve action which could not legitimately be directly achieved by the Commission and Council is barely disguised.[124] If

[120]In this context see Advocate General Darmon in Case 242/87, op. cit. note 12, at 1445. For details of the establishment of an Erasmus cooperation scheme see Cousins, "Hallmark and Pickup, Inter-University Co-operation and Erasmus", 44 *Higher Education Quarterly* (1990) 82–97.

[121]See also Shaw, J., "Twin-Track Social Europe: the Inside Track", in O'Keeffe, D. and Twomey, P., *Legal Issues of the Maastricht Treaty* (1993) London, Chancery Press, pp.295–311, at p.309.

[122]These are not the only two programmes adopted by the Community. It has also adopted the Comett programme on cooperation between universities and industry, the Tempus/Phare programmes on cooperation with the countries of Central and Eastern Europe and the Republics of the Former Soviet Union, the Petra programme on vocational training for young people and the Youth for Europe Programme.

[123]Case 242/87, op. cit. note 12, at para.32.

[124]See in this respect, OECD, *Financing Higher Education* (1990) Paris, at 8–13: "a funding mechanism is not merely a device for allocating resources from providers to users. It is also a system of control". See also, regarding changes in the curriculum in particular, *Higher Education and Europe*

Member States chose to avail of Community funds, they had to respect the conditions which the Community had attached to the use of such funds. Furthermore, the programme required legislative amendments in a number of Member States in that it required the payment of maintenance grants by the Member State of origin for study abroad though some Member States previously restricted the payment of grants to the national territory. It further provided that tuition fees would be paid in the Member State of origin not the host Member State. Furthermore, there is a wide discrepancy in the average level of grant received across the Member States.[125] Finance was conditional on the fulfilment of certain criteria, and priority in this respect was given to programmes which conformed with the conditions favoured by Erasmus. If the rewards of Erasmus were to be reaped, changes had to be made at national level. Though they were not directly mandated by Community legislation they were a direct consequence of it. Furthermore, the ECTS system required participating universities to recognise the periods of study and course units of all other participating universities. Such recognition, without any prior harmonisation of courses, directly opposed the traditional autonomy of national educational systems and their institutions. In a number of Member States, national law exercises complete control over courses of study. Thus in Belgium, traditional university degrees in medecine, pharmacy, dentistry, law, engineering etc. were previously issued after successful completion of a legally defined programme of education. Such national legislation, which excluded the possibility of concluding agreements with other universities recognising study periods and crediting these periods as part of the overall degree award, had to be altered if national universities wished to participate in Erasmus. Although the Member States continue to be responsible for the general funding of higher education, they themselves increasingly point to the responsibilities of the Community for funding activities with a European dimension. They have also claimed that the funding of EC programmes is inadequate and have suggested the possibility of drawing on structural funds.[126] If the European dimension of education (language training, mobility etc.) becomes more and more costly, arguments based on the principle of subsidiarity may support rather than detract from increased Community competence and activity in the field of education. Thus, although Articles 126 and 127 may be expressions of subsidiarity, it may, nevertheless, turn out that supplementary and supportive measures are best and most effectively taken at Community level. As such, incentive measures would be an

---

after 1992, op. cit. note 5 at p.3: "Community resources and support available through these programmes [Erasmus, Lingua, Comett, Esprit] are, and will, constitute a powerful incentive for universities to engage in new types of activities. The actual amount of the resources is less important than their political impact and dimension."

[125]See "Erasmus est passé par Maastricht", *Le Monde*, 7 January 1992, which explains that the division of funds from Brussels between Member States "se fait en fonction de la population étudiante de chacun et non du nombre des candidatures". Thus, it ranges from ECU 71 per month for students from Ireland, to ECU 488 for students from Italy. See Erasmus, Student Support Systems in the EC Member States 1987–88, 8. Could this be unlawful discrimination?

[126]Commission (Education, Training, Youth), *The Outlook for Higher Education in the EC: Responses to the Memorandum*, Studies no.2, at p.37.

expression of the positive obligations on Member States which also flow from sub-sidiarity. If incentive measures, of which Socrates is one, are viewed from this per-spective, it is arguable that they may include more and stronger measures than if subsidiarity were external to Articles 126 and 127.[127]

Socrates

The Socrates programme was adopted in April 1995 to "contribute to the develop-ment of quality education and training and the creation of an open European area for cooperation in education" (Article 1).[128] The programme attempts to rationalise and improve the Community's previous action in the field of vocational training and to adopt new instruments on the basis of its new competence in the field of education in Article 126. It is comprised of the following areas of action: higher education (Erasmus); school education (Comenius); and horizontal activities re-garding language skills (Lingua), open and distance learning and the exchange of information and experience. Since the scope of Socrates is not limited to general education, it has been adopted on the basis of Articles 126 and 127. Its preamble reiterates the limits placed on Community action by the principle of subsidiarity and Article 3 recalls that the programme will encourage cooperation and support and supplement the action of Member States "while fully respecting their respons-ibility for the content and teaching and the organization of educational systems, and their cultural and linguistic diversity". The programme seeks variously to de-velop the European dimension of education so as to strengthen European citizen-ship, to promote the learning of language, to promote cooperation between educational institutions and to encourage mobility and recognition of diplomas and periods of study etc. The Commission will be assisted by a committee, which will help to implement the detailed "actions" annexed to the Decision.

The chapter of the Socrates programme on higher education addresses the pro-motion of the European dimension in education, student mobility and the financing of Erasmus grants. It develops the previous Erasmus techniques and relies on arrangements like the inter-university cooperation programmes. Chapter 1 of the Socrates programme also confirms the trend identified with respect to the Erasmus programme, the use of Community funds to encourage educational institutions to comply with conditions concluded at Community level. Institutions which permit students to study abroad and recognise that period, who promote the ECTS system, who engage in joint curriculum development, who permit staff to work in an insti-

---

[127]See Besselink, L.F.M., Albers, H.S.J. and Eijsbouts, W.T., "Subsidiarity in Non-Federal Contexts: The Netherlands and the European Union", Dutch Report, 16th FIDE Congress, *Le principe de subsidiarité* (1994) Rome, pp.365–409, at 408.

[128]Decision no.819/95, OJ 1995 L87/10. For the background to the adoption of Socrates see the Commission's original proposal in COM (93) 708; the first opinion of the European Parliament, OJ 1994 C128/479; the common position adopted by the Council, OJ 1994 C244/51; the decision of the European Parliament, OJ 1994 C323/50; COM (94) 502 final; the opinion of the ECOSOC, OJ 1994 C195/29; and the opinion of the Committee of Regions, OJ 1994 C217/18.

tution abroad and who set up intensive short-term course will be in a favourable position to receive financial assistance.[129] Action 1 also refers to Community support and Community assistance, but it is unclear whether this is synonomous with financial assistance. Action 2.1 sets out the conditions which must be fulfilled to ensure that study-abroad periods benefit students. It also provides that "the Community will continue to develop a system of direct financial aid to students who complete a period of study in another Member State". It devises a formula to determine how Community funds for student mobility will be divided between the Member States. The formula is based on the number of students at university, the number of young people between 18 and 25, the difference in the cost of living between the host Member State and the Member State of origin and the cost of travel.[130] Member States are obliged to continue to make grants or loans available at national level available to Erasmus students. The Erasmus section of Socrates is entitled to over 55 per cent of the available funds. The school education chapter aims to establish multilateral school partnerships as part of a European education project. The latter also involves language training, projects of European interest, mobility of pupils, exchange of material and information (Action 1.1). Priority for financial aid will also be given, in this field, to projects promoting the European dimension in the manner outlined in Action 1.2 of Chapter II. In addition the Comenius section of Socrates addresses the education of migrant workers children and the children of occupational travellers and gypsies (Action 2) and seeks to update and improve the skills of teaching staff (Action 3). Chapter III establishes horizontal measures for language teaching, open and distance learning and the exchange of information and experience. The Socrates programme is accompanied by an updated Youth for Europe III programme and an action programme for the implementation of an EC vocational training policy,[131] otherwise known as Leonardo da Vinci, which is based on Article 127. It is estimated that 150,000 students and 22,000 university institutions will be involved in the Socrates programme.[132]

5.6. Vocational Training and Education Following the Treaty on European Union

In Title VIII and IX of the Union Treaty Article 128 EEC has been replaced by Articles 126, 127 and 128 on education, vocational training and youth and culture, respectively. Article 126 provides that "the Community shall contribute to the development of quality education by encouraging cooperation between Member States and, if necessary, by supporting and supplementing their action, while fully respecting the responsibility of the Member States for the content of teaching and

---

[129]Action 1.A. on inter-university cooperation.
[130]Action 2.2(b).
[131]Decision 94/819, OJ 1994 L340/8.
[132]*Agence Europe* no.6432, 3 March 1995.

the organisation of education systems and their cultural and linguistic diversity". The objectives of the provisions are to develop the European dimension in education (particularly through teaching and the dissemination of language), encourage mobility, (by encouraging academic recognition of diplomas and periods of study), to promote cooperation between Member States, to develop exchanges of information and expertise on issues common to education systems and to encourage the development of youth exchanges. Article 126 does not aim to establish a common educational policy. However, it does represent a step forward since it is an independent legal basis which is not limited to higher education. "Incentive measures" may be adopted to contribute to the achievement of the objectives in Article 126, but they do not include harmonisation of the laws and regulations of the Member States. Measures adopted pursuant to Article 126 will be adopted according to the codecision procedure in Article 189(b). The adoption of the Socrates programme demonstrated how long-winded this procedure can be.

Incentive measures do not figure in the list of measures which Community institutions may adopt in Article 189. Lenaerts claims that incentive measures, unlike the recommendations also available under Article 126(4), are binding.[133] The purpose of incentive measures under Article 126 is to encourage cooperation between Member States in the fields covered. There is some debate about whether the list in Article 126 is exhaustive. The European Parliament considers that it is not and that the list is simply an example of the measures which the Council can adopt:

> [The European Parliament] considers that the fields of action referred to in Articles 126 and 127 are not exhaustive, but are rather in the nature of examples and that the new treaty forms a solid basis, while respecting the areas of responsibility of the Member States and/or regions, for action in the areas of responsibility of the Member States and/or regions, for action in the areas referred to and in other areas in which action proves necessary, to bring about the necessary cohesion between measures to be taken in the field of education and training by the Community and in the political sphere by the Member States.[134]

It is certainly arguable that incentive measures and recommendations are not exhaustive of the type of Community action permissible on the basis of Article 126, since they are adopted to *contribute* to these objectives.[135] Recommendations, on the other hand, are to be adopted by a qualified majority acting on a proposal from the Commission.

It is debatable, however, whether these measures can be regarded as sources of Community *law*.[136] Unlike Regulations, Directives and Decisions, Article 189 does

---

[133]Lenaerts, op. cit. note 109, at 31. See also Bekemans, L. and Balodimos, A., "Le traité de Maastricht et l'éducation, la formation professionelle et la culture", *Revue du Marché Unique Européen* (1993) 99–141.

[134]Resolution A3-0139/92, 15 May 1992 on education and training policy in the run-up to 1993, OJ 1992 C150/366, at 368.

[135]Article 126(4), emphasis added. For an alternative view, see Bekemans and Balodimos, op. cit. note 133, at 109.

[136]See generally, Lasok, D. and Bridge J.W., *Law and Institutions of the EC*, 5th edn. (1991) Oxford, Butterworths, at pp.153 *et seq.*

not confer binding force on Recommendations. Their role is said to be "persuasive and constructive in the formulation and execution of the policies of the Community," and they are regarded as auxiliary elements of the law-making process.[137] In *Grimaldi* v. *Fonds des Maladies Professionelles* the Court stated that recommendations are not binding, are generally adopted when the Community institutions do not have power to adopt binding measures, or when they consider that it is not appropriate to adopt more mandatory rules and they cannot enjoy direct effect.[138] Nevertheless, it also held that national courts are bound to take them into consideration in order to decide disputes submitted to them, particularly when they assist in the interpretation of national measures, or where they are designed to supplement binding Community provisions. Community "soft law" may not have binding effect, but it may clearly influence Community and national practice.[139] Article 128 EEC previously provided for the "lay[ing] down of general principles for implementing a common vocational training policy". With reference to that provision, the Court in *Erasmus* held that "the Council is entitled to adopt legislative measures providing for Community action in the sphere of vocational training and imposing obligations of cooperation on the Member States". Article 126 is far more specific with respect to permissible action in the field of education. It permits the Community to adopt supplementary and incentive measures to encourage Member States to act in a certain manner, but according to Lenaerts, it would appear that obligations of cooperation are also in line with this provision. The difference with the former Article 128 EEC is that Article 126(1) may be used to specify limits to the extent of those obligations. An examination of the provisions of the Socrates programme would seem to support Lenaerts's argument with respect to obligations of cooperation.

Article 127, in contrast with Article 126, refers to the implementation of a vocational training *policy* which shall support and supplement the action of the Member States, while fully respecting Member States' responsibility for the content and organisation of vocational training. Article 127 does not introduce a new Community competence, but simply reorganises an existing one, while specifying certain limits to Community action. Its power of action in this sphere is wider than in the fields of education and culture. Measures adopted to implement the Community's vocational training policy also exclude any harmonisation of the laws and regulations of Member States (Article 127(4)). Recommendations are not specifically mentioned. The provisions of Article 127 appear to be more geared to training in an industrial and employment context. It aims, therefore, to facilitate industrial changes, the integration and reintegration into the labour market and cooperation on training between educational establishments and firms. Development of the Community's

---

[137]See Soldatos, P. and Vandersanden, G., "La recommandation, source indirecte du rapprochement", in De Ripainsel-Landy, D. *et al.*, *Les instruments du rapprochement des legislations dans la CE* (1976) at pp.95 *et seq.*

[138]Case C-322/88 [1990] ECR I-4402.

[139]Snyder, F., "The Effectiveness of European Community Law: Institutions, Processes, Tools and Techniques", 56 *Modern Law Review* (1992) 19–54, at 32.

vocational training policy is thus an essential aspect of economic and social cohesion and the growth of the competitiveness of European industry.

Are the powers of action under the new articles narrower or wider than the "general principles" under the former Article 128 EEC which were widely defined in the *Erasmus* case? The jurisprudence of the Court of Justice has progressivly evolved in this sphere. It would therefore be surprising if this codification does away with the Court's concerted efforts to build up a wide definition of the scope and powers of the Community under Article 128 EEC. Nevertheless, the provisions specifically recognise the Member States' continued competence with respect to the content and organisation of education and underlines the limitations on the powers of the Community which were sometimes, but not always, voiced by the Court of Justice. The legislative powers permitted by the Union Treaty are weak since the Community can only resort to recommendations and incentive measures and harmonisation is expressly excluded. The scope of incentive measures and recommendations could be interpreted in conjunction with strong Community functional objectives in the field of free movement and citizenship, however, it remains to be seen whether the "subsidiarity *specialis*" in these Articles would preclude such interpretations. It is also possible that the Court will embark on a similar voyage of expansive teleological interpretation as it did before when confronted with the relatively weak text of Article 128 EEC. Thus, the Community "soft law" permitted by Articles 126 and 127 could be preparatory steps for future and more positive Community legislative action.[140] Any reluctance to teleologically expand the provisions of the Union Treaty on the part of the Court will be due to the fact that the Union Treaty reflects the political negotiations of Member States and their fears of the threat which Community action in education poses. The analysis of the effects of the Community's present approach in the field of education demonstrate that some of these fears are not unfounded. The principle of subsidiarity is, therefore, of considerable importance in terms of the development of Community action in education and vocational training and it appears that Germany, in particular, might seek to contain the Community's powers in the field of education at the forthcoming intergovernmental conference.[141]

5.7. National Identity, Citizenship and Community Citizenship

National citizenship is regarded as a legal relationship between the state and the individual, which can entail a number of civil and political, as well as economic, social and even fundamental, rights (and duties). Increased international migration and the conclusion of a number of international agreements such as the European Convention of Human Rights, or the International Covenant of Civil and Political Rights, have reduced the paramountcy of state membership as the criterion for en-

---

[140]See Van Craeyenest, F., "La nature juridique des résolutions sur la co- operation en matière d'éducation", in De Witte, op. cit. note 15, pp.127–133, at p.127.
[141]See *Agence Europe* no.6438, 11 March 1995, at p.5.

titlement to rights. However, citizenship is still not an irrelevant consideration. In the specific context of education, it may be relevant to the extent that (i) some states restrict the social and economic advantages attached to education and which facilitate its enjoyment to their own citizens and (ii) due to the fact that education still serves as a vehicle for the transmission of aspects of national identity, culture, history and, in some cases, ideologies or policies which are peculiar to that state, or considered representative by it.[142] The right to education is guaranteed in various forms in a number of Member States. It is, however, normally available to all within the jurisdiction. Thus, Article 42 of the Irish Constitution recognises the educational rights of parents not citizens and the state's duty to educate children not junior citizens. Nevertheless, the brief survey in Section 5.4.2 of national student support systems underlines the continuing relevance of state membership.[143] Insistence on the possession of medical insurance and sufficient resources in the three Directives on residence also underline the general unwillingness of Member States to admit non-nationals to their social welfare benefits. With respect to the second quality, that of socialising and educating a state's citizens in terms of a particular philosophy, ideology or culture, education has been regarded as an imperative right without which the exercise of other citizenship rights is rendered more difficult, if not impossible.[144] Indeed, Chapter 4 noted, with reference to Member States' traditional control of entry and residence, closure was regarded as a means to preserve national identity and culture. Education has generally been considered as one of the primary means by which state values and culture can be preserved and transmitted. Indeed, the 'Socrates' programme has identified the importance of more European-oriented education for the future of European citizenship.

An extensive assertion of competence by the Community in the field of education is feared by many precisely because of its potential influence on national identity and culture. The Community's activities in cultural fields have included financial support, tax relief for cultural foundations and conservation projects, the general application of a specific social security scheme for self-employed cultural workers, assistance from the European Social Fund and European Regional Development Fund, awards of Community scholarships and grants etc.[145]

[142]See Lonbay, J., *Fundamental Rights as Citizenship Rights: Towards Fundamental Rights for Community Citizens*, Federal Trust Working Group on European Citizenship, London, 4–6 October 1990.

[143]See also Plant, R., "Social Rights and the Reconstruction of Welfare", in Andrews, G., *Citizenship* (1991) London, Lawrence and Wishart, at p.56, who states in general that: "citizenship as a status confers some rights to resources such as income, health care, social security and education".

[144]See Bendix, R., *Nation Building and Citizenship: Studies of Our Changing Social Order* (1977) Berkeley, University of California Press; and Gellner, E., *Thought and Change*, cited in Hammar, T., *Democracy and the Nation State: Aliens, Denizens and Citizens in a World of International Migration* (1990) Ethnic Relations Series, Aldershot, Avebury, at p.63, to the effect that modern nations are shaped in schools where national languages and cultures are taught and developed. In Gellner's view, it is not nationalism that brings about homogeneous culture, but the other way round.

[145]See Rasmussen, H., "Structures and Dimensions of EC Cultural Policy. L'Europe des bonnes volontés culturelles", in Ress, E. and Schwarze, J. (eds.), *The Dynamics of European Community Law* (1987) Baden-Baden, Nomos, pp.185, at pp.186–187; see also the solemn declaration by the Heads of State and Governments in Stuttgart in 1983, Bull. EC. 6/83, para.3.3, at 28.

Surprisingly, despite the extensive case law outlined in Section 5.3, the Court has demonstrated awareness of the need to protect national educational and cultural peculiarities in the face of the functional dynamics and objectives of free movement. In Ireland, for example, the government relies on the national system of education as a means to promote and preserve the Irish language and as a means to express national identity and culture. This policy has been held by the Court of Justice to be compatible with the Treaty and Article 3(1) Regulation 1612/68, with respect to the imposition of a language requirement for teachers, in the *Groener* case. The Court held that "The EEC Treaty does not prohibit the adoption of a policy for the protection and promotion of a language of a Member State ... The importance of education for the implementation of such a policy must be recognised."[146] The Advocate General regarded the protection of national language as striking at the very heart of cultural identity and regarded the problem with which the Court of Justice was faced as one of "drawing a line between the powers of the Community and those of the Member States and of considering whether or not a policy of preserving and fostering a language may be pursued, having regard to the requirements of Community law".[147] The decision also demonstrates Community recognition of the importance of national education systems and policies for national identity and membership: "The importance of education for the implementation of such a policy [a policy on national languages] must be recognised. Teachers have an essential role to play, not only through the teaching which they provide but also by their participation in the daily life of the school and the privileged relationship which they have with their pupils." The Court's decision recognised the continued importance of national authorities and the importance which they wish to attribute to cultural heritage. In this respect *Groener* could be regarded as an early judicial expression of the principle of subsidiarity which is now the subject of considerable debate.

5.7.1. Education and the Principle of Subsidiarity

Article F(1) of the Union Treaty provides that "The Union shall respect the national identities of its Member States". The new Article 128 also requires the Community to respect national and regional diversity in its aims to bring a common cultural heritage to the fore. Action in the field of culture and education is limited to cooperation between Member States and the role of the Community is to support and supplement that action by improving the knowledge and dissemination of the culture and history of Europe, the conservation and protection of European cultural heritage, cultural exchanges of a non-commercial nature and artistic and

---

[146]Case C-379/87, Groener [1989] ECR 3967, at paras.19 and 20. See also Article 13(3) of the International Covenant on Economic, Social and Cultural Rights, 1966, which guarantees the state's role in regulating the right to education in order to "ensure such minimum educational standards as may be laid down or approved by the state".

[147]Ibid., at 3982.

literary creation. The Community is to take cultural aspects into account in the action it takes under the new Article 128. Thus, the Commission has described the measures in culture and education as complementary, in the sense that both are to support national measures.[148]

Article 3(b) of the Union Treaty provides that "in areas which do not fall within its exclusive competence, the Community shall take action, in accordance with the principle of subsidiarity, only if and in so far as the objectives of the proposed action cannot be sufficiently achieved by Member States and can therefore, by reason of the scale or effects of the proposed action be better achieved by the Community" (para.2). Furthermore, "any action by the Community shall not go beyond what is necessary to achieve the objectives of this Treaty."[149] Article 3(b) does not determine what competences are attributed to the Community, but the manner in which non-exclusive competences are exercised. With respect to non-exclusive competences, the principle of subsidiarity requires the Community to perform only those tasks which cannot be performed more effectively at national level. It can alternatively enable the Community to assert its competence to take action with respect to an area which, for example, by virtue of its "scale or effects" (Article 3(b) para.2) can be better achieved by the Community. The origins, justiciability and usefulness of the principle of subsidiarity are not of specific concern here. This section discusses the relationship between Article 3(b) and the Community's incremental and expansive approach to date in the field of education and its relevance with respect to the new provisions on education in the Union Treaty.[150]

In its communication on subsidiarity, the Commission stated that the Treaty gave the institutions a great deal of latitude with respect to vocational training, but that the chosen method of implementing Community competence had been supportive measures such as the Erasmus programme.[151] This assessment underestimates the effect of Erasmus on national educational systems. The issue of subsidiarity had arisen some years ago in the context of the adoption of the Lingua programme, which included a proposal to include foreign language training in the national curricula, as well as determination at Community level of the scope of certain educational exchanges. The British government and German *Länder* argued against Lingua being a Community action programme and the part of the programme dealing with school exchanges was eventually deleted and Member States

---

[148]See Communication of the Commission to the Council and the European Parliament on the Principle of Subsidiarity, *Agence Europe* nos. 1804/1805, 30 October 1992, at 10.

[149]One of the recitals of the Union Treaty provides that "resolved to continue the process of creating an ever closer union among the peoples of Europe, in which the decisions are taken as closely as possible to the citizen in accordance with the principle of subsidiarity".

[150]For a general discussion of subsidiarity see Toth, op. cit. note 34; Cass, D.Z., "The Word that Saves Maastricht? The Principle of Subsidiarity and the Division of Powers within the European Community", 29 *CMLRev* (1992) 1107–1136; Sir Leon Brittan, *Subsidiarity in the Constitution of the EC*, Robert Schumann Lecture, European University Institute, 11 June 1992, Florence; and Constantinesco, V., "Who's Afraid of Subsidiarity?", 11 *YEL* (1991) 33–55.

[151]See Communication of the Commission to the Council and European Parliament on the principle of subsidiarity in *Agence Europe* nos. 1804/05, 30 October 1992 at 10 of the annex.

were left to determine how to integrate foreign languages into their national curricula.[152] Similarly, although the Council affirmed the existence of Community educational policy in 1989, Community action was nevertheless to respect cultural and
linguistic diversity and "must respect the fundamental powers of the Member
States in matters of general educational policy".[153]

The new provisions on education and vocational training contained in the Union
Treaty are clearly wary of excessive legislative intervention by the Community in
this field. Harmonisation of national legislation is expressly excluded and
Community action in the form of recommendations is merely intended to supplement the action of the Member States. Will the introduction of Article 3(b) and the
explicit enforcement of the principle of subsidiarity in the Union Treaty dramat-
ically alter the actions of the Court of Justice and Commission, in particular, with
regard to vocational training and education? Reference to the *Grimaldi* decision
suggests that although the Community may be limited to recommendations and cooperative action following the Union Treaty, national courts will still be required
to interpret national law in accordance with the underlying objectives which these
recommendations embody. It is not clear whether this principle is justiciable[154]
and, therefore, the determination of which level of authority is more suitable to
deal with a specific problem may ultimately depend on a political decision. If one
assumes that the completion of the internal market and, consequently, the effective
operation of the four freedoms is one of the exclusive competences of the
Community, activity in the field of vocational training, mutual recognition of diplomas and even the free movement of students on the basis of Article 6, could all be
linked in some way to the furtherance and completion of the internal market and,
therefore be regarded as constituent parts of an exclusive competence. As Toth
points out, no one has ever suggested that the completion of the internal market is
not an exclusive competence of the Community.[155] With reference to Articles 126
and 127, he has further argued that although these provisions appear to indicate
that the drafters did not intend to confer exclusive competence on the Community
in these matters, "many of these policies are inextricably linked with the internal
market and also with one another".[156] As such, he claims that Article 100A should
continue to provide for any necessary harmonisation to the extent that these matters relate to the establishment and functioning of the internal market. Shaw also

[152]See Wilke, M. and Wallace, H., *Subsidiarity: Approaches to Power-Sharing in the EC*, RIIA
Discussion Paper no.27, at pp.33–34.

[153]Conclusions of the Council and the Ministers for Education Meeting within Council of 6
November 1989, on cooperation and Community policy in the field of education in the run up to 1993,
OJ 1989 C277/5.

[154]Certainly, the general expression of the principle in Article B of Title I of the Union Treaty is
not justiciable by the Court of Justice by virtue of Article L which provides that "the powers of the
Court of Justice ... shall apply only to the following provisions of this Treaty: (a) provisions amending
the Treaty establishing the EEC with a view to establishing the EC ... (b) the third subparagraph of
Article K.3(2)(c); (c) Articles L to S.

[155]Toth, op. cit. note 34, at 1094.

[156]Ibid., at 1094.

points out that "[I]t remains a moot point ... whether other provisions of the Treaty such as Articles 100, 100a and 235 could be used as a legal basis for harmonization measures should this prove necessary in the future either to facilitate the completion of the internal market or to attain one of the Community's objectives."[157] The establishment of Union citizenship and strengthening the rights and interests of Union citizens is one such objective. In addition, fragmenting policies according to whether they are linked, or not, to the internal market may not be wise. Indeed, cultural considerations are to be taken into account throughout the Community's decision-making processes,[158] which would suggest that policies in education and vocational training should not be divided up according to whether they come within the internal market or not.

This chapter has already recalled the far-reaching effects which the objectives of the Community have often had when read in conjunction with its implied powers. Toth argues that "Measures to be adopted in the future relating to matters already legislated upon in the past and thus brought within exclusive Community competence cannot be subject to the principle of subsidiarity, even if they fall within one of the 'new policy areas'." Article B supports this reasoning since it specifically sets out the objective of "maintain[ing] in full the *acquis communautaire* and build[ing] on it".[159] It is undeniable that the new provisions are more restrictively framed, but in the light of this objective of maintaining the *acquis*, it seems unlikely that the jurisprudence built up on the basis of the general principles in the former Article 128 EEC will be made redundant. Furthermore, the potential practical and financial consequences of the free movement of students, the increasingly vibrant nature of Community education programmes and the scale or more likely the effect of Community action so far, may in fact necessitate a more intimate involvement by the Community in future, whether it be by means of Member State and Community cooperation or powerful judicial persuasion following further expansive decisions by the Court of Justice.[160] A definitive answer to the question of the relationship between education and vocational training in the Union Treaty and the principle of subsidiarity is impossible at this stage. In the words of one commentator: "The concept of subsidiarity is not a hard and fast rule in constitutional law, as comparative studies have demonstrated. It is like quick sand and allows only for short respite."[161] This uncertainty about the future of subsidiarity in

---

[157]See also Shaw, op. cit. note 121, at p.309.

[158]Article 128(4) provides that "the Community shall take cultural aspects into account in its actions under other provisions of this Treaty".

[159]Indeed Article B envisages building on the existing *acquis communautaire* "with a view to considering ... to what extent the policies and forms of cooperation introduced by this Treaty may need to be revised with the aim of ensuring the effectiveness of the mechanisms and the institutions of the Community". See also Curtin, D., "The Constitutional Structure of the Union: A Europe of Bits and Pieces", 30 *CMLRev* (1990) 17–69, at 19. See also the Presidency Conclusions, Edinburgh European Council, 11–12 December 1992, pt.A Annex 1, Basic Principles, *Agence Europe* 13–14 December 1992.

[160]See Section 5.5.

[161]See the editorial, "Subsidiarity: Backing the Right Horse?", 30 *CMLRev* (1993) 241–245, at 244.

the field of education and vocational training also emerged in the responses to the Commission's memorandum on education. Some Member States and educational institutions regarded it as a guarantee of national identity and independence and an obstacle to over-formal harmonisation. However, others feared that an overly strict interpretation of the principle of subsidiarity might impede the implementation of policies and programmes adopted at Community level and might restrict desirable European innovations.[162] Furthermore, subsidiarity is not the only Community principle of relevance here. Unmitigated application of the principles underlying the four freedoms might work against poorer regions unless they are counterbalanced by Community policies which provide economic activity in those regions, since the four freedoms encourage people to immigrate.

5.8. Conclusions

The purpose of this chapter is to assess the scope of the Community's competence and the principle of equal treatment in the field of education. It examines the Court's incremental but active assessment of the scope of Community policy in the sphere of vocational training and its application of equal treatment to the rights of migrating students, Community workers and their families. The *Gravier* decision, for example, required a dramatic change in the organisation and financing of education in some Member States. Nevertheless, the Court has never seriously addressed these consequences in detail, nor have the Community institutions generally sought to deepen their understanding of the type of symbiosis which should have emerged in the Community/Member State relationship *vis-à-vis* education.

The Community claims to exercise limited competence as regards education, excluding matters concerning the organisation, policy making and financing of education. In practice, however, its judgments have a considerable impact on these matters. Attempts by national governments to organise education in a certain manner (*Commission* v. *Belgium*), or to reduce the financial effects of innovative Community decisions (*Gravier*) have generally been rejected by the Court of Justice (*Barra*). However, differences between Member States concerning public expenditure as percentages of the total national or educational budget reflect national financial and social perspectives on higher education and explains the Member States' inability and unwillingness, in certain situations, to financially endorse the Community's perspectives on free movement and education. It remains to be seen how long maintenance grants will be explicitly excluded from the scope of Community law and Article 6. The effects of *Gravier* are not equally felt in all Member States and a mechanical downward harmonising of educational systems could be feared in the absence of better Community legislative coordination, with

---

[162]See Commission (Education, Training, Youth), *The Outlook for Higher Education in the EC: Responses to the Memorandum*, Studies no.2, at p.10.

respect to which the Community institutions and Member States deny that the Community is competent. The Court of Justice has actively developed the Community's competences in this area. However, if it is concluded that greater Community participation in education is a desirable or necessary consequence of the Community's action to date, or of the situation in Member States, Community legislative action may be preferable. Subsidiarity, in such circumstances, may not prove to be the ally of all Member States, since some have demonstrated support for greater Community involvement in this field. However, if student mobility in the Community is to increase, equity between Member States must be done and be seen to be done. In the words of one author: "in its efforts to prevent discrimination against students, the Court has created a system which discriminates against Member States ... These problems illustrate the danger of policy-making by judicial decision. It would have been better for the Court of Justice to leave the Council to adopt a policy on migrant students. Such a policy would no doubt take time to develop, but the end result would probably have been preferable from the educational point of view."[163]

The Community institutions have, until now, endorsed half-baked solutions in the field of education. Thus, equal treatment operates selectively with respect to certain conditions of access only and they unconvincingly deny competence in certain respects, in particular, with regard to the organisation and financing of education. Free movement of students might be more suitably promoted by requiring Member States to finance the true economic cost of the education which their nationals receive in other Member States. The European Parliament proposed a similar solution with respect to maintenance expenses of students in the context of Directive 90/366. It proposed that if students did become a burden on the host Member State that the costs were to be met by the student's Member State of origin.[164] Host Member States would not therefore have to face the inequitable unbalancing of their national education systems by other Member State nationals. A disadvantage of this solution is that Member States may consequently be required to finance their own migrating students beyond what they normally do with respect to students who do not migrate. A solution could no doubt be reached with respect to such discrimination by establishing loans rather than grants. Such a system of payment by the Member State of origin may be preferable to the *a priori* exclusion of Member State nationals from the education systems of other Member States if they are unable to maintain themselves. This solution does preserve a nationality criterion contrary to the general practice of Community law and it may be difficult to determine the Member State of origin. Is it the Member State of nationality or last residence? It also interferes with the policy choices of some Member States not to export educational benefits. However, this solution might iron out the mobility imbalances which have emerged so far and the overall effect on "importing"

---

[163]See Green *et al.*, op. cit. note 70, at pp.192–193.
[164]See Article 3 of the draft Directive, OJ 1990 C15/71, at 80.

Member States in the field of education and on the quality of education which they can afford to offer is likely to be far less detrimental than the current haphazard approach.

Admittedly, this approach also undermines the social dimension of citizenship which was discussed in Chapter 4 and which would, if extensively interpreted, entail some degree of social solidarity between Community citizens. However, the relationship between national systems of education and Community law is clearly controversial at present. This controversial relationship underlines some of the intractable and difficult questions posed by the creation of a supranational concept of citizenship. It vividly depicts the issues of national versus Community identity and the protection of social rights at national level compared to the Community's almost total impotence to positively legislate in this respect. One of the solutions in the area of the free movement of students which was mentioned above – Member States paying for the cost of the education of their migrating students – may have the dual effect of encouraging governments to improve the quality of their educational courses as elements of educational "competition" enter the educational market, while protecting the quality of national education by not subjecting it to an open-ended and undetermined influx of foreign students uncatered for in the national organisation and financing of education. Furthermore, it is the pragmatic resolution of a situation whereby, according to the demands of free movement, the Community has a role to play in education, but economic, political and structural factors limit its competence for the moment and its own financial position means it cannot at present foot the bill for a Community-orientated distribution of education benefits.

Chapter 6

Equal Treatment and Political Participation (I)

6.1. Introduction

Electoral rights, namely the right to vote and to stand as a candidate for election, have traditionally been limited to persons enjoying the nationality or citizenship of a particular state. Indeed some writers regard political participation as the essence of citizenship, which they define as "the possession by the person under consideration, of the highest or at least of a certain higher category of political rights and (or) duties".[1] As a result, individuals resident in a state other than their own have generally been in an unfavourable political position compared to nationals of the state of residence. The traditional limitation cum prohibition of non-national political participation stemmed from the close identification, in legal and political thought, of the concept of state closure and the status of citizenship with rights of political participation.

European Community Member States were no exception to this rule regarding the exclusion or limitation of the role of non-nationals in political life. Before the adoption of the Union Treaty, for example, Member States could roughly be divided into three categories according to their attitude to non-national participation in municipal elections: (i) those who extended electoral rights at municipal level to Member State and third country nationals on the basis of residence (Denmark, Ireland, the Netherlands, Sweden and Finland); (ii) those who extended electoral rights to the nationals of states with whom they enjoy a special (historical) relationship (Portugal, United Kingdom); and (iii) those who reserved electoral rights to their own nationals. In order to understand some of the controversy excited by the adoption of Community legislation with respect to electoral rights at local level,

---

[1] See Koessler, M., "'Subject,' 'Citizen,' 'National,' and 'Permanent Allegiance'", 56 *Yale Law Journal* (1946–47) 58–76, at 61.

which will be discussed in detail in Chapter 7, this chapter analyses how some Member States regulated municipal electoral rights prior to the adoption of the citizenship provisions and how they have accommodated Community law obligations in the field of electoral rights since then.

Despite the predominantly economic underpinnings of the Treaty of Rome, Community law did demonstrate, from the start, that it was not totally immune to the issue of civil and political rights. Article 138(3), for example, provided that the Parliament was to draw up proposals for the direct election of the European Parliament in accordance with a uniform procedure in all Member States. Elections by direct universal suffrage were subsequently established in 1976. However, little progress has been made with respect to the formulation and adoption of a uniform electoral procedure and the Community's prolonged failure to adopt any such procedure for elections to the European Parliament. This chapter will discuss the issues surrounding the extension of electoral rights in European Parliament elections to all Member State nationals on the basis of residence and the legal changes which the Union Treaty has instigated in this respect. It will also briefly refer to the Parliament and Council's failure to adopt a uniform electoral procedure.[2] Note, however, that the legislative procedure for the adoption of electoral rights in Article 8(b)(2) differs from that designed for the adoption of a uniform electoral procedure on the basis of Article 138(3). This could be a result of the failure of the Parliament and Council to formulate and adopt a coherent proposal for a uniform electoral procedure. However, this amendment, which gives the Commission the right of legislative initiative with respect to proposals on electoral rights for the European Parliament, could also be interpreted as an attempt to minimise the Parliament's input, although the issue of electoral rights clearly affects its prerogatives.

6.2. Participation in Political Life by Resident Non-nationals

Chapter 1 describes how the parallel development of the nation state and democracy led to an intimate association between political participation and involvement in national sovereignty. Sovereignty was located within the nation, which in turn provided the foundations for a level of ethnic and cultural homogeneity which allowed people to push ahead with democracy. Since aliens were not part of the ethnic or cultural homogeneity of the nation, their political activity was regarded as capable of perverting the *ordre public* of the host state. In other words, if they were

---

[2]The purpose of this part of the book is to analyse the rights which Union citizens enjoy on the basis of the principle of equal treatment. The following part (Chapter 8) goes beyond the principle of equal treatment and examines whether a direct link has been forged between Union citizens and the Union on the basis of Union citizenship and the type of rights which Union citizens enjoy vis-à-vis the Union. Discussion of the adoption of a uniform electoral procedure is more appropriate, therefore, to Chapter 8 and Section 8.3.2 in particular. Nevertheless, since rights to political participation are being discussed in detail in this chapter, the uniform electoral procedure will be discussed herein and its importance for the establisment of a direct link between the Union and its citizens will be reiterated in Chapter 8.

allowed to participate in political life they would have been participating in the for-mulation of the sovereignty of a nation/state to which they did not belong. Consequently, political activity by non-nationals was regarded as a possible ground for their expulsion.[3] Their perceived lack of allegiance to the host state was the basis for the threat to the public order and their exclusion from political activity was justified in terms of the host state preserving its own "basic conception of a political community" to which aliens did not belong.[4] Given the relationship be-tween the exercise of political rights and national sovereignty, the political status of aliens and their rights of political participation were left to be determined by the domestic law of each individual state.[5] The fact that national sovereignty was thought to require social, legal, cultural and political borders reinforced arguments in favour of the political exclusion of non-nationals.[6]

However, the nation state is now a more debatable point of reference and the po-litical exclusion of non-nationals is consequently more difficult to justify. Indeed, the exclusion of long term residents from political life confuses the foundations and rationale behind political participation since it depicts it as an expression of alle-giance and as an aspect of state sovereignty. Political participation could, or should, be regarded, in the alternative, as the exercise of a democratic right by persons who are governed, which in turn legitimises the position and decisions of those govern-ing them. In the context of the European Community, for example, Habermas points out that "an increasing number of measures decided at a supranational level affect more and more citizens over an ever-increasing area of life. Given that the role of citizen has hitherto only been institutionalised at the level of the nation state, cit-izens have no effective means of debating European decisions and influencing deci-sion-making."[7] The Community's democratic deficit is subject to criticism precisely because more and more far-reaching decisions are being made at a certain level of government which those affected cannot debate or influence. This tradition of pe-nalising the political activity of foreigners gave way, in time, to a more liberal ap-proach in some European countries but, in general, political activity by foreigners has been regarded suspiciously. In France, for example, trade union activists could be expelled for not respecting political neutrality until 1981. Non-Community na-tionals are still required to observe political neutrality.[8]

    [3]See generally Evans, A.C., "The Political Status of Aliens in International, Municipal and European Community Law", 30 ICLQ (1981) 20–41.
    [4]*Dunn* v. *Blumstein* 405 US 330 (1972) and *Sugarman* v. *Dougal* 413 US 634 (1973); see also the comparative reports in Frowein, J.A. and Stein, T. (eds.), *The Legal Position of Aliens in National and International Law* (1987) Max Planck Institute, Springer Verlag, Part 2, at pp.2016 and 2017.
    [5]See Miller, M.J., *Foreign Workers in Western Europe: An Emerging Political Force* (1981) New York, Praeger, at p.143.
    [6]See Wihtol de Wenden, C., *Citoyenneté, Nationalité et Immigration* (1987) Paris, Arcantère, at p.25; and Hammar, T., *Democracy and the Nation State*, Research in Ethnic Relations Series (1990) Aldershot, Avebury, at p.57.
    [7]See Habermas, J., "Citizenship and National Identity: Some Reflections on the Future of Europe", 12 *Praxis International* (1992) 1–19, at 9.
    [8]See Baldwin-Edwards, M., "The Socio-Political Rights of Migrant Workers in the EC", in Room, G. (ed.), *Towards a European Welfare State* (1991) Bristol, SAUS Publications, pp.189–234, at p.215.

Increased international protection of human rights and the emergence of international conventions which specifically address the position of aliens have done little to alter their exclusion from political life. Citizenship or nationality have generally survived as the necessary preconditions, if not the essential preconditions, for the enjoyment of political rights.[9] Thus, although Article 16 of the European Convention of Human Rights does not prevent Contracting States from admitting non-nationals to the political arena, it does permit them a discretion to withhold the level of protection secured for the other guarantees of rights and freedoms in the Convention when it comes to political rights.[10] Article 21 of the Universal Declaration of Human Rights states that "everyone has the right to take part in the Government of his country, directly or through freely chosen representatives".[11] The text of the Declaration is not binding, but the resolutions of the General Assembly reflect the opinions of the different participating governments and Article 21 can be regarded as an authoritative interpretation of the principles of the Charter. Article 21 is of limited use, however, since it refers to rights to vote and to stand for election in one's "country". Article 25 of the International Covenant on Civil and Political Rights also guarantees every citizen the right and opportunity "to vote and to be elected at genuine periodic elections which shall be by universal and equal suffrage and shall be held by secret ballot, guaranteeing the free expression of the will of the electors". However, this provision is also limited to citizens.[12]

The implicit and explicit restrictions contained in other international conventions also support the conclusion that, in general, non-nationals have not been allowed or encouraged to integrate into the political climate in which they are resident. Thus, the Geneva Convention on the Status of Refugees contains no provision on political rights. However, refugees are obliged to comply with national law and, in particular, to maintain public order. Political rights do not appear in the International Labour Conventions either. The 1948 Declaration on the Universal Rights of Man recognises a right to take part in public affairs in Article 21, but this right is only guaranteed for nationals. Despite the fact that states are required to "facilitate" the entry and residence of nationals of other Contracting Parties in Articles 1 and 2 of the European Convention on Establishment,[13] Article 3 permits expulsion on grounds of an offence against *ordre public*. Protocol III(a) states that this includes expulsion for "political reasons". Article 5(c) of the International Convention on the Elimination of all Forms of Racial Discrimination requires that all persons are treated equally as regards participa-

---

[9]See generally Rosberg, G., "Aliens and Equal Protection: Why Not the Right to Vote?", 75 *Michigan Law Review* (1977) 1092–1136.

[10]Article 16 provides: "Nothing in Articles 10,11 and 14 shall be regarded as preventing the High Contracting Parties from imposing restrictions on the political activity of aliens."

[11]UN General Assembly, Resolution 217(111).

[12]See Steiner, H.J., "Political Participation as a Human Right", 1 *Harvards Human Rights Yearbook* (1988) 77–134.

[13]ETS 19.

tion in elections. However, Article 1(2) of the Convention provides that its terms are not applicable to distinctions or exclusions made by a state party between citizens and non-citizens.[14]

6.3. Early Community Law and Rights of Political Participation

The provisions on the free movement of persons introduced by the Treaty of Rome did little initially to alter this traditional perception of the restricted political rights of migrant workers or resident nationals from other Member States. In *Van Duyn* v. *Home Office*, for example, the plaintiff was refused admission to the United Kingdom on the ground that her association with the Church of Scientology was considered contrary to public policy.[15] The Court held that reliance on the public policy proviso was permissible and pointed out that Article 48(3) was a derogation from a fundamental principle of Community Law and that, as such, it had to be interpreted strictly. Its scope was not to be determined unilaterally by each Member State. However, it further held that "the particular circumstances justifying recourse to the concept of public policy may vary from one country to another, and it is therefore necessary in this matter to allow the competent national authorities an area of discretion within the limits imposed by the Treaty".[16] *Van Duyn* gave rise to the wide proposition that Member States could rely on public policy, although the activity in question, when attributable to its own nationals, would not have given rise to repressive measures.

The Court softened the effects of this decision in *Rutili* v. *Minister of the Interior*.[17] It reiterated the need for the concept of public policy as a derogation from free movement and the principle of equal treatment, to be interpreted strictly, so that its scope could not be determined unilaterally by each Member State. However, it also held that the conduct of the individual in question "must constitute a genuine and sufficiently serious threat to public policy" for the exclusion or expulsion order to be justified. Drawing on principles enshrined in the European Convention of Human Rights, the Court held that measures taken under Article 48(3) must, all other conditions being satisfied,[18] be shown to be "necessary in a

---

[14]Cmnd 4108; and generally, Ruzié, D., "Les droits publiques et politiques des travailleurs étrangers", in *Les travailleurs étrangers et le droit international*, Societé Française pour le droit international, Colloque de Clermont-Ferrand 25–27 May 1978, (1979) Paris, A. Pedone; and Ozsunay, E., *The Participation of Aliens in Public Affairs (Political and Associational Life)*, Funchal-Madeira, 17–19 October 1983 (1985) Council of Europe.

[15]Case 41/74 [1974] ECR 1337.

[16]The Court went on to identify Article 3(1) of Directive 64/221, the principle of proportionality and the principle of equal treatment as three possible limitations, but failed to apply any of them in the instant case.

[17]Case 36/75 [1975] ECR 1219.

[18]See Simon, D., "Ordre public et libertés publiques dans les Communautés Européennes: à propos de l'arrêt *Rutili*", 195 RMC (1976) 201–223.

democratic society".[19] To an extent, the Court thus conceded that respect for political freedoms in a democracy is a factor, if not the determining factor, in the event of an exclusion or expulsion order being made. As a result of *Rutili*, Member States may not expel Community nationals on the basis of the public policy proviso for getting involved in political activity. However, it is unclear to what extent *Rutili* prevents Member States from *restricting* the political activity of nationals from other Member States. In Germany, for example, non-nationals cannot found political parties and the number, or rather percentage, of non-nationals in political parties is restricted. Thus, although a national from another Member State may not be expelled from Germany for getting involved in political activity, it is still unclear, even following *Rutili*, to what extent the host Member State can subject that activity to sanctions. *Adoui and Cornuaille* v. *Belgian State* simply requires that sanctions should not be discriminatory.

A recent case before the European Court of Human Rights is of some interest in this respect. In *Dorothée Piermont* v. *France*, a German national was expelled from French Polynesia for taking part in a peaceful demonstration against nuclear testing.[20] The plaintiff relied on her right to freedom of expression under Article 10 of the European Convention on Human Rights, while France sought to justify the expulsion with reference to Article 16 of the Convention. The Commission of Human Rights noted that Article 16 reflected the predominant idea at the time when the Convention was adopted that the political activity of foreigners could and should be restricted. However, it held that the Convention "is a living instrument, which must be read in the light of the living conditions of the world today and the evolution of modern society".[21] Given that the plaintiff had acted in her capacity as a Member of the European Parliament, she could not be considered a "foreigner" within the meaning of Article 16. The Court confirmed the decision of the Commission in April 1995. Although it held that it could not assess the impact of Union citizenship, it reaffirmed that France could not rely on Article 16 in the circumstances of the case.

However, limited civil and political rights emerged in other areas of free movement also. Article 8 Regulation 1612/68, for example, also provides that migrant workers "shall enjoy equality of treatment as regards membership of Trade Unions

---

[19]See also Joined Cases 115 and 116/81 *Adoui and Cornuaille* [1982] ECR 1665. For a discussion of the concept of public policy and its effect on the free movement of persons generally see Woolridge, F., "Free Movement of EEC Nationals: The Limitation Based on Public Policy and Public Security", 2 *ELRev* (1977) 190–207; Seché, J.C., "Free Movement of Workers under Community Law", 14 *CMLRev* (1977) 385–409; Tomuschat, C., "L'ordre public. Menace pour la libre circulation", CDE (1975) 302; Jacobs, F.G., "The Free Movement of Persons Within the EEC", 30 *Current Legal Problems* (1970) 123–139; Dorlodot, M.F.X., "Les exceptions aux règles de la libre circulation des personnes dans le traité CEE", *Administration Publique* (1981) 241–252; Evans, A.C., "Ordre public, Public Policy and UK Immigration Law", 3 *ELRev* (1978) 370–381; and Evans, A.C., "Ordre public in French Immigration Law", *Public Law* (1980) 132–149.
[20]Requêtes no.153773/89 and 15574/89, Rapport de la Commission, adopted on 20 January 1994.
[21]Ibid., at para.59.

and the exercise of rights attaching thereto, including the right to vote".[22] In *ASTI* v. *Chambre des employés privés* the Court of Justice was asked whether national legislation which denied the right to vote to Community workers in elections for the ruling body of a professional association was contrary to Community law and, in particular, Article 8(1) Regulation 1612/68.[23] Affiliation with the association was obligatory and the purpose of the association, which exercised a consultative role at a legislative level, was to defend the interests of the workers. The Court underlined that Article 8(1) was a specific expression of the principle of non-discrimination and that its scope could not be limited according to the specific legal form which the organisation in question took. The exercise of trade union rights pursuant to Article 8(1) does not simply apply to trade union organisations strictly speaking, but includes the participation of workers in those bodies which, although not trade union bodies *per se*, carry out similar functions, such as the defence and representation of the interests of the workers. In the instant case, the right to participate in the election of the ruling body of a professional organisation was considered a trade union right within the meaning of Article 8(1) and there was no need, for that provision to apply, to specifically determine whether that organisation was a trade union or not.[24] Furthermore, the exclusion of non-nationals could not be justified by the fact that some of that organisation's activities might involve exercising a public law function.[25] However, this quasi-political activity by Member State nationals is only protected to the extent that they are involved in the exercise of one of the freedoms provided in the Treaty. Indeed, prior to the adoption of the Union Treaty, Community competence to adopt legislation with respect to electoral rights for Member State nationals on the basis of residence was highly controversial both with respect to municipal and European elections.

6.4. European Parliament Elections

The Treaty of Rome did not explicitly provide for Community competence to regulate electoral rights for European Parliament elections. It did, however, establish a legal basis (Article 138(3)) which allowed the European Parliament and Council to devise and adopt proposals for a uniform electoral procedure. Electoral rights for persons who had availed of their free movement rights were regarded then as an aspect of a uniform electoral procedure. This section discusses European Parliament proposals on the inclusion of electoral rights on the basis of nationality

---

[22]See Evans, A.C., "Development of EC Law Regarding the Trade Union Rights of Migrant Workers", 28 ICLQ (1979) 354–366; and Betten, L., *The Right to Strike in Community Law* (1985) Amsterdam, North Holland.

[23]Case C-213/90 [1991] ECR I-3057.

[24]Ibid., at para.17.

[25]Ibid., at paras.19–20. See also Case C-118/92 *Commission* v. *Luxembourg*, judgment of 18 May 1994, nyr. ECR, with regard to the exercise of trade union rights and participation in the management of bodies governed by public law.

or residence within the scope of its proposals on a uniform electoral procedure. At least some of the difficulties encountered in the formulation of a uniform electoral procedure related to the issue of electoral rights in European Parliament elections for nationals from other Member States. However, such a procedure has not been adopted to date and the difficulties surrounding its adoption will be briefly discussed herein also.

6.4.1. The Failure to Adopt a Uniform Electoral Procedure

Disagreement within the European Parliament and with the Council have made it impossible to date to adopt a uniform procedure for elections to the European Parliament. The European Parliament has produced several reports which have tried to resolve the legal and highly political issues involved in the establishment of a uniform electoral procedure. Disagreement has essentially centred on how uniform the procedure drawn up with respect to Article 138(3) has to be.[26] Do the rules adopted have to be identical in all Member States, for example, or does the establishment of a number of common principles satisfy the requirements of Article 138(3)?[27] The proposals on European Parliament elections in the 1960s, in particular the Dehousse Report, focused on the partial direct election of members of the European Parliament and opted simply for a set of common principles with respect to the other aspects of the electoral procedure. However they rejected the idea that the electoral systems in all Member States had to be identical. The European Parliament has consistently held since then that there is no need for the provisions adopted pursuant to Article 138(3) to be identical in all Member States.

Debate with respect to direct elections and a uniform procedure began in earnest in the 1970s, following the accession of Denmark, Ireland and the United Kingdom. Ironically, the accession of the United Kingdom also made the task of adopting a uniform procedure considerably more difficult, since its first past the post system differs significantly from the electoral systems in other Member States. The Patijn Report, for example, sought to achieve direct elections in the first in-

---

[26]On the issue of a uniform electoral procedure see Sasse, C., et al., *The European Parliament: Towards a Uniform Electoral Procedure for Direct Elections* (1981) OPOCE/EUI; Quintin, Y., "Vers un procedure électorale uniforme. Essai d'explication d'un échec", 267 RMC (1983) 269–272; De Lobkowicz, W., "Une élection européenne ou des élections nationales?" 909 *Revue Politique et Parlementaire* (1984) 85–107; Van den Berghe, G., "Direct Elections in Accordance with a Uniform Procedure", *ELRev* (1979) 331–340; Lodge, J., "The 1984 Euro-Election Tour: The Quest for Uniformity?", 64 *The Parliamentarian* (1983) 204–212; Vedovato, G., "Legge Elettorale Europea Uniforme", 51 *Rivista di studi politici internazionali* (1984) 609–615; Scarpa, R., "Considerazioni in ordine a una procedura uniforme per l'elezione dei deputati all'assemblea del parlamento europeo", 13 *Affari Sociali Internazionali* (1985) 61–67; Ameglio, F., "Una proposta per l'Europa. Una procedura elettorale uniforme per l'elezione del Parlamento Europeo", 14 *Affari Sociali Internazionali* (1986) 65–74; Silvestro, M., "L'élection des membres du Parlement Européen au suffrage universel et direct", 333–342 RMC (1990) 216–218; Millar, D., "A Uniform Electoral Procedure for European Elections", 9 *Electoral Studies* (1990) 37–44; and the House of Lords Select Committee for the European Communities, *Uniform Electoral Procedure for the Elections of Members of the European Parliament*, session 1982–83, 5th report.

[27]See Van den Berghe, op. cit. note 26, at 332.

stance on the basis of national electoral systems, but also proposed that the European Parliament should proceed to introduce a uniform system by stages.[28] However, the primary objective of the Patijn Report was to establish a framework for direct elections, which explains why the potentially more controversial issues with respect to a uniform procedure were dealt with tentatively and with a view to their gradual establishment.

The Parliament and its Committees have varied, however, with respect to the common principles necessary to establish a uniform procedure pursuant to Article 138(3). The 1975 draft convention which followed the Patijn Report, for example, seemed simply to require "the fundamental principles of democratic elections i.e. elections must be equal, free, universal, direct and secret". However, once again, it seems that this restrictive interpretation was favoured in order not to endanger agreement on the 1976 Act on Direct Elections. A broader interpretation of common principles would seem to include standardisation of the system of proportional representation in European Parliament elections. This position was favoured in the Seitlinger Report, which held that "uniform ... means having a common denominator of all the fundamental features of electoral law without necessarily being identical in every respect".[29] However, this standardisation in turn raises the question whether Member States would be obliged to adopt a lists system, for example, or a single transferable vote system. In other words, how far should standardisation of electoral rights go? Whatever is adopted, as Van den Berghe points out, must "take into account national and regional characteristics and interests".[30] This is confirmed by Article F(1) of the common provisions of the TEU which obliges the Union to respect the national identities of its Member States, whose systems of government are founded on the principles of democracy. At the moment, however, there are few parallels between the Member States in the field of electoral procedure[31] and in the absence of a uniform procedure, the other areas where a common approach is desirable – the size and the drawing up of constituencies, admission of parties, eligibility, voting age, nomination of candidates, obligatory or optional vote, electoral thresholds, postal or proxy votes, campaign rules, financing of electoral expenses and access to the media – are left to the discretion of the Member States. However, these are precisely the issues which raise fundamental questions about "easy access to the system, the 'grip' of the political parties and the fairness of the electoral system"[32] and which determine whether the exercise of electoral rights by Union citizens in European Parliament elections enhances their status of citizenship.

In 1979 two different approaches to a uniform procedure were proposed by the Political Affairs Committee of the European Parliament. The Rey proposal was based on two fundamental and minimalist principles – proportional representation

---

[28]See the Draft Convention on Direct Elections adopted on the basis of the report, OJ 1975 C32.
[29]Debs. EP, 10 March 1982.
[30]See Van den Berghe, op. cit. note 26, at 340.
[31]See De Lobkowicz, W., op. cit. note 26, at 101, where he surveys the various national systems.
[32]See Van den Berghe, op. cit. note 26, at 339.

and the right to vote for all Member State nationals. Accompanying measures with a view to establishing a uniform procedure, it was argued, could be introduced by the Parliament over time.[33] The Seitlinger Report, on the other hand, was initially based on the system of election to the German Bundestag, so that some members of the Parliament (30 per cent) would be directly elected by a first past the post system and would represent constituencies, while others would be elected on the basis of proportional representation from national lists. However, this "additional member" system was not supported by all political groups within the Political Affairs Committee and an additional working group had to be set up. Agreement was eventually reached on the basis of a "regional lists" proportional representation system, which formed the basis of the Proposal for a Decision embodying a Draft Act which was adopted by the plenary.[34] Candidates were to be elected by proportional representation from lists in multi-member constitutencies. Seats were to be allocated to each list or combination of lists with reference to the d'Hondt system, which is an averaging process which ensures that the number of votes needed by each party to win a seat is the same.[35] Member States were free to establish the electoral threshold as well as the use of the single transferable vote and the establishment of electoral lists. However, neither a working group set up by the Council to consider the draft act, nor the Council itself, were able to reach agreement on the provisions of the Seitlinger document and a conciliation meeting between the Parliament and Council simply revealed the depth of disagreement in the Council with regard to a uniform procedure.[36] The Council simply promised to pursue attempts to introduce a uniform procedure for the 1989 direct elections and called on Member States to permit Member State nationals to vote either in their Member State of origin or their Member State of residence. The Seitlinger project was beset by two difficulties in particular – the refusal of the United Kingdom to accept a system of proportional representation and French fears that a uniform procedure, in particular a national one district system, would threaten the indivisibility of the French Republic and other principles of constitutional value.[37]

The Seitlinger Report was followed by the Bocklet Report[38] which reiterated the main principles of the Seitlinger Report and which insisted that a uniform electoral procedure did not imply an identical electoral procedure in all Member States. The electoral system was to be proportional, based on constituency lists established at Member State level and seats were to be allocated according to the d'Hondt sys-

---

[33]The proposal was unsuccessful because the majority of the committee members felt that the lack of uniformity left by such an approach might be open to challenge before the Court of Justice.

[34]OJ 1982 C87.

[35]For further details see Millar, op. cit. note 26, at 39. See also the House of Lords Select Committee for the European Communities, op. cit.

[36]Bull. EC. no.4-1983, at pt.2.4.9.

[37]See Alvarez Conde, E. and Arnaldo Alcubilla, E., "De Nuevo Sobre el Procedimiento Electoral Uniforme", 86 *Revista de Estudios Politicos* (1994) 39–69, at 48; and Lodge, J., "The 1984 Euro-Election Tour: The Quest for Uniformity", 64 *The Parliamentarian* (1983) 204–212, at 205 *et seq.*

[38]Doc. A2-1/85, 22 March 1985

tem according to the order of names on each list, unless a Member State had chosen to introduce preferential voting. Member States were free to adopt such a preferential voting system if they wished and to set the electoral thresholds. However, discussion of this report was complicated by the fact that the Committee on Legal Affairs had also produced a report, which differed in some respects and by the fact that the imminent accession of Spain and Portugal meant that some members wished to delay the report anyway.[39] In the event, the report was never discussed by the European Parliament. The fact that members of the European Parliament were fully aware of the opposition of the United Kingdom to the introduction of a system of proportional representation and were unprepared to spend time drafting and discussing a report whose passage through the Parliament would only by blocked by the British members seemed to doom the Bocklet Report. However, as Millar argues, there was still work to be done with regard to further definition of preferential voting systems, the financing of elections, democratic rules to govern the adoption of candidates etc.[40] The Parliament could have pressed ahead with these aspects regardless of British opposition to proportional representation.

The 1991 De Gucht Report and subsequent guidelines suggest that the European Parliament is still tenaciously trying to establish a uniform procedure. However, its success seems to depend not simply on agreement in the Council, but also in the European Parliament itself which, like the electoral systems of the Member States, is still divided along party lines. The De Gucht Report has left the determination of electoral circumscriptions to Member States, allowing them to decide on a single national district or on a system of regions or plurinominal circumscriptions. It also favours a system of proportional representation and establishes rules with respect to electoral campaigns, electoral expenses and the transmission of information and pamphlets at election time. The report achieved a significant degree of consensus in Parliament, which has since adopted a further set of almost identical principles in March 1993, although the electoral rights of Union citizens no longer feature in this proposal.[41] This reaffirmation of the 1991 guidelines soon after the adoption of the Union Treaty was seen by some as an attempt to safeguard Parliament's prerogative to initiate legislation pursuant to Article 138(3). It feared that the adoption of Article 8(b)(2) might indicate that the Commission could preempt the powers of the Parliament in this sphere.[42] One positive aspect introduced by the TEU is the amendment of Article 138(3) so that the Council will lay down the appropriate provisions for a uniform electoral procedure, on the basis of the proposals drawn up by Parliament as before and, in addition, after having obtained its consent.

[39]The regional structure of Spain was expected to cause some difficulties and was the principal reason for the delay.

[40]Millar, op. cit. note 26, at 43.

[41]OJ 1993 C115/121.

[42]OJ 1993 C115/121.

6.4.2. *Electoral Rights as Part of a Uniform Electoral Procedure*

Despite the provision of explicit competence in Article 138(3) it took the European Parliament and the Council sixteen years to agree on the establishment of direct elections to the European Parliament. The Act on Direct Elections adopted in 1976 resembled a Treaty or Convention rather than a piece of Community legislation. This enabled national parliaments to debate the provisions of the Act in depth rather than have to rubberstamp a Council decision.[43] Article 7(2) of the Act provided that until a uniform electoral procedure had been worked out and entered into force, the electoral procedure was to be governed in each Member State in accordance with national provisions.[44] Article 8 of the 1976 Act also provided that "no-one may vote more than once in any election of representatives to the Assembly". In the light of Article 7(2) of the Act and pending agreement between the Member States, the issue of electoral rights remained a matter for individual Member States.[45] The European Parliament limited itself to adopting a resolution recommending that Member State governments and parliaments should ensure that all Community nationals who fulfilled the remaining voting conditions, apart from residence, be allowed to vote in their Member State of origin.[46] The Council subsequently adopted a report on voting *in loco*.

The issue of electoral rights in elections to the European Parliament was tackled in the Seitlinger Report for the Parliament's Legal Affairs committee. It initially proposed that the right to vote be granted in the Member State of origin to persons who had not resided for more than five years in another Member State and in the Member State of residence once five years outside the Member State of origin had been exceeded.[47] The right to stand for election was to be guaranteed in the Member State of nationality alone. This was regarded as having the double advantage of championing universal suffrage while applying the principle of residence only where this was truly justified on the basis of long term residence.[48] Parliament rejected this approach, however, opting for the right to vote in the Member State of nationality while allowing the individual to stand for election in his country of residence after five years.[49] This proposal was clearly flawed. Parliament was treating

---

[43]Council Decision 76/787, OJ 1976 L278/1. See generally, Forman, J., "Direct Elections to the European Parliament", 1 *ELRev* (1976) 35–41.

[44]The 1960 Dehousse Report, OJ 1960 no.834, 2 June 1960 had proposed that Member States grant voting rights to their nationals resident in another Member State. The 1975 Patijn Report (Doc. 368/74) chose to separate the issues of direct election and a uniform procedure; see also the resolution of the European Parliament following the Patijn report, OJ 1975 C32/15.

[45]See Mr Patijn speaking in a debate on Doc. 43/77, at 145. He was in favour of a general appeal to Member States to resolve the problem of disenfranchisement.

[46]OJ 1977 C163/39, 11 June 1977. See also OJ 1988 C262/222, 10 October 1988.

[47]Doc. 1-988/81.

[48]See De Lobkowicz, op. cit. note 26, at 96.

[49]Articles 5 and 6, respectively, OJ 1982 C87/62. The extension of eligibility on the basis of residence entailed constitutional difficulties for some Member States. Article 138(3) para.2 recognises, however, that a uniform electoral procedure can only be adopted once these difficulties have been resolved. See also the submissions of the French Délégation pour les Communautes Europeennes du

the right to vote and the right of eligibility as two independent rights in granting one on the basis of nationality and the other on the basis of residence. Hence, an individual could stand for election in a Member State where he or she was not entitled to vote, which seems absurd.[50] The debate on the report in Council had first proceeded on the basis of voting in the Member State of residence to be transmitted *mutatis mutandis* to the right to stand for election.[51] It soon became clear, however, that Member States were not universally in agreement with the idea of modifying their electoral systems[52] and a compromise was in order, allowing both criteria of nationality and residence to co-exist, depending on the choice made by the individual Member State.[53] The European Parliament condemned the Council for its failure to reach a decision on the proposal.[54] The Bocklet Report for the Parliament's Political Affairs Committee later represented a further compromise, providing generally for the right to vote on the basis of nationality, but when agreed by a Member State, on the basis of residence.[55] Articles 2 and 3 of the proposal provided that these conditions were to apply equally to the right to stand for election. The criterion of nationality gained favour not only because it was thought to safeguard national sovereignty in the vital context of elections, but also because of the existence of pre-established Member State quotas based on the number of eligible voting nationals.[56] However, as Section 6.4.1. pointed out, the Bocklet Report, for a number of reasons, was never discussed in a plenary session of Parliament.

Prior to the adoption of the TEU, there was still a clear lack of consensus in Parliament about which criterion, nationality or residence, was to be employed for the enjoyment of electoral rights. Thus, the De Gucht interim report on behalf of the Institutional Affairs Committee maintained nationality and residence as alternatives.[57] However, in its resolution on guidelines for the draft uniform electoral procedure, the European Parliament ultimately proposed that

---

Senat, Doc. Senat no.427, 25 June 1982 where, at p.36, it recalled that: "l'octroi du droit de vote aux ressortissants des Etats- membres, même sous condition de résidence, souleverait des difficultés analogues dans la mesure ou notre Constitution, dans son article 3 alinea 4, réserve la qualité d'électeur aux seuls nationaux".

[50]Criticised in Debs. EP no.1-296/50, 8 March 1983.

[51]The Council had set up a working party of experts at its meeting on 26 and 27 April 1982, see Question no.68 N-184/82, Debs. EP no.1-286/181, 16 June 1982.

[52]See Question no.19 H-683/82, Debs. EP no.1-294/164, where the Council reported a meeting between its President and the European Parliament where it had become clear that agreement on active and passive voting rights was impossible. The Council stated, however, that it intended to continue its work in this area to achieve what it regarded as a Community objective, namely, a uniform electoral procedure for European elections; see Debs. EP no.1-296/48, 8 March 83; the Council statement presented to Parliament on 7 June 1983, PE 85.037, reported in OJ 1983 C152/37, particularly the submission of Mr Seitlinger, at p.55.

[53]See Quintin, op. cit. note 26, at 271.

[54]See OJ 1983 C96/28.

[55]EP Doc. A2-1/85.

[56]See the opinion of the Legal Affairs Committee attached to the Bocklet Report, at p.27. Article 138(2) details the number and division of delegates. It has been the subject of revision due, *inter alia*, to the reunification of Germany and the acession of new Member States. See Decision 93/81, OJ L33/15.

[57]Doc. A3-0152/91, 29 May 1991, at p.9.

"any national of a Member State ... shall be entitled to vote and stand for election to the European Parliament in the Member State in which he has had his main residence for at least the previous year ... The Member States shall cooperate to make it easier to exercise the right to vote and the right to stand for election ... and to prevent any voter from casting two votes in an election. Any citizen may stand for election in any Member State."[58]

Since the adoption of Article 8(b)(2) the issue of electoral rights is no longer discussed in the context of the adoption of a uniform electoral procedure.

6.5. Electoral Rights in European Parliament Elections Following the Treaty on European Union

Article 8(b)(2) provides that "every citizen of the Union residing in a Member State of which he is not a national shall have the right to vote and to stand as a candidate in elections to the European Parliament in the Member State in which he resides under the same conditions as nationals of that state". At first sight, Article 8(b)(2) appears to restrict electoral rights in European Parliament elections to Community nationals resident within the Communities. Such a limitation is consistent with the general choice of residence in Article 8(b) as the basis for the enjoyment of electoral rights by Member State nationals who wish to exercise them in a Member State other than their own. However, such an interpretation of the requirement of residence in Article 8(b)(2) is problematic for some Member States whose nationals who are permanently resident in a third country retain the right to vote in various elections, including European, presidential and national elections and referenda.[59] Previous proposals for a uniform electoral procedure accommodated individual Member State's electoral provisions for their own nationals.[60] This point seems to have been resolved in Directive 93/109, which clearly provides in Article 1(2) that "Nothing in this Directive shall affect Member States' provisions concerning the right to vote or to stand as a candidate of its nationals who reside outside its electoral territory".[61] The Directive addresses the electoral rights of Union citizens residing in a Member State of which they are not nationals and where they wish to vote. The rights extended under national law to Member State nationals resident in third countries are not inconsistent with Article 8(b)(2). Nevertheless, that these rights in European Parliament elections are not subject to

---

[58]Point 2(iii), OJ 1991 C280/141.

[59]This is the case in Italy and Spain. Italians resident in a third country were granted the right to vote in European Parliament elections in 1979. In the Netherlands, a similar system of voting for non-resident nationals operates at the request of the person involved; see Articles B.3, K.7 and L.9 of the Electoral Laws (Kieswet), which deal with voting by proxy and Article M, which deals with postal voting.

[60]Thus, for example, the 1991 European Parliament resolution on the guidelines for the draft uniform electoral procedure (which followed the interim De Gucht Report), op. cit. note 58, at pt. 2(iii) provided: "Those resident outside the Community shall be subject to the national legislation of their Member State of origin."

[61]OJ L329/34, 30 December 1993.

the same Community constitutional guarantee as the rights of Member State nationals resident in the Community, who wish to vote and stand for election in a Member State other than that of their nationality.

The objective of the inclusion of electoral rights within the scope of Union citizenship was to allow Member State nationals resident in a Member State other than their own to participate in matters which affect them in their daily lives. It was also a reflection of the essential role which political participation plays in any definition of citizenship. Union citizenship, it will be remembered, was partly conceived as a means to reduce the Community's democratic deficit and enhance European identity.[62] The link between national citizenship and the exercise of the highest level of political rights at national level is undisturbed by the creation of Union citizenship since Article 8(b) does not extend to national parliamentary elections. The latter are thought to be too closely related to matters of national sovereignty and policy with which non-nationals, even if they are from Community Member States, should not be involved. Some commentators argue, however, that the European Parliament deals with issues which, in terms of national importance, rival those confronting national legislatures. They question the logic of including European Parliament elections within the scope of the Community's attempts to extend electoral rights to non-nationals and enhance their integration, while national elections are excluded. The legislative role of the Parliament has clearly been improved following the adoption of the cooperation procedure in the SEA and co-decision in the Union Treaty and its budgetary powers are considerable.[63] Furthermore, the Court of Justice has championed the Parliament's input in Community decision-making[64] and increasing the powers of the European Parliament was a key element of many national proposals prior to the Maastricht Treaty. These proposals are likely to reemerge in the negotiations and discussions preceding the 1996 intergovernmental conference.[65]

These arguments emphasise the incoherent rationale behind the limited extension of voting rights at Community level to local and European but not national parliamentary levels. In the context of the debate for a uniform electoral procedure, however, the advisory as distinct from the legislative role of the European

---

[62]See COM (93) 534, at 8.

[63]See Weiler, J., *Symposium on the European Parliament in the Community System*, organised by the European Parliament and the Trans-European Policy Studies Association. Research and Documentation Papers, November 1988, where he states, at p.114: "Its budgetary powers are probably greater than those of any similar parliament in Europe. Its legislative powers, which are quite weak, are still greater than those of some national chambers". See also Quinty, D. and Joly, G. "Le rôle des parlements européens et nationaux dans la fonction legislative", 2 *Revue du droit public* (1991) 393–436, on the evolution of the European Parliament's legislative role in the Community.

[64]Case C-300/89 *Commission* v. *Council* [1991] ECR I-2867.

[65]See, for example, the Martin Report on the functioning of the Treaty on European Union with a view to the 1996 IGC – Implementation and Development – which calls for equal status with the Council in all fields of European Union legislative and budgetary competence, increased scrutiny of the second and third pillars and broader rights of action before the Court of Justice, Article 23 (iii), (iv) and (v), Doc. A4-0102/95, adopted at plenary on 17 May 1995.

Parliament has been underlined.[66] Furthermore, the low turn out at European Parliamentary elections is attributed to the qualitative difference between these and national elections and the voter's perception that the political powers which matter remain in the hands of Member State parliaments.[67] The European Parliament's legislative input and political weight has undoubtedly improved. However, the participation of nationals from other Member States in European elections does not pose the same challenge to national sovereignty as their participation in national elections would and this participation is not thought to interfere with or upset national bonds of allegiance, which states assume their own nationals recognise and respect.

The proposals forwarded by the Commission pursuant to Article 8(b)(2) were adopted unanimously by the Council after consulting the European Parliament. By dividing the issues of electoral rights and a uniform electoral procedure as it does, the Union Treaty has deprived the European Parliament of its former right of initiative in a matter which directly concerns it. Article 8(b)(2) applies "without prejudice to Article 138(3)", but it is difficult to envisage how the Commission's right to submit a proposal under the former has not prejudiced Parliament's powers under the latter. The Parliament may still draw up its own proposals for a uniform electoral procedure in accordance with Article 138(3), but the Commission's obligation is merely to consult the European Parliament and it is not obliged to take its proposals into account. Although the European Parliament's attempts to formulate a uniform electoral procedure have not been harmonious,[68] this change in procedure is arguably due to the politically sensitive nature of the subject matter and the fact that Member States may encounter a number of constitutional and domestic difficulties when implementing Article 8(b). However, the European Parliament's prerogative to participate as fully as possible in the regulation of its own elections has clearly been undermined. This is surprising in the light of the Court's decisions on the essential legislative role of the European Parliament: "participation [of the European Parliament] was the reflection at the Community level of a fundamental democratic principle, according to which people were to take part in the exercise of power through the intermediary of a representative assembly".[69] The European Parliament was also clearly unhappy with the limitation of its role under Article 8(b)(2).[70]

---

[66]See the House of Lords Select Committee on the European Communities, *Uniform Electoral Procedure for the Election of Members of the European Parliament*, op. cit. note 26, at xvii.

[67]See Stephanou, C.A., "Identité et Citoyenneté Européenne", 343 RMC (1991) 30–39, at 37.

[68]See, for example, the fairly vitriolic debate surrounding the choice of nationality for the exercise of the right to vote and the choice of residence for the right of eligibility in Parliament's 1982 proposal, OJ 1982 C87/62 in Debs. EP no.1-296/50, 8 March 1983.

[69]Case C-300/89, op. cit. note 64, at para.20.

[70]See the Resolution of the European Parliament following the Froment-Meurice Report, OJ 1993 C329/30; and the report itself Doc. A3-0537/93, at p.5: "It is highly regrettable that, in view of the major political significance of this directive for Parliament, Parliament should only be consulted on the matter. The Treaty should be modified on this point in 1996."

6.6. Directive 93/109 on Electoral Rights in European Parliament Elections

Article 8(b)(2) provided that detailed arrangements were to be adopted unanimously by the Council on a proposal from the Commission following consultation of the European Parliament. The 31 December 1993 was set as the deadline for the adoption of these detailed arrangements to enable Union citizens to exercise their new rights in the fourth direct elections scheduled for June 1994. The Commission presented its formal proposal in October 1993.[71] Even before the Union Treaty had entered into force, however, it had drawn up a working document which it had circulated to the Council and European Parliament.[72] The Parliament and Council held preliminary discussions on the implementation of Article 8(b)(2) on the basis of this document.

The Commission proposal first outlined some of the differences which existed between Member States as regards the right to vote. Prior to the adoption of the Directive all Member States, except Ireland, permitted their nationals to vote even if they were resident abroad. Some Member States limited this right to nationals resident in another Member State (Denmark, the Netherlands, Portugal), some to residence in Council of Europe states, or to residence in a third country for less than ten or twenty years (Germany and the United Kingdom), while others made no residence specifications. In four Member States (Belgium, Ireland, the Netherlands and the United Kingdom) nationals from other Member States were entitled to vote on the basis of residence, subject to certain conditions. Ten Member States reserved the right to stand for election to their own nationals, even if they were resident in another Member State, or a third country. British citizens, Commonwealth citizens and Irish nationals could stand for election in the United Kingdom, while Italy permitted nationals from other Member States to stand in Italy even if they were not resident.

According to the Commission a directive was the most suitable legal instrument to implement the guarantee in Article 8(b)(2). It was also the instrument which would interfere least with the prerogative of national parliaments. The choice of a directive and a careful limitation of its provisions to what was necessary to achieve the guarantee in Article 8(b)(2) were in line with the Community principles of proportionality and subsidiarity in Article 3(b) of the Union Treaty. The purpose of Article 8(b) and the arrangements adopted thereunder is not, after all, to harmonise national electoral laws on European Parliament and municipal elections. That provision simply requires that the principle of equal treatment is extended to these elections so that Union citizens can vote on the basis of their residence in a Member State other than their own on the same conditions as nationals of that state. The purpose of Article 8(b) is thus to ensure that the requirement of nationality, which in most Member States conditions the exercise of electoral rights, would not

---

[71]COM (93) 534 final.
[72]SEC (93) 1021 final.

exclude the participation of Union citizens in European Parliament and municipal elections. The preamble of Directive 93/109 also identified electoral rights in European Parliament elections on the basis of residence as a corollary of the right to freedom of movement and residence which Union citizens also enjoy on the basis of Article 8(a).[73]

6.6.1. General Provisions of Directive 93/109

Article 1 of the Directive specifies that its scope is limited to giving Union citizens resident in a Member State other than their own the choice of voting and standing as a candidate in elections to the European Parliament. It does not apply to the electoral rights of Union citizens residing in their Member State of origin, or Union citizens who wish to exercise these rights in a Member State other than that of their origin or residence, or indeed the electoral rights granted by a Member State to persons resident in their territory who are not Union citizens such as, for example, Commonwealth citizens in the United Kingdom.[74]

Article 2 of the Directive establishes the definitions of the essential terms used in the Directive. Thus, "elections to the European Parliament" and "electoral territory" are defined with reference to the 1976 Act on Direct elections and the national legislation adopted pursuant to it in each Member State. "Member State of residence" means the Member State where a person resides but is not a national, whereas home Member State is defined with reference to nationality. Given differences in the manner in which the electoral register is organised at national level, Article 2(7) simply refers to the register drawn up by the competent authorities of the Member State of residence and in order to include Member States which do not have an electoral register, but which rely on the general register.[75] The "reference date" is the day or days on which Union citizens must satisfy the conditions for voting and eligibility in their Member State of residence according to the law of that state. It is up to the Member States whether the same day applies for both rights. Finally, a "formal declaration" for the purposes of the Directive is one "inaccuracy in which makes that person liable to penalties, in accordance with the national law applicable." This definition also indicates that the Directive is not intended to harmonise what amounts to a formal declaration. The Commission, for example, points to the difference between a British statutory declaration and a sworn statement under German law. It emphasises that it is up to the Member State

---

[73]OJ 1993 L329/34, at recital 3.

[74]See COM (93) 534, at pp.2 and 9; and Doc. A3-0537/Part B, at pt.2.1.

[75]Member States vary from a system of automatic registration (Spain, Italy, Belgium, Denmark, Germany, Luxembourg, the Netherlands, the United Kingdom and Ireland) to a system of registration on request (France and Greece) to a mixed system (Portugal). In those Member States where registration is automatic, it is based on information from another public register, or on information collected by the registration officer. In most Member States the register is periodically revised once a year. In some, however, it is subject to revision the year before each election (Belgium, Germany and the Netherlands).

to determine, in conformity with the loose definition in Article 2(9), what constitutes a formal declaration. The Commission also interprets the relevant legislation for determining liability for an inaccurate statement (i.e., "the national law applicable") as that of the Member State of residence. However, it is strange that the Directive does not specify that the legislation of the Member State of residence is intended as it does elsewhere whenever the Member State of residence is in question. Furthermore, this point is of some relevance, since it determines whether the declaration of a United Kingdom national applying to exercise his electoral rights in Germany, where he is resident, should comply with German or British standards. Since the Directive mentions the possibility of penalties it seems that the Member State of residence was intended since that is where such penalties could be enforced, but the Directive could have been clearer in this regard.

Article 3 establishes the conditions to be met by Union citizens who wish to enjoy the rights guaranteed by Article 8(b)(2) and the Directive: the applicant must be (i) a Union citizen/Member State national and (ii) must be resident in a Member State of which he is not a national and must satisfy the conditions which that Member State imposes on its own nationals. The Commission states that reference to Article 8(1) is recognition that the determination of Member State nationality does not fall within the scope of Community law and that, with reference to the declaration on nationality annexed to the Union Treaty, Member States are entitled to determine who their nationals are and, consequently, who can exercise electoral rights pursuant to Directive 93/109. The residence condition in Article 3(b), like that in Article 5, is not defined uniformly, to avoid unnecessary interference with the way residence is defined at national level for the purpose of participation in elections. It must also be remembered that the Community institutions were under considerable pressure to reach agreement on the proposal in order to adopt the Directive in time for the fourth direct elections, which might explain why compromise on issues such as residence was so essential. The provision requires resident Union citizens to be treated in the same way as nationals of the Member State of residence. It does not require that the conditions for voting or eligibility established in one Member State have to be the same in another. Although the minimum voting age is 18 in all Member States, the minimum age to stand as a candidate varies from between 18 to 25 years of age. Application of the principle of equal treatment permits Member States to maintain their administrative requirements as long as they do not discriminate against non-nationals. If nationals of the Member State of residence are required to reside for a minimum period in the constituency in which they wish to vote, the same condition can be legally applied to resident Union citizens. Finally, Article 3 para.2 deals with the requirement imposed by some Member States that candidates must have been nationals for a certain minimum period in order to stand. If such a condition is imposed on nationals, resident Union citizens are deemed to have fulfilled it if they have been naturalised in their home Member State for the same period.

The rights to vote and to stand for election established in the Directive are based on choice. Union citizens may choose whether they exercise these rights in their home Member State (if that Member State permits it), or their Member State of residence. However, once they do choose, they may only exercise the right in one election in one Member State.[76] Article 5 does not specify what is meant by residence, but provides that, if nationals in the Member State of residence are required to have resided there for a minimum period then Union citizens are deemed to have fulfilled this condition if they have completed an equivalent period in another Member State. This provision is designed to prevent Union citizens being placed in a less favourable position than nationals of the Member State of residence. It does not mean that specific conditions of residence in a particular locality or constituency cannot be imposed. However, any such condition must not be discriminatory. The purpose of a constituency residence condition is to ensure that voters or candidates have sufficient knowledge of the place in which they are about to cast their vote or stand for election, which is a legitimate interest which Member States can oblige Union citizens to respect, provided it is non-discriminatory.

Pursuant to Article 6, anyone who is debarred from standing as a candidate under either the law of the Member State of residence or the home Member State, cannot stand as a candidate in elections for the European Parliament in the Member State of residence. Individual criminal or civil law decisions are listed in the provision as grounds for being deprived of the right to vote and the right to stand for election. The Commission does not regard this concurrent application of grounds for ineligibility as discriminatory. The aim of such concurrent application is, instead, to prevent any possible distortions arising from the differences which exist between the Member States' ineligibility rules. Some Member States such as Denmark, Ireland, the Netherlands and the United Kingdom have a fairly liberal approach towards electoral disabilities while in France and Belgium they are taken very seriously. In France, for example, persons can be disqualified on the basis of mental illness, or political crimes and the issue is highly sensitive. Although the "liberal" Member States regarded concurrent application of disabilities as excessively bureaucratic, a solution had to be found to accommodate Member States where the issue was not so lightly regarded. The Commission further justified the application of two sets of disqualification rules by stating that a person who has been disqualifed in his home Member State should not be able to recover his right simply by taking up residence in another Member State.[77] The European Parliament recognises that "exporting" electoral disqualifications may seem excessive. However, it also points to difficulties which the wide disparities between Member States on grounds for disqualification may cause. Like the Commission, it regards safeguarding the credibility and reputation of the European Parliament as the paramount consideration. As a result, in order to prove eligibility, persons submitting an application to stand as a candidate must provide, in addition to the supporting documents required by Article 10(1), an attestation from the competent

---

[76]Articles 4(1) and (2). The ban on double voting was previously established in Article 8 of the 1976 Act.

[77]COM (93) 534, at pp.14–15.

authorities in their home Member State that they have not been deprived of their right to stand as a candidate there.[78] Article 6(2) provides that an application is declared inadmissible if the candidate cannot furnish this attestation.

However, the rules on the disqualification of voters are more flexible than those for candidates. The host Member State may check whether a Community voter has been disqualified in his Member State, but it is not obliged to do so. This flexibility is further reflected in Article 9(3)(a), which provides that the Member State of residence may require Community voters to state in their declaration under Article 9(2) that they have been disqualified, but this is not an obligatory element of the declaration required of them. If Member States decide to check whether a Community voter has been disqualifed it may notify the home Member State, informing it of the declaration made by the Community voter. The home Member State must reply to these inquiries in good time and providing all relevant information which is normally available. Article 7(2) is concerned with the protection of the personal data of the applicant Community voter, since only information relevant to the application of Article 7 and necessary for its application is to be communicated by the home Member State and used by the Member State of residence. Article 8 reiterates the freedom to choose where to vote in Article 4. Article 8(1) provides, in particular, that a Community voter will only be entered on the electoral roll of his Member State of residence if he expresses his wish to vote there. Registration is not automatic. However, once he has expressed his wish to do so, he is subject to the same rules on compulsory voting as nationals of that Member State, if in fact voting is compulsory.

6.6.2. Exercise of the Right to Vote and the Right to Stand for Election

Member State rules on the time to apply for entry on the electoral register vary considerably. Article 9(1) does not interfere with national rules on registration, but provides that Member States shall take whatever measures necessary to enable a Community voter to be registered sufficiently in advance of the polling day. The Commission states that Member States which revise their rolls periodically will thus be able to register Community voters during the established period or, in exceptional circumstances, outside that period on the same conditions as nationals. Where the roll is automatically revised, Community voters should be entitled to apply within a reasonable period before the closure of the register. Presumably, when transposing the Directive into national law Member States will have to define what the appropriate period is. Furthermore, the "necessary measures" in Article 9(1) would seem also to include a sufficiently clear and extensive publicity campaign. Article 12 supports this conclusion, since it provides that Union citizens must be advised of their rights in good time. Community voters are required to provide the same documents as nationals in order to register. In addition, they must

---

[78]Article 10(2).

provide a formal declaration stating name and address in the electoral territory of the Member State of residence, the locality or constituency in which they were last registered in the home Member State and a statement that they will only exercise their right to vote in one Member State. In addition, the Member State of residence may require Community voters to state that they have not been disqualified in their home Member State, to produce valid ID and to indicate since when they have been resident in that Member State (Article 9(3)). The purpose of these obligatory and optional documents is to verify the identity of the applicant Community voter and to prevent double voting. Community voters remain on the register until they request to be removed, or until they no longer satisfy the conditions which they must fulfil in order to enable them to vote. A Community national who wishes to stand as a candidate must also produce the same supporting documents as national candidates and a formal declaration similar to that in Article 9(2). Unlike Union citizens who simply wish to exercise their right to vote, candidates for election must submit an attestation from the competent authorities of their home Member State that they have not been disqualified from standing as candidates there. They may also be required to produce valid ID and to state for how long they have held the nationality of a Member State.[79]

Community voters and candidates for election must be informed in good time of the action being taken with respect to their applications. It is up to individual Member States to decide whether they notify the persons concerned individually or by publishing the information along with the electoral roll. On the basis of the information given to them, Article 11(2) provides that Community voters and candidates are entitled to the same legal remedies as the legislation of the Member State of residence prescribes for its national voters and persons entitled to stand as candidates. Article 13 provides for the exchange of information between the two Member States concerned regarding the electoral roll. The home Member State is to take whatever measures possible to ensure its nationals do not vote twice or stand in more than one Member State.

6.6.3. Derogations and Transitional Provisions

The derogations permitted in Article 14 on the basis of the second sentence of Article 8(b)(2) were incorporated in the Directive with reference to the exceptional position of Luxembourg and the special electoral regime which exists between Ireland and the United Kingdom, although these Member States are not specified. The proportion of Community nationals resident in Luxembourg is about 29 per cent of the total potential electorate. This proportion reaches approximately 50 per cent in some electoral districts such as La Rochette, where there is a large Portuguese community. In other Member States, the percentage of Community nationals is between 0.3 per cent and 6 per cent. In the light of these circumstances,

---

[79]Article 10(3).

Article 14(1) provides that a Member State may derogate from Articles 3, 9 and 10 if the proportion of the non-national Community population of voting age resident in that Member State exceeds 20 per cent of the total number of Union citizens residing there who are of voting age. Once this percentage has been exceeded, the Member State of residence may restrict the exercise of the rights guaranteed in the Directive to Union citizens who have resided there for a minimum period. This period may be no longer than one term of office (five years) in the case of the right to vote and two terms in the case of the right to stand for election. This derogation may not apply, however, to nationals of other Member States who, by reason of their residence in another Member State and/or the duration of that residence, are no longer permitted to exercise these rights in their home Member State as, for example, in Ireland.

Article 14(2) addresses the special relationship which exists between the United Kingdom and Ireland in the field of political rights. Irish nationals resident in the United Kingdom have been entitled to participate in parliamentary and local elections there since 1948 and in European Parliament elections since 1979. British nationals resident in Ireland have enjoyed reciprocal rights in parliamentary elections since 1985. All non-national residents in Ireland have been entitled to vote in local elections since 1963. Irish nationals resident in the United Kingdom and British nationals resident in Ireland, who are entitled to vote, normally appear on the electoral register for parliamentary elections which are established by automatic registration in both Member States. The electoral register for European Parliament elections is also established automatically on the basis of the parliamentary register. The Directive does not interfere with this special relationship and provides that Irish and British nationals, although they are not specified, are exempt from the conditions provided in Articles 6 to 13.

The Commission had argued that the clause permitting derogations in Article 8(b)(2) was concerned with derogations from the arrangements for the exercise of the rights guaranteed in the Treaty, rather than a derogation from the guarantee itself. As such, the derogation in Article 14 will be subject to review eighteen months before each election and the Commission is to submit a report to the European Parliament and Council on whether the derogation is still warranted by circumstances in the Member States or whether adjustments are required.[80] The European Parliament was also anxious to delete Article 14(1) para.2, which provides that "These provisions are without prejudice to appropriate measures which [the derogating] Member State may take with regard to the composition of lists of candidates and which are intended in particular to encourage the integration of non-national citizens of the Union." Essentially this meant that derogating Member States could also control the number of Community citizens on the electoral lists. The Froment-Meurice report argued that this aspect of the derogation was unacceptable and discriminatory and that Luxembourg members of the European

---

[80]Article 14(3).

Parliament might find themselves at risk if national legislation implementing this derogation was impugned before the Court of Justice.[81] It wanted the derogation to carry an explicit rider stating that national authorities were not empowered to act in a discriminatory manner on this basis. Lundberg suggests that this derogation means that nationals from other Member States may be prevented from setting up separate lists of candidates in elections to the European Parliament.[82] In the event, it appears that Luxembourg will rely on this derogation to ensure that a certain minimum per cent of party lists are comprised of nationals.

Given the tight schedule for implementing the Directive in time for the 1994 elections, Article 15 also provided for a number of transitional arrangements which took into account problems facing certain Member States. Some of these arrangements only succeeded in diffusing the problems faced in the 1994 elections and it remains to be seen what will happen next time round. The Commission is required, pursuant to Article 16, to review the experience gained from the implementation of the Directive. It may, as a result, propose any amendments it considers necessary which the Council may adopt pursuant to the procedure established in Article 8(b)(2). At the time of writing, the Commission has not yet produced this report. The deadline for the transposition of the Directive was 1 February 1994, in order to ensure that it would be in force in time for the fourth direct elections in June 1994. The Member States were obliged to refer to the Directive when transposing it into national law.

A review of the proposals of the Commission, the report of the Parliament's Institutional Affairs Committee and the final text adopted by the Council reveals that there was little institutional disagreement on the text of the Directive. This is rather surprising for a proposal of such magnitude, which had caused considerable controversy when discussed as part of a uniform electoral procedure. However, this lack of disagreement was no doubt due to the fact that before the Commission presented its formal proposal and indeed before the Union Treaty had been adopted, the European Parliament and Council had been discussing a working document which the Commission had submitted to them. The Froment–Meurice Report had proposed a slight amendment to the text of Article 4(2) and Article 14(1) second paragraph (on non-nationals and party lists). It also regretted that the Parliament should only be consulted on a matter which is of major political concern to it. As a result, it called for a modification of the legislative procedure in Article 8(b)(2) in the forthcoming 1996 intergovernmental conference. However, its main objection was to the three-part derogation in the Directive, which was to deal with the exceptional situation of Luxembourg. It accepted the residence conditions in Articles 14(1)(a) and (b), but rejected the Commission's justification of the provision on the composition of electoral lists. The Commission had argued that

<hr>

[81]Doc. A3-0537/93 part A, at p.7; and EP Resolution OJ C329/130, at p.131.
[82]See Lundberg, E., "Political Freedoms in the European Union", in Antola, E. and Rosas, A. (eds.), *A Citizens' Europe: In Search of a New Order* (1995) London, Sage Publications, pp.113–134, at p.132.

the latter came within the scope of the uniform electoral procedure and that derogations were from the arrangements for the exercise of the guarantee in Article
8(b)(2) and not from the guarantee itself. However, the report held that "any limitations of the rights of citizens to stand for election necessarily call into question a
fundamental freedom, and not merely an electoral procedural rule".[83] It also argued that if Luxembourg adopted discriminatory provisions regarding the composition of electoral lists, those rules would be open to challenge before the Court of
Justice and the election of European Parliament members in Luxembourg might be
deprived of a legal basis. In its resolution adopted on the basis of the Froment–
Meurice Report the European Parliament also "Express[ed] its opposition to the
derogation provided for in Article 14 of the proposal for a Directive as contrary to
the spirit and letter of Article 6 of the EC Treaty".[84] It also called for a degree of
approximation between Member State rules on electoral disqualification and that
all derogations should cease by 2004.[85]

6.6.4. The Fourth Direct Elections to the European Parliament and the Implementation of Directive 93/109

Statistics compiled by the Commission reveal that only one non-national European
Union candidate was successful in the 1994 elections (Table 6.1). They also indicate
that there is still a great disparity between the potential number of non-national
European Union voters and the percentage actually enrolled. In France, for example,
1,100,000 Member State nationals resident in France are entitled to vote. However,
only 47,632 were enrolled prior to the 1994 elections.[86]

It is impossible to examine the implementation of the Directive in all Member
States (see Table 6.3). Particular attention is paid here to France to highlight the
difficulties encountered there and which may arise in other Member States. The
Directive was transposed into French law a few days after the deadline established
therein, 1 February 1994, had passed.[87] The definition of residence for the purposes of the Directive presented particular difficulties in France. Member State nationals qualify as residents if they have an effective or real domicile, or if their
residence is continuous. The first project presented in Parliament referred to Article
11 of the Electoral Code for a definition of residence. That provision extends beyond real residence or domicile to persons who appear for the fifth time, the year
of the application for enrolment, on the register of municipal rates and who have

---

[83]Froment–Meurice Report, part B, pt. 3.2.

[84]OJ 1993 C329/131, at pt.5.

[85]See also Arnaldo Alcubilla, E., "El derecho de sufragio de los extranjeros en las elecciones locales", 12 *Revista Española de Derecho Constitucional* (1992) 67–97, at 93.

[86]See the statistics (Table 6.2), which were presented at Nationality and Citizenship Status in the
New Europe, organised in London by the Institute for Public Policy Research/Abo Akademi University,
Turku, 9–10 June 1995.

[87]See *Loi* no.94/104, Journal Officiel 8 February 1995, which completes *Loi* no.77/729, 7 July
1977; and Decree law no.94/206, 10 March 1994.

Table 6.1 EP Election 1994: presentation of non-national EU candidates

	Deadline	EU candidates	Successful EU candidates
Belgium	1 April 1994	18 (out of 534)	None
Denmark	4 weeks before election	1	None
France	27 May 1994	5	None
Germany	66 days before election	12	1
Greece	20 days before election	5	None
Ireland	7–14 May 1994	1	None
Italy	39 days before election	2	None
Luxembourg	60 days before election	8 (out of 120)	None
Netherlands	27 April 1994	2 None	
Portugal	4–18 April 1994	None	
Spain	4–9 May 1994	1	None
United Kingdom	17.2 – 29 March 1994 (prolongation until 22 April 1994)	2 (0.37 per cent)	None

declared their desire to exercise their electoral rights there. Parliament rejected this second paragraph of Article 11 as an unsuitable definition of residence for the purposes of Directive 93/109. It felt that it would leave open the possibility that nationals from other Member States with a second residence in France would vote there. Both Houses of Parliament insisted on limiting the definition of residence to the first paragraph of Article 11 of the Electoral code. Thus Community nationals who can prove effective residence in a French municipality will have established residence for the purposes of the Directive, even if that municipality is not where they wish to vote, or is not where they pay their municipal rates. Chalteil suggests that the law is discriminatory, since it introduces a criterion for applicant Member State nationals – payment of municipal rates – which does not apply to nationals, but that the need to combat double voting justifies this discrimination.[88] However, she also points out that the French legislation insists on the same type of residence condition for candidates for election. This requirement may be less justifiable, since Article LO 127 of the Electoral Code regards all French nationals, regardless of residence, as eligible.

Union citizens must also enrol voluntarily on a complementary electoral list, if they wish to participate in European Parliament elections in France. In addition, the legislation establishes a number of mechanisms to avoid European Union citizens who have been deprived of the right to vote in their Member State of nationality, being able to enjoy that right in France. In order to avoid double voting, which the Directive prohibits, Member States will have to develop a rapid system for exchanging information. The French National Institute of Statistics and Economic Studies is responsible for processing the necessary information in France. It is clear, however, that the Directive has been transposed, in the main, almost word for word into French national law.

---

[88]See Chalteil, F., "La loi française sur le droit de vote des citoyens européens aux élections européennes", 381 RMC (1994) 528–532. For the Spanish situation see Martín Lopez, A., "La Unión Europea y el derecho de sufragio de los extranjeros comunitarios", 119 *Noticias de la UE* (1994) 11–23.

Table 6.2 EP Election 1994: participation of non-national EU-voters

	Deadline for registration as voter	General participation in elections	Potential non-national EU voters	Non-national EU voters enrolled (and percentage of non-national electorate)	Information campaign
Belgium	7.2 – 31 March	90.7 per cent (total electorate: 7,096,273)	471,000	24,000 (5.1 per cent)	Press conference by the ministry of the interior, responsibilities for information lay with municipalities Individual letters
Denmark	9.3 – 28 April	52.9 per cent (total electorate: 3,994,200)	27,042	6,719 (24.85 per cent)	Private associations
France	14.3 – 15 April	52.7 per cent (total electorte: 38,160,000)	1,100,000	47,632 (4.35 per cent)	
Germany	8.1 – 28 March	60 per cent (total electorate: 60,473,927)	1,369,863	80,000 (5.84 per cent)	Decentralised information responsibilities (municipalities), measures varying from German language folders to individual information in different languages
Greece	8.1 – 28 March	71.2 per cent (total electorate: 9,485,495)	40,000	628 (1.57 per cent)	One TV spot sponsored b government.
Ireland	24 May 1994	44 per cent (total electorate: 2,639,000)	Ca 17,000 (excluding British nationals)	6,000 exluding British Nationals 35.29%)	Press release and public notice
Italy	12.2–12.3 – 24 March	74.8 per cent (total electorate: 48,372,726)	99,100	Ca 2,000 (2.02 per cent)	Press
Luxembourg	1 March 1994	88.5 per cent (total electorate: 198,370)	105,000	6,907 (6.58 per cent)	Information leaflet published in five languages
Netherlands	Deadline for opt out until 19 May	35.6 per cent (total electorate: 11,618,677)	160,000	15,000 (9.37 per cent)	Individual letters
Portugal	1 – 15 March	35.5 per cent (total electorate: 8,555,733)	30,519	715 (2.34 per cent)	Press announcements, radio, TV
Spain	3.1 – 15 February	59.1 per cent (total electorate: 18,664,053)	172,466	24,277 (14.05 per cent)	Radio spots, press anmouncement, poster all sponsored by government
United Kingdom	17.2 – 29.3 (late claims for registration were accepted until 22 April)	36.4 per cent (tota electorate: 43,770,000 including Irish citizens)	Ca 400,000 (excluding Irish citizens)	7,755 excluding Irish citizens (1.94 per cent)	Press release, official statement, information campaign by private associations, information of embassies and consultates

Table 6.3 Implementation of Council Directive 93/109/CE

Member States	Directive implemented by
Belgium	Loi du 11 April 1994 modifiant la Loi du 23 mars 1989 relate à l'élection du PE et portant exécution de la directive du Conseil des Communautés Européennes 93/109 du 6 December 1993 in MB no.10288 du 16 April 1994
Denmark	Law no.1086 of 22 December 1993 modifying law no.746 of 7 December 1988 concerning the election of Danish representatives to the European Parliament (L); Notification of the Ministry of Interior no.79 of 31 January 1994 concerning the deletion of persons from the Danish electoral roll who are registered on the electoral roll of another Member State (N79); Notification of the Ministry of Interior no.80 of 31 January 1994 concerning the registration of Union citizens as voters for the elections of the European Parliament (N80).
Spain	Ley Organica 13/94 of 30 March 1994 in BOE no.77, 102259 of 31 March 1994 (LO); Real Decreto 2118/93 of 3 December 1993 in BOE no.290, 34662 of 4 December 1994 (RD); Orden del Ministerio de Economia y Hacienda 30393 of 20 December 1993 in BOER no.305 of 22 December 1993 (O30) and Orden del Ministerio de Economia ya Hacienda de 28 January 1994 in BOE no.25 of 29 January 1994 (O20).
France	Loi no.94-104 du 5 février relative à l'exercice par les citoyens de l'Union Européenne résidant en France du droit de vote et de l'éligibilité au Parlement Européen (L); Décret no.944-206 du 10 mars 1994 pour l'application de la loi 94-104 du 5 février 1994 (D).
Germany	Drittes Gesetz zur Änderung des Europawahlgesetzes of 8 March 1994 in BGBl 1994, I, p.419 f of 12 March 1994, Zweite Verordnung zur Änderung der Europawahlordnung of 15 March 1994 in BGBl 1994, I, P.544 of 17 March 1994.
Greece	Loi no.2196 du 22 mars 1994, Journal Officiel du Gouvernement Grec, Vol.1, Serie 41 du 22 mars 1994.
Ireland	Electoral Act 1992 (EA); European Parliament elections Regulation 1994 of 31 December 1994 (EPER); Second Schedule Electoral Act 1992 (SSEA); European Parliament Elections Act 1993 (EPEA); First schedule European Assembly Elections Act 1977 (FSEAEA).
Italy	Decreto Legge no.128 del 21 February 1994 in GU no.47 of 26 February 1994.
Luxembourg	Loi du 28 janvier 1994 fixant les modalités de l'élection des représentants du Grand Duché de Luxembourg au Parlement Européen.
Netherlands	Wet van 26 januari 1994 houdende wijziging van de Kieswet ter uitvoering van richtlijn no.93/109/EG van 6 December 1993 tot vaststelling aan de wijze van uitoefening in de Lid-staat van verblijf van het actieve en passieve kiesrecht bij de verkeizingen van het europese parlement, Staatsblad, 1994, 58.
Portugal	Lei 3/94 de 28 February 1994 (RE); Lei 4/94 de 9 March 1994 (PE) in Diario da Republica Serie A no.57 de 9 March 1994.
United Kingdom	European Parliamentary Elections (Changes to the Franchise Qualification of Representatives) Regulations 1994 of 17 February 1994.

6.7. The Regulation of Electoral Rights at Municipal Level

The Treaty on European Union did not confine itself to an extension of the principle of equal treatment to European Parliament elections. Whether or not free movement had been a success in numerical terms, the fact remained that those who availed of their Community free movement rights, often found themselves disenfranchised. They were excluded from voting in their Member State of origin because they did not reside there and were not generally permitted to participate in elections in their Member State of residence, which generally required persons participating in elections to possess nationality.[89] The debate surrounding the extension of the principle of equal treatment to electoral rights in municipal elections was one of the most far-reaching examples of the Community asserting competence over the legal rights of Community citizens detached from the exercise of an economic activity. In order to discuss the adoption of a Community Directive on electoral rights in municipal elections, which will be discussed in detail in the following chapter, this section examines the constitutional and legal changes which some Member States have had to adopt to accommodate Article 8(b)(1). It contrasts the position in other Member States where no constitutional or legislative amendments were necessary. The Member States discussed reflect some, but not all, of the national reactions to supranational involvement in a matter traditionally determined at national level and which, in certain Member States, was regarded as constitutive of state sovereignty and national identity. No conclusions will be drawn at the end of this chapter, since discussion of equal treatment with respect to electoral rights will continue in Chapter 7.

6.7.1. The Consequences at National level of Community Competence in the Field of Electoral Rights

With reference to entry, residence and eligibility for national welfare benefits, Chapter 4 discusses the fact that free movement poses a major challenge to exclusive and closed concepts of citizenship. Indeed, once migrants and their families have achieved a certain level of integration in their host Member State, their focus generally switches from the availability of work and residence permits to rights to participate in local and/or parliamentary decision making on the basis of the links they have acquired in their Member State of residence through work, residence, payment of taxes, attendance at school etc.[90] The European Community has not been immune to this aspect of the integration process. This section outlines the legislative and constitutional position regarding the exercise of electoral rights by Member State nationals resident in a Member State other than their own prior and subsequent to the adoption of the Union Treaty. A comprehensive review and analysis of the legal position in all twelve Member States is beyond the scope of the book. Language restrictions also make it difficult to deal with the primary or doctrinal sources in certain Member States.[91] Specific attention is paid to Ireland,

---

[89]In its proposal for the Directive on municipal elections the Commission calculated that 4 million Member State nationals resident in a Member State other than their own were disenfranchised, while about 2.6 million lost their rights in their Member State of origin if they were resident abroad, COM (94) 38 final, citing Eurostat population statistics, 1992.

[90]See Arnaldo Alcubilla, op. cit. note 85, at 69.

[91]On the legal position in individual Member States see generally, Council of Europe, *Study of Civic Rights of Nationals of Other Member States in Local Public Life* RM-SL (82) 55 revised; *Symposium on the Participation of Foreigners in Municipal Elections in the EEC Member States*, Louvain-la-Neuve, 28 February 1978, reproduced in 49 *Studi Emigrazione* (1978) 3–175; Casagrande, M., "Les immigrés et les elections communales dans les pays de la CEE", 10 *Objectif Europe* (1980) 38–47; Bull. EC. suppl. 7/86; Situazione del diritti di voto alle elezioni communali degli Stati Membri della CEE al 1989, 17 *Affari sociali internazionali* (1989) 231–233; Sieveking, K., Barwig, K. and

the Netherlands, Spain and France. The situation in these Member States is thought to reflect the diverse spectrum of common and civil law based systems, different constitutional backgrounds and different political and legal philosophies as regards the political participation of non-nationals. They vary in size, historical tradition, immigrant population, homogeneity and electoral organisation. Their reactions to the Union Treaty provisions on electoral participation have varied accordingly.[92]

Ireland

All persons, regardless of nationality, who are 18 years of age and who are ordinarily resident in the local electoral area, may register to vote in local elections in Ireland.[93] This extension of electoral rights on the basis of residence applies equally to Community and non-Community nationals. However, British citizens are privileged in that they may vote in national parliamentary elections.[94] This liberal local electoral regime precedes Ireland's accession to the European Communities. The small number of non-nationals affected by such legislation and the absence generally of a national immigration debate may partly account for the lack of controversy surrounding the participation of non-nationals in elections in Ireland.[95] It is submitted, in addition, that the Irish legislature possessed a fundamentally different approach than that of the French, for example, to electoral rights and their relationship with national citizenship. The juridical and political debate surrounding the constitutional guarantee of electoral rights for non-nationals and the subsequent adoption of parliamentary voting rights for United Kingdom nationals and other Community nationals on a reciprocal basis is a useful means of illustrating this point.

In 1983, a bill was introduced in the *Oireachtais* (Houses of Parliament), attempting to confer rights to vote in Dáil (the primary Parliamentary chamber) elections on British citizens. The bill was referred to the Supreme Court by the

---

Lorcher, K. and Schomacher, C. (eds.), *Das Kommunalwahlrecht fur Auslander* (1989) Baden Baden, Nomos; Rath, J., "Voting Rights" in Layton Henry, Z., *The Political Rights of Migrant Workers in Western Europe* (1990), London, Sage Modern Politics Services Vol. 25, pp.127–157, who focuses additionally on national political parties' reaction to the non-national voting rights debate; and the survey by the Citizens' Europe Research Project under the auspices of the BIICL, the Institute of Advanced Legal Studies and the Federal Trust for Education and Research on *Citizenship Rights in National Law*.

[92]Layton Henry suggests that these factors influence the willingness of a country to accept non-nationals as participants in the political system.

[93]See s.5(2)(a) of the Electoral Act, 1963 as amended by s.1 of the Local Elections Act, 1972 and s.2(a) of the Electoral (Amendment) Act, 1973.

[94]For details of the extension of the national franchise, see Anglo-Irish Joint Studies presented to both Houses of the Oireachtais by Dr. Garrett Fitzgerald on 11 November 1981; the Electoral (Amendment) Bill, 1983; Article 16.1.2 of the Constitution as amended in 1983; and s.2(1A)(a) of the Electoral (Amendment) Act, 1985.

[95]Cf. Breillat, D., "Le vote des étrangers en Europe du Nord" in Turpin, D., *Immigrés et réfugiés dans les démocraties occidentales. Défis et solutions*, (1989) Presse Universiatire d'Aix-Marseille/ Economica, at p.139, who believes that securing voting rights for non-nationals is usually the consequence of a large immigration debate.

President, in order to determine its constitutionality prior to promulgation.[96] The Supreme Court held that Article 16 of the Constitution, which lays down the conditions for the parliamentary franchise, was comprehensive in its provision of the mechanism by which the people could choose and control their legislators.[97] To interpret Article 16[98] to include non-nationals was considered contrary to the comprehensive electoral code specifically provided for therein. Support for this interpretation was found in Article 6 of the Constitution, which proclaims that all powers of government derive from the people and, further, that it is the people's right to designate the rulers of the State and decide all questions of national policy.[99] According to the Irish Supreme Court, Article 6 did not contemplate the sharing of powers with persons who do not come within the constitutional conception of the Irish people.

A referendum in 1984 adopted the 9th amendment to the Constitution which amended Article 16 so that the right to vote in national elections was extended to "such other persons as may be determined by law". Irish electoral legislation was amended accordingly in 1985, specifically enabling British citizens to vote and stand for election in national elections. The Minister for Justice was additionally enabled to issue an order entitling nationals of Member States of the Community who admit Irish nationals as electors in national elections on similar conditions as their own nationals, to vote in parliamentary elections in Ireland.[100] The reasoning of the Supreme Court, which attributed national sovereignty to the "Irish people", is not totally redundant, however, since non-nationals were still excluded from presidential and senate elections and from referenda. In the context of national elections, however, the Court's conception of Irish people no longer seems to apply. The amendment of Article 16 and the enactment of legislation implementing it has surely altered the concept of national sovereignty in Article 6. The text of Article 6 remains the same, but if read in conjunction with other constitutional provisions, it has been reduced in the electoral context to the expression of the national will in presidential elections and referenda.

This fluid concept of "the people" bears more relation to American jurisprudence than jurisprudence on electoral rights in France and Germany. Although the liberal regime governing electoral rights in Irish law predated accession to the

[96]In accordance with the pre-promulgation procedure in Article 26 of the Irish Constitution. The presidential reference in 1983 was tacitly supported by the government which wished to avoid constitutional difficulties stemming from the reform which might threaten the validity of subsequent elections.

[97]See *In the Matter of Article 26 of the Constitution and the Electoral (Amendment) Bill, 1983* [1984] Irish Law Reports Monthly 539. Prior to amendment, Article 16.1.1 provided that: "Every citizen without distinction of sex who has reached the age of eighteen years who is not disqualified by law and complies with the provisions of the law relating to the election of Dáil Eireann, shall have the right to vote at an election for members of Dáil Eireann."

[98]And consequently Articles 16.1.1 and 12.4.1, which refer to the right to stand for election in Dáil and Presidential elections, respectively.

[99]It states as follows that: "All powers of government, legislative, executive and judicial, derive, under God, from the people, whose right it is to designate the rulers of the State and, in final appeal, to decide all questions of national policy, according to the requirements of the common good."

[100]See s.2(IB) of the Electoral (Amendment) Act, 1985.

Communities, this silent and subtle change in the Irish constitutional conception of national sovereignty and the possibility of extending national electoral rights to Community nationals can partly be attributed to the state's subsequent accession to the Communities.[101] This view is supported by the singling out of nationals of the Member States of the Community in the 1985 legislation for possible reciprocal arrangements for the enjoyment of voting rights in national elections. If Community membership was irrelevant to this extension of voting rights, the specification of Community nationals in the 1985 Act would be meaningless and the provison would perhaps have referred to the member countries of the Council of Europe, or some other more general grouping. If this view is accepted, the effect of Community membership on national conceptions of sovereignty and state definition is nothing short of revolutionary, even if the traditionally liberal Irish perception of political participation means that its effect went unobserved at national level. Unlike the French, whose opposition to the Union Treaty largely centred on the Treaty's perceived interference with national sovereignty, the provisions of Article 8(b)(1) have excited little discussion in Ireland.

However, the Union Treaty could arguably have some effect on Ireland's electoral regime, in particular, on the rights which United Kingdom nationals resident in Ireland may enjoy in parliamentary elections. On the basis of a broad interpretation of the principle of equal treatment which has been discussed in other chapters, Ireland could arguably be obliged to extend this favourable treatment presently restricted to British nationals, to other Community nationals. In *Matteucci* the Court of Justice held that a bilateral agreement (reserving educational scholarships to the nationals of two Member States) cannot prevent the application of the principle of equal treatment between national and Community workers.[102] This was the case even though cultural agreements like that in question fall outside the scope of the Treaty. Can Ireland limit application of the principle of equal treatment on the basis of reciprocity as it does in s.2(IB) of the 1985 Electoral Act? Application of the principle of equal treatment in *Matteucci* was determined with reference to the position of the applicant rather than the subject matter of the agreement in question. Also relevant to a possible application of the principle of equal treatment to nationals of other Member States resident in Ireland but ineligible in national elections is the *Cowan* case.[103] That case extended the principle of equal treatment to national legislation on criminal injuries compensation schemes which did not come within the scope of the Community, but which, since it affected the rights of recip-

---

[101]See, for example, Frowein, J.A. and Stein, T. (eds.), *The Legal Position of Aliens in National and International Law* Pt. 2 (1987) Max Planck Institut/Springer Verlag, at p.2017: "A process of integration in the European Communities whereby nationals of Member States would gain access not only to market, but also to parliamentary elections was recommended. In the speaker's opinion, the traditional principle embodied in many constitutions that resident aliens are refused participation in national elections fails to honour their contributions to public funds and collides with one of the basic democratic values: the claim that taxation must be linked to parliamentary representation." The speaker was Mary Robinson.

[102]Case 235/87 [1988] ECR 5589.

[103]Case 186/87 [1989] ECR 195.

ients of services who were in a situation "governed by Community law", could not be applied in a non-discriminatory manner.

Although national legislation permitting Community nationals to vote in parliamentary elections is not required by Article 8(b)(1) and does not come within the scope of Community law, Article 6 could arguably be applied to prevent the discriminatory application of such national legislation "in a situation governed by Community law" when it affects the rights of resident Community nationals. Provision for the possibility of extending national electoral rights has already been made in the Irish Constitution and subsequent legislation. However, the element of reciprocity required by the 1985 Act for the adoption of a ministerial order to admit other Member States' nationals would be lacking if such an eventuality is provoked by judicial proceedings using a combination of Articles 8 and 6 of the EC Treaty. In such a situation, Ireland would be required to allow resident nationals from other Member States to vote in national elections purely because it operated a more liberal regime than its neighbours, despite the fact that similar treatment would not be enjoyed by Irish nationals resident in other Member States. Mechanical interference of this kind with Member State legislation should be avoided. It is unlikely, however, that the principle of equal treatment will be permiited to operate in this manner. Directive 93/109, for example, has recognised that more open and liberal electoral regimes exist in certain Member States and has provided that the limited rights provided for in Article 8(b)(2) and the arrangements adopted thereunder are not intended to interfere with such regimes.[104]

Netherlands

Article 130 of the Dutch Constitution, which was promulgated in 1983, provided that electoral rights could be granted by statute to non-Dutch residents in local elections.[105] This provision is to be found in Chapter 7 of the Constitution on provincial, local and decentralised government, whereas Article 4, which confers voting rights on nationals, is located amongst the basic rights listed in Chapter 1 of the Constitution. Consequently, a difference exists in Dutch law, at least from a theoretical perspective, between non-national voting rights and the parallel rights enjoyed by Dutch nationals.

The Dutch reform was not easily achieved, however.[106] The rules for amending the Dutch Constitution require that elections take place between the first and sec-

---

[104]See, for example, Article 14(2).

[105]See Groenendijk, C., Dutch Report to the Louvain-la-Neuve symposium, op. cit., at p.134, where he gives details of the original 1975 proposal to grant electoral rights to non-nationals. The Netherlands had also experimented with "partial town councils" for foreign residents; an immigrant advisory council (Migrantenraad) operated in Utrecht and advisory committees in Gouda and Zaanstad: Council of Europe report, op. cit., at p.39; and Rath, J., "Political Participation of Ethnic Minorities in the Netherlands", 17 *International Migration Review* (1983) 445–469. An exception is made, however, as regards residents in the service of a foreign state or international organisation, see Turpin, op. cit., at p.149.

[106]For further details see Rath, J., "Voting Rights", in Layton Henry, op. cit. note 91, at p.137.

ond reading of the bill proposing the amendment. With respect to the bill proposed in 1975[107] and considered in Parliament in 1976, the second reading could only take place in 1981, provided the Parliament served its full term. Article 46 of the Charter of the Kingdom of the Netherlands (*Koninkrijksstatuut*) provided that representative bodies should be elected by Dutch nationals resident in the Netherlands. This article was amended in 1985 as were the relevant provisions of the Dutch Electoral Act.[108] Non-nationals, including third country nationals, may vote if they have attained 18 years of age, are resident in the relevant municipality and have been legally resident in the Netherlands for five years prior to the elections, in accordance with Articles 9 and 10 of the Aliens Act (Vreemdelingenwet), the EC Treaty or the Treaty establishing the Benelux Economic Union. Article 3(d) of the European Election Act allows other Member States' nationals to vote in European Parliament elections in the Netherlands if they are eligible to exercise the right to vote in their own country. Only Dutch nationals may stand for election in the Netherlands.

There had been some debate in the early 1980s concerning extension of electoral rights at provincial and national level to non-nationals. Foreign policy and defence arguments were used to block these proposals with respect to national elections, while the involvement of provincial bodies in the election of the Eerste Kamer, which plays a legislative role similar to the House of Lords, dissuaged politicians from extending the franchise in provincial elections. Current proposals for revised provisions on naturalisation in the Nationality Act make political participation at national level dependent on the acquisition of Dutch nationality.[109] The period of residence required for the purposes of naturalisation is generally five years.[110] The required period of residence for the enjoyment of electoral rights in local elections was related to the duration of one term of municipal office in the 1988 proposal on electoral rights in municipal elections. Article 8(b)(1) and Directive 94/80 do not specify any particular period of residence. If one term term of office is used, the required period could be anything from three years upwards, depending on the Member State. Is it possible that Community nationals will find it easier, in certain Member States, to naturalise and therefore acquire voting rights in national elections than to acquire local electoral rights in Member States which require a long period of residence pursuant to Directive 94/80? It will be unfortunate if Member States empty the content of citizenship of its meaning by insisting on long periods

[107]Bijl. Hand. II 1975–76, 13991.

[108]See D'Oliveira, H.U.J., "Electoral Rights for Non-Nationals", 31 *Netherlands International Law Review* (1984) 59–72, at 59–60. The present basis for the right to vote for non-nationals in local elections is Article B.3, s.2 of the Elections Act (*Kieswet*) of 28 September 1989, Staatsblad 1989, 423 as amended in Staatsblad 1989, 480.

[109]See D'Oliveira, H.U.J., (1991) Nederlands Juristenblad 1734–1741, for details of the previous state of the law. A similar solution is favoured in Belgium, see Mabille, X., "Droit de vote et nationalité", 1279–1292 *Courrier Hebdomadaire* (1990), at 13–14 *et seq.*

[110]See Turpin, D., op. cit. note 95, at p.203 for details of the various naturalisation time limits and their sources in national legislation. The five year residence period was also applied by the United Kingdom, France, Belgium (*petite naturalisation*) and Italy; see also de Rham, G., "Naturalisation: The Politics of Citizenship Acquisition", in Layton Henry, op. cit. note 91, pp.158–185, at 158 *et seq.*

of residence. At issue are municipal not national elections. It is not necessary to limit electoral rights at this level on the basis of stricter criteria than other Member States employ with reference to naturalisation and participation in national elections. In Italy, for example, naturalisation legislation allows Community nationals to be accorded Italian nationality after they have resided for only four years.[111]

Spain

Article 13 para.2 of the 1978 Spanish Constitution provided that only Spanish nationals could enjoy the rights established in Article 23, with the exception of active electoral rights in municipal elections established on a reciprocal basis by Treaty or law.[112] In Decision 112/91, the Constitutional Court emphasised that this possibility was limited to the extension of rights to vote (active electoral rights) and did not include the right to stand for election (passive electoral rights).[113] Furthermore, in response to arguments based on Community law, the Court held that no Community legal norm yet existed which regulated the electoral rights of Community nationals. Indeed, the Court argued that, whatever the value and scope of such a hypothetical Community norm might be, all that existed was a proposal for a Directive, which was not legally binding. The Court was only concerned with legislation with binding force and what the Community and Member States might do in future was another matter.

Legislation on voting rights was not enacted on the basis of this provision for all Community nationals prior to the adoption of the Union Treaty. In 1990, Spain concluded a Treaty on local voting rights with Denmark and the Netherlands and subsequently, in 1991, with Norway and Sweden.[114] What is interesting about Spain is the manner in which Articles 8(b)(1) and (2) were received in Spain and the legislative and political debate which surrounded the adoption of the necessary amendments to the Constitution and secondary legislation. The Spanish delegation to the intergovernmental negotiations on political union were the most progressive supporters of European citizenship. They said that they regarded citizenship as a means to enhance the Community's democratic legitimacy.[115] It was not to be expected, therefore, that Spain's difficulties with the Union Treaty would centre on the issue of granting electoral rights at local level to other Member States' nationals.

In July 1992, the Spanish Constitutional Court was asked whether the Union Treaty was compatible with the Spanish constitution. It held that, in the main, the Union Treaty did not require prior constitutional amendments, but that constitutional reform was necessary as regards the grant of active electoral rights to

[111]Law no.91, 5 February 1992, JO no.38, 15 February 1992.
[112]See also Article 176 of the Organic Law on the General Electoral Regime of 19 June 1985; Article 5(2) of the Organic Law 7/1985 of 1 July 1985, on the rights and freedoms of foreigners in Spain; and Article 18.2 of the Law establishing the basis for local authorities.
[113]Published in supplement no.146 of the Spanish Official Journal, 9 June 1991.
[114]See Arnaldo Alcubilla, E., op. cit. note 85, at 85 and 86.
[115]See Co. Doc. SN 3940/90, 24 September 1990.

Member State nationals resident in Spain.[116] The Constitutional Court examined Article 8(b)(1) for its compatibility with Article 13(2) of the Constitution and Article 23, which confers on "citizens" the right to succeed to political office on an equal basis in accordance with conditions laid down by law. The Court held that the latter was a specific expression of the principle of equal treatment applicable to citizens and contained nothing capable of prohibiting electoral rights from being extended to the citizens of the European Union. However, Article 1.2 of the Constitution states that national sovereignty resides in the Spanish people. In the view of the Court, granting electoral rights to foreigners could only contradict this provision if the rights in question related to authorities whose "powers flow directly from the Constitution and the Statutes of Autonomy and which therefore are connected with national sovereignty, which is not the case for municipal authorities" (author's own translation). The question remained, however, whether Article 8(b)(1) could be ratified without prior revision of the Constitution, or whether ratification of the Treaty could proceed by means of a normal organic law pursuant to Article 93.[117] This proved impossible, since the Court also held that Article 13(2) did not permit the right to stand for election being extended to non-nationals. Although it conceded that the Constitution did not define who Spanish citizens are and that, in the context of Article 13(2), it is for the legislator to do so: "it could not, without incurring unconstitutionality, fragment, parcel or manipulate that condition recognising only certain effects for it with the sole objective of conceding to non-nationals a fundamental right, such as the right to stand for election, from which they are expressly excluded by Article 13(2)" (author's own translation). The Government had argued that the Constitution did not define "Spanish" and, therefore, did not impede European Union citizens being treated as "Spanish" for the purposes of Article 8(b)(1) and local elections. However, since the Court held that there was a contradiction between Article 13(2) of the Constitution and Article 8(b)(1) of the Union Treaty, the only means to rectify it was an amendment of the Constitution in accordance with the general or ordinary means to amend the Constitution envisaged in Article 167.

There was considerable debate in Spain about how to accomodate Article 8(b)(1). Some commentators preferred an organic law pursuant to Article 93 of the Constitution, which would have reformed the existing electoral laws.[118] The Court's decision indicated that this was clearly an insufficient means to constitutionally accommodate the provisions of the Union Treaty. A consultative referendum for the ratification of the Union Treaty was not regarded as juridically necessary, however, and parliamentary reform of the Constitution via Congress

---

[116]See the decision of the Spanish Constitutional Court, 1 July 1992; reproduced in 19 *Revista de Instituciones Europeas* (1992) 633.

[117]Article 93 authorises the ratification of treaties via organic laws which attribute to international organs or institutions the exercise of competences derived from the Constitution.

[118]See the opinion of the Council of State of 20 June 1991, no.850/91/seccion 2a, which held that there was no need to reform the Constitution and that authorisation for the ratification of the Union Treaty could be given in accordance with Article 93.

and the Senate was preferred. Those in favour of parliamentary reform of the Constitution drew attention to Spain's very recent accession to the Community when, they argued, it must have realised some of the Community's more long term objectives. This is in contrast to the position of founding Member States, such as France, which acceded to a very different Community which professed almost exclusively economic objectives and which could not then have foreseen the dynamic nature of the Community's construction. However, a consultative referendum had not been considered necessary when Spain acceded to the Communities and one was not considered necessary to confirm its continued accession after the conclusion of the Union Treaty.[119] All that was regarded as necessary following the Constitutional Court's decision was the addition of the words "passive" (in the sense of the right to stand for election) to the pre-existing provision which admitted active voting by non-nationals on the basis of reciprocity.[120]

The Spanish constitutional philosophy regarding the political participation of foreigners is clearly not as restrictive as the French. However, the Constitutional Court denied foreign participation in municipal elections having any effect on national sovereignty which, according to Article 1.2, only resides in the Spanish people. Furthermore, it took a Community Treaty amendment to provide the impetus for the actual implementation of the neglected possibility enshrined in Article 13.2 of the Constitution and to widen the parameters of that constitutional provision to allow Community nationals to stand for election in municipal elections. Some problems appear to have survived in Spain since Article 13.2 of the Constitution provides that "on the basis of reciprocity, the right to active and passive elecoral rights in municipal elections may be granted to citizens of other states by means of a treaty or a law". This condition of reciprocity subsequently appears in *Real Decreto* 202/1995, of 10 February 1995. It is unclear whether the latter is designed to transpose Directive 94/80, since no explicit mention is made of the Directive. However, this condition of reciprocity has been translated into Spanish secondary legislation to limit electoral rights to those Union citizens whose Member States of nationality have concluded the necessary agreements with Spain and which comply with the remaining conditions established in the Royal Decree.[121] This Royal Decree which appears, in principle, to be incompatible with the guarantee in Article 8(b)(1) will be discussed in Chapter 7.4.4.

France

Article 3 of the 1958 French Constitution provides that all adult French citizens who enjoy civil and political rights may vote according to the conditions determined

---

[119]See *El Pais*, 3 July 1992, at 1 and 15.

[120]See the adopted text in BOE no.207, 28 August 1992; and the amendment of the Electoral Law, BOE no.77, 3 March 1994.

[121]The situation is further confused in Spain by the fact that the 1991 amendment of the Organic Law on the General Electoral Regime provided that the condition of reciprocity could derive from "a Treaty or Community law". Organic Law 8/1991, 13 March 1991, amending Article 176.1 of the 1985 law.

by law. Article 3(1) further stipulates that national sovereignty belongs to the people, who exercise it through their representatives. Prior to the adoption of the Union Treaty all non-nationals were excluded from voting in French elections on this basis. Municipal elections feature separately in Article 72 of Title IX of the Constitution, however, which refers to: "ces collectivités [territoriales] s'administrent librement par des conseils élus et dans les conditions prévues par la loi". It has been argued that the position and wording of the latter provision indicated that national sovereignty was not at issue in municipal elections. As a result, it was suggested that municipal elections could be regulated on the basis of ordinary legislation, regardless of the reservation of voting rights to nationals in Article 3(1).[122] The French *Conseil constitutionnel* has held, however, that "il resulte des articles 3 de la Constitution et 6 de la Déclaration de 1789 que la qualité de citoyen ouvre le droit de vote et l'éligibilité dans les conditions identiques à tous ceux qui n'en sont pas exclus pour une raison d'âge, d'incapacité ou de nationalité ... Ces principes de valeur constitutionelle s'opposent à toute division par catégories des électeurs ou des éligibles pour tout suffrage politique."[123] Municipal elections were implicitly included within the scope of this reasoning. Furthermore, Article L280 of the Electoral Code provided that the Senate was elected by an electoral college which comprised of delegates of the municipal councils. Since the Senate does form part of the expression of national sovereignty and since delegates from municipal authorities participate in electing the Senate, participation in the election of municipal councils was restricted to nationals, who are the repositories of national sovereignty according to Article 3.

Given the absence of an explicit exclusion of non-nationals in Article 3, this conclusion could have been avoided, however, by reforming the Senate electoral college to exclude municipal councils, or foreign members of municipal councils. The election of the Senate is determined by ordinary law and this reform need not have been difficult to perform. Indeed, ordinary legislation could even have provided that the Senate be elected by direct universal suffrage.[124] In the alternative, the structure of municipal councils could have been revised to allow for the creation of distinct national and non-national electoral colleges. The former alone would have been involved in the election of the Senate, or the designation of the *grands électeurs* in the senate elections.[125] This could only have occured if local

---

[122]See the Derosier Report for the Délégation de l'Assemblée Nationale pour les CEs, "Le droit de vote et l'éligibilité des ressortissants des Etats membres de la CEE aux élections municipales", 31 May 1989, at p.273. The exclusion of municipal authorities from the definition of national sovereignty was also discussed by the Spanish Constitutional Court.

[123]Décision no.82-146 DC du 18 November 1982; and see Masclet, J.C., *Droit Electoral* (1989) Paris, PUF, at pp.12, 22 and 47.

[124]See Luchaire, F., "L'Union Européenne et la Constitution (I)", *Revue du droit public et de la science politique en France et à l'étranger* (1992) 589–616, at 597; Luchaire points to the law of 27 October 1946, whereby the first Council of the Republic (parliamentary assembly representing local councils) was elected by universal suffrage.

[125]This would have required amendment of Articles 2 and 44 of the Electoral Code and Articles 121-128 of the Municipalities Code. In support of this view see Bockel, "La Constitution Française et les

elections were not regarded as political elections within the meaning of Article 3, so as to exclude the equal treatment consequences of the 1982 decision of the *Conseil constitutionnel*, or if the link between citizenship and voting in political elections were disgarded. French legal doctrine on the issue of non-national voting rights generally suggested, however, that such a change was not possible in the forseeable future: "le caractère très vite passionel pris par le débat relatif au droit de vote ne permet pas de penser que l'étranger pourra en jouir dans un proche avenir".[126] The Commission was also of the view in its 1986 report on voting rights, that constitutional amendment was necessary in France to accomodate voting rights for Community nationals resident in France, even if the initiative for change came from the Community.[127]

Attempts to extend the franchise were abandoned by the Mitterrand government in the early 1980s in the face of considerable opposition.[128] Following the elections in May 1981, the government introduced a bill to parliament on the subject of local voting rights.[129] French public opinion, the CGT unions, and the conservative and communist parties refused to support the bill and there was no majority for the proposal in the Senate. It was dropped as a consequence. The issue of voting rights re-emerged in 1985 when, in a speech to the Congress of the League of Human Rights, President Mitterrand announced that he personally viewed such an extension as just, but that he was unwilling to expose the government to the nation's general lack of comprehension on the matter.[130] The depth of the controversy excited in France by the provisions of the Union Treaty on electoral rights for Community nationals in local elections was remarkable. However, given French views on the relationship between electoral rights and national sovereignty and citizenship, the reaction was not surprising. A survey in 1981 by SOFRES had revealed that more than 60 per cent of those interviewed were against the extension

étrangers" in *Les droits des immigrés*, Association des juristes pour la reconnaissance des droits fondamentaux des immigrés, (1983) Aix-en-Provence, at p.39: "par modification du Code Electoral ... les étrangers pourraient participer aux élections municipales ... rien *a priori*, dans la Constitution ne s'y oppose."

[126]See Breillat, D., "Les droits politiques de l'étranger en France", in *La condition juridique de l'étranger, hier et aujourd'hui*, Actes du colloque organisé à Nimegue 9–11 May 1988 par les Facultés de droit de Poitiers et de Nimegue, (1988) Faculteit Der Rechtsgeleerdheid, at p.82.

[127]See Bull. EC. 7/86.

[128]For details of legislative proposals in France in the late 1970s and 1980s see De Lobkowicz, W., "Un droit de vote municipal pour tous les européens. Commentaire de la proposition de Directive du 22 June 1988", 322 RMC (1988) 602–613, at 603, fn.15; see also Wihtol de Wenden, C., "Les immigrés et le discours politique municipale", 4–5 *Recherches sur les migrations internationales* (1982) 68, who details individual French political party support or opposition to electoral rights proposals for non-nationals, at 69 *et seq.*; and *Hommes et Migrations*, 998, 15 October 1980. See also socialist party support, "Les socialistes et l'immigration", *Documentation Socialiste*, 2 sp.l, September 1980, at 3; and the Déclaration faite à l'association internationale des maîtres des capitales francophones, Bruxelles, 15 October 1979, which received the support of the then Mayor of Paris, Mr Chirac.

[129]Known as the Creteil programme. It proposed voting rights for foreign residents after five years' residence. Supported by Claude·Cheysson on a visit to Algiers in August 1981: see *Le Figaro*, 10 August 1981 and *Le Monde*, 11 August 1981. See also Layton-Henry, op. cit., at p.130; and Breillat, D., "Le Vote des Etrangers en Europe du Nord", in Turpin, op. cit.

[130]Cited in Luchaire, F. and Conac, G., *La Constitution de la République Française* (1987) Economica, 2nd edn., at p.206.

of the franchise to non-nationals. Admittedly, the debate at that time was not limited to the extension of voting rights to Community nationals and at least some of the difficulties encountered in France were related to fears that an extension of voting rights to Community nationals was a forerunner of the extension of voting rights to all resident non-nationals.[131] Moreover, extension of voting rights alters the French constitutional conception of the people as the sole repositories of national sovereignty as defined with reference to citizenship, political participation and electoral rights.[132] Essential conditions for the exercise of national sovereignty have been defined by the *Conseil constitutionnel* as – assuring respect for national institutions, the continuation of the life of the nation and the guarantee of the rights and freedoms of citizens.[133] A general constitutional facelift had been forecast by Mitterrand before the Union Treaty was concluded. However, the French public and political class seemed to resent progress being foist upon them by the intergovernmental conference. Nevertheless, in a press conference following the conclusion of the Union Treaty in December 1991, it became clear that the French government was prepared to act in accordance with Article 8(b)(1) and did not intend to seek refuge in the possibility of derogations provided therein.[134]

Article 54 of the French Constitution provides that if the *Conseil constitutionnel* declares that an international commitment carries with it a clause contrary to the Constitution that authorisation for that ratification of that commitment, or for its approval, can only take place after the Constitution has been revised.[135] However, Article 55 provides that once a treaty has been ratified or approved, it is superior to ordinary law, but not the Constitution. Difficulties regarding constitutionality were not expected in France with respect to European Parliament elections. However, the issue of local electoral rights was extremely controversial because it altered the link between national citizenship and political participation and, once again, it was feared that it might be extended in future to all resident non-nationals.[136]

---

[131]With respect to the Union Treaty see the fears expressed by some deputies in the national assembly, Chalteil, op. cit. note 88, at 331.

[132]See, for example, the position of the Communist party with respect to electoral rights for non-nationals in the early 1980s reported in L'Humanité, 27 December 1980: "Le PCF demande un statut démocratique en tenant compte à la fois de leur [immigrés] situation de travailleur en France et de celle de citoyen de leurs pays auquel ils restent attachés."

[133]See the decision of the Conseil constitutionnel of 22 May 1985; and Boulouis, J., *Actualité Juridique et Droit Administratif* (1983) 80, who defined national sovereignty as a: "concept abstrait lié à l'existence du corps politique, le citoyen en est la composante elementaire, dont l'interchangeabilité garantit, avec la parfaite homogeneité du corps, l'indivisibilité de la souveraineté dont il est titulaire".

[134]"L'indispensable réforme de la Constitution", *Le Monde*, 12 December 1991: "certes le projet de traité prevoit que des dispositions derogatoires pourront être prévues lorsques des problèmes specifiques à un Etat le justifieront. Mais M. Mitterrand n'a pas l'intention d'user de cette possibilité, puisqu'au cours de sa conférence de presse, à l'issue du conseil européen, il a déclaré à ce sujet: 'On prendera les moyens qu'il faudra'."

[135]For a detailed description of these procedures see Oliver, P., "The French Constitution and the Treaty of Maastricht", 43 ICLQ (1994) 1–25.

[136]See Paris, G. and Robert-Diard, P., "On va donc accorder aux Européens ce que l'on refuse aux Corses", *Le Monde*, 13 December 1991; denied by Mitterrand, *Le Monde*, 17 December 1991; feared, however, by Chirac, "Maastricht simple étape", *Le Monde*, 21 December 1991 at p.9. The foreign pop-

Furthermore, a policy of decentralisation has operated in France since 1983, which has considerably increased the power of local authorities and rendered the issue of non-national access to such elections even more sensitive.[137]

Political opinion was divided on the issue.[138] An undertaking was made when the Union Treaty was concluded in December 1991 that a constitutional referendum would take place in order to reform the Constitution and regularise this transfer of sovereignty to the Community and the admission of non-nationals to electoral rights.[139] Article 89 of the French Constitution provides for two alternative amendment procedures – parliamentary or popular. A government or parliamentary bill proposing the amendment must be passed by the two Assemblies in identical terms. The President may then choose to submit it to the people or to parliament, which is convened in congress. The proposal is approved by the latter if it is accepted by a three fifths majority of the votes cast.[140] Article 11 of the Constitution is also relevant, in that it allows issues dealing with the organisation of public authorities to be submitted to referendum without parliamentary debate.[141] However, the subject matter of the proposal must not be contrary to basic law and the incompatibility of Article 8(b)(1) with certain French constitutional provisions seems to have prevented recourse to the Article 11 procedure. If the French Constitution was reformed to accommodate the provisions on electoral rights, the President could then choose to ratify the Union Treaty by a parliamentary vote or by a direct referendum, once again with reference to Article 11, but this time the incompatibility in question would have been remedied. In the event, the Union Treaty was referred to the people and was passed by a slim majority on 20 September 1992.

The French *Conseil constitutionnel* was asked by the French President pursuant to Article 54, whether ratification of the Union Treaty first required a revision of the Constitution. The Court stated that Article 3 of the Constitution specified that national sovereignty belonged to the people and that only French nationals were

---

ulation in France has more than doubled from 1,744,000 in 1946 to 4,488,000 in 1984. Less than half are nationals of Community Member States; see Guimezanes, N., *La circulation et l'activité économique des étrangers dans la CE, Droit communautaire, Droits nationaux* (1990) Nouvelles Editions Fiduciaires, at p.44.

[137]See Rath, J., "Voting Rights", in Layton Henry op. cit. note 91, at p.131.

[138]The Rassemblement pour la republiqué (RPR) and National Front were against, while the Union democratique française (UDF), Parti socialiste (PS) and Parti communiste française (PCF) supported the reform; see "La citoyenneté européenne divise l'opposition", *Le Monde*, 14 December 1991 at 10; and *Le Monde*, 14 January 1992.

[139]See *Le Monde*, 14 January 1992, where President Mitterrand announced the likely revision of the Constitution to cater for non-national electoral rights and the transfer of sovereignty in the Union Treaty.

[140]For a detailed discussion of the amendment procedure with particular reference to the Union Treaty see Luchaire, F., "L'Union Européenne et la Constitution (II)", 4 *Revue du droit politique* (1992) 933–981, at 935–937.

[141]Article 11 provides for a referendum procedure for treaties which "sans être contraire à la Constitution, aurait des incidences sur le fonctionnement des institutions" which is the case with respect to European and local elections. This procedure was used by De Gaulle with respect to the election of the President of the Republic by direct universal suffrage.

electors.[142] It further held that local authorities are created by law and that they are to be administered under conditions provided by law (Article 72). The Court held that pursuant to Article 24 and given the fact that the Senate represents local authorities, it must be elected by an electoral body which itself is representative of local authorities and, therefore, local councillors must have an influence on the election of the Senate. Given this fact, it held that: "to the extent that the Senate participates in the exercise of national sovereignty, only nationals can participate in the election of the deliberating bodies of local authorities. The Constitution must therefore be revised to permit the ratification of the Treaty."[143] The Court reiterated its previous decision that the European Parliament does not interfere with the exercise of national sovereignty and thus, that no amendment of the Constitution was required in this respect to accommodate Article 8(b)(2). The decision was based on the fact that the European Parliament was a product of the Treaties, not the French Constitution, and it was not, therefore, an institution in which the sovereign will of the French people was expressed pursuant to Article 3. Its decision was also based on the fact that the European Parliament "does not constitute a sovereign parliament enjoying general powers, nor does it seek to compete with the exercise of national sovereignty". It was necessary, in the light of the Court's decision, to amend the Constitution to permit non-national participation in local elections.

Following the decision of the *Conseil constitutionnel* the government presented its project for constitutional reform to the two assemblies. Once the constitution was revised, the government favoured ordinary legislation to modify the relevant provisions of the electoral law which is normally contained in ordinary legislation. The opposition parties preferred an organic law due to the importance of the subject matter involved. Organic laws are laws of an institutional nature which are provided for in the Constitution. In the end, the project for constitutional revision was accepted, but on condition that subsequent legislative changes be introduced by organic laws, which by virtue of Article 46, requires the Senate's agreement with regard to aspects of the proposed legislation which concern it. This political compromise could have meant and could still mean that the Senate will be able to block or render extremely difficult the passage of any organic law providing for the conditions for the exercise of electoral rights under the Union Treaty. The constitutional law relating to the electoral rights in the Union Treaty was promulgated in France on the 25 June 1992.[144] Article 88-3 of Title IV of the constitutional law provides that

> "Sous réserve de reciprocité, et selon les modalités prévues par le traité sur l'Union Européenne signé le 7 February 1992, le droit de vote et d'éligibilité aux élections municipales peut être accordé aux seuls citoyens de l'Union résidant en France. Ces citoyens ne peuvent exercer les fonctions de maire ou adjoint ni participer à la desig-

---

[142]Décision no.92-308 DC of 9 April 1992, JO 11 April 1992, 5354; and the observations by Jacqué, J.P., "Commentaire de la décision du Conseil Constitutionnel no.92-308 DC du 9 avril, 1992", 28 RTDE (1992) 251.

[143]Author's own translation of recitals 24-27; see Jacqué, op. cit. note 142, at 260.

[144]*Loi-Constitutionelle* no.92-554 of 25 June 1992.

nation des électeurs sénatoriaux et à l'élection des sénateurs. Une loi organique votée dans les mêmes termes par les deux Assemblées determine les conditions d'application du présent article.

The reciprocity condition appears to stem from the 15th recital in the preamble to the Constitution which provides that France will consent to limiting its sovereignty, so far as it is necessary for the organisation and maintenance of peace, on a reciprocal basis.[145] The amendment of the Constitution was followed by the adoption of implementing legislation and the ratification by the President. The advice of commentators like Vedel and Luchaire that the constitutional amendment could authorise ratification directly, was not followed.

Although Union citizens are allowed to participate in municipal elections, they are excluded from participating in senatorial elections or in the designation of the senatorial electoral college. However, the mere fact of participating in local elections and electing local representatives (even if they are French nationals) would appear to suggest that Union citizens indirectly participate in the election of the senate. The decree calling for a referendum was adopted by the President on 1 July 1992 with the text of the bill which would amend the Constitution annexed to it. In the event, the project was passed by a tiny majority in September 1992.[146] In the meantime, the *Conseil constitutionnel* had been reconsulted about non-national participation in local elections.[147] It held that the proposed constitutional project was compatible with the Union Treaty and that the organic law to be adopted thereunder must respect the provisions of Community law. Furthermore, it cleared up the ambiguity mentioned above – the fact that non-nationals could vote in local elections meant their automatic "participation" in the election of the senate via their elected members. The Court stated that the phrase "election of senators" and, therefore, the point when national sovereignty becomes involved, can be interpreted as beginning only after the appointment of the grand electors to the senate electoral college.[148]

---

[145]See Oliver, op. cit. note 135, at 12.
[146]See Law no.92-1017.
[147]In accordance with Article 54 of the Constitution, sixty senators seised the court.
[148]See Décision no.92-312 DC, 2 September 1992; and Luchaire, F., "L'Union Européenne et la Constitution (IV): Le Référendum", 6 *Revue du droit public* (1992) 1587–1609, at 1593.

Chapter 7

Equal Treatment and Political Participation (II)

7.1. Introduction

Prior to the adoption of the Union Treaty, no clear and uncontested legislative basis existed for the adoption of a Community instrument on electoral rights at municipal level. As a result, this chapter first locates the issue of municipal electoral rights in the context of the "special rights" campaign and the development of Community citizenship. In conjunction with proposals for a general right of residence detached from the exercise of an economic activity, electoral rights at municipal level for Community nationals on the basis of residence, was one of the twin prongs of the Citizens' Europe campaign. In 1988, notwithstanding the absence of a clear-cut legal basis, the Commission presented Council with a draft proposal for a directive on the basis of Article 235. The adoption of Article 8(b)(1) overtook the 1988 proposal and provided an explicit legal basis for the adoption of a Community instrument. However, Article 8(b)(1) has been the subject of considerable controversy both during and after the ratification of the Union Treaty. In particular, an analysis of the substantive content of the Directive on municipal elections, which was adopted in 1994, suggests that problems in this respect have not yet been totally resolved. First of all, the incorporation of a series of fairly extensive derogations in the text of the Directive itself undermines the extension of the principle of equal treatment to the rights of Union citizens in the field of municipal elections. Furthermore, the implementation of Directive 94/80 in some Member States appears to be incompatible with the provisions of Article 8(b)(1) since the rights of Union citizens have been made conditional on the existence of reciprocity.

7.2. Community Law and Electoral Rights at Municipal Level

The right to participate in local elections on the basis of residence was identified in the 1970s as an essential step in the creation of what was known as a Citizens'

Europe.[1] The Heads of Government meeting in Paris in 1974 established a working group to examine the possibility of granting "special rights" to Community citizens in their capacity as members of the Community.[2] The Commission subsequently identified civil and political rights, enjoyed on an equal treatment basis with nationals, as the "special rights" envisaged by the Paris summit. In its view, proposals with respect to such rights were to include voting rights and a right to stand for election at municipal level.[3] Apart from some cautious attempts to identify a legal basis within the Treaty text,[4] the following decade witnessed little fresh legal or political input in the electoral rights debate.[5]

The Scelba[6] and Macciochi[7] Reports both addressed the issue of voting rights. According to the former, the Community principle of equal treatment of all citizens included the grant of political rights. However, this general principle, expressed negatively in Article 6 in terms of non-discrimination, was limited to the scope of application of the Treaty. To argue in 1977 that the exercise of political rights was related to the exercise of free movement and, therefore, came within the scope of Community law and the principle of non-discrimination required cogent supporting arguments which the Scelba Report failed to provide. At that time, Articles 2 and 3 effectively circumscribed the objectives of the Treaty and the means available for their accomplishment.[8] Despite the adoption of the SEA and the considerable non-economic additions to Community law in the meantime (the environment, health and safety), heated debate still persisted as to whether the ob-

---

[1]See Debs. EP (1972–73) nos.148–150, Mansholt at 107, 19 April 1972. In bringing the European citizen "into the construction of Europe", Belgian and Italian Prime Ministers Eyskens and Andreotti were keen to admit migrant workers to local political participation, provided they fulfilled certain residence conditions, Bull. EC 11/1972 vol.5, 37 at 39 and 43, respectively.

[2]Bull. EC 12-1974, at 10 and 11. For further details of the role of the European Council in this regard see Macciochi Report, Doc. 1-121/83, at 10. On the subject of political rights generally, see Debs. EP, 11 June 1974; and Debs. EP, 17 January 1975.

[3]Towards a "Europe for Citizens", Bull. EC. (8) 1975 II nos.7/8, 12; The Protection of Fundamental Rights in the EC, Bull. EC. suppl.5/76; and the Commission's Action Programme for Migrant Workers, 18 December 1974.

[4]See the Commission's reply to Oral Question no.H-87/79, Debs. EP OJ Annex 245, sitting of 27 September 1979, 268 and 269, where it stated that: "Articles 2, 3(c) and 235 EEC could provide the legal basis for introducing the right to vote and to be elected in local elections."

[5]The issue was primarily consigned to Written Questions and debates in the European Parliament; see Written Question no.181/77, OJ 1977 C200/29; the submissions of Mr Ruffini, Debs. EP (1979–80) 248–252, 16 January 1980; Written Question no.779/79, OJ 1979 C299/25; Annex to OJ no.245, September 1979, 268; Council statement on Italian presidency in Annex to OJ no.250, January 1980, at 133; Debs. EP (1981–82) 268–271, 8 April 1981; Written question no.1041/81, OJ 1982 C12/10; EP Resolution on the rights of citizens of a Member State residing in a Member State other than their own to stand and vote in local elections, OJ 1984 C184/28.

[6]Doc. 366/77, 25 October 1977, EP Working Docs. 1977–78; and see Ceccarelli, A., "Il voto dei lavoratori migranti nella Comunita Europea", Il Mulino (1992) 366.

[7]Doc. 1-121/1983, EP Working Docs. 1983–84, 29 April 1983.

[8]For discussion of the changing objectives and scope of Articles 2 and 3 see Mattera, A., Le Marché Unique Européen. Ses règles, son fonctionnement (1990) Jupiter, at p.11; Vogel-Polsky, E. and Vogel, J., L'Europe sociale 1993. Illusion, alibi ou realité? (1991) Etudes Européennes, Editions de l'Université Libre de Bruxelles; and specifically in this context, the House of Lords Select Committee on the European Communities, Voting Rights in Local Elections, session 1989–90, 6th report, 6 February 1990, at 17.

jectives of the Community in Article 2 extended to non-economic activity.[9] When the Scelba report appeared in 1977, Article 236 was generally regarded as the only appropriate legal basis for Community action in the field of electoral rights.[10] The Parliament's resolution which followed the report accepted that the necessary conditions for recourse to Article 235 might not be fulfilled[11] and that recourse to a Treaty amendment pursuant to Article 236 might be necessary.[12]

The Macciochi Report cited the Treaty's preamble and Articles 2 and 3 in support of the proposition that integration of migrant workers into the social and political life of the Member States was one of the objectives of the Treaty. In the event that a formal proposal was to be requested by Parliament, the Legal Affairs Committee, on whose behalf the report was compiled, regarded Article 235 as the correct legal basis.[13] Problems concerning the definition of the level of government to which the proposal related, the possibility of the inclusion of regional elections and the constitutional difficulties which various Member States faced if such a proposal was adopted, led the majority of the Committee to the conclusion that the time was not politically ripe for a concrete legislative proposal.[14] According to a European Parliament resolution adopted following the report, complete equality of treatment with regard to political rights was an essential inherent Community objective and was to be located in the preamble of the Treaty and Article 2, which was said to extend to social matters.[15] In the absence of specific powers to act in this respect, Parliament now believed that the conditions for the application of Article 235 had been fulfilled.[16]

The Adonnino Report to the Milan European Council in June 1985, urged continued discussion on electoral rights.[17] However, the report categorically stated that the question fell within national jurisdiction. An intergovernmental approach

---

[9]See, for example, the House of Lords Select Committee on the European Communities, *Approximation of Laws*, session 1977–78, 22nd report, to the effect that use of Article 235 should be limited to the "economic and financial purposes provided for by Article 2 of the Treaty".

[10]Articles 236 provides: "The government of any Member State or the Commission may submit to the Council proposals for the amendment of this Treaty." See the Scelba Report, Doc. 346/77, at p.19: "As far as the procedural problems involved in writing 'special rights' into the Treaties are concerned, the Commission rightly regards Article 235 of the EEC treaty as an unsuitable legal basis since the granting of special rights does not constitute one of the objectives of the Community within the framework of the common market as mentioned by that Article."

[11]Similarly agreed by the Member States in COREPER in 1976, cited by the House of Lords Select Committee, op. cit. note 8, at p.12; and see the Commission's first comprehensive study of the voting rights issue in Bull. EC. 7/86, at 11.

[12]See the European Parliament's resolution on the granting of special rights to the citizens of the EC, which was to implement the decision of the Paris Summit of December 1974, OJ 1977 C299/26: "To press for an agreement between the Member States, on the basis of Article 235 and, possibly, Article 236 of the EEC Treaty."

[13]Doc. 1-121/83, point F, at 7.

[14]See Doc. 1-121/83, at recital 17-18 of the explanatory memorandum. The Political Affairs Committee, under the direction of Mr Mommersteeg, PE 81.688/fin/Ann IV, requested, however, that a proposal be drawn up by the end of 1983.

[15]OJ 1983 C184/28.

[16]Acting on behalf of the Commission, Mr Narjes failed to take up the request for a proposal but promised a report on the matter by the end of 1983, OJ Annex No. 1-300, 76.

[17]Bull. EC. Suppl. 7/85, point 2.2, at 20 and 21.

was therefore preferred by Council.[18] In 1985, the Danish delegation of the European Council proposed that two new articles be inserted into the Treaty.[19] The proposal was discussed at a preparatory meeting for the Intergovernmental conference on 30 and 31 October 1985. In the event, however, it was omitted from the amendments adopted in the SEA, which could be interpreted alternatively, as the abandonment of the intergovernmental approach to electoral rights, a belief that the SEA altered competences anyway, or simply lack of concern or commitment in this regard.

In 1986, three years later than promised, the Commission published its report on Voting Rights in Local Elections for Community Nationals.[20] The report carried a detailed demographic survey which assessed the numbers which would be involved if voting rights were extended to Member State nationals resident in a Member State other then their own. Only 39 per cent of foreigners then resident in the Community were Member State nationals, which represented a figure of some five million out of a total foreign resident population of thirteen million. The report claimed to establish a correlation between demographic statistics relating to the number of Community residents in each Member State and the political problems likely to be faced by the Member States in accepting a proposal to extend voting rights to Community nationals. In Belgium, for example, Community nationals represented approximately 9 per cent of the population. This percentage and their concentration in specific areas was said to have a definite impact on the political balance in the event of the right to vote being extended to Community nationals. The situation was even more extreme in Luxembourg, where foreign residents represent over a quarter (26.3 per cent) of the population and 92.7 per cent of these non-nationals are from Community Member States. The report argued that any extension of the electorate would alter the traditional political balance in these Member States.

The report also contained details of the constitutional obstacles faced by a number of Member States if the franchise were extended to non-nationals. In the view of the Commission, however, these constitutional and legal obstacles were not in-

---

[18]This position was confirmed by the Council in response to Written Question no.2747/86, OJ 1987 C177/70, where it was asked what action it intended to take regarding the voting rights of Dutch nationals resident in Spain. The Council was of the view that the reciprocity, non-reciprocity and grant of voting rights generally was a matter for the determination of individual Member States. Spain later agreed, of its own accord, to grant voting rights to Dutch nationals resident in Spain for more then three years; cited in Rath, J., "Voting Rights", in Layton-Henry, op. cit., at p.134.

[19]The proposed Articles 66a and 66b provided that: "Workers, the self-employed and their families shall be entitled to vote and stand in local and regional elections in their country of residence if they have lived there for at least three years."

[20]Bull EC Suppl. 7/86; for the interim debate before publication of the report, see the Marinaro report on the Commission's migration policy, Doc. 2-4/85 and the subsequent EP Resolution, OJ 1985 C259/2; Resolution on a People's Europe, OJ 1985 C345/27, at 30; EP Resolutions on the rights of nationals of other Member States to vote and stand in local government and European Parliament elections in their country of residence, OJ 1986 C345/82 and 83. Commissioner Ripa di Meana, who took part in the debate preceding adoption of the resolutions, had undertaken to ask the Commission whether the time was right to present a proposal for a Directive, OJ Annex no.2-332, 107, Doc. A2-133/85.

surmountable, since all constitutions permitted review procedures. It considered that the problem with local electoral rights was the difficulty involved in reaching political consensus rather than the legal implementation difficulties which such a proposal would entail.[21] However, the procedure for constitutional review in some Member States involves difficult parliamentary procedures, if not the temporary suspension of Parliament. The question involved was not simply political, since a successful proposal would have fundamentally altered the political and legal philosophies in some Member States regarding the link between political participation and national citizenship. Furthermore, the assertion that such a proposal could and should be adopted on the basis of Articles 235 had very real and significant legal consequences, namely, a considerable extension of what could be regarded as coming within the scope of the Treaty and as necessary for the completion of the common market.

The interim Vetter Report, published in 1987 on behalf of Parliament's Legal Affairs Committee, was extremely critical of the Commission's failure to present a legislative proposal in this context.[22] It rejected the Commission's attempts to tie electoral rights in local elections to the issue of a uniform electoral procedure for elections to the European Parliament. This was regarded as Commission subterfuge, excusing its own legislative procrastination by referring to the Parliament's lack of success or inertia with respect to the uniform electoral procedure. Prior to the adoption of the Union Treaty the right of legislative initiative with respect to the former lay with the Commission on the basis of Article 235, independent of the progress of the European Parliament under Article 138(3).

A proposal for a Directive was finally presented to the Council in 1988 on the basis of Article 235.[23] It is doubtful, however, whether the criteria for the use of Article 235 were fulfilled with respect to the adoption of legislation with regard to local voting rights in 1988?[24] If they were what, it may be asked, explained the change in the applicability of Article 235 in the field of electoral rights, or was the original assessment of its non-applicability wrong or simply based on a lack of

---

[21]See the evidence of Dr Taschner (Commission) to the House of Lords Select Committee, op. cit. note 8, at p.6: "we are here in this area where it is more a political question than a legal question".

[22]PE Doc. A2-197/87. During the EP debate of 14 February 1987, Commissioner Ripa di Meana had undertaken to present the Commission with a proposal for a Directive on voting rights in the first half of 1988, Debs. EP 2-359, December 1987. See also the Piquer Report of the Parliamentary Political Affairs Committee, Doc. A2-0197/87/Ann, 26 November 1987, which regarded the issue of voting rights as "attractive" in terms of the promotion of European Citizenship. The EP subsequently adopted another resolution urging the Commission to submit a proposal, OJ 1988 C13/33.

[23]COM (88) 371 final; OJ 1988 C246/3.

[24]On the use of Article 235 see generally Marenco, G., "Les conditions d'application de l'article 235 du Traité CEE", RMC (1970) 156; Schwartz, I.E., "Le pouvoir normatif de la Communauté, notamment en vertu de l'article 235. Une compétence exclusive ou parallèle", RMC (1976) 280; Usher, J., "The Development of Community Powers after the SEA", in White, R. and Smythe, *Current Issues in European and International Law* (1990) Sweet and Maxwell; Usher, J.A., "The Gradual Widening of EC Policy on the Basis of Articles 100 and 235 of the EEC", in Schwarze, J. and Schermers, H.G. (eds.), *The Structure and Dimensions of European Community Policy*, op. cit.

political consensus?[25] Justifying legislative recourse to Article 235 depends on whether one takes a restrictive or expansive view of the Community's competence and objectives.[26] Though the assessment of necessity thereunder may entail a considerable degree of political discretion, the subject matter in question must, nevertheless, be connected with the operation of the common market. Reliance on Article 235 need not be linked to the economic efficiency of the common market. However, although disenfranchisement may affect the quality of integration open to Member State nationals who have availed themselves of free movement, only with difficulty could it be said to affect the choice of free movement itself.[27] It is the latter, not the former with which the common market and, consequently, Article 235 is concerned.

The Commission proposal relied on the SEA as a major qualitative change in the field of electoral rights. However, a Danish proposal had been tabled and disregarded during the intergovernmental negotiations prior to the adoption of the SEA. In the light of this rejection, or omission, it is difficult to contend that broad references to common principles of democracy in the preamble of the SEA were a sufficient basis for the proposal on electoral rights and the type of national constitutional amendments which were required. In some Member States, such as France, national constitutional provisions relevant to electoral rights had been the subject of Supreme Court decisions which had underlined their fundamental relationship with national sovereignty and their exclusivity to nationals.[28] Article 31(2) of the Vienna Convention of 1967 on the Law of Treaties states that "for the purpose of the interpretation of a Treaty, (the context) shall comprise, in addition to the text, including its preamble and annexes".[29] A preamble must be precisely formulated for its provisions to be useful in the interpretation of a Treaty text.[30] The Court of Justice has referred, on occasion, to the preamble of the Treaty of Rome in determining, for example, whether Article 85 has been infringed.[31] The object-

---

[25]See Bull. EC (8) 1975 II no.7/8; Oral Question no. H-87/79, Debs. EP OJ Annex 245, sitting of 27 September 1979, at 268 and 269; Bull. EC. Suppl. 7/85.

[26]See Sasse, C. and Gourow, "The Growth of Legislative Power in the European Communities" in Sandalow, T. and Stein, E., *Courts and Free Markets* (1982) Clarendon Press, vol.1, p.92, at p.95; and Lesguillons, H., "L'extension des compétences de la CEE par l'article 235 du Traité de Rome", AFDI (1974) 886, who favours a liberal approach but states, at 903, that: "éducation et culture, défense ou politique étrangère sont sans doute des objets à ce point nouveaux qu'il conviendrait de les insérer aujourd'hui dans la Communauté de recourir à la procedure de révision edictée par l'article 236. Autrement dit, lorsqu'elles recourent à l'article 235, les institutions de la Communauté doivent se situer dans le cadre des grands objectifs économiques du Traité."

[27]In its evidence to the House of Lords Seclect Committee, the Commission accepted that a direct and fundamental link in this sense between voting rights and free movement did not exist, op. cit. note 8, at p.13.

[28]See *supra* Section 6.7.1.

[29]L.N. Doc. C. M. 13. 1931; reproduced in 63 *American Journal of International Law* (1969) 875, at 885.

[30]See Scherpers, S., "The Legal Force of the Preamble to the EEC Treaty", 6 *ELRev* (1981) 356–361.

[31]See Case 32/65 *Italy* v. *Council and Commission* [1966] ECR at 405, where it states: "Article 85 lays down the rules on competition applicable to undertakings ... Artice 85 as a whole should be read in the context of the provisions of the preamble to the Treaty which clarify it". Case 43/75 *Defrenne*

ives of the Treaty expressed in the preamble are precisely echoed in Article 85. However, it is the lack of a specific Treaty provision on the subject of civil and political rights which forced the Commission back on the vague democratic aspirations expressed in the preamble to the SEA. The preamble, however, is the enunciation of a general principle in abstract terms and apart from its interpretative value, it cannot act alone as a legal basis for Community legislation. Neither Articles 2 nor 3 specify political action as one of the Community's objectives or functional powers, hence they could advance the Commission no further when read in conjunction with the preamble. Surely such a considerable redivision of sovereignty required explicit negotiation and acceptance and in the absence of such, the Commission's 1988 proposal was premature. It is arguable that if the Community is to act in accordance with the rule of law, it must base its legislation within the scope of its powers and not stretch those powers to include policies which the opaque dynamics of European integration, in this specific context, Community citizenship, subsequently deem to be desirable. The incorporation of electoral rights in the Union Treaty has rendered the issue of reliance on Article 235 redundant. However, the controversy which some of the provisions of the Union Treaty have excited, the provisions on citizenship included, suggest that the 1988 proposal was indeed premature.

7.3. Electoral Rights at Municipal Level in Article 8(b)(1)

Article 8(b)(1) of the Union Treaty provides that "Every citizen of the Union residing in a Member State of which he is not a national shall have the right to vote and to stand as a candidate at municipal elections in the Member State in which he resides, under the same conditions as nationals of that State." This right is to be exercised according to "detailed arrangements" to be adopted by the Council before 31 December 1994. The legislative procedure envisaged by Article 8(b)(1) resembles that in Article 235 – unanimous adoption in Council of a Commission proposal, with the prior consultation of Parliament. However, Article 8(b)(1) also expressly provides that the arrangements to be adopted for electoral rights in both European and local elections may permit derogations where warranted by problems specific to a Member State.

The choice of legal instrument, or the nature of the "detailed arrangements" adopted to implement Article 8(b)(1), were not necessarily straightforward. Prior to the presentation of the Commission's 1988 proposal, suggestions about the legal form it would take included a Treaty amendment,[32] a resolution of the Member

---

[1976] ECR 455, at para.10; and, for example, the Council Resolution on a European Community programme to promote youth exchanges: "Having regard to the EEC Treaty objective of laying the foundations for ever closer cooperation between the peoples of Europe", OJ 1983 C184/21.

[32]See the Scelba Report and the Danish proposals in the run up to the conclusion of the SEA.

States,[33] or an international agreement.[34] A Directive has obvious advantages.[35] Article 189 stipulates that directives are binding as to the results to be achieved, but leave the choice of form and methods to the national authorities. In this particular context, they allow Member States to take the constitutional or legislative action necessary to render national law compatible with Community law prior to transposition.[36] The choice of a directive is also in line with the principle embodied in the declaration attached to the SEA in the context of Article 100A, whereby the Commission is to give precedence to the use of directives if harmonisation involves the amendment of legislative provisions in one or more Member States. A directly applicable instrument like a regulation, which leaves no room for manoeuvre for Member States in the application of Community law, might have experienced extreme difficulties in Council, since Member States would have been forced to register their concerns at the negotiation stage and as an integral part of the law. There would be little room for them to exercise any discretion with respect to the substance of the instrument at the implementing stage. Thus, in the context of Article 8(b)(1), the choice of directive and the legislative procedure laid down in that provision cannot be criticised on the grounds that the requirement of unanimity reduces, if not cancels, the possibility of national parliamentary control in a matter which directly affects national parliamentary prerogatives, as was the case with respect to the 1988 proposal.[37] In this sense, a directive is clearly in line with the principle of subsidiarity and the ratification of the Union Treaty at national level should have avoided the subsequent transposition of directives into internal law being regarded as a means to limit the prerogatives of national parliaments.[38] In the event the Council has successfully adopted both the Directives on European Parliament and municipal elections before the deadlines established in Article 8(b) elapsed.

It remains to be seen how the Commission and Court of Justice will deal with delayed or incorrect transposition of these Directives and how the Member States themselves will respond to their adoption. Germany provides an excellent example of the implementation difficulties regarding electoral rights which may be encountered at national level by at least some Member States. Prior to the adoption of the Union Treaty, the German Federal Constitutional Court examined the question of

---

[33]Recommendation of the House of Lords Select Committee on the European Communities, *Voting Rights in Local Elections*, op. cit. note 8, at p.18.

[34]See the French report by Chapus, R. in the *Symposium on the Participation of Foreigners in Municipal Elections in the Member States of the EEC*, Louvain-la-Neuve, 28 Febuary 1978, op. cit., at 116; and the Report of the Commission of the Belgian Senate cited in Mabille, X., "Droit de vote et nationalité", 1279–1292 *Courrier Hebdomadaire* (1990), at 11.

[35]For the problematic nature of directives as legislative instruments in the context of, for example, social policy, see Vogel-Polsky and Vogel, op. cit. note 8, at p.193.

[36]See De Burca, G., "Giving Effect to European Community Directives", 55 *Modern Law Review* (1992) 215, at 219.

[37]See the French Délégation de l'Assemblée Nationale pour les Communautés Européennes, *Conclusions sur le droit de vote et l'éligibilité des ressortissants des Etats membres de la CEE aux élections municipales*, 31 May 1989, at 7.

[38]Ibid., at p.7.

voting rights for non-nationals in the case of legislation introduced by the land of Schleswig-Holstein, which allowed foreigners to participate in local elections on a reciprocal basis.[39] The Parliament of the city-state of Hamburg also reformed its electoral law in February 1989 to allow non-nationals who had been resident for eight years to participate in local district councils. At issue in both cases was the constitutionality of giving the right to vote to non-nationals. In the Schleswig–Holstein case the Court confirmed that Article 20(2)(1) of the Basic Law and the concept of national sovereignty which it entails is a fundamental constitutional principle incapable of being amended pursuant to Article 79 para.3. Article 20(2)(1) states that "all state authority emanates from the people". The reference to "the people" in Articles 20(2)(1) and 28 of the Basic Law was held to refer exclusively to Germans, who alone could participate in political elections.[40] Even in the Hamburg case, which involved a borough election, the Court held that the definition of popular sovereignty in the German constitution prevented an extension of the vote to aliens in such elections. Extension of the franchise beyond "the people" would render the elections undemocratic within the meaning of the Constitution. It was unclear from these decisions how open the German legal order would be to such developments at Community level in the field of electoral rights.[41] Although Germany has subsequently ratified the Treaty on European Union, its Constitutional Court decision at that time also expressed the opinion that a constitutional state requires a certain cultural homogeneity of the people.

Considerable national debate was excited in Germany about the appropriate means to implement Article 8(b)(1), given the established sanctity of Article 20(2)(1) of the Basic Law. In addition, in non-unitary states like Germany, amendment of *Land* constitutional provisions is also necessary.[42] Implementation of Directive 94/80 will thus depend on legal and political reactions to the extension of

---

[39]For background details see Rath, J., "Voting Rights", in Layton Henry, op. cit., at 133; and Arnaldo Alcubilla, op. cit., at 72 *et seq.* This provision would have benefited Swedish, Danish, Dutch, Irish and Swiss residents.

[40]See Bundesverfassungsgerichts 2 *BvF* 2/89, 12 October 1989; Article 28 para.1(2) further provides that "in each Lander, counties and communes, the people must be represented by a body in general, direct, free, equal and secret elections." The homogeneity of the text of Article 28 is thought to extend the restriction to "the people" in Article 20(2)(1) to *Länder*, county and municipal elections. Article 79 para.3 provides that: "An amendment of this Basic Law affecting the division of the Federation into *Länder*, the participation in principle of the *Länder* in legislation, or the basic principles laid down in Articles 1 and 20, is inadmissible."

[41]See Neuman, G.L., "'We are the people': Alien Suffrage in a German and American Perspective", 13 *Michigan Journal of International Law* (1992) 259–335, at 289: "one could read the Court's nod to the EC narrowly, as implying only that an amendment [of the Constitution] could sacrifice homogeneity and remove local governments from the sphere of direct popular sovereignty."

[42]The constitutions of six *Länder* clearly restricted electoral rights in all elections to Germans: Baden-Wurttemburg, Article 26(1); Bavaria, Article 4/2(1); Berlin, Article 2(1); Hesse Article 73(1); Rhein-Palatinate Article 50 para.1; and Saarland, Article 66(1)/64. Five other *Länder* refer simply to "the People" in the same manner as the Basic Law: Bremen, Article 55 s.1/66 para.1; Hamburg, Article 3(2); Lower Saxony, Article 2(1); North Rhine-Westphalia Article 2; Schleswig-Holstein, Article 2 s.1. In Switzerland, the Federal Constitution leaves the regulation of local voting rights entirely to cantonal constitutions, hence the Neuchatel and Jura anomalies, where resident foreigners can vote.

the franchise, which vary from one *Land* to the next. In the event that a *Land* reluctantly or tardily implements the arrangements adopted pursuant to Article 8(b)(1), Community law sanctions should equally apply.[43] Disagreement persists in Germany between the *Länder* regarding the extent to which they can admit Community nationals to the franchise. It appears that Bremen has decided to admit Union citizens to elections for the parliament of this city state and that the Federal Government is willing to take action against Bremen for what it regards as an unconstitutional extension of the franchise. The applicability of Article 8(b) to direct democracy is also being discussed in Germany, where some *Länder* wish to admit Community nationals to referenda. Finally, some *Länder* may refuse to make use of the mayor/deputy mayor derogation. This could lead to claims of discrimination by Community nationals resident in *Länder* which do make use of this restriction.

Constitutional amendment might have been avoided in Germany prior to the Union Treaty if "the people" had been interpreted to include non-nationals, or if non-nationals had been admitted on the basis of ordinary legislation. Proponents of alien suffrage pointed to Germany's conversion into a *de facto* immigration country and the possibility of transferring sovereignty to the EC, for example, pursuant to Article 24.[44] Thus, in the German case, it is suggested that the Court could have avoided constitutional difficulties if attention had been focused on the institutional guarantee of local autonomy in Article 28 para.2 of the Basic Law.[45] This entails the constitutional right for each local authority to regulate its affairs in accordance with applicable legislation. This constitutionally guaranteed autonomy may not allow an interpretation of "the people" distinct from that in Article 20(2)(1), but the inapplicability of Article 20(2)(1) could have been established by underlining the administrative or non-sovereign quality of local elections. To interpret Article 28 para.2 in this way would have left the path open for similar amendments to *Land* constitutions where necessary. Such a liberal interpretation proved impossible in Germany and would be impossible in other Member States where constitutions, or constitutional courts, insist on the political and fundamental nature of these rights.[46] In addition, to alter the nature of these rights from a constitutional to an ordinary legislative basis is an unsatisfactory means to deal with fundamental political and constitutional rights and an unstaisfactory way to render national law compatible with Community obligations.[47] This solution was also rejected by the Spanish Constitutional Court, which refused to devise an artificial definition of citizen simply to allow Community nationals to stand as candidates in municipal elec-

---

[43]See, for example, Case 103/88 *Fratelli Costanzo SpA* v. *Commune di Milano* [1990] ECR 1839, where the Court of Justice held that all organisations of the administration, including decentralised authorities such as municipalities, are obliged to apply the provisions of the Community's directives.

[44]See Neuman, op. cit. note 41, at 272–273.

[45]See Sasse, C., *Kommunalwahlrecht fur Auslander* (1974).

[46]See Blumann, C., "L'Europe des citoyens", 346 RMC (1991) 283–292.

[47]See Curtin, D. and Meijers, H., "The Principle of Open Government in Schengen and the European Union: Democratic Retrogression?", 32 *CMLRev* (1995) 391–442, at 439: "An important consequence of a fundamental right status is that ... more rigorous standards have to be met than with respect to legal rights generally."

tions and avoid constitutional amendment. On a theoretical level at least, the result of such a move would be electoral rights for nationals and non-nationals on a different legal and constitutional basis.

7.4. Analysis of Directive 94/80 on Electoral Rights for Union Citizens in Municipal Elections

Much of the preamble and many of the provisions of Directive 94/80 are identical to the text adopted by the Council with respect to electoral rights in European Parliament elections. The Directive is also similar, in a number of respects, to the Commission's 1988 proposal on local electoral rights.[48] This section will try not to overlap and will draw the reader's attention to the provisions of Directive 93/109, where necessary.

7.4.1. General Provisions of Directive 94/80

Article 1, like Article 1 of the Directive on European Parliament elections, specifies that the Directive addresses the municipal electoral rights of Union citizens resident in a Member State other than that of their nationality. It does not, therefore, apply to the electoral rights of Union citizens resident in their Member State of nationality. Article 1(2) specifies that the Directive does not interfere with a Member States' rules on the electoral rights of its nationals in the home territory, even if they are resident abroad, or with the electoral rights of third country nationals resident in a Member State. The Commission interprets this provision as permitting a Union citizen who retains his rights in his home Member State and who acquires new rights in his Member State of residence to exercise these rights in separate elections. It regards the elections involved as legally and politically separate proceedings. This type of parallel voting does not, therefore, amount to double voting, which has been prohibited in European Parliament elections. Since national legislation generally requires evidence of stable links with the municipal government for which one wishes to vote or to stand for election, the Commission regards the practical importance of parallel voting as very limited.[49] Its impact is further reduced by the manner in which principal residence is determined for the purposes of the Directive. Admission of the possibility of parallel voting is also a result of the difficulties which would have been entailed in the exchange of information necessary to prevent it. Difficulties relating to the exchange of information would have been exacerbated by the fact that a decentralised level of authority is at issue. Finally, it was not considered proportionate to the gravity of the problem to spend

---

[48]For a detailed analysis of the 1988 proposal see O'Leary, S., *The Evolving Concept of Community Citizenship: From the Free Movement of Persons to Union Citizenship* (1993) EUI Doctoral Thesis, Chapter 8.

[49]COM (94) 38 final, at 17–18. The 1988 proposal eliminated the possibility of parallel voting by requiring applicants to prove that they could no longer vote in their Member State of residence.

time and money establishing the administrative machinary necessary to exchange information and to prevent parallel voting throughout the Union, given that only a few Member States (Germany, France, Italy and Spain) allow their nationals to vote in their home Member State if resident abroad.

One of the most difficult tasks of the Directive was to define the level of government to which the Directive applies. As recital 7 points out: "the way in which government operates in the different Member States is a reflection of different political and legal traditions and is characterised by an abundance of structures". The term municipal election does not mean the same thing in every Member State. The Directive had to specify, therefore, the level of government in question, the type of election covered and the offices open to non-nationals. The level of government chosen by the Community institutions is called the "basic level of government unit" and is defined as "administrative entities ... which, in accordance with the laws of each Member State, contain bodies elected by direct universal suffrage and are empowered to administer, at the basic level of political and administrative organisation, certain local affairs on their own responsibility".[50] The administrative entities in question are listed in an annex to the Directive. This loose definition, which refers back to national legislation, combines a number of common features which the Commission felt are shared by local authorities in the Member States – a defined territory, a measure of independence, a representative body elected by direct universal suffrage, created by law, either statutory or constitutional.[51] The Directive's definition is also related to the definition of local government in European Charter of Local Self-Government, agreed in the Council of Europe framework in 1985. The reference back to national law in the Directive ensures that Member States themselves determine what administrative bodies form the basic level of government according to the law of that Member State. The Commission emphasises that a basic local government unit may often have to act as an administrative unit for central government. However, the essential point is that they are bodies which enjoy political and administrative independence on the basis of law and that, in their own sphere they manage public affairs of local interest on their own responsibility. They are not to be confused with decentralised government agencies which provide a number of services at local level. Finally, basic local government units are usually run by a representative council which can take decisions and by an executive body. Some basic local government units are subdivided into administrative units which are subordinated to it. These units have governing bodies elected by direct universal suffrage. Subordinate units are regarded as forming an integral part of the basic unit. These subdivisions are also listed in the annex. Article 2(2) provides for amendment of the annex when a Member State notifies the Commission that, by virtue of national law, a local government unit listed in the annex is replaced by another, or that existing units have been abolished, or new ones created. The local government units affected by the

---

[50]Article 2(1)(a).
[51]COM (94) 38, at 3–4.

Directive in Sweden, Finland and Austria are absent from the annex. By permitting Member States to determine the relevant level of municipal government the possibility remains for considerable diversity between Member States.

The principle of equal treatment operates within the territory of each Member State and not throughout the Community as a whole. The diversity permitted by leaving the definition of local government to national law cannot, therefore, be challenged on the basis of Article 6.[52] The rights granted to a resident Irishman in the Netherlands on the basis of the Directive are not relevant to the position of a Frenchman resident in Portugal. Leaving this choice to the national law of each Member State is clearly dictated by subsidiarity, but it also reflects a reluctance on the part of Member States regarding the extension of electoral rights and their inability to reassess the criteria on which those rights are granted. Directive 94/80 is clearly innovative, in that it recognises residence as the basis for the extension of electoral rights. However, the object throughout the Directive and particularly with reference to the derogations in Article 12 seems to be to limit the disturbance caused by non-national political participation.[53] This attempt at "damage limitation" is also evident in the arguments sometimes used to justify the extension of electoral rights to nationals from other Member States. Electoral rights are phrased in terms of a vague notion of a People's Europe, European identity and solidarity, rather than the classic argument of "no taxation without representation". The latter would apply equally to Community nationals and third country nationals, which may be why the Citizens' Europe and European identity aspect is stressed. The identification of electoral rights as an incident of Union citizenship also helps to justify the exclusion of non-Community nationals. Indeed the rationale behind the extension of the franchise to non-nationals seems not to be their participation in and contribution to the local civic and economic community as much as an under-defined notion of membership in a supranational legal order which claims to favour the involvement of citizens.

The structure and organisation of government vary considerably from one Member State to the next. The terms local government, local authority, borough, district, commune, municipality, province and region are all political divisions reflecting different levels of government and different degrees of political participation in the national legislative process.[54] In Germany, for example, lower level government is divided between municipalities (*Gemeinden*), independent municipalities (*Kreisfreiestadte*) and counties (*Kreise*). Legislation governing their election is determined by the various *Länder* and, as Section 7.3 reveals, that there is a

---

[52]See Weatherill, S., "The Scope of Article 7", 15 *ELRev* (1990) 334–341, at 336.

[53]See D'Oliveira, H.U.J., "Electoral Rights for Non-Nationals", 31 *Netherlands International Law Review* (1984) 59–72 with respect to the debate about electoral rights for non-nationals prior to the adoption of the TEU.

[54]See generally, Buxton, R., *Local Government*, 2nd edn., (1973) Harmondsworth, Penguin; Batley, R. and Stoker, G., *Local Government in Europe: Trends and Developments* (1991) London, Macmillan; and Conseil de L'Europe, *La repartition des competences aux niveaux local et regional d'administration dans les Etats Membres du Conseil de l'Europe* (1988) Strasbourg.

possibility that the *Länder* will diverge in their extension of the franchise. The notion of "municipal election" does not exist at all in Belgium.[55] In the United Kingdom, local government is divided into an array of councils, districts and boroughs. Different administrative arrangements exist for England and Wales, Scotland and Northern Ireland which may constitute grounds for future claims of discrimination. Danish nationals refused admission to regional government, or its equivalent, in England, may not claim discrimination *vis-à-vis* the admission of British nationals to this level of government in Denmark. However, since the United Kingdom represents one territorial unit for the purposes of Community law, they may have better and justifiable claims if Danes resident in Scotland are allowed to participate more fully in the local administration than Danes in England.

Some national anomalies also exist. Paris is both a municipality and a department and its municipal council also exercises some of the competences of the General Council. The German city states, Bremen, Hamburg and Berlin, present similar problems. The Directive clearly permits Member States to determine what level of local government comes within its scope to avoid the apparent harmonisation of political participation at national level by Community law. However, if the political participation of resident Community nationals varies from parish to local to regional government in different Member States, a lowest common denominator as regards political rights may have been achieved, but it may be a denominator of little political value and consequently one which resident foreigners may choose not to use. Further, major qualitative differences concerning the status, competence and importance of local government exist amongst the various Member States. In civil law systems the structures and operation of local government are often featured in the constitution, entitling it to a certain level of legal and constitutional protection.[56] This is not the case in the United Kingdom and Ireland, where local authorities are established on a statutory basis and where the policy of central government, in the United Kingdom at least, has been to dismantle and weaken the apparatus and competences of local government. In addition, the civil law doctrine of general competence, whereby local government authorities have a general power of jurisdiction over the affairs of their area and its inhabitants, contrasts with the strict application of the doctrine of *ultra vires* in common law Member States. Though the Council of Europe report reveals a certain homogeneity in the type of issues dealt with at local level, significant differences nevertheless exist. The branch of government vested with competence to deal with issues such as electoral registers, policing, education, social assistance and public health, varies from one Member State to the next. In England and Wales, the electoral register is dealt with by the various local level authorities (London borough councils, metropolitan district councils and non-metropolitan district councils) while in Scotland, the matter

---

[55]See Misson, L., Belgian report the 1992 FIDE conference, *The New Developments of the Free Movement of Persons Towards European Citizenship* (1992) Lisbon, at p.62.

[56]Thus in Germany, Article 28(2) of the Basic Law gives a "guarantee of local self-government autonomy"; and Article 102(2) of the Greek constitution expressly provides for the election of local government.

falls to regional as distinct from district councils. General policing is a matter for the mayor of the municipality and the chairman of the general departmental council in France. It is similarly exercised by the first and second levels of government in Germany and the United Kingdom. The construction and maintenance of educational facilities is dealt with locally and regionally in France, Germany and the United Kingdom. The same applies to employment in education, with the exception of France, where it is a matter for central government. Social assistance (discretionary, and compulsory grants and housing grants) is awarded in France by local, departmental and central government. In Germany it is a matter for local government, while in the United Kingdom it is determined at both local and regional levels.[57] In some Member States intermediate levels of authority have considerable powers in health, social security and secondary education. These are matters directly affecting the lives of residents, which is part of the reason why the franchise is being extended in the first place. However, depending on the unilateral Member State definitions of local level government, resident Community nationals may or may not acquire a right to participate in the local decision-making which directly affects them and on which basis it is argued that they should be given political rights in the first place.

The definition of "municipal election" in Article 2(1)(b) is limited to elections by direct universal suffrage to appoint members of the representative council and the head and members of the executive of that unit, if the latter is permitted by national law. This definition does not include elections *inside* the local representative council. As a result, the election of the head and members of the local executive by the Council itself, which occurs in Denmark, Greece, Germany, France, Ireland and the United Kingdom, is not affected by the Directive. Furthermore, given the limitation of the scope of the Directive to elections to the representative council and not within it, the Directive does not affect national legislation dealing with the powers and responsibilities of the Council and its members. Nor does it affect the direct or indirect election of members of parliament by local councillors. Member States are permitted to exclude members of the Council who are nationals from other Member States, from taking part in such elections.

The suggestion that equal treatment in Article 8(b)(1) extends only to the election of municipal councils and does not extend to the functioning and operation of those councils thereafter is open to criticism. This seems to be another means to reenforce the exclusion of non-nationals from the posts of mayor and assistant mayor, or even of disqualifying them from the exercise of certain functions as ordinary councillors. Equal treatment should not be limited solely to the election of local councils, for if the functions of non-national councillors are diminished thereafter, the votes of the non-nationals and even those of a Member State's own nationals will be considerably undermined. To globally exclude the principle of equal treatment once the elections themselves have taken place is also inconsistent with

---

[57]See, in addition, the tables detailing the division of competences between the various levels in the report of the Council of Europe, op. cit. note 54.

the approach which the Court adopts with respect to Article 48(4). In this respect Member States have argued that the exclusion of foreign nationals from certain posts was necessary to avoid those nationals from being involved in a career which might later involve duties and responsibilities involving the exercise of powers conferred by public law.[58] Member States are allowed to rely on the public service exception to free movement with respect to "posts which involve direct or indirect participation in the exercise of powers conferred by public law and duties designed to safeguard the general interests of the State or of other public authorities."[59] However, the Court has rejected the global application of Article 48(4) on the grounds that it goes further than the provision requires and would have the effect of excluding foreign nationals from the totality of posts in the public service on the basis of "phantom" promotion possibilities. Thus, equal treatment is to apply to Member State nationals once they have been admitted to the public service until the nature of the post changes and meets the conditions laid down in Article 48(4).[60] Member States should not be allowed to unilaterally employ this type of reasoning to exclude the principle of equal treatment from applying to local councils once elected.

Although the type of judicial activism witnessed in *Cowan* is unlikely to extend to the field of political rights,[61] the logic and legislative scope of Article 6 does not stop at local elections, or matters which fall directly within the scope of the Treaty. Once voting rights become a Community law issue, it could be argued that Community law enters the field generally. National elections, according to this thesis, are excluded as a derogation from the general principle that political rights are relevant to the Community in the context of political union. They are excluded on the grounds that they relate too closely to the exercise of national sovereignty. This type of reasoning has considerable potential, given the narrow manner in which derogations must be construed and the possibility of assessing their compatibility with the general principles of Community law. The Court of Justice adheres to the principles embedded in the European Convention of Human Rights in accordance with "the structure and objectives" of the Community.[62] Article 8(b) now incorporates political participation amongst the Community's objectives. In terms of the operation of the common market and now political union, what is the legal qualitative difference between expansive or restricted enfranchisement? The principle of subsidiarity would argue against Community competence with respect to national

---

[58]See Case 149/79 *Commission* v. *Belgium* (no.1) [1980] ECR 3881.

[59]Case 149/79 *Commission* v. *Belgium* (no.1) [1980] ECR 3881.

[60]See O'Keeffe, D., "Judicial Interpretation of the Public Service Exception to the Free Movement of Workers", in O'Keeffe, D. and Curtin, D (eds.), *Constitutional Adjudication in European Community and National Law: Essays in Honour of Mr Justice T.F. O'Higgins* (1992) London, Butterworths, pp.89–106, at p.103.

[61]Some commentators state, however, that "it may be that judges are somewhat less constrained by such (political) conditions and may be in a position to contribute to the legal developments on which changes in those conditions may be partly dependent." D'Oliveira, H.U.J. and Evans, A.C., *Nationality and Citizenship*, in Cassese, A., Clapham, A. and Weiler, J.H.H., *Human Rights and the EC: Methods of Protection*, in *European Union: The Human Rights Challenge*, Vol.2 (1991) Baden Baden, Nomos, at p.326.

[62]See Case 11/70 *Internationale Handelsgesellschaft* [1970] ECR 1125, at 1134.

elections and the exclusion of Community competence with respect to national elections is understandable. What is less understandable, however, is the limited nature of the political rights which have in fact been extended on the basis of residence and the devaluation of these rights if based on artificial notions of a common European identity and a narrow selective application of the principle of equal treatment. The principle of equal treatment allows resident Community nationals to participate in the same manner, or almost the same manner, as nationals at local level. However, the fact that nationals compensate for the possibly weak political input of local level participation by expressing themselves at one, if not two, higher political levels should not be forgotten.

The definitions of residence, nationality, electoral roll, reference date and formal declaration in Articles 2(1)(c),(d),(e),(f) and (g), respectively, are identical to those in Article 2 of Directive 93/109. Article 3 goes on to establish the right to vote and stand for election in municipal elections on the basis of residence and the conditions governing the exercise of these rights. These electoral rights are subject, however, to the remaining conditions established in the Directive. Thus, for example, as Article 2(1)(f) specifies, it is up to Member States to determine what is the relevant reference date for Union citizens to comply with these conditions. The conditions established in Article 3 are identical to those for European Parliament elections: (i) nationality of a Member State; and (ii) residence in a different Member State. The 1988 proposal had stipulated, in addition to nationality and residence, that the Directive's beneficiaries "enjoy the civic rights stemming from that nationality" (Article 1). This condition does not appear in the 1994 Directive. Furthermore, the Commission declined to uniformly define the concept of residence. In particular, it rejected determining a uniform minimum period of residence in the territory of the host Member State. One of the grounds for the exclusion of this option was the rejection of the Commission's suggestion to this effect in the course of the intergovernmental proceedings.[63] Furthermore, the Commission felt that specifying a minimum period would deprive a number of Union citizens of the rights guaranteed under Article 8(b)(1), since they would not be able to establish residence in the host Member State for that period. This would be regrettable, since those Union citizens would still be subject to the decisions of a local government in which they would be unable, for a time, to participate.

Article 4 also deals with the condition of residence and also refrains from defining that term uniformly. To ensure that the principle of equal treatment is effectively applied to municipal elections, however, Article 4(1) provides that Member States must take into account periods of residence which voters and persons entitled to stand for election have passed in other Member States. In contrast, Article 4(2) is designed to prevent discrimination against national voters and candidates for election who are, in general, required to fulfil a condition of residence in the local government territorial unit where they wish to vote or to stand for election. If national legislation requires national voters and candidates to fulfil such a condition,

[63]SEC (91) 500 in CONF.UP 1740/91.

then voters and candidates from other Member States must do so also. This provision is to ensure that proper administrative requirements are observed and to guarantee that voters and candidates are familiar with the issues affecting the local government unit where they wish to exercise their rights. As a result, Union citizens with a permanent centre of interest in another Member State cannot be eligible under the provisions of the Directive simply by demonstrating mere residence in the territory of the host Member State. If nationals are required to prove residence in the specific geographical unit of government where the elections take place, nationals from other Member States must do so also. The Commission is of the opinion that this condition will, in general, lessen the incidences of parallel voting which are possible under Article 1. The absence of a fixed period of residence in Directive 94/80 contrasts with the five year period chosen by the Council of Europe Convention.[64] That Convention further provided that contracting states could "stipulate that the residence requirements laid down in Article 6 are satisfied by a shorter period of residence (Article 7)". The explanatory report on the Convention explains that residence means anywhere in the state since (i) states which already accord voting rights to residents do not require residence in the municipal district, and (ii) states without internal registration procedures would find it difficult to verify whether applicants had been resident in the municipal district for the required period.

Article 5 deals with the position of Union citizens who are legally debarred from standing for election. The provisions on ineligibility with respect to municipal elections are identical to those established in Article 6 Directive 93/109 with respect to European Parliament elections, except that Article 5(2) provides that an application to stand will be declared inadmissible not only if the applicant fails to produce, when necessary, the attestation from the competent authorities of his home Member State, but also a formal declaration to that effect pursuant to Article 9(2)(a). Articles 5 (1) and (2) are intended to safeguard the reputation of the representative councils of local governments and, in some Member States, their municipal executives. It is a formal control measure taken before elections take place, when any decision on ineligibility is desirable, in order to preserve the legal certainty and legitimacy of the electoral process. However, it does not substitute any national rules on disqualification which check the substance of the successful candidates' applications after the election. Surprisingly, Article 5(3) also deals with what is, in principle, a derogation from the rights guaranteed in Article 8(b)(1). However, no reference is made to this fact in the provision. It provides that "Member States may provide that only their own nationals may hold the office of elected head, deputy or member of the governing college of the executive of a basic local government unit if elected to hold office for the duration of his mandate". A similar provision was explicitly listed as a derogation in the 1988 proposal. Temporary or interim performance of these functions may also be restricted by the Member State of residence to its own nationals. However, in implementing these

---

[64]Article 6 ETS 144, Strasbourg, 5 November 1992.

provisions the Member State of residence is only permitted to take the proportionate and necessary steps to ensure that the reservation is applied and whatever steps they take must be compatible with the Treaty and general legal principles. To exclude these posts automatically would have been disproportionate, since the nature of these offices varies considerably between Member States.[65] The Directive could, however, have introduced functional criteria into the text of Article 5(3) along the lines of the jurisprudence of the Court of Justice under Article 48(4), to enable Member States to determine which posts can be reserved in accordance with Community law. Posts should only be reserved with reference to their substance and not their institutional title. Thus, Member States where mayors and deputy mayors do not play a role which would qualify for exception pursuant to Article 48(4) should not be allowed to rely on this provision automatically.

Article 2(1)(b), which defines municipal elections, does not apply to elections inside the representative council. Member States are entitled, therefore, to take whatever steps necessary to ensure that Union citizens elected to the representative council do not take part in the "designation of delegates who can vote in a parliamentary assembly, nor the election of the members of that assembly" (Article 5(4)). This reservation is in line with the provisions in Articles 48(4) and 55, which exclude posts involving the exercise of official authority and which safeguard the general interest, from the scope of the free movement provisions. France has declared in an annex to the Directive that Article 5(4) in no way jeopardises the electoral rights arising out of Article 8(b)(1) and the Commission and Council made a similar declaration with respect to Article 5(3).

Unlike the Directive on European Parliament elections, Article 6 of Directive 94/80 addresses the issue of incompatibility and provides that non-nationals are subject to the same rules on incompatibility as the Member State of residence applies to its own nationals. Furthermore, the office which a non-national holds in another Member State could be deemed incompatible with holding elected office in the Member State of residence, if it is equivalent to an office which, if held by a national of the Member State of residence, would be incompatible. This provision may also help to reduce the incidence of candidates with double mandates, since holding local government office in another Member State may be a ground of incompatibility in the Member State of residence. The Directive does not attempt to harmonise Member State laws on incompatibility, however, so that where incompatibility is treated in some states as a ground of ineligibility, it will be dealt with under Article 5.

7.4.2. Exercise of the Right to Vote and the Right to Stand for Election

The provisions of Article 7 on compulsory voting and registration on request respect the voters' freedom of choice and are identical to Article 8 of Directive

---

[65]See North, A., "Western European Government in Perspective", in Batley and Stoker, op. cit. note 54.

93/109. Article 8 of Directive 94180 further provides for the conditions which an applicant voter must fulfil to be entered on the electoral roll. It is similar to Article 9 of the Directive on European Parliament elections and only slight differences between the two provisions will be addressed here. The general rule is that a voter who qualifies on the basis of Article 3 will produce the same documents to be entered on the electoral roll as national voters. They may also be required by the Member State of residence to produce valid ID and a formal declaration stating their nationality and address in that Member State. These documents are obligatory for European Parliament voters, who must also specify the locality or constituency where they were last entered on the electoral roll in their host Member State and state that they will not double vote. Given the admission of parallel voting in municipal elections, the latter condition is not necessary under Directive 94/80. Voters remain on the electoral roll until they request to be removed, or until they are no longer eligible. The requirements for persons who wish to stand as candidates are more rigourous. Although they are subjected to the same conditions as nationals, they must also produce a formal declaration stating their nationality and their address in the Member State of residence. They may also be required, in the formal declaration, on the request of the Member State of residence, to state that they have not been deprived of the right in their home Member State, that they hold no incompatible office and to indicate their last address in their home Member State and produce valid ID. In addition, if there is some doubt about the declaration on ineligibility, or if the law of the Member State of residence requires it, they may have to provide an attestation on ineligibility from the competent authorities in the host Member State (Article 9(2)(b)). The Commission states that, if necessary, the competent national authorities may simply state that no ground for disqualification is known to them.[66] Articles 10 and 11 on appeals and the provision of information, respectively, are identical to the provisions which address these issues in the Directive on European Parliament elections.

7.4.3. Derogations and Transitional Provisions

The derogations in Article 12 are identical to those established for elections to the European Parliament. Derogations from the provisions of the Directive are only permissible where the proportion of resident Union citizens of voting age exceeds 20 per cent of the total number of citizens of the Union residing there who are of voting age.[67] The right to vote may be restricted to persons who have resided for longer than a term of the representative council and the right to stand for election to two terms.[68] The relevant residence periods will vary from one Member State to the next, depending on the length of the term of the representative council of the

---

[66]COM (94) 38, at 27.

[67]This is an improvement on Article 8 of the 1988 proposal, which referred to the proportion of resident nationals from other Member States compared to the total population.

[68]Article 12(1)(a) and (b).

basic local government unit. These derogations are not as generous as Article 9 of the 1988 proposal which, in addition, permitted derogating Member States to stipulate, in the first two elections, that non-national councillors could not occupy more than 25 per cent of Council seats. However, the 1994 Directive does provide derogations specific to certain Member States, Belgium, for example, has been allowed, pursuant to Article 12(2), to restrict the right to vote to a limited number of local government units. It must inform the Commission of which units come within the scope of the Article 12(2) derogation one year before the elections in which it intends to rely on the derogation. Belgium has stated that this derogation will be applied restrictively. A similar provision with respect to the special relationship between Ireland and the United Kingdom to that adopted for European Parliament elections has been adopted in Article 12(3).[69]

Section 6.6.3 noted that the Commission justified the derogation for Luxembourg on the grounds that the proportion of Community nationals of voting age resident in Luxembourg would constitute about 29 per cent of the total electorate. This proportion was said to reach almost 50 per cent in some districts. A demographic analysis of the situation in Luxembourg in 1988 revealed that only 14.55 per cent of the total foreign Community population would have been entitled to vote and 10.72 per cent would have been eligible for election. Furthermore, the average foreign resident population of 24.4 per cent was only surpassed in 26 out of 118 municipalities, 9 of which were not dominated by the Portuguese.[70] It is not clear, in these circumstances, whether the extension of the franchise would lead resident nationals from other Member States to dominate or upset the political balance in Luxembourg's municipal elections. The Community's arrangements to grant votes to disenfranchised Community residents may consequently give with one hand what they take away with the other, via overbroad and unnecessarily restrictive derogations which claim to safeguard national political balances, but which, in reality, prevent effective non-national political participation.

The derogations in Article 12 underline the confused rationale lying behind the Community's enfranchisement of resident Community nationals. The extension of the electorate should be a means to improve the democratic involvement of the resident, tax-paying, participating population. If the political balance is altered, it is precisely because the democratic makeup of the country has altered.[71] As a criterion for determining national political prerogative, nationality is said to have fallen into decline, to be replaced by a criterion of territoriality. Thus, D'Oliveira argues that:

---

[69]In support of this provision see the European Parliament's Resolution with respect to the 1988 proposal: "under no circumstances does this Directive impose restrictions on Member States which have already adopted more far-reaching legislation on voting rights, or which intend to do so in the future."

[70]See Lobkowicz, W. de, "Un droit de vote municipal pour tous les européens", 313–322 RMC (1988) 602–613, at 613.

[71]See Rath, J., "Voting Rights", in Layton Henry, Z. (ed.), *The Political Rights of Migrant Workers in Western Europe*, op. cit. at p.127.

only comparatively recently has the link between political rights and nationality been accepted as a matter of course, and it is already being eroded. The advent of the nation state and the sovereignty of the people have led to the establishment of a more precise definition of the bearers of such sovereignty, as a result of which discrepancies have arisen between the legalistic definition of the population and its sociological basis in reality.[72]

The state, has traditionally been the reference point for the enjoyment of rights and has been used to justify the exclusion of foreigners from the enjoyment of the rights of nationality and citizenship, in particular, political rights. As the state declines as the sole reference point for individual rights, it is increasingly difficult to maintain the insistence on nationality, or citizenship, as preconditions for the exercise of political rights. The potential future voter in the European Community is someone who, through residence over a specified number of years, payment of taxes and subjection to the obligations imposed on him by the state generally,[73] has shown a sufficient level of attachment and interest in the welfare of the state to be accorded a basic right to vote in, at least, municipal elections. To refuse to extend traditional citizenship rights to non- nationals, particularly in the context of the European Community's own elections to its parliament, could undermine the right of the host state to impose on foreigners general obligations which are attached to their residence, such as the payment of rates and taxes.[74] The right to vote should be seen first and foremost as a democratic right and not as the expression of a link of allegiance to a state.[75] To that extent, residence is a sufficient, if not the most suitable, criterion for the exercise of this limited right of political participation, which should not be unduly burdened or devalued by derogations.[76]

Union citizenship at least recognised that a Community which expresses a profound commitment to representative government[77] cannot disenfranchise over four million members simply because they avail of their rights of free movement under Community law.[78] However, it is assumed in the 1994 Directive that migrant work-

[72]See D'Oliveira, op. cit. note 53; and Rosberg, G., "Aliens and Equal Protection: Why not the Right to Vote?", 75 *Michigan Law Review* (1977) 1092, who undertakes a historical analysis of aliens and the right to vote. He concludes that, originally, residence was seen as the correct reference point for the right to vote. Voting as an incident of citizenship only emerged in subsequent years. See also Held, D., "Between State and Civil Society: Citizenship", in Andrews, G., *Citizenship* (1991) Lawrence and Wishart, at p.24: "The historical moment seems to have passed for trying to define citizens' claims and entitlements in terms of membership of a national community."

[73]See Layton Henry, op. cit. note 71, at vi of the introduction.

[74]See Ruzié, op. cit.; and Walzer, M., "The Distribution of Membership", in Brown, P. and Shue, H., *Boundaries: National Autonomy and its Limits* (1981) Totowa, NJ, Rowan and Littlefield.

[75]See Wihtol de Wenden, C., *Citoyenneté, nationalité et immigration* (1987) Paris, Editions Arcantère.

[76]De Lobkowicz, (1988) op. cit. note 70, contends that we no longer have to ask whether the right to vote in local elections comes within the ambit of the Common Market. He sees the extension of political rights as "un complément politique de la notion d'espace sans frontières".

[77]The preamble to the SEA refers in three different recitals to the principle of democracy. The preamble of the Union Treaty confirms the Member States' "attachment to the principles of liberty, democracy and respect for human rights and fundamental freedoms and the rule of law".

[78]According to Layton Henry: "The presence of large numbers of residents who are excluded from political decision-making means representative government is no longer truly representative."

ers, in particular, and resident Community nationals, in general, are more affected by decisions taken at municipal level. The everyday preoccupations of the average citizen – housing, education, social welfare, health – are all matters under the care of local councils. However, the interdependence of the various levels of government means that it is artificial to restrict the franchise in relation to resident foreigners to local level only. Furthermore, an increasing centralisation of government in some Member States means that local decisions taken on housing, education, social welfare and health are highly influenced by the policies of central government and the latter generally has control over the national purse strings and consequently determines available expenditure for the programmes which do affect the average citizen, though formulated at a local level. Voting by migrants in elections in the Member States will upset their traditional political balance precisely because the European Communities and the migration patterns in Europe in the post-war years have changed the make-up of these states so that "traditional" political balances no longer apply. The German Constitutional Court's ruling in 1986, for example, was based on a reconstruction of the constitutional texts and the intended meaning of Article 20(2)(1). The result was that the inclusion of non-nationals was held to make the electoral process undemocratic, since democratic representation could only stem from "the people", in other words, Germans. However the text, as interpreted, was not persuasive. Although the Court held that the inclusion of non-nationals was not consistent with democracy, the Court did not really tackle what the essence of democracy is.

The derogations permitted by Article 8(b) must be compatible with the Community's general principles of law, including the principles enshrined in the European Convention, which form a fundamental part of the Community system. Article 3 of Protocol no.1 of the European Convention of Human Rights states that "The High Contracting Parties undertake to hold free elections at reasonable intervals by secret ballot, under conditions which will ensure the free expression of the opinion of the people in the choice of the legislature." Article 3 is said to guarantee, in principle, the right to vote and the right to stand as a candidate in the election of a legislative body.[79] The "people" in Article 3 could be interpreted as eligible members of the electorate as determined by the state, or, in this instance, the state subject to the overall requirements and objectives of the Community.[80] The Commission of Human Rights has held that Article 14, read in conjunction with Article 3, protects every voter against discrimination directed at him as a person on the grounds mentioned in Article 14. It has also stated that this does not imply the same as protection of equal voting influence for all voters.[81] This was

---

[79]App. nos.6745/74 and 6746/74 *X and others* v. *Belgium* Decisions and Reports 2, 110; see also App. no.6420-23/74, 15 July 1974, where the right is classified as an individual right.

[80]In a concurring opinion in Appln. nos.14234/88 and 14235/88 *Open Door Counselling et al.* v. *Ireland*, 7/3/1991, Schermers, H.G. (20), defined the notion of "democratic society" in the convention as "the European democratic society".

[81]App. no.8765/79, 18 December 1980, Decisions and Reports 21, 211 (223–225); *Mathieu-Mohin and Clerfayt* v. *Belgium* [1988] European Human Rights Reports 1.

held, however, in the context of an application to determine if a state was obliged to introduce a particular electoral system and does not mean that the arrangement of party lists on grounds of nationality is compatible with the Convention.

When asked, however, whether a municipal council, established according to Dutch law, was invested with such normative power that it could be considered a "legislative body" within the meaning of Article 3, the Commission did not find it necessary to determine the question in the context of the case.[82] In the context of regional councils in Belgium, which do not enjoy legislative power but merely give advisory opinions, the Commission held that Article 3 did not apply.[83] Similarly, local authorities in Northern Ireland have been held not to fall within the meaning of "legislature" in Article 3.[84] Article 3 may not, therefore, be of any use in limiting the derogations, since many of the local bodies designated thereunder would not constitute "legislatures" within the meaning of Article 3.[85] Furthermore, it has been argued that this provision is aimed at a country's own nationals and does not require states to grant foreign residents a right to vote.[86] Article 3 Protocol no.1, like the other provisions of international law discussed previously, reflects the traditional suspicion of political participation by foreigners and a consequent reservation of these benefits to nationals. Nevertheless, the spirit informing this provision is arguably a fundamental desire to protect free elections and the Court of Justice could adhere to this fundamental principle as regards the Community's new role in political rights, ensuring that the derogations which the Commission and Council implement are not disproportionate to the objective sought to be achieved and that they do not effectively undermine, devalue or destroy, the substance of the right extended to Community citizens under Article 8(b). Thus, Article 12 also permits derogating Member States to "(c) take appropriate measures with regard to the

---

[82]App. no.8348/78 and 8406/78 *Glimmerveen et Hagenbeek* v. *Netherlands*, 11 October 1979, Yearbook XXIII, 366 (384); Decisions and Reports 18, 187 (196–197).

[83]App. no.6745/74, 6746/74, op. cit. note 79; App. no.8042/77, 15 December 1977. Decisions and Reports 12, 202 (205); App. no.8802/79, 7 May 1980.

[84]App. no.6420-23/74, 15 July 1976; See also App. no.5155/71, *X* v. *United Kingdom*, Decisions and Reports no.6, 13, 12 July 1976, where the Commission held that Article 3 of the Protocol does not apply to local authorities whose legislative function is confined to the making of by-laws, is rigidly limited by statute and which have no powers to make rules other than in accordance with the powers conferred by Parliament.

[85]The Commission of Human Rights regards councils in certain city-states as legislative, which indicates the legal diversity which the new Community rights may provoke; *X* v. *Federal Republic of Germany*, 4 January 1961, Digest 5, 83 (West Berlin) and App. no.6850/74 *Associations X* v. *Federal Republic of Germany*, 18 May 1976, Decisions and Reports 5, 90 (Hambourg).

[86]See working party responsible for preparing a draft opinion on the preliminary draft convention on the participation of foreigners in public life at local level, Strasbourg, 13 September 1989, Restricted CDDH (89) 30. In App. no.7566/76 *X* v. *United Kingdom* 11 December 1976, Decisions and Reports 9, 121, the Commission observed that "among the conditions commonly imposed in Convention countries on the possession or exercise of a right to vote in Parliamentary elections, are citizenship, residence and age". Though this reasoning called for further examination in App. no.7730/76 *X* v. *United Kingdom*, 28 February 1979, Decisions and Reports 15, 137, in the light of "attempts ... to create political rights for non-citizens in the country of their habitual residence", citizenship has not yet been disregarded. In App. no.11123/84 *Tête* v. *France*, op. cit. the Commission stated that what must be ensured under Article 3, Protocol no. 1 "is the principle of equality of treatment of all citizens".

composition of lists of candidates to encourage, in particular, the integration of citizens of the Union who are nationals of another State". This allows Member States to arrange party lists and it is questionable whether this provision is compatible with the guarantee in Article 3 Protocol no.1. Furthermore, given the decision of the Court of Human Rights in *Dorothée Piermont*,[87] it is arguable that the nature of modern society, or the development of the European Union in particular, does not warrant a restrictive interpretation of Article 16 of the European Convention and its supposed derogation with respect to political rights and freedoms.

In conclusion, given that Article 12 relates to derogations from the fundamental guarantee in Article 8(b)(1), it is subject to review in 1998 and every six years thereafter. However, these derogations are problematic and dilute the content and value of Union citizenship since they qualify and limit the rights of Union citizens. The final provisions are the same as those for Directive 93/109, although the deadline for the implementation of the municipal elections' Directive is 1 January 1996. In particular, the Commission is to pay attention to any changes in the electorate following the implementation of the Directive which might create specific problems for certain Member States.

7.4.4. Implementation of Directive 94/80

Section 6.7.1 discussed the amendment of Article 13.2 of the Spanish Constitution. A reciprocity condition also figures in Article 88.3 of the French Constitution, as amended. Prior to the local elections in May 1995, the Spanish government adopted a Royal decree law for the establishment of the electoral census of foreign residents in Spain for municipal elections.[88] Article 1 provides that foreign residents with whom Spain has concluded an agreement and who fulfil the basic conditions established therein, may enrol on the electoral register. Member States are obliged to implement Directive 94/80 by 1 January 1996 and, pursuant to Article 14 para.2, they should refer to the Directive in national implementing legislation. No such mention of Directive 94/80 appears in the Royal decree law. However, if this legislation is intended to implement the rights of Union citizens under Article 8(b)(1) and to subject that right to a reciprocity condition, then it appears to be incompatible with Community law.[89] Although Spain has not yet infringed Community law, since the deadline for implementation has not passed, it has clearly acted contrary to the spirit of Article 8(b)(1). Indeed, the Council was fully aware of the 1995 municipal elections in Spain when negotiating the Directive; the European Parliament had proposed an amendment to the text of Article 14 to the effect that each Member State would adopt whatever legislation and administrative provisions necessary to

---

[87]See *infra* Section 6.3.
[88]*Real Decreto* 202/1995, BOE no.38, 14 February 1995.
[89]There has been some suggestion that other legislation is being prepared to implement the Directive, *El Pais* 21 February 1995. Indeed, it appears that the Directive was not implemented in time for the May 1995 elections for political reasons – fear that the resident non-national population would favour the opposition party.

comply with the Directive before the first local elections celebrated in 1995 and not later than 1 January 1996. This amendment was not accepted by Council, but the latter did point out that a failure to apply the Directive to elections to be held in 1995 would constitute a failure to comply with the spirit of the Treaty and would delay the first step towards Union citizenship in those Member States until the next century.[90] Almost 90 per cent of European Union citizens resident in Spain have been deprived of their electoral rights under Article 8(b)(1), although they fulfil the remaining conditions established in the decree law – 18 years of age, possession of a Spanish residence card, residence in Spain for over three years.

The compatibility of this reciprocity condition with Community law has become even more interesting in the light of a recent decision of the Supreme Court of Valencia, one of Spain's autonomous regions. That Court has recognised the municipal electoral rights of all Union citizens resident in Spain on the basis of Article 8(b)(1) and has annulled the local elections in one of the municipal districts in Valencia where French nationals were prevented from exercising their rights pursuant to Article 8(b)(1) because no reciprocal agreement had been concluded with France.[91] The Supreme Court held that Article 8(b)(1) was to be applied immediately and that the condition of reciprocity "implicitly applies in all Union Member States as an imperative requirement". In other words, it was not necessary to insist on an agreement of reciprocity with other Member States since such agreement was an implicit consequence of Article 8(b)(1). The Court only examined and annulled the elections in this municipal district because an amendment of the register could have produced different results in the elections, which was not the case in the complaints presented to it with respect to other districts. Article 8(b)(1) does not comply with the conditions for direct effect outlined in Chapter 4.6.1. Nevertheless, the Supreme Court in Valencia seems to have followed the recent jurisprudence of the Court of Justice in *Francovich*, *Wagner and Miret* and *Faccini Dori* on the invocability of subjective rights in Community law. The primary consideration in the case in Valencia was not whether Article 8(b)(1) complies with the conditions of direct effect, but whether the Court should interpret national law in line with the spirit and objectives of the Treaty with respect to the electoral rights of Union citizens. If the provisions on Union citizenship are similarly interpreted by other national courts, there may be more potential in the concept of Union citizenship than at first appeared possible.

7.4.5. Specific Problems with the Exercise of Municipal Electoral Rights

In addition to guaranteeing electoral rights on the basis of residence in Article 6, the Council of Europe Convention on the Participation of Foreigners in Local Elections also guarantees freedom of expression, assembly and association on the

[90]*El Pais*, 21 February 1995.
[91]See *El Pais*, 2 July 1995.

same terms as nationals to foreign residents.[92] It is clear that the electoral rights guaranteed to Union citizens in Article 8(b) will be genuinely and effectively exercised only when Union citizens can enjoy the political freedoms which should accompany these rights. Most Member States grant nationals and non-nationals freedom of expression at constitutional level. In Spain and Ireland, where there is no constitutional guarantee of freedom of expression for non-nationals, they seem to enjoy this freedom in practice. In contrast, only the Netherlands guarantees freedom of assembly and association for non-nationals at constitutional level.[93] Although Union citizens may, in practice, enjoy these freedoms when resident in a Member State other than their own "a lack of explicit statutory guarantees ... results in a weaker and more unstable basis for the exercise of freedom of assembly and association by non-nationals, especially as far as sensitive areas such as organised political activities are concerned".[94] Non-nationals encounter difficulties in some Member States, such as Portugal and Germany, as regards the right to form or join a political party. Furthermore, although political parties are primarily concerned with political affairs at national level, nevertheless, they tend to permeate the municipal and European levels of political participation as well. As a result, the exclusion or restriction of non-national participation in parties at national level, is likely to influence and ultimately weaken their role at local and European level. As Lundberg points out, the right to nominate candidates for European Parliament elections is restricted to political parties, or equivalent bodies, in Denmark, Greece, Germany and the Netherlands. In addition, these bodies often enjoy favourable terms of access to the media and sometimes receive financial support for their campaigns. Given that electoral rights in Article 8(b) are a specific expression of the principle of equal treatment, it is questionable whether national legislation preventing non-nationals from other Member States to form or join political parties can survive the adoption of the Union Treaty. Furthermore, the statement in Article 138(a) that political parties at Community level should contribute to the formation of a European awareness and expression of the political will of Union citizens suggests that national legislation should not be allowed to restrict the formation of transnational parties. Article 138(a) originally ranked among the rights and duties of citizenship in Article 8. Its removal suggests that Member States wanted to avoid the possibility of a directly effective right developing. It should not be forgotten that those who drafted and approved or rejected these provisions are the very persons who would be affected by the development of transnational political parties. Is it possible that the proponents of a free market economy do not want political parties themselves to be subject to cross-border competition?

---

[92] Article 3.

[93] Articles 7 and 9 of the Dutch Constitution.

[94] See Lundberg, E., "Political Freedoms in the European Union", in Antola, E. and Rosas, A. (eds.), *A Citizens' Europe: In Search of a New Legal Order* (1995) London, Sage Publications pp.113–134, at 120.

7.5. Political Rights and the Public Service Exception

The public service in Western liberal democracies represents one of the strongest and most symbolic aspects of state power. The admission of non-nationals to its ranks has traditionally been seen as an interference with state sovereignty and as an inadvisable opening of the national labour market in a sphere which could otherwise be protected and reserved in favour of nationals in times of economic downturn. Thus, states traditionally reserved jobs in policing, defence, justice, finance, tax and foreign affairs to their own nationals, who they regarded as more loyal to the national "political community" and, implicitly, more worthy of employment.[95] Article 48(4) provides that the provisions on the free movement of persons do not apply to employment in the public service.[96] The purpose of this section is not to examine in detail the operation of this exception in relation to free movement and the principle of non-discrimination.[97] Instead, this section addresses the effects of the Union Treaty on the public service exception and questions whether the latter requires any alteration in the application and interpretation of the public service exception.[98] The admission of other Member States' nationals to national political life on the basis of residence, even at the lowest level of political life, is a dramatic alteration of the traditional relationship between political participation and national sovereignty. Non-nationals may automatically become involved in a section of the public service either directly as future councillors, if successfully elected, or indirectly in their capacity as voters. What life is left in the public service exception in these circumstances? The Union Treaty contains no express reference to the public service exception. However, the inclusion of a right to stand for election in Article 8(b)(1) may require a change of heart as regards the scope of the exclusion of non-nationals from the public service and may also require constitutional amend-

---

[95]In a statement concerning its action in respect of the application of Article 48(4), the Commission considered specific functions in the armed forces, police, judiciary, tax authorities, ministeries, regional government authorities and local authorities as covered by Article 48(4), OJ 1988 C72/02.

[96]Similarly, Article 55 provides that the Treaty provisions on establishment and, by reference, services, shall not apply to activities which in a Member State are connected, even occasionally, with the exercise of official authority. For the purposes of our discussion, the two derogations will be treated similarly.

[97]In this respect, see Lenz, B., "The Public Service in Article 48(4) EEC with Special Reference to the Law in England and in the FRG", *LIEI* (1989) 75–118; Handoll, J., "Article 48(4) and Non-National Access to Public Employment", 13 *ELRev* (1988) 223–241; Dubouis, L., "La notion d'emplois dans l'administration publique et l'accès des ressortissants communautaires aux emplois", 3 RFDA (1987) 949–962; Chapus, R., "Nationalité et exercise de fonctions publiques, service public et liberté", in *Mélanges Offerts au Professeur R.E. Charlier*, Edition de l'Université et de l'enseignement moderne, at p.19; Druesne, G., "La liberté de circulation des personnes dans la CEE et 'les emplois dans l'administration publique'", 17 RTDE (1981) 286–300, at 286; and O'Keeffe (1992), op. cit. note 60.

[98]See Mancini, G.F., "The Free Movement of Workers in the Case-Law of the Court of Justice", in O'Keeffe and Curtin, op. cit. note 60, pp.67–77, at p.77, who, arguing against the Commission's proposals to harmonise what is permissible within the terms of the exception, stated the "principal danger ... is the ossification of a process which, since it is linked to the objective of political union of the Member States, should be allowed to continue in as unrestricted a manner as possible".

ment in those Member States which restrict the holding of public office to their own nationals.[99]

As a derogation from the fundamental principle of free movement and non-discrimination between Community nationals in the area of employment, Article 48(4) is to be strictly construed.[100] Posts which are exempted on the basis of Article 48(4) are those which involve direct or indirect participation in the exercise of powers conferred by public law[101] and duties designed to safeguard the general interests of the State or of other public authorities.[102] Community law thus recognises that certain employed activity depends on the existence of a special relationship of allegiance between the state and the employed persons and the reciprocity of rights and duties which are regarded as forming the foundation of the bond of nationality.[103] These criteria are regarded as cumulative[104] and although the Court has not succeeded in applying a purely Community law definition of public service employment, it has rejected unilateral national definitions[105] and applies the derogation functionally and not institutionally, relating it to the actual functions and characteristics of the post in question,[106] irrespective of the nature of the legal relationship involved.[107] Interpretations of the public service based on domestic law alone, which might obstruct the unity and efficacy of Community rules, are not permitted. Nevertheless, the case-law of the Court is said to have "overcome only to a modest extent and only in relation to the lower and middle levels of employment, the resistance on the part of state to the employment of foreigners in the public administration".[108]

Article 8(b)(1), despite the possible limitations and derogations which it permits, provides that Member State nationals resident in a Member State other than their own should be allowed to serve as elected members of local or municipal authorities, on the same conditions as nationals. Consequently, it directly impinges

---

[99]In Belgium (Article 6(2)), Denmark (Article 27(1)), Greece (Article 4(4)), Italy (Article 51), Portugal (Article 15(2)), Luxembourg (Article 11(2)) Germany (Article 33(4) and (5)) and implicitly in France (Article 6 of the 1789 Declaration), non-nationals are constitutionally excluded from civil service posts.

[100]See Case 149/79 *Commission* v. *Belgium* [1980] ECR 3881; Case 152/73 *Sotgiu* v. *Deutsche Bundespost* [1974] ECR 153; Case 66/85 *Lawrie-Blum* [1986] ECR 2121; Case 225/85 *Commission* v. *Italy* [1987] ECR 2625; and Case 147/86 *Commission* v. *Greece* [1988] ECR 1637.

[101]Lenz suggests that these are the power of enjoying prerogatives outside the general law, the privilege of official powers and the power of coercion over citizens, op. cit. note 97, at 103. The Court of Justice has thus far refrained from giving any specific guidelines on the content of this criterion. However, these suggested criteria are undoubtedly fulfilled by local council members.

[102]See Case 149/79, op. cit. note 100, at para.10(3900).

[103]See the German submissions in Case 152/73, op. cit. note 100, at 156–157; Lenz, op. cit. note 97, at 78; and Handoll, op. cit. note 97, at 231;

[104]Case 66/85, op. cit. note 100; Case 33/88 *Allué and Coonan*; Case C-4/91 *Bleis* [1992] ECR I-5627; and O'Keeffe (1992), op. cit. note 60, at p.96. For an alternative view see Handoll, op. cit. note 97, at 230, who interprets Case 225/85 as a rejection of the cumulative approach.

[105]Case 149/79, op. cit. note 100, at para. 18(3903).

[106]Case 307/84 *Commission* v. *France* [1986] ECR 1725.

[107]Case 152/73.

[108]See Mancini, op. cit. note 98, at p.77.

on the issue of who is entitled to be admitted to a Member State's public service. If Member State nationals are able to serve on local and perhaps regional elected bodies, what justification will exist for excluding them from public service posts which, though performed at a low level of the administrative hierarchy, are claimed to be linked to national security or sovereignty. It is submitted that the criteria introduced in *Commission* v. *Belgium* may have to be more stringently applied following the adoption of the Union Treaty to permit exceptions to the free movement of persons. Thus, the exclusion of nightwatchmen, stock- controllers and architects from the provisions of the Treaty on free movement is less justifiable if the applicant may be elected as a representative of the municipal council, which is itself responsible for the appointment of these employees![109] There may be justifiable limits on this development of the relationship between Community and national law, such as for example, when the local council is responsible for the appointment of members of the local police, military or judiciary. However, municipal councils are often responsible for the appointment of public service posts. The fact that Article 8(b)(1) permits Member State nationals to directly and indirectly appoint public service personnel must surely also entitle them to be appointed to a variety of posts which, to date, have fallen outside the scope of free movement on the basis of Article 48(4). The electoral rights of Union citizens invests them with rights to be appointed to local authority posts on the same basis as nationals and to have access to higher level posts previously denied them. In addition, traditional justifications for the imposition of a nationality requirement for employment in the public service – that non-nationals lack the necessary psychological and cultural link with the state which breeds a degree of loyalty, or that non-nationals pose a threat of foreign interference with the public administration of the state of residence,[110] become less convincing with regard to certain public service posts to the extent that non-nationals will in future be free to elect and be elected to local and perhaps regional councils. It is not contended that all public service posts should be open to non-nationals on the basis of their admission to local level politics. Rather, their political eligibility undermines their exclusion from certain posts, particularly those selected at local level, which to date have come within the scope of Article 48(4).

Furthermore, the public service derogation is based on a conception of the state and of state sovereignty which suggests that the state's legitimate interests are best served by its own nationals, to the exclusion of the nationals of other states. Nevertheless, as Chapter 2 suggests with reference to the effects of Community law on the determination of nationality, this view may be "founded on a conception of nationality which may face increasing strain".[111] The rights essential to Union citizenship and other rights which were developed on the basis of the free movement of persons prior to the Union Treaty, go quite some distance in detaching the enjoyment of rights from the possession of individual Member State nation-

---

[109]See the type of jobs at issue, for example, in Case 149/79 (no.2) [1982] ECR 1845.
[110]See Handoll, op. cit. note 97, at 223; and Dubouis, op. cit. note 97, at 955.
[111]See O'Keeffe, op. cit. note 60, at p.105.

ality. This development further weakens any continued reservation of posts to a Member State's own nationals via the public service exception. It is clear that certain high level political and judicial offices will continue to be reserved. However, in a Community which is now moving in the direction of common foreign and security policy and monetary union, it is difficult to deny that the bonds of nationality are under increasing strain. Finally, Chapter 4 also argues that the "constitutionalistion"[112] of Union citizenship implies a greater need to control use of public policy and public security exceptions. A similar tightening of judicial control is necessary with respect to the public service exception. It has been argued in the past that a fundamental change in the application of Article 48(4) will only occur if the significance of the nationality link between individual and State declines.[113] Article 8(b)(1), despite its limited scope and the admission of derogations, alters national conceptions of sovereignty, state membership and political participation in the requisite manner. Since the Union Treaty does not register any alteration in the public service exception in Article 48(4), it may be up to the Court of Justice to ensure that the effective exercise of Union citizens' rights are not adversely affected, or restricted, by this omission.

7.6. Conclusions

Article 8(b) represents a significant departure from the traditional exclusion or limitation of the rights of non-nationals in the field of political participation. Union citizens are to enjoy electoral rights in European Parliament and municipal elections in the Member State where they reside on the same conditions as the nationals of that Member State. Nevertheless, they may still choose whether or not to exercise these rights in their Member State of origin, if national law permits, or in their Member State of residence on the basis of Article 8(b) and the Directives adopted thereunder. The ratification of the Treaty on European Union and the adoption of these Directives required a number of Member States to amend their constitutional provisions with respect to the exercise of electoral rights by non-nationals. The importance of these amendments of national conceptions of sovereignty, what it entails and who can exercise it, should not be underestimated. Although France, for example, denies that Union citizens participate in the exercise of national sovereignty by virtue of their rights under Article 8(b)(1), the fact remains, nevertheless, that they have been permitted to exercise rights which have traditionally been seen as the essence of national citizenship.

However, the adoption and implementation of the rights of Union citizens pursuant to Article 8(b) is not without its difficulties. That provision specifically provides for the possibility of derogations with respect to the application of the

[112]See COM (93) 702 final, Commission report on Union Citizenship.
[113]Handoll, op. cit. note 97, at 241.

principle of equal treatment in municipal and European Parliament elections. These derogations have been elaborated in the implementing legislation. Although their objective is to take into account problems specific to certain Member States, in particular those with a large proportion of resident Union citizens, they detract, nevertheless, from the extension of the principle of equal treatment. In addition, problems are likely to arise in some Member States where certain regions within the state favour a broader extension of electoral rights for Union citizens than others, or in Member States where national constitutional or secondary legislation insists on a condition of reciprocity. It will be interesting to see whether the political rights of Union citizens and the political freedoms which should support them, will be effectively protected by Community law at Community and national level.

Part III

COMMUNITY CITIZENSHIP: BEYOND THE PRINCIPLE OF EQUAL TREATMENT

Chapter 8

Beyond the Principle of Equal Treatment: The Relationship Between Union Citizens and the Union

8.1. Introduction

Part I of this book established a framework in which to analyse the evolution of Community citizenship. It first developed a rough model of citizenship to assess whether the extension of individual rights to Member State nationals could be qualified as a form of citizenship. Thereafter it clarified the basis on which Union citizens can enjoy "citizenship-like" rights in the Community, namely, possession of Member State nationality and involvement in an economic activity. Although Union citizenship appears to require only the fulfilment of the former, Chapter 3 argued that the scope and implementation of Union citizenship to date has demonstrated that Member State nationals who are engaged in some sort of economic activity may enjoy certain rights and benefits which are not available to their economically inactive counterparts.

Part II then examined the extent to which the principle of equal treatment applies to Union citizens. It emerged that the bulk of the rights of Union citizenship enumerated in Article 8, for example, the right of free movement and residence and electoral rights at European and local level, are extended on the basis of the principle of equal treatment, within limits and subject to certain conditions, to Union citizens who reside in a Member State other than their own. The sense which Member State nationals have of living in a "community" may have been enhanced as a result, since they will now enjoy rights and benefits on the basis of Union citizenship which they would otherwise only have enjoyed at the discretion of the host Member State in question. Admittedly, however, one of the most significant rights of Union citizenship, the right of free movement and residence, already existed before the creation of Union citizenship. The privileges bestowed on Community nationals resident in a Member State other than their own are emphasised by the fact that third country nationals who are legally resident in Member States of the Union are excluded from the enjoyment of these rights and benefits. If they do benefit, they do so on the basis of national law, not Community law. However, it is important to remember that the Community itself does not create the rights and benefits which are extended to other Member State nationals on the basis of the principle of equal treatment. These rights and benefits are the product of national law and the Community principle of equal treatment simply operates to extend these rights to resident Union citizens from other Member States only to the extent that the rights "come within the scope of application of this Treaty" (Article 6) and to the extent that the individual is in a situation governed by Community law.[1] Furthermore, simply because one Union citizen enjoys certain rights on the basis of Article 6, for example, does not mean that all other Union citizens are entitled to identical treatment. There may be factors, such as present or past employment, which place one citizen in a better position than others and which justify the host Member State discriminating between them. A case of justifiable discrimination emerged in the *Lair*[2] and *Brown*[3] cases, with respect to the applicability of equal treatment to maintenance grants. Since Ms Lair was regarded as a worker for the purposes of Community law, she was entitled to maintenance grants, as well as tuition fees, on the same conditions as nationals of the state in which she was resident. Mr Brown qualified as a Community worker but the rights which he could claim in the host Member State on the basis of the principle of equal treatment were more limited than those available to Ms Lair since the work he undertook was purely to prepare for a course of study.

The purpose of this chapter is to go beyond the rights (and duties) which Union citizens enjoy on the basis of the principle of equal treatment. In particular, this chapter seeks to determine what rights Union citizens are able to claim, on the basis of Community law, against their own Member States and against the Community or Union. In its first report on Union citizenship, the Commission claimed that "For the first time, the Treaty has created a direct political link between the citizens of the Member States and the European Union such as never existed with the Community."[4] It suggested that the purpose of creating such a link was to foster a sense of identity with the Union. By looking closely at the other rights enumerated in Article 8 and the rights which Union citizens enjoy on the basis of other Treaty provisions, this chapter questions whether a link, political or otherwise, exists between the Union and its citizens and whether they can develop a "sense of identity" with the Union. This inquiry is necessary, since the model of citizenship outlined in Chapter 1 defined citizenship as a juridical condition which describes membership of and participation in a defined community. This juridical link was said to imply a series of rights (and duties) which are an expression of the political, legal

---

[1] See Case 186/87 *Cowan* [1989] ECR 195.
[2] Case 39/86 [1988] ECR 3161.
[3] Case 197/86 [1988] ECR 3205.
[4] COM (93) 702 final, which was compiled pursuant to Article 8(e).

and even historical link between the individual and the state. Does Community citizenship reflect the expression, at Community level, of the political and legal link between Community citizens and the Community or Union?

As a preliminary, the rights which Member State nationals can claim against their own Member States on the basis of Community law are tackled, in particular, the issue of reverse discrimination is examined with a view to determining whether the creation of Union citizenship in Article 8 alters the relationship between Member States and their nationals. It is questionable whether reverse discrimination can survive the establishment and progressive development of the rights of Union citizenship pursuant to Article 8. The most immediate example where reverse discrimination may no longer be tenable is with respect to the right of free movement and residence in Article 8(a). Two previous cases of the Court of Justice which discussed reverse discrimination are analysed. It appears that the Court of Justice has only been prepared to prohibit reverse discrimination when economic considerations relating to the fundamental Community objective of free movement were at stake. Given that Article Article 8(a) provides for a "constitutional" right of free movement and residence "within the territory of the Member States" is the economic rationale behind the Court's previous jurisprudence still tenable? Discussion of reverse discrimination reveals that although Union citizenship complements and does not substitute national citizenship,[5] it may be possible that it will progressively alter the relationship between the Member States and their nationals, since the latter now enjoy rights on the basis of Community law which they have traditionally enjoyed within the context of their Member State of origin and on the basis of national law.

The rights which Union citizens can claim against the Community or Union on the basis of Community law are also addressed. Article 8(d), for example, establishes rights to petition the European Parliament and a right to appeal to an Ombudsman. The procedures which have been adopted with respect to these non-judicial mechanisms of protection will be introduced and discussed in some detail. However, the specific object of this section is to establish whether these rights will effectively protect the other rights which Union citizens enjoy and whether, as rights in themselves, they can be said to enhance the position of Union citizens and to create a direct relationship between them and the Union. Unlike the right to free movement and residence, or electoral rights in European and municipal elections, these rights are the creation of Community law and are regulated by Community legal instruments.[6] The adoption of a uniform electoral procedure for European

---

[5]See the Decisions of the Heads of State and Government, meeting within the European Council, concerning certain problems raised by Denmark on the TEU, OJ 1992 C348/2, 31 December 1992; and the unilateral declaration by Denmark, OJ 1992 C348/4, 31 December 1992.

[6]The right to diplomatic protection is rather anomalous in this respect. On the one hand, it is not necessarily a *right* of Union citizens, since it is regarded in some states as a privilege bestowed at the discretion of the state and Article 8(c) simply requires that Union citizens be given protection "on the same conditions as the nationals of that state." On the other hand, Article 8(c) extends the principle of equal treatment, in limited circumstances, to the sphere of diplomatic protection.

Parliament elections is also discussed in this context. Electoral rights in European Parliament elections are rights of Union citizenship *par excellence*; however, the European Parliament's elections are presently subject to the individual electoral rules in each Member State. What effect does this failure to adopt a uniform procedure, for which the competence exists, on the relationship between the Union and its citizens.

To conclude this discussion about whether Union citizenship establishes a direct link, or fosters a sense of identity, between the Union and its citizens, the final section examines a further set of rights, fundamental rights, which Union citizens enjoy, both against their own Member States and against the Union. Fundamental rights cannot be restricted, either in theory or practice, to Community nationals, since they are rights which inhere in everybody, not simply Union citizens. However, the manner in which these rights are protected in the Community limits their enjoyment to those persons and situations which come within the scope of Community law, which effectively means Community or Union citizens. The discussion of fundamental rights thus seeks to determine whether the means of protection of fundamental rights in the Community diminishes the subjective content of these rights. Given the absence of an explicit bill of rights in Community law, or a justiciable provision guaranteeing the respect for fundamental rights in the Community and Union, the Court of Justice has been forced to legitimise the Community system generally and the legitimacy of its own jurisdiction in particular. This need to emphasis legitimacy may have detracted from the position of individual Community citizens and from the protection of their rights in the Community. It is argued that an explicit link should have been forged between the protection of fundamental rights and the establishment of Union citizenship. Guaranteeing the fundamental rights of Union citizens does not imply that the rights of non-citizens are not respected. Despite the rhetoric of the Union Treaty, Community citizens still do not feel directly involved in the Community's integration processes and until they do feel that they are at the centre of the Community's integration equation, it is arguable that it is impossible to forge a sense of identity with the Union, or indeed with fellow Union citizens. Expressing respect for the most fundamental of all rights could have been a starting point for the development of a higher standard of protection and the development of a truly supranational citizenship.

Many of the rights discussed in Part II could have developed anyway on the basis of the free movement provisions and Article 6. Indeed, many of them were in place before an article on citizenship was introduced into the Treaty. They can be regarded as the gradual and natural results of the Community's integration process and as the inevitable consequences of an application of the principle of *effet utile* to the free movement of persons. It was inevitable that once Community nationals secured a minimum of economic rights, their minds would then turn to social and even political rights. It must be asked, therefore, whether the status of citizenship, as it stands, contributes to the creation of a link between Union citizens and the Union, whether it enhances their position in the Union and whether, either now or in the future, it will contribute to a sense of European identity and to the creation of

a European polity. If Union citizenship cannot proceed beyond a limited and sometimes incoherent extension of the principle of equal treatment, it is suggested that it
is precisely because Union citizens do not share this sense of "community" and it
is arguable that little opportunity has been afforded in the citizenship provisions,
for such a sense of "community" or solidarity to develop.

8.2. Rights which Union Citizens Enjoy *vis-à-vis* their own Member States

8.2.1. The Principle of Reverse Discrimination

Reverse discrimination implies that a Member State's own nationals may receive
less favourable treatment on their home ground than nationals of other Member
States who have travelled to that Member State and who have thus availed of the
provisions of free movement.[7] The principle of reverse discrimination feeds on a
distinction between Community cases and internal cases. The former involve situations which come within the scope of Community law and which demonstrate a
connection with one of the situations envisaged and provided for by Community
law. Internal cases, on the other hand, involve facts which do not disclose any factor connecting the case with Community law, but refer, on the contrary, to situations which fall entirely within the law of a Member State.[8] In the *Singh* case, for
example, the Advocate General listed a number of cases – *Saunders*, *Morson and
Jhanjan* and *Moser* – where the facts of the case revealed situations purely internal
to the Member States. He pointed out that in such internal cases, the persons relying on provisions of Community law had not, in reality, exercised any professional
activity or apprenticeship in another Member State and that it was clear, therefore,
that in the absence of any element connecting their case with Community law, that
their situation did not enter within the scope of application of the Treaty.[9] Thus,
only where Member State nationals have availed of the free movement provisions will Community law enter the field to ensure that they enjoy at least the same

---

[7]See, for example, Joined Cases 35 and 36/82 *Morson and Jhanjan* [1982] ECR 3723, discussed
infra; and generally Pickup, D., "Discrimination and the Freedom of Movement of Workers", 23
CMLRev (1986) 135–156; Kon, S.D., "Aspects of Reverse Discrimination in European Community
Law", 6 *ELRev* (1981) 75–101; and Druesne, G., "Discriminations à rebours. Peuvent-elles tenir en
échec la liberté de circulation des personnes?", 15 RTDE (1979) 429–439.

[8]There is a long and increasing line of case-law dealing with this issue: Case 175/78 *Regina* v.
Saunders [1979] ECR 1129; Case 298/84 *Iorio* [1986] ECR 247; Case 20/87 *Gauchard* [1987] ECR
4879; Case 147/87 *Zaoui* [1987] ECR 5511; Case 204/87 *Bekaert* [1988] ECR 2029; Joined Cases C-
297/88 and C-197/89 *Dzodzi* v. *Belgian State* [1990] ECR I-3763; Joined Cases C-54/88, C-91/88, C-
14/89 *Nino* [1990] ECR I-3537; Case C-60/91 *Morais* [1992] ECR I-2085; Case C-61/89 *Bouchoucha*,
op. cit.; Case C- 332/90 *Steen* [1992] ECR I-341; Case C-153/91 *Petit* [1992] ECR I-4973; Case C-
206/91 *Ettien Koua Poirrez* [1992] ECR I-6685; and Joined Cases C-29/94 to C-35/94 *Jean Louis
Aubertin and Others*, judgment of 16 February 1995.

[9]Case C-370/90 *The Queen* v. *Immigration Appeal Tribunal and Surinder Singh* [1992] ECR I-
4265, at 4282.

treatment when re-entering their Member State of origin as a national from another Member State would on the basis of Community law.[10] Nationals of Member States generally enter and reside in the territory of their Member State of origin by virtue of rights attendant on their nationality and not by virtue of those conferred on them by Community law.[11]

Thus, the Court of Justice prohibits reverse discrimination with respect to persons who have availed of the free movement provisions and who now wish to work in their Member State of origin. Compare, for example, *Knoors* v. *Secretary of State for Economic Affairs*[12] with *Morson and Jhanjan*. Mr Knoors was a Dutch national who had trained, worked and resided in Belgium for a number of years. He applied to the relevant Dutch authorities for permission to exercise his profession in the Netherlands but was refused on the grounds that he did not possess the professional qualifications required by Dutch law. The Court was asked whether the provisions of the relevant secondary legislation, Directive 64/427,[13] also applied to persons possessing the nationality of the host Member State. In other words, whether the relevant provisions of Community law can be relied upon by Member State nationals against their own Member States. The Court held that the Directive could apply to all persons who found themselves in the conditions described by the Directive, regardless of their Member State of nationality. Moreover, it held that the fundamental freedoms of Community law in Articles 48, 52 and 59 could not be fully realised if Member States could refuse reliance on Community law to their nationals who availed of the free movement provisions and who acquired professional qualifications in a Member State other than that of their origin.[14] The Member States argued that if their nationals could rely on Community law rights against their own Member States then they could bypass and possibly abuse the requirements established by national law with respect to vocational training qualifications. Although the Court recognised these legitimate fears, it held that the precise conditions established in the Directive would counteract the possibility of such abuse and pointed out that it was still open to the Council to adopt legislation harmonising vocational training qualifications.

The *effet utile* of the free movement provisions was clearly at issue in *Knoors*. If Member State nationals could not rely, in certain circumstances, on Community law rights of free movement and residence against their own Member State, then they would be deterred from exercising their free movement rights and working, training and residing in a Member State other than their own. In contrast with the *Knoors* case, Mrs Morson and Mrs Jhanjan were Surinamese nationals who sought entry and residence in the Netherlands on the basis of Article 10 para.1 Regulation 1612/68. The latter confers derivative rights on the spouse, chidren who are under

---

[10]Ibid., at para.23.
[11]Ibid., at para.22.
[12]Case 115/78 [1979] ECR 3999.
[13]JO 1964 p.1863.
[14]Case 115/78, at paras.20 and 24.

21 or dependent, and dependent relatives in the ascending line to install themselves with the worker. Their children were Dutch nationals who worked and lived in the Netherlands. Given the fact, however, that their children had never exercised their rights of free movement within the Community, the Court held that the case did not come within the scope of application of Community law and that the applicants could not, therefore, rely on Article 10 para.1.[15] Had their children moved to another Member State to carry out an economic activity, or had they returned to the Netherlands after having carried out a professional activity in another Member State, Mrs Morson and Mrs Jhanjan would have had a right to install themselves with their children on the basis of Community law in either Member State. The *effet utile* of the free movement provisions was not damaged if the right to install themselves with their children was denied the applicants. The workers in question had not freely moved in the Community and were not, therefore, workers for the purpose of Community law. A refusal to admit their parents to the Netherlands on the basis of Community law encouraged, rather than deterred free movement, since they could enjoy such a right of family reunification on the basis of Article 10 para.1 if they moved to another Member State.

It is arguable, however, that the object of free movement is not only to promote an integrated labour market within the Community, but also to allow Community nationals to "pursue the activity of their choice within the Community".[16] These objectives can also be fulfilled if Community nationals choose to stay put in their Member States of origin. Indeed, nothing in the text of Articles 8 or 48 suggests that Member States should be allowed to discriminate against their own nationals.[17] The Court of Justice has disregarded the reference to this choice in recital three of the preamble to Regulation 1612/68 and Member State nationals do not generally enjoy rights on the basis of Community law vis-à-vis their own Member States.

8.2.2. Reverse Discrimination and the Internal Market

However, reverse discrimination has become increasingly anomalous in the context of an internal market without frontiers.[18] Though the borders themselves may not disappear in the internal market, a transborder element seems illogical if physical and technical barriers are to be reduced or suppressed. Furthermore, the notion of an effect on inter-state trade under the competition provisions allows practices which appear to take place within a single Member State to be caught by

---

[15]Joined Cases 35 and 36/82, op. cit. note 7, at paras.15–17.
[16]Third recital of Regulation 1612/68.
[17]See also Evans, "Union Citizenship and the Equality Principle", in Antola, E. and Rosas, A. (eds.), *A Citizens' Europe: In Search of a New Order* (1995) London, Sage Publications, pp.85–112, at p.89.
[18]See D'Oliveira, H.U.J., "The Community Case: Is Reverse Discrimination Still Admissible under the SEA?", in *Forty Years On: The Evolution of Postwar Private International Law*, 5 Centruum voor Buitenlands Recht en Internationaal Privaatrecht (1990) Dordrecht, Kluwer, pp.71–86, at pp.82 *et seq.*, who rejects the Court's insistence on a transborder element in Community cases.

Community law.[19] The criterion of an effective link was discussed in Chapter 2 as a means to determine who should benefit from Community law, in particular, whether Member State nationality could survive as the sole condition precedent for the enjoyment of free movement and Community or Union citizenship. Use of an effective link criterion might also open up the rights contingent on free movement to Community nationals who are involved in situations which can be regarded as demonstrating an effective link with Community law including, where appropriate, a national employed in his own Member State. Indeed in *ex parte Singh*, Advocate General Tesauro did not seem opposed to the idea of Community law being a more generous source of rights than national legislation.[20] A genuine or effective link criterion might also provide a means by which third country nationals resident in the Community could gradually gain access to the rights and duties of Community citizenship. It would thus displace nationality at both national and Community level as the predominant, if not the only, basis on which an individual can enjoy rights on the basis of Community law. As D'Oliveira points out, the distinction between Community and internal cases can no longer hold water once internal frontiers are abolished. The fact that the existence of internal borders is the material on which this unnecessary discrimination has fed emphasises its legal and logical weakness as a means of delimiting the scope of Community law.

8.2.3. Reverse Discrimination, Union Citizenship and the Principle of Equality

The importance of the principle of equal treatment to the development of Union citizenship further undermines the survival of reverse discrimination. Reverse discrimination is arguably unacceptable if, as they should be, equal treatment and more complete free movement are considered prerequisites of Community citizenship.[21] The crux of maintaining the distinction between Community and internal cases is the assertion of which level of authority – Community or national – remains competent to regulate an individual's rights.

Reverse discrimination has only been prohibited to date when it would compromise one of the objectives of Community law: "l'interdiction de discrimination à rebours, lorsqu'elle existe, est, en realité, un prolongement fonctionnel des libertés économiques qui etançonnent le Marché Communautaire plûtot que une application

---

[19]See Sir Leon Brittan, *Subsidiarity in the Constitution of the EEC*, Robert Schuman Lecture, European University Institute, Florence, 11 June 1992 at pp.11 and 12, on the issue of "Community" and "internal" cases in the context of merger control; and Advocate General Mancini in Case 352/85 *Bond van Adverteerders* [1988] ECR 2085, at para.8, in the context of broadcasting services.

[20]See Case C-370/90, op. cit. note 9, at para. 13.

[21]See the Italian report by Adam, R., *The New Developments of the Free Movement of Persons: Towards European Citizenship* (1992) Lisbon, FIDE, pp.249–271, at p.250: "Du point de vue juridique, on pourrait au contraire envisager des repercussions d'ordre général sur l'interprétation de certaines situations juridiques individuelles règlées par le droit communautaire: étant reconnues au citoyen de l'Union, elles pourront être plus difficilement considerées comme des 'situations purement internes' et donc 'étrangères au domaine d'application des règles du Traité', quand elles seront faites valoir à l'egard de son propre Etat."

en ligne directe du principe d'égalité".[22] However, following the establishment of Union citizenship can Community law still only protect Union citizens against their own Member States to the extent that such protection facilitates the complete integration of the market? The possible effects of Union citizenship and the principle of equal treatment on reverse discrimination should not be underestimated. In the *Wolf and Dorchain* case,[23] for example, the Court held that Member State nationals can invoke the provisions of Community law with respect to the free movement of persons against their own or another Member State if national law threatens the *effet utile* of the provisions of Community law. Following this case, Lenaerts has argued that equal treatment no longer applies on the basis of nationality but that what counts is "la qualité de ressortissant de la Communauté qui, en tant que tel, possède le droit de ne pas être reparti en catégories incompatibles avec l'esprit du Traité".[24] Does this reasoning extend to Union citizens and a right to rely on Article 8(a) to establish a right of residence in their own Member States? To deny them this right would surely interfere with the *effet utile* of a Community law provision, which would go against the *Wolf and Dorchain* decision. The spirit of the Treaty in creating Union citizenship was to strengthen and protect the rights of Union citizens and they enjoy a right of free movement pursuant to Article 8(a) within the territories of the Member States. As the Advocate General argued in *Singh*, in certain circumstances Community law can be the source of more extensive rights than national law for persons who come within its scope. Furthermore, the introduction of Article 8 means that the free movement of persons in the Community is now no longer dependent on the economic rationale and requirements of purely market integration. As a result, the type of reasoning evident in the *Werner* case[25] might no longer be so easily applied. In that case a German dentist who had acquired his qualifications in Germany and exercised his profession in Germany, but who lived in the Netherlands claimed discrimination contrary to Article 52, because a higher tax regime was imposed on him by German law than would have applied if he had been resident there. However, the Court and Advocate General emphasised that the only element which brought the case outside of the internal sphere of Germany was the plaintiff's residence in another Member State. Furthermore, the Advocate General emphasised that the right in Articles 48 and 52 to move freely within the Community was with a view to exercising an economic activity in the Member State of residence.[26] However, Articles 48, 52 and 59 are now not the only Treaty bases on which to enjoy a right of residence and it is arguable that the Court of Justice may not be able to maintain this distinction between internal and Community cases. How can *Werner* be described as an internal case if Mr Werner resided in a Member State other than that of his origin and exercised his profession in a Member State other than that of his residence. Quite apart from his involvement in an economic activity

---

[22]See Lenaerts, K., "L'égalite de traitement en droit communautaire", CDE (1991) 3–41, at 19.
[23]Joined Cases 154-155/87 [1988] ECR 3897.
[24]See Lenaerts, op. cit. note 22, at 32.
[25]Case C-112/91 [1993] ECR I-429.
[26]Ibid., at paras.29–31.

in his Member State of origin he was exercising his constitutional right to reside in a Member State other than his own pursuant to Article 8(a). The case was, therefore, no longer internal to Germany.[27] Although the rights of Union citizenship may not yet be relevant in the area of tax law, which was what Mr Werner's objection was all about, nevertheless, Article 8(a) means that the Court's statement that the case is internal to Germany is no longer correct.

Further support for a departure from the Court's market-oriented limitation of reverse discrimination can be gained from the Opinion of the Advocate General in the *Saunders* case, where a national penal measure restricted the freedom of movement of a national of that Member State for acts committed within the territory of that state. In his view, the *dictum* of the Court in *Knoors* to the effect that the Treaty does not apply to cases purely internal to a Member State cannot be applied globally in the sense that *no* Treaty provision on the free movement of persons can apply in a case wholly internal to a Member State.[28] In his view, Article 6 forbids discrimination by a Member State against its own nationals as much as it prohibits discrimination against the nationals of another Member State. In support of this interpretation Evans argues that "it would seem incompatible with [Article 8(a)] for a national of a Member State wishing to acquire a right under the Treaty to reside in his own Member State to have first to move to another Member State. It might also be argued that it would be inconsistent with the definition of the internal market in Article 7a of the Treaty for rights to depend on the prior crossing of frontiers which are supposed to have been abolished at the end of 1992."[29] He also argues that the problem with respect to Union citizenship and reverse discrimination is more a political than a legal one, since the effect of prohibiting reverse discrimination with respect to Union citizens would be to extend a right, such as residence, which traditionally Member State nationals enjoyed on the basis of national law, to Member State nationals in their own state on the basis of Community law which would be extremely intrusive. Nevertheless, the logic of Union citizenship, which should be all about equality and the abolition of frontiers, does not preclude such an intrusion.

8.3. The Creation of a Direct Link Between Union Citizens and the Union

8.3.1. Non-Judicial Mechanisms for the Protection of the Rights of Union Citizens

Article 8(d) provides that every citizen of the Union shall have the right to petition the European Parliament in accordance with Article 138(d) and the right to apply

---

[27]The Court is right to point out that although Mr Werner resided in a different Member State he was still subject to the laws of Germany since he exercised his profession there. However, the point here is that the case was not an internal case and the establishment of Union citizenship may produce many more cases like this.

[28]Case 175/78, op. cit. note 8, at 1141.

[29]See Evans (1995), op. cit. note 17, at p.91.

to the Ombudsman who is to be established in accordance with Article 138(e). The following section discusses how these rights have been implemented and assesses whether they provide effective means to vindicate and protect the rights of Union citizens and whether, as constituent rights of Union citizenship in themselves, they help to forge a link between the Union and its citizens.

Complaints to the Omdudsman

The right to apply to the Ombudsman is elaborated in Article 138(e)[30] and in the secondary legislation adopted thereunder.[31] Article 138(e)(4) had provided that the European Parliament shall adopt the regulations and general conditions governing the performance of the Ombudsman's duties and that it was to do so after seeking the opinion of the Commission and with the approval of the Council, which was to act by a qualified majority. This provision is a significant departure from the normal distribution of legislative powers between the Community institutions and it underlines the close, albeit independent, relationship which the Ombudsman is to share with the European Parliament. Article 138(e) provides that any citizen of the Union, or any natural or legal person who resides or has their registered office in a Member State, may complain to the Ombudsman "concerning instances of maladministration in the activities of the Community institutions or bodies, with the exception of the Court of Justice and the Court of First Instance acting in their judicial role".[32] Thus, although the right to complain to the Ombudsman figures in Article 8(d) as a constituent right of Union citizenship it is, in fact, open to all natural and legal persons resident in the Community Member States. The only distinction between Union citizens and third country nationals is that the former can complain to the Ombudsman regardless of whether they reside in or outside the Union, since they are Union citizens on the basis of their nationality, not their place of residence. In contrast, third country nationals can only enjoy this right if they reside in a Member State.[33] Note, however, that Article 2(2) of the Decision on the Ombudsman

[30]See also Article 20(d) ECSC; and Article 107(d) EAEC.

[31]See Decision 94/262 of the European Parliament which determines the general conditions for the exercise of the Ombudsman's duties (hereafter, the Decision), OJ 1994 L113/15, 4 May 1994. The Decision of the European Parliament was subsequently approved by a qualified majority of the Council, Decision 94/114 of the Council, OJ L54/25, 25 February 1994.

[32]Marias suggests that instances of maladministration include administrative irregularities, administrative omissions, abuse of power, administrative action taken as a result of negligence, administrative actions based on illegal procedures, violation of the notion of equity, malfunction, incompetence, delay or lack of response. See Marias, E.A., "Mechanisms of Protection of Union Citizens' Rights", in Antola and Rosas, op. cit. note 17, pp.207–233, at p.221. See also Pierucci, A., "Les recours au mediateur européen", in Marias, E.A., *European Citizenship* (1994) Maastricht, EIPA, pp.103–117; and Gosalbo Bono, R., "Maastricht et les Citoyens: le Mediateur Européen", 64 *Revue Française d'Administration Publique* (1992) 639–649.

[33]This provision is less flexible than some national Ombudsman provisions, which allow individuals to complain to the Ombudsman regardless of nationality or residence. However, it is considerably more generous with respect to third country nationals than other provisions of the Treaty which generally exclude them from the benefits of Community law.

provides that all natural and legal persons who reside or have their registered office in a Member State of the Union can apply to the Ombudsman. This provision suggests that Union citizens must also be resident in the Union to avail of the right to apply to the Ombudsman. Given that Union citizenship is intended to strengthen the rights and interests of Union citizens, the text of the Treaty should prevail, so that non-resident Union citizens can avail of the right established in Articles 8(d) and 138(e).

The Ombudsman is to be appointed by the European Parliament after each election of the European Parliament and for the duration of its term of office, which at present is five years.[34] The Ombudsman must be a Union citizen, must enjoy his or her civil and political rights to the full, must offer guarantees of his or her total independence while in office and must be eligible for the highest judicial office in his or her Member State of origin, or have outstanding experience and competence which makes him or her eligible to exercise the office of Ombudsman.[35] The office of Ombudsman is completely independent and is to be performed, according to Article 9 of the Decision, in the interests of the Community and Union citizens. The Ombudsman is not to take instructions from any government or any organisation or body, is not allowed to engage in other professional activity during the term of office and is to abstain from any act which is incompatible with the nature of his or her functions as Ombudsman. To preserve the independence required by Article 9, the Ombudsman can only be dismissed by the Court of Justice at the request of the European Parliament and only on grounds that he or she no longer fulfils the necessary conditions for the performance of the duties of Ombudsman, or if he or she is guilty of serious misconduct.[36]

Article 138(e) only specifies the nature and organisation of the duties of the Ombudsman to a limited extent. Paragraph 2 of Article 138(e) provides that the Ombudsman shall conduct inquiries if he or she finds that there are grounds for the complaint. Presumably, the Ombudsman will first conduct a preliminary inquiry on the basis of the facts presented. If the Ombudsman is required to investigate all complaints in some depth in order to establish their admissibility, there is a risk that the office will become overloaded.[37] The Ombudsman may conduct inquiries of his or her own initiative, or as a result of complaints from natural or legal persons which are forwarded to the Ombudsman directly, or through a member of the European Parliament. It has been suggested, in addition, that the Ombudsman should also deal with complaints transmitted by national agencies, such as the national Ombudsman, or by members of national parliaments.[38] The Ombudsman is not allowed to conduct inquiries where the grounds for the complaint are, or have

[34]See Article 6 of the Decision.
[35]Article 6(2).
[36]Article 8.
[37]See also O'Keeffe, D., "Union Citizenship", in O'Keeffe, D. and Twomey, P. (eds.), *Legal Issues of the Maastricht Treaty* (1994) London, Chancery Press, pp.87–107, at p.102.
[38]Ibid., at p.101.

been, the subject of legal proceedings. Where the Ombudsman establishes that the complaint is justified and that there has been an instance of maladministration, he or she is to consult the institution in question. The latter has three months to reply to the Ombudsman. A report is then forwarded by the Ombudsman to the institution in question and to the European Parliament. The natural or legal person who lodged the complaint is also to be informed of the outcome of the inquiry, but it is unclear from the text of the Treaty whether the complainant has access to the report in question.

Article 138(e)(1) of the Treaty and Article 2 of the Decision specify the institutions and bodies which the Ombudsman can investigate to determine whether there has been an instance of maladministration, namely, the institutions and bodies of the Community. However, the Court of Justice and the Court of First Instance are excluded from the scope of the Ombudsmans' investigations when they are exercising their judicial function. No other authority or person may be investigated by the Ombudsman. The Ombudsman is not competent, therefore, to investigate institutions, bodies, or committees which belong to the Union rather than the Community. As D'Oliveira points out, what is at issue, therefore, is Community not Union citizenship, since there is no provision for complaints about the third pillar activities, or about the activities of Community institutions not acting within their Community capacity.[39] This means that the activities of bodies such as the Consultative Committee provided for in Article K.4 of the Third Pillar on Cooperation in the Fields of Justice and Home Affairs, does not come within the scope of the Ombudsman's competence. That Committee, which is not subject to judicial or parliamentary control, may submit opinions to the Council at the Council's request, or on its own initiative. It may also prepare the Council's discussions with respect to any of the issues listed in Article K.1, *inter alia*, police cooperation, judicial cooperation in civil and criminal matters, combating fraud and drug addiction, family reunion and access to employment for third country nationals and the conditions of entry and movement of third country nationals. These are precisely the sort of issues which may threaten the rights of Union citizens. O'Keeffe regrets, in addition, that the Ombudsman cannot investigate maladministration by national bodies acting in pursuance or violation of Community law and suggests that this was the intention of the Commission and, presumably, some Member States, when they proposed the creation of individual national Ombudsmen during the course of the intergovernmental conference prior to the adoption of the Union Treaty.[40] In contrast, the European

---

[39]See D'Oliveira, H.U.J., "European Citizenship: Its Meaning, Its Potential", in Monar, J., Ungerer, W. and Wessels, W. (eds.), *The Maastricht Treaty on European Union: Legal Complexity and Political Dynamic* (1993) Brussels, European Interuniversity Press, pp.81–106, at p.99.

[40]See O'Keeffe, op. cit. note 37, at p.107; the Commission's submissions to the 1992 IGC, SEC (91) 500; and Article 9 of the Spanish proposal on European Citizenship, which proposed the creation of an Ombudsman in each Member State, whose duty it would be to defend the rights of Union citizens before the administrative authorities of the Union and its Member States, reproduced in XLIII *Revista Española de Derecho Internacional* (1991), at 265.

Parliament's Committee on Petitions supported this limitation of the scope of the Ombudsman's investigations.[41]

When a complainant applies to the Ombudsman, the object of the complaint must be clear, as must the name of the complainant, who may request that the application remains confidential (Article 2(3)). Complaints must be presented within two years of the complainant becoming aware of the facts surrounding the complaint and the complainant must have previously made suitable applications to the institutions or bodies involved. The Ombudsman may advise complainants to direct their complaint to another authority (Article 2(5)) and applications to the Ombudsman does not stop time running in parallel administrative or judicial proceedings (Article 2(6)). The Ombudsman is obliged to declare inadmissible or to terminate complaints with respect to which judicial proceedings have taken place or are taking place (Article 2(7)). If the Ombudsman proceeds to investigate possible cases of maladministration, on his or her own initiative, or as a result of a complaint, the Community institution or body in question must be informed of the investigation and must be entitled to make whatever observations which it considers useful (Articles 3(1) and (2)). Community institutions and bodies are obliged to facilitate the Ombudsman with whatever information requested and to give him or her access to the relevant documents on the case. The Ombudsman can only be denied access to these documents for reasons of confidentiality which are duly justified. However, the prior agreement of Member States is necessary before the Ombudsman can have access to documents from Member States which have been classified as confidential (Article 3(2) para.2). Even with respect to unconfidential material from Member States, the Ombudsman is still obliged to inform Member States of the reason for the investigation. Civil servants and agents of the Community institutions can be required to give evidence before the Ombudsman if necessary. Member States are also required, via their Permanent Representatives, to furnish the Ombudsman with whatever information necessary to clarify whether or not there has been maladministration on the part of Community institutions and bodies (Article 3(3)). However, Member States are not required to divulge information which is deemed confidential, or which is covered by any other provision which prevents it from being transmitted. The Ombudsman will then only have access to the information in question if he promises not to divulge its contents. Indeed, the Ombudsman and his staff are obliged not to divulge the information they encounter in the course of their investigations[42] and the Ombudsman is required to take a solemn oath to exercise his or her duties with the utmost independence and impartiality and to respect the obligations of the office, in particular, honesty and discretion, when accepting duties after he or she has ceased to be in office (Articles 9(1) and (2)).

---

[41] See the Opinion of the Committee on Petitions, annexed to the Martin Report on the results of the IGC and the TEU, Doc. A3-123/92, at 125-126.
[42] Article 4(1).

The Ombudsman may inform the European Parliament if Member States deny the assistance requested by the Ombudsman and the European Parliament can then take the matter further (Article 3(4)). The primary function of the Ombudsman throughout the course of the investigation is to look for a solution with the Community institution or body in question which would elimante the instance of maladministration and satisfy the complainant (Article 3(5)). When the Ombudsman finds that the complaint is justified, he or she shall address his findings and recommendations to the body in question, which has three months within to return a detailed report. The Ombudsman then submits a report to the European Parliament and the institution in question, which may, but does not have to, include recommendations (Article 3(7)). The complainant must also be informed by the Ombudsman of the results of the investigation, of the "motivated opinion" made by the Ombudsman and of whatever recommendations the Ombudsman has made, if in fact he or she has made any. Pursuant to Article 138(e) para.3 of the Treaty and Article 3(8) of Decision 94/262, the Ombudsman must submit a report on the results of his or her investigations to the European Parliament at the end of every annual session. The Bindi report also suggested that the European Parliament could, in turn, request the Committee on Petitions to examine the report of the Ombudsman.[43] To improve the efficiency of his or her investigations and to enhance the protection afforded to the rights and interests of complainants, the Ombudsman may cooperate with corresponding authorities at national level, in accordance with the applicable national legislation. However national authorities which cooperate with the Ombudsman are not allowed to have access to the confidential information dealt with pursuant to Article 3 simply because they are cooperating with the Ombudsman (Article 5).

The right to apply to the Ombudsman is clearly one of the innovative aspects of Union citizenship. During the course of the intergovernmental conference it was strongly supported by the Danish[44] and Spanish delegations and by the Commission. All recognised in the creation of a European Ombudsman, whether at European or national level, an extra-judicial, inexpensive and accessible means to vindicate the rights of Union citizens and a democratic basis for further Community cooperation. Indeed the Spanish proposal saw the Ombudsman as a means to enforce the rights of Union citizens before judicial bodies on the initiative of the Ombudsman, or as a means to intervene on behalf of complainants. However, the right introduced by Article 138(e) and implemented by Decision 94/262 is problematic. In particular, the rights and interests of Union citizens generally and third country nationals, in particular, are considerably weakened by excluding the activities of institutions acting with respect to the Union, from the scope of the Ombudsman's investigations. The intervention of the Ombudsman may be particularly

---

[43]See the Bindi Report on the Ombudsman, Doc. A3-0298/92, at p.11.
[44]The Danish proposals are reproduced in Laursen, F. and Van Hoonacker, S., *The Intergovernmental Conference on Political Union* (1992) Maastricht, EIPA, at p.297.

necessary in this field of Union law, where both the Court of Justice and the European Parliament cannot intervene. O'Keeffe argues that the Union's single in-stituitional framework pursuant to Article C TEU could be used to extend the Ombudsman's investigations to any act of the institutions, whether they are acting on behalf of the Community or the Union.[45] This interpretation is possible in the light of the Rules of Procedure adopted by the European Parliament with respect to petitions, however, it is likely to cause a considerable stir, if not outright political controversy among some institutions. Further problems may emerge, over time, from the fact that the office of the Ombudsman has not always attracted the unan-imous support of the European Parliament.[46] The provisions of Article 138(e) and the 1994 Decision on the Ombudsman reveal that cooperation between these two institutions is vital if the office of the Ombudsman is to effectively solve the com-plaints and guarantee the rights of Union citizens. The effect of the Ombudsman's solution of complaints, recommendations and annual reports will largely depend on the extent to which the European Parliament is prepared to bring matters fur-ther, either legally or politically. On its own, the Ombudsman can issue no legally binding measures or sanctions. It will be regrettable if this non-judicial mechanism of protection suffers from rivalry within the European Parliament between the value of the office of Ombudsman versus the Committee on Petitions. However, the European Parliaments' lack of conviction with respect to the Ombudsman is re-flected in the fact that the Ombudsman was only elected mid-1995 due to differ-ences between the different political groups in the European Parliament. As a result, in the run up to the 1996 IGC, when the provisions on Union citizenship be amended or extended for the first time, Union citizens have still not been able to avail of one of the only innovative rights introduced in 1992 for their benefit and one of the rights which was to secure openness in the administration and to serve as a guarantee of the other rights of citizenship.

Petitions to the European Parliament

Article 138(d) provides that "any citizen of the Union, and any natural or legal per-son residing or having his registered office in a Member State, shall have the right to address, individually or in association with other citizens or persons, a petition to the European Parliament on a matter which comes within the Community's fields of activity and which affects him directly".[47]

Like the office of ombudsman, national parliamentary petitions' committees were set up to guarantee the extra-judicial protection of citizens' rights. The right

---

[45]See O'Keeffe, op. cit. note 37, at p.101.

[46]See the reservations of the Committee on Petitions expressed in its annual report on the delibera-tions of the Committee during the parliamentary year 1990–91, Doc. A3-0122/91; and OJ 1985 C175/273, where the differences between national legal systems was felt to deter the introduction of a European Ombudsman.

[47]See generally, Marias, op. cit. note 32; Marias, E., "The Right to Petition the European Parliament After Maastricht", 19 *ELRev* (1994) 169–181; and Pliakos, A., "Les Conditions d'Exercice du Droit de Petition", CDE (1993) 317–349.

to petition introduced in Articles 8(d) and 138(d) simply codifies a system of petitions which was already operating in the Community. The right to petition in the Community dates back to 1953, when the European Coal and Steel Assembly incorporated petitions in its Rules of Procedure. Since then the European Parliament has supported codification of this right for Member State nationals[48] and it amended its own Rules of Procedure accordingly in 1981 in order to allow Member State nationals to submit petitions. However, the European Council stopped short of adopting a legal basis for a right to petition following the Adonnino Report on a Citizens' Europe and simply acknowledged the political significance of petitions for Member State nationals.[49] Despite the absence of an explicit legal basis for the right to petition the European Parliament, the Parliament's Committee on Petitions was created in 1987.[50] The authority of this Committee to receive and examine petitions was recognised in an Interinstitutional Declaration signed by the Presidents of the Parliament, the Council and the Commission.[51] However, until the adoption of the Union Treaty the Rules of Procedure of the European Parliament did not give rise to a right which Member State nationals could enjoy on the basis of Community law and the Interinstitutional Declaration merely recognised a *custom* of Member State nationals to petition the European Parliament.[52]

Articles 8(d) and 138(d) now provide a legal basis for the right to petition the European Parliament and have thus converted a recognised custom of Community law into a legally enforceable right. The adoption of a specific legal basis has also facilitated the work of the Committee on Petitions, since it may now rely on the cooperation of the other Community institutions, in particular, the Commission.[53] Apart from supporting the custom of petitions the 1989 Interinstitutional Declaration recognised that the Parliament could send requests for assistance and information to the Commission. However, the Declaration was not legally binding and regardless of the duty of cooperation in Article 5, which binds Member States and arguably obliges them to provide information when requested, the European Parliament was still highly dependent on the cooperation of the Commission in the first instance. Now that Union citizens enjoy a legal right to petition, the European Parliament can request information directly from the Member States. Furthermore, the Commission is now under an obligation to assist the European Parliament in its inquiries and must assist in the protection of the rights of Union citizens, given its role as guardian of the Treaties.

Petitioners, like complainants to the Ombudsman, must establish their name, occupation, permanent residence and, in the case of legal persons, the address where their offices are registered and information about the activities pursued

---

[48]OJ 1977 C299/26.
[49]Bull. EC. Supplement 7/85
[50]See Articles 156, 157 and 158 of the European Parliament's Rules of Procedure, 1987.
[51]OJ 1989 C120/90.
[52]See Marias (1995) op. cit. note 32, at p.213; and Marias (1994), op. cit. note 32, at 170.
[53]See Marias (1995) op. cit. note 32, at p.217.

(Article 128 para.2). Petitions which comply with these conditions and which are, therefore, formally admissible, are entered in the petitions' register. They are then sent to the Committee on Petitions to be further examined.[54] The right to petition, like the right to apply to the Ombudsman, is not a right which is exclusively enjoyed by Union citizens. All natural and legal persons resident in the Community, or who have a registered office in the Community, have a right to petition pursuant to Article 138(d).[55] Some commentators have underlined the apparent confusion in enumerating the right to petition and the right to apply to the Ombudsman as Union citizenship rights on the one hand, and the extension of these rights to third country nationals on the other. However, this ambiguity is explained by the fact that Union citizenship has developed in the context of a community of sovereign states and, as a result, is far from the traditional notion of citizenship which exists or existed within individual states. In Durand's view, Union citizenship: "se résume essentiellement en l'octroi de droits que les ressortissants des Etats membres, en tant qu'individus, peuvent faire valoir et exercer a l'échelon de la Communauté".[56] However, it has also been argued that the inclusion of third country nationals in Articles 138(d) and (e) indicates that the right to petition and the right to apply to the Ombudsman have been dissociated from the other political rights of Union citizenship,[57] or that the Community/Union will be under increasing pressure to extend rights to third country nationals, now that they have extended some of the rights of Union citizenship to them.

Furthermore, Marias points out that it is unclear from the reference to residence in Article 138(d), a criterion which has proved difficult to define in other areas of Community law such as political rights, whether illegal immigrants are also entitled to submit petitions and suggests that this matter is for the European Parliament's Committee on Petitions to decide. He argues, however, that the European Parliament will find it very difficult to ignore the petitions of illegal residents. First of all, the Parliament's Declaration on Human Rights and Fundamental Freedoms extended the right to everyone within the Community.[58] Secondly, the Parliament had already discussed a preference for determining admissibility with respect to the substance of petitions, rather than on the basis of the persons submitting them. After all, the essential objective of the right to petition is to ensure greater access to the Community's administration and to enhance the Community's democratic legitimacy, which implies that more value should be accorded the substance than the form of the petition, or the standing of the petitioner.[59] Finally, and perhaps most controversially, the Rules of Procedure amended for the purpose of

---

[54]Articles 156(4) and (5) of the Rules of Procedure of the European Parliament.
[55]For a discussion of the types of legal persons deemed admissible see Marias (1994), op. cit. note 32, at 176.
[56]See Durand, A., "Le traité sur l'Union européenne. Quelques réflexions", *Le droit de la CEE. Addendum* (1992) Bruxelles, ULB, Vol.2, at p.438.
[57]See Pliakos, op. cit. note 47, at 320.
[58]See OJ 1989 C120/56.
[59]See also Pliakos, op. cit. note 47, at 324.

Article 138(d) already include a right of petition, in certain circumstances, for natural and legal persons not resident in the Community which the Committee can examine such petitions at its own discretion.[60] Unlike residents and Union citizens these non-residents do not even have to demonstrate that the subject of the petition affects them directly and the guidelines issued by the Committee on Petitions relating to the submissions of persons outside the scope of Article 138(d), suggest that the Committee should examine petitions relating to the free movement of persons, the right of residence and asylum and human rights in third countries. This extension of the personal scope of petitions and the subject matter which the Committee is being advised to examine suggest that a similar right for illegal immigrants on the basis of the Rules of Procedure may materialise, particularly since the European Parliament has interpreted the scope of petitions to include the Unions' activities and Article K.1(3)(c) specifically refers to unauthorised immigration, residence and employment on the territory of the Member States.

Article 138(d) provides that petitions are limited to the Community's fields of activities, which is identical to the wording of Article 128(1) of the Parliament's previous Rules of Procedure. Nevertheless, paragraphs 1 and 4 of Article 156 of the new Rules of Procedure stipulate that petitions should fall within the sphere of the European Union's activities. It is unclear whether this provision is compatible with Article 138(d), or whether, in practice, the European Parliament will examine petitions relating to Union activities. What is clear, however, is that widening the scope of the activities which can be examined in this way will undoubtedly favour Union citizens in the first instance, since the Committee is allowed to protect their rights within a broader field of activity.[61] However, it will probably benefit third country nationals to an even greater extent, since their rights and interests are threatened by actions under the third pillar to a far greater extent than those of Union citizens.

Both Article 138(d) of the Treaty and Article 156 para.1 of the Rules of Procedure have introduced a more restrictive legal right to petition than previously existed on the basis of custom. Both require that the subject of the petition affects the petitioner directly. However, neither the Treaty nor the Rules of Procedure provide any indication of what is meant by this condition. This restriction of the right to petition has been criticised by the Committee itself, which fears that it will restrict citizens' rights.[62] If this is the case, it seems incompatible with the purpose of Union citizenship as expressed in Article B para.3 TEU, which is to increase and strengthen the rights and interests of Union citizens and conflicts with the guarantee

---

[60]See Article 156 para.9 of the Rules of Procedure of the European Parliament; and previous Parliamentary support for this extension of the *ratione personae* of the right to petition, OJ 1989 C158/482.

[61]See also the Reding Report on the deliberations of the Committee on Petitions during the Parliamentary year 1989–90, at p.13.

[62]See the Annual Report of the Committee on Petitions, Doc. A3-0122/91.

[63]See the Opinion of the Committee on Petitions on the results of the IGC and the TEU, which was annexed to the Martin Report, Doc. A3-123/92.

in Article B para.5 TEU that the Union shall maintain the existing *acquis commu-nautaire* and to build on it. The Committee is of the opinion, however, that this condition should not be interpreted restrictively.[63] A previous version of Article 138(d) required that the petitioner be concerned directly and individually, but this proposal was eventually rejected on the grounds that it would greatly restrict the exercise of the right to petition. Nevertheless, the condition incorporated in Article 138(d) is reminiscent of the "direct and individual concern" condition which is im-posed on natural or legal persons who wish to institute proceedings against a Community decision on the basis of Article 173 para.4. The Court of Justice has held that "individual concern" in this context means that "persons other than those to whom a decision is addressed may only claim to be individually concerned if that decision affects them by reason of certain attributes which are peculiar to them or by reason of circumstances in which they are differentiated from all other per-sons and by virtue of these factors distinguishes them individually just as in the case of the person addressed".[64] However, as Weatherill points out, the terms of Article 173 invite a creative approach, since they do not lay down a detailed set of rules and the Court has been willing, as a result, to adjust its approach in accor-dance with the challenge before it.[65] According to the Court the direct concern ele-ment of Article 173 para.4 requires the existence of a direct causal link between the challenged Community act and the impact on the applicant[66] and if discretionary powers are invested in national authorities by the Community legislature it is un-likely that the Court will recognise direct and individual concern.

   The condition that the subject matter of the petition directly affects the peti-tioner appears to restrict the scope of Articles 8(d) and 138(d). It is unlikely, in practice, that the European Parliament will interpret this condition restrictively, as the Court has done pursuant to Article 173 para.4. The Court's restriction of indi-vidual standing pursuant to that provision was influenced by a policy choice which preferred individuals to use the Article 177 reference procedure than to take direct actions before the Court of Justice.[67] It is possible that the direct effect condition with respect to petitions could result in more active use of the Ombudsman. However, given the Parliament's reticence with respect to the Ombudsman in the first place, it will be in its interests to extend the scope of petitions by interpreting this condition generously and, as a result, to promote itself as the promoter of cit-izens' rights. However, there is a risk that the European Parliament will emphasis its role in the process too much and will, therefore, emphasis the objective value of petitions as a means to reinforce the role of the Parliament and its democratic con-trol of the other Community institutions,[68] rather than the subjective quality of pe-

---

[64]See Case 25/62 *Plaumann* v. *Commission* [1963] ECR 95.

[65]See Weatherill, S., *Cases and Materials on European Community Law*, 2nd edn. (1992) London, Blackstone, at p.511; and see Case 294/83 *Parti Ecologiste 'Les Verts'* v. *Parliament* [1986] ECR 1339.

[66]See Joined Cases 41-44/70 *International Fruit Co.* v. *Commission* [1971] ECR 411.

[67]See also Rasmussen, H., "Why is Article 173 Interpreted Against Private Plaintiffs?", 5 *ELRev* (1980) 112–127, who argues that the Court of Justice is reshaping the judiciary to allow itself to act as a high court of appeals of Community law.

[68]See Doc. P.E. 200.760, 29 April 1992, at p.6.

titions as an individual right of Union citizens. As Pliakos points out, the drafters of the TEU wanted to create an individual right which would serve to protect personal interests, while the European Parliament "tend à privilegier, par l'intermediaire des petitions collectives, le caractère politique du droit de petition, en associant leurs auteurs à l'exercice de ses pouvoirs".[69] The tendency of the European Parliament to emphasis its own role is evident in its opinion that the fact that the Ombudsman is seised of a particular issue does not limit the possibility of setting up Committees of Inquiry to investigate the same issue.[70] These committees, which can be set up by members of the European Parliament pursuant to Article 138(c) para.1, can investigate alleged contraventions or maladministration in the implementation of Community law. The scope of its investigations could, therefore, be considerably wider than those of the Ombudsman, which can only investigate Community institutions or bodies. However, the purpose of Committees of Inquiry is not necessarily to promote and guarantee the rights of Union citizens, which is what should guide the Ombudsman in the exercise of his functions.

8.3.2. European Parliament Elections and the Relationship Between the Union and Union Citizens

Chapter 6.4.1. discussed the unsuccessful attempts by the European Parliament to adopt a uniform electoral procedure. This failure can be attributed to the fact that it has proved legally and technically very difficult to design such a procedure while taking into account the character and traditions of each Member State and the obligation to respect their national (democratic) identities.[71] Furthermore, these proposals tend to be politically sensitive. They have been blocked within the European Parliament itself, or in subsequent discussions in the Council by members of national political parties, or by Member States themselves, which will not accept any alteration of fundamental aspects of their electoral systems.

The rights which Union citizens exercise on the basis of Articles 138(3) and Article 8(b)(2) should be the supreme example of citizenship rights and of a direct relationship between the Union and its citizens. However, Union citizens do not yet enjoy these rights fully, equally and effectively on the basis of Community law. The failure to adopt a uniform procedure means that direct elections to the European Parliament are presently conducted at national level in accordance with national rules of procedure. They are not, as a result, truly European elections, since this reliance on national rules of procedure has encouraged national rather than Community issues to predominate in the electoral debates preceding European elections. Union citizens will not enjoy these electoral rights on the basis of Community law and vis-à-vis the Community until these elections are organised uniformly throughout the Community on the basis of Community law.

[69]See Pliakos, op. cit. note 47, at 334.
[70]Seee the Musso Report on Parliamentary Committees of Inquiry, Doc. A3- 0302/92, 14 October 1992, at p.17.
[71]See Article F(1) TEU.

One of the fundamental considerations when establishing a uniform procedure is that it should create and favour a direct link between the Members of Parliament and Union citizens. This was clearly the intention of the drafters of the Treaty, although they did not then speak of Union citizens, with respect to the establishment of direct elections in accordance with a uniform procedure pursuant to Article 138(3). The adoption of a uniform procedure can be seen as one of the important steps in the democratization of the European Parliament. The latter is the only Community institution which is capable at present of reflecting the general will of Union citizens and which consists, as Article 137 states, of representatives of the peoples of the States *brought together in the Community*. Without a uniform procedure there is a risk, however, that the will of Union citizens is distorted via national rules of procedure. The classic example is the United Kingdom, where in the first direct elections in 1979 the Conservative Party won sixty seats on the basis of 6.5 million votes, compared to seventeen seats for the Labour Party with 4.3 million votes and no seats for the Liberal Party with 1.7 million votes.

The most negative aspect of the organisation of European elections on a national basis is thus the detrimental effect which such a system has on the expression and debate of European issues and the development of a European polity and European public opinion. Without the development of such debate and of such a polity the construction of a European Union cannot be subject to the necessary examination by the persons affected by it, nor can it win their support. Direct elections so far have proved to be an arena for national rather than European issues. Bogdanor argues that the nature of the party system in the Member States themselves prevents elections to the European Parliament from performing the function of reflecting popular opinion (both negative and positive) towards the Community.[72] First of all, European elections in almost all Member States are fought along national not Community lines. As a result, "the structure of the party system ... allows few deductions to be made from the outcome of direct elections about the distribution of opinion amongst the electorate on Community issues".[73] The exception is Denmark, which operates a separate Euro-party system parallel to the parties which operate at national level.[74] Secondly, the principal supporter of European integration in the European Parliament is the coalition between the socialists and the Christian democrats and it has proved impossible at Member State level to vote for or against the continuation of this coalition. As the powers of the European Parliament grow, Union citizens are likely to become more and more disenchanted with the fact that their voices carry little weight, since the need to create a nexus between the voter and the representative does not play centre stage and since strong coalitions between parties in the Parliament itself tend to over-

---

[72]See Bogdanor, V., "Direct Elections, Representative Democracy and European Integration", 8 *Electoral Studies* (1989) 205–215, at 208.

[73]Ibid., at 209.

[74]It is no coincidence that Denmark was one of the few Member States which offered its citizens the opportunity to express their opinion on the TEU.

power citizen activity when it does manifest itself. It does seem to be the case that the failure of the direct elections to create popular support for European integration can be located in the manner in which parties are organised at national level and the fact that in only one Member State have separate parties been established to address European issues. Furthermore, it is arguable that if the members of the European Parliament are to reflect the democratic will of Union citizens and are to operate as an effective European chamber, the distribution of seats must be revised, since the present system unfairly favours the smaller Member States. Some other system, such as the introduction of a second chamber or a regional assembly might have to be contemplated in future if the European Parliament is to evolve a truly democratic and representative role in the European Union. This two- chamber system might allow a more proportionate distribution of seats between the Member States with reference to their populations, without endangering the particular and minority interests of smaller Member States.

In conclusion, Chapter 6.4.1. asked how far the European Parliament should go in standardising the electoral procedures of the Member States in order to establish a uniform electoral procedure. The answer to this question must surely lie in the provisions on Union citizenship and Articles 137 and 138(a). Electoral procedures should be standardised to the extent necessary to ensure that Union citizens can participate effectively in European Parliament elections and that the Parliament does develop as the representative of the peoples of the Union in accordance with Article 137. A uniform electoral procedure should favour the creation of a direct link between the European Parliament and an emerging European polity which is armed with a sufficiently well-defined right on the basis of Community law, to express its opinion about European affairs. In conclusion, proposals for a uniform procedure should also encourage and facilitate the development of transnational parties, or at least the operation of separate Euro-parties at national level. As Article 138(a) emphasises "political parties at European level are important as a factor for integration within the Union. They contribute to forming a European awareness and to expressing the political will of the citizens of the Union."

8.4. The Protection of Fundamental Rights and Union Citizenship[75]

Article B TEU states that one of the explicit objectives of the Union Treaty is "to strengthen and protect the rights and interests of the nationals of the Member States through the introduction of a citizenship of the Union". The drafters of the Union Treaty have arguably correctly identified citizenship as an effective and proven means to protect and enumerate the rights of individuals vis-à-vis the authorities which govern them. Citizenship provides its beneficiaries with the instruments –

---

[75]Parts of this section first appeared in 32 *CMLRev* (1992) 519–554.

rights to political participation and representation – which enable them collectively to protect their rights from untoward state interference and to participate in the legal and political order of which they are members. In particular, Article 8(b) has extended electoral rights at local and European level to Union citizens who reside in a Member State other than their Member State of origin. Given that one of the central objectives of a legal order which protects fundamental rights is also to protect the individual from abuse of their fundamental rights by both private and public sectors, it is curious that Union citizenship, as established in Article 8, omits any explicit reference to the protection of the fundamental rights of Union citizens.[76] The Commission, European Parliament and certain Member States attempted to expressly include fundamental rights in the Union Treaty's citizenship package.[77] The European Parliament, for example, argued that a notion of Community citizenship could not succeed without reference to fundamental rights, since the latter are an essential part of the former.[78] However, the latter were relegated to a common provision in Title I of the Union Treaty which, pursuant to Article L, does not come within the jurisdiction of the Court of Justice. Article F(2) undoubtedly commits the Union to respecting fundamental rights as guaranteed by the European Convention of Human Rights and Fundamental Freedoms (hereafter the European Convention) and the constitutional traditions common to the Member States, but no specific consequences seem to have been drawn from that commitment in the context of Union citizenship. Indeed this commitment has been specifically divorced from the concept of citizenship introduced in the Union Treaty.

There is, therefore, a type of tension in the Union Treaty with respect to individual rights. The absence of both a justiciable provision on fundamental rights and an explicit reference to the protection of the fundamental rights of Union citizens seems to contradict the reason given in Article B for the creation of citizenship, namely, to strengthen and protect the rights of Union citizens. It is questionable whether Union citizenship is, in fact, intended to enrich the subjective rights and status of individual Community citizens. Since the bulk of the citizenship rights discussed in Part II already existed and those which did not exist could eventually have been adopted either by amending the Treaty without establishing a status of citizenship, or on the basis of Article 235, the answer to this question is far from clear. It is suggested that by analysing the relationship between Community citizenship and the protection of fundamental rights in the Community legal order, the real contribution which Community or Union citizenship has made, or which it has failed to make so far, to the protection of the individual's subjective rights in

---

[76]The rights which constitute Union citizenship need not, of course, be restricted to the express provisions of Article 8. The latter specifically provides that Member State nationals enjoy "the rights conferred by the Treaties" generally.

[77]See "Union Citizenship", Contributions of the Commission to the Intergovernmental Conferences, SEC (91) 500, Bull. EC Suppl. 2/91, at p.79 and Article X.2, p.85; the Bindi Report on Union Citizenship to the European Parliament, PE Doc. A3-0300/91, 6 November 1991; and Closa, C., "The Concept of Citizenship in the Treaty on European Union", 29 *CMLRev* (1992) 1137–1169, at 1153.

[78]See the Bindi Report, op. cit. note 77, at p.4.

Community law and their relationship with the Community or Union. It is also hoped in this way to proceed beyond a mere recital of the rights listed in Article 8 and the possible legal consequences which may flow from that provision to a deeper understanding of the purpose of citizenship in the Union, its relationship with fundamental rights in particular and ultimately the value, if any, of establishing an explicit constitutional status of citizenship in Community law. The construction of a relationship between Union citizenship and the protection of fundamental rights in Community law would seem to detract, at first sight, from the orthodox enjoyment of citizenship rights on an exclusionary basis and the present privileged position of Member State nationals, since fundamental rights are available to all, not simply privileged citizens of the Union. However, it is argued now, as it was in Chapter 2, that displacing nationality as the principal condition precedent for the enjoyment of citizenship rights and fundamental rights in the Community and promoting the individual as the key to the creation and enforcement of rights in the Union may promote a higher standard of rights protection than is possible under the present arrangement. Making individuals central to the construction of the European Union and effectively guaranteeing their rights is arguably the only means by which a sense of identity with the Union could be forged.

8.4.1. Methods of Protection of Fundamental Rights in Community Law

The absence in Community law of an enumerated or codified bill of rights is one of the Treaty's most visible lacunae.[79] The original reference by the Court of Justice to the Community's adherence to fundamental rights came as a consequence of national judicial opposition to the supremacy of Community law in the absence of such a codified bill of rights.[80] The Court of Justice initially avoided specifying a definitive list of the fundamental rights protected in the Community and referred simply to international treaties and the constitutional traditions common to the Member States as sources of inspiration for the protection of fundamental rights in the Community.[81] Having regard to these chosen sources of inspiration, a rough list of fundamental rights to which the Community adheres would include rights to due process, personal security and autonomy, limited rights to political participation, equality and, more controversially, a right to enjoy certain minimum economic and social benefits. Community fundamental rights have generally been relied upon by individuals to determine the compliance of Community legislation and of the actions of Community institutions with fundamental rights. Their availability against the action of Member States has proved far more controversial and is limited to instances when the Member State is implementing Community law

---

[79]See, *inter alia*, Mancini, G.F., "Il contributo della Corta di Giustizia allo sviluppo della democrazia nella Communita", *Rivista di Diritto Europeo* (1992) 713–725, at 714.

[80]Once again, see Mancini, G.F., "The Making of a Constitution for Europe", 26 *CMLRev* (1989) 595–614, at 611.

[81]See the second *Nold* Case 4/73 [1974] ECR 507, at para.13.

(for example, *Wachauf*)[82], or acting pursuant to one of the derogations permitted by Community law (*Rutili*[83] or *ERT*).[84]

This limitation of the Court's jurisdiction with respect to fundamental rights reflects the fact that the Community and Union are based on delicate political compromises and only partial integration. To advance on *ERT* and further incorporate Community fundamental rights standards with respect to the action of Member States requires a degree of political integration which the Community has not yet reached, or as is perhaps evident from the Union Treaty, which Member State governments are not yet willing to admit.[85] It is clear from cases like *Grogan* that the Court of Justice is not willing to endanger or sacrifice the relationship of cooperation which it has developed with national courts and on which the reference procedure in Article 177 heavily depends. However, precisely because the Court is now faced with the resolution of more sensitive cases, commentators argue that it must develop "a consistent and principled justification for both the development and limitation of its 'human rights role'".[86] Yet the legitimacy of the Court's role, like the future development of citizenship, depends on the legal and political order which is being constructed around it. An opportunity was presented to the Community institutions and Member States in the course of the intergovernmental conferences to reassess the "socio- legal contract" on which their legal and political relationship is based.[87] One important aspect of the revision of the Treaty could have been clarification of the scope and content of the protection of fundamental rights by and in the Community, or the adoption of an explicit stance as regards its relationship with the European Convention.[88] This opportunity was wasted and reference to fundamental rights has curiously been confined to Article F(2) and other unjusticiable provisions of the third pillar.[89] Indeed, the failure to recognise an explicit link between fundamental rights and the scope and operation of Community citizenship and to explicitly guarantee the protection of fundamental rights in a justiciable provision of the Treaty could be seen as an attempt to foreclose any judicial expansion of the rights of Union citizens.

Opinions on whether a reference to fundamental rights should have been included in the Treaty are divided. Some commentators suggest that including a cata-

---

[82]Case 5/88 [1989] ECR 2609.

[83]Case 36/75 [1975] ECR 1219.

[84]Case C-260/89 *Elliniki Radiophonia Tileorassi* v. *Dimitiki* [1991] ECR I-2925. See generally Weiler, J.H.H. and Lockhart, N., "Taking Rights Seriously — Seriously: The European Court and its Fundamental Rights Jurisprudence", 32 *CMLRev* (1995) 7–49 and 579–677.

[85]See Lenaerts, K., "Fundamental Rights to be Included in a Community Catalogue", 16 *ELRev* (1991) 367–390, at 373.

[86]See De Burca, G., "Fundamental Human Rights and the Reach of Community Law", 13 *Oxford Journal of Legal Studies* (1993) 283–319, at 304.

[87]See also Weiler, J.H.H., "Journey to an Unknown Destination: A Retrospective and Prospective of the Court of Justice in the Area of Political Integration", 31 JCMS (1993) 417–446, at 439.

[88]See De Witte, B., "Community Law and National Constitutional Values", *LIEI* (1991) 1–22, at 18: "the new Constitution of the European Union might help to solve some of the structural value conflicts indicated above by increasing the democratic character of Community decision-making and by codifying the fundamental rights guarantees."

[89]Articles J.1.2. and K.2.1. of the Union Treaty.

logue of fundamental rights within the concept of citizenship would not have added significantly to the status of Member State nationals, whose rights are consistently guaranteed at national level.[90] Furthermore, extending citizenship rights to Member State nationals is said to be one thing, but potentially widening the category of beneficiaries to non-Member State nationals by establishing citizenship on a fundamental rights basis is another.[91] It could also be argued that fundamental rights incorporate a set of inalienable higher rights which are inherent in the human person, whereas citizenship generally refers to the civil and political rights of certain individuals to participate in a given society. A reference to fundamental rights in the citizenship provisions might have prejudiced the position of third country nationals even further, since fundamental rights should be available to everybody and not just a privileged few. However, the inclusion of such a reference to fundamental rights could have preserved the coherency and integrity of the Community's concept of citizenship as a means of protecting individual rights and could have guaranteed increased judicial protection in areas of law which can and do increasingly come within the ambit of the Community and therefore the Court of Justice, given its duties under Article 164. By not including fundamental rights in the Community notion of citizenship the Member States have lost the opportunity, perhaps deliberately, to allow citizenship to evolve as a higher standard for the protection of individual rights. This higher standard was one of the purposes which Lenaerts suggested for the development of a Community catalogue of fundamental rights, which was to include a status of Community citizenship.[92] The position of third country nationals would not have been prejudiced if, in addition to securing the fundamental rights of Union citizens, a general guarantee of respect for fundamental rights, such as that in Article F(2), had been maintained. Not to include fundamental rights in the concept of citizenship is also to ignore the fundamental jurisdictional conflict which exists between the Community and national legal orders as regards who is now competent to protect what rights, in what circumstances and to what extent. This conflict was at the heart of the Court's decision in *Internationale Handelsgesellschaft*, where it held that respect for fundamental rights "must be ensured within the framework of the structure and objectives of the Community".[93]

8.4.2. The Link Between Citizenship and the Protection of Fundamental Rights in Community Law

It is not immediately obvious how to construct a relationship between the protection of fundamental rights in Community law and Community or Union citizen-

---

[90]See Closa, C., "Citizenship of the Union and Nationality of the Member States", in O'Keeffe D. and Twomey, P. (eds.), *Legal Issues of the Maastricht Treaty* (1993) London, Chancery Press, pp.109–119, at pp.111–112.

[91]See Verhoeven, J., "Les citoyens de l'Europe", 2 *Annales de Droit de Louvain* (1993) 165–191, at 188–189.

[92]See Lenaerts, op. cit. note 22, at 376.

[93]See Case 11/70, *Internationale Handelsgesellschaft* [1970] ECR 1125, at 1134.

ship. First of all, the two categories of rights appear to be inherently opposed. A commitment to protect fundamental rights does not seem to fit easily within the citizenship package, since citizenship refers to persons who belong to a certain privileged category on the basis of specific conditions. Secondly, fundamental rights are protected in a particular fashion in the Community and subject to certain jurisdictional and perhaps political limits. Thus, the protection of fundamental rights in the Community legal order is limited to situations and individuals "who are parties to legal relationships under Community law" – such as economically active Member State nationals and their dependants.[94] Furthermore, fundamental rights are ensured, as the Court held in *Internationale Handelsgesellschaft*, within the framework of the structure and objectives of Community law. In general, therefore, the Community legal order only protects the fundamental rights of those persons who would also come within the scope of Article 8 – Member State nationals. The Community legal order is not enhanced by the fact that the fundamental rights of non-Community nationals are not protected when they come within situations which derive from Community law, such as refugees or asylum seekers under the Schengen and Dublin Conventions.[95] Indeed, it has been argued that this limitation of fundamental rights and, it could be said, citizenship, prejudices the deeper values inherent in the "community" vision of integration, (community in the sense of a community of states and peoples sharing values and aspirations and sharing competence in a select number of fields): "Nationality as a referent for interpersonal relations, and the human alienating effect of *Us* and *Them* are brought back again, simply transferred from their previous intra-Community context to the new inter-Community one. We may have made little progress if the *Us* becomes European (instead of German or French or British) and the *Them* becomes those outside the Community or those inside who do not enjoy the privileges of citizenship."[96] The Court of Justice cannot legitimately, in the absence of a clear constitutional provision, exercise jurisdiction over matters which do not come within its competence, such as, the general legal protection of third country nationals. However, the social legitimacy of the Community legal order and Union citizenship is undermined by the fact that the fundamental rights of persons affected by Community integration, and free movement in particular, are not expressly guaranteed.

---

[94]See Case 106/77, op. cit., at para.15.

[95]The preamble of the Schengen Implementation Agreement provides that "the aim pursued by the Contracting Parties coincides with that objective" (i.e., the creation of an area without frontier controls). In addition, the Dublin Asylum Convention (Bull. EC 6- 1990) refers to "the joint objective of an area without internal frontiers in which the free movement of persons shall, in particular, be ensured" and states that the measures it adopts with respect to asylum are "in pursuit of this objective". For a rejection of "second class" Community citizens see also Garth, "Migrant Workers and Rights of Mobility in the EC and the US: A Study of Law, Community and Citizenship in the Welfare State", in Cappelletti, Secombe and Weiler (Eds.), *Integration Through Law: Europe and the American Federal Experience*, Vol.1 Book 3, (1986) Berlin, Walter de Gruyter/EUI, at p.123.

[96]See Weiler "Problems of Legitimacy in Post 1992 Europe", 46 *Aussenwirtschaft* (1991) 411–437, at 433–436.

8.4.3. Fundamental Rights as General Principles

Does the classification of fundamental rights as general principles of Community law[97] favour their operation as genuine subjective rights? General principles of Community law are the juridification of rights and do not constitute the rights themselves. They are, as Dauses said, a definition of the structural foundations of the legal order.[98] Loosely translated, for example, the principle of proportionality seeks to achieve a reasonable relationship between the ends chosen by the legislature and the objective sought to be achieved. It attempts to locate the correct balance in the legislative and judicial process between the individual interest and the general interest, the balance which best suits the social and legal objectives of the constitutional order in which it is based. Since the Community's tasks and the means to achieve them (Articles 2 and 3) primarily address the Member States and seek broad objectives of economic and now limited political cohesion, it is difficult to imagine circumstances in which an individual interest will proportionally outweigh a Community measure claimed to infringe the fundamental rights to which the Community adheres. Thus in the *Hauer* case, the Community's general prohibition on the planting of new vines was justified by the objectives of general interest pursued by the Community and did not infringe the substance of the plaintiff's right to property "in the form in which it is recognised and protected in the Community legal order",[99] In the *Heylens* case the Community's fundamental principle of free movement coincided with the claims of the plaintiff and the Court classified free access to employment as a fundamental right for which national authorities were required to give effective protection "under the best possible conditions".[100] However, the purpose and origin of this need to effectively protect individual rights was also the need to safeguard the effectiveness of Community law (defined in *Simmenthal* as part of "the very essence of Community law"[101] and the cohesion of the Community's free movement policies. This is the same type of reasoning which led to the prohibition by the Court of Justice of reverse discrimination in certain circumstances. The effect of this classification of fundamental rights as general principles is further reflected in the immediate connection consistently made in Community law between general principles and the structure and objectives of Community law.[102] Thus, the Court of Justice has developed the

---

[97]See Article F(2) and Case 26/69 *Stauder* [1969] ECR 419.

[98]Dauses, "The Protection of Fundamental Rights in the Community Legal Order", 10 ELRev (1985) 398–419, at 406.

[99]See Case 44/79 [1979] ECR 3727, at para.30.

[100]Case 222/86 *UNECTEF* v. *Heylens* [1987] ECR 4097, at para.18.

[101]Case 106/77 *Amministrazione delle Finanze dello Stato* v. *Simmenthal* [1978] ECR 629, at 644.

[102]See Case 11/70, op. cit. note 93; Case 44/79 op. cit. note 99, at para.14; Case 5/88, op. cit. note 82, at para.18; and Mancini, *Safeguarding Fundamental Rights: The Role of the Court of Justice of the European Communities*, Bologna, John Hopkins University, Occasional Paper no.62, March 1992: "[T]he Court does not have to go looking for maximum, minimum or average standards. The yardstick by which it measures the approaches adopted by the various systems derives from the spirit of the Treaty and from the requirements of a Community which is in the process of being built up."

principles of supremacy and direct effect to attain the objectives laid down in the Treaty and to resolve material conflicts which emerged as a result of the integration of the national and supranational legal orders. It is arguable that the rights of individual Member State nationals have been protected within the context of the promotion of those objectives.

8.4.4. Legal Certainty, the Protection of Fundamental Rights and the Community System

In the absence of a codified bill of rights, the Court of Justice has tended to develop the Community's adherence to fundamental rights incrementally on the basis of unenumerated general principles. There is thus little legal certainty as regards whether a right is considered fundamental in the Community. Furthermore, the Community's protection of fundamental rights is somewhat fragmentary, since the Court is generally obliged to rely on cases reaching it via references from national courts and cannot control the type of cases which reach it.[103] The latter are not always eager to expose national issues which touch fundamental rights to the Community judicial arena where the Court of Justice and Community law are preeminent.[104] In the *Grogan* case the Court of Justice held that, although abortion was a service, the absence of a link between the providers of information and the providers of the service of abortion meant that a prohibition on abortion information did not come within the scope of Article 59. As a result, the Court did not have to address the fundamental rights issue raised by the case. As a result of this decision, it is not clear whether the right to information is protected as a corollary of the free provision of services, or to what extent freedom of expression is protected in the context of Community law. The Court of Justice must await another reference from a national court in order to clarify these aspects of Community law.

Neither is there any certainty about the content of the fundamental rights protected in Community law. This was one of the Commission's principal considerations when it advocated formal adherence by the Community to the European Human Rights Convention.[105] Thus, a right to property may fall within the Court of Justice's fundamental rights catalogue with reference to the constitutional traditions common to the Member States, but the Member States protect that right in several different manners, to several different degrees and with several different

---

[103]See De Burca, op. cit., at 318; and Barrington, D. "The Emergence of a Constitutional Court", in O'Reilly, J. (ed.), *Human Rights and the Constitution: Essays in Honour of Justice Brian Walsh* (1992) Dublin, Roundhall Press, pp.251–261, at p.253, who notes that the legislature may have a policy in mind and may choose the means to bring it to fruition, but that the judiciary has no choice in the matter and has to decide whatever cases appear before it.

[104]See for example the uneasiness of the Irish Supreme Court as regards the Article 177 reference in *Society for the Protection of the Unborn Child* v. *Grogan* [1990] 1 CMLR 689.

[105]See "Accession of the Communities to the European Convention on Human Rights", Bull. EC. Suppl. 2/79, at para.5; Cf. Capotorti, "A propos de l'adhésion éventuelle des Communautés a la Convention Européenne de droits de l'homme", in *Das Europa der Zweiten Generation. Gedachtnisschrift fur Christoph Sasse* (1981) Kelh-am-Rhein/Strasbourg, Engel Verlag, Vol.1.

objectives in mind.[106] As De Witte has cogently argued "Constitutions are not mere copies of a universalist ideal, they also reflect the idiosyncratic choices and preferences of the constituents and are the highest legal expression of the country's value system."[107] The protection of any single fundamental right in concrete circumstances thus involves a legislative or judicial definition of the balance to be struck between the interests of the individual and the interests of society. This balance may vary from one Member State to the next and may vary with time. The content and protection of a particular right may vary depending on the perspective of "right" which a particular political and legal system chooses and will thus depend on the legal context within which the right is to be protected.

The complicated division of competences between the national and supranational levels means that the Court of Justice, when faced with a decision on fundamental or individual rights may have to solve a different equation than that which faces national courts in a similar internal case. The balance which it strikes in defining the fundamental right at stake must take into account not only the interests of the individual and the Member State, but also those of the supranational legal order in which the Member State is located. What, for example, did the Court mean in *Hauer* that the plaintiff's right to property was not infringed "in the form in which it is recognised and protected in the Community legal order"? When assessing the interaction of common constitutional traditions with the structure and objectives of the Community's legal order, the Court is not confronted with a value free task: "It [the Single Market programme] is ... a highly politicized choice of ethos, of ideology and of political culture: the culture of the Market .... the indispensable need for the success of the Single Market ... manifests a social (and hence ideological) choice which prizes market efficiency and European wide neutrality of competition over other competing values."[108] Given this ideological framework, the protection of a right to property, as *Hauer* demonstrated, will be subjected by the Court to the Community principles of market efficiency and competition. Although these principles may seem to favour the right to property, the Court's "first loyalty [will be] to the concept of Community integration. If a conflict arose it might give a different emphasis to the conflict between the interests of the Community on the one hand, and the protection of the individual on the other, than the balance that might be adopted by another tribunal, a human rights tribunal."[109] Hervey provides another example when she discusses the tensions involved in classifying sex equality or non-discrimination as a fundamental personal human right in Community law, since sex equality provisions refer both to fundamental personal rights and to the creation of an equal playing field in a competitive mar-

---

[106]See, for example, the text of the constitutional provisions cited in Case 44/79, op. cit. note 99, at para.20.

[107]See De Witte, op. cit. note 88, at 7.

[108]See Weiler (1991), op. cit. note 96, at 430–431.

[109]See Jacobs, *The European Convention on Human Rights, Two New Directions; EEC: UK* (1980), at p.17.

ket.[110] This does not, it must be added, automatically detract from the decisions of the Court of Justice. In general, the values which it reflects are those which have developed over the years in the Member States. Furthermore, when striking a balance between the protection of fundamental rights and the requirements of the general interest, national courts also refer to the values inherent in their own constitutional orders. But is there not an essential difference between the Community and national legal orders in this context? National courts operate within the context of political and constitutional systems which are not marked by the same democratic or representative deficit as the Community. In the end, the difference boils down to the availablility, even if limited, of national political consensus, representation and accountability at national level and the yawning gap which persists and which the Member States maintain, between the Community institutions, the Council included, and Community citizens. Can Union citizenship really be heralded, in this context, as a direct (political) link between the Union and its citizens? Given this framework for the resolution of fundamental rights issues, the position of the Court of Justice is sensitive, to say the least and it is possible that its more suspect decisions are the result of undue deference to Member State sensibilities rather than to a lack of commitment to the protection of individual rights. This situation is further aggravated by the fact that the decisions of the Court of Justice, unlike the decisions of national courts, are not subject to review by any higher authority.

8.4.5. Community Teleology and the Protection of Fundamental Rights

As Section 8.4.4 argued, the protection of fundamental rights in the Community are inevitably influenced by the nature of the legal system in which these rights are developed. As a result, Phelan has animatedly argued that "by reference to its economic and federal teleology of Community objectives, [the Court] has evolved certain legal techniques applicable to human rights which will point the Community in new normative directions. These techniques ... are used to control the three dimensions of conflict between state and federal competences, between a moral and economic ideal of what is fundamental, and between different legal doctrines of justification."[111] The author's criticism of the need to recharacterise the rights with which it deals, in order to bring them within the mainly economic parameters of Community law may be well-founded. This does not automatically imply, however, that what is fundamental in the Community legal order differs from what is fundamental in the Member States, nor that the Court's technique will necessarily point the Community's protection of fundamental rights in different normative directions.

---

[110]See Hervey, T.K., "Legal Issues Concerning the *Barber* Protocol", in O'Keeffe and Twomey, op. cit. note 37, pp.329–337, at p.336.
[111]See Phelan, D.R., "The Right to Life of the Unborn v. Promotion of Trade in Services: The European Court of Justice and the Normative Shaping of the European Union", 55 *Modern Law Review* (1992) 670–689, at 670.

What should be subject to criticism is not that in a case like *Grogan* the Court held that abortion is a service and that the Advocate General went further in holding that the Member State could act as it did only within the context of a justifiable restriction of Community law in the public interest. The latter technique was precisely a means to protect a justifiable national objective. For the Court to ensure that such an objective does not unduly restrict other important fundamental rights which come within the Community's field of activity does not imply that it arrogates the role of the national courts. As regards the protection of fundamental rights it was surely more objectionable for the Court of Justice to deny any jurisdiction with respect to the fundamental rights aspect of the case on the specious grounds that the legal relationship in question was not based on economic criteria. The problem is not therefore the involvement of Community law in sensitive cases. Rather it is the uncertain jurisdiction of the Court of Justice, its over-deference in some cases to national courts and the fact that the objectives and legal principles it employs have not yet been freed from the economic and structural limitations which oblige it, on occasion, to determine the fundamental rights balance with the limits of Articles 2 and 3 in mind. These limitations could interfere with what should be the essential commitment of a Community based on the rule of law to the protection of individual rights. The development of citizenship was precisely a vehicle which could have helped to move the Community beyond the market-oriented objectives which some authors have found so objectionable. However, it is arguable that for it to develop as a series of higher rights, standards and objectives, the Community should have attached citizenship to the mast of fundamental rights protection. If the quest for greater political union is to succeed it must surely be located within the framework of consensus and shared values and expectations and although the fundamental rights protected by the Member States may differ, they are, at their most basic, a reflection of a certain historical, political and social similarity.

Conclusions

Having examined the evolution of various of the rights attached to Community citizenship, is it possible to claim that an effective and meaningful citizenship-like status exists at Community or Union level? If the model of citizenship suggested in Chapter 1 is applicable to the Community, then the civil and political, socio-economic and fundamental rights which it entails should ensure that individual Community citizens are constitutent members of the Community or Union. Thus, the rights of Community citizenship, if effective and effectively protected, should be the basis for some sort of relationship between the Union and its citizens, a relationship which will, in turn reflect back on the Union and enhance its legitimacy.[1] Community citizenship should thus be able to demonstrate some sort of social contract or solidarity between the Union on the one hand and Union citizens on the other. Citizenship at Community level need not necessarily demonstrate cultural, historical or political homogeneity. However, there should be a minimum consensus about what Community citizenship does and should entail and thus consensus about the Community's integration project as a whole. Without this, it will be difficult, if not impossible, for European public opinion, or a European polity to develop and therefore for the relationship between Union or Community citizens and the Union to mature. Do the provisions analysed in the course of this book suggest that such a relationship exists at present, or that it could develop in the future?

The rights analysed in Chapters 2 to 8 demonstrate the weaknesses and limitations of Community citizenship as it stands. In addition, it is suggested that Union citizenship, as established in the TEU and implemented thereafter, has not achieved

---

[1]See Habermas, J., "The European Nation State: Its Achievements and its Limits. On the Past and Future of Sovereignty and Citizenship", PLS 2 (1995), 1–10, at 3 and 4: "in the course of [the] spread of political participation, there emerged a new level of a *legally mediated solidarity* among citizens, while the state, by implementation of democratic procedures, at the same time tapped a new secular source for *legitimation* ... citizenship gained the additional political and cultural meaning of an achieved belonging to a community of empowered citizens who actively contribute to its maintenance."

many of the objectives which were assigned to that status when created. Some of the possible reforms of Union citizenship which are being discussed, or which could be discussed, in the course of the 1996 intergovernmental conference, are outlined. In conclusion, however, it is suggested that the evolution of an effective and meaningful status of citizenship will depend on whether a rights-based approach is adopted with respect to this status.

Weaknesses and Limitations of Community Citizenship

Given the reference to limitations and conditions in Article 8(a)(1), there has been considerable debate about whether or not that provision and, therefore, the right of residence therein, is directly effective. Some Community officials and commentators suggest that the existence of implementing legislation renders the issue of direct effect irrelevant. However, Chapter 4 argues that some of the provisions of the 1990 residence Directives, the conditions on medical insurance and sufficient resources in particular, are incompatible with the right established in Article 8(a). As a result, the recourse which Union citizens have to their national courts may prove the only and essential means for them to vindicate their rights of residence. The Court of Justice has established in other areas of Community law that subjective rights which may be derived from Treaty provisions which lack direct effect may, nevertheless, be invoked by individuals in national courts. National Courts are thus obliged to interpret those rights in line with the spirit and objectives of Community law. The limitations on free movement and residence established in the Treaty and secondary legislation should not be permitted to cancel the fundamental constitutional right of residence which the Treaty confers on Union citizens. Indeed the jurisprudence of the Court of Justice on effective judicial protection and the enforceability of rights should equally apply in this area. This approach to the effectiveness of the rights of Union citizens is in line with the decision of the Court of Justice in the students' residence case which was discussed in Chapter 4. Some German *Länder* were opposed to the use of Article 6 precisely because of the possible consequences which might flow from a generous interpretation of Article 6 by the Court of Justice. The fact that the rights of Community citizenship are intimately linked with an extension of the principle of equal treatment may mean, however, that this possibility may and should become a reality.

Added to the problems surrounding the interpretation and implementation of the right of free movement and residence in Article 8(a) is the controversy which continues with respect to the implementation of the free movement of persons generally. The latter, as foreseen by Article 7(a), has not yet been achieved and Member States have found it impossible to reach agreement on what exactly Article 7(a) entails. The Commission's proposals in its original White Paper on the internal market met with little success.[2] As a result, it has opted since then for an intergovernmental

---

[2]COM (85) 310 final.

approach to the adoption of measures with regard to the free movement of persons – the Schengen convention which came into force on the 1 March 1995, the Dublin Asylum convention and the, as yet, unsuccessful External Frontiers Convention which is now being adopted on the basis of third pillar provisions. These conventions were negotiated outside the framework of Community law and are not therefore subject to the scrutiny of the European Parliament and do not come within the jurisdiction of the Court of Justice. The Commission's failure to adopt legislative proposals with respect to the free movement of persons has led the European Parliament to institute legal proceedings against it on the basis of Article 175. Despite the provision of a right of free movement and residence in Article 8(a), however, the fact remains that free movement issues have been divided between the first and third pillars of the Union Treaty and that free movement has not yet been achieved. Until the Member States and Community institutions determine which issues belong to which pillar, effective free movement will remain a distant possibility. The Commission adopted three proposals for directives regarding completion of the free movement of persons in an internal market in July 1995, but these proposals require unanimity at Council level.

The exercise of electoral rights by Union citizens pursuant to Article 8(b) are also likely to cause some problems. The provisions permitting Member States where Union citizens of voting age represent over 20 per cent of the total electorate to opt out of the provisions of the Directives for a certain period should be explicitly recognised as a fundamental derogation from the principle of equal treatment. Furthermore, as the European Parliament suggested, this derogation should be subject to a specific time limit. The rationale behind the derogation is that these Member States would otherwise be confronted with a significant alteration of their electoral balance. However, the fact of the matter is that their electoral balance should change in line with their resident population and their membership of the Union is precisely one of the forces behind this change. It is understandable that Luxembourg, for whom the derogations in the Directives were designed, wishes to preserve some of the traditional aspects of Luxembourg politics. Nevertheless, it is ironic that a Member State which has twice fought to retain the European Parliament within its territory[3] and which prevents a common accord from being reached on the seat of the Parliament will not permit Union citizens to participate in European Parliament or municipal elections. Many of these Union citizens are resident in Luxembourg because of the establishment of a number of Community institutions there. This is the type of attitude which will prevent even a limited concept of Union citizenship from developing effectively. Finally, the extension of electoral rights to Member State nationals also suggests that the public service exception in Article 48(3) may have to be revised or interpreted more restrictively since Union citizens may now clearly be involved in the exercise of official authority.

---

[3]See Case 108/83 *Grand Duchy of Luxembourg* v. *European Parliament* [1984] ECR 1945; and Joined Cases C-213/88 and C-39/89 *Luxembourg* v. *European Parliament*, judgment of 28 November 1991.

⌐ Union citizenship, as Chapter 2 established, is limited to Member State nationals. Nationality is, in turn, to be unilaterally determined by Member States. This is confirmed by a declaration on nationality annexed to the Treaty on European Union and by part of the decision of the Court of Justice in *Micheletti*. Union citizenship is thus dependent on how nationality is defined at national level. Given this fact, is it possible to claim, as the Commission does, that Union citizenship creates a direct political link between the Union and Member State nationals?[4] The fact of the matter is that citizenship as established in Article 8 does little more than codify the existing state of play with regard to Community nationals and essentially concerns the rights which they can enjoy on the basis of the principle of equal treatment when in another Member State. It has little to say about the rights which Community nationals enjoy *vis-à-vis* their own Member States, since reverse discrimination appears to survive the Treaty on European Union, or *vis-à-vis* the Union itself. A uniform electoral procedure, which could enhance the democratic participation of citizens in the Union via the election of a truly European representative assembly, has not yet been adopted. Furthermore, the rights which Union citizens can assert directly against the Union on the basis of Community law – a right to petition and a right to apply to the Ombudsman – do not result in binding legal decisions and the usefulness of the office of Ombudsman remains to be seen. In addition, there may be some rivalry between the work of the Committee on Petitions and the Ombudsman. In these circumstances it is premature to argue that a direct link, political or otherwise, has been created between Community citizens and the Union. This is one of the, if not the most, fundamental limitation of the scope and content of Union citizenship.

Furthermore, Community or Union citizenship was designed to encourage Union citizens to foster a sense of identity within the Union. However, the exclusion of long term legally resident third country nationals from some or all of the benefits of Union citizenship, suggest that a particular type of identity is being favoured which bears little relation to the composition of Member States which have been receiving immigrants for years. This attempt to limit a developing European identity to Judaeo-Christian and humanist traditions is open to criticism. If an aspect of Union citizenship is specifically to exclude third country nationals not only from the enjoyment of rights, but also from the formation of and involvement in a developing European identity, the discriminatory nature of this limitation of the rights of Union citizenship is further emphasised by the fact that nationals from EEA states may enjoy some of the rights contingent on Union citizenship, such as free movement to take up an economic activity and equal treatment within the scope of the EEA agreement.

The survival of sufficient resources and medical insurance as conditions precedent for the enjoyment of the right of residence under Article 8(a) suggest that the social dimension of Union citizenship is extremely weak. If the latter was intended to improve the legal protection and rights afforded Member State nationals it is

---

[4]COM (93) 702 final.

surprising that few, if any, socio-economic rights were made explicit on this basis. Community legislative activity in the field of social policy generally has been slow to develop and has been the subject of considerable controversy. The enjoyment of social rights at national level has generally been based on claims of entitlement based on "traditional community ties of autonomy and obligation".[5] Furthermore, social rights are often expressed in aspirational and non-justiciable terms. They are positive rights which confront states with a considerable legislative and financial burden to ensure their full and effective enforcement. They require active intervention rather than simply that the state desist from a certain line of action. The Community has been caught for years between a commitment to social progress and denial of the legislative competence necessary to adopt independent policies in the sphere of social policy. These limitations are evident in the EC Treaty, where the legal bases for action in social policy are limited and where other provisions, such as the pinciple of non-discrimination are interpreted by the Court of Justice while stopping short of considerably interfering with Member States' competence in this sphere. Thus, for example, in the *Brown* case on whether Article 6 on non-discrimination was applicable to tuition fees and maintenance grants, the Court re-iterated its decision in *Gravier* to the effect that Member States could not discriminate with respect to tuition fees and conditions of access. However, it held that maintenance grants do not come within the scope of conditions of access and non-discrimination. This distinction between tuition fees and maintenance grants protects Member States from having to foot the bill for the education of other Member State's nationals. However, it also undermines the extension of the principle of equal treatment with respect to Union citizens who are not economically active.

The Community is thus caught between promoting social progress and developing Community integration beyond purely market integration and being denied the legislative power to adopt its own independent policies. The preamble to the SEA, for example, declares that the Member States are determined to "work together to promote democracy on the basis of the fundamental rights recognised in the constitutions and laws of their states, the European Convention on Human Rights and the European Social Charter. No mention has been made of the European Social Charter in a Treaty text since then, although the *Blaizot* case mentioned it as part of the general principles of law which the Court of Justice is bound to protect. The Community charter of fundamental social rights was addressed to workers, but it did include as fundamental rights – free movement, fair remuneration, improved living and working conditions, adequate social protection, access to vocational training, sufficient social and medical assistance. Although the charter is not legally binding, it reflects the type of rights which the Member States consider common fundamental standards in the socio-economic sphere. The absence of socio-economic rights in the Union Treaty reference to fundamental rights and in the provisions on citizenship suggests that the Community is not yet prepared to take a

---

[5]See Culpitt, *Welfare and Citizenship: Beyond the Crisis of the Welfare State?* (1992), at p.1.

rights-based approach to social policy.[6] However, imaginative use of Article F(2) in future, or the accession of the Communities to the European Convention on Human Rights could result in inclusion of social rights and enforcement of these rights as general principles of Community law.

Perhaps most importantly of all, the survival of Member State nationality as the basis for the enjoyment of Union citizenship suggests that Member State sovereignty, rather than individual rights are central to the determination of the scope and content of Union citizenship. This limitation, which is informed by the desire of Member States to preserve their ultimate say in matters traditionally thought essential to the nation state means that there is a risk that Union citizenship has and will be phrased and implemented in terms of the relations between Member States in a political union, rather than in terms of the rights of individuals who reside in and are affected by that Union.

The 1996 IGC and the Reform of Union Citizenship

The reform or modification of European Union citizenship is likely to emerge in the course of the forthcoming Intergovernmental Conference, in particular, the issue of a charter of rights or accession to the European Convention on Human Rights. However, if citizenship is to evolve as an effective status entailing the enjoyment of a number of rights (and duties), a number of issues have to be addressed.

First of all, the Community must persist in its attempts to improve the openness and accountability of the Union. In a declaration annexed to the Union Treaty in 1992 the Member States provided that "The Conference considers that the transparency of the decision making process strengthens the democratic nature of the institutions and the public's confidence in the administration." However, little progress has been made in this regard.[7] This fundamental principle of transparency was also the subject of proceedings before the Court of First Instance where the *Guardian* newspaper acted against the Council for refusing it admission to the minutes of Council meetings. There is no doubt that if citizenship is to enhance the democratic legitimacy of the Community's decision-making process and if decision-making is to be brought closer to the citizens, then they must be aware of how and what decisions are being made. As counsel for the Guardian newspaper argues "it is of the essence of democratic government that the public should have the right to be informed of the circumstances in which decisions are being taken in their name and at least have an opportunity to express their views, and that the quality of those decisions will be improved not only by the public's contribution to the decision-making process but perhaps even more by the know-

---

[6]See Shaw, J., "Twin-Track Social Europe: The Inside Track", in O'Keeffe, D. and Twomey, P. (eds.) *Legal Issues of the Maastricht Treaty* (1993) London, Chancery Press.

[7]See Curtin, D. and Meijers, H., "The Principle of Open Government in Schengen and the European Union: Democratic Retrogression", 32 *CMLRev* (1995) 391–442.

ledge of the decision-makers that they are acting in the public view". The Dutch standing committee of experts on international immigration, refugee and criminal law also supports the addition of a provision on openness to the existing provisions on citizenship. It has suggested the adoption of the following provision: Article 8(f) "The Citizens of the Union shall have a right of access to information at the disposal of the institutions. The Council shall, in accordance with the procedure established in Article 189B, specify the categories of information to which the citizen shall not have access and the grounds upon which such access may be denied." This provision seeks to constitutionalise commitment to public access to an open European government.

As Community or Union citizenship stands, it has failed, or been prevented from, achieving the objectives assigned to it in 1992, which were mentioned in Chapter 1. It has not succeeded in forging a direct political link between Member State nationals and the Union, since European Parliament elections are still not organised along the lines of a uniform electoral procedure. Such a direct political link does not follow either from the Directive on electoral rights in municipal elections, since Member State nationality is the essential precondition for the enjoyment of the rights thereunder. Furthermore, the civil and political rights introduced by citizenship do not necessarily reduce the Community's democratic deficit or improve citizen participation in decision-making. The powers of the European Parliament are still, after all, far too limited and the involvement of Member State nationals in municipal elections on the basis of residence has nothing to do with enhancing Community decision-making processes. As regards the improvement of the efficiency and completion of the internal market, the constitutionalisation of a right of residence and electoral rights may be some help, but the unsatisfactory division of free movement issues between the first and third pillars has to be resolved. It is too early to identify whether Union citizenship is stimulating a European identity, but its initial reception in countries like France and Denmark do not augur well.

In order to fulfil these objectives, the Member States must determine what sort of European (political) society they wish to construct. This will ultimately determine the content and shape of Community or Union citizenship. Their failure to decide on this fundamental issue has arguably been one of the main limitations which the evolution of Community citizenship has encountered to date. As a result of this lack of decision, Article 8 does not disassociate Union citizenship from Member State nationality and the content of that provision reflects the smallest common denominator on which Member State delegations could reach agreement in 1992. The Member States still face a number of important questions which will determine how Community citizenship evolves. Does it, for example, extend beyond civil and political rights? Will it, at some stage, involve a direct political link between the Union and citizens? What is the position of third country nationals? How are fundamental rights to be protected and what about equality between the sexes, education and culture? How will the Union develop while respecting and preserving the historical, social and cultural identities of Member States? In order to answer these questions the 1996 IGC will have to address, *inter alia*, whether nationality should be the only basis for the enjoyment of the rights of Union citizenship; whether the time has come for a general principle of non-discrimination on grounds of race, sex, age, handicap, religion; whether a provision on racism and xenophobia should be inserted in the Treaty; whether a charter of fundamental rights is necessary for the constitutional and legitimate development of Community law;[8] and whether social rights will figure in such a charter.

Community Citizenship and Legitimacy: Possible Guidelines for the Evolution of Community Citizenship

The individual rights protected by Community law can usefully be divided into two categories. The first category refers to the subjective aspects of rights – rights which the legal order confers on the individual as a means to protect his rights and interests generally, such as freedom of movement, freedom to exercise an econmic activity, freedom to participate in political life and the civil and fundamental rights which enable persons to do so, namely freedom of expression, association or religion. A second category of rights or principles enshrine values of a more objective nature. These rights can be regarded as the means by which the political and legal order seeks to safeguard its own legitimacy and essentially its authority over the lives of individuals. They do so by setting basic standards which bind the legal and political conditions in which individuals live.[9] An example might be the right of access to the courts, the right to equal treatment, the right to have one's legitimate expectations upheld, or the right to be treated in accordance with the principle of proportionality. These two categories of rights are intrinsically different but the purpose behind them is essentially the same, to give the individual the means to safeguard his or her rights and to ensure that the legal and political order in which he or she lives respects those rights.

With reference to this objective category of rights the Court of Justice has tried to validate and legitimise the authority of Community law and the emergence of a new legal order which alters, to an extent, the relationship between the Member States and their nationals and which relies, with magnificent effect, on the principles of supremacy and direct effect. The development of the Community's obligation to adhere to fundamental rights is the most outstanding example of this phenomenon. As Weiler has suggested "even if the protection of human rights *per se* need not be indispensable to fashioning a federal-type constitution, it was crit-

---

[8]See, in particular, the proposals of the Spanish government regarding the adoption of a charter of justiciable fundamental rights and accession to the European Convention on Human Rights, *La Conferencia Intergubernamental de 1996. Bases para una Reflexión*, Madrid, 2 March 1995.

[9]See generally Diez-Picazo, "Una Constitución sin Declaración de Derechos? (Reflexiones constitucionales sobre los derechos fundamentales en la Comunidad Europea)", 32 *Revista española de derecho constitucional* (1991) 135–155; and Ferrajoli, "Cittadinanza e diritti fondamentali", 9 *Teoria Politica* (1993) 63–76.

ical to the acceptance by courts in the Member States of the other elements of constitution-building".[10]

This strong "objective values" approach as a means to assert the legitimacy of the Community legal order is perhaps inevitable, since any assertion of jurisdiction by the Court, or any assumption of competence by the Community institutions, implies a reduction in the exclusive sphere of action of the Member States. Furthermore, it is not novel for a legal and political order to rely on the protection of rights, citizenship rights and fundamental rights in particular, as one of the pillars of its constitutional construction, legal legitimacy and political power.[11] What is peculiar to the Community context is that in relying on fundamental rights, in particular, as a means of introducing an objective legitimising scale of values into Community law, the protection of subjective rights in concrete cases may have been neglected in favour of reaffirmation of the legitimacy of the Community legal order, protection of its primarily economic concerns and constant reappraisal of the division between Community and national competences. This neglect may also be reflected in the limited scope of Union citizenship, in the failure to link that set of rights to an effective fundamental rights framework and in the marked absence of what Habermas calls, "those discursive processes of opinion – and will-formation through which the sovereignty of the people can be exercised",[12] namely, representative parliamentary and political processes. The Court of Justice itself has recognised "the fundamental democratic principle that people should take part in the exercise of power through the intermediary of a representative assembly"[13] and has linked this aspect of democratic legitimacy to the rights of access of individuals to judicial proceedings which it vindicated in *Van Gend en Loos*.[14] This fundamental principle of democracy has not flourished at Community level given (i) the limited representative role of the European Parliament and (ii) the accumulation of decision making in Community matters in the hands of the Council and Commission and the lack of accountability to national parliaments.

It is suggested that the construction of relationship between Community citizenship and fundamental rights could hold the key to the successful evolution of a status of citizenship peculiar to the European Union. In establishing Community citizenship, the Member States have cleverly recognised that given the functions of government which the Community and Union are increasingly shouldering, the persons subject to that government, Member State nationals in particular, have to be accorded some visible non-economic rights. Otherwise, the Community could be charged with disregarding the fundamental principles of democracy and the rule of law. Recognition of fundamental rights is an essential aspect of the foundational

---

[10]See Weiler, "The Transformation of Europe", 100 *Yale Law Journal* (1991) 2403–2483, at 2418.
[11]See on this subject Habermas, "Human Rights and Popular Sovereignty: The Liberal and Republican Versions", 7 *Ratio Juris* (1994) 1–13, at 1-2.
[12]Ibid., at 13.
[13]See Case 138/79, *S.A. Roquette Frère* v. *Council* [1980] ECR 3360, at para.33.
[14]Case 26/62 *Van Gend en Loos* v. *Administratie der Belastingen* [1963] ECR 1. See also Mancini and Keeling, "Democracy and the European Court of Justice", 57 *Modern Law Review* (1994) 175–191, at 184.

pact between government and the governed and the legal and political value of fundamental rights is also their potentially integrationary and legitimizing function in a given legal order.[15] Fundamental rights and popular sovereignty coincide where the former dictate the conditions in which the "forms of communication necessary for politically autonomous law-making can be legally institutionalised".[16] Article F(2) reaffirms the commitment of the Union to fundamental rights, while Article 8 attempts to add a political gloss to the Community's previously market or consumer citizenship which was based on the fulfilment of certain economic objectives dictated by the integration of the market. Fundamental rights were first cited in the Community when the Court found that it had to affirm the supremacy of Community law in the face of Member State opposition. To legitimise its extensive involvement in socially sensitive fields of activity, the Community can no longer refer to the supremacy of Community law and to the original socio-legal contract and transfer of sovereignty with its Member States. The Community must now demonstrate some sort of social and political consensus amongst its members and a reaffirmation of fundamental rights and the establishment of citizenship may be the tools being used to forge such a consensus, or the appearance of such. The absence of any relationship between Community citizens and a European Community polity is an obstacle to the development of such a consensus and may ultimately weaken some of the rights of citizenship discussed in this book.

In this regard, it is useful to refer to a distinction drawn between the need for formal legitimacy and the need for social legitimacy in a given legal order.[17] Formal legitimacy "implies that all the requirements of the law are observed in the creation of the institution or system". This condition seems to be fulfilled in the Community where the Treaties and now the Union Treaty have been approved either directly by European citizens or by their national parliaments. Social legitimacy, however, "connotes a broad empirically determined societal acceptance of the system ... legitimacy occurs when the government displays a commitment to, and actively guarantees values that are part of the general political culture, such as justice, freedom and general welfare". This is the unclear aspect of the European bargain. As Weiler argues, although integration between Member States may lessen the democratic input of individual Member State nationals, since they become smaller fish in a bigger pond, the success of integration depends, not just on reducing the democratic deficit by increasing the input of the European Parliament. Enhancing the legitimacy of the Community and, therefore, improving the ultimate success of the integration process, depend, in addition, on achieving some level of shared aspirations and social values between the Community's members. Thus, in order to fulfil a social integrative function, Habermas also argues that democratic citizenship must be more than a legal status and must become the focus of a shared

---

[15]See also Lenaerts, K., "Fundamental Rights to be Included in a Community Catalogue", 16 *ELRev* (1991) 367–390, at 368.

[16]Habermas, op. cit. note 1, at 13.

[17]Weiler, J.H.H., "Problems of Legitimacy in Post 1992 Europe", 46 *Aussenwirtschaft* (1991) 411–437, at 415 *et seq.*

political culture.[18] Developing a type of Community citizenship may indeed have been correctly identified as a means to redress (or perhaps divert attention from), the democratic deficit in the Community and to develop a degree of social consensus sufficient to justify continued integration.

However, if Community citizenship is confined to a reciprocal extension of limited civil and political rights on an equal treatment basis, it will not succeed in moving the Community far beyond its present commitment to market integration. In its present form it merely pays lip service to the ideal of greater social legitimacy and consensus among the Community's members. By relating it to fundamental rights and effectively promoting it as a fundamental objective of Community law, the rights of individual members of the Community might indeed receive more effective protection. Citizenship was established and fundamental rights are protected at state level not merely as instruments to achieve some form of economic integration and hybrid confederation of states. They developed on the basis of common values and interests and were means to protect individuals' rights and permit individual participation and access to the political and legal system. This is the third aspect of citizenship. Beyond its extension of political rights and rights of economic participation, citizenship also refers to the formation of some sort of identity based on shared values and expectations.[19] In the process of forming such an identity, citizenship developed in many states in the wake of revolution and conflict. It has been established in the Community in Article 8, however, without reference to the individuals who are now said to enjoy this status. Given the ideological charge which citizenship carries, the evolution of a status of citizenship at Community level is not without its dangers and its difficulties. The meaning and content of citizenship may be used by different sectors to promote different interests. It is suggested, however, that identifying a relationship between the objectives of Community citizenship and the protection of fundamental rights in the Community would be an effective safeguard against Community citizenship being ideologically abused. Indeed, it may be more dangerous to allow the Community's hegemony of economic interests to develop without recognition of the important consequences which such a hegemony may have for the rights and interests of individual members of the Community.

In conclusion, the protection and furtherance of individual rights should be the central objective of both Community citizenship and the adherence to fundamental rights in Community law. Both categories of rights have been weakened by the failure to recognise this essential purpose of the protection of individual rights in and against the national and supranational legal orders. Community citizenship should be relied on in future to establish a more direct legal and political relationship between the Community and its citizens and as a vehicle to represent their interests. Fundamental rights should also be enforced in conformity with the Court's powerful principle of effective judicial protection. Otherwise, both categories of

[18]See Habermas, op. cit. note 1, at 7.
[19]See Nauta, "Changing Conceptions of Citizenship", 12 *Praxis International* (1992) 20–33, at 29.

rights will merely be a means to cover up for the lack of accountability and legitimacy in the Community's political and legislative processes. Fundamental rights and citizenship could be a means to redefine a European polity and, on that basis, to assert greater social legitimacy as Community integration proceeds. However, if the protection of the individual is not increasingly identified as the central element of the Community's social contract with Member States and their nationals, it is difficult to see how the Community's social legitimacy can be enhanced. The process of integration to date has opted for free market efficiency and competition, ideologies which at national level have been fiercely debated and which have had marked social, political and even historical consequences. To proceed, even at this stage of integration, without deepening the social legitimacy of the Community would be a grave error. To ignore the essential role which individual Member State nationals should play in defining the content and limits of this new European polity on which the future of the Communities and Union so much depends would be even graver. The construction of a relationship between fundamental rights and Community citizenship could be the means to ensure the steady evolution of an effective and meaningful rights-orientated status of citizenship in the Community.

Bibliography

Ackers, L., "Women, Citizenship and European Community Law: The Gender Implications of the Free Movement Provisions", *The Journal of Social Welfare and Family Law* (1994) 391–406.

Adinolfi, A., "Aspetti innovativi in tema di soggiorno e di trattamento dei cittadini di stati membri della Comunitá Europea", 73 *Rivista di diritto internazionale* (1990) 105–113.

Adjei, C., "Human Rights Theory and the Bill of Rights Debate", 58 *Modern Law Review* (1995) 17–36.

Adonnino, P., "L'Europa dei cittadini. Considerazioni e prospettive", 17 *Affari esteri* (1985) 438–449.

Alexander, W., "The Law Applicable to Nationals of Third Countries in the Absence of Agreements Between the Community and their Country", *Actualités du droit* (1994) 285–298.

Allington, N., "Funding arrangements for universities and students in the European Communities", 6 *European Access* (1991) 10–12.

Ameglio, F., "Una proposta per l'Europa. Una procedura elettorale uniforme per l'elezione del Parlamento Europeo", *Affari sociali internazionali* (1986) 65–74.

Andersen, N., "Free Movement of Labour within the Nordic Countries and within the European Communities", 5 *Nordic International Law Journal* (1988) 384–392.

Anderson, M., den Boer, M. and Miller, G., "European Citizenship and Cooperation in Justice and Home Affairs", in Duff, A., Pinder, J. and Pryce, R., *Maastricht and Beyond: Building the European Union* (1994) London, Routledge, pp.104–122.

Andrews, G., *Citizenship* (1991) London, Lawrence and Wishart.

Antola, E. and Rosas, A., *A Citizens' Europe: In Search of a New Order* (1995) London, Sage Publications.

Arnaldo Alcubilla, E., "El derecho de sufragio de los extranjeros en las elecciones locales", 12 *Revista española de derecho constitucional* (1992) 67–97.

Arnull, A., *The General Principles of EEC Law and the Individual* (1990) Leicester, Leicester University Press.

Arnull, A., "Owing up to Fallibility: Precedent and the Court of Justice", 30 *Common Market Law Review* (1993) 247–266.

Baldwin-Edwards, M., "The Socio-Political Rights of Migrants in the EEC", in Room, G. (ed.), *Towards a European Welfare State* (1991) SAUS Publications, pp.189–234.

Balibar, E., "Sujets ou citoyens?" 452/3/4 *Les temps modernes* (1985) 1726.

Barbalet, J.M., *Citizenship* (1988) Milton Keynes, Open University Press.

Barnard, C., annotation of Case C-300/89, 17 *European Law Review* (1992) 127–133.

Barry, B. and Goodin, R.E., *Free Movement: Ethical Issues in the Transnational Migration of People and Money* (1992) New York, Harvester Wheatsheaf.

Batley, R. and Stoker, G., *Local Government in Europe: Trends and Developments* (1991) London, Macmillan.

Beaud, O., "Le droit de vote des étrangers. L'apport de la jurisprudence constitutionelle allemande à une théorie du droit de suffrage", 8 *Revue française du droit administratif* (1992) 410–424.

Bebr, G., "A Critical Review of Recent Case Law of National Courts", 11 *Common Market Law Review* (1974) 408–431.

Bebr, G., "How Supreme is Community Law in the National Courts?", 11 *Common Market Law Review* (1974) 3–37.

Beddard, R. and Mittall, D., *Economic, Social and Cultural Rights* (1990) London, Macmillan.

Bekemans, L. and Balodimus, A., "Le Traité de Maastricht et l'éducation, la formation professionelle et la culture", *Revue du Marché Unique Européen* (1993) 99–141.

Belloni, "A Common Policy on Migration: A Step Towards a Citizen's Europe", *Il politico* (1987) 437–451.

Benard, C., "Migrant Workers and European Democracy", 93 *Political Science Quarterly* (1978–79) 277–299.

Bendix, R., *Nationbuilding and Citizenship* (1977) Berkeley, University of California.

Bengoetxea, J., *The Legal Reasoning of the European Court of Justice: Towards a European Jurisprudence* (1993) Clarendon Press.

Benot, Y., "Des droits politiques aux immigrés", 452/3/4 *Les temps modernes* (1984) 1754.

Bercusson, B., "Fundamental Social and Economic Rights", in Cassese, A., Clapham, A. and Weiler, J.H.H. (eds.), *European Union: The Human Rights Challenge. The Substantive Law* Vol.3 (1991) Baden Baden, Nomos.

Berlin, "Interactions Between the Lawmaker and the Judiciary in the EC", *Legal Issues of European Integration* (1992) 17–48.

Bernhardt, R. and Jolowicz, J.A., *International Enforcement of Human Rights*, Colloquium of the International Association of Legal Science, Heidelberg 28 July–3 August 1985 (1987) Springer Verlag.

Betten, L., *The Right to Strike in Community Law* (1985) Amsterdam, North Holland.

Betten, L. (ed.), *The Future of European Social Policy*, European Monographs 1 (1991) Deventer, Kluwer.

Bickel, A.M., "Citizenship in the American Constitution", 15 *Arizona Law Review* (1973) 369–387.

Bieber, R. and Ress, E. (eds.), *The Dynamics of European Community Law* (1987) Baden Baden, Nomos.

Bieber, R., "The Settlement of Institutional Conflicts on the Basis of Article 4 of the EEC Treaty", 21 *Common Market Law Review* (1984) 505–523.

Bieber, R. *et al.*, "Implications of the Single Act for the European Parliament", 23 *Common Market Law Review* (1986) 767–792.

Blackburn, R. (ed.), *Rights of Citizenship* (1993) London, Mansell Publishing.

Blake, C., "Citizenship, Law and the State: The British Nationality Act, 1981", 45 *Modern Law Review* (1982) 179–197.

Blanc, H., "Schengen. Le chemin de la libre circulation en Europe", 351 *Revue du Marché Commun* (1991) 722–726.

Blanpain, R., *Labour Law and Industrial Relations of the EC Maastricht and Beyond: From a Community to a Union* (1992) Deventer, Kluwer Law and Tax Publishers.

Bleckmann, A., "Considérations sur l'interprétation de l'article 7 du Traité CEE", 12 RTDE (1976) 469–481.

Bleckmann, A., "The Personal Jurisdiction of the EEC Treaty", 9 *Common Market Law Review* (1972) 467–478.

Blumann, C., "L'Europe des citoyens", no.346 *Revue du Marché Commun* (1991) 283–292.

Bockel, "La Constitution Française et les étrangers", in *Les droits des immigrés* (1983) Aix-en-Provence.

Bogdanor, V., "Direct Elections, Representative Democracy and European Integration", 8 *Electoral Studies* (1989) 205–216.

Bohning, W.R., "The Scope of the EEC System of the Free Movement of Workers: A Rejoinder", 10 *Common Market Law Review* (1973) 81–84.

Bohning, W.R. and Werquin, J., *Some Economic, Social and Human Rights Considerations Concerning the Future Status of Third Country Nationals in the Single European Market* (1990) Geneva, ILO Working Paper.

Bolly, A., "Droit d'entrée et de séjour des ressortissants communautaires. Développements récents", 3 *Actualités du droit* (1990) 735–748.

Bouder, A., "New Forms of Employment and their Use in the Employment Policies of the Member States of the European Communities", 5 *International Journal of Comparative Labour Law and Industrial Relations* (1989) 1–16.

Boulouis, J., "Note sur le non-effet de l'élection au suffrage universel direct de l'Assemblée des Communautés Européennes", *Pouvoirs* (1981) 111.

Bourrinet, J., "Vers une citoyenneté européenne. Aspects économiques", 362 *Revue du Marché Commun* (1992) 772–776.

Bouza i Vidal, N., "El ambito personal de aplicación del derecho de establecemiento en los supuestos de doble nacionalidad", 20 *Revista de instituciones europeas* (1993) 563–581.

Bowen, H.R., *The Costs of Higher Education* (1980) San Francisco, Carnegie Council on Policy Studies in Higher Education, Jossey-Bass.

Boyce, B., "The Democratic Deficit of the European Community", 46 *Parliamentary Affairs* (1993) 458–477.

Bradley, K. St. C., "The European Court and the Legal Basis of Community Legislation", 13 *European Law Review* (1988) 379–402.

Breillat, D., "Les droits politiques de l'étranger en France", in *La condition juridique de l'étranger. Hier et aujourd'hui* (1988) Faculteit Der Rechtsgeleerheid, Katholieke Universiteit Nijmegen.

Brittan, L., *Subsidiarity in the Constitution of the European Communities* (1992) Robert Schuman Lecture at the European University Institute, Florence.

Brons, R., "An Investigation into the Structure of Higher Education in Europe", 44 *Higher Education Quarterly* (1990) 142–153.

Brown, P. and Shue, H., *Boundaries: National Autonomy and its Limits* (1981) Rowman and Littlefield, Totowa NJ.

Brubaker, W.R. (ed.), *Immigration and the Politics of Citizenship in Europe and North America* (1989) NewYork and London, Lanham, University Press of America.

Bullain, I., "Ciudadania y Union Europea", 38 *Revista vasca de administración pública* (1994) 57–75.

Burban, J.L., "Des élections encore peu européennes", 878 *Revue politique et parlementaire* (1979) 18.

Buxton, R., *Local Government* (1973) Harmondsworth, Penguin.

Callovi, G., "L'Europe des douze au défi de l'immigration", 11 *L'evénèment européen* (1990) 27–46.

Capotorti, F. (*et al.*), *Du droit international au droit de l'integration. Liber Amicorum Pescatore* (1987) Baden Baden, Nomos.

Cappelletti, M. and Golay, D., "The Judicial Branch in the Federal and Transnational Union: Its Impact on Integration", in Cappelletti, M., Seccombe, M. and Weiler, J.H.H., *Integration Through Law: Europe and the American Federal Experience* Vol.1 Book 2 (1986) Berlin, Walter de Gruyter/European University Institute, p.261.

Carens, J.H., "Aliens and Citizens: The Case for Open Borders", 49 *Review of Politics* (1987) 251–273.

Casagrande, M., "Les immigrés et les élections communales dans les pays de la CEE", 10 *Objectif Europe* (1980) 38–47.

Cass, D.Z., "The Word that Saves Maastricht? The Principle of Subsidiarity and the Division of Powers within the EC", 29 *Common Market Law Review* (1992) 1107–1136.

Cassese, A., Clapham, A. and Weiler, J.H.H. (eds.), *European Union: The Human Rights Challenge* Vols.1–3 (1991) Baden Baden, Nomos.

Ceccarelli, A., "Il voto dei lavoritori migranti nella Comunitá Europea", *Il Mulino* (1992) 366–372.

Cellamare, "Il diritto di voto dei cittadini italiani all'estero", *Rivista di diritto europeo* (1979) 260.

Chaltiel, F., "La loi française sur le droit de vote des citoyens européens aux élections européennes", no.381 *Revue du Marché Commun* (1994) 528–532.

Chapus, R., "Nationalité et exercise de fonctions publiques, service public et liberté", in *Mélanges Offerts au Prof. R.E. Charlier*, Edition de l'université et de l'enseignement moderne.

Churches' Commission for Migrants in Europe, *The Use of International Conventions to Protect the Rights of Migrants and Ethnic Minorities* (1994) Strasbourg.

Cini, M., *Local Government and the EC* (1990) 16 European Dossier Series, London, PNL Press.

Clapham, A., "A Human Rights Policy for the European Communities", 10 *Yearbook of European Law* (1990) 309–366.

Clapham, A. and Waaldijk, K. (eds.), *Homosexuality: A European Community Issue* (1993) Deventer, Martinus Nijhoff/Kluwer.

Closa, C., "The Concept of Citizenship in the Treaty on European Union", 29 *Common Market Law Review* (1992) 1137–1169.

Closa, C., "Citizenship of the Union and Nationality of Member States", 32 *Common Market Law Review* (1995) 487–518.

Closa, C., "Citizenship of the Union and Nationality of the Member States", in O'Keeffe, D. and Twomey, P. (eds.), *Legal Issues of the Maastricht Treaty* (1993) London, Chancery Press, pp.109–119.

Close, G., "Definitions of Citizenship", in Gardner, P. (ed.), *Hallmarks of Citizenship: A Green Paper* (1995) Institute for Citizenship Studies and the British Institute of International and Comparative Law, pp.3–18.

Clute, R.E., "Nationality and Citizenship", in Wilson *et al.* (eds.), *The International Law Standard and Commonwealth Developments* (1966) Commonwealth Studies Center, Duke University Press, pp.100–136.

Coenen, H. and Leisink, P. (eds.), *Work and Citizenship in the New Europe* (1993) Aldershot, Elgar Publishing.

Cohen-Jonathan, G., "La Cour des Communautés Européennes et les droits de l'homme", *Revue du Marché Commun* (1978) 74.

Cohen-Jonathan, G., *La convention européenne des droits de l'homme* (1989) Economica/Presse Universitaire d'Aix-Marseille.

Cohen-Jonathan, G., "Le parlement européen et les droits de l'homme", *Revue du Marché Commun* (1978) 384.

Colvin, C.M., "*SPUC* v. *Grogan*: Abortion Law and the Free Movement of Services in the European Community", 15 *Fordham International Law Journal* (1991–92) 476–526.

Commission E.C./Catholic University of Louvain, *The Future of the European Social Policy* (1994) Louvain.

Constantinesco, V., *La distribution des pouvoirs entre la Communauté et ses états membres. L'equilibre mouvant de la compétence legislative et le principe de subsidiarité* (1990) Working paper at the annual conference of the College of Europe, Bruges.

Constantinseco, V., "L'article 5 CEE, de la bonne foi à la loyauté communautaire", in *Liber Amicorum Pierre Pescatore. Du droit international au droit de l'integration* (1987) Baden Baden, Nomos, p.97.

Constantinesco, V., "L'Europe en formation", 256 *Les cahiers du fédéralisme* (1984) 53.

Constantinesco, V., "Who's Afraid of Subsidiarity?", 11 *Yearbook of European Law* (1991) 33–55.

Coote, A. (ed.), *The Welfare of Citizens* (1992) London, IPPR/River Oram Press.

Coppell, J. and O'Neill, A., "The European Court of Justice: Taking Rights Seriously?", 29 *Common Market Law Review* (1992) 659–692.

Costa-Lascoux, J., "Droits des immigrés, droits de l'homme et politique de l'immigration", 113 *Regards sur l'actualité* (1985) 20.

Costa-Lascoux, J., "Nationaux seulement, ou vraiment citoyens?", 204 *Projet* (1987) 45–57.

Costa-Lascoux, J., "De l'immigré au citoyen", 4886 *Notes et études documentaires* (1989) Secretariat du Gouvernement, Direction de la Documentation Française.

Council of Europe, *Proceedings of the Colloquium about the ECHR in relation to other International Instruments for the Protection of Human Rights* (1979) Strasbourg.

Council of Europe, *Conférence des pouvoirs locaux et regionaux* (1978) Strasbourg.

Council of Europe, *Allocation of Powers to the Local and Regional Levels of Government in the Member States of the Council of Europe* (1988) Strasbourg.

Council of Europe, *Study of Civic Rights of Nationals of Other Member States in Local Public Life* RM-SL (82) revised, 25 October 1982, Strasbourg.

Council of Europe, *Les droits de l'homme des étrangers en Europe* (1985) Strasbourg.

Cousins, M., "Free Movement of Workers and Period of Unemployment Requirements in the Irish Social Welfare System", 8 *Irish Law Times* (1990) 258.

Cousins, M., "Equal Treatment and Social Security", 19 *European Law Review* (1994) 123–145.

Cousins, R., Hallmark, H. and Pickup, I., "Inter-University Cooperation and Erasmus", 44 *Higher Education Quarterly* (1990) 83–97

Cristofanelli, L., "Equaglianza di trattamento e frequenza di corsi scolastici e di formazione professionale nella CEE", 15 *Affari sociali internazionali* (1987) 11–28.

Cruz, A., "La compétence communautaire *vis-à-vis* des ressortissants des pays-tiers", Document du travail du comité des églises auprès des migrations en Europe (CEME), no.5, Bruxelles.

Culpitt, I., *Welfare and Citizenship: Beyond the Crisis of the Welfare State?*, Politics and Culture (1992) London, Sage Publications.

Curtin, D., "Directives: the Effectiveness of Judicial Protection and Individual Rights", 27 *Common Market Law Review* (1990) 709–739.

Curtin, D., "The Province of Government: Delimiting the Direct Effect of Directives in the Common Law Context", 15 *European Law Review* (1990) 195–223.

Curtin, D., annotation of Case C-159/90 *Grogan*, 29 *Common Market Law Review* (1992) 585–603.

Curtin, D., "The Constitutional Structure of the Union: A Europe of Bits and Pieces", 30 *Common Market Law Review* (1993) 17–69.

Curtin, D., "The Decentralised Enforcement of Community Law: Judicial Snakes and Ladders", in O'Keeffe, D. and Curtin, D. (eds.), *Constitutional Adjudication in European Community and National Law: Essays in Honour of Mr Justice T.F. O'Higgins* (1992) London, Butterworths, pp.33–49.

Curtin, D., "Constitutionalism and the European Communities: The Right to Fair Procedures in Administrative Law", in O'Reilly, J. (ed.), *Human Rights and Constitutional Law: Essays in Honour of Justice Brian Walsh* (1992) Round Hall Press, Dublin, p.293.

Cvetic, G., "Immigration Cases in Strasbourg, the Right to Family Life Under Article 8 of the ECHR", 36 *International Comparative Law Quarterly* (1987) 647–655.

Dahl, R., "A Democratic Dilemma: System Effectiveness versus Citizen Participation", 109 *Political Science Quarterly* (1994) 23–34.

Dahrendorf, R., "Citizenship and the Modern Social Contract", in Holme, R. and Elliot, M., *1688–1988: Time for a New Constitution* (1988) London, Macmillan.

Dalichow, F., "Academic Recognition Within the EC", 22 *European Journal of Education* (1987) 39–58.

Dallen, R.M., "An Overview of the European Commmunity Protection of Human Rights, with some special reference to the UK", 27 *Common Market Law Review* (1990) 761–789.

D'Armont Francois, A., "L'Unione Europea e la politica sociale", 20 *Affari sociali internazionali* (1992) 407.

Daubler, W., *Market and Social Justice in the EC: The Other Side of the Internal Market. Strategies and Options for the Future of Europe* Basic Findings 3 (1991) Bertelsmann Foundation Publishers, Gutersloh.

Dauses, M.A., "The Protection of Fundamental Rights in the Community Legal Order", 10 *European Law Review* (1985) 398–419.

De Burca, G., "Giving Effect to European Community Directives", 55 *Modern Law Review* (1992) 215.

De Burca, G., "Fundamental Human Rights and the Reach of EC Law", 13 *Oxford Journal of Legal Studies* (1993) 283–319.

Dehousse, F., "Les élections européennes au suffrage universel direct", 3 *Les nouvelles* (1969) 285.

De Lobkowicz, W., "Un droit de vote municipal pour tous les européens", 313–322 *Revue du Marché Commun* (1988) 602–613.

De Lobkowicz, W., "Des élections européennes aux municipales. Un droit de vote pour certains étrangers?" 900 *Revue politique et parlementaire* (1982) 55.

De Lobkowicz, W., "Une élection européenne ou des élections nationales?" 909 *Revue politique et parlementaire* (1984) 85–107.

De Lobkowicz, W., "Quelle libre circulation des personnes en 1993?" 334 *Revue du Marché Commun* (1990) 93–101.

De Lobkowicz, W., "The Dublin Convention: A Useful Complement to International Humanitarian Law", 10 *Objectif Europe* (1990) 7.

Denza, E., "Le passeport européen", 260 *Revue du Marché Commun* (1982) 489–493.

De Moor, A., "Article 7 of the Treaty of Rome Bites", 48 *Modern Law Review* (1985) 452–459.

Desolre, G., "De la notion au concept communautaire de travailleur", CDE (1979) 38.

Detter de Lupis, I., *International Law and the Independent State* (1987) Aldershot, Gower Publishing.

De Witte, B. (ed.), *European Community Law of Education* (1989) Baden Baden, Nomos.

De Witte, B., "The Impact of EEC on Culture and Sport", in *Le football et l'Europe*, 3–5 May 1990, European University Institute/European Cultural Centre, Florence.

De Witte, B. and Post, H., "Educational Rights and Cultural Rights", in Cassese, A., Clapham, A. and Weiler, J.H.H. (eds.), *Human Rights and the EC* (1991) Baden Baden, Nomos.

De Witte, B. "The Scope of the Community Powers in Education and Culture in the Light of Subsequent Practice", in Bieber R. and Ress, E. (eds.), *The Dynamics of European Community Law* (1987) Baden Baden, Nomos.

De Witte, B., "Cultural Policy: the Complementarity of Negative and Positive Integration", in Schwarze, J. and Schermers, H.G., *The Structure and Dimensions of EC Policy* (1988) Baden Baden, Nomos, pp.195–204.

De Witte, B., "Community Law and National Constitutional Values", *Legal Issues of European Integration* (1991) 1–22.

De Witte, B. and Forder, C. (eds.), *The Common Law of Europe and the Future of Legal Education* (1992) Deventer, Kluwer Law and Taxation Publishers.

De Zwaan, "The SEA: Conclusion of a Unique Document", 23 *Common Market Law Review* (1986) 747–765.

Diez Picazo, L.M., "Una constitución sin declaración de derechos? Reflexiones constitucionales sobre los derechos fundamentales en la Comunidad Europea", 32 *Revista española de derecho constitucional* (1991) 135–155.

Diez Picazo, L.M., "Reflexiones sobre la idea de constitución europea", 20 *Revista de instituciones europeas* 533–559.

D'Oliveira, H.U.J., "Electoral Rights for Non-Nationals", 31 *Netherlands International Law Review* (1984) 59–72.

D'Oliveira, H.U.J., "Foootball and Nationality in Europe", in *Le football et l'Europe*, 3–5 May 1990, European University Institute/European Cultural Centre, Florence.

D'Oliveira, H.U.J., "Plural Nationality and European Union", forthcoming Martinus Nijhoff.

D'Oliveira, H.U.J., "The Community Case: Is Reverse Discrimination Still Admissible Under the Single European Act?", in *Forty Years On: The Evolution of Postwar Private International Law*, 5 Centruum voor Buitenlands Recht en Internationaal Privaatrecht, Universiteit van Amsterdam (1990) Dordrecht, Kluwer, pp.71–86.

D'Oliveira, H.U.J., "European Community Refugee Policy", 6 *Migrantenrecht* (1991) 76–82.

D'Oliveira, H.U.J., "European Citizenship: Its Meaning, its Potential", in Monar, J., Ungerer, W. and Wessels, W. (eds.), *The Maastricht Treaty on European Union: Legal Complexity and Political Dynamic* (1993), Brussels, European Interuniversity Press, pp.126–146.

D'Oliveira, H.U.J., "Expanding External and Shrinking Internal Borders: Europe's Defence Mechanisms in the Areas of Free Movement, Immigration and Asylum", in O'Keeffe, D. and Twomey, P. (eds.), *Legal Issues of the Maastricht Treaty* (1993) London, Chancery Press, pp.261–278.

Dolle, S., "Refugees and Family Reunion of Immigrants: the Strasbourg Case-Law", in *Proceedings of the Colloquium on Human Rights Without Frontiers* (1990) Council of Europe, Strasbourg (30 November–1 December 1989, DH-ED (89) 20).

Donner, R., *The Regulation of Nationality in International Law* (1983) The Finnish Society of Sciences and Letters.

Dorlodot, M.F.X., "Les exceptions aux règles de la libre circulation des personnes dans le traité CEE", 5 *Revue du droit public et des sciences administratives* (1981) 241–252.

Druesne, G., "La liberté de circulation des personnes dans la CEE et 'les emplois dans l'administration publique'", 17 RTDE (1981) 286–300.

Druesne, G., "Liberté de circulation des personnes, les prolongements de la libre circulation des salariés. Droit de séjour et progrès social", 18 RTDE (1982) 556–567.

Druesne, G., "La réserve d'ordre public de l'article 48 du Traité de Rome", 12 RTDE (1976) 229–258.

Druesne, G., "Liberté de circulation des personnes, l'ordre public. A nouveau comme la punition des filles de Danaos?", 18 RTDE (1982) 706–722.

Druesne, G., "Discriminations à rebours: peuvent-elles tenir en échec la liberté de circulation des personnes?", 15 RTDE (1979) 429–437.

Druesne, G., "Ordre public et garanties procedurales offertes aux travailleurs migrants", 16 RTDE (1980) 428–437.

Drzemczewski, A., "The Domestic Application of the European Human Rights Convention as European Community Law", 30 *International Comparative Law Quarterly* (1981) 118–140.

Drzewicki, K., Krause, K. and Rosas, A. (eds.), *Social Rights as Human Rights: A European Challenge* (1994) Institute of Human Rights, Turku.

Dubouis, L., "La notion d'emplois dans l'administration publique et l'accès des ressortissants communautaires aux emplois", 3 *Revue française de droit administratif* (1987) 949–962.

Dummett, A. (ed.), *Towards a Just Immigration Policy* (1986) London, The Cobden Trust.

Dummett, A. and Nicol, A., *Subjects, Citizens, Aliens and Others: Nationality and Immigration Law* (1990) Law in Context Series, London, Weidenfeld and Nicolson.

Durand, A., "European Citizenship", 4 *European Law Review* (1979) 3–14.

Edens, D.F. and Patijn, S., "The Scope of the EEC System of the Free Movement of Workers", 9 *Common Market Law Review* (1972) 322–328.

Espada Ramos, M.L., "Asilo e inmigración en la Unión Europea", 86 *Revista de estudios políticos* (1994) 71–98.

European Commission, *The Future of European Social Policy* (1994) Louvain, Louvain University Press.

Evans, A.C., "Nationality Law and European Integration", 16 *European Law Review* (1991) 190–215.

Evans, A.C., "Ordre public, Public Policy and United Kingdom Immigration Law", 3 *European Law Review* (1978) 370–381.

Evans, A.C., "Ordre public in French Immigration Law", (1980) *Public Law* 132–149.

Evans, A.C., "The Political Status of Aliens in International, Municipal and European Community Law", 30 *International Comparative Law Quarterly* (1981) 20–41.

Evans, A.C., "Development of European Community Law Regarding the Trade Union and Related Rights of Migrant Workers", 28 *International Comparative Law Quarterly* (1979) 354–366.

Evans, A.C., "European Citizenship: A Novel Concept in Community Law", 32 *American Journal of Comparative Law* (1984) 679–715.

Evans, A.C., "EC Law Regarding the Trade Union and Related Rights of Migrant Workers", 28 *International Comparative Law Quarterly* (1978) 354.

Evans, A.C., "European Citizenship", 45 *Modern Law Review* (1982) 497–515.

Evans, A.C., "Freedom of Trade under the Common Law and EC Law: the Case of Football Bans", 102 *Law Quarterly Review* (1986) 510–548.

Evans, A.C., "Nationality Law and the Free Movement of Persons in the EEC: with Special Reference to the British Nationality Act 1981", 2 *Yearbook of European Law* (1982) 173–189.

Evans, A.C., "Entry Formalities in the European Community", 6 *European Law Review* (1981) 3–13.

Evans, A.C., "Union Citizenship and the Equality Principle", in Antola, E. and Rosas, A. (eds.), *A Citizens' Europe: In Search of a New Legal Order* (1995) London, Sage Publications, pp.85–112.

Evans, A., "Third Country Nationals and the Treaty on European Union", 5 *European Journal of International Law* (1994) 199–219.

Everling, U., "Reflections on the Structure of the European Union", 29 *Common Market Law Review* (1992) 1053–1077.

Evrigenis, D., "Recent Case-Law of the ECHR on Articles 8 and 10 of the ECHR", 3 *Human Rights Law Journal* (1982) 121.

Fenwick, K., "Making the Most of Overseas Students", 41 *Higher Education Quarterly* (1987) 126–137.

Fernández-Martín, J.M.F., "La legitimación activa restringida del parlamento europeo en el recurso de anulación (comentario à la sentencia del TCJE 'Chernobyl' de 22 de mayo de 1990)", 17 *Revista de instituciones europeas* (1990) 911–933.

Fernández Martín, J.M., "El efecto directo de las directivas y la protección de los derechos subjetivos comunitarios en la jurisprudencia del Tribunal de Justicia", *Noticias de la UE* (1995) 1–13.

Fernhout, R., "Schengen and the Internal Market: an Area without Internal Frontiers also without Refugees?", *International Spectator* (1990) 683–689.

Ferrajoli, L., "Cittadinanza e diritti fondamentali", 9 *Teoria politica* (1993) 63–76.

FIDE, *The New Developments of the Free Movement of Persons Towards European Citizenship* (1992) Lisbon.

FIDE, *Legal Aspects of Community Action in the Field of Culture* (1988) Thessaloniki.

Finnie, W., "The Location of Fundamental Rights in the Community Treaty Structure", *Legal Issues of European Integration* (1982) 89–99.

Flora, P. and Heidenheimer, A., *The Development of Welfare States in Western Europe*, (1981) New Brunswick and London, Transaction Books.

Flynn, J., "Vocational Training in European Law and Practice", 8 *Yearbook of European Law* (1988) 59–85.

Fogg, K. and Jones, H., "Educating the European Community: Ten Years On", 20 *European Journal of Education* (1985) 293–300.

Forman, J., "Direct Elections to the European Parliament", 2 *European Law Review* (1977) 35–41.

Fransman, L., *British Nationality Law* (1989) London, Fourmat Publishing.

Fransman, L., "Supranationality: The Fall of the Empire and the Rise of Europe", 4 *Immigration and Nationality in Law and Practice* (1990) 28–34.

Freeman, G.P., "Migration and the Political Economy of the Welfare State", *Annals of the American Academy of Political and Social Science* (1986) 51–63.

Frowein, J.A., *Study of Civic Rights of Nationals of Other Member States in Local Public Life*, Council of Europe, Steering Committee for Regional and Municipal Matters, RM-SL (82) 55 revised.

Frowein, J.A., "Fundamental Human Rights as a Vehicle of Legal Integration in Europe", in Cappelletti, M., Seccombe, M. and Weiler, J.H.H. (eds.), *Integration Through Law* Vol.1 Book 3 (1986) Berlin, Walter de Gruyter/EUI, pp.231–248.

Frowein, J.A. and Stein, T. (eds.), *The Legal Position of Aliens in National and International Law* Part 2 (1987) Max Planck Institute/Springer Verlag.

Gaja, G., *I lavoratori stranieri in Italia* (1984) Società editrice Il Mulino.

Gaja, G., "New Developments in a Continuing Story: the Relationship Between EEC Law and Italian Law", 27 *Common Market Law Review* (1990) 83–95.

Garcia, S., "Europe's Fragmented Identities and the Frontiers of Citizenship", RIIA Discussion Papers (1992) 45.

Garcia, S. (ed.), *European Identity and the Search for Legitimacy* (1993) London, The Eleni Nakou Foundation/RIIA.

Gardner, J.P., *A Review of the Role of Nationality in Public International Law*, Discussion paper prepared for the 1st international workshop, 2–3 February 1989, BIICL.

Gardner, J.P. et al., "European Citizenship: Does a Comparative Review of National Laws Concerning Citizenship Rights Help?", Paper presented at the 2nd international workshop, 6–7 July 1989 and to the W.G. Hart Legal Workshop, *The Single European Market and the Development of EC Law*, 1989, IALS, London.

Gardner, J.P., *What Lawyers Mean by Citizenship*, BIICL.

Gardner, J.P. and the BIICL, *Introduction to the Nationality Provisions in the Constitutions of the Member States of the EEC*, paper prepared for the 2nd International workshop/BIICL, London, 6–7 July 1989.

Garrone, P., "Les droits du citoyen européen. L'acquis communautaire et l'apport du traité de Maastricht", 3 SZIER (1993) 251–271.

Garrone, P., "La discrimination indirecte en droit communautaire. Vers une théorie générale", 30 RTDE (1994) 425–449.

Garrone, P., *La libre circulation des personnes. Liberté de mouvement, égalité, liberté économique. Etude du droit Communautaire et Suisse* (1993) Zurich, Schulthess Collection de droit européen 8.

Garth, B., "Migrant Workers and Rights of Mobility in the EC and the US: A Study of Law, Community and Citizenship in the Welfare State", in Cappelletti, M., Secombe, M. and Weiler, J.H.H., *Integration Through Law: Europe and the American Federal Experience*, Vol.1 Book 3 (1986) Berlin, Walter de Gruyter/EUI, pp.85–163.

Ghandi, S., "Interaction Between the Protection of Fundamental Rights in the EEC and Under the European Convention of Human Rights", *Legal Issues of European Integration* (1981) 1–33.

Glazer, M. (ed.), *Clamor at the Gates: the New American Immigration Policy* (1985) San Francisco, Institute for Contemporary Studies Press.

Goebel, R.J., "Employee Rights in the EC: a Panorama from the 1974 Social Action Program to the Social Charter of 1989", 17 *Hastings International and Comparative Law Review* (1993) 1–95.

Goodwin-Gill, G., *International Law and the Movement of Persons Between States* (1978) Clarendon Press.

Gosalbo Bono, R., "Maastricht et les citoyens. Le médiateur européen", 64 *Revue française d'administration publique* (1992) 639–649.

Goy, R., "La garantie européenne du droit à de libres élections legislatives. L'article 3 du premier protocole additionnel à la Convention de Rome", 102 *Revue du droit public et de la science politique en France et a l'étranger* (1986) 1275–1326.

Goybet, C., "Le manque d'une politique européenne d'immigration", 351 RMC (1991) 685–687.

Grahl, J. and Teague, P., "Economic Citizenship in the New Europe", 65 *The Political Quarterly* (1994) 379–396.

Green, L.C., "Is World Citizenship a Legal Practicality?", 16 *Annuaire canadien du droit international* (1987) 151–185.

Green, N., Hartley, T.C. and Usher, J.A., *The Legal Foundations of the Single European Market* (1991) Oxford, Oxford University Press.

Greenwood, C., "Nationality and the Limits on the Free Movement of Persons in EEC Law", 7 *Yearbook of European Law* (1987) 185–210.

Grewe, Rupp and Schneider, *Europaische Gerichtsbarkeit und nationale Verfassungegerichtsbarkeit* (1981) Baden Baden, Nomos.

Grief, N., "Domestic Enforcement of the ECHR as Mediated Through Community Law", *Public Law* (1991) 555–567.

Groenendijk, C.A., "D'étranger à concitoyen. La signification symbolique du droit de vote pour les immigrés aux Pays-Bas", 40 *MRAX Information* (1985) 23.

Groenendijk, C.A., "Contrôle de l'immigration en Europe. Moyens, effets, craintes", 55 *Revue du droit des étrangers* (1989) 223.

Grusser, S., White, S. and Dorn, N., "Free Movement and Welfare Entitlement: EU Drug Users in Berlin", 5 *Journal of European Social Policy* (1995) 13–28.

Guarneri, G., "Les moyens non judiciaires de protection et de promotion des droits de l'homme. L'action du Conseil de l'Europe", *Affari sociali internazionali* (1983) 53–64.

Guimezanes, N., *La circulation et l'activité économique des étrangers dans la CE. Droits communautaires, droits nationaux* (1990) Nouvelles éditions fiduciaires.

Habermas, J., "Human Rights and Popular Sovereignty: The Liberal and Republican Visions", 7 *Ratio Juris* (1994) 1–13.

Habermas, J., "Citizenship and National Identity: Some Reflections on the Future of Europe", 12 *Praxis International* (1992–93) 1–19.

Habermas, J., "The European Nation State: Its Achievements and its Limits: On the Past and Future of Sovereignty and Citizenship", PLS 2 (1995) 1–10.

Hagen, J., "University Cooperation and Academic Recognition in Europe: the Council of Europe and the Communities", 22 *European Journal of Education* (1987) 77–83.

Hailbronner, K., "Perspectives of a Harmonization of the Law of Asylum after the Maastricht Summit", 29 *Common Market Law Review* (1982) 917–939.

Hailbronner, K., "The Right to Asylum and the Future of Asylum Procedures in the European Community", 2 *International Journal of Refugee Law* (1990) 341–359.

Hamer, L.D.H., "Free Movement of Persons: An Exploration from a Dutch Perspective", *Legal Issues of European Integration* (1989) 49–59.

Hammar, T., "Citizenship: Membership of a Nation and a State", 24 *International Migration* (1986) 735–748.

Hammar, T., "Dual Citizenship and Political Integration", 19 *International Migration Review* (1985) 438–450.

Hammar, T., *Democracy and the Nation State: Aliens, Denizens and Citizens in a World of International Migration* (1990) Research in Ethnic Relations Series, Aldershot, Avebury.

Hammar, T., *European Immigration Policy: A Comparative Study* (1985) Cambridge, Cambridge University Press.

Hammar, T., "Civil Rights and Political Participation of Immigrants", in *The Changing Course of International Migration*, OECD, Rome, 13–15 March 1991.

Hand, G., Georgel, J. and Sasse, C., *European Electoral Systems Handbook* (1979) London, Butterworths.

Handoll, J., "Foreign Teachers and Public Education", in De Witte, B. (ed.), *EC Law of Education* (1989) Baden Baden, Nomos, pp.31–50.

Handoll, J., "Article 48(4) EEC: Non-National Access to Public Employment", 13 *European Law Review* (1988) 223–241.

Hartley, T.C., "Nationality and the Right to Vote in Elections for the European Parliament", 4 *European Law Review* (1979) 50–52.

Hartley, T.C., "Federalism, Courts and Legal Systems: The Emerging Constitution of the EEC", 24 *American Journal of Comparative Law* (1986) 229.

Hartley, T.C., *EEC Immigration Law* (1978) Amsterdam, North Holland.

Hartley, T.C., "Public Policy and Internal Freedom: a Critical Commentary on the *Rutili* decision", *European Law Review* (1975–76) 473–479.

Hartley, T.C., "The Internal Personal Scope of the EEC Immigration Provisions", 3 *European Law Review* (1978) 191–207.

Hartley, T.C., "Are British Immigration Rules Contrary to Community Law?", 6 *European Law Review* (1981) 280–283.

Hartley, T.C., "La libre circulation des étudiants en droit communautaire", 25 *Cahiers de droit européen* (1989) 327–344.

Heater, D., *Citizenship: The Civic Ideal in World History, Politics and Education* (1990) London, Longman.

Heater, D., "Citizenship: A Remarkable Case of Sudden Interest", 44 *Parliamentary Affairs* (1991) 140–156.

Heiserman, R.G., "The Changing Significance of Nationality under the New US Immigration Law", 18–19 *California Western Law Journal* (1987–88) 157.

Heisler, M.O., "Transnational Migration as a Small Window on the Diminished Autonomy of the Modern Democratic State", 483–485 *Annals of the American Society of Political and Social Science* (1986) 153–166.

Held, D., *Political Theory and the Modern State* (1989) London, Polity Press.

Held, D., "Citizens and Citizenship", in Hall, S. and Jacques, M., *New Times: the Changing Face of Politics in the 1990s* (1989) London, Lawrence and Wishart, p.173.

Hennis, E., "Access to Education in the European Communities", 3 *Leiden Journal of International Law* (1990) 35–44.

Hepple, B., "Social Rights in the EEC: a British Perspective", 11 *Comparative Labour Law Journal* (1990) 425.

Hepple, B.A., *The Making of Labour Law in Europe: A Comparative Study of Nine Countries up to 1945* (1986) London, Mansell Publishing.

Herdegen, M., "Maastricht and the German Constitutional Court: Constitutional Restraints for an 'Ever Closer Union'", 31 *Common Market Law Review* (1994) 235–249.

Hervey, T.K., "Legal Issues concerning the *Barber* Protocol", in O'Keeffe, D. and Twomey, P. (eds.), *Legal Issues of the Maastricht Treaty* (1993) London, Chancery Press, pp.329–337.

Hochbaum, I., "The Federal Structure of Member States as a Limit to Common Educational Policy: The Case of Germany", in De Witte, B. (ed.), *European Community Law of Education* (1989) Baden Baden, Nomos, p.145.

House of Lords, *Approximation of Laws*, House of Lords Select Committee for the European Communities, session 1977–78, 22nd report.

House of Lords, *Uniform Electoral Procedure for the Members of the European Parliament*, House of Lords Select Committee for the European Communities, session 1982–83, 5th report.

House of Lords, *Easing of Frontier Formalities*, House of Lords Select Committee for the European Communities, session 1983–84, 4th report.

House of Lords, *Youth Training in the EEC*, House of Lords Select Committee for the European Communities, session 1983–84, 24th report.

House of Lords, *Recognition of Higher Education Diplomas*, House of Lords Select Committee for the European Communities, session 1985–86, 22nd report.

House of Lords, *1992: Border Control of People*, House of Lords Select Committee for the European Communities, session 1988–89, 22nd report.

House of Lords, *Voting Rights in Local Elections*, House of Lords Select Committe for the European Communities, session 1989–90, 6th report.

House of Lords, *Free Movement of People and the Right of Residence in the EC*, House of Lords Select Committee for the European Communities, session 1989–90, 7th report.

House of Lords, *Vocational Training and Re–Training*, House of Lords Select Committee for the European Communities, session 1989–90, 21st report.

House of Lords, *Social Policy After Maastricht*, House of Lords Select Committee for the European Communities, session 1991–92, 7th report.

House of Lords, *Human Rights Re-Examined*, House of Lords Select Committee for the European Communities, session 1992–93, 3rd report.

House of Lords, *Community Policy on Migration*, House of Lords Select Committee for the European Communities, session 1992–93, 10th report.

House of Lords, *Visas and Control of External Borders of the Member States*, House of Lords Select Committee for the European Communities, session 1993–94, 14th report.

Hondius, F.W., "Legal Aspects of the Movement of Persons in Greater Europe", 10 *Yearbook of European Law* (1990) 291–307.

Hoogenboom, T., "Integration into Society and Free Movement of Non-EC Nationals", 3 *European Journal of International Law* (1992) 36–52.

Hubeau, B. and Van Put, R., "Les compétences des Communautés en matière d'immigration", 58 *Revue du droit des étrangers* (1990) 71–79.

ILO, *Informal Consultation Meeting on Migrants from Non-EEC Countries in the Single European Market after 1992*, 27–28 April 1989, Geneva.

Iglesias Buigues, J.L., "Entrada, permanencia y trabajo en Espana de nacionales de Estados Miembros de la Comunidad Europea", 3 *La Ley-Comunidades Europeas* (1986) 25.

Ignatieff, M., "The Myth of Citizenship", 12 *Queen's Law Journal* (1987) 399–420.

Iivonen, J. (ed.), *The Future of the Nation State in Europe* (1993) Aldershot, Elgar.

Institute for Public Policy Research, *Nationality and Citizenship Status in the New Europe* London, 9–10 June 1995.

Ireland, P.R., "Facing the True 'Fortress Europe': Immigrants and Politics in the EC", 29 *Journal of Common Market Studies* (1991) 9–33.

BIBLIOGRAPHY   327

Jacobs, F.G., *European Law and the Individual* (1976) Amsterdam, North Holland Publishing Co.
Jacobs, F.G., "The Free Movement of Persons Within the EEC", 30 *Current Legal Problems* (1977) 123–139.
Jacqué, J.P., "Commentaire de la décision du Conseil constitutionnel no.92-308 DC du 9 avril 1992", 28 RTDE (1992) 251.
Jaeger, M., "La notion 'd'emploi dans l'administration publique' au sens de l'article 48, paragraphe 4, du Traité CEE, à travers la jurisprudence de la Cour", 30 *Rivista di diritto europeo* (1990) 785–802.
Janowitz, M., "Observations on the Sociology of Citizenship: Observations and Rights", 59 *Social Forces* (1980) 1–29.
Jimenez Piernas, C., "La protección diplomática y consular del ciudadano de la Union Europea", 20 *Revista de instituciones europeas* (1993) 9–49.
Kaiser, F. *et al.*, *Public Expenditure on Higher Education*, Center for Higher Education Policy Studies, University of Twente (1992) Jessica Kingsley Publishers.
Kampf, R., "La Directive 90/366/CEE relative au droit de séjour des étudiants communautaires: sa transposition en France", 357 *Revue du Marché Commun* (1992) 307–316.
Killerby, M., "Nationalité et statut personnel dans la nouvelle loi sur la nationalité britannique", in Verwilghen, M. (ed.) *Nationalité et statut personnel. Leur interaction dans les traités internationaux et dans les legislations nationales* (1984) Brussels, Bruylant, pp.239–260.
King, D.S., *The New Right: Politics, Markets and Citizenship* (1987) London, Macmillan.
King, D.S. and Waldron, J., "Citizenship, Social Citizenship and the Defence of Welfare Provision", 18 *British Journal of Political Science* (1988) 415–443.
Koessler, M., "Subject, Citizen, National and Permanent Allegiance", 56 *Yale Law Journal* (1946–47) 58–76.
Koopmans, T., "*Stare Decisis* in European Law", in Schermers, H.G. and O'Keeffe, D. (eds.), *Essays in European Law and Integration* (1982) Deventer, Kluwer.
Koopmans, T., "European Public Law" (1991) *Public Law* 53.
Koopmans, T., "The Roots of Judicial Activism in Protecting Human Rights: The European Dimension", in *Studies in Honour of G.J. Wiarda* (1988) Carl Heymans, p.317.
Koopmans, T., "The Future of the Court of Justice of the European Communities", 11 *Yearbook of European Law* (1991) 15–32.
Kon, S.D., "Aspects of Reverse Discrimination in Community Law", 6 *European Law Review* (1981) 75–91.
Koslowski, R., "Intra-EU Migration, Citizenship and Political Union", 32 *Journal of Common Market Studies* (1994) 369–402.
Kovar, R. and Simon, D., "La citoyenneté européenne", 3–4 CDE 83–315.
Krogsgaard, L.B., "Fundamental Rights in the European Community after Maastricht", *Legal Issues of European Integration* (1993) 99–112.
Kravaritou-Manitakis, P., "L'emploi selon le Traité de Rome et l'action communautaire. Textes et realités", 16 *Rivista di diritto europeo* (1976) 20–36.
Kravaritou, Y., *New Forms of Work: Labour Law and Social Security Aspects in the European Community*, European Foundation for the Improvement of Living and Working Conditions (1988) OPOCE.
Kritz, M., Keely, C.B. and Tomas, S.M., *Global Trends in Migration: Theory and Research on International Population Movements* (1981) Center for Migration Studies, Staten Island, NY.
Labayle, H., "Vers une citoyenneté europénne? Le point de vue communautaire", 76 *Petites affiches* (1992) 23.
Lachman, "Some Danish Reflections on the Use of Article 235", 18 *Common Market Law Review* (1981) 447–461.

Lagarde, P., "La participation des étrangers aux élections municipales", 49
    Etudes/Migrations (1978).
Lanfranchi, M.P., *L'entrée et la circulation des travailleurs migrants ressortissants d'états
    tiers dans la communauté européenne*, Thèse pour le doctorat en droit (1992) Université
    de droit, d'économie et de sciences politiques d'Aix-Marseille.
Lary, H. de, "Libre circulation et immigrés à l'horizon 1992", 43 *Revue française des
    affaires sociales* (1989) 93.
Laske, C., "The Impact of the Single European Market on Social Protection for Migrant
    Workers", 30 *Common Market Law Review* (1993) 515–539.
Laslett, J., "The Mutual Recognition of Diplomas, Certificates and Other Evidence of
    Formal Qualifications in the European Communities", *Legal Issues of European
    Integration* (1990) 1–66.
Lasok, D., "Deporting Unemployed Immigrants", 86 *Law Society Gazette* (1991) 17–18.
Laursen, F. and Van Hoonacker, S (eds.) *The Intergovernmental Conference on Political
    Union* (1992) Maastricht, EIPA.
Layton-Henry, Z., *The Political Rights of Migrant Workers in Western Europe* (1990)
    London, Sage Modern Publishing Series/ECPR.
Lebon, A., "Ressortissants communautaires et étrangers originaires des pays tiers dans
    l'Europe des douze", 6 *Revue européenne des migrations internationales* (1990)
    185–202.
Leca, J., "Questions sur la citoyenneté", 171–180 *Projet* (1983) 112–124.
Leca, J., *Une conceptualisation politique de l'Europe du Traité du Maastricht* (1993)
    Barcelona, Institut de Ciencies Politiques i Socials.
LeClercq, J.M. and Rault, C., *Les systèmes educatifs en Europe. Vers un espace communau-
    taire?* (1989) La documentation française.
Lee, L.T., *Consular Law and Practice* (1991) Oxford, Clarendon Press.
Leibfried, S., "The Social Dimension of the EU: En Route to Positively Joint
    Sovereignty?", 4 *Journal of European Social Policy* (1994) 239–262.
Leibfried, S. and Pierson, P., "Prospects for Social Europe", 20 *Politics and Society* (1992)
    333–365.
Lenaerts, K., "ERASMUS: Legal Basis and Implementation", in De Witte, B. (ed.),
    European Community Law of Education (1989) Baden Baden, Nomos, pp.113–125.
Lenaerts, K., "Fundamental Rights to be Included in a Community Catalogue", 16
    European Law Review (1991) 367–390.
Lenaerts, K., "Some Reflections on the Separation of Powers in the European Community",
    28 *Common Market Law Review* (1991) 11–35.
Lenaerts, K., "Education in EC Law After Maastricht", 31 *Common Market Law Review*
    (1994) 7–41.
Lenaerts, K., "L'égalité de traitement en droit communautaire", CDE (1991) 3–41.
Lenz, B., "The Public Service in Article 48(4) with special reference to the Law in England
    and in the Federal Republic of Germany", *Legal Issues of European Integration* (1989)
    75–118.
Lesguillons, H., "L'extension des compétences de la CEE par l'article 235 du traité de
    Rome", AFDI (1974) 886.
Lhoest, A., "Le citoyen à la une de l'Europe", 189 *Revue du Marché Commun* (1975)
    431–435.
Linan Nogueras, D.J., "De la ciudadania europea a la ciudadania de la union", D-17 *Gaceta
    juridica de la CE* (1992) 63–99.
Lippolis, V., *La cittadinanza europea* (1994) Universale Paperbacks Il Mulino.
Llobera, J.R., "The Role of the State and the Nation in Europe", in Garcia, S. (ed.),
    European Identity and the Search for Legitimacy (1993) London, RIIA/The Eleni Nakou
    Foundation, pp.64–79.

Lodge, J., "Citizens and the EEC: the Role of the European Parliament", 58 *The Parliamentarian* (1977) 176.

Lodge, J., "The 1984 Euro-Election Tour: the quest for uniformity?" 64 *The Parliamentarian* (1983) 204.

Lodge, J., *The EC and the Challege of the Future* (1989) London, Pinter.

Loewnfeld, E., "Nationality and the Right to Protection in International Law", 42 *The Grotius Society* (1956) 5–22.

Loman, A. *et al.*, *Culture and Community Law: Before and After Maastricht* (1992) 2 European Monographs, Deventer, Kluwer.

Lonbay, J., "Education and Law: The Community Context", 14 *European Law Review* (1989) 363–387.

Lonbay, J., "Rights in Education in the ECHR", 46 *Modern Law Review* (1983) 345.

Lonbay, J., "Educational Rights", W.G. Hart Legal Workshop, *The Single European Market and the Development of European Community Law*, 6 July 1989, London, Institute of Advanced Legal Studies.

Lonbay, J., Fundamental Rights as Citizenship Rights. Towards Fundamental Rights for Community Citizens, Federal Trust Working Group on European Citizenship, 4–6 October 1990, London.

Lonbay, J., "Free Movement of Persons, Recognition of Qualifications and Working Conditions", 39 *International and Comparative Law Quarterly* (1990) 704–707.

Loschak, D., "Les ressortissants de la Communauté Européenne", 5 *Droit social* (1976) 83–88.

Louis, J.V. and Waelbroeck, M. (eds.), *Le parlement européen dans l'évolution institutionelle* (1989) Bruxelles, Université Libre de Bruxelles.

Lucchese, A., "Le droit de vote aux étrangers pour les élections locales en Europe", 309 *Revue du Marché Commun* (1987) 473–492.

Luchaire, F., L'Union Européenne et la Constitution, Parts (I), (II), (III) and (IV), *Revue du droit public* (1992) 589–616, 933–981 and 1587–1609, respectively.

Luckhaus, L., EEC, "Social Security and Citizenship", in the W.G. Hart Legal Workshop on *The Single European Market and the Development of European Law* IALS (1989) London.

Lyon-Caen, A., "La libre circulation des travailleurs dans la Communauté Economique Européenne", 7–8 *Droit social* (1989) 526–540.

Mabille, X., "Droit de vote et nationalité", 1290 *Courrier hebdomadaire* (1990) 3–28.

MacDonald, I., *Immigration Law and Practice* (1983) London, Butterworths.

Macedo, S., *Liberal Virtues: Citizenship, Virtue and Community in Liberal Constitutionalism* (1990) Oxford, Clarendon Press.

MacKenzie Stuart, A.J., "Problems of the EC: Transatlantic Parallels", 36 *International Comparative Law Quarterly* (1987) 183–197.

MacKenzie Stuart, A.J., "Recent Trends in the Decisions of the European Court: Towards the Creation of a Community Citizenship", 21 *Journal of the Law Society of Scotland* (1976) 40–44.

MacKenzie Stuart, A.J., "Brussels 1992 – Philadelphia 1787" (1989) *Denning Law Journal* 131.

MacKenzie Stuart, A.J. and Warner, "Judicial Decision as a Source of Community Law", in Grewe, Rupp and Schneider, *Europaische Gerichtbarkeit und nationale Verfassungsgerichtsbarkeit* (1981) Baden Baden, Nomos.

Maestripieri, *La libre circulation des personnes et des services dans la CEE* (1972) UGA, Heule.

Mageira, S. (ed.), *Das Europa der Burger in einer Gemeinschaft ohne Binnengrenzen* (1990) Baden Baden, Nomos.

Maihofer, W., "Culture politique et identité européenne", in Schwarze, J. and Schermers, H.G. (eds.), *The Structure and Dimensions of EC Policy* (1988) Baden Baden, Nomos, pp.215–228.

Maillet, P., "A nouvelles ambitions, nouvelles priorités nouvelles répartitions des compétences", 346 *Revue du Marché Commun* (1991) 267.

Mairet, G., *Discours d'Europe ou souveraineté, citoyenneté et démocratie* (1989) Edition La Découverte.

Majone, G., "The European Community Between Social Policy and Social Regulation", 31 *Journal of Common Market Studies* (1993) 153–170.

Mancini, G.F., "Politica comunitaria e nazionale delle migrazioni nella prospettiva dell'Europa sociale", *Rivista di diritto europeo* (1989) 309–319.

Mancini, G.F., "The Making of a Constitution for Europe", 26 *Common Market Law Review* (1989) 595–614.

Mancini, G.F., "The Free Movement of Workers in the Case-Law of the European Court of Justice", in O'Keeffe, D. and Curtin, D. (eds.), *Constitutional Adjudication in European Community and National Law: Essays in Honour of Justice T.F. O'Higgins* (1992) London, Butterworths, pp.67–77.

Mancini, G.F., "Il contributo della corta di giustizia allo sviluppo della democrazia nella communita" (1992) *Rivista di diritto europeo* 713–725.

Margue, T.L., "L'action culturelle de la Communauté Européenne", *Revue du Marché Unique Européen* (1993) 171–185.

Marias, E.A., "The Right to Petition the European Parliament After Maastricht", 19 *European Law Review* (1994) 169–181.

Marias, E.A. (ed.), *European Citizenship* (1994) Maastricht, EIPA.

Marin Lopez, A., "La Union Europea y el derecho de sufragio de los extranjeros comunitarios", 119 *Noticias de la CEE* (1994) 1–23.

Marshall, T.H., "Citizenship and Social Class", in *Class, Citizenship and Social Development* (1977) Chicago, University of Chicago Press.

Martin, P.L. and Houston, M., "The Future of International Labour Migration", 33 *Journal of International Affairs* (1979) 311.

Martin, P.L. and Miller, M.J., "Guestworkers: Lessons from Western Europe", *Industrial and Labour Relations Journal* (1980) 315.

Martinello, M., "Vers une citoyenneté multiculterelle de l'Union Européenne", 119 *Cahiers de Clio* (1994) 78–94.

Martinello, M., "European citizenship, European identity and migrants: towards the post-national state?", in Miles, R. and Thranhardt, D. (eds.), *Migration and European Integration: The Dynamics of Inclusion and Exclusion* (1995) London, Pinter, pp.37–52.

Martinello, M., "Citizenship of the European Union: a Critical View", in Baubock, R. (ed.), *From Aliens to Citizens: Redefining the Status of Immigrants in Europe* (1995) Avebury, Aldershot, pp.29–47.

Masclet, J.C., *Droit électoral* (1989) Paris, PUF.

Masclet, J.C., "Document. Les politiques d'immigration dans la Communauté", 947 *Revue politique et parlementaire* (1990) 59.

Masclet. J.C., "Le Parlement Européen devant ses juges", 270 *Revue du Marché Commun* (1983) 518.

Matscher, F. and Petzold, H., *Protecting Human Rights: The European Dimension. Studies in Honour of E.J. Wiarda* (1988) Koln, Carl Heymanns Verlag KG.

Mattera, A., "Un espace sans frontières, le défi de l'Europe '93", *Revue du Marché Unique Européen* (1992) 5.

Mattera, A., *Le Marché Unique Européen. Ses règles, son fonctionnement* (1990) Jupiter.

Mattera, A., "La libre circulation des travailleurs à l'interieur de la CE", *Revue du Marché Unique Européen* (1993) 47–108.

Meehan, E., "European Citizenship and Social Policies", in Vogel, U. and Moran, M. (eds.), *The Frontiers of Citizenship* (1991) London, Macmillan, pp.125–154.

Meehan, E., "Citizenship and the European Community", *The Political Quarterly* (1993) 172–186.

Meehan, E., *Citizenship and the European Community* (1993) London, Sage Publications.

Meijers, H. (ed.), *Schengen: Internationalisation of Central Chapters of the Law on Aliens, Refugees, Security and the Police* (1991) Dordrecht, WEJ Tjeenk Willink/Kluwer.

Mendelson, "The European Court of Justice and Human Rights", 1 *Yearbook of European Law* (1981).

Mertens de Wilmars, J., annotation of Case 186/87 *Cowan*, 26 CDE (1990) 387–402.

Mertens, de Wilmars, J., "Réflexions sur les méthodes d'interprétation de la Cour de Justice des Communautés Européennes", 22 CDE (1986) 5–20.

Metropolis, D.G., "Human Rights, Incorporated: The European Community's New Line of Business", 29 *Stanford Law Review* (1992) 131–164.

Miaille, M., "Droit et politique à propos des immigrés", in *Le droit et les immigrés*, Vol.2, Journées de travail de 1985 (1986) Edisud.

Milas, R., "La concurrence entre les bases legales des actes communautaires", 283–292 *Revue du Marché Commun* (1985) 445.

Millar, D., "A Uniform Electoral Procedure for European Elections", 9 *Electoral Studies* (1990) 37–44.

Miller, M.J., "The Political Impact of Foreign Labor: A Re-Evaluation of the Western European Experience", 16 *International Migration Review* (1982) 27–60.

Miller, M.J., *Foreign Workers in Western Europe: An Emerging Political Force* (1981) New York, Praeger.

Minor, J., "The Abolition of Non-Discriminatory Obstacles to Free Movement", *Actualités du droit* (1994) 209–225.

Misson, L., "Le minerval perçu à charge des étudiants étrangers face au droit communautaire", *Revue du droit des étrangers* (1988) 48.

Mohr, B. (ed.), *Higher Education in the EC: The Student Handbook* (1990) European Commission.

Montani, G., "Cittadinanza europea e identità europea", 36 *Il Federalista* (1994) 95–126.

Moor, A. de, "Article 7 of the Treaty of Rome Bites", *Modern Law Review* (1985) 452.

Moran, M. and Vogel, U. (eds.), *The Frontiers of Citizenship* (1991) London, Macmillan.

Morris, G., Fredman, S. and Hayes, J., "Free Movement and the Public Sector", 19 *The Industrial Law Journal* (1990) 20–28.

Moulier Boutang, Y., "Resistance to the Political Representation of Alien Populations: The European Paradox", 19 *International Migration Review* (1985) 485–492.

Naudet, J.Y., "Analyse economique de la mobilité des salariés", 344 *Revue du Marché Commun* (1991) 88–93.

Nauta, L., "Changing Conceptions of Citizenship", 12 *Praxis International* (1992) 20–33.

Neel, B., "L'accord de Schengen", AJDA (1991) 32.

Neuman, G.L., "'We are the People': Alien Suffrage in German and American Perspective", 13 *Michigan Journal of International Law* (1992) 259–335.

Neunreither, K., "The Democratic Deficit of the European Union: Towards Closer Cooperation between the European Parliament and the National Parliaments", 29 *Government and Opposition* (1994) 299–314.

Neuwahl, N. and Rosas, A. (eds.), *Human Rights and the European Union* (1995) Martinus Nijhoff.

Neville Brown, L. and Jacobs, F.G., *The Court of Justice of the European Communities* (1977) Sweet and Maxwell.

Nowak, M. (ed.), *Progress in the Spirit of Human Rights: Festschrift für Felix Ermacora* (1988) Kehl am Rhein, NP Engel Verlag.

O'Connell, D., *International Law* Vol.2 (1970) London, Stevens and Sons.

OECD, *Financing Higher Education: Current Patterns* (1990) Paris.

OECD, *Reviews of National Policies of Education: Education Policies in Perspective: An Appraisal* (1979).

O'Keeffe, D., "Practical Difficulties in the Application of Article 48 of the EEC Treaty", 19 *Common Market Law Review* (1982) 35–60.

O'Keeffe, D., annotation of Case C-357/89 *Raulin* and Case C-3/90 *Bernini*, 29 *Common Market Law Review* (1992) 1215–1228.

O'Keeffe, D., "Equal Rights for Migrants: the Concept of Social Advantages in Article 7(2) Regulation 1612/68", 5 *Yearbook of European Law* (1985) 93–123.

O'Keeffe, D., "Trends in the Free Movement of Persons", in O'Reilly, J. (ed.), *Human Rights and Constitutional Law: Essays in Honour of Justice Brian Walsh* (1992) Dublin, Round Hall Press, pp.263–291.

O'Keeffe, D., "Legal Implications of East Germany's Membership of the EC", *Legal Issues of European Integration* (1991) 1–18.

O'Keeffe, D., "The Schengen Convention: A Suitable Model for European Integration?", 11 *Yearbook of European Law* (1991) 185–219.

O'Keeffe, D and Curtin, D. (eds.), *Constitutional Adjudication in European Community and National Law: Essays in Honour of Mr Justice T.F. O'Higgins* (1992) London, Butterworths.

O'Keeffe, D., "The Free Movement of Persons and the Single Market", 17 *European Law Review* (1992) 3–19.

O'Keeffe, D., "The Agreement on the European Economic Area", *Legal Issues of European Integration* (1992) 1–27.

O'Keeffe, D., "Union Citizenship", in O'Keeffe, D. and Twomey, P. (eds.), *Legal Issues of the Maastricht Treaty* (1993) London, Chancery Press, pp.87–107.

O'Keeffe, D., "The Emergence of a European Immigration Policy", 20 *European Law Review* (1995) 20–36.

Oldfield, A., *Citizenship and Community: Civic Republicanism and the Modern World* (1990) London, Routledge.

Oldfield, A., "Citizenship: An Unnatural Practice?", 61 *The Political Quarterly* (1990) 177–187.

O'Leary, S., *The Evolving Concept of Community Citizenship* (1993) EUI, Doctoral Thesis.

O'Leary, S., "The Court of Justice as a Reluctant Constitutional Adjudicator: an Examination of the Abortion Information Case", 17 *European Law Review* (1992) 138–157.

O'Leary, S., "Nationality and Citizenship: A Tale of Two Unhappy Bedfellows", 12 *Yearbook of European Law* (1992) 353–384.

O'Leary, S., annotation of Case C-295/90 *European Parliament* v. *Council*, 30 *Common Market Law Review* (1993) 639–651.

O'Leary, S., "A Case Study of the Community's Protection of Human Rights, with particular reference to the free movement of persons", *Actualités du droit* (1994) 429–462.

O'Leary, S., "The Social Dimension of Community Citizenship", in Antola, E. and Rosas, A. (eds.) *A Citizens' Europe: In Search of a New Order* (1995) London, Sage Publications, pp.156–181.

O'Leary, S., "Aspects of the Relationship Between Community Law and National Law", in Neuwahl, N. and Rosas, A. (eds.), *Human Rights and the European Union*, forthcoming Martinus Nijhoff.

O'Leary, S., "The Relationship Between Community Citizenship and the Protection of Fundamental Rights in Community Law", 32 *Common Market Law Review* (1995) 519–554.

Oliver, D., *Government in the United Kingdom: The Search for Accountability, Effectiveness and Citizenship* (1991) Milton Keynes, Open University Press.

Oliver, P., "Non-Community Nationals and the Treaty of Rome", 5 *Yearbook of European Law* (1985) 57–92.

Oliver, P., "The French Constitution and the Treaty of Maastricht", 43 *International Comparative Law Quarterly* (1993) 1–25.

O'Reilly, J. (ed.), *Human Rights and the Constitution: Essays in Honour of Justice Brian Walsh* (1992) Dublin, Roundhall Press.

Orzack, L.H., "The General Systems Directive: Education and the Liberal Professions", in Hurwitz, L. and Lequesne, C. (eds.), *The State of the EC: Politics, Institutions and Debates in the Transition Years 1989–1990* (1991) Boulder, Lynne Rienner, pp.137–151.

Ozsunay, E., "The Participation of the Alien in Public Life", in *Human Rights of Aliens in Europe* (1985) Dordrecht, Martinius Nijhoff.

Page, E.C. and Goldsmith, M.J., *Central and Local Government Relations: A Comparative Analysis of West European Unitary States* (1987) London, Sage.

Perez Vera, E., "La ciudadania europea en el tratado de Maastricht", in *Hacia un nuevo orden internacional y europeo. Homenaje al Prof. M Diez de Velasco* (1993) Madrid, Tecnos.

Perez Vera, E., "El tratado de la unión europea y los derechos humanos", 20 *Revista de instituciones europeas* (1993) 459–484.

Pertek, J., "La reconnaissance mutuelle des diplômes d'enseignement supérieur", 25 RTDE (1989) 623–646.

Pertek, J., "L'Europe des diplômes", 334 *Revue du Marché Commun* (1990) 167.

Pertek, J., "L'Europe des universités", 46 *Actualités juridiques* (1990) 233–241.

Pertek, J., "The Europe of Universities", 11 *Yearbook of European Law* (1991) 257–271.

Pescatore, P., "Le problème des libertés dans l'ordre juridique des communautés européennes", 9 *Jus Gentium* (1972) 1–9.

Pescatore, P., "Les objectifs de la communauté européenne comme principes d'interprétation de la jurisprudence de la cour de justice", in *Mélanges Ganschof van der Meersch* (1972) Bruylant, p.325.

Pescatore, P., "Une revolution juridique. Le rôle de la Cour de Justice européenne", 59 *Commentaire* (1992) 569.

Pescatore, P., "Fundamental Rights and Freedoms in the System of the European Communities", *American Journal of Comparative Law* (1970) 348.

Pescatore, P., "The Protection of Human Rights in the European Communities", *Common Market Law Review* (1972) 73–79.

Pescatore, P., "Les exigences de la démocratie et la legitimité de la communauté européenne", Faculté internationale de droit comparé et le centre international d'études et de recherches européennes (1974) Luxembourg.

Peuchot, "Droit de vote et condition de nationalité", *Revue du droit public* (1991) 481.

Phelan, D.R., "Right to Life of the Unborn v. Promotion of Trade in Services: The European Court of Justice and the Normative Shaping of the European Union", 55 *Modern Law Review* (1992) 670–689.

Philip, C. (ed.), *L'enseignement supérieur et la dimension européenne* (1989) La documentation française, Paris, Economica.

Pickup, D., "Discrimination and the Freedom of Movement of Workers", 23 *Common Market Law Review* (1986) 135–156.

Pierrucci, A., "Les recours au médiateur européen", in Marias, E.A., *European Citizenship* (1994) Maastricht, EIPA, pp.103–117.

Pieters, D. (ed.), *Social Security in Europe*, Miscellanea of the Erasmus programme of studies relating to social security in the EC (1991) Bruylant, MAKLU Uitgevers.

Pittau, F., "Verso l'Europa del 1992 con prospettive innovative in materia elettorale", 17 *Affari sociali internazionali* (1989) 117.

Plant, R., "Social Rights and the Reconstruction of Welfare", in Andrews, G., (ed.), *Citizenship* (1991) London, Lawrence and Wishart, pp.50–63.

Plender, R., "An Incipient Form of European Citizenship", in Jacobs, F.G. (ed.), *European Law and the Individual* (1976) Amsterdam, North Holland, pp.39–53.

Plender, R., *International Migration Law*, 2nd edn. (1988) Dordrecht, Martinus Nijhoff.

Plender, R., "Competence, European Community Law and Nationals of Non-Member States", 39 *International Comparative Law Quarterly* (1990) 599–610.

Plender, R., "In Praise of Ambiguity", 8 *European Law Review* (1983) 313–324.

Pliakos, A., "Les conditions d'exercice du droit de petition", CDE (1993) 317–349.

Quentin, J.P., "L'élection du parlement européen au suffrage universel direct", 307 *Problèmes politiques et sociaux* (1977) La documentation française.

Quintin, Y., "Vers un procédure électorale uniforme. Essai d'explication d'un échec", 267 *Revue du Marché Commun* (1983) 269.

Quinty, D. and Joly, G., "Le rôle des parlements européen et nationaux dans la fonction legislative", *Revue du droit public* (1991) 393–436.

Rasmussen, H., "Why is Article 173 Interpreted Against Private Plaintiffs?", 5 *European Law Review* (1980) 112–127.

Rasmussen, H., "Structures and Dimension of European Community Cultural Policy: L'Europe des bonnes volontés culturelles", in Schermers, H.G. and Schwarze, J. (eds.), *Structure and Dimensions of European Community Policy* (1988) Baden Baden, Nomos.

Rath, J., "The Political Participation of Ethnic Minorities in the Netherlands", 17 *International Migration Review* (1983) 445–469.

Raulet, G., "Citoyenneté, nationalité, internationalité", 11 *L'évènement européen* (1990) 165–179.

Reich, C., "Le rôle du parlement européen dans le développement institutionnel de la Communauté Européenne", 340 *Revue du Marché Commun* (1990) 587.

Rist, R.C., "The EEC Manpower: Policies and Prospects", 33 *Journal of International Affairs* (1979) 201–218.

Rocco, F., "Evoluzione recente della normativa CEE in materia di lavoro e sicurezza sociale", 9 *Rivista italiana di diritto* (1990) 134.

Roche, M., *Rethinking Citizenship: Welfare, Ideology and Change in Modern Society* (1992) London, Polity Press.

Rogers, R., *Guests Come to Stay: The Effect of European Labour Migration in Sending and Receiving Countries* (1985), Boulder, Col., Westview Press.

Room, G. (ed.), *Towards a European Welfare State* (1991), Bristol, SAUS Publications.

Rosas, A., "Democracy and Human Rights", in Rosas, A. and Helgesen, J. (eds.), *Human Rights in a Changing East-West Perspective* (1990) London, Pinter, pp.7–57.

Rosas, A., "Nationality and Citizenship in a Changing World Order", in Suksi, M. (ed.), *Law Under Exogenous Influences* (1994) Turku.

Rosberg, G., "Aliens and Equal Protection: Why not the Right to Vote?", 75 *Michigan Law Review* (1975) 1092–1136.

Rousseau, D., "Chronique de jurisprudence constitutionelle", *Revue du droit public* (1992) 37–108.

Ruzié, D., "Les droits publics et politiques du travailleur étranger", in *Les travailleurs étrangers et le droit international*, Société française pour le droit international, Clermont-Ferrand, 25–27 May 1978 (1979) Paris, Editions A. Pedone, pp.343–366.

Ruzié, D., "Nationalité, effectivité et droit communautaire", 97 *Revue Générale de droit international public* (1993) 107–120.

Saggio, A., "Rapports entre droit communautaire et droit constitutionnel italien", *Rivista di diritto europeo* (1991) 327–337.

Sandalow, T. and Stein, E., *Courts and Free Markets*, Vol.1 (1982) Clarendon Press.

Sasse, C., Brewe and Huber, H. *Towards a Uniform Electoral Procedure for Direct Elections* (1981) OPOCE/EUI.

Sasse, C., *Kommunwahlrecht für Auslander* (1974) Bonn, EU.

Saunders, O.O.R., "Tourism and the Treaty of Rome: Some Recent Developments", 1 *European Business Law Review* (1990) 69.

Scarpa, R., "Considerazioni in ordine a una procedura uniforme per l'elezione dei deputati al Parlamento Europeo", 13 *Affari sociali internazionali* (1985) 61–67.

Schauer, F., "Community, citizenship and the search for national identity", 84 *Michigan Law Review* (1985–86) 1504–1517.

Schepers, S., "The Legal Force of the Preamble to the EEC Treaty", 6 *European Law Review* (1981) 356–361.

Schermers, H.G., "The Communities under the ECHR", *Legal Issues of European Integration* (1978) 1–8.

Schermers, H.G. and Waelbroeck, M., *Judicial Protection in the European Communities* 5th edn. (1992) Deventer, Kluwer.

Schermers, H.G., "The European Communities Bound by Fundamental Human Rights", 27 *Common Market Law Review* (1990) 249–258.

Schermers, H.G., "The Effect of the Date 31 December 1992", 28 *Common Market Law Review* (1991) 275-289.

Schermers, H.G., "The Scales in the Balance: National Constitutional Court v. Court of Justice", 27 *Common Market Law Review* (1990) 97–105.

Scheuner, "Fundamental Rights in EC Law and in Constitutional Law", 12 *Common Market Law Review* (1975) 171–191.

Schmitter Heisler, B. and Heisler, M.O., "Transnational Migration and the Modern Democratic State: Familiar Problems in a New Form or a New Problem?", 485 *Annals of the American Society of Political and Social Science* (1986) 12.

Schockweiler, F., "La portée du principe de non-discrimination de l'article 7 du Traité CEE", *Rivista di diritto europeo* (1991) 3–24.

Schockweiler, F., "La dimension humaine et sociale de la Communauté Européenne", *Revue du Marché Unique Européen* (1993) 11–45.

Scholsem, J.C., "A propos de la circulation des étudiants. Vers un fédéralisme financier européen", 25 *Cahiers de droit européen* (1989) 306–324.

Schuck, P.H. and Smith, R.M., *Citizenship without Consent: Illegal Aliens in the American Polity* (1985) New Haven, Yale University Press.

Schuck, P.H., "Immigration Law and the Problem of Community", in Glazer, M. (ed.), *Clamor at the Gates: The New American Immigration* (1985) Institute for Contemporary Studies Press, San Francisco, p.285.

Schutte, J., "Schengen, its Meaning for the Free Movement of Persons in Europe", 28 *Common Market Law Review* (1991) 550–571.

Schwartz, I.E., "Article 235 and Law-Making Powers in the European Community", 27 *International Comparative Law Quarterly* (1978) 614.

Schwartz, I.E., "Le pouvoir normatif de la Communauté notamment en vertu de l'article 235", *Revue du Marché Commun* (1976) 280.

Schwarze, J. and Schermers, H.G. (eds.), *The Structure and Dimensions of European Community Policy* (1987) Baden Baden, Nomos.

Seche, J.C., "Free Movement of Workers under Community Law", 14 *Common Market Law Review* (1977) 385–409.

Shaw, J., "Twin-Track Social Europe: the Inside Track", in O'Keeffe, D. and Twomey, P. (eds.), *Legal Issues of the Maastricht Treaty* (1993) London, Chancery Press, pp.295–311.

Sica, M., "Diritto di voto ai cittadini comunitari", *Comuni d'Europa* (1988) 9.

Sica, M., *Verso la cittidinanza europea* (1989) Florence, Le Lonnier.

Sica, M., "Involvement of the Migrant Worker in Local Political Life in the Host Country", 15 *International Migration* (1977).

Sieveking, K., Barwig, K., Lorcher, K. and Schomacher, C. (eds.), *Das Kommunal-wahlrecht fur Auslander* (1989) Baden Baden, Nomos.

Silvestro, M., "L'élection du parlement européen au suffrage universel et direct", 335 *Revue du Marché Commun* (1990) 216.

Silvestro, M., "Le droit de vote et éligibilité aux élections municipales", 370 *Revue du Marché Commun* (1993) 612–614.

Simmonds, K., "Immigration Control and the Free Movement of Labour: A Problem of Harmonisation", 24 *International Comparative Law Quarterly* (1972) 307.

Simmonds, K., "The British Nationality Act, 1981 and the Definition of the Term National for Community Purposes", 21 *Common Market Law Review* (1984) 675–686.

Simmonds, K.R., annotation of Case C-355/89 *Barr*, 29 *Common Market Law Review* (1992) 799–806.

Simon, D., "Ordre public et libertés publiques dans les communautés européennes", 195 *Revue du Marché Commun* (1976) 201–223.

Simon, G., "Une europe communautaire de moins en moins mobile", 7 *Revue européenne des migrations internationales* (1991) 41–61.

Skouris, W., "La formation professionelle dans la jurisprudence de la Cour de Justice des communautés européennes", in Schwarze, J. and Schermers, H.G. (eds.), *The Structure and Dimensions of European Community Policy* (1987) Baden Baden, Nomos, p.205.

Smith, A.D., "National Identity and the Idea of European Unity", 68 *International Affairs* (1992) 55–76.

Snyder, F., "The Effectiveness of European Community Law: Institutions, Processes, Tools and Techniques", 56 *Modern Law Review* (1993) 19–54.

Solbes Mira, P., "La citoyenneté européenne", 345 *Revue du Marché Commun* (1991) 168–170.

Spicker, P., "The Principle of Subsidiarity and the Social Policy of the European Community", 1 *Journal of European Social Policy* (1991) 5–14.

Stangos, P.N., "Les ressortissants des états tiers au sein de l'ordre juridique communau-taire", 3–4 CDE (1992) 306–347.

Stanley, A. and Rowlands, M., *The Rights of Third Country Nationals in the New European* (1994) London, Immigration and Nationality Research and Information Charity.

Starkle, G., "Extension du principe de non-discrimination en droit communautaire au ressortissant d'un Etat Membre licitement installé dans un autre Etat Membre", 5–6 CDE (1984) 667–695.

Stefanini, P. and Doublet, F., "Le droit d'asile en Europe. La convention relative à la deter-mination de l'état responsable de l'examen d'une demande d'asile presentée auprès d'un Etat Membre des communautés européennes", 347 *Revue du Marché Commun* (1991) 391–399.

Stein, E., "Lawyers, Judges and the Making of a Transnational Constitution", 75 *American Journal of International Law* (1981) 1.

Stein, E., "The European Communities in 1983: A Less Than Perfect Union", 20 *Common Market Law Review* (1983) 641–656.

Steiner, H.J., "Political Participation as a Human Right", 1 *Harvard Human Rights Yearbook* (1988) 77–134.

Steiner, J., annotation of the *Gravier* case, 10 *European Law Review* (1985) 348–352.

Steiner, J., "The Right to Welfare: Equality and Equity under Community Law", 10 *European Law Review* (1985) 21–41.

Steiner, J., "From Direct Effect to Francovich: Shifting Means of Enforcement of EC Law", 18 *European Law Review* (1993) 3–22.

Stephanou, C.A., "Identité et citoyenneté européennes", 343 *Revue du Marché Commun* (1991) 30–39.

Straubhaar, T., "International Labour Migration within a Common Market: Some Aspects of EC Experience", 27 *Journal of Common Market Studies* (1988) 45–62.

Streeck, W., "From Market-Making to State-Building? Reflections on the Political Economy of European Social Policy", DOC. IUE. 76/94 (col.27) presented at *European Law in Context: Constitutional Dimensions of European Economic Integration*, 14–15 April 1994.

Szyszczak, E., "Social Policy: a Happy Ending or a Reworking of the Fairy Tale?", in O'Keeffe, D. and Twomey, P. (eds.), *Legal Issues of the Maastricht Treaty* (1993) London, Chancery Press, pp.313–327.

Taylor, P., "The Nation-State in the European Communities: Superficial Realities and Underlying Uncertainties", 39 *International Journal* (1983–84) 577.

Teague, P., *The European Community Social Dimension: Labour Market Policies for 1992* (1989) London, Issues in Human Resource Management no.4, Kogan Page.

Teichler, U. and Dalichow, F., *Higher Education in the EC: Survey of "Joint Study Programmes"* (1986) Luxembourg, OPOCE.

Temple Lang, J., "The Sphere in Which Member States are Obliged to Comply With the General Principles of Law and Community Fundamental Rights Principles", *Legal Issues of European Integration* (1991) 23–35.

Temple Lang, J., "New Legal Effects Resulting from the Failure of States to Fulfill Obligations under European Community Law: The *Francovich* Judgment", 16 *Fordham International Law Journal* (1992–93) 1.

Temple Lang, J., "Community Constitutional Law: Article 5 EEC Treaty", 27 *Common Market Law Review* (1990) 645–681.

Timmermans, C.W.A., "German Unification and Community Law", 27 *Common Market Law Review* (1990) 437–449.

TMC Asser Institute, *The Free Movement of Persons in Europe: Problems and Experiences* (1993) Dordrecht, Martinus Nijhoff.

Tomuschat, C., "A United Germany Within the European Community", 27 *Common Market Law Review* (1990) 415–436.

Tomuschat, C., "L'ordre public. Menace pour la libre circulation", CDE (1975) 302.

Toth, A.G., *Legal Protection of the Individual in EC Law*, Vols.1, 2 (1978) Amsterdam, North Holland.

Toth, A.G., "The Legal Status of the Declarations Annexed to the SEA", 23 *Common Market Law Review* (1986) 803–812.

Toth, A.G., "The Principle of Subsidiarity in the Maastricht Treaty", 29 *Common Market Law Review* (1992) 1079–1105.

Traversa, E., "L'interdiction de discrimination en raison de la nationalité en matière d'accès à l'enseignement", 25 RTDE (1989) 45–69.

Tung, Ko-Chih R., "Voting Rights for Alien Residents: Who Wants it?", 19 *International Migration Review* (1985) 451–467.

Turack, D.C., *The Passport in International Law* (1972) Lexington, Lexington Books.

Turner, B.S., *Citizenship and Capitalism: The Debate over Reformism* (1986) Controversies in Sociology Series no.21, Allen and Unwin.

Turner, B.S., "Outline of a Theory of Citizenship", 24 *Sociology* (1990) 189–217.

Turpin, D., *Immigrés et refugiés dans les démocraties occidentales. Défis et solutions* (1990) Economica/Presse Universitaire d'Aix-Marseille.

Twine, F., *Citizenship and Social Rights: The Interdependence of Self and Society* (1994) London, Sage Publications.

Twomey, P., "The European Union: Three Pillars Without a Human Rights Foundation", in Monar, J., Ungerer, W. and Wessels, W. (eds.), *The Maastricht Treaty on European Union* (1993) Brussels, European Interuniversity Press, pp.121–131.

Usher, J., "The Scope of Community Competence: Its Recognition and Enforcement", 24 *Journal of Common Market Studies* (1985) 121–136.

Usher, J., "Measures of the organs intended to develop competences and legal instruments", in Bieber, R. and Ress, E., *The Dynamics of European Community Law* (1987) Baden Baden, Nomos, p.343.

Van Craeyenest, F., "La nature juridique des résolutions sur la cooperation en matière d'éducation", in De Witte, B. (ed.), *European Community Law of Education* (1989) Baden Baden, Nomos, p.127.

Van den Berghe, G. and Huber, H, "European Citizenship", in Bieber, R., Bleckmann, A. and Capotorti, F. (eds.), *Das Europa der Zweiten Generation. Gedachtnisschrift fur Christopher Sasse* (1981) Kehl-am-Rhein/Strasbourg, Engel Verlag, pp.755–774.

Van den Berghe, G., "Direct Elections in Accordance with a Uniform Procedure", 4 *European Law Review* (1979) 331–340.

Van den Berghe, G., *Political Rights for European Citizens* (1982) Aldershot, Gower.

Van Gerven, W. and Van den Bossche, P., "Freedom of Movement and Equal Treatment for Students in Europe: An Emerging Principle", in *Free Movement for Persons in Europe: Problems and Experiences*, Proceedings of the TMC Asser Institute Colloquium, The Hague, 12–13 September 1991 (1992) Dordrecht, Martinus Nijhoff.

Van Gunsteren, H., "Notes on a Theory of Citizenship", in Birnbaum, P., Lively, J. and Parry, G. (eds.), *Democracy, Consensus and Social Contract* (1978) London, Sage Modern Politics Series, Vol.2, pp.9–35.

Van Nuffel, P., "L'Europe des citoyens. Vers un droit de séjour generalisée", *Revue du Marché Unique Européen* (1991) 89–109.

Van Praag, Ph., "Aspects économiques à long terme des migrations internationales dans les pays de la CEE", 9 *Migrations Internationales* (1971) 126–136.

Varat, J.D., "State Citizenship and Interstate Inequality", 48 *University of Chicago Law Review* (1981) 487–572.

Vedovato, G., "Legge elettorale europea uniforme", 51 *Rivista di studi politici internazionale* (1984) 609–615.

Verhoeven, J., "Les citoyens de l'Europe", 2 *Annales de droit de Louvain* (1993) 165–191.

Verscheuren, H., "L'arrêt *Rush Portuguesa*. Un nouvel apport au principe de la libre circulation des travailleurs dans le droit communautaire", 60 *Revue du droit des étrangers* (1990) 231–237.

Verzijl, J.H.W., *International Law in Historical Perspective*, Vol.5 (1972) Leiden, A.J. Sijthoff.

Villani, U., "Osservazioni sull'elettorato passivo al Parlamento Europeo", 28 *Diritto comunitario e degli scambi internazionali* (1989) 349.

Vincenzi, C., "European Citizenship", in *The Single European Market and the Development of European Law*, W.G. Hart Legal Workshop (1989) London, Institute of Advanced Legal Studies.

Vincenzi, C., "Aliens and the Judicial Review of Immigration Law", *Public Law* (1985) 93–114.

Vincenzi, C., *Immigration Rights for Community Nationals: A Basis for Citizenship?*, 4–6 October 1990, London, Federal Trust Workshop on European Citizenship.

Vincenzi, C., "Challenging a Refusal of Entry: EEC Workers", 2 *Immigration and Nationality Law and Practice* (1987) 2–6.

Vincenzi, C., "Freedom of movement in the single market: an Irish solution?", 140 *New Law Journal* (1990) 664–669.

Vogel-Polsky, E., *L'Europe sociale 1993. Illusion, alibi ou realité* (1991) Etudes européennes, Bruxelles, Editions de l'Université Libre de Bruxelles.

Vogel-Polsky, E., "L'acte unique ouvre-t-il l'espace social européen?", 2 *Droit Social* (1989) 177.

Walter, M.R., "The Alien's Right to Work and the Political Community's Right to Govern", 25 *Wayne Law Review* (1979) 1181–1215.

Watson, P., "Wandering Students: Their Rights under Community Law", in O'Keeffe, D. and Curtin, D. (eds.), *Constitutional Adjudication in European Community Law and National Law: Essays in Honour of Mr Justice T.F. O'Higgins* (1992) London, Butterworths, pp.79–88.

Watson, P., annotation of Case 344/87 *Bettray*, 14 *European Law Review* (1989) 415–422.

Watson, P., "The Community Social Charter", 28 *Common Market Law Review* (1991) 37–68.

Watson, P., "Social Policy After Maastricht", 30 *Common Market Law Review* (1993) 481–513.

Weatherill, S., "Discrimination on Grounds of Nationality in Sport", 9 *Yearbook of European Law* (1989) 55–92.

Weatherill, S., "The Scope of Article 7", 15 *European Law Review* (1990) 334–341.

Weiler, J.H.H., "The Dual Character of Supranationalism", 1 *Yearbook of European Law* (1981) 267–306.

Weiler, J.H.H., "Parlement Européen, integration européenne, démocratie et legitimité", in Louis, J.V. and Waelbroeck, M., *Le Parlement Européen dans l'evolution institutionelle* (1989) Bruxelles, Université Libre de Bruxelles, p.325.

Weiler, J.H.H., "The Transformation of Europe", 100 *Yale Law Journal* (1991) 2403–2483.

Weiler, J.H.H., "Protection of Fundamental Human Rights Within the Legal Order of the European Communities", in Bernhardt, R. and Jolowicz, A.J. (eds.), *International Enforcement of Human Rights* (1986) Berlin, Heidelberg, NY.

Weiler, J.H.H., *Symposium on the European Parliament in the Community System*, organised by the European Parliament and the Trans-European Policy Studies Association, Research and Documentation Papers, November 1988.

Weiler, J.H.H. and Lockhart, N., "'Taking Rights Seriously' – Seriously: The European Court and its Fundamental Rights Jurisprudence", 32 *Common Market Law Review* (1995) 7–49 and 579–677.

Weiler, J.H.H., "Thou Shalt Not Oppress a Stranger: On the Judicial Protection of the Human Rights of Non-EC Nationals – A Critique", 3 *European Journal of International Law* (1992) 65–91.

Weiler, J.H.H., "Journey to an Unknown Destination: A Retrospective and Prospective of the Court of Justice in the Area of Political Integration", 31 *Journal of Common Market Studies* (1993) 417–446.

Weiler, J.H.H., "Problems of Legitimacy in Post-1992 Europe", 46 *Aussenwirtschaft* (1991) 411–437.

Weis, P., *Nationality and Statelessness in International Law*, 2nd edn. (1979) Alpen aan den Rijn, Sijthoff and Noordhoff.

Welsh, J.M., "A Peoples' Europe? European Citizenship and European Identity". EUI Working Paper ECS No.93/2.

Werner, H., "Free Movement of Labour in the Single European Market", 25 *Intereconomics* (1990) 77–81.

White, R. and Hampson, F., "British Nationality Law: Proposed Changes", 30 *International Comparative Law Quarterly* (1981) 247–259.

Whiteford, E., "Social Policy After Maastricht", 18 *European Law Review* (1993) 202–222.

Wiessner, S., "Blessed be the Ties that Bind: The Nexus Between Nationality and Territory", 56 *Mississippi Law Journal* (1986) 441–533.

Wihtol de Wenden, C., *Citoyenneté, nationalité et immigration* (1987) Paris, Arcantère.

Wihtol de Wenden, C. (ed.), *La citoyenneté* (1988) Paris, Edilig Foundation Diderot.

Wihtol de Wenden, C., "Les immigrés et le discours politique municipal", GRECO 13, (1982) nos.4–5 *Recherches sur les migrations internationales* 68.

Wilkinson, B., "Abortion, the Irish Constitution and the EEC", *Public Law* (1992) 20–30.
Wishart, D.A., "Allegiance and Citizenship as Concepts in Constitutional Law", 15
    Melbourne University Law Review (1985–86) 662–707.
Woolridge, F., "Free Movement of EEC Nationals: the Limitation Based on Public Policy",
    2 *European Law Review* (1977) 190–207.
Wyatt, D., "The Social Security Rights of Migrant Workers and their Families", 14
    Common Market Law Review (1977) 411–433.
Young, I.M., "Polity and Group Difference: A Critique of the Ideal of Universal
    Citizenship", 99 *Ethics* (1988–89) 250–274.
Zilioli, C., "The Recognition of Diplomas and its Impact on Educational Policies", in De
    Witte, B., (ed.), *European Community Law of Education* (1989) Baden Baden, Nomos,
    pp.51–70.

Index